# The
# Tender
# Mercies
## of
# Personal
# Revelation

*Guy Laing*

i

This collection of stories does not completely represent the doctrines of the Church of Latter-day Saints. Many of the quotes are from apostles, prophets, and the Holy Scriptures; the balance of the experiences is from Christian disciples of Christ.

"For they that are wise and have received the truth, and have taken the Holy Spirit for their guide, and have not been deceived ..." (D&C 45:57)

Dedicated to my expansive family, friends, peers, and those who have the gift of believing on the testimony of others:

"To some it is given by the Holy Ghost to know that Jesus Christ is the Son of God, and that he was crucified for the sins of the world. To others it is given to believe on their words, that they also might have eternal life if they continue faithful." (D&C 46:13-14)

# The Tender Mercies
# of Personal Revelation

Copyright © 2019 by Guy Laing
Cover design by Hyrum Rappleye
ISBN: 9781796408263

Guy's Books
3813 S 5800 S, Roy, UT 84067
guym@xmission.com
www.guylaing.blogspot.com

First Printing, 2019
Printed in the United States of America

# Contents

# Contents

# PREFACE

## Experiences from Christian Disciples of Christ, the Holy Scriptures, and Apostles and Prophets

I have attempted to *"liken the scriptures"* to ourselves throughout this work to show that everyday people can have experiences and miracles in their lives—similar to the apostles, leaders, and prophets. Countless Christians and righteous people over the eons have had similar situations in their lives regarding their respective realms of responsibilities.

The revealed *Come Follow Me* program is exactly that: likening the scriptures unto ourselves. Through the weekly lessons in *Come Follow Me*, the user is reminded to ponder, pray, and seek the personal revelation that helps one better apply the scripture teachings throughout their respective responsibilities and lives in order to come closer and return to our Savior and Father in Heaven.

> "... do as the prophet Nephi counseled: *liken the scriptures* to yourselves so that it will be for your profit and learning." (See 1 Ne. 19:23-24) (Ezra Taft Benson, GC, April 1984)

My hope is that this collection of Christian stories along with spiritual experiences from Saints serving in the backgrounds—to apostles and prophets that walk/walked the earth will give you encouragement and desires to do more.

Some stories show the brutal battle Saints slog through on this Telestial terrain. You will find stories of success in overcoming opposition by seeking the Holy Ghost and Christ. Heavenly Father's love and care for all His children is evident.

May these experiences enhance the Holy Ghost and Light of Christ throughout your lives by connecting with the stories of your peers. Enjoy the merciful manifestations of tender mercies. May this book bountifully bless your lives and carry convicting spiritual truths into you hearts.

# ACKNOWLEGEMENTS

Mountains of gratitude are due the many disciples of Christ who have contributed their personal experiences and testimonies through the years. Thank you to all our family, friends, leaders, relatives, and peers.

Thank you to Jill Laing and Tracy Decker for their help with editing and advising. Thanks to my wife, Tamara Laing, for her suggestions and support.

Huge thanks go out to all of our journals which helped record and store forgotten memories of great importance. "A short pencil is better than a long memory." (Anonymous)

> Please follow the counsel you have been given in the past and maintain your personal journals. Those who keep a book of remembrance are more likely to keep the Lord in remembrance in their daily lives. Journals are a way of counting our blessings and of leaving an inventory of these blessings for our posterity. (President Spencer W. Kimball, GC, April 1978)

## ABBREVIATIONS USED:

*CR*: Conference Report
*DS*: Doctrines of Salvation
*GC*: General Conference
*HC*: History of the Church
*JD*: Journal of Discourses
*JSH*: Joseph Smith History
*JST*: Joseph Smith Translation
*TPC*: Teachings of Presidents of the Church
*TPJS*: Teachings of the Prophet Joseph Smith

**Bold**, *Italics*, <u>Underline</u> added for emphasis throughout

"The Lord's tender mercies do not occur randomly or merely by coincidence. Faithfulness, obedience, and humility invite tender mercies into our lives, and it is often the Lord's timing that enables us to recognize and treasure these important blessings." (David A. Bednar, *Tweet*, 12/17/18)

"... I will tell you in your mind and in your heart, by *the Holy Ghost*, which shall come upon you and which shall dwell in your heart. Now, behold, this is the *spirit of revelation*...." (D&C 8:2-3)

"The most valuable inspiration will be for you to know what God would have you do. If it is to pay tithing or to visit a grieving friend, you should do it. Whatever it is, do it. When you demonstrate your willingness to obey, the Spirit will send you more impressions of what God would have you do for Him. As you obey, the impressions from the Spirit will come more frequently, becoming closer and closer to constant companionship. Your power to choose the right will increase." (Henry B. Eyring, GC, Oct 2015)

> If thou shalt ask, thou shalt receive revelation upon revelation, knowledge upon knowledge, that thou mayest know the mysteries and peaceable things— that which bringeth joy, that which bringeth eternal life. (D&C 42:61)

*Third Hour* tweeted on 3/9/2019 "It's all about the stories! 'Only 5% of people remember any statistics after they are shared, while 65% of people remember the stories told.'" (Matt Luhn)

"I love the Random Sampler stories in the Ensign magazine. Here is an entire book of stories to love!" TAL

*Over 700 stories from contributors ages 3–90+*

# Introduction

Our Heavenly Father showers down bounteous blessings upon His children throughout all climes. Personal revelation is available to one and all. These heavenly messages can come to all mankind through a myriad of methods offering them a plethora of possible pathways.

> "I have learned that strong, impressive spiritual experiences do not come to us very frequently." (Boyd K Packer, *That We May All Be Edified*, 337)

I have realized the very same thing through the decades. The majority of personal revelation is communicated to many of us through peaceful, quiet, and simple ways. Throughout the millennia that same Spiritual member of the Godhead continues to communicate through a still ... small ... voice.

> And there are many among us who have many revelations, for they are not all stiffnecked. And as many as are not stiffnecked and have faith, have communion with the Holy Spirit, which maketh manifest unto the children of men, according to their faith. (Jarom 1:4)

> The Lord gives to many of us the still, small voice of revelation ... it comes to each man, according to his needs and faithfulness, for guidance in matters that pertain to his own life ... It isn't position, it is not education that gives the commandments of God; but it is keeping the commandments of the Almighty God. (Heber J Grant, *TPC*, 20.182)

Pure revelation will, at times, fly in the face of "common sense" and not follow normal patterns of thought or tradition. When promptings and whisperings are incongruent with our normal habits and usual patterns we need to become more like the rejected prophet Alma and *return speedily* into the firestorm and unknown. We often operate on assumptions and suppositions; while the Godhead fully functions on light and truth. Therefore, "Trust in the Lord with all thine heart; and lean not unto thine own understanding. In all thy ways acknowledge him, and he shall direct thy paths." (Proverbs 3:5-6)

I recently heard some wise counsel to the effect of: "If you just sit around and wait for revelation to come to you, you will be greatly disappointed."

1

... men should be anxiously engaged in a good cause, and do many things of their own free will, and bring about much righteousness; For the power is in them, wherein they are agents unto themselves. And inasmuch as men do good they shall in nowise lose their reward. (D&C 58:27-28)

"And let us not be weary in well doing; ... let us do good unto all men ..." (Galatians 6:9-10)

*When we go about serving others, fulfilling our callings, filling the temples, pondering and praying, studying the scriptures, and doing good wherever, the subtle promptings and still ... small ... voice will be enhanced and increased to help one even better minister to many of God's children. Faith is an action verb; when we rise from our knees and go forward, the Lord will turn us into **His ministering tools**.*

I do desire, and it is something you should desire, to have that humility, and that meekness, and that simplicity to enjoy the spirit of revelation. It is your privilege, every one of you, to have enough of the spirit of revelation to know exactly what to do. (President Lorenzo Snow, *TPC*, Chapter 4)

A person may profit by noticing the first intimation of the spirit of revelation; for instance, when you feel pure intelligence flowing into you, it may give you sudden strokes of ideas, so that by noticing it, you may find it fulfilled the same day or soon; ... those things that were presented unto your minds by the Spirit of God, will come to pass; and thus by learning the Spirit of God and understanding it, you may grow into the principle of revelation, until you become perfect in Christ Jesus. (*TPJS*, 151)

What power shall stay the heavens? As well might man stretch forth his puny arm to stop the Missouri river in its decreed course, or to turn it up stream, as to hinder the Almighty from pouring down knowledge from heaven upon the heads of the Latter-day Saints. (D&C 121:33)

# 1. When I Was a Child

"When I was a little girl in Primary I loved the Primary songs. When we would sing it felt like my heart enlarged and bubbly spray was going through my veins." (A peer)

―――――●◆●―――――

*The resurrected Savior was visiting and ministering to the righteous Nephites and Lamanites in Bountiful. Christ had healed ALL their sick and raised one man from the dead:*

> … on the morrow that the multitude gathered themselves together, and they both saw and heard these children; yea, even babes did open their mouths and utter marvelous things; and the things which they did utter were forbidden that there should not any man write them. (3 Ne. 26:16)

―――――●◆●―――――

It was thrilling to listen to a father relate this story about his three-year-old youngster recently, as they knelt by the crib in the usual manner for the little fellow to say his simple bedtime prayer. Eyes closed, heads bowed, seconds passed, and there were no words spoken by the child. Just about the time Dad was going to open his eyes to check the lengthy delay, little Tommy was on his feet and climbing into bed. "How about your prayers?" asked Dad.
"I said my prayers"
"But son, Daddy didn't hear you."
"But Daddy, I wasn't talking to you."
Even three-year-olds have personal, private matters to discuss with Heavenly Father from time to time. (Robert L. Simpson, CR, April 1970)

"If He comes to a little child, He will adapt himself to the language and capacity of a little child," (Joseph Smith, HC, 3:392).

―――――●◆●―――――

When a very young child in the home of my youth, I was fearful at night. I traced it back to a vivid dream in which two Indians came into the yard. I ran to the house for protection, and one of them shot an arrow and hit me in the back. Only a dream, but I felt that blow, and I was very

3

much frightened, for in the dream they entered … and sneered and frightened mother.

I never got over it. Adding to that were the fears of mother, for when father was away with the herd or on some mission, mother would never retire without looking under the bed, so burglars or men who might enter the house and try to take advantage of mother and the young children were real to me.

Whatever the conditions, I was very much frightened. One night I could not sleep, and I fancied I heard noises around the house. … I became terribly wrought in my feeling, and I decided to pray as my parents had taught me.

I thought I could pray only by getting out of bed and kneeling, and that was a terrible test. But I did finally bring myself to get out of bed and kneel and pray to God to protect mother and the family. And a voice as clearly to me as mine is to you, said, "**Don't be afraid. Nothing will hurt you**." Where it came from, what it was, I am not saying. You may judge. To me it was a direct answer and there came an assurance that I should never be hurt in bed at night. (David O. McKay, *TPC*, 9.2)

My father and brothers had been digging under the house to replace something and had made a very large pile of dirt by the side of the house in the shade of the locust trees. This was a great place for two little boys to play with cars and trucks.

My mother had given me a quarter for some reason. A quarter was a lot of money for a six-year old in 1952; I kept it in the center pocket of my bib overalls. I thought of all the things I could buy with it if I ever got to go to town with mom. Back then a quarter would buy enough candy to make you and your friends sick.

We were playing in the dirt pile when Mom called us in for lunch. Just before I got up to go in to the house for lunch I checked my pocket to see if my quarter was still there. It was missing! I was pretty panicked and started searching in the dirt for the quarter. David helped me but we couldn't find it anywhere.

Then I remember what Sister Flinders, my Primary teacher, had taught us about prayer. I knelt right down in the dirt and asked Heavenly Father to help me find the quarter; with full expectation that He would answer my prayer. When I opened my eyes, there lying on the ground between my knees and on top of the dirt was the quarter. I was really impressed.

I knew at the tender age of six that our Heavenly Father answered prayers. The faith of a child had taught me a powerful lesson that I would never forget. (Fellow Missionary)

————◆————

Seven-year-old Jamie loved her mother dearly. The family had known for nearly a year that their wife and mother was dying of cancer. The father and seven children fasted and prayed; they pled with the Lord to heal her. Everything possible was done for their mother, yet at the end of three painfully difficult months, she passed from this life.

In the first hours following her death, the father brought the grieving family together. After prayer, the children went to their own rooms to prepare for bed. Jamie, who had spent many hours with her mother and was devoted to her, knelt at her own bedside. "Heavenly Father," she prayed through her tears, "we thank thee for the great mom you gave us. We thank thee for helping us try to make her well. Help us to be good so we can live with her again." Without a hint of bitterness, this little seven-year-old girl continued for several minutes in a sweet attitude of peaceful prayer, reflecting her understanding and acceptance of her mother's death.

Jamie was a child at peace. How did she come to that peace? She had been prepared by parents with spiritual understanding. Such preparation brings peace. (Michaelene P. Grassli, GC, Oct 1988)

————◆————

One Saturday, I was to drive to the airport for a flight to a stake conference in California. But the cow was expecting a calf and in trouble. The calf was born, but the cow could not get up. We called the veterinarian, who soon came. He said the cow had swallowed a wire and would not live through the day.

I copied the telephone number of the animal by-products company so my wife could call them to come and get the cow as soon as she died.

5

Before I left, we had our family prayer. Our little boy said our prayer. After he had asked Heavenly Father to "bless Daddy in his travels and bless us all," he then started an earnest plea. He said, "Heavenly Father, please bless Bossy cow so that she will get to be all right."

In California, I told of the incident and said, "He must learn that we do not get everything we pray for just that easily."

There was a lesson to be learned, but it was I who learned it, not my son. When I returned Sunday night, Bossy had "got to be all right." (Boyd K. Packer, GC, Oct 2009)

An eight or nine year-old primary girl shared her family's experience. Our family came home and we were locked out of our house. No one had a key to get in. We decided to say a prayer for help. After the prayer we walked around the house to see if there was any way we could get in.

I tripped and fell down. From the ground I could see down to my brother's window and saw that it was cracked open. We were able to get in. I am glad Heavenly Father answered our pray. (Young friend)

President Benson receives many letters from children. Sometimes they are humorous, other times tender. When President Benson was hospitalized and the doctors provided a pacemaker to help regulate his heart, one little girl wrote in and said, "Dear President Benson, I know you will be all right because the Bible says, 'Blessed are the pacemakers.'" (Thomas S. Monson, GC, Oct 1986)

"When I was 10 years old, in the shadows of the Salt Lake Temple I first read the Joseph Smith story and received a powerful testimony of the truthfulness of the Restoration." (Glenn L. Pace, GC, April 2000)

When I was around eleven-years old an issue arose in my young life. Up to this point my friends and I usually rotated staying over in each other's backyards in sleeping bags during some summer nights. Small towns don't have a lot of lights and we really enjoyed clearly seeing the countless stars covering the night sky. We had a lot of fun and enjoyed one another's company. I felt a little guilty about taking low hanging apples above sidewalks. With a little salt, even the green apples weren't bad. We were careful not to eat too many green ones after hearing stories of how sick some people got from overeating green apples.

During one of our sleepovers, my two best friends started talking about doing vandalism to personal and business property during our night outings. My conscience made me feel that their new plan was bad. I was very uncomfortable about the situation and wasn't sure what to do about it. I mulled it over again and again in my young mind. I did not want to tell my parents because they would say I couldn't sleep out anymore and not let me play with my friends. I knew for sure that my five younger sisters would tell on me if I shared my dilemma with any one of them. My dad would then punish me for even thinking about doing something wrong: "*Just in case you do it in the future!*" If I told my friends I did not want to participate in illegal activities, they might make fun of me and/or not want to do things together anymore with me. I just did not know what to do and contemplated my options, pondering possible outcomes, none of which seemed workable to me.

I decided to sleep in our backyard all by myself the following Friday night and privately think on how to figure this out. While laying alone in the darkness, pondering the problem, I recalled Primary lessons about praying for answers when we had a question, we did not know what to do, or were scared. So I knelt down atop my sleeping bag in the darkness of our back yard and explained it all to God through prayer. I laid out my issues and asked which idea would be the best. I was sure surprised when a voice in my mind clearly and quickly said, "**Change friends**." It was just like I was talking to somebody and they had answered my question right then and there in front of me!

That answer was not one of my choices and following that advice actually worried me. I was simply unsure about making a change with my best friends. The challenge seemed difficult and problematic. If I tried to change friends I might end up with no friends at all! By the next day I decided to follow the council, figuring that I had asked for a solution and received an answer directly from Heaven! I'd better be obedient to that advice.

When those friends talked about sleepovers and activities, I began making up excuses until they stopped calling anymore. Over the next few months I was surprised as to how easy it actually was to make new friends. This new group of buddies continued to enjoy lots of fun, while staying out of serious trouble in the mean time. A simple prayer saved me from a lot of possible problems. We can all be helped in our quandaries by following inspired direction, which is available to all mankind.

This experience is a great example of how the Light of Christ and the Holy Ghost can work together for the benefit of mankind. Everyone born into this world receives a free and wonderful gift of the Light of Christ. Many people refer to the Light of Christ as our conscience. We feel that things are wrong or amiss through the Light of Christ; then when we ask in faith, we can receive answers on how to best resolve those questions through inspiration from the Holy Ghost. Both forms of communication could be considered personal revelation to each recipient. The Light of Christ and the Holy Ghost appear to work in tandem in a spiritually synergistic pattern. Many in the church, including leaders, feel that the Holy Ghost is able to work in and through the Light of Christ.

> For behold, the Spirit of Christ is given to every man, that he may know good from evil; wherefore, I show unto you the way to judge; for every thing which inviteth a man to do good, and to persuade to believe in Christ, is sent forth by the power and gift of Christ; wherefore ye man know with a perfect knowledge it is of God. (Moroni 7:16)

> "It is important for a teacher or a missionary or a parent to know that the Holy Ghost can work through the Light of Christ." (Body K. Packer, *Ensign*, April 2005)

> "By using the Light of Christ to discern and choose what is right, we can be led to an even greater light: the gift of the Holy Ghost." (Robert D. Hales, *Ensign*, May 2002)

One of my early recollections was having a frightening nightmare as a small child. I still remember it vividly. I must have screamed in fright during the night. My grandmother woke me up. I was crying, and she took me in her arms, hugged me, and comforted me. She got a bowl of some of my favorite rice pudding that was left over from dinner, and I sat on her lap as she spoon-fed me. She told me that we were safe in our house because Jesus was watching over us. I felt it was true then, and I still believe it now. I was comforted in both body and soul and went peacefully back to bed, assured of the divine reality that Jesus does watch over us. (James E. Faust, GC, Oct 2000)

I recall an August morning when I was 10 or 11 years old, following a night of unusually strong winds, being greeted by friends as I left my home. They were obviously excited by something and inquired, "Did you hear the wind last night?"

When I said that I had, they proceeded to tell me what they had discovered—the wind had blown down sections of the fencing surrounding the Lyonses' home. I could not understand why this would cause so much excitement and asked them to explain the significance.

They responded with even greater enthusiasm: "We have access to the apple trees!"

I was still very cautious and asked, "But what about Mr. Lyons?"

"Mr. and Mrs. Lyons are not at home; they are away visiting relatives."

"Where is the dog?" I probed.

"The family has placed him in boarding kennels," came the reply.

My friends had certainly carried out detailed research. So, reassured by their words, we headed for our target with all haste. Entering the grounds we climbed trees and hurriedly plucked fruit, filling our pockets and also the space between our shirts and our bodies. My heart was pounding and my pulse racing since I feared that any moment the dog or Mr. Lyons, or both, would appear in the garden and apprehend us. We ran from the scene of our trespass to a secluded place in a nearby wooded area and, after regaining our composure, began to consume the apples.

It was August, and the apples were not yet ripe enough to eat. In fact, they had a very bitter taste, but the tartness of these green apples did not deter us as we enthusiastically consumed our spoils, acting out of a compulsion I cannot now explain. After devouring a significant number, I contented myself with taking a bite out of each remaining apple and throwing the remnants of the fruit into the nearby bushes. The frivolity diminished as our bodies began to gradually react to the invasion they had experienced. The chemical reaction between my gastric juices and the unripe apples caused me to experience stomach cramps and to feel nauseated. As I sat regretting what I had done, I realized that a feeling within me was producing even more discomfort than the unripe apples.

The greater discomfort resulted from the realization that what I had done was wrong.

When my friends had proposed that we invade the garden, I had felt uncomfortable but lacked the courage to say no and so suppressed my feelings. Now, after the deed had been accomplished, I was filled with remorse. To my regret, I had ignored the promptings warning me of the error of my actions. (Kenneth Johnson, GC, Oct 2002)

———•◆•———

I remembered the phone call when my daughter called to let us know Brian had proposed. While we were watching *Fried Green Tomatoes*, Marita called with so much excitement in her voice that I knew she was engaged even before she told me. Before she said good-bye she said, "Mom, it was Brian after all!"

She was referring to a dream she had when she was four years old and saw how it would be on her wedding day. She had described her dress to me back then and the car they drove off in after the temple wedding. She knew from the dream that her husband would be named Brian.

I wrote down what she told me of her dream and saved it all of those years. (A peer)

"... I will pour out my spirit upon all flesh; and your sons and your daughters shall prophesy ... your young men shall see visions." (Joel 2:28)

———•◆•———

I remember as a child listening to the testimonies given by adults in my ward. Those testimonies entered my heart and inspired my soul. Wherever I go throughout the world—no matter the language, no matter the culture—I thrill to hear the testimonies of the Saints. (Joseph B. Wirthlin, GC, Oct 2000)

———•◆•———

*A Primary-aged girl in our ward was bearing her testimony about an experience with prayer. She was only 8-9 years old:*

I had been looking forward to the bike parade for a long time and couldn't wait to participate. The day for the bike parade finally came and I was so excited! Then my dad told me that grandpa was really sick and our family needed to go visit him. He was so sick that this might be the last time we would see him alive, dad told me. I told him that I only wanted to go to the bike parade and didn't want to visit grandpa.

*The bike parade was an annual activity started by my wife, when she was the Primary president. This Presidency desired to help celebrate the July 24th pioneers. So few people owned wagons any more that they felt, to be all inclusive, it would be best for the youth to decorate wagons, bikes, trikes, and scooters, etc. This activity was very popular with the ward children and other neighborhood kids who all loved the police escorts, cotton candy, snow cones, face painting, etc.*

My dad told me that it was more important to visit grandpa and that was final! I went up to my room mad and frustrated. I decided to pray about my problem.
I little voice said to me, "**Just relax**"; so I thought to myself "what do I do to relax … well, I usually read a book."
So I found a book and started reading it and I felt better. After awhile, my dad came to my room and told me that the plans had changed and that we were going to see grandpa the next night. So I got to go to the bike parade and to see grandpa and everything was okay.

*This innocent story of personal revelation touched me more than most. I thanked this young woman a decade later, before she left for her foreign mission, for her testimony. I explained how much her experience had touched me and how it teaches us that our Heavenly Father is aware of everybody's issues and problems, no matter how old or young they are. She thanked me for reminding her of an experience she had forgotten. I suggested she record it in her missionary journal so that she wouldn't forget it again.*

————————◆◆◆————————

*Another young girl was sharing an experience during her sacrament meeting talk recently:*

I wanted to make a really special Mother's Day card for my Mom and I finally got it all done and put it away until Mother's Day. When it was Mother's Day I couldn't find the card anywhere. I looked all over the place and could not find it! I was very disappointed and went into the kitchen and told my Mom about not being able to find the special card I made for her.

She suggested I pray about my situation. So I went to my room and said a prayer to help me find the lost card. I had a thought come to my mind to "**read a book**" and that confused me. I thought my brain was messing with me. Then I decided to go ahead and find a book to read. I grabbed a book and opened it up to a page and there was the Mother's Day card I had made!

---

The first time I had a major experience with the Holy Ghost was when I was ten years old. My dad taught the plan of salvation with a flannel board. It seemed magical to me, and the room filled thick with a permeating feeling that told me it was true.

At the time, my best friend was the daughter of a pastor. I excitedly told my friend about how we lived in heaven before we came, and how there were three heavens after we die, with the best people going to the Celestial Kingdom.

The next day I visited my friend, we were playing downstairs, and her father came half-way down the stairs, so he towered over me. Among other things, he practically shouted that there was only one heaven and one hell, and that I was a very confused little girl. This did not shake me except that I was afraid he would not let me be friends with his daughter anymore. Luckily, we stayed friends, and I kept my budding testimony of the gospel of Jesus Christ because I had felt it, and no yelling or name calling could remove what I knew in my heart to be true. (A relative)

---

I was driving home after finishing a three-day sales trip and needed to grab some lunch before traveling three more hours to arrive at my final destination. I came upon a tiny town in Wyoming called Marbleton. It is truly a one-horse town. There was one small gas station with limited food.

I ordered some fried chicken and sat down in one of five empty tables with my back to the other four tables. I was tired and feeling a little down, wishing I was already home. I was staring out the window and eating slowly.

Then all of a sudden and to my surprise a small boy climbed up onto the chair next to me at my table and exclaimed, "Hi, I'm J J!"

Following that a little girl hopped into the chair on the other side of me and said, "Hi, I'm K K!"

Then another young girl came and sat in the last chair and said, "Hi, I'm Crystal."

I replied, "Oh, I thought you would be G G."

Then this intelligent smaller girl straightened me right out stating, "I'm K K and I'm four. That's J J and he's three. Crystal is five and she's not our sister—silly!"

I was quite surprised that she caught my humor.

"Well how did you three get here?"

"In 'da Durango!"

"Who was driving the Durango?"

K K, the obvious spokesperson for the young group, replied, "Jamie."

"Well, where's Jamie?"

They were not sure where Jamie was. We had a full table and I was now alert and happy amongst these small earthly angels. They were entertaining, delightful, and bright. Jamie didn't show up, so I helped them unwrap their corn dogs while saying, "Let's get eating." So we ate together and visited.

As we finished eating, Jamie finally showed up and apologized. I explained that I loved little children and that they love me. We were fine and I told her that her little ones really cheered me up and made my day.

She thanked me as we parted. I was alert and happier, than before lunch, for the drive home. I believe there are millions of babies and small children who are earthly angels, in one way or another, who minister to us older folks through various ways. (Journal 5/23/2010)

> "... Suffer the little children to come unto me, and forbid them not, for of such is the kingdom of God." (Mark 10:14)

> When I was a little girl I participated in a program here in the Tabernacle. At that time an impression came to me that I have never forgotten, even though I did not understand it then. I was filled with an awareness that sometime I would stand before a vast congregation of the Church in this building. I thought this vision of my childhood was realized in the 1974 Relief Society conference when I was sustained as the general president of the Relief Society. But now I feel certain that *this* is the day I saw. (Barbara B. Smith, GC, April 1984)

During kindergarten recess I was telling a girl the Joseph Smith story. This was in California. Then our family moved to Utah. Years later, who should be in my chemistry class—that same girl I told the Joseph Smith story to in kindergarten! She had joined the church. I have no idea if I had any influence over her, but I was sure surprised!

In Utah there was another primary-aged girl that I shared the Gospel with. I ran into her in college and she was on a dance scholarship. She had not joined the church. However, later that year she did become a member. Again, I don't know what influence I had on her, if any. (A relative)

Now, we will compare the word unto a seed. Now, if ye give place, that a seed may be planted in your heart, behold if it be a true seed ... behold, it will begin to swell within your breasts ... this is a good seed ... the word is good, for it beginneth to enlarge my soul; ... (Alma 32:28)

---

We were meeting in a rented building for church in Germany. We had to haul everything in and then take everything out afterwards because we couldn't leave anything in the building. There were only tables and chairs there for us to use. I was serving as the Primary president and we still went to Primary during the week back then.

I sat my stack of books and papers on top of my car and loaded my two young children in then drove off. When we arrived at the church I did not have any materials. I asked my son, who was 7 at the time, if he didn't remember me carrying a stack of books and manuals to our car. He confirmed that I did have a bunch of books in my arms.

My seven year old son said, "Mom, we need to pray to Heavenly Father so we can find your books." Here was my son, teaching me again.

I said, "You're the one with the faith, will you say the prayer?"

He gave a very nice prayer, like children often do. I had the thought to retrace our route and dreaded what we'd find! I pictured finding the books all scattered and torn, lying in a gutter.

As we drove back, my son exclaimed, "Look Mom, there's your books and He even stacked them for you!" On the sidewalk in a perfect pile were all my materials. (A friend)

*We don't know exactly who stacked the books so orderly, though it must have been either a considerate earthly angel or a heavenly being who was inspired to answer this child's faithful prayer.*

---

*Our daughter shared the following:*

When I was eight years old we were sitting in Primary and singing the songs.
A voice said to me, "**Amber, you have a beautiful voice**."
I looked around to see who said that and all the other children were singing. I looked at the adults and they were all singing and none of them were looking at me. I did not realize until later that this was the first time I heard the Holy Ghost speak to me.
*Amber truly does have an angelic voice.*

*Our daughter Amber was asked to sing His Hands, by Jenny Jordan Frogley & Kenneth Cope, at a recent sacrament meeting where a young friend was reporting his mission. She sang angelically and perfectly as the audience felt the love and charity of our Savior portrayed in this beautiful song. There was nary a dry eye in the audience. The Spirit was very strong as the song was a special witness of our Savior Jesus Christ. (Journal 8/9/18)*

---

Joe Lee sat quietly in conference listening to the people who spoke. He couldn't understand all they said, but he loved singing the songs with them. He thought how wonderful it would be if he could go up on the stand and tell everyone how exciting it was to be a member of the Church. Joe was an eight-year-old Korean-Hawaiian boy who had just been baptized. Joe and his mother were members of the Church, but his father had no interest in it at all. Joe had such a good feeling that he wanted his father to become a member of the Church too.
That night after conference Joe told his mother the thoughts that had come to him during the meeting and later she told Brother Murphy, who was conducting the conference, what her young son had said. During the next session of conference Joe suddenly heard his name called. Brother Murphy was inviting him to go up to the pulpit and speak. Joe quickly stood up, and while he was walking up

to the pulpit, someone on the stand hurried to get a little chair. ...

Joe stood on the chair and spoke in the microphone. A breathless hush came over everyone as Joe began, "Aloha everybody!" He paused only a moment. Then in a clear calm voice he went on, "I know that Jesus is God's own Son. I know that Joseph Smith is a prophet."

Tears filled many eyes when Joe said, "My father is not a member of the Church. Please pray that he will become one so he can take Mother and our family to the temple. Then we will all be together in the next world."

Joe's prayer and the prayers of others were answered a short time later when Joe's father was baptized. One of the happiest days of Joe's life was about a year later when his father took his family to the temple at Laie, where they were sealed as a family. (True Stories from Hawaii, *Friend*, July 1973)

----------◆----------

When Tate and Morgan were little we were staying at my in-law's home, taking care of their youngest child while they were out of town. But this story took place when we were there alone, just the three of us.

While in the basement, Tate had seen me lock the bathroom door and pull it shut, to keep little Morgan out of the bathroom (I kept a Q-tip close by to open the door). Upstairs, Tate followed my example when he locked a door and pulled it shut, but Morgan was locked inside and the door did not open with a Q-tip. Instead it required a special tool that could turn the tiny knob inside the door. Morgan was locked in a toy room by herself which was okay, because she seemed content in there while we were searching for the special tool. But I was worried because I couldn't check on her to make sure she wasn't choking on a small toy, etc. So while we were looking for the special tool I would talk to her through the door and asked her if she was ok. The funny thing is that she would always respond with a calm, "no," but hearing her answer was all I needed to know that she was ok.

At this point Morgan had been locked in the room by herself for about 30 minutes, which is a long time for a tiny girl. We definitely needed help. I knew there had to be a tool in the house somewhere, we just couldn't find it. Then

I had an idea. I knew Tate had gotten us into this predicament and that he knew it too. I told Tate we should say a prayer asking Heavenly Father to help us find the tool. As we knelt down together right outside that locked door, Tate said a prayer asking Heavenly Father for help. I had faith that Heavenly Father would answer Tate's first sincere prayer requesting help. As soon as we finished the prayer, Tate stood up and walked straight down the hall and into my father-in-law's bathroom. He walked right up to the sink, opened the middle drawer, and pulled out a tiny screwdriver and asked me if the tool would work. It was the perfect size to open the door.

While I had faith that God would answer Tate's prayer, I was still amazed that Tate found the perfect tool immediately following the prayer. It was a defining moment in Tate's young life. A story that I hope he'll never forget. I believe he was about 5 years-old at the time. (A relative)

---

*Elder David B Haight shares this youthful experience:*

My father died when I was nine years old, leaving my mother to raise our family. My mother was wise. She believed that boys and girls should have things to do. Some of my chores were chopping wood for the cook stove, raking leaves, and mowing the lawn.

Mother knew we needed to have more to do in our lives that just work and play. Together we read the great stories from the Bible. She taught us to sing, to enjoy church, and to pray.

Mother always kept a cow so that her sons would have what she called "some real responsibility." This included milking the cow every morning and every night, pitching hay down into the stall for the cow to eat, and watering her morning and night at a nearby stream. Unless we did these chores, the cow would be hungry and thirsty.

There were times when I would be a little late getting home, and I'd wish I didn't have to take care of that cow. One evening when I returned home, I found that she had broken down the fence and run away. I looked in all of the usual places, but I could not find her. I looked everywhere imaginable—but no cow.

It started to grow dark, and I was desperate. I knew that my mother would be worried if she knew the cow was lost. We sold milk to some of our neighbors, and I could picture them waiting for me to take them their fresh milk.

How well I recall that evening! I had been taught to pray, and I knew I could ask the Lord for help. There was a little clump of bushes near the canal, and so I took off my cap, got down on my knees, told the Lord my problem, and asked Him to help me find our cow.

After my prayer, I started walking down the canal bank. And only a few yards from where I had prayed, I found our cow. She was almost hidden in the tall willows by the canal because she was about the same color as the willows. I was grateful my prayer had been answered and that our Heavenly Father had guided my footsteps down the canal bank to where she was.

The many nights my mother knelt by my bed to teach me how to pray helped me learn to talk to our Father in heaven. Ever since, the night I prayed for help by that clump of bushes, I have continued to pray for His guidance. And I know the Lord answers our prayers. (*Friend*, Mar 1973)

———————◆———————

And about the time Ammaron hid up the records unto the Lord, he came unto me. (I being about ten years of age, and I began to be learned somewhat after the manner of the learning of my people) and Ammaron said unto me: I perceive that thou art a sober child, and art quick to observe. (Mormon 1:2)

*As a young boy, Mormon was entrusted with the holy records. That is an impressive young man! Ammaron did instruct Mormon to wait until he was twenty four before he retrieved them from a mountain side. This sounds somewhat similar to another young man's experience involving sacred records hidden in a hillside.*

*Another young man, Joseph Smith, also had a challenging assignment to guard and protect sacred records from many who attempted to steal them from him. Ironically it was Mormon's son Moroni, now an angel leading the following event:* "I made an attempt to take them out, but was forbidden by the messenger, and was again informed that the time for bringing them forth had not yet arrived; neither would it, until four years from that time ..." (*JSH* 1:53)

Our son is six and autistic. He was tired of living in an apartment; he wanted to live in a home with a backyard for his special activities.

He told us that he prayed for a new home within 60 days so that he could have the things he needs. We had an idea of what we wanted in a home and those homes were always out of our price range. A house came on the market that fit our list to a "T" and that was within our price range. We made an offer and it was the only offer. We didn't have to haggle in a bidding war, even though the housing market was tight. They accepted our offer. We were able to close and move into our new home within six weeks of our son's faithful prayer.

This experience really boosted our son's faith in prayers and he prays all the time for things. I have been trying to teach our children to pray when they're: thankful, lonely, scared, confused, or have a question.

Our autistic son gets very frustrated, exclaiming, "I can't control myself!" Now he prays to Heavenly Father to calm down and to reduce his levels of frustration. And those prayers really do help. (A peer)

I was just a young girl when I gained my testimony. I was eight or nine and we were singing in sacrament meeting. The song was "I know that my Redeemer Lives" *(Hymns, no. 136)*.

I was just sitting there and started crying. The Spirit just ran through my body and was so powerful. It went through my soul. I recognized the Spirit and could identify with it and I knew what had happened.

My mom looked at me and asked, "What's wrong honey?" (A Peer)

"Each of us may feel the influence of the Holy Ghost differently. His promptings will be felt in different degrees of intensity according to our individual needs and circumstances." (Robert D. Hales, GC, April 2016)

I was so excited to move into our new house when I was around five years old. I remember the smell of newness from the floor covering and the fresh paint. And, of course, what little girl wouldn't be in love with the white kitchen countertops that sparkled with gold flecks!

Most little girls love jewelry as well. I had a cheap silver ring with fake diamonds set in the pattern of a flower. It must have come from a vending machine because the band was adjustable on the back by squeezing it together or pulling it apart. But, oh, how I loved my sparkly ring!

One late afternoon while playing out on the graveled area near the shed, the ring slipped off my finger. It must have fallen off a few moments before I noticed it because when I looked around within a few feet of where I was standing, I could not find it. Gravel can come in many colors, but this gravel was a nice gray color that even sparkled in the sunshine. The rocks were certainly camouflaging my ring! The sun was starting to set and I had searched for what must have felt like an eternity to a small child.

I resorted to crying and thought, 'I am never going to find my ring!'

At that moment, I believe the Holy Ghost brought to my mind a story I had probably heard in Primary about someone losing something, praying for help, and then finding it. So I said what must have been a very simple prayer.

I opened my eyes after saying, "Amen," and looked into the gravel near my feet and saw my ring! Do you think I believed that Heavenly Father answers prayers? You bet I did! That was the beginning of many prayers that have been answered throughout my life. (A friend)

———•◆•———

As John started down the hill toward home, fog mixed with smoke rolled over him in smothering waves. The frightened ten-year-old boy sat down to try to light the lantern Mr. West had loaned him to use in just such an emergency, but the dampness blew out the flame of the matches. John stood up, pulled his oilskin coat tighter about him, and tried to see ahead through the fog and darkness of the late afternoon.

Earlier that day John's mother had sent him with a basket of food to the home of an old shepherd who lived alone about three miles northeast … It was the first time Mother had ever let John go on this errand alone, and he was both proud and excited. But he had stayed at Mr. West's home too long, and when a dark cloud blacked out the sun before a soft rain started, John jumped up quickly and said goodbye to his old friend.

Mr. West offered to walk back with the boy to Milnthorpe, but John shook his head. "This is my first trip alone," he explained, "and my mother wouldn't let me come alone again if you had to take me home."

Now, John wished that Mr. West were with him. He imagined all kinds of strange sounds and movements in the fog that closed in thick around him. He had no idea where he was. Suddenly he came to a big iron gate that marked the end of the road, and from beyond the gate came the frightening growl of a dog.

John was almost paralyzed with fright. Then he remembered that his mother had told him that God was always near, even though he might sometimes think that he was all alone.

John dropped down to his knees and asked for help. As he did so, all his fear left; and he was not surprised a few minutes later to hear a voice call out of the mist, "Johnny, I've come to take you home." It was Mr. West!

The young boy was John Taylor, who became the third president of the Church. Although he lived to be eighty years old, he never forgot the quick answer to his prayer as a frightened boy on that lonesome foggy evening. (A Voice from the Mist, *Friend*, 1972)

---

This happened to me when I was twelve years old. My family was living in Phoenix, Arizona. My two older sisters had recently married and had left to start their lives. My parents purchased a business and our family was moving from my childhood home to Yuma, Arizona. I would be starting school at a different school in a new community. I had attended my previous school from Kindergarten through 7th grade. My world had been very comfortable, safe, and secure. Starting a new life in a new community and new school was extremely scary for me.

My first day at my new school was challenging for me. I knew no one and I felt very alone. I went to my 1st Period class, Social Studies with Mr. Riley. I noticed a boy sitting across from me, wearing an Alta-Ski Utah shirt. As I looked at the shirt and the boy a very distinct and clear thought came into my head. **"That boy is just like you. He is a Mormon. He holds the Aaronic Priesthood and is a deacon just like you."**

I, being extremely shy, did not say anything at this point; however as the year went by Jimmy Estes and I became friends. We rode the same bus home and I would often help him with his Science homework. He was an answer to a prayer that I likely never uttered, but the Lord knew my heart and what I needed. Tragically at the end of the school year he lost both of his parents in a plane crash and moved away to live with his older sister to attend high school.

Years later he returned to Yuma and to this day, I still refer to that first spiritual experience as the *"Jimmy Estes Test"* and use it as a litmus test to ensure that the promptings I receive are comparable to what happened with my friend Jimmy Estes. Here, as a child, I learned that the Spirit is real and that God uses it to bless his children with the things they need, no matter how small and trivial we may think they are. (A relative)

"Now, we have the Holy Ghost….There is nothing mysterious about it to people who learn to be guided by the Spirit. The voice of the Lord has come into my mind, in sentences, in answer to prayer." (Marion G. Romney, GC, Oct 1961)

Eleven-year-old John Roothoof lived in Rotterdam, Holland. He had once been happy going to school and church, playing with his friends, and doing all the things a boy enjoys. Then, without warning, a painful eye disease caused him to lose his sight. No longer could he go to school or read. …. Each day was filled with darkness and suffering.

Word reached the Latter-day Saints in Holland that President Joseph F. Smith was coming to visit them. John thought about this for a long time, and then he said to his mother, "The prophet has the most power of any man on earth. If you take me with you to the meeting he can look into my eyes, I believe I'll be healed."

At the close of the meeting the next Sunday, President Smith went to the back of the small chapel to greet the people and shake hands with each one. Sister Roothoof helped John, his eyes bandaged, go with the others to speak to their beloved leader.

President Smith took the blind boy by the hand and then with great tenderness lifted the bandages and looked into John's pain-filled eyes. The prophet blessed John and promised him he would see again.

Arriving home, John's mother took the bandages from his eyes so she could bathe them as the doctors had told her to do. As she did so, John cried out with joy, "Oh Mamma, my eyes are well. I can see fine now—and far too. And I can't feel any pain!" (*Friend,* Aug 1973)

---

Back in the day when we use to rent videos we made a lot of trips back and forth to the video stores. When the VCRs first came out, one had to rent the VCR machine along with the movies! It was a cold, snowy weekend so we decided to rent several family films to enjoy during the storm. Our two young daughters came with us because it was their turn to help with the choices. We found some good-looking movies and headed back up the steep hill to get back to our community. Halfway up this long, steep hill the car completely died. I was able to use the momentum of the vehicle to pull it over, into the deep snow on the side of the road. There were no businesses or homes along the incline on either side of the road, just lots of snow covering steep snowy hillsides.

I got out and couldn't find anything wrong, such as a dropped drive line or leaking fluid.

Sometimes a broken water pump will stop your car on the spot and leak a lot of anti-freeze. I checked the engine and there were no piston rods sticking through the block and the battery was still good. Narrowing down the mechanical culprits and the few breakdowns that will halt a vehicle, I surmised, "It must be the timing chain and we're not going anywhere. I feel like what we need to do is say a prayer and ask Heavenly Father for help."

Our daughters excitedly exclaimed, "We already prayed Daddy! In fact, we said 2 prayers!!"

I replied, "Well that ought to do it. The faith of a child is powerful."

Just as I was complimenting our young girls for remembering to pray, some lights appeared behind our car. A new Suburban, with a young family, pulled up to see if we needed help. I explained how our car was non-drivable and that we would need a tow truck. Obviously, we had no working heater, were getting quite cold, and desired to get our young ones home. They had plenty of room in their spacious vehicle and were able to take all of us home, which was about 4 miles.

It was quite snowy and cold so upon arriving home we offered our rescuers hot chocolate, which they readily accepted. Then they told us what they were doing that evening. They had been shopping and were ready to go home and get their young ones out of the storm and into bed. The Spirit told them to go the opposite way and they did not know why they were driving away from home, until they saw our car. The Spirit confirmed to them that our stalled car was the reason they were prompted to drive in the wrong direction.

During our daughters' prayers for help, the car (with lots of extra room) was driving up, led by the Holy Spirit, to lend assistance. More often than not, our prayers are answered through *"earthly angels."* (Journal 1/21/1996)

"Children are a heritage from the Lord: and the fruit of the womb is his reward." (Psalm 127:3)

Our young daughters had borrowed a video tape from their grandparents and the youngest one put the VHS tape in the wrong machine. The tape became totally jammed and every button they pushed did not work. No matter what they tried to free the video tape from the machine's tight grasp it didn't work.

My older daughter began yelling at the younger one; telling her "You ruined grandma's movie and now they can't even watch it!"

My little one came upstairs crying and explaining what had happened through her teary eyes. Then she said, "I'm going to pray about it." So she said a prayer and then went downstairs and pushed one button. The tape came right out, undamaged! Afterwards she said to me, "Prayer really does work, doesn't it mommy?" (Our friend)

The summer was almost over when on Saturday morning, Dad said, "I know a fishing hole I think we'll visit this afternoon." The boys' eyes lighted up in happy anticipation and right after lunch they all started for Willow Creek. When they reached the stream, Dad turned off the main gravel road onto a steep dirt one.

The road was narrow and full of curves but finally widened out along the creek bank. After Dad helped the boys untangle their lines and bait their fishhooks, he went a short distance downstream to find a good fishing hole.

James and Joseph didn't notice the sun clouded over until a loud clap of thunder startled them. ... heavy rain began to fall. They hurried back to the car, wet and frightened.

The downpour of rain had turned the dirt road into a sea of mud. Dad tried to plow through it but the wheels began to spin out of control. Each spin edged the car closer to the embankment.

The anxious moments ticked slowly by while they all thought of their comfortable home. Father suggested that the boys kneel on the seats of the car while they all prayed for help.

The rain continued to splatter the windows of the car until it seemed as if the car were on an isolated island. But soon, above the noise of the pelting storm, they heard the roar of a motor and saw a four-wheel-drive jeep come into view.

The jeep pulled up alongside the stalled car, and a man jumped out. It was an answer to prayer when he called, "We knew someone needed help in this storm!" (*Friend,* June 1974)

---

When I was five I was sick and I don't know what I was sick with. I had a high fever. I got a blessing from my dad and my grandpa. I remember receiving the blessing and my fever/sickness seemed to just go away. This was the first time I recognized the Spirit. I knew the Gospel was true. I found a belief for the power of the priesthood. (A young friend)

---

My little sister and I were walking home from school, from the bus stop. Then we took this shortcut and started running. I had this extreme prompt to "*STOP!*" dead in my tracks. It was like a voice inside my mind and also there was a force to my body or all my senses to stop. I stopped immediately and my sister stopped right behind me. A second later a sharp lightning bolt hit the path right in front of us. The lightning bolt looked as big around as when I hold my arm in a circle. It felt like a dream or an out-of-body experience because it was so bizarre!

We ran even faster all the way home and ran inside the house. We were so shocked and didn't talk to anyone about it for 2 weeks. Whenever I start doubting the Gospel or wondering if there is a God; I go back to that experience when I was 8-years old and it has carried me forward all my life. (A friend)

"God sent his holy angel to stop us by the way." (Alma 36:6)

————————————

My friend shared a neat story with me.  She said, My young daughter and I were waiting to cross a street.  My daughter stepped off the curb and then she stepped back up onto the sidewalk.  Just then a vehicle came speeding by and he was right next to the gutter! That made my heart jump.
"Why did you step back onto the curb?"
"Because you told me to Mommy."
"But honey, I didn't say a word." (A close friend)

————————————

Josiah was eight years old when he began to reign, and he reigned thirty and one years in Jerusalem. And his mother's name was Jedidah, the daughter of Adaiah of Boscath. And he did that which was right in the sight of the LORD, and walked in all the way of David his father, and turned not aside to the right hand or to the left. (2 Kings, 22:1-2)

————————————

My sister and I had very small toy bears we were throwing up in the air after church. Then we would have fun finding them on the extra large lawn. I lost my bear and couldn't find it. Dad yelled for us to go, so we got in the car and left. That night I prayed to God to help me find my bear. They were only about 1" tall. The next time we were at church I found my bear and thanked God for helping me find it. (A family member)

————————————

Lealand and John were hot and tired. A large feedbox stood near the corral … they decided to lift the heavy lid and see what was inside. The boys were fascinated when they saw crickets. 'Let's catch them,' one of the boys suggested.
The feedbox … was barely large enough for the two boys to squeeze inside. But it didn't take them long to slip of their shoes … and help each other into the box. Just at that moment a cow … nearby … tossed her head and flipped the

lid back over the box. A lock on the outside caught, and Lealand and John were imprisoned.

Except for a thread-like crack ...the box was airtight ... they frantically called for help ... no one heard them.

Then eight-year-old John said, 'Oh, Lealand, let's pray. No one else can hear us, but our Heavenly Father can.' The boys took turns whispering desperate prayers.

A few minutes later Lealand's four-year-old brother, Wesley, noticed the shoes on the ground ... he climbed up on his little wagon to see if the older boys were hiding from him inside the box. Somehow he managed to undo the lock.

... They were almost too weak to climb out, but when the fresh air rushed in, they felt a new surge of strength. Wet with perspiration, they got out of the box and staggered gratefully toward home." (The Feedbox, *Friend,* Jun 1974)

"Take heed that ye despise not one of these little ones; for I say unto you, That in heaven their angels do always behold the face of my Father which is in heaven. (Matt. 18:10)

*This is a fascinating story about great faith in God, a prayer of two young boys, and the answer that was literally lifesaving coming as their curious little earthly angel brother, age 4! Surely the toddler was led and inspired by the Holy Spirit and/or an angel.*

A good friend and I played together quite often until he moved to California. There was a construction area behind his house that had a sandy steep slope that was between five and ten feet high. It had been just a hill, but construction vehicles had hauled away soil from it to create a cliff that stretched about fifty feet. Many of the neighborhood kids often played there.

One Saturday, Tom and I took a bunch of toy cars to play at the cliff. It was threatening rain, so we found a sheet of plywood and leaned it against the cliff to form a sheltered play area. We got busy making all kinds of roads in the sand. The wall was sandy stuff, so it was easy to carve roads for our cars in the wall. We made switchbacks, caves, and mines for "our construction vehicles."

It started to rain. Suddenly I got this eerie feeling, like something was not right. I asked Tom if he thought everything was okay. I could see that he was sensing something too, but he figured it was okay. Besides, the rain was picking up; if we left our shelter we'd get wet. So we continued playing. A few moments later I felt it again. Tom did too. We both thought, "We had better clean up and go."

Somehow we both sensed that urgency was required. Instead of putting the cars nicely into the container as we usually did; we grabbed them and chucked them in as fast as we could. We then darted out from under the plywood. Tom was just behind me. His foot was just inches from the plywood when a sizeable section of soil on the wall above the plywood broke loose and completely buried the plywood!

We didn't stop running but made a beeline for Tom's house. His neighbor was working in his backyard and said he watched what had happened. He said, "It's very dangerous over there and I'm glad you boys are safe. That large amount of dirt that buried the plywood would have likely killed you both!"

We went into Tom's basement and straightened out all our cars while our hearts were still pounding. I'm grateful for the warning of the Spirit that kept us safe on that day, and I'm glad we finally listened. (A relative)

———— •◆• ————

There was a huge extra warmth surrounding the day of my baptism. After my baptism we had a family dinner. I had taken a large portion of Jell-O salad, with the ball-like noodles.

"Those are frog eyes!" my brother teased. Thus the name *frog eye salad*.

My grandma confirmed that was really the name of this salad that became very unappealing to me.

Upon my Aunt noticing my reluctance to eat her salad, I told her I was simply saving the best for last. Oh, how awful and sour I felt. With a low disappointment the Spirit hit me. It was only a tiny lie, to save my Aunt's feelings. But even then, at eight years old, the Spirit was teaching what to do and NOT do to keep myself clean and close to Him. (A relative)

My wife, Tamara, was teaching the five-year olds in Primary. This Sunday their lesson was on prayer. Little Vic had the hiccups and his problem was disrupting the class. Children were laughing and making comments every time he hiccupped.

Vic said, "Why don't we say a prayer to make my hiccups go away?" Vic wanted to say the pray and when he was done, the hiccups were all gone. The class was back to order. What an awesome object lesson!

When I was very little I got a circus wagon for Christmas. It had wooden animals with plastic legs that were connected by brads so they moved. I loved that wagon and it made me want real animals. I remember leaving the wagon in my sisters' room. I prayed really hard that God would change those animals into real animals. In the morning I found the circus wagon just as I left it, unchanged. I learned that sometimes God says no when it is not the best for us. (A family member)

Some years ago, some close friends of ours loaned us their cabin in Island Park, Idaho. When we arrived at the cabin, we found that the key that we had been given to unlock the front door didn't work. We tried to undo windows and pry open screens, all to no avail.

Suddenly our son Steven, who was about seven years old at the time, shouted to us that he had just successfully opened the front door. Steven, with a big grin on his face, was standing triumphantly inside the front doorway. I was amazed. I asked him how he did that.

He responded with wonderful, childlike spontaneity: "I bowed my head and prayed. When I looked up, my eyes spotted this big rock by the front steps, and I thought, 'There is a key under that rock.' And sure enough there it was." The prayer of a child had been heard. I thank the Lord for his mother who had taught him to find keys in moments of crisis. (L. Edward Brown, GC, April 1997)

*In first Samuel 1 we read about a sorrowful woman, Hannah, who was barren. Hannah was: provoked, not eating, weeping, grieving in her heart, in bitterness of soul, feeling afflicted, and forgotten. While outside the temple, on their yearly visit, she made a promise to the Lord; she would give her child unto the Lord for the rest of her child's life. Hannah's barren*

29

womb was blessed and she finally cherished and nurtured her own baby boy, whom she named Samuel. I cannot begin to fathom the emotions that ran through Hannah's heart, mind, and soul, before, during, and after Samuel's birth. After Samuel was weaned, she took him to the temple and turned him over to the prophet Eli.

*As a young man, Samuel had the following experience:*

... Samuel was laid down to sleep ... the Lord called **Samuel**: and he answered, Here am I. And he ran unto Eli, and said, Here am I; for thou didst call me. And he said, I called not; lie down again ... the Lord called yet again, **Samuel**. And Samuel arose and went to Eli, and said, Here am I ... And he answered, I called not, my son, lie down again.
Now Samuel did not yet know the Lord ... And the Lord called Samuel again the third time. And he arose and went to Eli, and said, Here am I; for thou didst call me. And Eli perceived that the Lord had called the child.
Therefore Eli said to Samuel, Go, lie down ... if he call thee ... say, Speak, Lord; for thy servant heareth ... And the Lord came, and stood, and called ... **Samuel, Samuel**. ... (1 Samuel 3:3-10)

*This was the beginning of Samuel's call to be a future prophet over Israel. Samuel was a young boy ministering for Eli the priest. The Lord gave Samuel a very difficult assignment "And Samuel feared to show Eli the vision." (1 Samuel 3:15)*

*The young lad did reveal to his master a destructive vision, one that would bring down the house of Eli. In the near future Eli, his two wicked sons, and a daughter-in-law all died. The prophecy given to Samuel as a boy was pronounced per Eli's request and subsequently fulfilled.*

*Now as for the blessings from sacrificing a son unto the service of the Lord: Eli the priest blessed Elkanah and Hannah; Hannah went on and gave birth to three more boys and two girls, Samuel became a great prophet, and Samuel would eventually ordain King Saul and King David.*

*We would all do well to learn a great lesson from Hannah in remembering to praise the Lord with gratitude after our prayers are answered.*

And Hannah prayed, and said, My heart rejoiceth in the Lord, mine horn is exalted in the Lord: my mouth is enlarged over mine enemies; because I rejoice in thy salvation. There is none holy as the LORD: for there is none beside thee: neither is there any rock like our God. (1 Samuel 2:1-2)

━━━━●◆●━━━━

Another child in our day had a similar experience: Julina [Smith] had three daughters but no sons, and so she went before the Lord and, like Hannah of old, "vowed a vow." Her promise: that if the Lord would give her a son, "she would do all in her power to help him be a credit to the Lord and to his father." The Lord hearkened to her prayers, and she kept her promise to him; and he also manifest to her, before the birth of the man child, that her son [Joseph F. Smith] would be called to serve in the Council of the Twelve. (Bruce R. McConkie, *Ensign*, Aug 1972)

━━━━●◆●━━━━

*Spencer W. Kimball shares a prophecy that his father made:*

"Spencer, your father was a prophet. He made a prediction that has literally come to pass ... Your father talked with me at the corral one evening, I had brought a load of pumpkins for his pigs. You (Spencer) were just a little boy and you were sitting there, milking the cows, and singing to them as you milked.

"Your father turned to me and said, 'Brother, that boy, Spencer, is an exceptional boy. He always tries to mind me, whatever I ask him to do. I have dedicated him to be one of the mouthpieces of the Lord—the lord willing. You will see him some day as a great leader. I have dedicated him to the service of God, and he will become a mighty man in the church.'" (CR, Oct 1943)

━━━━●◆●━━━━

When I was nine-years-old we were living in Boise, ID. Several of us had planned to go to the swimming pool one summer day. My mother had warned me to stay away from the deep end as I had had not yet learned to swim and I agreed with her.

After playing in the shallow end for some time I needed to get a drink of water. This required walking around the deep end of the pool. There were kids everywhere and a lifeguard on a tall platform. She simply could not keep an eye on everyone at once. As I was walking by the deep end and older boy decided to have some fun and shoved me several feet out into the deep end, twelve feet of water.

All I could think to do was to hold my breath and I immediately sunk like a rock to the bottom. By this time panic had set in. I flailed my arms and legs and finally managed to get my head up a little out of the water but not far enough to get a breath of air. I realized that I was all alone as no one noticed the trouble I was in. I sank a second time and couldn't get myself back up enough to get a breath.

I started sinking for a third time and my young life started flashing before me like playing on a fast-moving movie reel. It happened very quickly but my entire life to that point was shown to me. I just knew I was going to drown.

Suddenly I felt an arm around my neck and I was lifted out of the pool and gently set down on the edge of it. I quickly turned around to thank whoever saved my life. There was no one there! Not one person had noticed or acknowledged me in any way.

It was years later that I realized an unseen angel had literally saved my life. This incident had such a profound effect on me that I would not go near the water for over three years. Later I learned to swim. The fact of the angel preserving my young life has remained as a cherished memory throughout my life. (A peer)

When I was twelve years old we were at a youth conference where we could participate in some, but not all, of the activities that the fourteen and over kids could do. My dad and I were there while my older siblings attended special events like dances, etc. We were all able to attend the fast and testimony meeting and it was good! I felt a special spirit and that's where my testimony really began. (A Relative)

In the camp of the Willie Company, a young man had a dream in which he saw the rescue party coming down Rocky Ridge into the camp the next evening. He told members of the company about his dream the next morning. Many of those who heard it took courage ... That evening the rescue party came into camp just as he had seen in his dream. (*Remember*, 1997, pg. 148)

We were returning through Yellowstone Park after a youth temple trip to Idaho Falls, Idaho. My wife and I had four or five "Beehives" in our large van, young girls, mostly twelve years old. We had previously told their parents that we should be arriving in Cody, Wyoming, about 6 pm where they could pick up their respective children at the church.

We were listening to some church songs on a cassette tape and having a great time, following a wonderful temple experience. The panel lights started flickering and then dimming. I immediately turned off the headlights and the radio/cassette player. We were going downhill and I declared, "We have a problem with the car; the car will die the next time we have to stop." I could tell that the alternator was going out.

These wonderful young girls immediately started praying for help. About fifteen minutes later we came to a junction with a stop sign. No other cars were there so I blew through the stop sign and coasted to a closed service station lot. Our entire caravan was ahead of us, except for one other vehicle, which stopped behind us.

Jack Kelley, the other vehicle's driver and I dismantled the alternator; we both had toolboxes in our vehicles. But now what?

Just then a tow truck rumbles up towards us, stops, and this vibrant young man jumps out. He exclaimed, "I was going the other way, but something told me to turn around. How can I help?" He glowed with so much light that he could have been a translated being. Regardless of that possibility, this sharp young man was a direct answer to these young girls' faith and all of our prayers!

"We need a new alternator for our van."

"Well I have keys to this gas station, let's take a look."

They had only three alternators available and one was the exact model we needed! The holes matched up perfectly!

Jack and I reinstalled the new alternator as quickly as possible. The young man gave us a jump from his truck battery and we were off down the road once again. Our car battery fully recharged as we worked our way home three hours later than planned. There was no way we could call anyone. Everything was closed and there were no payphones; cell phones wouldn't have worked even if someone had owned a very early model.

We left a note inside the gas station, thanked them, and asked them to send us a bill for the alternator. We couldn't contact anyone else except our Heavenly Father. We finally found a payphone, around Fishing Bridge and called all the parents to let them know we would be dropping their girls off at their respective homes, late that night—they were safe.

We thanked those young girls for their faith and prayers and then we discussed the miraculous answer: The right person— at the right time—

with the right keys— the right tools—and the exact part actually being available at a small closed business! This experience was a tender mercy for every one of us. (7/12/1992)

———————————◆——————————

I think maybe I was around ten or eleven years of age. I was with my father out on a farm away from our home, trying to spend the day busying myself until my father was ready to go home. Over the fence from our place were some tumbledown sheds that would attract a curious boy, and I was adventurous. I started to climb though the fence, and I heard a voice as clearly as you are hearing mine, *calling me by name* and saying, **"Don't go over there!"** I turned to look at my father to see if he were talking to me, but he was way up at the other end of the field. There was no person in sight. I realized then, as a child, that there were persons beyond my sight, for I definitely heard a voice." (Harold B. Lee, *Stand Ye in Holy Places*, 139)

———————————◆——————————

*My favorite scripture:*

And he spake unto the multitude, and said unto them: **Behold your little ones**. And as they looked to behold they cast their eyes towards heaven, and they saw the heavens open, and they saw angels descending out of heaven as it were in the midst of fire; and they came down and encircled those little ones about, and **they were encircled about with fire; and the angels did minister unto them**. (3 NE 17:23-4)

*WOW!!*

Few groups of children of all time have been so honored and blessed as were those Lamanite and Nephite little ones who were taken into the arms of our Redeemer and blessed by him. What a privilege! They were encircled by fire and angels ministered to them, but the greatest of all was the actual embrace by the Son of God while their exultant parents watched and prayed and bore record. (Spencer W. Kimball, GC, April 1949)

34

# 2. Thou Art But a Youth

As I brought that young man up out of the waters of baptism, he surprised me by throwing his arms around my neck and whispering in my ear, tears streaming down his face, "I'm clean, I'm clean." That same young man, after we laid our hands on his head with the authority of the Melchizedek Priesthood and conferred on him the Holy Ghost, said to me, "When you spoke those words, I felt something like fire go down from the top of my head, through my body, all the way to my feet." (Henry B. Eyring, GC, April 2005)

———————◆———————

When I was around fourteen, a couple of new boys moved into our neighborhood and ward. They were from a far away state and they looked, dressed, and even talked differently than we did.  Most kids simply stared at them, while others poked fun at them. I felt sorry for our new classmates and decided I was going to befriend them. I introduced myself to them and invited them over to my house; soon a great friendship developed between the three of us.

At fifteen we could legally drive motorcycles and that was a great incentive to work at whatever jobs we could to afford our variety of fun. We loved to fish, hunt, lift weights, and play games.  Chess became our favorite indoor game. These brothers had older sisters and after awhile I got to know them and also their parents.  We were in each other's homes quite often, but primarily in their home because I had 5 younger sisters at my house.  Their sisters were all older and moved out, so we had their basement to ourselves—just the guys.

Their parents would often invite me to stay for dinner and Sister Noakes made the most scrumptious cinnamon rolls for dessert, frequently. My two new friends and I hung around at church, school activities, after school events, and weekends— really enjoying our newfound camaraderie.

One night we were laughing and having a jolly old time down in their basement.

Sister Noakes called downstairs and asked if just I would come up for a surprise she had for me. She had a large, freshly frosted, warm cinnamon roll on a plate, with glistening frosting dripping off the sides, and a tall, cold glass of milk just for me.  After I *"snarfed"* the treat down and guzzled the milk, she stated, "I hope you enjoyed that cinnamon roll because it's the last one you're ever going to get from me!"

I was taken back and didn't know what to say.

She then proceeded to lay into me as she ripped me up one side and down the other! She continued, "I love my boys and they are starting to make mistakes and some bad choices. I feel like they're slipping away from me. I believe your frivolity and silliness is dragging them down and I don't want you to see them anymore. You are a bad example for them! I don't want you in my house or on my property! I don't want your motorcycle in my driveway or yard! I don't even want to hear your motorcycle driving by our home!

(I couldn't get a word in edgewise as I sunk lower in my chair.)

She sternly demanded that I avoid her entire family altogether. She explained that I was not to talk to them, especially not to her boys at: church, seminary, school, or activities. "I don't want you associating with them in any manner! Don't be calling them on the phone! Just stay away," she exclaimed! And then she continued, "Don't go back downstairs, just leave, get out right now! Go!" as she pointed a stiff finger towards the door. "And don't ever come back!!"

I pushed my motorcycle off their property; kick started my ride, and drove home slowly, my mind swimming in confusion, while bearing a broken heart. She was a large and powerful woman and had actually frightened me. I chose not to tell my family or my other friends and quietly kept this berating beat down to myself. I wasn't quite sure why this had happened.

Over the next few weeks I avoided these two friends as instructed and made plans with other friends only. My five younger sisters were instructed to answer these two boys' phone calls with, "I'm sorry, Guy's not here." I told them to not ask why. It was quite difficult and very frustrating.

Finally, at school one day, these two brothers, my former friends, cornered me in a hallway and asked me what was going on.

"Why don't you have time for us anymore?"

"I'm sorry, go home and ask your mother about it."

They incredulously responded with, "What?!"

I walked away leaving them with, "Really, I'm serious!"

They both cornered me again the next day and shared their findings. They had asked their mother what the big problem was. She explained how she was so concerned about their lives and futures. She shared with them how much she loved them. She was worried that I was a detrimental factor with a predetermined path leading them in the wrong direction for their successful futures.

They replied to her, "Mom, Guy isn't trying to ruin us—he's trying to save us! His rules are: No drinking, no drugs, no sex, no dirty jokes, no vandalism, no marijuana, no breaking the laws. He's the best example we have amongst our friends!"

Later that week I received a phone call from Sister Noakes who said, "Hi Guy, I've made a very terrible mistake! I really need to apologize to you and I feel so awful about the entire thing. To start my amends, I have two warm cinnamon rolls with your name on them, sitting on my kitchen table right now. If you would please be so kind to forgive me and come over to just visit with us and talk about it I would really appreciate it."

I told her thank you and that I would come right over.

She swallowed me up with a huge hug as we shed some heartfelt tears, mostly hers. Once again she pled for my forgiveness. I forgave her, beginning a decades-long friendship that never wavered. She realized that I was the type of friend that was actually interested in her boys just like she was. We had many good times with every member of the Noakes family. I was elated to see them all once again in Powell, WY, during and after brother Noakes funeral.

> The inspiring influence of the Holy Spirit can be overcome or masked by strong emotions, such as anger, hate, passion, fear, or pride. When such influences are present, it is like trying to savor the delicate flavor of a grape while eating a jalapeño pepper. Both flavors are present, but one completely overpowers the other. In like manner, strong emotions overcome the delicate promptings of the Holy Spirit. (Richard G Scott, GC, Oct 2009)

When we had our second wedding reception in my home town of Powell, Wyoming, guess who was right there to help my mother with every detail: Sister Betty Noakes. We visited with sister Noakes in October, before our late December reception in my home town. She had everything very organized. Sister Noakes would make the wedding cake and handle the reception for us. She had become a second mother to me. Ours is an eternal relationship I cherish. My mother was busy sewing five bridesmaids' dresses for my five younger sisters and sending out all the announcements. (Journal 12/28/1980)

Years later, I was honored to be able to attend Sister Betty Noakes funeral in the Avenues above SLC, UT. As my wife and I sat in the audience we recognized a deep voice from the pulpit. It was Bruce Lindsay from KSL TV; more recognizable by his voice than his face, to me. He was conducting the funeral and mentioned Sister Noakes famous cinnamon rolls.

We were able to visit with Brother Lindsay afterwards and I commented, "I feel like we have a bond now with those famous cinnamon rolls. Ever since I was a little boy growing up in northern Wyoming watching KSL news, I've wanted to tour the KSL studios."

Brother Lindsay, promised, "Give me a call some day and I'll hook you up."

It was enjoyable just to hear him talk with his beautiful 'radio voice' in person.

A few years later I had a thought to call KSL studios. I was able to visit over the phone with Brother Lindsay and he set up a time for our tour during their early evening newscast. We visited KSL studios and they surely surprised us with a small bench placed right on the set just for us! It was closer than a bird's-eye view! All the other visitors were up a level sitting behind extra thick glass in a soundproof room full of seating. What an honor to receive KSL's VIP treatment!

These newscasters we'd grown to know over the decades were right there in front of us; visiting with us … when the recording light was off. They were so warm and congenial that we felt like good friends. Deanie Wimmer and Kevin Eubank were awesome and genuinely gracious too. I have never felt a better *spirit of goodness*, in a business, than with this group. We were allowed to stay and witness the entire newscast and see how it all functioned. That humongous green screen was the most interesting; with Kevin Eubank pointing to various areas where we saw nothing but a large, bright green wall—from our vantage point.

We were very pleased after the broadcast, when Bruce Lindsay said, "Now let me show you the rest of KSL." That was totally unexpected.

KSL Studios is a very large building with many long hallways. We were headed down a long hall on the way to tour KSL Radio. This gave us time to visit. I asked Brother Lindsay if he'd like to hear the cinnamon roll story. I shared the *full story* of Sister Noakes cinnamon rolls and myself with Brother Lindsay as we walked onward.

Afterwards he replied, "That's a good story."

Then I experienced a most interesting discernment and basically blurted out, "Are you going to retire from KSL and are you and your wife going to be Mission Presidents next July?"

Brother Lindsay inquired, "How could you know that?! … We are, but it's not official until this Friday. I'm retiring from KSL and all I can say is that my wife and I are going to a place that is very far away."

In a week or so the news came out that Brother Lindsay was retiring from KSL and that he would be serving, with his wife, as the Mission President of the Perth Australia Mission, that coming July. We still enjoy hearing Brother Lindsay's voice as he narrates the Book of Mormon through our iPhones on the LDS Library app. We are grateful to mutually know saintly sister Noakes. (Journal 2/19/2012)

In high school I love to run cross country. We met every day at three o'clock to run cross country. As I was making my rounds, visiting some of my teachers I had a distinct prompting to grab my cross country clothes. I followed the prompting and grabbed my gear. I had not heard that our coach had changed that day's run to 2:30 pm. When it was announced that the cross country team was leaving right away I was prepared. It was so simple, but I was ready to go and didn't miss out on that day's trip. (A young friend)

When I was 14, I remember realizing what the Spirit was for the very first time. I loved going to church, especially sacrament meeting. I always felt so warm and peaceful. This was the Spirit. I'm not sure I knew how important it was. I just knew it made me feel good. As an adult, I've learned that it not only makes us feel good, it teaches and testifies ... It can warn us of danger and help us remember things. (Carol B. Thomas, GC, April 2001)

When I was a young man I wanted to be good and grow up to someone important and useful. Our family was always active in the Gospel. We were often encouraged to read the Book of Mormon. Like most youth I made several attempts and would always stall in 2nd Nephi somewhere in the Isaiah chapters. When I was ordained a teacher I made another attempt to read the Book of Mormon and stopped at Jacob 5 that time.

*After reading the Book of Mormon about fifty times I finally felt the spirit and understood parts of the allegory of the tame and wild olive trees in Jacob chapter five. Elder Spencer W. Kimball said,* "Richard (G. Scott) you used a scripture from the Book of Mormon today that I had never thought of using that way. ... And to think that I have read that book more than seventy-six times." (Spencer W. Kimball, TPC, 6.61)

Many of you probably remember President Benson and his strong push to read the Book of Mormon and protect us from condemnation. Later in my fifteenth year I set a goal to complete the entire Book of Mormon and it took about eight months. Some days I would read ten or fifteen chapters and others days maybe only half of one chapter. When I finished it I decided to pray about the truthfulness of the Book of Mormon and also to learn if Joseph Smith was a true prophet of God.

I prayed often and didn't receive any feelings or revelation. I continued to pray day after day. One Sunday while sitting in sacrament meeting we were listening to a return missionary bear his testimony of the Book of Mormon and the Prophet Joseph Smith. At that moment the Spirit ran completely through my body twice. I had received undeniable answers to my two questions.

I have relied on those strong witnesses throughout my life in callings of service and leadership. (A peer)

And when ye shall receive these things, I would exhort you that ye would ask God, the Eternal Father, in the name of Christ, if these things are not true; and if ye ask with a sincere heart, with real intent, having faith in Christ, he will manifest the truth of it unto you by the power of the Holy Ghost. (Moroni 10:4)

When our daughter Emi was 15, she made a decision. One morning I noticed her Book of Mormon opened to Alma, chapter 48. She had marked the verses that describe Captain Moroni: "Moroni was a strong and a mighty man; he was a man of a perfect understanding. ... Yea, and he was a man who was firm in the faith of Christ" (Alma 48:11, 13) In the margin she had written, "I want to marry a man like Moroni." Seven years later, she did! Emi gained her vision for her future husband as she read the scriptures and listened to the promptings of the Holy Ghost. (Elaine S. Dalton, GC, April 2003)

Have expectations for your children. We had a curfew and told our sons that the Holy Ghost goes to bed at midnight. When they didn't come home, a few times the Holy Ghost told me to go out and find them. That surprised a few of their dates! We laugh about that now—but I must admit, laughter comes easier as they have grown older. (Bonnie D. Parkin, GC, Oct 2005)

When I was sixteen there was a girl visiting from out-of-town that I became enamored with. She showed up at church and told us she was staying with a cousin who was a non-member.

We hit it off; I asked her out and she sweetly said, "Yes."

I had a Honda motorcycle that we would mostly use for transportation to various activities. When double-dating my father would loan us one of his many vehicles.

It was a sad day when this young woman had to return to her hometown which was in the same state, but about as far apart as one could get in our state—over 375 miles away! We wrote letters mostly and spoke by phone a little. I wanted to see her and after much convincing and pleading I talked my parents into allowing me to take a long motorcycle ride. I promised to stop and visit an aunt and uncle along the way and then stay with a cousin's family in my destination city.

I had a small motorcycle, Honda 250 or 350, at the time. It did have a sissy bar that allowed me to strap a sleeping bag along with my backpack and I used that combination as a seatback. This makeshift seat was a real help over the many miles. I soon found out that smaller bikes are not great for long road trips however; they vibrate too much and rattle your bones to the core! I also had chrome glass pack mufflers and one of them rattled free from its mounting bracket due to excessive vibrations. The special exhaust pipe mounted weld simply rattled apart!

My aunt had a lunch fit for a king. I had never seen a larger lunch before (she is Scandinavian) and being a very hungry young man, enjoyed the meal immensely. I couldn't stop thanking her; it was all so scrumptious! My Uncle had a friend with a shop directly across the street from their home. He took my bike and its separated muffler to his mechanic buddy who welded it back on for free. That was awesome because I did not have much spare change. (Later in married life **this ministering aunt** stopped by to say hi on a Saturday. I was cutting up a large elk on the table and she sat down, visited cheerfully, and helped me cut up the entire elk for three to four hours! What a relief. We had a great time.)

I headed out for three more hours driving. Back then we could drive pretty fast legally and that helped some. The bike ran pretty well at 70-75 mph. Finally I arrived at my cousin's home. I was so impressed with the spirit of her, her husband, and their young brood of children. They and their home absolutely glowed with the Spirit. I watched their family closely and looked for reasons why it made me feel so wonderful in their midst. I made mental notes of what to look for in a companion. I also noticed things that I wanted to add in my future home; tangibles and intangibles. My home was good and had a nice spirit; their home literally glowed with the Spirit. They were so happy and wholesome, wonderful examples of righteous living.

The next day I met my girlfriend and she had all kinds of places lined out for us to go on my motorcycle. I was pleased that she liked my ride. We enjoyed some awesome tourist sites, took a great hike, and ended up back in town at A&W. She already figured out that was my favorite place to eat: Teen Burger, Root Beer Freeze, & Tater Tots. There was a local university with many options for young people too. We were having a very enjoyable time.

The second night my cousins announced they had to make a sudden trip out-of-state and asked me if I knew anyone else in town that I could stay with. The only other people I knew were my girlfriend's family. I talked to them and they said they liked me and that I could stay in their missionary son's room.

I thought, "Great, I'll get to see my girlfriend even more often!" So I packed up my backpack and swapped homes. Hers was a good home too, but not bright like my cousins.

The next day was Sunday, so I attended church with her and her family and she introduced me to her girlfriends.

After church she asked if I remembered the real cute little blonde friend of hers. I responded that I did notice her.

My girlfriend then explained, "I have to go to work and my friend has agreed to make you lunch and visit with you at the city park, so you won't be lonesome."

I replied, "Okay, we'll get together then when you're off."

Her friend was very cute and equally as nice. We had no trouble making conversation; it almost felt like we were kindred spirits. She provided me a great lunch and we shared each other's companionship over a beautiful afternoon. We visited on the swings, took a walk around the park, and sat at the picnic table a lot.

After three or four hours, she asked, "Don't you wonder why you are with your girlfriend's best friend? Doesn't that seem a little odd to you?"

"I just thought you were being nice, besides you're really cute, and I appreciate it."

"Well our mutual friend is not at work. She's with her local boyfriend, who's older, and she is doing absolutely everything her mommy doesn't want her to do! That's why you're with me. I'm doing her a favor."

Wow! What a shock! My mind was really racing, attempting to reel in all this newfound information.

As to leave no questions in my mind, she continued, "She is drinking, smoking, doing marijuana, and having sex!"

Oh my! This really changes things!

She told me that she felt very sorry for me and the deceptive hand I was dealt.

We parted from the park early evening and I returned to my former girlfriend's home. After I brushed my teeth I got ready for bed; pajama bottoms only because it was so hot with no A/C. All the recent naughty news was circling through my mind like something scurrying around a racetrack. My main thought was, "I need to get out of here ASAP." My ex-girlfriend had still not come home yet. I was lying on the bed, starting to sweat and wondering how I was going to get to sleep amidst all these racing thoughts and the heat.

Then her mother called me from my room to talk. We met in the hall and she appeared very serious. She really laid into me, ripping me up one side and down the other. She yelled, "I cannot believe you! The audacity to come into our home and stay with us and eat our food and date our daughter; then spend the rest of today with her best friend! You are a two-timing twit! You're a nobody! You're worthless! How could you do this to our family?! People from our ward have been calling me because they saw you in church with my daughter and then saw you at the park with her cute little friend all day! You are the worst! I was so embarrassed by your actions! What did you think you were doing? Oh my! I cannot believe you!"

I was floored, and then she continued after taking a deep breath: "I'm so embarrassed. You've embarrassed us and our home and I don't want anything to do you with! You need to leave first thing in the morning and don't look back. Don't call, write, or contact our daughter. Don't contact our family ever again! This is just terrible what you have done!" She went on and on and on, shaking her finger at me, and then she proceeded poking my bare chest as she was trembling. She had made her point!

Once this frustrated mother ran totally out of breath and energy from the lengthy railing, I found courage to respond to her. I was trembling and emotional as I explained to her that her daughter had lied about working. I informed her about her daughter's true whereabouts. I explained how her daughter had also set up the picnic and *park date* intentionally. I told her exactly what the cute little blonde said about "doing everything a good little Mormon girl shouldn't be doing." And then I explained what her little girl was actually doing.

Now this poor mother's heart was brashly broken as the shattered dreams for her daughter were scattering throughout her mind. She was just beginning to process the horror as I was starting to come to grips with the situation myself. This flustered mother dropped her jaw and gave me a big, long hug as she sobbed and trembled; and I cried along with her.

Since she was in her nightgown and I was shirtless, I became a little uncomfortable from too long of a hug and started to back away.

After this distraught mother gained her composure, she pleaded, "Please help me save my daughter! Oh … but you probably don't want to have anything to do with her now, do you?"

I confirmed the same. I did not want any further contact with her daughter and I promised to be gone early in the morning. I had a lot more to think about on the long, oscillating drive home, than I did on the equally long ride to that very educational visit.

Her daughter and I had a brief visit the next morning and I asked her why she was so good and modest around me. She replied, "Because you said you wanted to serve a mission. I did not want to get in the way of that."

> "An individual … who lets his or her emotions influence decisions will not be powered by the Spirit." (Richard G. Scott, GC, April 2012)

*I have been guilty of this too. Sometimes emotions and the Spirit are very close in the way they feel in our bodies and can lead to confusion at times. Emotions for me are like goose bumps on the skin and exhilaration; the Holy Ghost and Light of Christ are more internal and gently electrify through or from within the body, heart, and mind.*

———————◆———————

*I remember a general-authority seventy sharing the following, paraphrased:*

> While in the church office building I became aware of a brand new mission opening up in areas that use to be part of Russia. Our daughter had just put in her mission papers and I received this tremendous feeling in my body. I just knew she would be called to and faithfully serve in this brand new mission.
>
> I shared this excitement with my wife and we gratefully anticipated our daughter's future mission call.
>
> The day of truth came when most of our entire family and close friends witnessed her open her mission call. Her call was not to the new mission.
>
> I came to realize that my feelings were high emotions and not the Spirit witnessing truth. I had mistaken emotions for the Holy Ghost.

———————◆———————

> There was this woman in our ward and she was very, very old. One day the Spirit prompted me to write her a letter. I

found a picture of the Savior and wrote a note to her saying; "I know you are a daughter of God and I love you, etc." I went to her house and gave them to her.

She said it was so special to have a picture of Christ given to her. She fell on my neck and hugged me, crying. I never felt so much profound love before. (A young friend)

"Honor widows that are widows indeed." (1 Timothy 5:3)

━━━━◆━━━━

And when the servant of the man of God was risen early, and gone forth, behold, an host compassed the city both with horses and chariots. And his servant said unto him, Alas, my master! how shall we do?

And he answered, Fear not: for they that *be* with us are more than they that *be* with them.

And Elisha prayed, and said, LORD, I pray thee, open his eyes, that he may see. And the LORD opened the eyes of the young man; and he saw: and, behold, the mountain *was* full of horses and chariots of fire round about Elisha. (2 Kings 6:15-17)

━━━━◆━━━━

Throughout my younger years I had this reoccurring thought, "if I ever got pregnant as a teenager, I'd give the baby up for adoption." Because we had an adopted a child in our family and I saw how much she blessed our lives. I also knew that she was so much better off in our family than where she came from.

Now I never planned on getting pregnant, but when I was seventeen I did get pregnant. I started filling out the adoption papers right away and nine months later I was talking to possible candidates.

When I was introduced to this one family, the spirit burned within me and confirmed this was the best place for my baby to live.

The baby's father did not want to give the baby up for adoption. This was really a big issue. He wasn't interested in me, but he wanted to keep the baby.

I prayed that his heart would be softened and that he would be touched by the spirit. I asked the baby's father if he would just talk to these people.

After he agreed and did talk to them, he told me, "This will be the best place for our baby. I feel really good about it."

His strong confirmation is exactly what I needed. Normally he would have fought for the opposite. I knew Heavenly Father had answered my prayer and He helped direct every single part of my situation. (A friend)

"... Be strong and of a good courage; be not afraid, neither be thou dismayed: for the LORD they God is with thee withersoever thou goest." (Joshua 1:9)

---

I was a newspaper carrier when I was about thirteen-years-old. I had a five mile paper route which I did on my bicycle. I lived in Payson, UT, and had to ride approximately two miles to the center of town to pick up my newspapers and start my route.

Before leaving home my mother gave me a sealed envelope with a $20 bill inside it to mail. I threw it in my paper bag and when I got to town I had forgotten to go to the post office and mail it. I picked up my papers and did my entire route without thinking anymore about the letter. When I got home my mom asked me if I had mailed the letter and that's when it hit me—no, I didn't mail the letter—I forgot to! I went out and looked in my paper bag and no, it wasn't there. Twenty dollars was a lot to my parents back in 1945 and I had failed them. That is when I found a place to pray and pray I did, harder than I had ever prayed before. Then I hopped on my bike and retraced my five-mile-route.

Not really expecting to find the envelope, I had gone approximately five blocks when I noticed an envelope on the ground. It was torn open with a white sheet of folded paper off to the side. Someone had opened the envelope, pulled out the folded paper, and didn't look inside! How often does that happen? The $20 was still inside! This was my very first answer to a pray. (Ward member)

---

We had only had a few people this day at the lake and brought only one machine, a 3-seater wave runner.

Our teenage son had pulled up and stowed the anchor and was waiting, in the water, while we were making lunch up at a picnic table. He was tired from a lot of wave running on a very hot day and laid atop the wave runner to rest his eyes.

Shortly after he was relaxed the still, small voice said, **"Look to your left."** He was very tired from all the wave running on a very hot day and ignored the prompting.

Then 10-15 seconds later the voice firmly repeated, **"Look to your left!"**

He looked to his left and saw some people playing in the water in the distance. Everything seemed fine. Then he looked closer and saw only two little hands barely making noticeable splashes above the water. He instantly dove in the water toward her. He picked the little girl up out from the lake and brought her to the shore and patted her back a bunch. Water started coming out and then she threw up.

He was surprised that she didn't have a life jacket or any "floaties" on. About that time her parents finally realized what was going on and came down to where they were on the waterfront.

Our son, an Eagle Scout, was very happy, as were we and her family, that he saved the young girl's life. (Journal 8/1/2010)

---

We lived in California when I was younger. My parents were not active in the church, but they would drive us five girls to church and drop us off. I was sixteen and working as a lifeguard at Balboa Beach.

One day as I was walking home from a friend's house, I heard the Spirit clearly say, **"Read the Book of Mormon and get your Patriarchal blessing."**

My dad worked in Costa Mesa, CA, not too far from the beach and he would drop me off and go to his job. He worked two hours longer than my shift. Dad would pick me up then park in the shade, where I would read the Book of Mormon in his car while I waited for him to get off work. I might be one of the few people who read the entire Book of Mormon in a bathing suit!

Our house was small and busy. I was the oldest of us five girls. After finishing the Book of Mormon, I remembered the promise of Moroni. I went into the bathroom, where it was quiet, and knelt by the bathtub to pray. I received a wonderful confirmation of the truthfulness of the Book of Mormon. After that I received my Patriarchal Blessing, and those experiences were the beginning of my conversion and testimony.

I am so grateful that Heavenly Father reached out to me in support at a critical time in my life. I truly love my Savior and Heavenly Father. (Our friend)

"Our Latter-day Saint students are wonderful examples of faith in action." (Thomas S. Monson, GC, Oct 1978)

———————◄◆►———————

When I was 17 years old, we lived on an island in southern Norway called Andabeloy. My father converted to the Church on Andabeloy, and I was baptized in the ocean there.

One day in 1941 we got a call from the doctor in Flekkefjord, to the north. A woman who lived about two hours away by boat needed immediate medical attention. Dr. Hoffman asked if I could take him to see her, but my parents were worried about a storm raging in the North Sea. We decided to pray, asking Heavenly Father what to do. We received an answer that **we should proceed**.

After picking up the doctor ... I steered through the storm until we got to a rocky inlet ... which led to our destination. The waves were so high I could not control the boat through the inlet ... "What should we do?" the doctor asked.

"We have to pray about it," I replied.

I paused and prayed to Heavenly Father for direction. As soon as I had said amen, an answer came to me clearly. I suddenly recalled a story an old fisherman had told me. He had been fishing in this same area during a bad storm ... he noticed a pattern in the incoming waves. After three great big waves washed in, a short period of calm followed.

I had fished many times in this area but had never noticed a wave pattern. Nevertheless, I brought the boat to the front of the inlet, where we waited and watched three big waves come in. Sure enough, a sudden calm followed. I glided the boat forward over the smooth water on the inner bay and brought Dr. Hoffman safely to shore.

When the doctor returned about an hour later, he declared, "We saved her life!" I bear witness that when we need help, we should pray. I know that Heavenly Father will answer. (Latter-day Saint Voices, *Ensign*, Oct 2014)

"And thine ears shall hear a word behind thee, saying, This is the way, walk ye in it, when ye turn to the right hand, and when ye turn to the left." (Isaiah 30:21)

———————◄◆►———————

In the early seventies an older cousin lived with us and worked at my father's photography business. My cousin had recently returned from a mission to Germany. We would often travel with my dad to help *shoot* wedding pictures in many different towns in Montana, Utah, and Wyoming. Sometimes we would stay with relatives.

The three of us were staying over at Thermopolis, WY, with my aunt and uncle on a work/visit trip. They had a small, congested home that was dark, with curtains drawn, and wreaked of smoke. Our uncle was a chain smoker and a master chess player. He would beat us so quickly we hardly knew what had happened. My aunt fed us well and always had a great chuckle to serve along with her meals.

My cousin and I were trying to sleep on a twin bed in a tiny room that was too hot. The smoke had agitated my asthma and I had trouble getting to sleep. Thankfully, my cousin took my mind off of my struggling breathing to teach me. He laid out the plan of salvation before me; my mind's eye was enlightened. God's plan for His children became alive in my mind as I was able to visualize our discussion. The Spirit was so strong in that uncomfortable, small, dark space.

That night I gained my testimony of the plan of salvation. I was around fifteen years old. Decades later I was thanking this cousin for bearing his testimony, teaching me, and helping me to feel the Spirit in abundance.

"Do you remember what you said afterwards?"

"Way back then, I don't remember what I said."

"You said, 'Wow, this makes it all worth it!'" (Journal 9/24/2017)

No matter how dark, deep, and miserable the muck and debris one finds himself wading through ... wishing he could climb out of; the Holy Ghost can reach and teach you. The Light of Christ can also find you amongst heights or depths and direct you to a better path.

"But the Lord was with Joseph, and shewed him mercy,
and gave him favour in the sight of the keeper of the prison
... because the Lord was with him, and that which he did,
the Lord made it to prosper." (Genesis 39:21 & 23)

Joseph was left in prison over two years. He was given responsibility for all the prisoners. Joseph was also blessed with the spiritual gift of interpreting dreams.

The Prophet Joseph Smith spent some unjust and uncomfortable time in jails. Sections 121 - 123 were written during the time he was incarcerated as a prisoner in the Liberty, MO jail. The Prophet spent 4 ½ months in inhumane conditions during the winter in late 1838 and early

1839. He also received and distributed revelations from the Lord. Once again, when at your worst please peruse this heavenly council:

> And if thou shouldst be cast into the pit, or into the hands of murderers, and the sentence of death passed upon thee; if thou be cast into the deep; if the billowing surge conspire against thee; if fierce winds become thine enemy; if the heavens gather blackness, and all the elements combine to hedge up the way; and above all, if the very jaws of hell shall gape open the mouth wide after thee, know thou, my son, that all these things shall give thee experience, and shall be for thy good.  The Son of Man hath descended below all. Art thou greater than he? (D&C 122:7)

When I was seventeen I heard about a trip to Africa, for service, that a lady we knew was planning. I had a desire to go to Africa ever since I was a little girl. I met with her and she explained how she takes groups over to Kenya and serves those people. I got super excited about the whole idea. Then I remembered I did a study and report, when I was younger, specifically on Kenya. I felt like I was drawn to the whole concept and idea!

The trip was really expensive and my parents thought I was crazy. The cost was $3,000 in 2015. I decided to fast for a long time and pray about it. After that, I had a feeling that I definitely wanted to do this. Now that I knew I was going, I decided to fast and pray again and ask for the Lord's help in raising the money.  I was terrified and had no idea how I was going to get that much money.  How was I going to do this? So I set goals and saved all my money from my job. And I received money for my birthday, Christmas, and graduation.  I, to this day, don't know how I saved up that much money in such a short time, but the Lord provided.  I was supposed to go on this trip.

The trip lasted two weeks and we lived with a tribe for some time, then we got to help at a girl's school.  The girls go there to run away from abuse and early marriages. I had so much fun serving the Kenyans and visiting with them in their dung huts. It was a wonderful two weeks.  But, after I got home, it was such a long plane ride that I was totally exhausted.  I got a priesthood blessing and there was something interesting in that blessing. It said, '**Strengthen**

**your relationships with those you served in Kenya**.' So then I started 'Face booking' and writing letters to contact my new friends in Africa and it has been wonderful!

The lady that plans the trips to Kenya informed me about another trip. I decided to fast and pray about this second trip. During my fasting and prayers I felt total peace. It was interesting though, because after the fast I started having doubts and became discouraged. I soon realized how close I was to the spirit while fasting and afterwards I was getting negative messages from a different source. It was easy to tell the difference between the two. We are now planning another trip to serve the Kenyans in 2017. I'm very excited about that! (A young friend)

"Peace I leave with you, my peace I give unto you: not as the world giveth, give I unto you. Let not your heart be troubled, neither let it be afraid." (John 14:27)

———•◆•———

When I was thirteen, growing up in an exceptionally large family (of 12 kids), being a teenager was sometimes rough. Responsibility was high and time for friends or individual support was limited. Being a teenager with identity crisis on top of that didn't help. I was feeling frustrated, scared, and alone.

The question racing through my heart was "When I try to be so good, why does it have to be so hard?!"

I felt prompted to open the Book of Mormon. I turned to 2 Nephi 2:11 where it reads "… there must needs be an opposition in all things …" I was filled with warmth from my head to my toes. It was an extreme feeling of love and understanding that I had never, ever, felt before. It was wonderfully filling and unforgettable.

In that moment I KNEW God lived, and that there was a Savior there to support and succor, and love me through anything.  And I learned if things were tough, it was actually a good sign that I was on the right path. (A relative)

"And the disciples were filled with joy, and with the Holy Ghost." (Acts 13:52)

———•◆•———

Let me tell you about a young man who has felt the evidence of this love. I first met Sione in New Zealand, He is a Tongan. A finer, more clean-cut, intelligent young man I have never met anywhere. Sione comes from a very modest background ...

"If a fourteen –year-old boy by the name of Joseph Smith would pray to God and have his prayer answered, why can't I?" So Sione dropped to his knees in the taro patch and opened his heart to his Heavenly Father and told him of his desire to become an educated person so he could improve the lot of his own people.

Well, Sione rose from his knees, went about his work, returned home and nothing happened for a while. Then one day an envelope came in the mail. In the envelope was the notice that Sione had received a full scholarship to the Church College of Hawaii, and he hadn't even applied for it! When I met Sione he had graduated; he had his degree. He was teaching school; he was a coach, one of the most loved and respected of all the teachers in the schools in Tonga. (Victor L. Brown, Speeches of the Year, "The Faith and Courage to Be True," May 5, 1970)

---

I will never forget the night I came home from high school to a dark house. No one was home and as soon as I walked in the door I could feel that something was wrong. This was before cell phones, so I just waited to hear from somebody, hopefully soon. The phone finally rang—it was mom, telling me that Grandpa Smith had just had a heart attack. They weren't sure if he was going to make it.

As soon as I got off the phone I knelt down and pleaded with my Heavenly Father that grandpa would be ok. I prayed, "Please don't let him die." I ended my prayer. As soon as I stood up I felt a very strong impression that this was not the right prayer. I found that a very interesting thought, because I had never thought of a prayer as being *wrong*.

But the strong impression continued to stay with me. So I knelt back down and this time it was a different prayer. I asked Heavenly Father to comfort us and bless grandpa with peace, if it was his time to go. Grandpa did pass away and we were all very sad. However I was comforted, knowing that Heavenly Father had heard my first prayer, but He had different plans for grandpa. (A friend)

"I will not leave you comfortless: I will come to you." (John 14:18)

---◆---

In the mid 70's President Spencer W Kimball made a visit to our large youth conference in Billings, Montana. We had driven up from Wyoming and were all staying at a college dorm in Billings. We had stayed up very late and sleepily arrived after everyone else was already seated in the large auditorium. What a surprise it was to run into people (body guards) escorting the Prophet down the hallway, right in front of us tardy attendees. President Kimball stopped, so his entourage stopped; he kindly said hello to us and shook our hands. I felt a very special feeling.

A few moments later we found some open seats among the throngs of our peers. President Kimball walked onto the stage and everyone stood up and started singing "We Thank Thee, O God for a Prophet" (*Hymns,* no. 19). The good feeling I had in my chest became very intense and made me feel wonderful. I don't remember ever feeling like that before. I thought, "Wow, this is a very special person and a prophet of God!" (Pre-Journal experience)

As a young woman, I came to downtown Salt Lake one wintery day. I had parked in front of the Church Administration Building and was just putting a nickel in the meter when I noticed a man leaving the building. He wore a dark overcoat and a wool hat. But he had something more: a spirit that stirred my soul. I could not take my eyes off him, and as he descended the steps, I suddenly realized he was President David O. McKay. He said nothing as he passed me; he merely smiled gently and tipped his hat. The Spirit literally filled my being. I knew I had seen a prophet of God. (Bonnie D. Parkin, GC April 1996)

---◆---

When I was a young man, I was on my way to a session of general conference when someone took my elbow. It was President David O. McKay. "Come with me, Joseph," President McKay said. "I'll help you find a good seat."
"I want you to know, Joseph," he said, "that the President of the Lord's Church does receive inspiration and revelation from the Lord Jesus Christ." At that moment, the Spirit whispered to my heart that President David O. McKay was telling me the truth. I knew then that he was truly a prophet of God. That testimony has remained with

me throughout my life, filling me with reverence and respect for the office our prophet holds. (Joseph B. Wirthlin, GC, Oct 1997)

---

I was serving as our Ward YW President at the time and was having a large fundraiser. The young men and women would decorate the cultural hall; we called it the *Spring Fling*. Then we sold tickets to their parents and fixed a really nice dinner. We had everything set up the afternoon of the activity.

I had all the money we had collected in a file folder; there were lots of checks and a lot of cash. This wasn't an envelope, but an open file folder. It was full of everything because everyone had to prepay. I also had the list of everything we had purchased along with everyone's names.

I was carrying a bunch of things to the car and set the folder on top of the car and drove away. I had a thought to look for it in our old station wagon and it wasn't there! We didn't have cell phones so I had to wait until I got home to call people.

I had a councilor with a daughter named Colleen. She was around sixteen and a Laurel. They had left the church just before me and they had gone to the grocery store.

Her daughter declared, "Mom, we need to go back to the church."

"What for?"

"I don't know. We just need to go back to the church."

As they got back to the church there was the folder lying on the ground. There it was with all the money and all the lists of everyone's responsibilities. It had everything in it!

I called my councilor and I was crying and explained to her that I had lost everything, including all the money for our fundraiser.

She exclaimed, "We have the folder!" Then she explained how Colleen was inspired to go back to the church.

I was so grateful because the way the wind blows around here, the checks, money, and papers could've been scattered all over the place. I was accountable for all of it and I was so thankful that Colleen listened to the Spirit. (A relative)

"The youth of today are wonderful. ... The youth of the Church are one of the most powerful forces for good on the earth today." (Vaughn J. Featherstone, GC, Oct 1987)

━━━━●◆●━━━━

When I was a teenager, my older sister was making some bad choices. I remember being really concerned and worried about my sister. My family always prayed for her too. I prayed that she would come back and that she would have peace. This is the first time I heard the spirit whisper to my mind. One night I prayed for her and a voice said, **"She's going to be okay; you don't need to worry anymore."** I remember that I stopped worrying because God told me not to worry anymore. And then she came back! (A family friend)

━━━━●◆●━━━━

Because of my great fear of public speaking I had graduated from high school without ever bearing my testimony or speaking at school. When I was supposed to give a 2 ½-minute talk in Sunday School, as a boy, I hid amongst the women's long coats in the coat closet at church. The bishop said over the pulpit, "I know you're here Guy, I saw you earlier." I remained hidden until the meeting was over!

Now fast-forward fourteen years and I was sitting with a group of young adults at the institute building. They were having a program and some treats. The leaders chose to open up a testimony meeting for the young crowd. I felt as if my inner torso was being mixed like a can of paint in a paint mixer like one sees at the hardware stores.

I was strongly stirred inside and was urged, seemingly pushed, to stand up, bare my soul, and bear a testimony through trembling lips. I have no idea what I said, but I will never forget the encouraging spirit!

"Yea, and thus saith the still small voice which whispereth through ... and often times it maketh my bones to quake while it maketh manifest ..." (D&C 85:6)

━━━━●◆●━━━━

*When Jacob's son Joseph, the youngest of twelve sons, was only seventeen years old, he had a couple of prophetic dreams.*

*First he dreamed:* "For behold, we were binding sheaves in the field, and , lo, my sheave arose, and also stood upright; and, behold, your sheaves stood round about, and made obeisance to my sheaf." (Genesis 37:7)

*His eleven brothers hated him for this dream, on top of being jealous of Joseph and his coat of many colors.*

*Then young Joseph had another dream as follows:*
Behold, I have dreamed a dream more; and, behold, the sun and the moon and the eleven stars made obeisance to me. And he told it to his father, and to his brethren: and his father rebuked him, and said unto him, What is this dream that thou has dreamed? Shall I and thy mother and thy brethren indeed come to bow down ourselves to thee to the earth? And his brethren envied him, but his father observed the saying. (Genesis 37:9-11)

*What an amazing son of God Joseph is! To remain positive and faithful through such difficult trials, Joseph is an epoch example for every one of us.*

*Look what Joseph faced while only a teenager and young adult: All eleven brothers envied and hated him, his father rebuked him, his brothers threatened to kill him, he was abandoned in a deep pit with no water, he was sold off as a slave by his own brothers for twenty pieces of silver, he was lied about so his parents thought he was dead, he was resold as a slave, he was sexually assaulted by an adulterous women, he was lied about and accused of accosting the lying woman, he was imprisoned due to a false witness, he lost a chance to get out of prison when the freed butler forgot about his dream, and he remained in prison two more years!*

*After all these possibly depressing events, Joseph always rose to the top of the pot in any circumstance: At Potiphar's house, down in prison, and eventually in Pharaohs' court. He skyrocketed to the number two position in all of Egypt; Joseph was second only to Pharaoh himself! All these many trials and triumphs of Joseph occurred over the space of a few years. He was now nineteen or in his early twenties.*

*In fulfillment of his teenage dreams we learn "… and Joseph's brethren came, and bowed down themselves before him with their faces to the earth." (Genesis 42:6)*

*Later, his parents and eleven brothers would all move to Egypt and be under his rule. Joseph and Pharaoh treated the seventy souls of Jacob's family generously.*

The year we studied the Book of Mormon in Seminary they passed out a chart where you could mark down for each day whether you had completed morning prayer, evening prayer, and scripture study. I put the chart up next to my bed. After about a month I looked at the chart and realized that I wasn't doing very well. I resolved to not miss one of those events and did very well over the next two months.

My Sunday school teacher, Brother Wheelwright, also challenged us to read the Book of Mormon, cover to cover and then to pray about it. I took him up on the challenge. After several months I had developed a regular habit of morning and evening prayer and scripture study. My efforts were not always the best quality, yet these habits have benefited me throughout my life.

It took months, but I finally finished the Book of Mormon. I didn't really need to ask whether it was true; by that time I had received manifestations from the Spirit throughout my reading that testified what I was reading was indeed true. Still, in order to complete the assignment, I went to my bedroom one Sunday evening and finished reading the book. I then knelt and prayed fervently about the book.

After about twenty minutes of sincere prayer I received an outpouring of the Spirit, more powerful than anything I had previously experienced. I knew that the Book of Mormon was true! I knew that the men whose words were in the book really existed; and that there had been true prophets on the American continent in ancient times.

As I was reveling in a magnificent spiritual experience that I cannot adequately describe in human language, the Spirit gave me much more than I had asked for. The Spirit poured over and throughout my soul impressing upon me in a way that I cannot fully explain that: the First Vision happened just as Joseph Smith said it did; Joseph Smith was a true prophet of God; his account regarding the gold plates and the translation of the Book of Mormon was true. I also knew then that the men that have succeeded Joseph Smith as presidents of the church have indeed been true prophets called of God, having His authority.

As noted, I cannot adequately describe the experience, but it was pure revelation from God. I cannot doubt the truthfulness of the things witnessed to me without sinning against the Holy Ghost and being dishonorable. If I am honest with myself I must admit that I know these things are true more than I know anything else in this life to be true. I truly received a divine manifestation of the Spirit. (A relative)

"... May the Spirit of the Lord be poured out upon you."
Mosiah 18:13

———◆———

When we were in high school, in the early 70's, hunting and fishing were common activities on Saturdays. Sometimes we would even take off after school during our off seasons from sports. We felt lucky to have early school-year birthdays and be part of the few sophomores that could legally drive within the first few weeks of school forward.

A good friend and I decided to go rabbit and duck hunting, since both seasons were open. After school, in the middle of the week, we grabbed our shotguns, 22 rifles, and knives. We hadn't found much game at all and just started talking about high school stuff when we both noticed an unused road; this little road was barely discernible. Travel on the road had been so light that tall grass was even growing in the dim wheel tracks.

We had a 4-wheel drive and my friend said, "This looks like a great place for some game. It looks like no one has been here for some time." So we veered off the main canal road and slowly took this drive through the bushes and trees. We came to a turn-around area and at the end we spotted our church leader's car parked at the furthest point, against the trees.

I said, "Oh great, he's already found this secluded hunting spot and beat us to it! Oh well, let's go see if we can find him." We grabbed our guns and headed down toward his car. We were not prepared for what we would find. Instead of our friend, we found his wife. She must've heard a twig snap and then stood up on her knees on the car seat, facing us. It was readily apparent that his wife didn't have a stitch of clothing on! What was even more shocking to our young minds was the fact that that the nude man under her was not her husband! She was so surprised and shocked to see guys with guns that I don't think she even recognized us. We did have hats and bright orange clothing on. We were thinking and saying to each other: *"What the heck?!"*

We started slowly backing away with our wide eyes firmly affixed on the *situation*. She nervously attempted to cover herself with one hand as she reached over the seat to retrieve her underwear. She tried to avoid eye contact with us. At first we were too stunned to move. The man stayed low so as to not be seen and possibly identified. We had witnessed too much! We still had no idea who this adulterous man was; we just knew who he wasn't! From his hair color and balding we knew he was someone else. We started getting scared and hurried back to our vehicle as we proceeded to process our discovery.

Even though we had guns and knives, we were still frightened by an adult man. As we loaded up in the rig we were still in shock and awe.

After we sat safely inside our locked vehicle and gathered ourselves, we noticed a sedan parked to the right, partially hidden under a weeping willow tree. We could only see the back of that car; we saw enough to jot down that car's license plate number, make, and model. Then we took off in a real hurry, spinning tires, while flinging dirt and grass up in a makeshift smokescreen, hoping to mask our own vehicle and license plate number from their view.

Back then, in small towns at least, the phone books also listed everyone's license plate number in the back pages. You could cross reference a license plate number with a phone number and address. So we did some detective work and made a scary discovery. The mystery car belonged to a high school administrator! Now we were even more frightened. We definitely did not want him to know who "caught them in the act" and threw a wrench in the middle of their tryst. And there is no way we wanted to tell anyone about our findings now. We carried this sordid secret between ourselves for a couple of weeks.

One day we drove around and talked privately about it. We used to "drag main" and drove an "L" shape down the highway going through town and then turning down Main Street, maybe 4 streetlights total, going around the block at the end and returning to the starting point. Just before the end of the U-turn on the highway was a popular A&W drive-in. As we would drive back and forth through town we would see our church leader sitting in his truck, alone, at the A&W. We kept talking to each other and saying to each other "we should tell him what we saw/know." Then we chickened out and wouldn't even pull into the drive-in so that we could avoid the very possibility of having talking to him. At church our lips were sealed.

Finally, following the third week of the "incident" we pulled into A&W on the other side. Our young men's leader noticed us and he waved us over. We climbed up into his truck and sat with him. He asked us how we were doing and how school was for us.

We told him we were doing great!

Then we asked him how he was doing and he replied, "Not so good." He seemed so sad.

Then our conversation turned to small talk as my friend and I started elbowing each other, meaning:

"You tell him."

"No, you tell him."

"No, you should."

"No, you!"

I dropped the bombshell relaying, "We have something important to tell you. We found you wife in your car totally naked with another man!"

He slammed the dashboard really hard with his fist as his face turned bright red.

"I knew it! I've suspected her! I just haven't been able to get any proof!"

"We got the license of the other car too."

"Good! Will you guys testify for me in court?"

"We will testify!"

"We will testify!"

"Thanks guys. Thanks for having the guts to share that with me. You better go now, I need to be alone."

We left his truck as we wished him the best. With that load off our shoulders and big sighs of relief we went back to dragging main. We really loved him and felt so sorry for his predicament.

A couple weeks later, after mutual/MIA, he pulled the two of us aside and confided, "Thanks for offering to go to court for me. She confessed to that affair and more. She will not contest. We'll be getting divorced as soon as possible. Court is not necessary. Besides she's already gone." That may be the only time we ever hugged our dear leader, in a congratulatory yet sorrowful way.

Over the years I have wondered why we had to have that experience. Why did we have to see all that at a young age? Why couldn't it have been a game warden or the local sheriff on patrol? The only thought regarding this incident that has come to my mind is that: we were earthly angels answering the pleadings, prayers, and broken heart of a concerned husband, friend, and leader.

I believe this harrowing happening was also meant to show us boys what type of a girl not to marry. Curvaceous and flirtatious was not what we should be looking for in our future temple-worthy companions. We both married ultra-modest young women. Maybe it was a lesson for our leader too? He also remarried an elect daughter of God, also very modest, that we are good friends with to this day.

————◆——

Katie is a young woman who did just that. Let me share her story with you. (Carol B. Thomas, GC, April 2001)

All my life I have wanted to be good, but I got to the point where I wondered, 'How can anyone really know if the Church is true?' I took Moroni's challenge and for five months prayed and read my scriptures every day. One night I sat on my bed almost in tears, giving up. I decided to pray. I said, 'Heavenly Father, help me to please just know you are there. I've done what Thou hast asked according to the

Church and I just really need to know.' Immediately I felt like someone had wrapped their arms around me. I didn't hear a loud voice or see an angel, but I felt Heavenly Father telling me, **"Sweet Katie, you've known all along."** It was like a kind and loving father comforting his little girl (letter).

---

I secretly overheard a perverted plan, during my junior year in high school, in the locker room. A new boy had moved into our sister ward and high school. All the girls were going gaga over him. He was dating a popular LDS student and they made a cute couple.

What I heard being whispered that day was chilling though: "I have a careful, 6-month plan to get her in bed with me. I will sweep her off her feet and into my arms—just watch me."

I was worried for her and had frightening thoughts of date rape if she resisted. She was such a good girl and this sordid situation was more than bothersome.

I did not share this with anyone. As I kept the nasty secret, the Holy Ghost began working on me. About every 3-4 hours, the spirit would clearly say, **"Warn her."** Before school, during lunch, after school and before going to bed; the same message steadily repeated itself, **"Warn her."** I would start to build up my confidence and then easily talk myself out of the task at hand.

She was a very popular girl and I was an unpopular boy. How could I talk to a girl about something like this? I would simple shun from my heaven-sent responsibility.

This spiritual message persisted for two-and-a-half days, about every 3 hours like clockwork, **"Warn her"**… **"Warn her"**… **"Warn her"** It was always the exact same two-word message. I was getting tired of being told to talk to her. Finally I mustered the courage to call her up on the third day and asked if I could come over and visit with her. I mentioned that I had something important that I needed to talk to her about.

> "… It is this spirit which rests upon us that is prompting us to do it, and it will not let us rest until these things are done." (John Taylor, JD 19:122)

I hopped on my motorbike and thought again, "How am I going to do this. I don't think I can handle it."

She greeted me on the porch and we sat down on her porch to visit, side by side (it was a small porch). We talked about high school, seminary, school sports, friends, siblings, teachers, etc.

I hemmed and hawed for half-an-hour, after which she exclaimed, "Guy, if you want to ask me out just say so!"

I chuckled and thought, "Wow, I think she'd say yes if I asked her out and stored that idea in my memory banks."

Her unexpected comment broke the ice and gave me courage to *get it all out.*

"No that's not why I came over today. I have something more important to say."

"Well, what is it?"

"Your boyfriend has a devious and evil plan for you and his endgame is to get you in bed with him within six months!"

"He was so perfect, such a gentleman—I felt there was something wrong, but I just couldn't put my finger on it! Thanks for telling me." She stood up quickly as she thanked me, rushed inside, and slammed the door really hard behind her.

I remained on the porch still pondering the situation; saying to myself, "surely she's not mad at me too?"

A few minutes later she cracked the door open and whispered, "Thanks again, I really need to be alone right now."

I nodded in agreement and then scooted on home, no longer pestered by a persistent Spirit, although grateful for the outcome.

A few weeks later this popular young man pulled me aside and I thought "Oh-Oh!"

Thankfully he was just confiding in me about his girlfriend breaking up with him. He asked if I'd heard anything as to why she didn't like him anymore.

I replied, "If there's one thing I've learned about women, it's that they change their minds often." He was satisfied and we parted. Whew!

During our senior year I did ask this young woman out on a date and she did say yes. My father really liked her family and that's the only date/day in 4 years of high school that my father allowed me to drive the *Grey Ghost*, his beloved '36 Chevy. This awesome antique had a push button start; six-volt battery, and thick metal spoke rims. It was all original. We had a blast cruisin' Main together and stopping off to eat at the popular A&W.

After my mission I was attending BYU and this same young woman and I ran into each other in the Provo, Utah, post office on a Saturday morning. She had married a tall, dark, and handsome young man in the temple and was now eight months pregnant. She let me feel the baby kicking in her tummy. She then thanked me for being brave and warning her of a danger she faced back in high school. The Spirit raced through me in what I can only describe as a *confirmation of goodness.* I was so grateful that I conjured up courage enough to give her that challenging, yet vitally important message to avoid a possibly terrible situation.

> Even though I dislike such a subject, I believe it necessary to warn the youth against the onslaught of the arch tempter who, with his army of emissaries and all the tools at his command, would destroy all the youth of Zion, largely through deception, misrepresentation, and lies. (President Spencer W. Kimball, GC, Oct 1980)

*The Grey Ghost* – 1936 Chevy Coupe

I was in the library during the middle of the week in my senior year of high school. I was in the tall aisles looking for homework answers. The library was not very busy and the librarian must have been away from his desk. Next to the tall glass windows on the north side were a couple round tables where students could study. There was a group of four to five boys and girls, also seniors, but they were doing anything but studying.

I started to overhear a devious design which I can only describe as a secret combination. I was able to find some missing books among two consecutive rows that granted me a double-slotted peephole which enabled me to barely see who was seated at the table of conspirators. Only until they leaned forward to talk to one another could I even see their faces. This table group was having quite a discussion.

The *spokesman* said, "Alright, we are all in agreement then. I'm so tired of her not drinking with us, as you are. Friday night we are going to get alcohol down her throat if we have to break her teeth!"

They all agreed and shook on it like a pact. "Good, so we're all in agreement then" he concluded. Next they all got up and walked out.

63

I buried my head within a big book in the back of an aisle and acted real focused. I don't believe they ever even knew I was there.

Now the Spirit persisted in pestering me again, every three hours I would clearly hear, **"Tell her."**

This LDS girl was also very modest, yet hung with a partying crowd; the most popular kids in school. They were the rich kids with the nicest clothes and cars. Once again I felt like I fell short and was incapable. She was so popular and wealthy. I was so unpopular and poor. I didn't feel like I could even talk to her. I felt so inadequate for the task at hand.

After constant reminders, **"Tell her"** ... **"Tell her"** every three hours for two-and-a-half days, I called her up to see if I could come over and talk. Hopping on my motorbike again, I rode from the poor side of town; across the canal and the railroad tracks, clear over to the expensive homes on the opposite side of town.

She had a large porch. We sat down and began a conversation about high school and church.

Then she challenged me, "So what did you really come over to talk to me about?"

Her comment broke the ice and I then explained the sinister plot that was brewing with her best buds and commented, "You know with friends like that, who needs enemies?"

She thanked me for warning her and said "I will deal with this!" And we parted.

Twenty years out of high school, this same woman was invited to be a consultant for the company I worked for. We were both sent to New York City to attend a major trade show. Afterwards, while waiting to fly home, to Wyoming, from LaGuardia Airport in Queens, NY, the two of us visited on an airport bench. Within this busy airport, there was only one topic she wanted to discuss with me.

She sincerely thanked me for coming to her home and warning her when we were seniors in high school two decades ago. She thanked me for protecting her from her *friends*.

Once again, the *Spirit of rightness* tingled strongly within my entire body. I was so grateful I finally followed the persistent promptings and could be her earthly angel. (Journal 1/28/1995)

"Such rewards come when the Spirit touches a heart for eternal good because someone like you was there. To share truth in difficult circumstances is to treasure it more." (Richard G. Scott, GC, Oct 2003)

"The Spirit voice of goodness, whispers to our hearts ..."
(Our Savior's Love, *Hymns*, no. 113)

*Many stories in "The Tender Mercies of Personal Revelation" are from members of the Church of Jesus Christ of Latter-day Saints and others are from non-members, other Christians, and believers. My all-time favorite story from a teenager who was a non-member is the following:*

> ... I kneeled down and began to offer up the desires of my heart to God. ... I saw a pillar of light exactly over my head, above the brightness of the sun, which descended gradually and fell upon me. ... When the light rested upon me I saw two Personages, standing above me in the air. One of them spake unto me, calling me by name and said, pointing to the other—This is My Beloved Son. Hear Him! (JSH 1:15-17)

> ... I betook myself to prayer and supplication to Almighty God. ... I discovered a light appearing in my room, which continued to increase until the room was lighter than at noon day, when immediately a personage appeared at my bedside, standing in the air ... He called me by name, and said unto me that he was a messenger sent from God to me, and that his name was Moroni ... (Testimony of the Prophet Joseph Smith)

# 3. Behold the Field is White

On my mission, we used sidewalk chalk. There are streets in the Ukraine where there are no cars, but lights and music, and people simply *'gulyat'* or stroll around and enjoy time together during the day. On Saturdays, when the street was the busiest, we would normally draw a large picture of the plan of salvation in chalk. We would then add a few quotes to bring people's attention to the artwork. This program brought up people's interest and we obtained a lot of contacts.

For weeks the idea of drawing the Book of Mormon on the sidewalk came again and again to me. I figured it was a silly idea, since our current drawing was working so well. Yet the feelings and thoughts only became stronger. These thoughts entered my mind at times when I wasn't even remotely thinking about Saturday chalking.

So, I finally brought these promptings up with our district and they agreed that even though it seemed simplistic; if the idea keeps returning we had better do something about it.

That Saturday we began drawing the Book of Mormon. We hadn't even finished drawing the book when a lady walked up to us and asked, in Russian of course, "Is this your book? I've been looking for you for 2 years!" Her friend had given her a copy and she couldn't remember where she'd gotten the book from. This lady had read the Book of Mormon cover to cover, over and over again. She was ready to hear the Gospel and was soon baptized. All because of following a prompting that didn't quite make sense to me at first. (A relative)

Faith means that we trust not only in God's wisdom but that we trust also in His love. … With this kind of faith, though we may not understand why certain things happen … we can know that in the end everything will make sense. (Dieter F. Uchtdorf, GC, Oct 2016)

---

*A sister shared the following from her mission, which began in Chicago:*

One day I wanted to knock on just one more door.

My companion said, "No, we need to go home."

Thinking my companion was being a little lazy I said a quick prayer and indeed felt she was correct—we needed to go home.

When we arrived at our apartment the zone leader called us and told me I was being transferred to San Diego and leaving at 5 am the next morning!

Since I heeded my companion's prompting, I had time to pack and prepare for my new assignment. Serving as a missionary to the deaf was very unique. Transfers were often to a new mission, mission president, and state! I loved the Chicago mission, but my companion's inspiration helped me know that the transfer was right. (My sister)

———————— • ◆ • ————————

Later in life I found myself single and living with my mother. I was playing with a couple of my grandchildren in the yard one day when a couple of young LDS missionaries walked up to talk to us. After visiting with them briefly I thought I would be coy and get rid of them for good. I said, "I will only talk to young girl missionaries, not young men!'

I had noticed young missionary pairs over the years and had never seen a couple of missionary girls so I felt safe. Was I ever surprised when two sister missionaries showed up the next week! They were so kind and simply got to know us over two months. I don't now how they knew that I didn't like anything quick or pushy.

After becoming friends, they finally suggested we consider the missionary discussions. I agreed and my mother listened in, too. We were both members of two different religions. The first time I stepped into an LDS chapel, a quiet voice said, **"You're home"**. After that I knew I was to be baptized back in 2001. It was the best decision I ever made. My mother was more stubborn, but she came along later and was also baptized. (Branch member)

———————— • ◆ • ————————

The most powerful spiritual experience I've had was when I went up into the mountains to pray about going on a mission or not. I was dating several boys that looked like possible good candidates for marriage. So I was praying about whether I should stay home and get married or go out and serve a mission.

As I was pondering both possibilities in my mind, a very strong impression came into my mind that there were people in a foreign land that needed to hear the gospel and that I was the one to teach it to them. If felt the Spirit so strong that I began crying; I just knew that's what I needed to do.

I had to call my parents because I was only a week into BYU and I had to drop all my classes and prepare for my mission. Everything I was enjoying did not feel right anymore. I didn't feel like I should be in my classes, my apartment with roommates, my ward, or on dates. It was just a really powerful witness that I wasn't supposed to be there and I was supposed to be somewhere else. I was called to northern England. (A Relative)

"Behold, my soul delighteth in the things of the Lord; and my heart pondereth continually upon the things which I have seen and heard." (2 Ne. 4:16)

I served a mission in Micronesia on various islands. My parents sent me this recipe for Reese's Peanut Butter Cups. These treats were always a favorite of mine as a kid. On P-day we bought all the ingredients. We were excited to try that so we whipped them up one morning after our studies. We figured the candies would 'set' while we were out teaching. This caused us to get out ten minutes later than we should have to begin our day.

We felt it was important to follow the rules, however: As we walked down the street we saw emergency vehicles. Exactly where we would have been walking ten minutes ago, a drunk driver came at high speed and smashed into a tree. The man was killed. The timeline was so close that I said, "That's a tender mercy in my book." (A peer)

"But behold, I, Nephi, will show unto you that the tender mercies of the lord are over all those whom he hath chosen, because of their faith, to make them mighty even unto the power of deliverance." (1 Ne. 1:20)

My family has always been a positive influence in my life. We all came from the land of Ecuador. Twenty-five years ago, the Lord led our family to New York City.

About three years ago, I was involved in a serious car accident. The miracle was that I walked away without a scratch. I pondered and prayed over what had happened. Then a few days later, I was home alone when I heard a knock on the door. It was two representatives from the Church, Elder Jeff Alexander and Elder Eric Medina. I knew and felt in my heart that their message was an answer from God. I was baptized July 24, 1994. My mother and father were not pleased with my decision to be baptized, but they had always taught me in my youth to do what is right. I knew this was the right thing to do, but it was not easy.

There was no support from my family. They did not want to hear anything about the Mormons. I was very discouraged for awhile. I found strength in exercising my faith in Jesus Christ and prayed fervently that their hearts would be softened. In the meantime, I attended all my meetings, went out with the missionaries, read my scriptures, served others in small ways, and of course made sure I enjoyed myself by keeping the commandments.

About this time I made up my mind to serve a full-time mission. My parents were very concerned about this, so they decided to do a little investigation of the Church themselves. They not only came to understand my desire to serve a mission, but they also gained a testimony.

I didn't know about any of this. The missionaries and ward members made sure I came to the meetinghouse the day of their baptism. I walked in to find my parents and best friend, Alejandra, sitting in white. My father took me in his arms. This was a very special day!

The Lord has bestowed miracle after miracle upon my family. On Sept. 19, 1997, my mom, Maria, and my father, George, were sealed in the Washington Temple." (Elder Robert Andrade, *Church News*, Dec 6, 1997)

"When your heart begins to tell you things that your mind does not know, then you are getting the Spirit of the Lord." (Harold B. Lee, *New Era*, Feb 1971)

*There is an inherent excitement of spirit amongst missionary labors and conversions. One might think of this wonderful spirit as a "Spirit of*

*Excitement." The profound missionary Paul describes missionaries and converts as thus:*

> "For what is our hope, or joy, or crown of rejoicing: Are not even ye in the presence of our Lord Jesus Christ at his coming? For ye are our hope and our glory." (1 Thes. 2:19-20)

As missionaries in New York, we went on splits and I was placed with a member of the ward. He was a really faithful home teacher and he home taught this couple that we would visit. They were a very unique couple; because the husband was a member of the Reorganized Church and his wife a member of the LDS Church. We went on splits together several times to this family.

We presented Lehi's dream and it was like all brand new knowledge to him; like he may have read it, but it never opened up to him. On our next visit he explained that his Sunday congregation really loved the story of Lehi's dream. He was one of the leading elders in the Reorganized Church of Jesus Christ of Latter-day Saints. He then went on to basically testify that, over time, the LDS Church would join with the Reorganized LDS church.

I guess you could say that I was bold, but I basically testified to him that that would not happen. I testified of the succession of our prophets, starting with Joseph Smith and Brigham Young. I simply stated the facts through testimony. I think the member was a bit surprised.

The next Sunday this member pulled me aside and said, "That sister we visited called me and said that when I was testifying there was a glow around me that was bright!" (A relative)

> "And all that sat in the council, looking steadfastly on him (Stephen), saw his face as it had been the face of an angel." (Acts 6:15)

We were working with an alcoholic man in Antrim, Northern Ireland. He wanted to change his life, but it was very hard for him.

One day as we were street contacting, I thought about him and wondered how he was doing that day. I had the thought that we should call him and ask him. At first, I rationalized, thinking that we saw him all the time and we didn't need to check up on him. I went back to talking to the people on the street. However, the thought persisted and I finally shared it with my companion. We called him during our lunch time.

It turned out that he was having a really rough day and was kind of depressed when we called him. We talked to him for a minute, and then asked if we could come to his home and give him a priesthood blessing. The senior missionary couple in our city came with us and he was able to get a priesthood blessing. It helped him a lot.

He said it was amazing that we knew to call him—we were able to teach him that God is so mindful of his life.

Sometimes those random thoughts that won't go away are actually the Spirit being persistent and trying to get us to do something. (Sister Missionary)

————•◆•————

A few days prior to the meeting, President Tateoka had an impression, a feeling in his heart, to invite *all* missionaries of that zone to the leadership meeting, instead of the prescribed small number of elder and sister leaders....

During this meeting a 9.0-magnitude earthquake and tsunami struck the region of Japan where the Japan Sendai Mission is located. Tragically, many coastal cities—including those from which the missionaries had been gathered—were devastated and suffered great loss of life. And the city of Fukushima suffered a subsequent nuclear event.

Although the meetinghouse where the missionaries were meeting that day was damaged by the earthquake, through following the promptings of the Holy Ghost, President and Sister Tateoka and all missionaries were safely assembled. They were out of harm's way and miles from the devastation of the tsunami and the nuclear fallout. (Gary E. Stevenson, GC, April 2017)

————•◆•————

We had a missionary sister, called to the Ukraine, come to our mission while she waited for her Visa to clear. We receive many missionaries who are called to foreign missions and they normally wait 7 weeks, or 14 weeks, and sometimes even 21 weeks until they're cleared to go to their respective countries.

This missionary sister was so desirous to get to her called labor of service, she questioned, "Why does the Lord want me in Ogden, UT, when I'm called to serve in the Ukraine?"

I advised her to work hard and promised that she would find her purpose in our mission.

She called me up 10 days later, saying, "President, I haven't found my purpose in my mission yet."

I replied to her, "Don't *face your fears, faith your fears* sister."

Two days later a Russian immigrant moved into our area. He was interested in the church and this sister was the only one in our entire mission that could speak Russian. He was baptized this weekend and this sister leaves for Ukraine in two days. There are no coincidences! (Mission President, Ogden Utah Mission, 2/2017)

———◦◆◦———

*President Gordon B. Hinckley discusses his mission to England, which began in Preston, England:*

I was not well when I arrived. Those first few weeks, because of illness and the opposition which we felt, I was discouraged. I wrote a letter home to my good father and said that I felt I was wasting my time and his money. He was my father and my stake president, and he was a wise and inspired man.

He wrote a very short letter to me which said, "Dear Gordon, I have your recent letter. I have only one suggestion: forget yourself and go to work."

Earlier that morning in our scripture class my companion and I had read these words of the Lord: "Whosoever will save his life shall lose it; but whosoever shall lose his life for my sake and the gospel's, the same shall save it." (Mark 8:35.)

Those words of the Master, followed by my father's letter with his counsel to forget myself and go to work, went into my very being. With my father's letter in hand, I went into our bedroom in the house at 15 Wadham Road, where we lived, and got on my knees and made a pledge with the Lord. I covenanted that I would try to forget myself and lose myself in His service.

That July day in 1933 was my day of decision. A new light came into my life and a new joy into my heart. The fog of England seemed to lift, and I saw the sunlight. I had a rich and wonderful mission experience, for which I shall ever be grateful, laboring in Preston where the work began and in other places where it had moved forward, including the great city of London, where I served the larger part of my mission. (*Ensign*, July 1987)

"... the Spirit of the Lord came upon them, and they were filled with joy ..." (Mosiah 4:3)

President David O. McKay shares a mission experience from his father: He accepted a call to a mission about 1880. When he began preaching in his native land and bore testimony of the restoration of the gospel of Jesus Christ, he noticed that the people turned away from him. They were bitter in their hearts against anything Mormon, and the name of Joseph Smith seemed to arouse antagonism in their hearts. ...

In a month or so he became oppressed with a gloomy, downcast feeling, and he could not enter into the spirit of his work. ... he went to the Lord and said, "Unless I can get this felling removed, I shall have to go home. I cannot continue my work with this feeling."

It continued for some time after that, then, one morning, before daylight, following a sleepless night, he decided to retire to a cove, near the ocean, where he knew he would be shut off from the world entirely, and there pour out his soul to God and ask why he was oppressed with this feeling ... He entered that place and said: "Oh, Father, what can I do to have this feeling removed? I must have it lifted or I cannot continue in this work"; and he heard a voice, as distinct as the tone I am now uttering, say: "**Testify that Joseph Smith is a Prophet of God.**"

... the whole thing came to him in a realization that he was there for a special mission, and that he had not given that special mission the attention which it deserved. Then he cried in his heart, "Lord, it is enough," and went out form the cave. (*Gospel Ideals*, 21-22)

In the mission home we enjoyed an amazing sacrament meeting. The speakers consisted of eight Elders who were all converted within fifteen months of entering the mission home. So they all had their respective awesome conversion stories. The spirit in that meeting was indescribable! (Missionary Journal, Feb 1976)

The "spirit of conversion" is extremely exciting and sated with strong spiritual experiences—cherished ones!

Brothers and sisters, this type of love, kindness, and thoughtfulness must— MUST—exist in our missionary and reactivation work. This "love of God" is the spirit of missionary work, and the spirit of reactivation. This "love of God" is the spirit of conversion. This "love of God" is the spirit of nurturing. "It is the most desirable above all things" and it is "the most joyous to the soul" (Yoshihiko Kikuchi, GC, April 1992)

Craig confided to me his deep and abiding love for his parents. He shared his innermost hope that somehow, in some way, his father would be touched by the Spirit and open his heart to the gospel of Jesus Christ. He pleaded earnestly with me for a suggestion. I prayed for inspiration concerning how such a desire might be rewarded. Such inspiration came, and I said to Craig, "Serve the Lord with all your heart. Be obedient to your sacred calling. Each week write a letter to your parents and, on occasion, write to Dad personally and let him know that you love him, and tell him why you're grateful to be his son."

He thanked me and, with his mother, departed the office. I was not to see Craig's mother for some 18 months. She came to the office and, in sentences punctuated by tears, said to me, "It has been almost two years since Craig departed for his mission. His faithful service has qualified him for positions of responsibility in the mission field, and he has never failed in writing a letter to us each week. Recently my husband Fred stood for the first time in a testimony meeting and said, 'All of you know that I am not a member of the Church, but something has happened to me since Craig left for his mission. His letters have touched my soul. May I share one with you?'

"'Dear Dad, Today we taught a choice family about the plan of salvation and the blessings of exaltation in the celestial kingdom. I thought of our family. More than anything in the world, I want to be with you and with Mother in that kingdom. For me it just wouldn't be a celestial kingdom if you were not there. I'm grateful to be your son, Dad, and want you to know that I love you. Your missionary son, Craig.'"

Fred then announced, "My wife doesn't know what I plan to say. I love her and I love our son, Craig. After 26 years of marriage I have made my decision to become a member of the Church, for I know the gospel message is the word of God. I suppose I have known this truth for a long time, but my son's mission has moved me to action. I have made arrangements for my wife and me to meet Craig when he completes his mission. I will be his final baptism as a full-time missionary of the Lord.'" (Thomas S. Monson, GC, Oct 1974)

---

On the very first day of my mission in the missionary training center I was grouped with the only other elder going to New York, all the rest were going to a western state. I was asked to be the senior companion and we began our evening study together.

I did not think of it much at the time, but I chose to read from Gospel Principles and I stopped on the chapter about chastity. We read and discussed the entire chapter. I made the comment, "Can you imagine trying to teach the law of chastity if we're not living it ourselves?" Well I had no clue, but my companion was not worthy to be a missionary.

Three days later my companion confessed to the Mission President and his parents were called to come pick him up. I escorted him to the curb and saw his mom get out of the car crying and hugging him; then he was gone. I didn't think I had promptings, but realized I was led right to that important section and to say certain things. Later in my mission I realized how subtle these spiritual promptings can be. Give me another missionary companionship whose first discussion is the law of chastity. I bet it doesn't happen often! (A Relative)

"For the Holy Ghost will teach you in the same hour what ye ought to say." (Luke 12:12)

---

Early in my mission to Sweden we were teaching Herr Degerfeldt and discussing the discourse in Alma 32 regarding faith.

Our investigator said, "Yes! I get it! It's just like my job; I can see dials and gauges and observe the machines running, but the inner parts I cannot see. I have to simply trust that they will work and function properly." He added, "Faith is just like a school teacher teaching students mathematics. The students need to believe in what the teacher is saying even though they don't know for sure that it's right."

This investigator was teaching us and I was very appreciative of that. He armed us with additional examples that other Swedes could relate to when discussing the principle of faith in their homes. I am grateful to have learned early on that we are not sent only to teach others; we are also meant to experience learning and growth from those we come in contact with. (Missionary Journal 5/14/1976)

◆

*Forty years after my mission, a fellow missionary informed me that I was an important part of his conversion in an unusual way. My curiosity was piqued until he shared the following:*

It was early into my second year as a missionary in Sweden in 1976. We met our new mission president at a Zone conference in Malmö, Sweden. His young age surprised many of us, and to our astonishment, he had been a missionary in Sweden just about fifteen years previously.

One elder wore a hat and at that conference President Oscarson decided that we would all wear felt hats when doing our missionary labors. This is something he had done on his mission in this very area. Our new hats were not to be knit or fur, but felt only. I thought, "Felt hats are not warm, especially in the cold winters!" That directive made no sense to me.

But the more I brooded on the subject, the more I was convinced that it was nonsense getting a felt hat. As the weeks went by I chose simply to refuse to get a felt hat. My arguments found a receptive audience with my companion. That wasn't the case with my mission leaders.

My District Leader would make it the first subject of our weekly phone calls: "Have you got your hats yet?" Then the Zone Leaders were getting in on applying the pressure. After awhile another Zone Conference was coming. We were the only companionship without hats. I finally succumbed, but on my terms. We chose felt hats that looked like the 1940's. (Think Newman & Redford in *The Sting*)

While we were at that Zone Conference, the Zone Leaders slipped out and organized everyone's coats and hats in a nice orderly manner on the coat rack and shelf. To me this was just a memory from our President's mission that the leaders were determined to force on us.

I can honestly say I have no recollection of anything that was taught or shared that entire conference. The Spirit was not with me and I didn't care! I stewed the entire conference.

One particular Elder (Elder Laing) I think loved goading me about hats. He made a comment that didn't make sense, "That will probably help us baptize about as much as our hats will."

Any talk about hats would set me off. I was doing the dishes a few days later and I started thinking about hats again. The District Leaders knew how I felt. I then went to the Zone Leaders who I felt used hats to further their prestige with the Mission President. I vented to the Assistants to the President and finally told our Mission President that I felt he was gratifying a nostalgic memory. But it didn't stop there ... I then went to the Missionary Committee thinking they couldn't figure out we need warm hats for cold weather.

Then I thought to myself, "Who's on the Missionary Committee?—none other than Apostles and a Prophet of the Lord."

I paused doing the dishes.

At that instant I did a complete 180-degree turnabout.

Hats would no longer be an issue for me. I knew I had turned a corner when that Elder in the District tried to provoke me one more time by saying, "It would help us baptize about as much as these hats will." I didn't get upset in the least. In fact, I thought to myself, "You don't know this, but this hat just might help get me a baptism more than you think!" Then I smiled.

By goading me on hats, that Elder provoked me to come to a crisis from which I could return. All these years later, forty, I wanted to let him know how thankful I was for him in a service he never would have imagined! (A fellow missionary)

When we were laboring in Aberdeen, Scotland, there was a sister who didn't have a companion for a week, so we were a trio with her. I was new to the area and didn't know my way around at all. The sister who was staying with us for a week had a car, but usually the missionaries in our area used public transportation.

The catch was the car didn't have a GPS; none of us knew the roads in Aberdeen. Accordingly, one day, we got hopelessly lost in the middle of a neighborhood (the kind where all the houses look the same).

Since we didn't have many options, we decided to try praying for directions. At every intersection we would say a quick prayer in our hearts and then go whichever direction we felt impressed to go: right, left, or straight ahead.

Amazingly, after about 10 minutes, we found our way back to a main road that we recognized. Looking at a map that evening, we discovered that we had zigzagged through the neighbor hood a bit, but we didn't make any incorrect turns.  We never had to turn around and were always heading in the general direction we needed to go. The Spirit really can guide us in all things. (Missionary Sister)

"Howbeit when he, the Spirit of truth, is come, he will guide you into all truth ..." (John 16:13)

During my mission to Guam we were working on a small island.

Our power had gone out and my companion said, "Let's pray." So we knelt down and he asked for power. As soon as he said "Amen", the power was restored.

Fast-forward a few months and we experienced a dry spell in the second wettest country on earth. We had a 20-gallon metal tub that caught rainwater for our needs. The container was empty due to the lack of rain. We were starting to get desperate. My companion and I went over to the clerk's office and noticed he was watching a rebroadcast of General Conference.

President Monson was telling the story about the military men floating in the ocean for days:

"For three days we floated about in enemy territory with ships all about us and planes overhead. Why they couldn't see a yellow group of rafts on blue water is a mystery," he wrote. "A storm came up, and waves thirty feet high almost tore our rafts apart. Three days went by with no food or water. The others asked me if I prayed. I answered that I did pray and we would indeed be rescued. That evening we saw our submarine that was there to rescue us, but it passed by. The next morning it did the same. We knew this was the last day [it would] be in the area. Then came the promptings of the Holy Ghost, **'You have the priesthood. Command the sub to pick you up.'** Silently I prayed, 'In the name of Jesus Christ, and by the power of the priesthood, turn about and pick us up.' In a few minutes, they were alongside of us. When on deck, the captain ... said, 'I don't know how we ever found you, for we were not even looking for you.' I knew." (President Thomas Monson, GC, Oct 2008)

After watching that with the clerk, I said, "we have the priesthood too, why don't we use it to ask for rain? We need to exercise our faith."

My companion agreed with my idea. We knelt in prayer again and using the priesthood we commanded the skies to open and release rain for the island. The rains came so heavily that our twenty gallon storage tank was overflowing. We had more than enough water. (A peer)

This area had been experiencing an especially dry season, and I believe many prayers had been sent heavenward over the preceding several weeks for much-needed rain. Unfortunately, it came just before the performance and stayed for the entire production! Despite the fact that the youth were soaked through with the rain and chilled from the cool temperature, we all felt the Spirit of the Lord. (President Thomas S. Monson, GC, April 2014)

----◆----

I was serving in the northeastern United States in Amish country at the time. There was a small, tiny branch that we served in. Essentially what happened is that I got a call in the middle of the night. I'm a deep sleeper and the first time it rang forever and began to wake me up, but I never answered it. Then the phone started ringing again. I picked it up and on the other end was this distraught woman. She was going on and on and apologizing and kept saying "I'm sorry." Eventually I realized she thought she was talking to the friend that had just raped her.

She was in a mind frame that it was her fault. It was an interesting phone call.

After she finally finished, I said, "This is not Max. I am a missionary from the Church of Jesus Christ of Latter-day Saints." I began teaching her the principles of the Gospel. She would back away and I would lighten up. Then I would teach some more. Then I convinced her that she needed to go to the hospital and get some things done that way.

I knew that this was no coincidence that she called me. Anyway, I had always wanted to meet her, but never did. She did send me a letter and thanked me for being there for her. It was such a unique experience. I feel like I helped the girl. A member was aware of the situation and got a Book of Mormon to her. I don't know if she was baptized, but a seed had been planted in a most desperate situation. (A Relative)

---

"On my mission I remember many times that my companion and I would pray together about where to go and who to visit or call. When we both got the same answer, we always knew it was right." (Family member)

"Wherefore, I the Lord ask you this question—unto what were ye ordained? To preach my gospel by the Spirit, even the Comforter which was sent forth to teach the truth." (D&C 50:13-14)

---

Early in my mission to Sweden I was still serving with my trainer. We had one investigator, Rolf Lundgren, who was very interested and had solid questions. He was just a few years older than we were.

As we visited after another discussion, he suggested, "I would like to go out into the woods and pray like Joseph Smith did. I would like you to go with me."

That sounded like an awesome idea and we asked him what he wanted to pray about.

He thought praying about Joseph Smith would be a good idea. "But," he revealed, "I don't really know how to pray."

We went through the steps for prayer and then found a secluded grove of trees to pray in, just outside of town. There are flurries of forests in Scandinavia. My companion suggested we kneel down in a circle and then take turns praying. We would all pray about the truthfulness of the Prophet Joseph Smith.

We both said consecutive prayers and then Rolf offered his humble, heartfelt, and faithful plea. He followed the steps we had taught him perfectly. What we didn't expect was the powerful answer we all received. There seemed to be a large column of light and the Spirit was as tall as the trees and as wide as the grove. It was nearly overwhelming! Rolf could barely finish his prayer and afterwards he fell to the ground crying. We were all overcome with extreme emotion and shed a flood of tears.

My companion and I remained on our knees, weakened by the strong spiritual feast. It was so strong that it seemed like an out-of-body experience. I felt like I was as tall as the treetops or as if my spirit was enlarged and expanded to encompass the entire height and width of the grove of trees!

> "... whether in the body, I cannot tell; or whether out of the body, I cannot tell: God knoweth ..." (2 Cor. 12:12)

God had given us an undeniable witness regarding the Prophet Joseph Smith's true mission. There was no doubt in any of our minds. No longer did I believe, I knew! My companion knew! Our investigator knew! I had the thought, "Joseph Smith is a lot more important than I ever realized." We gave Rolf additional council and taught him more, once we regained our composure, as we walked to his home from the woods.

During our next discussion Rolf exclaimed, "I don't know if I want to pray again—because I might blow to pieces!" That comment brought back a portion of that strong spirit we had experienced in the grove, to bask in once again. Even with that, Rolf was not ready to give up some of his addictions; even though he had at least two amazing witnesses. There were some powerful seeds planted in Rolf that day that I know blossomed in his future. What an unquestionable testimony booster for two young elders.

> "To the many missionaries ... I share the observation that the seeds of testimony frequently do not immediately take root and flower. Bread cast upon the water returns, at times, only after many days. But it does return." (Thomas S. Monson, GC, April 2003)

This early mission experience was one of the highlights of my mission and my life. I am eternally grateful for the perseverance and faithfulness of the Prophet Joseph Smith. (Missionary Journal, 6/7/1976)

> I was on my knees and jumped up and told him to hold on that I was not a learned man, and I thought that my ordination would injure the work. But presently the Holy Ghost came upon me till I thought that I should be burnt up. (Heber C. Kimball, JD 12:188)

> Here in mortality, we already know moments when because of the great goodness of God, there is a gushing out of many tears. Our joy is brim. Yet this is but a foretaste of the ultimate homecoming, when our cups will not only be brim, but will run over without ceasing. (Neal A Maxwell, GC, April 1988)

> Joseph Smith, the Prophet and Seer of the Lord, has done more, save Jesus only, for the salvation of men in this world, than any other man that ever lived in it. In the short space of twenty years, he has brought forth the Book of Mormon, which he translated by the power of God, and has been the means of publishing it on two continents; has sent the fulness of the everlasting gospel, which it contained, to the four quarters of the earth; has brought forth the revelations and commandments which compose this book of Doctrine and Covenants, and many other wise documents and instructions for the benefit of the children of men ... (D&C 135:3)

--------◆·-------

> My companion and I were fasting for someone to teach the Gospel to. We were seeking direction about where to labor because the Lord knows who's ready to receive the Gospel; we just need to find them.
> We had fasted for twenty-four hours and then looked at the map and I said, "Heavenly Father, we have prepared our hearts, where should we go? What street shall we tract or where can we find a family that is searching for the Gospel?" As we looked at the map, one of the streets showed up, it was emphasized to me. I knew that was the street we were supposed to go to.

We went to that street which is very long and we spent all day on that street. Hardly anyone was home and those that were home were not interested. We went clear down to the end and worked our way up the other side. We only had a half-of-a block left and it was looking dismal, but I knew this is where Heavenly Father wanted us to be. 'Where is the door we are supposed to find?'

Just as I was saying that, two twin girls showed up on the sidewalk and each one had a cupcake.

They said, "Hey Elders, we thought you'd like something."

After fasting, they tasted really good! That was the family we were supposed to meet. The twins introduced us to the rest of the family. We had already knocked on their door, but they weren't home. They had just returned from a soccer game and were getting ready to go somewhere else. We were able to make an appointment with them.

So it wasn't a door or even a house like we assumed. They met us on the sidewalk. We began teaching the family; the children that were of age were baptized. (A Relative)

"...with singleness of heart that thy fasting may be perfect, or, in other words, that thy joy may be full." (D&C 59:14)

———————•◆•———————

The little boat had been tossed by storms for more than six weeks as it made its way slowly from England to South Africa. Elder Franklin D Price, a young Mormon missionary ... became more worried because food and money were scarce ... no one was permitted in the country unless he had twenty dollars ... Elder Price did not have the required sum.

When the boat finally docked ... As he walked off the ship, he noticed a small folded piece of paper lying at the foot of the gangplank. Without thinking ... he picked it up, and automatically slipped the paper into his pocket.

... At the border, immigration officials came aboard ... Elder Price was worried about what would happen to him. ... When the men approached, Elder Price felt a moment of panic. Then, without even knowing why, he reached into his pocket and pulled out the piece of paper ... The man nodded his head and returned the paper to the astonished elder.

The paper was an endorsed check in the amount of twenty dollars ... tears of gratitude streamed down his face ... The mission president suggested the check be locked in a trunk ... when Elder Price unlocked the truck to show some elders, it was not there! It had disappeared as mysteriously as it had come! (True Stories from South Africa, *Friend*, April 1972)

———•◆•———

We were on a mission in Australia and one of the Elders felt so strongly that he had been sent to the wrong place. This Elder complained and talked about "his dilemma" often.

The Mission President and mission leaders became so tired of this Elder's bellyaching that they transferred him to Perth, Australia. This is about as far as you can physically get from Salt Lake City, UT, as far as an organized church.

This Elder and his companion were out tracting one day in an area where the people had their names on their doors. The carping Elder was drawn to this one door because it had the same peculiar surname that he had. He thought, "This is really weird, I've never seen my odd name anywhere before."

Upon asking the woman at the door about the odd name which matched his missionary nametag, she explained, "This is my dad's name and he's from Arizona. He abandoned the family when I was just three years old and they had no idea where he ended up." After comparing notes they realized they had the same father and were brother and sister! He no longer questioned why he was called to the Australian mission. (A Relative)

"Now the word of the Lord came unto Jonah ... Arise, go to Nineveh, that great city, and cry against it ... But Jonah rose up to flee from the presence of the Lord" (Jonah 1:1-3)

———•◆•———

Early on in my mission I was struggling with the language. We often repeated the 1st Discussion when meeting various people, so those discussions went well. As we were teaching a couple beyond the initial discussion, we were going over the steps of repentance prior to baptism. I was much less familiar with this latter discussion. As we were teaching this young couple, an enormous feeling of guilt swept over my mind and body.

We reviewed "restitution for any sins" where it was possible to: replace, repair, or repay any losses or damages to those that had been wronged.

I thought, "Man, what a hypocrite I am. I need to practice what I preach! I can't teach this before I live it myself!" My mind reverted to a childhood memory.

A friend and I loved the Matchbox series cars and trucks. These cool metal cars and trucks were fifty-five cents each. We had a devious little plan to avoid detection. We would always buy one car each, every time we came in to the five and dime store. We would also pocket one car each before buying our new cars. Our ingenious buy-one-get-one-free plan was simply shoplifting; buying one car and walking out with two. The store owner was a grumpy old man.

I felt terrible and justifiably unworthy to truthfully teach the principle of repentance to our investigators. My conscious was eating away at me and making me a miserable missionary.

I guesstimated how many toy cars I had stolen and added some extra dollars for a couple I may have forgotten. Then I added the 3% sales tax. I wrote a letter of apology and enclosed a check for my transgressions to the dime store owner. It would take some time to arrive from overseas. I never heard from the store. After repenting the guilt was gone and that was a great relief. (Journal 6/7/1979)

After my mission and upon returning to my home town, I went around to all the businesses to say hi. Dad had a photo studio right down town and we knew most of the retailers on our five-block main street. As I came into the Ben Franklin store, the old grump smiled and gave me a warm handshake and a hug! That was unexpected.

He exclaimed, "Welcome back, I have never had anyone send me a letter with money in it likes yours! And I know I've had a lot of little things walk out of my store over the years." We became fast friends.

Following my marriage and college graduation we moved back to this area to work for a gift and novelty company. The former town grump, turned warm friend, was an awesome test-market customer for our business. He would try anything we came up with, gladly paying for any product. Other accounts in a two-state area also tested products; most of those would only do products on consignment—paying us only for product they actually sold.

My new found friend would take various product lines and display them on prime shelving spots. That long overdue repentance/repayment and apology letter really paid off! The store owner did not seem grumpy any more. In retrospect, the best part was that the guilt vanished and I functioned as a much better missionary and a better person in the future, no longer the hypocrite.

> When "a mighty change" is required, full repentance involves a *180-degree turn,* and without looking back! Initially, this turning reflects progress from telestial to terrestrial behavior, and later on to celestial behavior. As the sins of the telestial world are left behind, the focus falls ever more steadily upon the sins of omission, which often keep us from full consecration. (Neal A. Maxwell, GC, Oct 1991)

When I was on my mission there was an emphasis to search for a service project weekly. Sometimes the projects found us. We were downtown and I was drawn to this woman in a phone booth who was making call after call. I went over and asked her if she was in trouble and needed someone to help her.

She told us that she was looking for people to help her plant her tomato plants. The reason she needed help is because she had 2,500 tomato plants! I explained to her that we were missionaries and tried to do service every week; we would be glad to help her. We hurried home and changed clothes and then met her at her home in the country. The crazy thing was that we were fasting that day. There was a hot summer sun beating down on us.

We were helping her children with all the planting and they would offer us snacks and water. We turned them down and then finally told them we were fasting. This was a Catholic family living an Amish lifestyle. They had no electricity and no running water. The woman was impressed with us because we were freely serving and fasting. She felt like we were a great example for her children, insomuch that she invited us to dinner. We were able to teach them the first discussion by lamplight, kind of like the Joseph Smith era.

The father and children were receptive, but the mother was not. Well, we planted some good seeds and a whole bunch of tomato plants! (A Relative)

Now, we will compare the word unto a seed. Now, if ye give place, that a seed may be planted in your heart, behold, if it be a true seed, or a good seed, if ye do not cast it out by your unbelief, that ye will resist the Spirit of the Lord, behold, it will begin to swell within your breasts; and when you feel these swelling motions, ye will begin to say within yourselves—It must needs be that this is a good seed, or that the word is good, for it beginneth to enlarge my soul; yea, it beginneth to enlighten my understanding, yea, it beginneth to be delicious to me. (Alma 32:28)

———————•◆•———————

At times ward and/or stake leaders will invite members to purchase Book of Mormons for around one dollar each. Back then we were asked to place a picture of our family along with our testimonies in each Book of Mormon we purchased. These books would then be handed to missionaries in various missions and then be given out to their investigators. We chose to participate each time this program was offered.

Out of the blue one day, a letter came from the California Ventura mission saying: "Thank you for your donation of a Book of Mormon. One of our investigators received your book with your family picture and testimonies. Johnny got baptized!"

We decided to send out many more Book of Mormons along with our family picture and testimonies. (Journal 4/26/1983)

———————•◆•———————

I was serving with another sister in the northeastern United States. We were teaching a doctor that was feeling very troubled. He was distraught and downtrodden due to a sin-filled life. He felt like there was no forgiveness for him, so why should he even try?

We prayed earnestly for a solution that would best help him in his quandary. I had the Holy Ghost whisper to me, **"Give him the *Miracle of Forgiveness*."** We had a member who sourced a copy and presented it to our investigator. This book changed his mind set and his life! The doctor realized that he could be forgiven and the *Miracle of Forgiveness* is the reason he chose to be baptized.

Besides the miracle of conversion, the real miracle occurred in our apartment one evening. Two pillars of brightness appeared in our room and we both witnessed the warm colors and experienced a positive energy that was so wonderful. We thought they may be two translated beings or special angels. The experience lasted for nearly thirty minutes. Before disappearing, we heard just two words—**"Thank you."**

Their positive influence and amazing spirit seemed to linger throughout our apartment for two-and-a-half days! We then surmised that the two enlightened beings were most likely righteous spirits from Paradise, the doctor's kindred dead that thanked us for following the Spirit and bringing their loved one around. (Our friend)

"When messengers are sent to minister to the inhabitants of this earth, they are not strangers, but from the ranks of our kindred, friends, and fellow-beings and fellow-servants." (Joseph F Smith, *Gospel Doctrine*, 435)

———◆———

When Elder Monson was ordained an Apostle of Jesus Christ and spoke in Conference, the Spirit said to me, **"He will one day be the Prophet."** It was such a strong feeling in my heart as the words came to my mind. This became an important witness to me that my husband was the right man for me when he told me, as we were dating, that President Monson came to his mission in Australia, just after being ordained an Apostle and as Elder Monson walked into the room, the Spirit told my husband **"He will one day be the Prophet."** At that time, I told my boyfriend that I had had the exact same witness. As we began our couple's mission 42 years later, that personal revelation became reality with our own special witness on our new missionary cards—authorized by President Thomas S. Monson. We felt such joy and increased faith in the Lord and His kingdom on earth going forth as ambassadors for His church! We headed out for Cle Elum, Washington.

We finally arrived during the night at Ensign Ranch in a continually ferocious snowstorm as the ranch sign swung fiercely in the wind. We were welcomed with loving kindness and shown to our little trailer where missionaries had previously hand shoveled a walkway, with five foot walls of snow, to our door. Once inside, we found welcoming handmade cards and cookies from the other missionary couples. Our warm welcome was a stark contrast to the threatening elements outside.

My husband was put to work the next day plowing snow, plowing snow, and plowing snow. I became snowed under in the office trying to decipher their dinosaur-era reservation process—all by hand with 12 different places to record information. I was feeling worthless and discouraged as I went to bed one night and the phone rang.

Our daughter was in intensive care for a full-blown asthma attack caused by a friend's cleaners as this friend helped clean their home. Our daughter was pregnant, too. I knew some natural remedies that helped as I had helped her through many attacks throughout her life; her three little girls knew me like a mother because they all lived in our home for a year. At one point the oldest girl suggested, "Grandma, could we just call you Mom and pretend like our mother is the babysitter?"

One of the girls is autistic; she loved me like her mother also and needed special care. There was no doubt in my mind that it was urgent that I return home. After all, I wasn't being of much use in the office! When I told my husband, he stated, "A prophet of the Lord has sent us here and HERE is where we are going to stay." We readied for bed and prayed for our family and the unborn child.

As my husband went to sleep, I began to start packing. I could be halfway to Provo, UT, by the time he woke up. As I was packing, the thought came into my mind, **"You should pray about going."** I hadn't even considered praying because I KNEW I was needed at my daughter's side! Knowing what the answer would be, I knelt down and asked the Lord. To my surprise these words came into my mind, **"Call your mother."** I thought, "It's 1:00 am in Arizona now! I can't call her." Again the words came into my mind, **"Call your mother."**

So I called my mom in the middle of the night and she answered! She was awake! I told mother what was happening and what I was about to do. Immediately a wave of power washed over me with certain knowledge that mother spoke the truth as she said with strong emphasis, "You can do more for your daughter by staying on your mission than you can by coming home!"

I hung up the phone and went to bed and fell asleep immediately with perfect calm and faith that all would be well. True to the promise of the Lord through my mother, our other married daughters, one by one, came to their sister's aide, from all across the west—two weeks at a time to feed, clean, and care for their nieces' needs. The closeness and love that bonded our daughters from this experience would have never happened if I had been there to take care of our ill daughter and her family. I see this increased connection of love between our daughters as a gift from God for our faithful missionary service. (Our friend)

"... And it is the Spirit that beareth witness, because the Spirit is truth." (1 John 5:6)

———————◆———————

I had a companion that did not want to be on a mission. His father promised him the keys to an expensive car if he would go on a mission. I was trying to help him have a good experience so he would have a desire to do missionary work. He wouldn't do door approaches; in fact, he wouldn't do much of anything.

So I was praying over the map of our area, seeking inspiration for where we could go so that he could have a great experience. This whole street just lights up on the map! This street went for miles and miles in a major city. There are thousands of houses on this extremely long street; they all look the same. But I knew that was where we were supposed to go.

I was so excited for the next morning. We got to the street and then I wondered if we should go left for miles or right for miles. I felt we should go a certain way; we chained up our bikes to the street sign. I was full of enthusiasm and we began knocking on doors. My companion wouldn't say anything. Sometimes he would step back or even be clear back in the street when I was knocking on a door. And it was a terrible day!

Every door we knocked on, they would: scream and yell at us, sick the dogs on us, and swear at us. Then we came to a door where an old drunk came out and threw a beer bottle at us and he was screaming anti-Christ vulgarities. We tracted all morning, had lunch and came back and the afternoon was even worse! It was a terrible day of tracting. I went home feeling just beat up.

At home I looked at the map and we hadn't even covered a tenth of the street. So we planned to go back there again. Now my companion refused to leave the apartment, so I couldn't leave. So I called the District Leader and they came and split with us; so the District Leader went out with me and his companion stayed in our apartment. This other elder hoped to do something constructive and encourage the lazy one.

We knocked all day long. I told this elder about how strongly I felt about this street.

At the end of the day we knocked on a door and this little man, about 4' something came to the door. And he says, "Thank you, I have been praying that you would come."

We sat down and explained about the Book of Mormon and how Christ came to the Americas. This man just started bawling and bawling.

We left him crying as he tearfully thanked us for bringing him the Book of Mormon. I asked him if we could come back the next day and he readily agreed. But we couldn't go because my companion wouldn't budge. He was sent home two days later. So this missionary I was trying to help never did get to meet our golden contact. I was able to go on splits with a member and we returned to this man's house.

We turned to 3 Nephi to read and discussed Christ's visit to America. Again, the man starting bawling and bawling and then I started cry. He told us that when he read 3 Nephi 11 the Spirit told him, "**My son, these things are true.**" Then a pillar of light and the Spirit entered the room swirling around and it was the choicest experience! The member, this investigator, and I were all bawling.

Once we stopped crying and our investigator could gather himself, he said, "I just heard these words again: '**My son, these things are true.**'"

It was a most amazing and beautiful experience! This man and his wife were both baptized one month later. (Our friend)

... Being weighed down with sorrow, wading through much tribulation and anguish of soul because of the wickedness of the people ... while Alma was thus weighed down with sorrow, behold an angel of the Lord appeared unto him saying: Blessed art thou, Alma, lift up thy head and rejoice ... (Alma 8:14)

And they ministered to the Lord, and fasted, the Holy Ghost said, **Separate me Barnabas and Saul for the work whereunto I have called them**. And when they had fasted and prayed, and laid their hands on them, they sent them their away. So they, being sent forth by the Holy Ghost, departed unto Seleucia; and from then they sailed to Cyprus. (Acts 13:2-4)

*This is a perfect example for all missionary callings and assignments. Leaders fast from the world and pray to seek counsel and guidance from the Holy Ghost regarding respective missionary duties: Apostles selecting mission presidents and laying hands on their heads, general authorities deciding worldwide missionary assignments, mission presidents inspired direction placing elders and sisters in leadership positions and/or the right area for specific times, and missionaries praying for direction on how and where to reach and teach people on various days in their different areas.*

---

*And, last but not least, please enjoy the following from one of our favorite, most successful, missionaries of all-time—Elder Wilford Woodruff laboring for the Lord in England:*

… in Herefordshire, there were people who had never seen a Latter-day Saint, and never heard of the Gospel. … I went one evening to the town of Hanley. There was a very large congregation and I had appointments out for two or three weeks in that town and adjacent villages. As I went to take my seat the Spirit of the Lord came upon me and said to me, **"this is the last meeting you will hold with this people for many days."** I was surprised, because I did not know, of course what the Lord wanted me to do. I told the assembly when I rose, "This is the last meeting I shall hold with your for many days." They asked me after the meeting where I was going. I told them I did not know. I went before the Lord in my closet and asked him where he wished me to go, and all the answer I could get was to go to the South.

"But this is not all; ye must pour out your souls in your closets, and your secret places, and in your wilderness." (D&C 34:26)

"And the angel of the Lord spake unto Philip, saying, **Arise, and go toward the south unto the way that goeth down from Jerusalem unto Gaza, which is desert.**" (Acts 8:26)

*Can you imagine being a missionary with two to three weeks of solid appointments, baptizing five or six people every evening, and then being told to leave the area?!*

I got onto a stage and rode eighty miles south, as I was led by the Spirit of the Lord ... I had learned that there were six hundred people there, under Elder Kington, called the United Brethren, and that they had been praying to the Lord for guidance in the way of life and salvation. Then I knew why the Lord had sent me to that place—he had sent them what they had been praying for. I commenced preaching the Gospel to them, and I also commenced baptizing ... and out of the six hundred belonging to Elder Kingston's body all were baptized but one in seven month's labor. I brought eighteen hundred into the church on that mission, and I will say that the power of God rested upon me and upon the people. (Wilford Woodruff, *JD* 342-3)

*Read and reread Paul's council to the Romans when you find yourself down and/or discouraged in your calling/s or missionary work.*

"And how shall they preach, except they be sent? as it is written, How beautiful are the feet of them that preach the gospel of peace, and bring glad tidings of good things!" (Romans 10:16)

---

"I have just had real, genuine joy and satisfaction in proclaiming the gospel and bearing my testimony of the divinity of Jesus Christ, and the divine calling of Joseph Smith, the prophet." (Heber J. Grant, CR, Oct 1942)

# 4. The Joy of the Saints

"And it came to pass that there was no contention in the land, because of the love of God which did dwell in the hearts of the people." (4 Ne. 1:15)

In the early 60's I enjoyed staying with my aunt and uncle in North Ogden, UT, for weeks at a time during the summer. Their family consisted of five boys while I lived with five younger sisters. To have boys to play with was a real treat. After awhile the allure of Easy Bake Oven, Barbie dolls, and all the other girl toys wore off.

My aunt's boys had a half-day of summer camp during the week. My aunt and uncle both worked full time, so I was left with a sitter each morning during the week. The lady in their ward that tended me appeared as an angel in my mind and was just as good as one! She treated me like one of her own children and made me feel so loved. She was very cheerful and full of charity. She glowed!

At that early age I even thought, "I'd like my future wife to be like her!" I really enjoyed being in her home. This is during the time I was ten, eleven, and twelve years old. Her fresh-picked cherries were the best I have ever tasted, along with other fresh fruit from her property.

Later in life, I asked my Aunt Joyce, "Who was that angelic, loving lady you left me with on those summer mornings when I lived with you guys?"

She replied, "Oh that's Michaelene Grassli. Sister Grassli is a wonderful women and she's served on the church's general boards for many years."

I learned that Sister Grassli served on the general Primary board, as a counselor and lastly as the Primary general president. She served in all three of those callings, consecutively from 1975—1994, serving faithfully for eight years as the general Primary president. Sister Grassli is a perfect example of charity that I classify as: *the Goodness of the Saints*.

"Then this Daniel was preferred above the presidents and princes, because *an excellent spirit was in him*; and the king thought to set him over the whole realm." (Daniel 6:3)

Jesus gave us a clear pattern to follow in fulfilling our responsibility to nurture and teach children. ... As he demonstrated, *our* physical presence and attention is vital to the children in our families, church, and communities.

We can know their needs and minister to them *when we spend time with them.* We can *behold* our children in their eternal perspective and see that they *all* know of the Savior and learn the significant truths of his gospel. We can help them witness marvelous spiritual events. They can hear our earnest prayers in their behalf. **We are their ministering angels on earth** if we follow the Lord's example. (Michaelene P. Grassli, GC, Oct 1992)

*One of the **sweetest ministering angels** I was blessed to be served by as a boy. She wonderfully walked the talk!*

———————•◆•———————

I remember when, as a young deacon, I would cover a portion of the ward on fast Sunday morning, giving the small envelope to each family, waiting while a contribution was placed in it, and then returning it to the bishop. On one such occasion, an elderly member, Brother Wright, welcomed me at the door and, with aged hands, fumbled at the tie of the envelope and placed within it a quarter. His eyes fairly twinkled as he made his contribution. He told me of a time years before when the Relief Society president, Sister Balmforth, with food collected from those who had given, carried to his home in a small red wagon food for his cupboard and provided gratitude for his soul. He described her as "an angel sent from heaven" I have not forgotten Eddie Wright. (Thomas S. Monson, GC, Oct 1996)

———————•◆•———————

Our family has been richly blessed and I was pondering how I could bless other people's lives. For the past three years, every time I am at a drive-through-window, I pay for the person's meal/s behind me.
Recently I pulled up to the drive-through to pay for my order and the carful behind me. Frantically searching through the car, I realized that I had forgotten my purse. I had no money!
The clerk noticed me being frazzled and informed me, "Calm down; the car ahead of you already paid for your meal!" (Our relative)

"… see that you are merciful unto your brethren; deal justly, judge righteously, and do good continually; and if ye do all these things then shall ye receive your reward; yea, ye shall have mercy restored unto you again ..."(Alma 41:13)

––––––––––◆––––––––––

Several years ago, a gold class ring from the 60's was found on a beach reservoir after the lake had receded. I had the ring for several years; when gold prices hit nearly $2,000/ounce in 2011/2012. I took the ring into a jeweler. He confirmed the ring was definitely gold and offered me an unacceptable price. I put the ring back on a shelf in a closet.

My old high school formed a Facebook group which enabled us to post information, obtain contacts, and see which of our classmates had passed away already. I noticed that ring on my shelf, which wasn't really mine, and wondered if that class had a Facebook page. I was able to find it—I posted a ring find on the out-of-state's high school page in 2016.

I received a call the summer of 2018 from a woman who claimed the ring belonged to her husband. After visiting with her husband, who turned out to be the previous owner, he exclaimed, "Oh that was probably one of my two ex wives who tossed my ring into the reservoir!" I obtained their address and told them I would be glad to send the ring to them with no remuneration.

Several months later I received a letter in the mail: "Dear Mr. Laing, thank you very much for finding and returning my class ring. It had been lost for a very long time. Here's a little something for you to get a nice steak dinner. Thank you so much." Enclosed was $50 in cash! (Journal 9/30/18)

––––––––––◆––––––––––

*Ezra Taft Benson shares an experience while working in Washington, DC:*

The Chicago business man explained "I told some of my business associates that I had been given the responsibility of coming down to Washington, D.C. to establish an office and employ a man to represent our corporation…. a man who is honest, a man of real integrity, a man who lives a clean live, who is clean morally, who, if married, is a devoted husband, and who, if unmarried, is not chasing lewd women. I would like a man who doesn't drink, and if possible I would prefer to get a man who doesn't even smoke."
"Well what you need is a returned Mormon missionary."
"Are there any Mormons in Washington?"
"I don't know, I suppose there are. They seem to be everywhere."

"Can you give me the names of three or four young men who meet the standards which I have just outlined?"

Well of course it was not difficult to give him the name of three or four dozen who fully met the standards he outlined. I mention this, my brethren and sisters and friends, because in the Church we have certain standards— standards of living, standards of morality, standards of character which are coming to be well known in the world. These standards are admired. People with such standards are sought after. These standards are based on true, eternal principles. They are eternal verities. (CR, April 1958)

In our local Care Center Branch there is a resident who is always positive and smiling. He has lost one leg and has had other surgeries and complications. Amidst what most would call serious issues he finds joy. He cheers everyone up. His glass is full to overflowing!

This saint will go around in his wheelchair to greet all the new residents. He visits with them and finds out what their favorite things are. He will then prepare little gifts, such as: gum, candy, $5 bill, or even cigarettes, and deliver them to the respective residents. He also takes time to get to know his long-term peers.

We were disappointed to learn that he was looking to go to another facility because this care center wanted more money from him. The next week we were very pleased to find out why he would not be moving out. The administrator of the facility told this happy man that his rate would stay low because of his excellent dealings with all the other residents. He boosted the morale of his peers and the workers. He was such a good influence to everyone there; the administration was willing to do whatever it took to keep him in their facility. We are grateful for the decision because this brother is an example for our branch presidency, its members, and visitors too! (Journal 1/14/2018)

*The children of Israel were sacrificing and worshipping for fourteen days when Solomon brought the ark and the covenant into the holy of holies in the temple.*

"On the eighth day he sent the people away: and they blessed the king, and went unto their tents joyful and glad of heart for all the goodness that the LORD had done for David his servant, and for Israel his people." (1 Kings 8:66)

We enjoyed playing church volleyball to the extreme that we decided to join the city leagues. After a few seasons, our LDS team would be vying for the championship and either win it all, or place second, and sometimes third. This was a co-ed division that we competed in along with our wives.

After several seasons and a fun match one night, we were walking down the long school hall towards the parking lot. I heard somebody running up behind me and was expecting them to pass us, figuring they must be hurrying to get somewhere. However, the quick footsteps suddenly stopped and I felt a tap on the shoulder.

A nice woman from another team asked if she could talk to me.

I said, "Sure." (I was the team captain).

She explained, "I would like to join your team, if you have room for me. I have watched you guys play and there's something different about all of you. What I really noticed is that you are all happy, even when your team loses! When the other teams lose, they kick, swear, get angry, and then go out and get drunk. I really like how your team carries itself and acts. I don't want to be on any of the other teams. I would like to play with your team."

I responded with, "Let me visit with my team and I'll get back with you; just give me your number."

After talking it over with our team, we all agreed that she could be an asset to our team; we could also provide a good atmosphere for her. We had not really noticed what she observed in us; we were simply being ourselves. After playing several matches together over the coming weeks she wanted to know more about us and why we acted like we did. We explained that we were all members of the Mormon Church and strived to live our religion 24/7.

She asked to know more; we told her about our missionaries and set up an appointment with the Elders for her family. She had an entire volleyball team as her fellowshippers!

She was divorced and had two school-age children. Her family took the discussions together, prayed about it, and chose to be baptized. Her daughter was baptized first. Our new friend was baptized at a later date because her parents were in such an uproar. We were elated as our volleyball team was all there to enjoy her family's special days.

This was definitely the highlight of our sports season! Her family's conversion was much more important than our team championship that year. Although we were also very grateful she helped us win those vital games. (Journal 7/10/1988)

"... I would desire that ye should consider on the blessed and happy state of those that keep the commandments of

God. For behold, they are blessed in all things, both temporal and spiritual; ..." (Mosiah 2:41)

———•◆•———

I was living at home and attending college in Arizona. Some of my friends were Mormon and they talked me into taking the missionary discussions. My mother was very much against this and shoved all the anti-Mormon literature at me. After many missionary discussions the elders challenged me to be baptized and I turned them down.

Sometime later my friends told me they were excited to hear from an Apostle of the Lord at an upcoming fireside. They convinced me to go with them. There was a new Apostle named L. Tom Perry talking to us and he explained there was a new prophet, Spencer W. Kimball, and he testified of the spirituality of that change in leadership. As Elder Perry was talking I witnessed a large, very white, rainbow above the speakers at the podium.

Afterwards, one of the young women asked, "did anyone notice something special about tonight's speakers?"

I responded timidly, "I did; I saw a white rainbow over them." No one else in the group noticed anything different. As we walked down the sidewalk I pondered these things. Then I had this swoosh of water, but it wasn't wet, run through my entire body. I knew that the church was true. I knew what I had been taught by the missionaries was true and I knew the church was lead by a prophet and apostles. (A peer)

"... The light which did light up his mind, which was the light of the glory of God, which was a marvelous light of goodness ..." (Alma 19:6)

*Note: Elder L. Tom Perry was called to be an Assistant to the Twelve in 1972 and to the apostleship in 1974. Elder Spencer W. Kimball was called by God to be His prophet in December of 1973.*

———•◆•———

I have been blessed to work with so many fine young men in the Boy Scouts of America. With over 35 years of leadership experience, I have crossed the paths of oodles of awesome youth! As an advancement chairman for a BSA District, for 18 years, I was able to help hundreds of young scouts with their Eagle Scout project approvals, board of reviews, and their resulting Court of Honors. Through all the training, campouts, and activities, there has not been a noticeable revelatory vein running through the years of my BSA life. We mostly enjoyed the outdoors, service, and laughs.

One Eagle Board of Review was especially enlightening however. We had a young man in our stake who was hit by a car while riding his bike at age 13. He was severely paralyzed. He remained active in Scouts and desired to learn and do everything. The Boy Scouts of America has an excellent program to accommodate any degree of challenges a young man might face. Brayden Howe accomplished, even though a quadriplegic on life support after the accident, a high school diploma, BS college degree, and job at Hill Air Force Base!

Braden had earned all the necessary merit badges (21) and completed his Eagle project and he was ready for his Eagle Board of Review. He was so positive and full of the Spirit. Braden glowed. From the hundreds of boards I have chaired, there never was a Board of Review like this was. Braden knew the BSA Law, Oath, Motto, and Slogan perfectly! He repeated them to me with glowing confidence and exuberance! His countenance filled the entire room with light and the spirit. It was an amazing experience, one that I will never forget! Braden taught me and many others a valuable lesson of remaining very positive amidst visibly harsh challenges.

As his mother confirmed, "Braden is an exceptional young man. Braden endured his disability by lifting others who were struggling."

Braden passed onto paradise in 2011, about 15 years after his accident. Braden has that same bright light and spirit with him as he now freely moves about serving Heavenly Father and His Son Jesus Christ.

> The radiation and chemotherapy made Jared very ill. The surgeries were difficult, but he always bounced back very quickly. Although he suffered much pain, the Lord blessed and sustained him. Jared had a special spirit that drew others to him. He never complained about how he felt or about having to be sick or about the treatments he had to have. When asked how he was doing, he always said, "Good," no matter how he felt. He was ever known for his contagious smile. The Light of Christ was in his eyes. (Thomas S. Monson, GC, Oct 1993)

> "Happy is that people, that is in such a case: yea, happy is that people, whose God is the Lord" (Psalms 144:15)

My three-year old son was saying, "Mom, the grass is happy."

"Why is the grass happy?" I asked.

He just kept saying it was so happy. Later we were up at the family cabin and he was telling us how happy the rocks were. He said the rocks were talking.

I asked him what the rocks were saying.

He said they are saying, "Thank you!"

Then I thought it was cool when we read about everything having a spirit and being created spiritually. Additionally, I thought about how all the creations, except for man, praise God all the time.

I went outside the cabin with my husband and my grandpa to pick huckleberries. While we were picking the huckleberries I had this amazing spiritual feeling overcome me. I exclaimed, "Grandpa, these huckleberries are very happy because they are *filling the measure of their creation*!"

He just laughed at me. (A relative)

"For after it hath filled the measure of its creation, it shall be crowned with glory, even with the presence of God the Father;" (D&C 88:19)

Following our home evening lesson and activities one night we felt impressed to visit some neighbors. We went to the end of our driveway pondering which direction would be best. We felt like walking east. Stopping by our friends with the triplets, no one was home. We then proceeded to another family's house and found only the wife home.

She said to us, "My husband and children are all gone and I was just sitting here wishing someone would come and visit me." (Journal 5/7/2006)

"Maybe we don't know a widow whose home needs paint or a new neighbor on our street. But promptings will come, encouraging us to do something good for someone." (JoAnn Randall, GC, Oct 1981)

When I was on my mission in Ohio we had an investigator that was coming along nicely. We also had a man in the town that was a very vocal anti-Mormon, holding meetings often. Our investigator's friends convinced her to attend a large meeting this detractor had advertised.

We were concerned and did not know how to handle this situation so we called our Mission President for some advice. We were surprised when he counseled us, "Go with her. These kinds of things always consume themselves over time."

"And the Spirit bade me go with them, nothing doubting." (Acts 11:12)

So we attended the anti-Mormon rally with our investigator and her friends. After this man's rants and ravings, including displays of sacred Mormon items, our investigator walked straight up to the presenter and exclaimed, "This is all a big pack of lies. I have Mormon neighbors that I would trust with anything! They are nowhere near the kind of people that you are talking about! They are truly good and happy."

She ended up joining the church. (A friend)

And now, as the preaching of the word had a great tendency to lead the people to do that which was just— yea, it had had more powerful effect upon the minds of the people than the sword, or anything else, which had happened unto them ... (Alma 31:5)

My wife invited me to attend a tradeshow with her in Pocatello, ID. The pre-registration numbers were rather low, making vendors wonder what their sale's outcomes would be. I prayed the night before the event: "Please bless my wife and others to have a successful show and I pray that I will be able to minister to a mother and her baby."

During the morning I listened to a little ruckus at the table behind ours. A young mother was attempting to try a product that took both hands, while keeping a baby boy sitting in her lap. He kept leaning forward trying to put both of his hands on the apparatus.

"Would it help if I held your baby?"

"Yes it would—but he'll scream."

"Let's just give him a try." (As I lifted him from her lap)

"He's not screaming."

"I'll just hold him right here until your done testing."

"Thank you so much!"

Later in the afternoon my attention was drawn to a mother and her baby. She was trying different things at various booths and would shift her baby boy from one arm to the other. I figured she had been packing him around since arriving at the tradeshow 8-9 that morning.

I discerned she could use some help. She was two aisles over on the right and started working her way back to the left. I figured I would be able to meet up with her if I took a perpendicular path on a side aisle. Sure enough we met at the intersection and she surprisingly turned immediately away from me at that juncture. I wondered what to do now and then noticed there was a large bowl of chocolate candies on a booth's table. The young mother was attracted to the assortment of candy and was grabbing some chocolate nougat.

I grabbed a pack of my favorites and said: "Mmm...M&M's!—What a handsome baby boy you have."

"Thank you."

"My personal best way to minister to people is to help care for their babies when needed. I would love to hold your baby if you would like a break."

"Well then! If that's the case, here you are." She placed her precious package atop my awaiting arms. He was very comfortable with me and me with him.

"I can hold him for 30 minutes or longer if you like."

"I'll set my phone timer for 30 minutes. I'll be in one of the classes."

"We'll likely end up at my wife's booth, which is over there." (Pointing)

Like clockwork, she returned in 30 minutes. "How are you two doing?"

"We are wonderful! Would you like a longer break?"

"I feel like I'm imposing. I hate to impose on people."

"Your baby's happy; you and he are making my day. We're great; you're not imposing at all."

"Okay thanks. I'll see you when the class is over."

The beautiful boy, 4-5 months, was finally getting a little restless, so I walked him around the event floor. People always assume I'm holding a grandchild, which is rarely the case. After a while he finally fell gently asleep and melted into my arms. I sat back down and thoroughly enjoyed the moment.

His mother returned and found him sleeping and asked if I wanted to keep him longer. I confidently confirmed her comment. My inspired wife suggested I get the mommy's cell phone number so we could communicate if the baby got hungry and/or cranky. We exchanged phone numbers and the mother was off to another class.

Sure enough, about half-an-hour later, the little one was getting hungry and became harder to console. I had held him for two enjoyable hours. I finally put him in his stroller, which mama had left, and pushed him around. The baby was still getting fussier; I then texted his mother. "Your baby is finally hungry and fussy."

"I'm on my way."

"Thank you so much for sharing your baby with me."

"Thank you for giving me a needed break." We parted and my soul felt nourished with positive energy. Later that evening the young mother sent me a text of love an appreciation for all my help that day. (Journal 10/21/18)

> "He has given us the ingredients for successful living: his gospel as a perfect plan for happiness and success for all who live it, the Church with inspired leaders, and the promptings of the Holy Ghost to guide us and warn us." (ElRay L. Christiansen, GC, Oct 1971)

---

> At my ten-year high school reunion a girl came up to me and said, "I let the missionaries in my door because of you and your friend's examples back in school. I remembered your happiness and attitudes impressed me. I am now a member of your church!" (A Missionary peer)

---

> Our grandson Ethan is 17. I was touched this summer when he told me that, inspired by his mother's example, he prays each day to have an opportunity to serve someone. As we spent time with his family, I observed how Ethan treats his brother and sisters with patience, love, and kindness and is helpful to his parents and looks for ways to reach out to others. I am impressed with how aware he is of the people around him and of his desire to serve them. He is an example to me. Doing as Ethan does—inviting the Lord to help us find ways to serve—will allow the Spirit to open our eyes to see the needs around us, to see the "one" who needs us that day, and to know how to minister to him or her. (Bonnie L. Oscarson, YM Gen Pres, GC, Oct 2017) *She's also my "mission mother."*

"And surely there could not be a happier people among all the people who had been created by the hand of God." (4 Ne. 1:16)

———————◆———————

Jayant loved the Church even before he became a member. He liked to listen to his uncle talk about the gospel and tell how he had been the first person from India to join the Church in Fiji.

After listening to the missionaries, Jayant asked his parents if he might join the Church. They gave him permission, and Jayant tried hard to be a missionary to his family by living the principles of the gospel and being a good example.

Before long, Jayant's father and brother were baptized, but his mother hesitated. Her grandfather had been an important Hindu priest in India, and she was worried about what her family would say if she became a Mormon. *Because of the example of her son*, however, she too finally joined the church.

Now all of Jayant's family is active in their branch in Suva, Fiji ... (A Good Example, *Friend*, Mar 1974)

———————◆———————

Early in our marriage we would buy old cars because they were affordable. We bought this big Lincoln Continental for a thousand dollars. We thought it was a pretty good deal for a car with 120,000 miles and no dents. We later found out it actually had 220,000 miles already racked up!

A few months later I was driving up an incline from our place and the drive line dropped to the ground. The car stopped right in front of a home where a sister in our ward lived. Her non-member husband offered to help me on a night we were both off work. I thanked him and set up a time.

On a determined evening we blocked the tires, jacked the car up enough to squeeze under it and prayed the heavy beast wouldn't slip of the jacks and blocks onto the dirt road that was inclined and scattered with gravel. As we worked to take off the attached end of the U-joint we discovered it was a double-universal joint. (On this model the two U-joints had different size small roller bearings and we had just mixed them up assuming they were all uniform. Another good sister's non-member husband helped me sort that greasy mess out.)

As we were finishing up attaching the U-joints and drive line under the car, on another evening still praying for safety and our lives, I blurted out, "You know I bet your wife would really appreciate it if you were to take her through the temple."

He was a cowboy and with tobacco chew in his mouth drawled, "Yeh, I 'spose she would."

The car was repaired and his good wife gave us some hot chocolate and cookies. Nothing much else changed.

What a delightful Spirit traveled through my heart, mind, soul, and spirit from a newsy phone call many moons later! A relative from our old stomping grounds told me that this brother had finally converted and took his wife through the temple, which she greatly appreciated and loved.

The cowboy finally retired and was piddling around their home. His ever-active wife suggested he help her with some of the widows in her ward with his extra time. He agreed and soon found God and the true gospel by serving God's children. He fell in love with the elderly widows and the service. Through the widows of the ward's needs and his good wife's decades of faithful service, example, and long patience, they were now both members of the Church of Jesus Christ of Latter-day Saints, just at different times. Not long after that, this friendly couple was sealed for time and all eternity in the Lord's house! (Journals 9/04/1983, 4/22/2018)

> "And it came to pass that we lived after the manner of happiness." (2 Ne. 5:27)

Our third child chose to come in the middle of the night. At 2 a.m. my wife called a sister in the ward to meet us in the hospital to take our children overnight. We rushed to the hospital as this couple waited for us to arrive. We all rode up in the elevator together along with our two little ones. During the elevator ride up I overheard the brother in a whiny whisper question his wife, "Why'd they call us?"

She positively responded, "I'm her visiting teacher!"

With that they took our two tired toddlers and a stuffed diaper bag. We excitedly awaited another precious package from paradise. Two hours later, our new baby girl arrived. (Journal 3/9/1986)

> "May we show our gratitude and love for God by **ministering with love** to our eternal sisters and brothers." (Jean B. Bingham, GC, April 2018)

I've heard people's miraculous stories about paying their tithing and being blessed. I have never had an experience like that. I always felt like if I paid my tithing I would be taken care of and that was my testimony. I always paid my tithing and likewise my needs were always met. I know it's a simple testimony, but I couldn't have a better one for me. (A friend)

"Every man according as he purposeth in his heart, so let him give; not grudgingly, or of necessity, for God loveth a cheerful giver." (2 Cor. 9:7)

———•◆•———

I was driving in a small town and I noticed something in the corner of my eye; something like a shingle fell off the roof of a home. As I drove by the home I noticed a small boy lying on the ground. Then it was impressed on my mind that this toddler had fallen from the second story. The building was a two-story complex and the windows had a ledge or outcropping below them.

I was about nine-months pregnant, but knew this little boy needed help. I pulled around the corner and came over to him and there was this massive dog that came out and wouldn't let me get near the boy. The dog was not happy with me. I thought, 'Oh my goodness, if I try to help this boy, the dog is going to get me!'

A person came out of the house that could approach the boy, so I took off. I ran my errand and then came back by the house and there was an ambulance there. I explained to the ambulance driver that I kind of saw what happened and wondered how the little boy was. He said the boy's mother had fallen asleep and the window wasn't latched. His grandma was asleep on a couch downstairs; but she was awoken right at the time the boy fell and she saw him fly by the window. So she ran outside and helped the little boy because the dog would have attacked me.

The little boy basically had the wind knocked out of him and had a slight concussion, but he was fine. I feel confident God woke the woman up to witness the event and take care of the dog that was going to eat a pregnant woman alive! I thought it was a miracle. (A friend)

"Because I have been part of miracles, large and small, I am a firm believer in what we have learned to call 'divine choreography'—those times when the Lord's hand is clearly involved in the details of our lives (A relative)

———•◆•———

The majority of our Roy, UT, ward families attended a camping activity at Martin's Cove, WY. It was a five to six hour drive, depending on who was driving. There were a mass of tents and campers set up with dozens of children running around. At this point in time, our ward was very young. We had around 180 members in attendance, an amazing turnout! We were camping over two nights.

The handcart experience was great for most everyone. I carried a small baby for a young family on the trail and my arms were burning by the end. My good wife has relatives from both the Willie and Martin companies that survived the ordeals. One of her relatives was also a rescuer to the stranded saints. This brother actually ended up marrying a woman he rescued on the frozen plains. This woman was also a relative of my wife's.

Another nice thing about the event was that the Wyoming winds subsided during our three-day stay. Different family groups were assigned to cook, clean, etc. We ate as a very large group around a campfire. The overall spirit that resides over this hallowed ground is amazing. Those that have been there know what I'm talking about.

On the closing evening we had a testimony meeting with special songs. A brother in the ward had written a song entitled, "**When the Angels Come.**" His song refers to certain member's journal entries referring to pushing their handcarts until they were fully spent; they would then feel their handcarts being pushed from behind when no one was there. This was the pinnacle of the meeting and a testimony-building experience for the entire ward. The Spirit was extremely strong in abundance. I was very grateful that we were all together as a family. We are all grateful for the extreme sacrifices of the pioneers. We could sense eternity that evening. (Journal 7/1/2001)

> Francis Webster testified: I have pulled my handcart when I was so weak and weary from illness and lack of food that I could hardly put one foot ahead of the other. I have looked ahead and seen a patch of sand or a hill slope and I have said, "I can go only that far and there I must give up, for I cannot pull the load through it."
>
> I have gone on to that sand and when I reached it, the cart began pushing me. I have looked back many times to see who was pushing my cart, but my eyes saw no one. I knew then that the angels of God were there.
>
> Was I sorry that I chose to come by handcart? No. Neither then nor any minute of my life since. *The price we paid to become acquainted with God was a privilege to pay, and I am thankful that I was privileged to come in the Martin*

*Handcart Company.* (President James E Faust, *Ensign*, Feb 2006; "Pioneer Women," *Relief Society Magazine* 35, 1)

———◆———

I was serving in Germany on a U.S. military base. The Relief Society president shared this story with my companion and me so that we could begin teaching someone. "Two women on the base were 'looking for religion' and a third woman, a non-member, overheard their conversation. She explained to them that if they were looking for a positive religion they should talk to this certain woman. She further explained to the two that 'this woman really loves and lives her religion! She is truly happy.'" The two ladies contacted the "happy woman" and were directed to the Relief Society president and then the missionaries. Both of them were baptized following the missionary discussions. (A relative)

"Their countenances shone, and the radiance from the presence of the Lord rested upon them, and they sang praises unto his holy name." (D&C 138:24)

———◆———

We were pleased to be invited to the Grand Opening of the new Marriott Hotel in downtown Salt Lake City, UT, in late 1981. We were recently married and attending college at the time. It was a warm autumn day; the hotel had an old fashioned root beer stand in one corner of the ballroom. The refreshing beverage helped take the edge off of the hot day. Maybe they hadn't gotten the air conditioning set right yet because it was noticeably warm in the expansive ballroom.

We had a humorous visit with LeGrand Richards and Secretary Haycock. After that I was pleased to see Elder Thomas S. Monson standing in the middle of the ballroom all alone. I thought, what a great opportunity to have a one-on-one with an Apostle of the Lord. He is a big man and his large hand swallowed up my hand as we shook. He was very congenial and enjoyable to visit with, also exhibiting a great sense of humor.

I noticed Elder Monson's dark three-piece suit as we visited and thought, "Man, if I'm hot, he must be dying!" I suggested that I could quickly bring him a cold root beer.

He said he appreciated the thought; then he taught me something, saying, "Whenever there is alcohol also served in a facility, we do not even hold an empty cup or glass in our hands—in order to never give the wrong impression."

Then I thought, "I'm glad I don't have to worry about that." However, in reality I should really think harder about what I say, what I do, and how I portray myself in private and public. What would an Apostle do? What would a Prophet do? What would Jesus do? That's what we should do. (Journal, 10/20/1981)

"Abstain from all appearance of evil" (1 Thes. 5:22)

━━━━━●◆●━━━━━

Raised Episcopalian, BYU professor of family life David C. Dollahite ... was introduced to the Church as a teen. Fascinated by the committed way many LDS families practice religion within their homes, he determined to research how families of various faiths do the same. Dollahite now serves as codirector of the American Families of Faith Project, a long-term study on how religion and family intersect. (BYU Magazine, *Families of Faith*, Spring 2017, pg 18)

━━━━━●◆●━━━━━

My wife was able to attend a trade show with me in the Seattle, WA area. We made some time to see the Space Needle and other tourist sites. At the end of the three-day show, we had an afternoon free and decided to attend the fairly-new Seattle Temple (Dedicated on Nov 17, 1980).

I put on my suit and my wife looked gorgeous in her maternity dress. She was approaching eight months with our second child. We boarded a congested city bus with standing room only. We really stood out, being over dressed and her obvious late-stage pregnancy protruding. A young businessman quickly offered his seat to my wife, which she gladly accepted.

That businessman was a sharp young stock broker. He explained that they, in their jobs, start early when the New York markets open and then end work early in the afternoon when those same markets close on the east coast. Then he proceeded to ask me why we were so dressed up and where we were going?

I explained that we were going to worship in a Holy Temple.

He was very professional and asked great questions. He wondered what we did in our temples.

I talked about our belief in life continuing after the grave. I mentioned how important families were to us and that we tied or linked families together to enjoy one another in the next life for eternity. I explained how we did work for people that had passed on and couldn't do the ordinances for themselves; such as: baptisms and eternal marriages.

Then I looked around the bus and was surely surprised to see that the entire bus crowd, sitting and standing, was locked onto our conversation. I was bearing my testimony of our Holy Temples and the plan of salvation to the entire bus load! Out of all those riders, no one else was talking except the business man and me. We were on a stretch of freeway so there were no stops for quite some time. I was able to answer all his great questions with suitable responses and I thank the Lord for His support in that endeavor. Finally we exited and the young man thanked us and we thanked him likewise. The Spirit was there in abundance on that bus and I know it touched people; healthy seeds of faith, light, and truth were planted in people during that bus ride. (Journal 2/9/1986)

> "Therefore, blessed are ye if ye continue in my goodness, a light unto the Gentiles, and through the priesthood, a savior unto my people Israel." (D&C 86:11)

---

> Several years ago I served as a temple worker in the Santiago Chile Temple. I left early … I prayed that the train I needed would be there so I could get home soon … I thought my prayer was answered … But as I approached … a passenger was experiencing a possible heart attack … my favorite hymn pierced my mind: *"Have I done any good in the world today?"* (*Hymns,* no. 223) I immediately felt impressed to help.
> I prayed to know what to do and pled with Heavenly Father to spare the young man's life … I held his hand and tried to help him remain calm. I assured him that he had a long life ahead and that God had a purpose for him … I felt I should stay with the young man until his family arrived. To my surprise, the paramedics decided I should come with them … to the hospital.
> … His mother broke into tears, threw her arms around me, and said she was glad there are still good people on earth. A week later I received a phone call from the young man. He told me the doctors said that remaining calm had been critical during that time before he reached the hospital.
> I was speechless when he exclaimed, "You saved my life, and I am forever grateful to you! Now I know there is a God." (Carla Sofia Gavidia, Ontario, Canada, Latter-day Saint Voices, *Ensign,* Mar 2014)

---

My buddy and I worked with a road crew on Hwy-14 on the eastside of the Bighorn Mountains in northwest Wyoming, after our missions. He worked at the base camp and I was out on a compactor, the machine that smoothes down dirt and gravel. At times various workers would sit down in the dirt on the roadside, with a few other employees, for a quick lunch.

One day it was just the flag girl and me sitting together on a long stretch of a dusty dirt road. As we visited over sandwiches, she commented, "You're different!"

"What do you mean?"

She shocked me with, "You haven't asked me to sleep with you."

"Why would I do that?"

"Well all the other guys have; they don't even care that I'm married and have two kids! You are definitely different. Why?"

I had a very nice visit with her about eternal marriage and being worthy for those blessings through an honest and chaste lifestyle. I talked to her about the importance of families and my belief in God and in his Son, Jesus Christ.

Our lunch turned into a very nice conversation, after which she stated, "Gee—that sounds really nice." Then she asked if we could eat lunch together from now on and I told her that would be fine. I personally did not enjoy being around the other crude construction workers either. (Summer 1978)

"Let no man despise thy youth; but be thou an example of the believers, in word, in conversation, in charity, in spirit, in faith, in purity." (1 Timothy 4:12)

When I was 16, I participated in a student foreign-exchange program for a year. I went from … Ukraine to … Arizona, USA, where I stayed with a Latter-day Saint family. I had never heard of Latter-day Saints before.

The exchange program didn't allow the family to preach to me … I chose to attend church with my host family and participate in all church activities. *I felt the Spirit with that family, and I felt much love at church.* At that time I didn't know that what I was feeling was the Spirit, but my heart was touched.

When I returned to Ukraine, I missed that feeling very much. About four years later some missionaries knocked on my door. I was so happy to see them. While they were out working, they had listened to the Spirit, which led them to my house … I was baptized and confirmed soon afterward … (Victoria Mikulina, Russia, Latter-day Saint voices, *Ensign*, Aug 2001)

Happiness is the object and design of our existence; and will be the end thereof, if we pursue the path that leads to it; and this path is virtue, uprightness, faithfulness, holiness, and keeping all the commandments of God. (*TPJS*, 255-256)

————— •◆•• —————

One of my favorite home teaching memories was as the home teacher to an elderly brother who hadn't attended Church for many years. I was a full-time college student and my wife and I sold our cars and bought bikes to conserve money. My assigned companion was not active and I would often ride my bike to visit brother Peay alone. I saw him regularly and was always cordially received, though he had no interest in attending church. I continued visiting him month-after-month, year-after-year.

One Sunday when I entered our chapel foyer I smelled the pungent aroma of mothballs; there in the chapel I found dear Brother Peay sitting reverently and quietly on the back pew. Having him back in church was a joy to me. It didn't matter a bit that he came wearing a mothball-infused suit that had been packed away many years.

People don't use mothballs much anymore, but if I ever get a whiff of that unmistakable smell, I immediately think of Brother Peay and the blessings and joy of priesthood service. (A relative)

"But brethren, we are bearers of the Holy Priesthood, after the Order of the Son of God!" (Dieter F. Uchtdorf, GC, Oct 2012)

————— •◆•• —————

Each of us had hands laid upon our head, and we received the priesthood of God. We have been given authority and responsibility to act in His name as His servants on earth. Whether in a large ward or a small branch, we are called upon to serve, to bless, and to act in all things for the good of everyone and everything entrusted to our care. Could there be anything more exhilarating? Let us understand, appreciate, and feel the joy of service in the priesthood. (Dieter F. Uchtdorf, GC, Oct 2012)

————— •◆•• —————

We had the wonderful opportunity as a family to walk through the Holocaust Memorial Museum in Washington, D.C. Overall the museum was a humbling experience with evolving emotions attached. Near the end of the tour there is a large, beautiful, memorial room with various pod platforms one can walk onto to mediate.

I chose to do this alone and as I pondered, I received a most precious, tingling, spiritual feeling. I actually questioned myself, "Why am I feeling a feeling that is similar to a special spirit one might experience in the temple—here?"

Then the thought came into my mind **"These are my people, whom I love."** These men, women, and children were a sizable group of the Lord's precious people. The feelings and spirit were so strong that I hated to leave. The murdered millions were all beloved children of God who had their earthly lives cut short. Some have, yet many have not, forgotten the six million plus Jews lost under tragic circumstances; their Father in Heaven has never forgotten them. (Journal 11/12/2006)

> And it shall come to pass that I will establish my people, O house of Israel. And Behold, this people will I establish in this land, unto the fulfilling of the covenant which I made with your father Jacob; and it shall be a New Jerusalem. And the powers of heaven shall be in the midst of this people; yea even I will be in the midst of you. (3 Ne. 20:21-22)

———————————•◆•◆———————————

> *A young adult woman in our stake shared her story:*
> I am a convert to the church. Before my conversion I began noticing a light in some people and not in others. When there was a group of people I noticed that had this light, I wanted to have what they had. I approached them and began to visit. I discovered they were members of the Church of Jesus Christ of Latter-day Saints. They were different, but in a good way.
> I didn't tell them about the light I saw, but that is the main part of my conversion: the light in members of the church.

> "Let your light so shine before men, that they may see your good works, and glorify your Father which is heaven." (Matt. 5:16)

———————————•◆•◆———————————

A younger mother in the ward took the time to write an encouraging three-page letter to my wife. During this time we were faced with difficult challenges due to the ramifications of a child's chronic illness. My wife was at a low point and this inspiring, uplifting script could not have been timed better. I thanked the sister later and asked her why she wrote it.

She thought my wife looked like she needed a lift. Even though this mother was very busy with five young boys, she still took time to serve another sister. We became good friends with their family over the years, starting with her selfless service.

---

A family member was in dire financial straits. Their credit cards were maxed out and there was around $10 cash to spare. Now their main vehicle needed $1,000 in repairs.

They came to ask me a question and I assumed it would be a request for money; those "family loans" that never seem to get repaid.

"I figured it out. We are going to pay our tithing first."

"Great! Paying tithing first is always the best financial plan in any situation."

Even though I complimented them for their religious maturity, I remained in doubt feeling like I would still be footing the bill.

Within 48 hours blessings started pouring in. An aunt called out of the blue and asked our family member to do some work at their vacation home for $500. They did such a good job that the pay was upped to $700.

Then, from a much deeper blue, an inheritance surfaced that no one was even aware of! This money trickled down through three generations and all the great-grandchildren received $500 each. I don't believe I've ever witnessed the windows of heaven being opened so quickly. (Journal 2/21/2010)

---

I received a very nice card at work one day from one of our younger employees. She was an older teenager and a delight to work with at our health food store. She thanked me for being her "Gospel Mentor" and for being such a great example.

I was taken by surprise. I asked her about this and she replied, "My mother is a former Mormon and has become very anti, as well as my dad!" She was trying to *find herself* and had just joined a student ward. She did not agree with her parents, yet she needed to find out for sure. She had been asking me a couple gospel-related questions each day that I gladly answered for her.

I had no idea what a critical environment she was exposed to. I was grateful that she could look up to me and gain strength from my lifestyle and testimony. (Journal 3/10/2002)

"... that ye may show forth good examples unto them in me, and I will make an instrument of thee in my hands unto the salvation of many souls." (Alma 17:11)

———————•◆•———————

I was an officer in the Marine Corps and only a few of the marines were LDS. More than twenty years later one of my men contacted me to tell me he was getting baptized. He thanked me for being such a good example to him.

He said, "You never berated me and always treated me fairly. You were different than my other leaders."

He said some missionaries came to his door and he wanted to hear their message because of my example back in the service. He told the young men he wanted to know about a religion that produced such good men. (A family friend)

"That ye may be blameless and harmless, the sons of God, without rebuke, in the midst of a crooked and perverse nation, among whom ye shine as lights in the world; ..." (Philip. 2:15)

———————•◆•———————

Spencer W. Kimball was visiting with a businessman on a train leaving New York City: "How much do you know about the church?"

"I know little about the church, but I know of its people."

He was developing subdivisions in New York.

"There is a subcontractor working for me. He is so honest and full of integrity that I never ask him to bid on a job. He is the soul of honor. If the Mormon people are like this man, I'd like to know more about a church that produces such honorable men." (*Faith Precedes the Miracle*, 240-241)

And they all cried with one voice, saying: Yea, we believe all the words which thou hast spoken unto us; and also, we know of their surety and truth, because of the Spirit of the Lord Omnipotent, which has wrought a mighty change in us, or in our hearts, that we have no more disposition to do evil, but to do good continually. (Mosiah 5:2)

———————•◆•———————

During the eighties I developed a great relationship with a true Christian, Dick Hammer. There was no other businessman that I enjoyed working with more than Dick. He owned Dick's Cafe in St. George, Utah. He also had a sizable gift shop within his cafe.

I was a sales representative for a gift and novelty company while attending BYU. We did a lot of business together and Dick was a great support in helping me to become established in my fledgling business. He would even help our company test market new product ideas.

Dick was so personable and fair in all his dealings. He shared his wisdom and advice with me, a "greenie" in business. He wasn't condescending in any way, simply an honest, good soul. I was so impressed with him. I was so delighted and equally surprised to hear Dick's story in General Conference!

Below we can get the "rest of the story" as reported by our prophet, President Monson:

> The proprietor of Dick's Cafe in St. George, Utah, is such an example. Dick Hammer came to Utah during the Depression years with the Civilian Conservation Corps. During that period, he met and married a Latter-day Saint young woman. He opened his cafe, which became a popular meeting spot. Home teacher to the Hammer family was Willard Milne. Since I knew Dick Hammer and had printed his menus, I would ask my friend Brother Milne when I visited St. George, How is our friend Dick Hammer coming?
>
> The reply would generally be, "Slowly."
>
> The years passed by, and just a year or two ago Willard said to me: "Brother Monson, Dick Hammer is converted and is going to be baptized. He is in his 90th year, and we have been friends all our adult lives. His decision warms my heart. I've been his home teacher for many years—perhaps 15 years."
>
> Brother Hammer was indeed baptized and a year later entered that beautiful St. George Temple and there received his endowment and sealing blessings.
>
> I asked Willard, "Did you ever become discouraged teaching for such a long time?"
>
> He replied, "No, it was worth the effort. I am a happy man." (Thomas S. Monson, *Ensign*, Nov 1997)

> "Finally, brethren … Be perfect, be of good comfort, be of one mind, live in peace; and the God of love and peace shall be with you." (2 Cor. 13:11)

# 5. Seek Ye Out of the Best Books

"Nevertheless, ye are blessed, for the testimony which ye have borne is recorded in heaven for the angels to look upon; and they rejoice over you, and your sins are forgiven you." (D&C 62:3)

*From New Zealand we enjoy the following story:*

I needed to get my car inspected for safety and emission standards; the line was nine cars long. I decided to pull out a copy of *"The Family Proclamation to the World"*, which I kept in my car. Eventually, my turn came to have my car inspected. One of the men who did inspections indicated that he would drive my car into the garage.

Time passed as I watched other customers come and go. After awhile I began to think that something was seriously wrong with my car. Finally the mechanic came … my car had passed. I paid the cashier and walked to my car and found the mechanic waiting for me.

"Miss," he said, looking at me intently, "can I please talk to you for a minute?"

Of course, I told him.

"I want to apologize for taking so long with your car inspection. … When I drove your car into the garage, I noticed a piece of paper on the passenger seat that talked about families. Instead of returning your car to you, I sat in the garage and read that piece of paper over and over."

He continued, "What is the church? What is this document on the family? Can I have a copy of it? It says it is written by Apostles. Do you mean to tell me that there are Apostles on the earth today just like in Jesus' time? Please, I need to know."

I told him there were indeed apostles and prophets on the earth … I told him about Joseph Smith and the restoration of the Gospel. I then gave him all of the Church materials I had in my car. He gave me his phone number so the missionaries could contact him.

I have never forgotten the look of eagerness in that man's eyes. This experience was an unforgettable lesson on the power of *"The Family: A Proclamation to the World"* …

(Angela Fallentine, Latter-day Saint Voices, *Ensign*, Mar 2013)

One Sunday in sacrament meeting the bishop announced the release and a "vote of thanks" for three brethren from the following four callings: Scoutmaster, deacon's quorum adviser, second counselor in YMs, and Scout committee chairman. Then the bishop asked for a sustaining vote for one brother to take on all four of those callings! There were literally gasps in the audience.

I thought to myself, "I don't have a truck or a tent; I guess things are going to change."

One brother firmly shook my hand afterwards and said, "I raised my hand to sustain you and I mean it! If you need a truck, some equipment, or assistance—all you have to do is ask." And he meant it! Ron Lynn was a great asset whenever we needed something special.

Many other members were also awesome at supporting our Scout troop. The Scout's parents were always assisting whenever asked to do so. I decided to throw myself into the work and these young men's lives.

I was also serving as the Stake Auditor during these new calls for another couple of years. Following my four new ward callings one of my auditors gave me back his unfinished audits stating, "I'm going on a sabbatical for an undetermined amount of time."

The only other brother helping with audits in the stake said, "I'm 77 and done!" (Journal 5/22/1988)

As we progressed through a few years I was totally impressed with this fine group of young men. I did receive a bounteous blessing of dedicated service however. I was the Blazer Leader/11-yr. old Scout leader for the previous three years and had worked all the boys up to the Star Rank. They all enjoyed Scouting and life in general.

I learned so much from these capable young men. Boy Scouts need 20 nights camping out, yet these young men had 40 campout nights! Scouts need to learn *knots and lashings*; our Scouts taught *knots and lashings*; they knew them so well. My older Scouts would train the younger scouts, allowing me time to work with the younger boys in the middle of their advancement. By working with them on Wednesday nights, weekend campouts, Eagle projects, and during Sunday lessons, I became very familiar with their likes, dislikes, families, strengths, weaknesses, and birthdays. I grew to love all of them and still do.

We had finished all the requirements and were now doing an Eagle project every two weeks for nine different Scouts. In Wyoming we would have a Stake Court of Honor for all Eagle Scouts. Many of our wards were twenty five to sixty five miles apart, with the outlying wards within thirty to forty five minutes of the Stake Center. We had fourteen Eagles from the stake and nine of them were *my boys*. I didn't realize it, but it was reportedly the largest Eagle Court of Honor in the State's history. The mayor came and a State Senator also attended, both being non-members. I was recognized also and received national awards.

These boys' parents were so grateful for the years of sacrifice for their young men that they threw me parties, had special dinners, and showered me with gifts. The other leaders and parents told me I was the best Scoutmaster ever!

The District leader from Billings, Montana said, "We rarely find a man that will work hard in Scouts that doesn't have his own boy in the program. Thank you!" (Our own three boys were all younger than 11).

All these awards, compliments, and gifts went to my head. I was thinking to myself, "Maybe they're right, maybe I am the best Scoutmaster in the State—Nation—World? I did a most awesome job!" My ego sustained a super boost.

I was enjoying some church literature one afternoon and came upon these timely, inspiring words: *"The cemeteries are full of people who thought themselves indispensable."* (*Postgraduate Medicine*, June 1948) Those words kept rolling over in my head again and again, "The cemeteries are full of people who thought themselves indispensable." They (when alive), like me, thought they were irreplaceable! Those words were personal revelation to me and ever so timely.

I prayed for forgiveness, attempted to not think of myself, and threw my support towards the new Scoutmaster who was doing a wonderful job in his own right.

I have now been a Boy Scout leader for over 35 years and still don't have that truck; thankfully almost every boy's father has had an available truck, so we could not have done it without them.

> Here is another important lesson of leadership: *Leaders are duty-bound and obligated to prepare others to take their place* at some future time. Brothers and sisters, the cemeteries are filled with leaders who thought they were indispensable. (Spencer J. Condie, GC, April 1990)

————— •◆• —————

> One day the mailman accidentally delivered an *Ensign* magazine to our mailbox. It belonged to our new neighbors ... I did not know anything about the LDS Church except what I had learned in school about the Mormon Trail ... I kept the *Ensign* for a week and read it cover to cover. That particular issue featured articles on the family. I was

overjoyed to find a church that believed what I did—that families are important and that it is our responsibility to care for them.

I truly believe the *Ensign* was delivered to our house for a purpose. The entire issue was devoted to the family, which was the very reason we had been searching for another church. As a result, I was able to listen to the plan of salvation with an open heart because I had felt the truth of the gospel in the pages I had read a year and a half earlier in the *Ensign*.

I gained a testimony and was baptized four months later. After my husband's baptism, we were sealed for time and eternity in the Washington, D.C Temple. (My Neighbor's Magazine, *Ensign*, Sep 2008)

"... With my fellowlabourers, whose names are in the book of life." (Philip. 4:3)

When we were having very difficult family issues and financial woes I found help in a book by Jon Huntsman, Sr. In one of his many books he talks about being newlywed and struggling. They decided to show their faith in the Lord by paying a very large fast offering. Back then $100 fast offering, every month, was a lot to pay and a big chunk of their budget. They witnessed windows of heaven being flung far wide open and blessing their lives. He became a self-made billionaire. Remember that the Lord's blessings from heaven, however, come in many different packages other then financial gain. (Brother Huntsman passed away on February 2, 2018).

My wife and I discussed their faith and decided we needed bounteous blessings to dig out of the turmoil and financial stress that seemed to be devouring us. Our daughter was mentally ill and our health insurance provider wouldn't cover her bills, which were enormous as were the insurer's seemingly useless high premiums! Our savings for missions, rainy days, and weddings were depleted by disasters. Then I was laid off from a great job. Things seemed dismal, at best!

We decided to greatly increase our faith in the Lord and fast offerings and pay $100 monthly. I started a new business servicing my existing clients and others in two additional states. Income was very minimal, if any, at first. It usually takes about three years to build your own brokerage.

Things started coming together and within three years we actually had tripled our previous savings and paid off our mortgage. We could not believe the bounteous blessings! If I had to show how the financial recovery worked on paper it would not be possible.

A gentleman in Chicago, a corporate president, called me up one day. He said, "I have had your resume sitting on my desk for six months and today it jumped out at me. I believe we would like to hire you to represent our company in the Rocky Mountains." [His experience is another good example of a great Christian man being prompted by the Holy Spirit. When I interviewed with them over dinner in a fine Chicago restaurant, the owners suggested I bless the food. I believe that blessing sealed the deal!]

I gladly accepted this additional line which ended up being an $8,000 raise; $8K per month, not per annum! We had so many blessings showered down upon us when all the doors and windows opened that we could hardly handle it all.

Tongue-in-cheek, I refer to this as the *"Huntsman Principle."*

> Will a man rob God? Yet ye have robbed me. But ye say, Wherein have we robbed thee? In tithes and offerings … Bring ye all the tithes into the storehouse … prove me know herewith, saith the Lord of hosts, if I will not open the windows of heaven, and pour you out a blessing, that there shall not be room enough to receive it … And I will rebuke the devourer for your sakes … (Malachi 3:8, 10-11)

---

> I read a book when I was first married and I cannot even remember the title other than: A wide river, a river runs through it, or something. But I learned a principle from that book, even though it was a novel. The Spirit talked to me clear as a bell.
>
> In the book this man got fed up with his wife because she was so *"naggy"* and he just couldn't deal with it anymore. The Spirit said to me, **"Never ask your husband to do anything that you can do for yourself."** My husband has been so busy and I have learned to only ask him for help when I really need it. Then he is more than happy to assist.
>
> I am glad I knew this before he was called to be a bishop. Everyone else was so demanding on his time. We have developed such a sweet relationship and it had a great deal to do with my following the Spirit's clear direction. I just needed to do my job and he needed to do his. We can learn so much from little things and observations around us. Everything is designed to bring us closer to God. (A friend)

*President Joseph Fielding Smith stated:* "It is contrary to the law of God for the heavens to be opened and messengers to come to do anything for man that man can do for himself." (*DS* 1:196)

———•◆•———

The Ensign magazine occasionally had writing contests for subjects pertaining to the Old Testament, New Testament, etc. A close friend of ours earned some money from her article she submitted to the Ensign.

Throughout the scriptures we witness Jesus Christ's perfect living example; yet other scriptures prove He had not achieved perfection in mortality. Obviously he did not have a perfect body until after His resurrection.

I felt bad writing about my idea, attempting to write a paper on the imperfections of our Savior. I gathered that Christ was perfect in most all areas while being not fully perfect in body, health, joy, and knowledge.

> "These are they who are just men made perfect through Jesus the mediator of the new covenant, who wrought out this perfect atonement through the shedding of his own blood." (D&C 76:69)

> "For man is spirit. The elements are eternal, and spirit and element, inseparably connected, receive a fulness of joy. And when separated, man cannot receive a fulness of joy." (D&C 93:33-34)

> "Their sleeping dust was to be restored unto its perfect frame, bone to his bone, and the sinews and the flesh upon them, the spirit and the body to be united never again to be divided, that they might receive a fulness of joy." (D&C 138:17)

> "And that same sociality which exists among us her will exist among us there, only it will be coupled with eternal glory, which glory we do not now enjoy." (D&C 130:2)

If you read the New Testament and Book of Mormon versions of the Sermon on the Mount which Jesus taught on both continents you will find one noticeable difference: Christ confirms that *only Father in Heaven is perfect* vs. the after resurrection addition of *I, or your Father is perfect*. (See Matt. 5:48 and 3 Ne. 12:48)

> And I, John, saw that he received no of the fulness at the first, but received grace for grace. And he received not of the fulness at first, but continued from grace to grace, until he received a fulness. And thus he was called the Son of God, because he received not of the fullness at first. (D&C 93:12-14)

This was a difficult paper to write. After hemming and hawing and sweating it out I finally submitted my version to the Ensign for consideration. I was interested as to what the Church might say. I wondered if the Church of Jesus Christ was ready for something of this nature.

I knew that the church was really ready for such a subject, when some time later an Apostle of the Lord talked about this same thought pattern in General Conference. I never heard back from the church on my similar article—an evil thought tickled my mind: "So this is one way the Apostles obtain ideas for their talks, they peruse what members submit to the Ensign!"

Not long after reading the Ensign article I was reading a business magazine and came upon the topic of: *Multiple Discovery/Simultaneous Discovery.* These terms refer to the phenomenon of people totally independent of one another coming up with the same ideas, discoveries, or inventions at basically the same time. Often these creators, inventors, and writers are from different states or even continents.

There was my answer! Elder Russell M. Nelson and I simply had similar ideas totally independent of one another at around the same time. Plagiarism was not in the spiritual picture at all! An apologetic repentance was needed once again due to my carnal thoughts. (Journal, Oct 1995)

*Written and spoken, similar to my submission, yet much better said than I could have ever done are portions of Elder Nelson's talk:*

> Just prior to his crucifixion, he said that on "the third day I *shall be perfected*" Think of that! The sinless, errorless Lord—already perfect by our mortal standards—proclaimed his own state of perfection yet to be in the future. His *eternal* perfection would follow his resurrection and receipt of "all power ... in heaven and in earth."
> That Jesus attained eternal perfection following his resurrection is confirmed in the Book of Mormon. ... He said, "I would that ye should be perfect *even as I*, or your Father who is in heaven is perfect." (3 Ne. 12:48; emphasis

added) This time he listed himself along with his Father as a perfected personage. Previously he had not. (See Matt. 5:48)

Resurrection is requisite for eternal perfection. Thanks to the atonement of Jesus Christ, our bodies, corruptible in mortality, will become incorruptible. … Our bodies will be sustained by spirit and become changeless and beyond the bounds of death. (Russell M Nelson, GC, Oct 1995; emphasis added)

Within the holy temples, that now dot the earth, are sacred records of every reported spiritual event involving each respective temple. This would involve any experience shared by the: Temple Presidency and/or their wives, matrons, patrons, sealers, and all temple workers inside and outside—volunteer and paid.

The temple recorder and assistant temple recorder normally maintain and update these private records. In the smaller temples, a counselor in the Temple Presidency is usually delegated to record spiritual events in those precious books.

Now those are books that I/you would absolutely love to read! Just ponder on the miraculous experiences and feelings you have had in the Lord's house and then multiply that by a million!

"And a book of remembrance was kept, in the which was recorded, in the language of Adam, for it was given unto as many as called upon God to write by the spirit of revelation." (Moses 6:5)

We were teaching a couple from the "Bible Belt" and we gave them my favorite article by Hugh B. Brown—*Profile of a Prophet*. We were trying to get them to come to church the next morning. They were picking up their parents up at the airport around midnight.

My mouth about dropped when they came in to church at 9:00 a.m. with their parents! Many members would have used that late night as an excuse not to show up! We expected their parents to council them, "Don't you have anything to do with these Mormons." Boy we were surprised!

This couple did accept baptism and then I was transferred. I have often wondered how far their conversion extended to their parents, siblings, future children, etc. (A relative)

"The best way to obtain truth and wisdom is not to ask it from books, but to go to God in prayer, and obtain divine teaching" (*TPJS*, 191)

*On the flip side, answers to prayers, your truths, are sometimes discovered within books and frequently found throughout the scriptures.*

━━━━◆━━━━

In most every Ensign following General Conferences each April one will find the small "Statistical Report" submitted by the Church Auditing Department. The presenter will generally close his brief comments something like the following: "The Church follows the practices taught to its members of living within a budget, avoiding debt, and saving against a time of need."

This "scripture" from our leaders is stressed from time to time in other presentations and manuals; the rich advice can be so valuable to families and individuals when followed. Our extended families have lived these sound principles as the rains and storms have periodically pounded down upon them and their loved ones with a wide variety of challenges and vengeances.

Following our faith's financial counsel has blessed our families. I was surprised to become unemployed twice, less than a year after being awarded the top national salesman in each company. When the paychecks suddenly stopped, we survived because we had budgeted, saved, and avoided debt for those rough and rainy days. We were able to get by, purchase what we needed without borrowing, and survive until new jobs were found. We are grateful that the LDS Church practices what it preaches by example and spirit. We really do reap blessings when we walk the talk.

"If we live in the Spirit, let us also walk in the Spirit." (Galatians 5:25)

━━━━◆━━━━

I was alone in our 1948 Chevrolet, waiting for my parents, when I became inescapably bored. In desperation I looked down at the seat and spotted my stack of free stuff. I picked up a pamphlet entitled *Joseph Smith Tells His Own Story* and began to read it.

I was riveted, and my heart was filled with joy. After completing it, I caught my reflection in the rearview mirror, and much to my surprise, I was crying. I didn't understand then, but I understand now. I had felt a witness of the Spirit. My parents weren't there. My sister wasn't there.

My Primary teacher wasn't there. It was just me and the Spirit of the Holy Ghost. (Glen L. Pace, GC, April 1978)

———————•◆•———————

I was baptized just a few weeks before my thirteenth birthday. I remember going to church four or five times within the next three years. The reason for this is because we lived 30 miles from town where the church was and part of this time we did not have a car. Our mode of transportation was a team and wagon.

My dad was baptized about the same time that I was, but he didn't take much interest in the church. My mother would read the Book of Mormon or Bible to us teenagers. This was most of my training in the church for the first three years.

My mother was very pleased when my dad decided to move the family to the Big Horn Basin in Wyoming to look for work in the oil fields.

*They lived on a dry ranch in Nebraska and sold their cattle for only $4 a head during the depression. The teenagers collected cow chips to burn for the family's heat.*

My mom was very pleased because they had several churches there so that we could go to church every week. The first thing that I noticed is they celebrated the 24th of July. The 4th of July was always a big day for our family in the past.

After we had settled in Lovell, WY, mother was desirous of me to receive a patriarchal blessing. She took me to the patriarch who was Cash Carlton.

He gave me a real nice blessing and after he was through, he said, "Fred these blessings are yours if you live for them."

He could tell that I didn't know very much about the church.

He told me to go to the Deseret Bookstore the next time I was in Salt Lake City, UT, to buy a certain book. The name of the book was *The Soul's Fire*, by Jeremiah Stokes.

This book lived up to its name and it would set your soul on fire. This old patriarch new this book would strengthen my testimony and it did. I have had a strong testimony ever since. (My father)

"There are special times when the spirit of a son or daughter is just right and the power of these great scriptures goes down into their heart like fire." (Neil L. Anderson, GC, Oct 1999)

My good wife suggested I keep a yellow-lined notebook and pen beside my bed to record the impressions, promptings, and dreams that come to me. She keeps loose journal pages on her side of the bed to record her inspired thoughts and dreams. By the time we get to our regular journals, many of our thoughts have flown the coop.

I have had many recurring dreams which I regard as reminders to make adjustments in my life and thoughts. It has become necessary to knock repeatedly on my skull to wake me up at times. At this point I begin to shed the sinful layers of my mind and purge pride in order to be worthy to receive the message(s) and direction from heaven.

When the personal revelation does come, the messages are often *journal-worthy*.

President Russell M. Nelson finished up his 2018 world-wide tour in Hawaii where his wife, Wendy Nelson, gave an awesome address:

During our 12 years of marriage I have been accustomed to my husband being awakened during the night with ideas for and refinements to general conference talks. ... But since becoming President of the Church, the frequency and abundance of the messages to him from heaven have increased exponentially. (Wendy Nelson, *LDS.org*, 4/25/18)

Sister Nelson also said that the Apostle, now Prophet, keeps a lined note book beside his bed to write down the important inspiration he is receiving. The process and power by which our prophet receives revelation is the same for us—our realms of responsibility are dynamically different however. We are able to receive revelation for our little lives while the president of the church is inspired with direction from Deity for the Church of Jesus Christ of Latter-day Saints and for the entire world! (Journal 5/6/18)

I again became acutely aware that God knows me. My mother-in-laws's family organization needed someone to write the history of Andrew Scott Hunter, a 2nd great-grandfather, an early pioneer settler and mayor of Provo, Utah.

When my husband told me of the search, from my own mouth came, "*I* will write it." I was as dumbfounded as my husband was at what had come unbidden from my lips, yet I was immediately wrapped in the warmth of the Spirit as confirmation came that the task ahead was *mine*. That undeniable conviction carried me through the five years it took to complete the project. (A relative)

We will receive a calm and unwavering certainty that will be the source of our testimony and conviction ... These promptings of the Spirit, rather than human logic alone, will be the true foundation upon which our testimony will be built. (Dieter F. Uchtdorf, GC, Oct 2006)

While working as a marketing manager we had a very successful novelty candy line. One day I was thumbing through an industry magazine and this tiny ad jumped right out of the page at me. The ad read something like, "Customize your company name or logo on our roll candy."

I thought, well why couldn't we place our novelty slogans on different flavors of roll candies as well? After researching the prices, case packing, shipping costs, and terms, I introduced my idea to the company president. He was enamored with the possibility and we went right to work creating different product ideas for humorous labels. We ended up selling over 11 million units!

That minute magazine advertisement injected energy and new life into our company. (Journal 12/22/1983)

My deacon's advisor had encouraged me to read the Book of Mormon; I finally opened up the book and slowly made my way through it. The Isaiah chapters in Second Nephi really baffled me, but I pushed forward. Once I reached the book of Alma I was really enjoying the story.

Interestingly, I had started reading non-LDS religious books. I was still learning about the doctrines of the gospel, and I wasn't sure how everything fit together.

I checked out a book from the library that talked about reincarnation and past lives, I can remember the dark feelings the book generated in me. I knew the Spirit was telling me, "This is false."

I returned the book and focused solely on finishing the Book of Mormon. I knew we would be studying it in ninth-grade Seminary, so I figured I would at least be ahead of the class.

When I finished reading the Book of Mormon, I wanted the spiritual confirmation that the prophet Moroni talked about at the end of the book. I knew Joseph Smith had prayed in a grove of trees, so I went into a field behind our house with tall grass and prayed for awhile, but all I got was a bunch of ant bites on my legs.

I reasoned that maybe it needed to be more challenging, so during a rainstorm I knelt in the mud in the backyard and prayed for 20 minutes, but all I received was a good drenching.

Deep down I knew the book was true and felt good when I read it, but I suppose I expected something along the lines of a heavenly messenger appearing to me.

I was now fourteen. One day I was praying in my bedroom, I got the impression **"Write in your journal."** As I started to do so, the Spirit rushed into the room. My chest was burning with a confirmation about the truthfulness of the Book of Mormon, and I was able to write these wonderful feelings down as they occurred.

The Spirit was so powerful that I started crying. As I described the experience, I wrote, "Thank you, Heavenly Father! I know without a doubt that the Book of Mormon is true!" (Chad Daybell, *Living on the Edge of Heaven*, Pgs. 36-37, used with permission.)

---

I have a severe bleeding disorder and so do four of our children. It is an inherited disease, but when I was young nobody knew about it. Every time I bore children it was life threatening because I would lose so much blood. One time the bleeding just wouldn't stop following childbirth.

My doctor declared, "You can have a hysterectomy and be here to raise these children or you can lie here and bleed to death."

My concern was, "Are there more children waiting to come to our family?"

We decided to go ahead with the hysterectomy.

I went in to do all the preliminary checks prior to surgery. I was so upset and out of sorts that I had to leave and I'm not like that; I am usually calm, cool and collective.

Hospitals don't even make me nervous at all. I thought, "This is really weird!" So I went down to my brother's and he gave me a blessing.

I couldn't ask my husband to bless me because he was too involved in the situation. My brother gave me just the sweetest blessing. In my blessing I was told that my body had done all it could do; surgery was okay. So I returned to the hospital and the difference was incredible.

I was lying on the table preparing for the spinal block and the surgeon stopped and remarked, "I have never seen the patient and everyone in the room so calm prior to a surgery."

I was as calm as if I were lying on a beach! There was such a Spirit in that room and the doctor even noticed it; it was all because of that blessing.

In addition to that experience we were in the hospital later with a daughter who was getting her tonsils out. I was sitting in the waiting room and thumbing through *Better Homes & Gardens*, reading "The 10 most misdiagnosed diseases in America." There was a list of things suggesting a visit to the doctor if you had those symptoms. I could check everything off on the list!

I visited her doctor before the tonsillectomy started and showed him the list and said, "That's me and that's my daughter. We have all these symptoms."

The doctor replied, "Well that is really rare, I don't know. What we can do is have a timed bleeding test."

So both my daughter and I took the test. I asked the nurse how long these tests took and she replied, "Oh, they are usually done within a minute." Fifteen minutes later the nurse said, "Ma'am, this is the longest I am allowed to let this test go!"

That's the day we discovered we had Von Willebrand disease, a lifelong bleeding disorder in which your blood doesn't clot well. There have been cases of children dying during tonsillectomies from the loss of blood. We could have very well lost our daughter that day if I hadn't found that article and our diagnosis in a magazine! Now they have medicines and treatments for this disease. Being led to that specific article in that one magazine has been a blessing to our entire family. I had blood tests done on everyone else and four of our nine children have the bleeding disease. (A friend)

———•◆•———

My daughter was kidnapped by my abusive husband and taken out of the country illegally. I showed my bishop, from my journals, recorded dates detailing improper behavior by my husband.

The bishop confided, "I cannot talk to you about what your husband and I have discussed, however I can confirm that what is recorded in your journals is true. Protect your journals as valuable evidence for your court case in winning back your daughter and getting a legal divorce." (A peer)

———•◆•———

Years ago I read in a Church magazine the story of a girl who was living away from home and going to college. She was behind in her classes, her social life was not what she had hoped for, and she was generally unhappy. Finally one day she fell to her knees and cried out, "What can I do to improve my life?" The Holy Ghost whispered, "**Get up and clean your room.**" This prompting came as a complete surprise, but it was just the start she needed. After taking time to organize and put things in order, she felt the Spirit fill her room and lift her heart. (Larry R. Lawrence, GC, Oct 2015)

———•◆•———

When we were engaged, my girlfriend still wondered what kind of a guy she was marrying. One day at my apartment she perused the back of my journal and found my pages of goals: 1 year, 5 year, 10 year, 20 year, couple, family, eternal, etc.

Once she read the list of goals that I felt were important to achieve approval to return to our heavenly parents she was relieved and felt like she kind of knew me. My journal helped secure our future temple sealing! (Journal 10/4/1980)

We have referred back to our respective journals for talks, lessons, spiritual experiences for my wife and my books, medical records, illness dates, important dates, or events, etc. Journals are our extra sets of family scriptures!

After perusing my journals for experiences and dates for this book I have been reminded of the hundreds of earthly angels that have blessed my family's and our extended family's lives.

Journal's can have other uses also. Many years ago, around 10 p.m., I heard a shrill shriek coming from my wife in the bedroom just as I was answering an important phone call. I hurried the call as much as I could and then rushed to save the young maiden in distress.

She was still shaking and pointing towards the bathroom towels. A very large black widow spider was on one of the towels. It was an ugly, frightening thing!

I had been writing in my journal before the phone rang and still had it in my hand. I grabbed some tissue and folded it inside my journal pages and snapped the journal shut on that dangerous insect. The journal helped slay the beast, the young maiden was relieved, and our babies were safe once again. (Journal 6/8/1987)

———————◆———————

We have so much collateral reading in this Church. With all due respect to those who write books, I think there is only one place where we can really get a testimony of the divine mission of the Prophet Joseph Smith, a testimony of the truth of the Gospel of Jesus Christ, and that is right back with the source material—the standard works of the Church. (Matthew Cowley, General RS Conference, Oct 1, 1952)

*If he only knew of today's overwhelming collateral reading, he'd be rolling over in his grave!*

———————◆———————

"For the names of the righteous shall be written in the book of life, and unto them will I grand an inheritance at my right hand." (Alma 5:58)

"He who overcomes will retain his name in the book of life, reach godhood, and be with Jesus as He is with the Father." (Revelation 3 heading)

# 6. Search the Scriptures

"Wherefore, I said unto you, feast upon the words of Christ; for behold, the words of Christ will tell you all things what ye should do." (**2 Ne. 32:3**)

"And whoso treasureth up my word, shall not be deceived." (**JST, Matt. 1:37**)

"… The rod of iron … was the word of God, which led to the fountain of living waters, or to the tree of life." (**1 Ne. 11:25**)

My wife, youngest son, and I are in three different stakes now. Our son goes to the young adult stake, my wife attends our local stake, and I serve in an out-of-area calling in a branch presidency at a large care center in a third stake. It seems very unusual for three members in one home to be in totally different stakes at three different times.

We still home teach in my old ward because this great grandma, and she's serious, said she'd stop receiving home teachers if her current beloved home teachers are released. She actually teaches us more than we teach her, which we consider a blessing. I also continue to receive updates from the secretary in our high priest group. My wife at least has a companion for her ward parties and dinners.

I received a text today about helping a sister in my old ward this evening. I kind of brushed it off since I'm not actually in that ward. Then I thought, "but she lost her husband" and this scripture came clearly to me.

"Pure religion and undefiled before God and the Father is this, To visit the fatherless and widows in their affliction, and to keep himself unspotted from the world." (**James 1:27**)

I explained to my wife that I needed an early dinner because I was changing into my work clothes and jeans to help this widow in her ward. I'm glad I did because only three high priests showed up. Thankfully a group of young men also showed up and saved our sixty-year old backs.

I felt good and tired afterwards and remembered we needed a car wash before our out-of-state trip the next day. The car was very dirty from our last trip to a far away funeral during a rainstorm. As I pulled into the self-help bay and got out to pay, I couldn't figure out if the machine took cash. The machine sounded like it was on already and read 9:30 minutes. "Oh, somebody overpaid and drove away," I thought to myself.

As I went through all the "free" choices of brushing, spraying, waxing, washing, etc., the time clock was actually advancing instead of decreasing. When I finally finished washing the car, the timer read 17:35 minutes remaining. The timer was running in reverse! Our car was now unspotted in the world.

I felt that I should tell the manager and pay for the car wash.

She replied with a large smile, "Well you got lucky!"

I joyfully replied, "Well I got blessed! Thank you!"

We do receive bounteous blessings in many different ways when serving the Lord by serving others. (Journal 3/11/2018)

The scriptures that teach me how to look to God as a believer have schooled me and I find in their words strength and direction. Daniel's three friends were ready to give their lives in the fiery furnace for the cause of God, though they came through unscathed. I recognize that their kind of outcome does not always result in the face of great adversity, but for me the miracle of their survival is not the most important part of the story found in **Daniel 3**. Rather, it is their three little words *"but if not"* (see vs. 18) that provide a great statement of submission to His will, whatever it might be. (A relative)

"Yea, and there was continual peace among them, and exceeding great prosperity in the church because of their heed and diligence which they gave unto the word of God ..." **(Alma 49:30)**

We always enjoy visiting other wards on our trips and vacations because we learn so much and witness different testimonies and cultures. In order to help keep the Sabbath Day better we plan our returning drives and/or flights on Saturdays or Mondays whenever feasible and/or possible.

At our son's ward in Redmond, Washington, we were taught a lot. A very intelligent older man was teaching gospel doctrine. The teacher told the class they could read the entire **Standard Works** in less than one year if they read five chapters a day. He promised we could even miss a day or two a month, as he did and had done. The rest of his class was very inspiring and very well worth it.

Obviously the importance of perusing and studying the scriptures by subject or story is often a better option. However, it is a wonderful experience to read every chapter in each book so that you do not miss one single story, nor miss many others that you could learn from and be inspired by.

As one who loves statistics, I decided to verify his claim. Now don't let nearly 1,600 chapters scare you off. Even reading the introductions to the books, one could finish the entire scriptures in 320 days or read exactly 4.35 chapters a day if you're a geek. Being a book geek myself, I read the Old Testament about once every ten years. This wonderful instructor was absolutely correct in his claim and experience. (Journal, 1/10/2016)

———————◆———————

> Every time I need help, a boost start, answers from God, I open the scriptures. It's like God talks to me through His scriptures. Without fail, no matter my situation, I hear his voice addressing my exact situation at the time. (A friend)

*Many Christians and saints have utilized this simple idea and followed the spirit for their own and/or for teaching others by simply opening the scriptures and reading from the first verse their eyes spotted.*

———————◆———————

> I was in the National Guard and they mobilized the National Guard. They said, "Raise your right hand—you are now in the regular army!" And just like that I was in the regular Army! They shipped us to Fort Lewis, Washington. And here I was a senior in high school and I still had 3 credits. I wasn't graduated; I was still a senior. But I went along. I graduated later when I got back. But when I got out there, there were only 2 or 3 other Mormons in the whole company.
>
> We went over to the Philippine islands and made three beach heads in the Philippine islands. We used to dig our fox holes in a five-pointed star with our feet together and our heads pointing out. One guy had to sit up—one guard all the time—sit up and watch. Then we'd take 2 hour shifts—one guy would sit up for two hours then he'd lay down and sleep. And another guy would sit up. That way, if you saw a [Japanese soldier] a sneakin' up, you could tap the guy's feet. You didn't dare talk, you know, you had to keep quiet. And at night we would take this wire and we'd stretch it about three feet off the ground all around our foxhole about 25-30 yards from our foxhole. So if a [Japanese soldier] snuck up he'd trip that wire. And we had

tied that wire to our hand grenade ring. Tripping the wire would pull the ring on the hand grenade ring and shoot the intruder. See ... that's how we protected ourselves at night.

I was the Squad Sergeant. That's how I found out I didn't know anything about my church. They were running my church down and I'll admit I never did read *The Book of Mormon*. So I read *The Book of Mormon* in the foxhole over there. I'd lay there in the foxhole and read *The Book of Mormon*. I read the whole thing over there, and learned about the church. That was quite a testimony to me, I gained a testimony there of the church.

Then my mom, she read a story someplace, where a soldier had a *Bible* with a little lead cover and it stopped a bullet. So my mom, she got me a copy of the *Bible* with a lead cover and I carried it in my pocket all the time but never got shot. The Army issued us a little *Book of Mormon* that same size. That's the one I read in the foxhole, the little tiny one, the one that fit in a shirt pocket. I still got those books home some place. I haven't seen 'em for years, but I still got 'em.

I gained a testimony that way by reading that **Book of Mormon**. Oh, the kids would say, "Come on Laing, let's go play ball." or something.

"No. I gotta read this book. It's an interesting book."

At first I just couldn't lay it down. Boy, I read 2 or 3 chapters every time I had time to read. I laid in my foxhole and read it. I got it all read before I come back, before I came home, so I'm a full-fledged member now!" (Our father)

At the beginning of our mission training we were in Salt Lake City, UT. We had the privileged opportunity to be on the third floor of the Salt Lake Temple in the solemn assembly room. All the Elders and Sisters were promised they could ask any question regarding the Holy Temple ordinances, rooms, clothing, etc. What was fascinating and surprising is that every question thrown out there was answered through **the**

**scriptures**, absolutely every single one. Elder O. Leslie Stone was an obvious scriptorian, because he could find the answers to simple and hard inquiries swiftly. We were duly impressed and grateful for the meeting. The first Temple experience for me was very confusing. I had no preparation whatsoever. This meeting was educational and did answer a lot of my questions, as I am sure it did for many of the other new "greenie" missionaries. (Missionary Journal, Feb 1976)

———◆———

> We were trying to decide if we should allow our seventeen-year-old son, who graduated early from high school, to move to a different state and work construction with an uncle. I was reading the bible about how David was anointed as a young man and left his family. David would play the harp and it calmed Saul. **(1 Sam. 16:23)** This scripture story was calming for me. I felt like God was telling me it was okay to send our son far away. The thought of Joseph being sold as a slave to Egypt also came to my mind. Young Joseph was Jacob's seventeen-year old son. Joseph was taken from his family, yet he became second to Pharaoh. (A relative)

———◆———

Lehi's family was blessed with a miraculous brass ball of curious workmanship. There were two spindles that pointed a direction they should travel, find food, etc. There were also plain writings on the ball from the Lord to teach the family that changed periodically. The Liahona was a personal revelatory tool beyond measure! However, the spindles and messages only worked when they were faithful and diligent. (**See 1 Ne. 16: 10, 26-30**)

We are likewise blessed with immeasurable gifts from our Heavenly Father that the Liahona is a type or foreshadowing of.

"Your Patriarchal Blessing: A Liahona of Light" (Thomas S. Monson, GC, Oct 1986)

> The ball, or Liahona … was prepared by the Lord … Wouldn't you like to have that kind of a ball—each one of you—so that whenever you were in error it would point the right way and write messages to you? … you all have. The Lord gave every boy, every man, every person, a conscience which tells him every time he starts going down the wrong path. … You must realize that you have

something similar, like the Liahona, in your own system. (President Spencer W. Kimball, GC, Oct 1977)

Now brothers and sisters, we have available to us a tool even more remarkable that the best GPS. Everyone loses his or her way at some point, to some degree. It is through the promptings of the Holy Ghost that we can be brought safely back onto the right path … (M. Russell Ballard, GC, April 1977)

… I would that ye should understand that these things are not without a shadow, for as our fathers were slothful to give heed to this compass (now these things were temporal) they did not prosper; even so it is with things which are spiritual. For behold, it is as easy to give heed to the word of Christ, which will point to you a straight course to eternal bliss, as it was for our fathers to give heed to this compass, which would point unto them a straight course to the promised land… is there not a type in this thing? For just as surely as this director did bring our fathers, by following its course, to the promised land, shall the words of Christ, if we follow their course, carry us beyond this vale sorrow into a far better land of promise. … Do not let us be slothful because of the easiness of the way …" **(Alma 37:43-46)**

*Therefore we have many insurmountable and immeasurable gifts from God to direct and guide us on routes of righteousness: The Light of Christ, The Holy Ghost, our Patriarchal Blessings, the Scriptures, and Apostle and Prophets. A perfect package of personal revelation available to anyone, depending on the heed and diligence they are willing to wager.*

As a teenager I got to go to girl's camp, like many of you. At the end of camp, as everyone who goes knows, there is a testimony meeting; where you're suppose to get up and give a tear-jerking testimony of what you learned at girl's camp.

A leader stood up and said, "Now, if you are feeling the Spirit, I want you to get up and tell everybody about what you are feeling."

I watched fifteen-to-twenty girls stand up and tell about how they felt the Spirit. And I didn't feel anything; I didn't feel anything negative, I just didn't feel anything at all.

I began thinking, "well these girls are just faking it; or there's something happening and I'm not a part of it." Neither of those options was good. I started doubting my testimony as a teenager. That can be really detrimental to understanding how the Spirit works. Now, as an adult, I can look back and realize that I was feeling the Spirit during that time.

The Scripture that really helped me understand the workings of the Holy Ghost is in **Galatians 5:22-23** "But the fruit of the Spirit is love, joy, peace, longsuffering, gentleness, goodness, faith, meekness, temperance: …"

I think when we talk about the Spirit that it is important to talk about the *fruits of the Spirit*. So I could look back at my teenage years and realize I was feeling the results of the Spirit and experiencing the fruits of the Spirit or results of goodness. (A peer)

"And behold, whosoever believeth on my words, them will I visit with the manifestations of my Spirit …" (D&C 5:16)

---

Bob's dad and mom were visiting us and staying the night. They were going to go home the next day. At five o'clock in the morning I heard thrashing and banging going on upstairs. My husband jumped out of bed to see what had happened. I stayed in bed and prayed.

I decided to take my bible, which I had been reading, upstairs with me where I found mom praying. Dad was alone on the bed and his eyes were rolled back and all I could see was white. I was in the **middle of Luke**, so I just opened the bible to that spot and started reading out loud to dad. All the scriptures were talking about Jesus healing people. I read the scriptures until Dad's eyes turned back and I could see his irises and pupils. I yelled, "He's back! He's back!"

Bob got hold of 911 and the EMTs came to take him to the hospital, about 45 minutes away. He was fine, just suffering from sleep apnea. Afterwards he would tell people that I healed him. I would remind them that I was only a vessel— "God healed you!" (A relative)

"The Master Healer can comfort and sustain us as we experience painful 'realities of mortality,' such as disaster, mental illness, disease, chronic pain, and death." (Carole M. Stephens, GC, Oct 2016)

One scripture in the New Testament really jumped out at me and then that scripture resonated in my mind. I gained a testimony of my heavenly heritage and knew, beyond a doubt, that I and all people are truly Heavenly Father's spirit children. (Missionary Journal) "The Spirit itself beareth witness with our spirit, that we are the children of God:" **(Romans 8:16)**

Another scripture that keeps me on the straight and narrow is this fact: For behold, I God, have suffered these things for all, that they might not suffer if they would repent. *But if they would not repent they must suffer even as I*; Which suffering caused myself, even God, the greatest of all, to tremble because of pain, and to bleed from every pore, and to suffer both body and spirit ... **(D&C 19:16-18)**

Christ atoned for every sin of omission and commission, all agonizing pains of body and spirit, and every terrible pain of our minds, etc. However, the Savior did not atone for unrepentant sinners. The Atonement needs to be claimed by our humility to avoid suffering ourselves.

Paul confirms to the Hebrews: "So Christ was once offered to bear the sins of many." **(Hebrews 9:28)** Many of mankind's host will not have to suffer as Christ suffered. Let us be good!

Now let's discuss how far-reaching the atonement is. The infinite atonement is so powerful that its healing balm reaches forward and backward in time. The atonement was efficacious even during the pre-existence!

The war in heaven was led by Michael (Adam) and his angels who fought against Satan and his dark angle force. Michael's team of pre-existent angels won the war, resulting in Satan and one third of the host of heaven being cast down to earth; they lost their first estate. "And they overcame him (Satan) by the blood of the Lamb, and by the word of their testimony ..." (Revelation 12:11)

The infinite atonement also reaches far beyond our world and universe as we know it. Poetically from the Prophet Joseph Smith:

And I heard a great voice bearing record from heav'n.
He's the Saviour and Only Begotten of God;
By him, of him, and through him, the worlds are made,
Even all that careen in the heavens so broad.

Whose inhabitants, too, from the first to the last,
*Are sav'd by the very same Saviour of ours;*
And, of course, are begotten God's daughters and sons
By the very same truths and the very same powers.
(Millenial Star, vol. 4, pp. 49-55)

---

Several years ago, I had a troubled mind while serving as a counselor in our ward bishopric. ... I was eligible to compete by written examination for the next pay level ... in my vocation. This was a very important step in my career.

I was serving in the bishopric, had a young family and very little time to study. What should I do? I had not discussed this with anyone except my Father in Heaven through prayer.

One special Sunday, while sitting on the stand and trying to push this concern out of my mind, the speaker quoted this scripture: 'But seek ye first the kingdom of God and his righteousness, and all these things shall be added unto you.' **(3 Ne. 13:33)** It was the answer to my prayers.

The Lord, however, did not just hand me the promotion, but He did help. I was called to serve on jury duty. Rather than watch TV, play cards, or just chat like the others did, I spent the time studying. I not only received the promotion, but previous to my retirement, I advanced two additional levels. (Living by the Scriptures, *Church News*, 2/24/96)

---

By the time I had been a parent for almost two decades, half of my six children were not active in the Church and in their testimonies. They were struggling with addictions of the world that led them to many wrong choices. Two of them spent time in jail for drug related crimes.

This all came to a climax for me and I felt despair and helplessness to get my children back on the right path. I was sure there was some concrete answer or miracle I could facilitate to bring them back, and I wanted it soon! I fasted and went to the Temple expecting an answer, from long experience of my Father hearing and answering my prayers very directly through the scriptures.

I arrived at the Temple early enough to have time to sit in the chapel with the scriptures. As was a familiar pattern in my life, the pages almost turned themselves to my answer. These are the words that jumped off the page, as though the Savior Himself was speaking to me: "FRET NOT THYSELF because of evildoers ... TRUST IN THE LORD ... Rest in the LORD, and wait patiently for him; fret not thyself ... fret not thyself." **(Psalms 37:1-8)** "Fret Not" being repeated three times in those verses rally caught my attention.

I knew these words were my answer. But I could hardly comprehend how that would be the solution. In my mind I cried out, "How can I not fret when my children's eternal exaltations are in jeopardy?"

I turned the pages to get my second witness, as is the pattern for such revelations I have had uncountable times in the past. **(1 Peter 3:14-15)** "... Be not afraid of their terror, neither be troubled; But sanctify the Lord God in your heart." I sat in shock and awe, knowing by the Spirit that I had received the exact answer I needed, but not knowing in the least how I was going to change my mind set to this new idea. I spent the next week pondering, wondering, and trying not to give in to the habit of fretting and worrying; until I almost gave up on my new path.

The following week I sat down prayerfully, admittedly fretting a bit, in the Temple chapel again, and opened my scriptures to: **(Luke 24:38-39)** and again the Savior gently taught me: "Why are ye troubled?   Behold my hands and feet that it is I myself ..." This third witness sealed it in my heart; I overflowed with joy at such a merciful answer to a prayer. I had been willing to go to hell and back to rescue my wayward children and here was the answer of the Redeemer. I thought to myself, "I can't save them, but the Lord can and will!" He had already been to hell and back for them and all mankind. He is the only one who can save them ... and he WILL!

I learned to let go of my unfaithful pattern of fretting and worrying. It was a difficult habit to break, but the peace that replaced it was an amazing gift from the atonement. (A family friend)

"As we read and ponder the scriptures, we will experience the sweet whisperings of the Spirit to our souls. We can find answers to our questions." (President Thomas S. Monson, *Ensign*, Nov 2013)

In May of 1996 our daughter departed for her mission to Arkansas. She loved the work and the people she was serving. ... Her doctors found a large brain tumor, and immediately she was flown home for emergency surgery. The tumor was blocking the nerve to her eye, and other vital parts of her brain would soon be affected. ... The evening before her surgery we went to the temple. Before going to bed, my husband and I read this scripture and it impressed us to focus on it through the surgery and during her recovery.

My son, peace be unto thy soul; thine adversity and thine affliction shall be but a small moment; And then, if thou endure it well, God shall exalt thee on high; thou shalt triumph over all thy foes. They friends do stand by thee, and they shall hail thee again with warm heart and friendly hands. Thou are not yet as Job; they friends do not contend against thee, neither charge thee with transgression, as they did Job. **(D&C 121:7-10)**

... Nine months after surgery, having faced many adversities and receiving many blessings, she is now back in the mission field serving the Lord and the people she has come to love. Her friends did stand by her, and did once again hail her with warm hearts and friendly hands. (Living by the Scriptures, *Church News*, 12/20/97)

Since President Monson's challenge six months ago, I have tried to follow his counsel. Among other things, I've made lists of what the **Book of Mormon** is, what it affirms, what it refutes, what it fulfills, what it clarifies, and what it reveals. Looking at the Book of Mormon through these lenses has been an insightful and inspiring exercise! I recommend it to each of you" (Russell M Nelson, GC, Oct 2017)

*Elder Nelson called me to repentance through his humble example of following the prophet. When I heard President Monson's challenge, a half a year ago, I was immersed in other scriptures. I had read the **Book of Mormon** many times already; surely I could wait until I read the **Bible, Doctrine & Covenants, and Pearl of Great Price** first. My pride and rationalization kept respective blessings Elder Nelson received, through his humble and simple obedience, from coming into my life.*

We have all read multiple scriptures and heard various prophecies regarding the Second Coming of our Lord and Savior Jesus Christ over the decades. Although neither man nor any angel knows the day of the second coming, we are closer than ever before. I believe General Conferences have a "theme" and my good wife doesn't believe there's a theme. We both strongly agree however that the talks are inspired by heaven's Godhead and we consider them scriptures also.

Weren't April 2018 General Conference talks and revelatory changes remarkably memorable? And if there is a theme or not, consider the following recent talks and scriptures; all were given at the aforementioned General Conference:

> Elijah committed the sealing keys of this dispensation. For those of us alive at this time, the increase in temples and family history work is phenomenal. *This pace will continue and accelerate until the Second Coming of the Savior*, lest the whole earth "be utterly wasted at his coming." (**D&C 2:3**, Elder Quentin L. Cook)

> What a wonderful blessing to live in a time on continual revelation from God! As we look forward to and embrace the "restitution of all things" (**Acts 3:21**) which has and will come through the prophesied events of our time, *we are being prepared for the Savior's Second Coming.* ... I gladly bear my personal witness that these revelatory changes are inspired of God and that, as we embrace them with willing hearts, *we will become better prepared to meet His Son, Jesus Christ, at His coming.* (Jean B Bingham, Relief Society General President)

> I witness that, as prophesied in the holy scriptures, including the **Book of Mormon, Another Testament of Jesus Christ**, the Lord's kingdom [is] once again established on the earth, *preparatory to the Second Coming of the Messiah.* (New Apostle, Elder Gerrit W. Gong)

> I bear you my witness that *the Lord has already begun a great step forward in His plan for us* to become even more inspired and charitable ... (President Henry B. Eyring)

> You will understand your identity as a son of God, called with a holy calling to do His work. And, *like John the*

*Baptist, you will help prepare for the coming of His Son.*
(Elder Douglas D. Holmes)

Now, brethren, will you please remain standing and join with our chorus in singing all three verses of "Rise Up, O Men of God."(*Hymns*, no. 324) While you sing, *think of your duty as God's mighty army to help prepare the world for the Second Coming of the Lord.* This is our charge. This is our privilege. I so testify in the name of Jesus Christ, amen. (President Russell M. Nelson)

*Our Savior and Redeemer, Jesus Christ, will perform some of His mightiest works between now and when He comes again.* We will see miraculous indications that God the Father and His Son, Jesus Christ, preside over this Church in majesty and glory. But in coming days, it will not be possible to survive spiritually without the guiding, directing, comforting, and constant influence of the Holy Ghost. (President Russell M. Nelson)

*We need to double our diligence and be better prepared throughout our bodies, families, homes, minds and spirits. The time of the Second Coming is knocking at our doors. Be ye prepared and please follow the following wise council/commandment from our new beloved prophet:*

I exhort you to study the messages of this conference frequently—even repeatedly—during the next six months. Conscientiously look for ways to incorporate these messages in your family home evenings, your gospel teaching, your conversations with family and friends, and even your discussions with those not of our faith. Many good people will respond to the truths taught in this conference when offered in love. And your desire to obey will be enhanced as you remember and reflect upon what you have felt these past two days. (President Russell M. Nelson, GC, April 2018)

One day in February 2009 I received an email from our friend Leslie, whom I had baptized six years earlier. She lives in another city now and has struggled with her new ward. She was having some troubling experiences and called me to further explain her concerns. I had been praying for guidance as to what I might say to her. The thing that came to mind was the parable of the olive trees in **Jacob 5** in the Book of Mormon. Toward the end of the chapter the master sends his servants out to make one last effort to get good fruit from the trees. He tells the servants to dig about the trees, to prune them and to dung them.

As I thought of that I was granted some enlightenment from the Spirit to understand what it all meant. The Lord has to turn things upside down for us, to break up the comfort zone so the Spirit can get to us. Then He has to cut back all the pride and the "fluff", to get down to the heart and core of us. Then he piles on the fertilizer to help us grow. Many times we wonder if we can make it through the trials we are given, but when we think life really stinks, that is when Heavenly Father is loading us up with fertilizer to help us grow! (A friend)

———— •◆• ————

Nearly thirty years ago I drove to Utah for the first time. I had been living a very unchristian life, but wanted to change. I just didn't know how. ... I stopped at a motel in a small town in southern Utah. As the lady in the office handed me a room key, I asked if she was a Latter-day Saint.

She pleasantly replied, "Yes, I am." Beaming, she added, "Have you read our wonderful book, the Book of Mormon?"

Both startled and enticed, I told her I had not.

"There's a copy in your room," she continued. "There's nothing exciting for you in this town, so you might as well get acquainted with this wonderful book."

I thanked her and took my luggage to my room. Once there I saw a maroon paperback titled the Book of Mormon on the nightstand. I casually opened the book near the center and read a few verses, but my mind went blank. I did not understand anything.

Disappointed, I put the book down and left my room ... drove around until I found a bar ... I went inside and felt instantly miserable, lonely, and hopeless ... turned around and strode out, determined to never again waste a moment of my life in any bar.

Invigorated, I returned to my motel room and picked up the Book of Mormon. I knelt before the Lord, whom I knew little about, and pleaded with Him to have mercy on me. I asked Him to forgive me for the mess I had made of my life.

I opened the book reverently and read the first verse I saw, 'I glory in plainness; I glory in truth, I glory in my Jesus, for he hath redeemed my soul from hell.' (**2 Ne. 33:6**) My heart burned and my tears fell. The words stood out with a wonderful light of hope—a light of Jesus Christ beckoning me to come unto him.

Weeping, I again knelt in prayer, begging the Lord to lead on ... I read until 2:00 the next morning; the Lord opening my understanding as I read. Six months later I was baptized a member of this wonderful, true Church." (Latter-day Saint Voices, *Ensign*, Sep 2014)

My husband received news that his request for a job transfer had been approved. We were happy and excited about this upcoming adventure. Nevertheless, the anticipated change was also physically and emotionally uncomfortable and stretching, even painful.

One Sunday a few weeks before we were going to move, I started out on my usual walk through the wooded path near our home. I poured out my heart to my Heavenly Father. I thanked Him for this great blessing, and I also shared my concern.

As I did so, I soon found myself overtaken with deep sadness at the thought of leaving people we had learned to love. I didn't want to feel regret. I didn't want to feel gloomy and depressed. I needed to be strong for our five children. So I pleaded with the Lord to remove this heartache from me.

As I expressed this desire for peace, my focus immediately turned to the trees ... A tree, as I remembered, is able to remove toxins from the environment and provide fresh oxygen in its place. I recalled how these toxins are removed through tiny windows, known as stomata which let carbon dioxide in and let oxygen out.

At that moment, I recalled a scripture I had recently read in the Pearl of Great Price, "And out of the ground made, the Lord God, to grow every tree naturally, that is pleasant to the sight of man; and man could behold it. And it became also a living soul. For it was spiritual in the day I created it; for it remaineth in the sphere in which I, God, created it, year, even all things which I prepared for the use of man ..." **(Moses 3:9)**

Next, the thought came into my mind and heart that the tree also had a spiritual purpose. Finding myself alone, I stretched out my arms and placed them around a tree trunk. With closed eyes and a sincere plea, I asked Heavenly Father to allow this "living soul" which He had created to take away the hurt I was feeling and to provide healing ... to soothe my soul with the Balm of Gilead. I asked Him to do spiritually for me what the tree does physically for the air. As I finished my prayer, and opened my eyes, the darkness was gone!

Words cannot describe how dark my mind felt before, and yet how full of light it had become. I felt a complete peace! I knew that the move would be good and right for our family. I know that the Savior can and WILL remove the great pains of everyday living and even more assuredly all of our sins, thanks to His great and eternal atonement. (A family friend)

———◆———

There was a business in SLC, UT, called Youth Developmental Enterprises or YDE. This company would fly nearly 1,000 young men to Hawaii on three large charter jets for summer jobs. I joined the YDE group and, along with a bunch of other boys, picked and planted pineapples for three months. The field labor became boring and very hot at times.

The weather was unbelievably enjoyable however, once one got use to the thick humidity. All the youth workers were bunked in cots at labor camps, for the loss of a better word. There was no air conditioning. We were on Lanai and an early morning city alarm blared to wake the entire town. Most locals also worked for Dole Pineapple and this island was covered with pineapple fields, with no noticeable tourists at that time (1975).

What I found amazing, coming from Wyoming, was that you could lie out on the grass, any time of day or night, and the temperature never seemed to change much at all. Previously I had gained a strong testimony of Joseph Smith and the **Book of Mormon** through a memorable experience reading the **Doctrine and Covenants**. I thought to myself, "It might be very difficult to testify on my mission about the Book of Mormon and the Prophet Joseph Smith. What are people going to think when I bear witness of the Book of Mormon and the investigators ask me if I've read it.

'Uh, no, but I know the Book of Mormon is true.'" I felt like that scenario would not fly very well at all.

So I decided to read the Book of Mormon in Hawaii, lying out on the grass, in my free time over the summer. I already had a testimony of the book; I simply needed to read it. What a wonderful experience I had when I could have been wasting my free time. After finishing the Book of Mormon in late summer, I knelt beside my cot and prayed about the book's truthfulness and if it really is the word of God. I received a tingling reassurance of the truthfulness of the Book of Mormon once again. Now I could go on my mission with confidence!

Mom, Dad, and I went to the SLC Temple after I received my mission call. Our new Ogden Temple was under construction. This was my first time here and they sat me on a front row in a waiting room. My parents were seated in the back of the room. I had been sitting there for a few minutes when Mom came up, handed me a Book of Mormon, and asked me to read some verses, it was **Alma 37:32-37:** "And now, my son, remember the words which I have spoken unto you; trust not those secret plans unto this people, but teach them an everlasting hatred against sin and iniquity. Preach unto them repentance, faith in the Lord Jesus Christ; teach them to humble themselves and to be meek and lowly in heart; teach them to withstand every temptation of the devil, with their faith on the Lord Jesus Christ.

"Teach them to never be weary of good works, but to be meek and lowly in heart; for such shall find rest to their souls. O, remember, my son, and learn wisdom in thy youth; yea, learn in thy youth to keep the commandments of God. Yes, and cry unto God for all thy support ... Counsel with the Lord in all thy doings ... when thou liest down at night lie down unto the Lord ... let thy heart be full of thanks unto God ..."

I cried as I read those words of inspired counsel, given to me by my mother. She was not a scriptorian, but she knew the Gospel. She had been praying for something that she could give or say to me that would be appropriate counsel for a parent to give a son who was leaving on a mission. As she sat down in the temple that evening there was a Book of Mormon in front of her. As she picked the book up, it fell open to that passage in Alma. As she read it, she knew she had an answer to prayer. How grateful I am for a loving mother who recognized the guidance of the Spirit. (A family friend)

——————◆——————

The struggles of being a stay-at-home mom with young children are overwhelming at times! It becomes monotonous, day after day, doing the same duties. As LDS women, we must deal with the pressures of perfection … and then feel we aren't up to such a standard. On such days, I was often reminded of "my calling."

As I worked at finding balance with family and other responsibilities, I would often look around and see a cluttered house, sink full of dishes, and clothes needing laundered. Many times I would find myself thinking, "I've wasted the whole day!" Luckily, the Lord provided me with His tender mercies through the scriptures, which I really needed. **"… be not weary in well-doing, for ye are laying the foundation of a great work."** (D&C 64:33) and **"… by small and simple things are great things brought to pass: and small means in many instances doth confound the wise."** (Alma 37:6) These scriptures seemed to literally jump out of the page to me! They were definitely personal revelation given to me from my Heavenly Father. They became my motto! I understood that being home with my children was important and it was making a difference.

I will be eternally grateful for all the tender mercies that Heavenly Father provided me when raising children. To have a personal witness that I was doing what I was supposed to do, that it was important, and that Heavenly Father was pleased with me, made it all worthwhile. By small and simple things, great things ARE brought to pass! (A friend)

——————◆——————

*Alma was astonished to meet the sons of Mosiah as they crossed paths on their ways to their various missionary areas:*

… Alma did rejoice exceedingly to see his brethren; and what added more to his joy, they were still his brethren in the Lord; yes, and they had waxed strong in the knowledge of the truth; for they were men of a sound understanding and **they had searched the scriptures diligently,** that they might know the word of God. **(Alma 17:2)**

We recently enjoyed a forty-year Swedish mission reunion with both of our mission presidents—still living! (They were called at 30 and 40 years old.) The extreme joy we felt was due to our leaders, companions, and friends remaining solid in the Gospel of Jesus Christ for four decades. One could easily witness that they had been greatly blessed for continued obedience; for their lights truly did shine! (Journal, 10/1/2017)

---

One of the hardest times in our life was when the ranch we worked and lived on was sold. We didn't know for sure what we would do. There was an opportunity for my husband to work for a former employee, but he would be stepping down from ranch manager to ranch hand.

He did find an opportunity to interview with another company some distance away. Our children would need to change schools and we would relocate to company housing. We wrote a list of pros and cons and they were about even. We had no clear answer. The only thing left to do was pray.

I received a very clear answer while reading the Bible, "This is not the way, neither is this the city." **(2 Kings 6:19)** We backed off our decision to move. Then we talked with the production manager of the new land owners.

He counseled us, "Wait a couple months and I think you'll be okay."

A couple of months later, the new company hired my husband to be their "ranch overseer" and offered him a company truck. He told them he already had a truck, so they pay for all his gas now. We could stay where we lived and our children wouldn't have to change schools. This new job was a huge pay raise. The Lord had blessed us every step of the way, even when we had no idea what the future held! We felt like we had received every blessing one could imagine. (A family member)

---

I was reading my **scriptures** in my bedroom and like out of nowhere this prompting comes to "**Get going on food storage.**" It was so strong that I have thought about and worked on our food storage for the past ten years. I have also had the calling two or three times to be the provident living specialist during that time. Through all my research and preparation I was able to help others get started or improve upon their own food storage. Because of the strong Spirit that came during scripture reading, I was able to prepare our family and many other families. (A relative) The best food storage is not in welfare grain elevators but in sealed cans and bottles in the homes of our people. What a gratifying thing it is to see cans of wheat and rice and beans under the beds or in the pantries of women who have taken welfare responsibility into their own hands. (President Gordon B. Hinckley, GC, Oct 2006)

I was reading my scriptures one night and this one verse really jumped out at me. "Seek not to declare my word, but first seek to obtain my word, and then shall your tongue be loosed; then, if you desire, you shall have my Spirit and my word, yea, the power of God unto the convincing of men" (**D&C 11:21**). Then the Spirit said to me, **"You are going to speak in Stake Conference tomorrow."** We were having Apostle David Bednar visit. I said, "That's insane! They don't call people out of the audience during Stake Conference, especially when there's an Apostle there." The next morning two people spoke; Elder Bednar stood up and called several of us out of the audience to bear our testimonies. (Sister missionary) (*Elder Bednar declared unto us this daughter of God:* "was like unto Nephi.")

Years ago my husband was the bishop in a tourist town. People from all walks of life would come through in droves during the summer months. As the 1st ward bishop all welfare needs were forwarded to him. The demand became so heavy and tiresome that the stake decided to share the love and have a different bishop handle traveler's welfare needs for a month each, on a rotating basis.

As my husband was taking the first month he got a call from a woman who needed help. We were all at the church already at our ward party. He suggested she come right over. Of course she shows up in a tank top and short shorts. She was a member and knew her ward and bishop. She knew all the necessary answers to receive help and he gave said help to her. A couple days later, my husband sat straight up in bed in the middle of the night. He said that this woman's face came into his mind along with the following scripture: "… *when saw we thee an hungered, and fed thee: or thirsty, and gave thee to drink?"* **(Matthew 25:37)**

He knew this woman was hungry but didn't know where she was. We left at 6 am and headed for town to look for her. She had mentioned a hotel when they had visited and that is where we found her. She had obtained a job, yet had not received a paycheck. She had not eaten for two days! We took her to a local restaurant and told her, "You eat all that you want!" Then he promised the owner that he would pay for all her meals, no questions asked.

After getting to know her we discovered she was a convert and was active in her ward in the Midwest. At first we just assumed this woman to be another drifter passing through town. This wonderful woman had just fallen on some hard times. (Our friends)

"**Scriptures** are like packets of light that illuminate our minds and give place to guidance and inspiration from on high." (Richard G Scott, *Ensign*, 11/2011)

━━━◆◆◆◆━━━

I remember watching the General Conference when President Monson announced the reduction in ages for young men and women to serve missions back in 2012. The Spirit tingled through me and I knew I would be going on a mission. I immediately started a mission savings account.

Now that I was finally old enough for the new age, I knew many young men that were out serving and one sister who was a special example to me. I was in the middle of a college year and received a strong impression to begin the mission process, even though I could earn my Associates Degree with just one more semester.

I called my father and told him of my strong prompting and he agreed to support me. Then I had trepidation and concerns about where I would serve. I wanted to feel good about my calling. Then I read this scripture and all fears dispersed: "Wherefore, go ye and preach my gospel, whether to the north or to the south, to the east or to the west, it mattereth not, for ye cannot go amiss." **(D&C 80:3)**

I couldn't go amiss! (Sister missionary)

━━━◆◆◆◆━━━

Although baseball was important to young Joseph Fielding Smith, he sometimes left games early, pulled away by an interest that was even more important to him. At such times, he could be found secluded "in the hayloft or in the shade of a tree to get back to his reading" of **the Book of Mormon**. "From my earliest recollection," he later said, "from the time I first could read, I have received more pleasure and greater satisfaction out of the study of the scriptures …" (Joseph Fielding Smith, *TPC*, 4)

"This book of the law shall not depart out of thy mouth; but thou shalt meditate therein day and night, that thou mayest observe to do according to all that is written: …" (Joshua 1:8)

───────◆───────

*We have often been told that the Godhead works with natural laws. Is it possible that Jesus performed the first Lasik eye surgery? During Lasik surgery, a thin flap in the cornea is created using either a blade or a laser. The surgeon then folds back the flap and removes some corneal tissue underneath using an excimer laser.*

And as Jesus walked by, he saw a man which was blind from his birth … he spat on the ground, and made clay of spittle, and he anointed the blind man with the clay. And said unto him, Go, wash in the pool of Siloam … He went his way therefore, and washed and came seeing. **(John 9:1, 6-7)**

*I always thought that Jesus used the coarseness of the clay to clean up the cornea and/or eye damage in that miracle—naturally.*

───────◆───────

As is seen fit, modern scriptures will update or expound upon older scriptures when so inspired. I would like to illustrate the first example with an experience in Gospel Doctrine. We all enjoyed our Gospel Doctrine teacher who was very well read and researched; even as far as to be adorned with the apparel of the era we were studying. The class thoroughly enjoyed his lessons and teachings.

While we were studying the New Testament, we came upon the third and fourth chapters of 1 Peter. Specifically we read, "For Christ also hath once suffered for sins, the just for the unjust, that he might bring us to God, being put to death in the flesh, but quickened by the Spirit: By which also he went and preached unto the spirits in prison." **(1 Peter 3:18-19)** Then our teacher bore a fervent testimony of Christ's preaching to His fallen brethren in spirit prison, following His resurrection.

I raised my hand and commented, "We know from modern revelation that Christ did not actually go to the wicked spirits in prison. This is found in the last section of the Doctrine and Covenants."

He asked, *Brother Scriptorian*, (an older man in the audience), "Is that true?"

The sage saint stated, "Yes, it sure is."

The teacher grumbled a bit and quickly moved on to the next section.

I had forgotten about this discussion until church was over and I went to my car. Leaning against my driver's door was our husky Gospel Doctrine teacher. He was the "army sergeant" type and a former chief of police. I thought, "Gee, I haven't had this happen since high school—He could probably kill me five different ways in two or three minutes, if he wanted to!" As I approached him he stuck out his large hand and quickly swallowed up my hand very tightly.

He placed his other hand firmly on my shoulder and said, "Brother Laing, I appreciate your comments in class." Then he briskly walked away.

> **But unto the wicked he did not go**, and among the ungodly and the unrepentant who had defiled themselves while in the flesh, his voice was not raised; Neither did the rebellious who rejected the testimonies and the warnings of the ancient prophets behold his presence, nor look upon his face. **(D&C 138:19-20)**

This last section, 138, is the great revelatory vision President Joseph F. Smith experienced while *pondering the scriptures* on October 3rd, 1918. I've always had an affinity for this revelation on my birthday.

This all makes sense in conjunction with Section 76 in the Doctrine and Covenants. The Holy Ghost is the only member of the Godhead who visits the Telestial Glory.

> These are they who shall not receive of his fulness in the eternal world, but of the Holy Spirit through the ministration of the terrestrial … And also the Telestial receive it of the **administering of angels** who are appointed to minister for them, or who are appointed to be ministering spirits for them … **(D&C 76:86, 88)**

*The following scripture was modified because circumstances changed over time.*

During the Sermon on the Mount the Saviors teaches us:

"Be ye therefore perfect, <u>even as your Father</u> which is in heaven is perfect." **(Matthew 5:48)** The JST verse reads exactly the same, no changes were made.

*Now let's look at Christ's similar discourse to the Nephite nation following His resurrection:*

"Therefore I would that ye should be perfect <u>even as I, or your Father</u> who is in heaven is perfect." **(3 Ne. 12:48)**

Even though Christ lived a perfect life, He was not perfected, in all things, until after His resurrection.

*Another great scriptural explanation of multitudinous references within the Bible and Book of Mormon is found in D&C 19. Throughout the scriptures hell is described as an everlasting life of misery and woe:*

"... that awful monster, death and hell, and the devil, and the lake of fire and brimstone, which is endless torment." **(2 Ne. 9:26)**

*Now the revelatory scripture:*

Nevertheless, it is not written that there shall be no end to this torment, but it is written endless torment. Again, it is written eternal damnation; wherefore it is more express than other scriptures, that it might work upon the hearts of the children of men, altogether for my name's glory.
Wherefore, I will explain unto this mystery ... For, behold, the mystery of godliness, how great it is! For, behold, I am endless, and the punishment which is given from my hand is endless punishment, for Endless is my name. Wherefore—Eternal punishment is God's punishment. Endless punishment is God's punishment." **(D&C 19:6-8, 10-12)**

We learn from the Doctrine and Covenants that eternal punishment, or everlasting punishment, does not mean that a man condemned will endure this punishment forever, but it is everlasting and eternal because it is God's punishment, and he is Everlasting and Eternal. Therefore, when a man pays the penalty of his misdeeds and humbly repents, receiving the gospel, he comes out of the prison house and is assigned to some degree of glory according to his worth and merit. (*DS*, 2:161)

*In other words, we now know that God's punishments do not last forever. In his mercifulness there comes a time of reprieve, of sorts, for all sinners, which durations only He will determine.*

In Revelations one reads:
"And before the throne there was a sea of glass like unto crystal: and in the midst of the throne, and round about the throne, were four beasts full of eyes before and behind." **(Revelation 4:6)**

*Joseph Smith received revelation describing the above symbolism and meaning as follows:*
What is the sea of glass …? It is the earth in its sanctified, immortal, and eternal state.
What are we to understand by the four beasts …? They are figurative expressions … describing heaven, the paradise of God, the happiness of man, and of beasts, and of creeping things, and of the fowls of the air; that which is spiritual being in the likeness of that which is temporal; and that which is temporal in the likeness of that which is spiritual … **(D&C 77:1-2)**

"And other sheep I have, which are not of this fold: them also I must bring, and they shall hear my voice; and there shall be one fold, and one shepherd." **(John 10:16)**

*Who are these other sheep Jesus taught about? Another Testament of Jesus Christ gives the answer. Jesus revealed to the righteous Nephites:*

"… ye are they of whom I said: Other sheep I have which are not of this fold; them also I must bring, and they shall hear my voice, and there shall be on fold, and one shepherd." **(3 Ne. 15:21)**

*Additionally Jesus explained to the Nephites regarding other sheep:*

"… I say unto you that I have other sheep, which are not of this land, neither of the Land of Jerusalem, neither in any of the land round about whither I have been to minister." **(3 Ne. 16:1)**

*And then He further reveals:*

"But now I go unto the Father, and also to show myself unto the lost tribes of Israel, for they are not lost unto the Father, for he knoweth whither he hath taken them." **(3 Ne. 17:4)**

---

One scripture is often paraphrased as such: "if a person gains more knowledge and intelligence they will have an advantage in the next life." **(D&C 130:19)** actually reads "And if a person gains more knowledge and intelligence in this life *through their diligence and obedience than another*, he will have so much the advantage in the world to come."

The most important part of this scripture is frequently omitted. Those who utilize the atonement and frequently repent will have the advantage. Saints who understand and live a life of charity will be ahead in the next life. Those whose lives mirror King Benjamin's wise counsel to serve God will wear their lives out by serving others. Men and women who diligently strive to live the first law of heaven will have the real advantage in the next world.

It is important to learn and study, yet even more important to peruse proper literature. Paul explains the problem with some educated people: "Ever learning, and never able to come to the knowledge of the truth." **(2 Tim. 3:7)**

There are treasures in the scriptures, the church magazines, and many good books that we can gain much from. However the most vital knowledge and intelligence one can obtain is through a life lived as Christ lives. This is how God's children can "... pass by the angels, and the gods, which are set there, to their exaltation and glory in all things ..." **(D&C 132:19)**

"The knowledge which we seek, the answers for which we yearn, and the strength which we desire today to meet the challenges of a complex and changing world can be ours when we willingly obey the Lord's commandments." (President Thomas S. Monson, *Ensign,* May 2013)

---

*What does the Lord do when an important event is missing from the scriptures?*

"And Jesus said unto them: How be it that ye have not written this thing, that many saints did arise and appear unto many and did minister unto them?" **(3 Ne. 23:11)**

*Many people arose from the dead, following Christ's resurrection, and the Church leaders forgot to record it. One of the most important and miraculous events in their history was missing from their scriptures. This is why it is important to keep records and journals.*

*In addition important items are sometimes removed from the scriptures:*

> ... They have taken away from the gospel of the Lamb many parts which are plain and most precious; and also many covenants of the Lord have they taken away. And all this have they done that they might pervert the right ways of the Lord, that they might blind the eyes and harden the hearts of the children of men. (**1 Ne. 13:26-27**)

> In 1830 Joseph Smith began working on a correct **translation of the Bible**. Sidney Rigdon was his scribe. In preparing this translation of the Bible, Joseph was not translating from an ancient language, as he did with the Book of Mormon, but was restoring the Bible to its original meaning. As Joseph studied and pondered the Bible, he was inspired through the power of the Holy Ghost to correct errors in it. (Primary 5:20)

———— •◆• ————

*The great and final sacrifice of the perfect Son ended the Law of Moses. All those scriptures and laws that had been faithfully followed for millennia were now done away with. As our resurrected Savior taught the Nephites he instructed:*

> Behold, I say unto you that the law is fulfilled that was given unto Moses. Behold, I am he that gave the law, and I am he who covenanted with my people Israel; therefore, the law in me is fulfilled, for I have come to fulfil the law; therefore it hath an end. For behold, the covenant which I have made with my people is not all fulfilled; but the law which was given unto Moses hath an end in me. (**3 Ne. 15:5-6, 8**)

———— •◆• ————

*At times I have marveled at the story of Noah's Ark. How could there be only one righteous family amongst all the children of men at that time? How did all the people become so wicked?*

"And God saw that the wickedness of man was great in the earth, and that every imagination of the thoughts of his heart was only evil continually." **(Genesis 6:5)**

*Once one considers the history of the people at the time, the scriptures also reveal that there were many righteous people upon the earth during Noah's pre-flood days. All the righteous patriarchs and their wives had passed away: Adam and Eve, Seth, Enos, Cainan, Mahalaleel, Jared, Lamech and Methuselah and their wives. These servants of God had lived for many centuries: 777 - 969 years old!*

*The remaining righteous were taken up in/with the City of Enoch, between Adam and Seth's passing.*

"... Zion, in process of time, was taken up into heaven ..." **(Moses 7:21)**

*Other righteous people, up to the time of the flood, also attained the City of Enoch.*

And Enoch beheld angels descending out of heaven, bearing testimony of the Father and Son; and the Holy Ghost fell on many, and they were caught up by the powers of heaven into Zion. **(Moses 7:27)**

*So it was actually not an absolutely wicked world flush with evil men and women as I/we use to think. The fact of the matter is that all the righteous people had been purposely removed from the earth; some enjoying paradise, while others lived in a translated state. The cream of the crop was probably enjoying the Celestial kingdom as just men and women made perfect. This necessitated only one living patriarch and his family remaining in righteousness amongst the throngs of wanton wickedness. The following scriptures put this idea more succinctly:*

"And it came to pass that the God of heaven looked upon *the residue* of the people, and he wept." **(Moses 7:28)**
"... upon *the residue* of the wicked the floods came and swallowed them up." **(Moses 7:43)**

*Following the death of all but one of the great patriarchs, their wives' deaths, the rest of the righteous passing away or being translated, and eight righteous souls inside the ark, all that remained on earth to experience the great flood was the residue—the wicked.*

161

*The event of Noah's ark could well be considered a foreshadowing of Christ's Second Coming, when the righteous will be separated from the wicked prior to their destruction. Only the wicked people will be left on the earth, once again, for the second cleansing. The residue will remain as prophesied.*

> And righteousness will I send down out of heaven; and truth will I send forth out of the earth, to bear witness of mine Only Begotten; his resurrection from the dead; yea, and also the resurrection of all men; and righteousness and truth will I cause to sweep the earth as with a flood, to gather out mine elect from the four quarters of the earth, unto a place which I shall prepare , an Holy City, that my people may gird up their loins, and be looking forth for the time of my coming; for there shall be my tabernacle, and it shall be called Zion, a New Jerusalem. And the Lord said unto Enoch: then shalt thou and all thy city meet them there, and we will receive them into our bosom ... **(Moses 7:62-63)**

*Everyone loves the stories of the two thousand stripling warriors and their faithful mothers. Those young men testified:*

> Now they never had fought, yet they did not fear death; and they did think more upon the liberty of their fathers than they did upon their lives; yea, they had been taught by their mothers, that if they did not doubt, God would deliver them. And they rehearsed unto me the words of their mothers, saying: We do not doubt our mothers knew it. **(Alma 56:47-48)**

*Only a mother who has lost a husband or child could begin to comprehend what these righteous women had been suffering through. Many of them had lost their husband and/or son/s, uncles, brothers, etc. to a war against the Lamanites. Now their younger boys wanted to go fight in bloody battles! The Lord must have blessed these dear women's hearts and souls with a great comfort.*

*The people of Ammon (former Lamanites) had buried their weapons of war and refused to fight again. Over 1,005 Ammonites were mowed down while praying to God.*

*This scene of merciless horror touched so many of their Lamanite brethren that the warriors ceased the carnage.*

"... the people of God were joined that day be more (men) than the number who had been slain ..." (Alma 24:26)

*Considering the communities demographics one discovers just over one thousand men being recently. All these hundreds of grieving widows were likely reunited in marriage with some of these new men over time. A woman could have feasibly married a Lamanite convert who unknowingly killed her husband and older son and now was sending off her younger boys to war against his old* friends!

---

*We have often heard talks and read stories about the gathering of Israel in the last days. Much of this prophecy has already happened, some of the prophecy is being fulfilled currently, and other parts of the prophecy relate to the future: Second Coming of Christ.*

... I, Nephi, spake much unto them concerning these things; yea, I spake unto them concerning the restoration of the Jews in the latter days. And I did rehearse unto them the words of Isaiah, who spake concerning the restoration of the Jews, or of the house of Israel; and after they were restored they should no more be confounded, neither should they be scattered again. **(1 Ne. 15:19-20)**

*Now compare the above scriptural prophecies with the following factual data from our time:*

In 1948, there were some 650,000 Jews in Israel, who represented about 5% of the world's Jews. Today, Israel's Jewish population has grown ten-fold and stands at about 6.8 million people. Some 43 percent of the world's Jews live in Israel: this population overtook American Jews several years ago and is now the world's largest Jewish community. (Daniel Gordis, *Bloomberg Review,* published in the *Standard Examiner,* Ogden, Utah, *4/21/2018, B10*)

*If that's not a gathering—I don't know what is!*

---

"Therefore those things which were of old time, which were under the law, in me are all fulfilled. Old things are done away, and all things have become new. " (3 Ne. 12:46-47)

"And there shall be a new heaven and a new earth; and they shall be like unto the old save the old have passed away, and all things have become new." (Ether 13:9)

*Is the first scripture a foreshadowing of the second scripture? Initially Christ was ending the Mosaic Law and lastly Christ will end the old heavens and earth; making "all things become new."*

My husband and I had been married for over three years and we had tried for that long to have our first child. Nothing we tried worked. We started spending money for special treatments. There were high costs with no positive results. We didn't know what to do. Obviously we had fasted and prayed; yet no definitive answer seemed to come to us. While I was reading in Ether one day I felt a need to change the manner of my prayers.

"And they did sing praises unto the Lord; yea, the brother of Jared did sing praises unto the Lord and he did thank the Lord all the day long; and when the night came, they did not cease to praise the Lord." **(Ether 6:9)**

I decided to go with prayers of gratitude instead of praying for what we didn't have. As I was praying with thankfulness in my speech and gratitude in my heart, the Spirit spoke clearly to me and suggested we adopt a child. I knew that this was how we would need to obtain our family we desired.

We immediately started the adoption process and that took some time. That energetic nine-year-old boy is the result of my scripture study and personal revelation. I simply needed to show gratitude and not always ask for what I wanted. (A friend)

"Being enriched in every thing to all bountifulness, which causeth through us thankfulness to God." **(2 Cor. 9:11)**

*One of my very favorite sections in the **Doctrine and Covenants is Section 76**. Our fourth-great grandfather was present when this section was given. He, Philo Dibble, refers to this section as "Vision of Glories."*

The vision which is recorded in the Doctrine and Covenants was given at the house of "Father Johnson", in Hyrum, Ohio, and during the time that Joseph and Sidney were in the spirit and saw the heavens open, there were other men in the room, perhaps twelve, among whom I was one during a part of the time—probably two-thirds of the time, I saw the glory and felt the power but did not see the vision.

Joseph would, at intervals say: "What do I see?" as one might say while looking out the window and beholding what all in the room could not see. Then he would relate what he had seen or what he was looking at. Then Sidney replied, "I see the same." Presently Sidney would say "and what do I see?" and would repeat what he had seen or was seeing, and Joseph would reply, "I see the same." This manner of conversation was repeated at short intervals to the end of the vision, and during the whole time not a word was spoken by any other person. Not a sound nor motion was made by anyone but Joseph and Sidney, and it seemed to me that they never moved a joint or limb during the time I was there, which I think was over an hour, and to the end of the vision. Joseph sat firmly and calmly all the time in the midst of a magnificent glory, but Sidney sat limp and pale, apparently as limber as a rag, observing which, Joseph remarked, smilingly, "Sidney is not used to it as I am." (Philo Dibble, *Life History*)

The greatest revelation the Lord, Jesus Christ, has ever given to man, so far as record is made, was given to the Prophet Joseph Smith ... known as **the 76th section** ... commonly called for years and still know as *"The Vision."* I say, this to my mind is the climax of all wonderful revelations that have come from the Lord from the days of Father Adam until the present moment. (Melvin J. Ballard, Three Degrees of Glory, 3-4)

———————— •◆•— ————————

The Lord has given us in **the standard works** the means by which we should measure truth and untruth. May we all heed his word (President Ezra Taft Benson, *Ensign*, Dec 1972)

# 7. My Soul Delighteth in the Song

"Be filled with the Spirit. Speaking to yourselves in **psalms and hymns and spiritual songs**, singing and making melody in your heart to the Lord;" (Eph. 5:18-19)

"Through the miracle of sacred music, the Spirit of the Lord descended upon us, and we were made ready for gospel instruction and worship." (Dallin H. Oaks, GC, Oct 1994)

I had just given birth to our daughter, Rebekah. My labor had been intense, and I was exhausted. When Rebekah was placed in my arms, I had the overwhelming feeling that I should sing my favorite, **"I am a Child of God"** (*Hymns*, no. 301). My initial response was, "No, I'm too tired. I'll sing to her later." But then the thought came again. So, even though I was exhausted, I began singing the first verse. My husband and my mother soon joined me.

When we finished the song, I felt a special feeling in the room. Even the doctor, who until that point had been professional and rather aloof, had tears streaming down her face. She thanked us for singing such a beautiful song. She said that in all the years she had been delivering babies, she had never felt as she did at that moment. (Latter-day Saint Voices, *Ensign*, April 2015)

My youngest sister and I attended a funeral for another sister's father-in-law. He was a former BYU professor. I was told that he had planned his funeral and estate in advance.

As our cute little niece walked in with the Children's Songbook I asked her why she had the book. "Oh, I'm playing the music for the grandchildren's song."

"So you're doing the regular 'I Am a Child of God', I'm guessing."

"No ... we're singing 'When He Comes Again.'"

"Oh, that's really nice!"

As I looked over the program and thought about the songs he had chosen the Spirit swept over me and witnessed that he was truly a disciple of Christ. I was so grateful that we attended and learned more about his service-filled life.

Following are the songs he chose: **"Our Savior's Love"** (*Hymns*, no. 113), **"Jesus, Savior, Pilot Me"** (*Hymns*, no. 104), **"When He Comes Again"**

(*Children's Songbook*, 82) and "**God Be with You Till We Meet Again**" (*Hymns*, no. 152). (Journal 3/4/2018)

———•◆•———

Another of our translators received the songbook *The Children Sing* to be translated into German. Music is most difficult to translate, and *The Children Sing* is no exception. In this case, however, the translator could not write fast enough to keep up with the flow of words as they came to her. There was no doubt in her mind as to the source of her inspiration. (Victor L. Brown, GC, April 1974)

———•◆•———

During the summer of 2006 I was having a lot of music go through my head: ads, radio, ice cream truck, etc. Certain tunes tended to stick in my head and I preferred they didn't. I have found that if I start *playing* a different song, that song will usually stick. My go-to song is my very favorite hymn "*I Stand All Amazed.*" (*Hymns*, no. 193)

Then I purchased a new CD of beautiful arrangements by Lex De Azevedo. I listened to this CD for a couple of weeks and now a new song was planted in my mind, playing over and over at times. However, I didn't mind because it was a very beautiful song.

Then all of a sudden I heard a different song. It was one of the hymns that I had not heard until I went on my mission. It was not in our old hymnbook, but it was in the German hymnbook. The music to it is from an old German folk song and the tune is kind of catchy. (*Hymns*, no. 266, **The Time Is Far Spent**) Now this was stuck in my head and I thought, that's fine, I like this one too. This song repeated so often that I felt a need to read the actual words to that hymn.

I got out our hymnbook and looked it up; as I read the words I began to cry. The fourth verse was exactly what I needed to hear at that time. I was struggling with some things that had recently come into my life. The fourth verse says, "Be fixed in your purpose, for Satan will try you; the weight of your calling he perfectly knows. Your path may be thorny, but Jesus in nigh you; His arm is sufficient, tho demons oppose."

My loving Father has given me reassurance through the words of a hymn that came into my mind. Quite a few times since then I have noticed a new hymn going through my mind; when I have gone and read the words I have found answers that are exactly what I need to hear at the time. (A friend)

———————◆———————

Peter looked around the strange hospital room. This was the first night he had ever been away from his mother and father, and he was frightened even though the nurses had promised to stay close by.

The hospital was large, but it was very crowded. The only bed available for Peter was in a little room at the end of the men's ward. All of those men were frightening to Peter. He pulled the bed sheet up around his chin and began to pray so he wouldn't feel so afraid and alone. After the prayer, there came into Peter's mind a song he and his friends had sung in Sunday School that begins **"Jesus loves me, this I know …"**

A nurse going by the door heard a small clear voice swell with the chorus of the familiar song. Peter's sweet singing could be heard throughout the men's ward. The men stopped their talking. They turned off their radios. Tears ran down the cheeks of some of them …

When Peter finished singing, he snuggled down in his bed. His song-prayer had brought him the comfort he needed. He was no longer lonely or afraid. (Our Praying Friends, *Friend*, June 1974)

"… I will sing with the spirit, and I will sing with the understanding also." (1 Cor. 14:15)

———————◆———————

On my mission to Sweden we had only a couple of actual chapels to meet in. They both had a piano and an organ, which was rare. While serving in the beautiful cities of Lund and Malmö, on P-days, my companion and I would spend a couple of hours on the piano and organ respectively at that meetinghouse. My companion was teaching himself to play the organ while I was trying to teach myself to play our hymns on the piano.

One Monday afternoon, after our laundry, shopping, and chores were done, we headed for the church building. As I sat there *plinking out* songs, one really touched my heart. **"I Stand All Amazed"** (*Hymns*, no. 193) seemed to sing to me from the piano and the message of the song sunk sweetly into my soul. It was the most spiritual experience I have ever had with a song. I seemed to obtain a miniscule understanding of the incomprehensible Atonement; yet more importantly, I felt the power and efficacy of God's love and charity for us all, His children. (Missionary journal 4/21/1976)

> "If ye have experienced a change of heart, and if ye have felt to sing the song of redeeming love, I would ask, can ye feel so now?" (Alma 5:26)

When I lived in the dorms at Utah State University (USU), I attended a church that everyone called the Golden Toaster. Trust me, if you saw it, you'd know why. (It was torn down in 2015. Google "Golden Toaster" to see the picture and story.)

There in the Golden Toaster was my first time in a student ward, so every Sunday was exciting. However, after a while I noticed that way too often we sang **"How Firm a Foundation"** (*Hymns*, no. 85) in sacrament meeting. It was getting on my nerves, so I finally asked the ward organist why we didn't sing other songs more often.

She explained that "How Firm" was one of the few songs she could play on the organ, and she felt that the organ was more appropriate than the piano for sacrament meetings. Sigh, I couldn't convince her to play other hymns, and that song tormented me all year long.

Little did I know that years later, whenever we sang that much used hymn at church, it transported me back to those wonderful, glorious days at USU. Now over thirty years later, I still remember the page number and can sing the first three verses by heart. (A relative)

As a young woman attending youth conference, I felt the Spirit bear witness to me of the truthfulness of the restored gospel. In preparation for a testimony meeting, we sang **"The Spirit of God."** Now, I had sung that hymn many times before in sacrament meetings. But on this occasion, from nearly the opening note, I felt the Spirit. By the time we sang, "The latter-day glory begins to come forth **'The Spirit of God'"** (*Hymns*, no. 2) I knew that these were more than nice lyrics; they were beautiful truths. (Vicki F. Matsumori, GC, Oct 2009)

A young couple in Brazil shares their experience: "When my wife and I married, I was unemployed. We had very little furniture, but we had a lot of love and faith. When I got my first job, it required me to work on Sunday afternoons. I had promised the Lord I wouldn't work on His day. But I was still responsible for providing for my family. Even so, the promise I'd made didn't leave my mind.

My answer came the next Sunday while singing *"Welcome, Welcome, Sabbath Morning"* (*Hymns*, no. 280) and realizing the importance of the Sabbath day. After learning that negotiating a new schedule wouldn't be an option, I quit my job.

We believed the Lord would help us. ... I utilized the Perpetual Education Fund ... Fifteen months after ... I got my current job. I am now a technician in electrical energy measurement. I work Monday through Friday, which I consider to be a miracle in this industry. (Employment: A Lot of Faith, a Little Furniture, *Ensign*, Aug 2016)

———•◆•———

I was on the high school ski team and we were all on a bus headed to a meet. We were seniors and took over the back of the bus. The conversation turned very off color. I soon found my mind in the gutter, even though I wasn't saying anything. I wanted no part of the filthy discussion.

I turned my face to the window and replaced the awful thoughts with a Primary song: *"A Child's Prayer"*, Children's Songbook, 12) I was able to replace those awful thoughts with this beautiful children's song." (A relative)

The standard is clear. If something we think, see, hear, or do distances us from the Holy Ghost, then we should stop thinking, seeing, hearing, or doing that thing. If that which is intended to entertain, for example, alienates us from the Holy Spirit, then certainly that type of entertainment is not for us. Because the Spirit cannot abide that which is vulgar, crude, or immodest, then clearly such things are not for us. Because we estrange the Spirit of the Lord when we engage in activities we know we should shun, then such things definitely are not for us. (David A. Bednar, GC, April 2006)

———•◆•———

My ears burned bright red with embarrassment as my teenage son, Derek, and I finished singing **'Be Still, My Soul"** (*Hymns*, no. 124) in sacrament meeting. I had not

My Soul Delighteth in the Song

properly warmed up before the meeting began, and as a result, when I tried to reach a high note, my voice cracked badly.

I slid back onto my bench, feeling uncomfortable … After the closing prayer I headed to my car to retrieve a lesson manual. A sister in our ward stood near the door; sobbing … the weeping sister called my name and expressed appreciation to me for choosing the hymn we sang and for performing it in a way that touched her deeply.

She explained that she had given birth to a stillborn baby several days earlier and had battled anger and despair ever since. As Derek and I sang the hymn, she had felt the Sprit wrap her aching soul in peaceful comforting warmth. It had filled her with the hope she needed to bear her cross of grief. (Latter-day Voices, *Ensign*, Sep 2013)

————— •◆• —————

When I was at Rick's College, I stayed for the summer semester. We were with a group of educator's at a cabin in Island Park, ID. One of the classes we took was geology and they would take us around to see specific geological wonders such as Yellowstone National Park.

The group went to a powerful geyser that shoots as high as the Old Faithful geyser. It is a spectacular geyser but is unpredictable and doesn't go off very often. As we traveled through the park we kept running into this Baptist youth group at the sites. Once again the Baptist youth were spread around this geyser spout as were a lot of other people. I said, 'We should sing a song that everyone would know; maybe we could get this geyser going?'

We decided a song most people would know was, "**How Great Thou Art**", (*Hymns*, no. 86). As a group of Rick's College youth we had our hymnals with us and pulled them out. We started singing and everyone joined us! So there are all these tourists, Baptist kids, and Mormon kids singing "My God how great Thou art." And honestly, right as the group song ended, the geyser erupted and went off! It was just spectacular and just the coolest experience with good music. I think heaven knew we all had the faith that that thing could go off, even though we were from many different religions. (A relative)

————— •◆• —————

I had a very dear friend whose wife had passed away and he had *lost his way*. He became inactive in church and was very unmotivated. He ended up marrying a woman who was actually an anti-Mormon. This did not seem to improve his situation and feelings. Life was just getting more and more difficult and he felt one day that he just needed to go to church.

At church they sang the song, *"Do What Is Right"*, (*Hymns*, no. 237). The chorus really hit him strong: "Do what is right; let the consequence follow."

He thought to himself, alright I am going to try and do what is right and see what follows. He began coming back to church and reactivated himself. Things turned around. It wasn't six months later that his wife was baptized.

That song helped totally change his life and her life. Doing what was right, the consequences were beautiful! (Our friend)

————•◆••————

Elder Monson oversaw the completion of the 1985 songbook, the first new edition in 37 years. ... Several older hymns were replaced by new ones, including *"Hark, All Ye Nations,"* (*Hymns*, no. 264) one of President Monson's favorites ... For Elder Monson, his involvement with the hymnbook was a treasured experience." (Thomas S Monson, *To the Rescue*, 419)

————•◆••————

I give it to all, in this forum, because of the activities of a few who evidently are seeking to lead others in the paths which they are following. I speak of those who advocate the offering of prayers to our Mother in Heaven. I quote from that earlier address:

This [practice] began in private prayer and is beginning to spread to prayers offered in some of our meetings.

It was Eliza R. Snow who wrote the words: "Truth is reason; truth eternal / Tells me I've a mother there." *(Hymns, 1985, no. 292.)*

It has been said that the Prophet Joseph Smith made no correction to what Sister Snow had written. Therefore, we have a Mother in Heaven. Therefore, [some assume] that we may appropriately pray to her.

Logic and reason would certainly suggest that if we have a Father in Heaven, we have a Mother in Heaven … That doctrine rests well with me.

However, in light of the instruction we have received from the Lord Himself, I regard it as inappropriate for anyone in the Church to pray to our Mother in Heaven.

The Lord Jesus Christ set the pattern for our prayers. In the Sermon on the Mount, He declared:

"After this manner therefore pray ye: Our *Father* which art in heaven, Hallowed be thy name." (Matt 6:9) (Gordon B. Hinckley, *GC*, Oct 1991)

---

I served a mission when sister missionaries were more rare than common. I had always desired to go on a foreign mission. I excitedly received my call and was internally disappointed because it was to the central United States.

I was sitting in sacrament meeting and the song *"I'll Go Where You Want Me to Go"* (*Hymns*, no. 270). *"It may not be on the mountain height Or over the stormy sea, It may not be on the battle's front, My Lord will have need of me."*

We tracted into a golden investigator; this does not happen very often. She was converted and baptized, went through the temple and is still a strong member today, serving in the temple. She has become my best friend and she's been a great support over the years.

Even though it was not where I wanted to go, it was where the Lord wanted me to go and where I was supposed to be. (A peer)

---

My most cherished and most undeniable experience was the following:

I was married to my high school sweetheart and we had three boys. I was 32 years old and teaching at the neighborhood Jr. High School. I lived close enough to the school that I walked to work every day.

This particular day was just like so many other mornings, however that day as I rounded the corner at 20th place, a conduit of sorts opened in my mind.

A voice came into my head and announced, **"You will be the bishop of the 3rd Ward."**

Then, an angelic choir began singing the chorus to hymn **#243 *Let Us All Press On*:** "Fear not, though the enemy deride; Courage, for the Lord is on our side. We will heed not what the wicked may say, But the Lord alone we will obey." It was if someone had put a set of headphones over my ears and then taken them off.

The one thing that impressed me most is that I must not be fearful. I must learn to trust God.

Once the word "obey" was sung, the conduit closed and then my thoughts returned to my own. Immediately I thought, "How can that be?" Our bishop has only been the bishop for two years—his time is not up yet up." Yet I could not doubt what had just happened to me, although I said nothing of this experience to anyone except my wife, not even the bishop; I was serving as his first counselor at the time.

A few weeks later I learned that the bishop had accepted a new position out-of-state and that he would be moving very soon. When the stake president called me to serve as the bishop of the 3rd Ward, he was amazed that I could give him the names of my two counselors and had an outline for several of the goals I intended to work on as bishop. I then shared with him the experience that I had. (A relative)

---

About 15 years ago my husband and I offered to bring two nephews into our home to attend high school here. Their parents had divorced, their mother was addicted to prescription drugs, and they had been living with their father who was overwhelmed and not doing much in the parenting department. Besides failing in school, they were running with a bad crowd and being taught nothing of the Gospel. I was teaching Seminary at the time, and I felt like the Spirit really told me they needed to live with us. After the initial 'honeymoon' period, however, reality kicked in. They found bad friends here, also, and they began to rebel somewhat against our family rules.

We had provided the older boy with a car to drive to school and even a gas credit card to use. After a few months, when I was paying the bills, I noticed some discrepancies and it was obvious it was being used several times on the same day— apparently to fill up the cars of his friends, also, or perhaps to provide gas in exchange for cigarettes or something— who knows? I was livid; especially when he denied all my accusations. Home life became difficult even having them around. I couldn't believe the audacity of such a thing when we had been so generous and accepting of them.

One morning, while at Seminary, I randomly chose an opening song "**Lord, I Would Follow Thee**." (*Hymns*, no. 220) I was also the pianist, so while playing and singing along, we came to verse 2 with these words: "Who am I to judge another when I walk imperfectly? In the quiet heart is hidden, sorrow that the eye can't see." It was as if a wave of guilt came over me. Seriously, who was I to judge so harshly when I had no idea what they had been through or how they may have learned to survive in the world? Tears came to my eyes and I had to compose myself to carry on with a lesson that day.

Since that time, hymn 220 has become a favorite— and I think of my nephews whenever we sing it. They didn't "turn out" exactly as I had hoped and dreamed, but they are now adults who are contributing to society and I think they actually have come to appreciate our small sacrifice in their lives. They are certainly in a better place than they were headed, and I think I really was inspired to bring them into our home for a few years. (A friend)

We had two small children and a baby when I was called to serve in the Young Women's presidency. My husband was working and going to college.

There was a youth conference coming up and I had no one to watch my little ones so they were in tow. After a full day of helping and tending to our small children, I was feeling overwhelmed. My husband was always so busy and loneliness was creeping up on me.

Often, my favorite part of girl's camp or youth conference was the testimony meeting. I desired to go but felt a need to take my children home and put them to bed. As I walked to the car, my feelings were overcoming me; the song, **"Come, Come, Ye Saints"**, (*Hymns*, no. 30) played in my mind. The following verses answered all my concerns and worries:

"Why should we mourn or think our lot is hard? 'Tis not so; all is right.

"Why should we think to earn a great reward If we now shun the fight …

"Gird up your loins; fresh courage take. Our God will never us forsake;

"And soon we'll have this tale to tell — All is well! All is well! "

I learned through the challenge all was right—it was in perfect order and I was not alone; the Lord was with me. I also needed to take courage and move forward in that courage. We will have tough experiences in our lives, but we can push forward in courage and trust while it may not be as we wish it was—all is well. (A relative)

---

I was a counselor in the Primary Presidency. I have always had a testimony of the Gospel and believed it was true simply because my parents said it was. But at this particular time in my life I needed to know for myself if the Church was true. So I started fasting and praying. I needed some kind of confirmation that this church I had belonged to all my life really was the true church and that all I had been taught was true. At first nothing happened. In fact, a week or so went by, and I didn't feel like I had gotten any kind of answer ... nothing at all. I got a little frustrated and started questioning ... did Heavenly Father even hear my prayers? Why would he not answer me? Was this not the true church?

That Sunday I attended the 'It's Great to be Eight' program at the church for all the children that would be getting baptized that year. We started singing, "I belong to **The Church of Jesus Christ** of Latter Day Saints ... I know who I am, I know Gods plan, I'll follow him in faith ..." (Children's Songbook, 77) It was then that I got my answer. As I sang those words I got goose bumps over my whole body, the spirit filled my soul, my heart beat harder, and my eyes started filling up with tears. Without a doubt, I knew that was my answer. Now, whenever I sing that song, it brings back the memory of that day, and the overwhelming feeling I had, that yes, the church is true! (Our friend)

"The hymns of the Restoration carry with them the spirit of conversion. They came as a result of sacrifice." (Jay E. Jensen, GC, April 2007)

---

The Holy Ghost can help us in many different ways, the experience I had was with the Holy Ghost testifying of a particular gospel truth.

I remember as a teenager singing the hymn "**Praise to the Man**" (*Hymns*, no. 27) from the hymnbook. It is a hymn about the prophet Joseph Smith. As I was singing the song and really thinking about the words I was singing, I had an overwhelming testimony born to me that Joseph Smith was not only a prophet of God, but a wonderful man who cared about me and loved me, even though he lived long before I was ever born.

Every time I sing or hear that hymn, I receive that witness from the Holy Ghost again just as strongly as I did the first time.

Since that first experience over twenty years ago, I have never once doubted that Joseph Smith was a prophet of God. That knowledge has been a great help to me in building my testimony of the Book of Mormon and other parts of the gospel. I read a talk once by President Hinckley where he described a similar experience he had in his youth while singing the same hymn. (A peer)

"For my soul delighteth in the song of the heart; yea, the song of the righteous is a prayer unto me, and it shall be answered with a blessing upon their heads." (D&C 25:12)

The First Presidency has said:

"Inspirational music is an essential part of our church meetings. The hymns invite the Spirit of the Lord, create a feeling of reverence, unify us as members, and provide a way for us to offer praises to the Lord.

"Some of the greatest sermons are preached by the singing of hymns. Hymns move us to repentance and good works, build testimony and faith, comfort the weary, console the mourning, and inspire us to endure to the end" (*Hymns*, 1985, p. ix).

"The singing of hymns is one of the best ways to put ourselves in tune with the Spirit of the Lord. I wonder if we are making enough use of this heaven-sent resource in our meetings, in our classes, and in our homes." (Dallin H. Oaks, GC, Oct 1994)

# 8. Served God with Fastings

As I was wrapping up my senior year at BYU in marketing, we felt a need to focus on the job market. My wife and I discussed our future desires and narrowed our job search down to three companies within six southwestern states. I was always interested in and also graduated in marketing and business.

We researched the three companies and laid out information on each with some pros and cons noted on the papers. We studied it out in our minds and then sought heavenly guidance. We decided to fast and pray for help in deciding which of these businesses to aggressively seek employment with.

Our apartment had a cherry tree on the property. We opted to end our fast with a fresh, homemade cherry pie a'lamode. As we were up in the large tree picking cherries, our phone rang. I hurried down from the tree to answer it.

My cousin, whom I was working for part-time as a sales representative, surprised me with: "We would like to hire you as our National Sales & Marketing Manager. We want your help taking our company national. You are our top salesman and we need you here right away!"

This was music to my ears and the Spirit ran through my entire body, from the top of my head to the bottom of my feet, resonating throughout my soul. I knew this was the answer to our fasting and prayers. Even though this was not one of our three choices, or one of the six states we hoped to live in, this offer was what the Lord knew was optimal for us at that point in time.

My wife Tamara also had a spiritual confirmation that God had answered her fasting and prayers in a specific way, also with the same solution neither of us had even anticipated. So we would end up moving farther north than we had planned to a job that did not exist a month ago. The Lord always knows what's best for us, if we will but listen. (Journal 7/11/1982)

> Behold, I say unto you they are made known unto me by the Holy Spirit of God. Behold, I have fasted and prayed many days that I might know these things of myself. And now I do know of myself that they are true; for the Lord God hath made them manifest unto me by his Holy Spirit; and this is the spirit of revelation which is in me. (Alma 5:46)

---

*I have always been impressed with King Darius in regard to Daniel and the lions' den. The Kingdom of King Darius was large, boasting 120 princes and three presidents, Daniel being promoted to the number one position of the three. All these other leaders conspired against Daniel. They sat a trap for Daniel and it worked. The King was forced to feed Daniel to the hungry lions.*

"Then the king went to his palace, and passed the night fasting: neither were instruments of musick before him: and his sleep went from him." (Daniel 6:18)

*The great lesson I find in this king's fast is that he fasted from more than food; he also fasted from worldly pleasures. The king's fasting should be an example/lesson for all of us.*

---

When I was on my mission, there was an incredible zone leader who stood out from all the other elders. I felt the Spirit like a pillar around me every time he stood up to speak. I found out later that he felt the same way about me. We had a spiritual attraction to each other and to me that was much more powerful than anything physical. After our missions we started dating. However, I was at BYU and he was at the U, so it was difficult to get together as often as we wanted.

We felt so highly about each other that we began to talk about marriage before we really knew each other that well. I even met his parents after only a couple of dates. I don't remember him truly proposing, but when we were practically engaged, we decided to fast for the Lord's approval. There wasn't anything I wanted more than to be married in the temple to a worthy man, so this was the most important fast of my life.

We spent the day together to fast, pray, and enjoy each other's company. The trouble was I kept forgetting that I was fasting. Then when I remembered that I was fasting, I forgot what I was supposed to pray about. I kept trying to get back on track because I wanted a YES answer. Then I'd forget again. It was the most obvious stupor of thought I'd ever had. I knew the answer was NO, and since I was so sure, I thought he'd be sure as well, but he was a little upset about my answer.

I had a difficult time breaking up with him because I loved having a boyfriend even though I knew in my heart that he wasn't the one. The Lord knew that this wonderful man wasn't for me. Four months after we broke up, he married someone else. It worked out for the best. (A relative)

A young girl in our ward had serious medical problems. She was born with a genetic defect in her pancreas. Following fasting, prayers, and many temple, doctor, and hospital visits, an experimental surgery was decided on. Our ward opted to hold a ward fast, which ended up being a super spiritual experience for many individuals and the ward as a whole. Her surgery was successful. She grew up to be a beautiful young woman and was able to serve a mission.

The first time I fasted for more than a day was when our young son broke his leg and was in traction for eighteen days. I decided to fast to get answers from the Lord. This was a very intense time for us. I felt guilty because I was sledding with him and the neighbor when the accident happened.

It was difficult to get someone to find someone to tend our one-year-old baby. I fasted for a couple of days.

The next day a minister I did not know walked in and offered to pray with me. He prayed for me to relax, be at peace, and wait for God.

In my mind I was screaming, "No, this is not what I want to hear!" After calming down I realized this was just what I needed to hear. I cut a yellow legal pad into pieces, wrote scriptures about healing on them, and placed them all around our son's hospital bed. His room was at the end of the hall with a view from an open door. Everyone came to see the cute little boy in traction at the end of the hall.

One afternoon this woman came to visit me and said she was in for gallbladder surgery and was very nervous. She saw our son's bed late at night and went in to look. She saw the scriptures around the bed and said that they blessed her and help to calm her down. You never know who you are going to effect. (A relative)

"And the peace of God, which passeth all understanding, shall keep your heart and minds through Christ Jesus." (Philip. 4:7)

Our teenage nephew was burned from a grease spill on his legs. The doctors told him he would need skin grafts to repair the severe damage to his skin. Our large family all held a family fast for this young man and for his doctors. The week after the fast, the burned boy went to the specialists to be informed on how they would take skin from one part of his body and graft that removed skin to his legs.

When the doctor and specialist examined his burned legs to know where best to work next, "We are amazed!" The burn specialist commented, "Your legs have miraculously healed and there is no need for any skin grafts."

This was an awesome testimony of fasting and prayer for our family! (Friends)

Grant was only six weeks old when his father ... was called to preside over the Southern Far East Mission. When Grant was three years old (1958) ... his neck became stiff, and there was pain in his chest. Soon he could not walk on his legs. ... Missionaries fasted and prayed, but still his condition grew worse.

Grant's father gave him a special blessing before taking him to the hospital. After tests, the illness was diagnosed as paralytic polio. The doctors said Grant would soon need an iron lung to help him breathe. Polio is not common among the Chinese ...

By the end of the week in the hospital, Grant was completely paralyzed. Only his eyes moved, and the little body that had seemed healthy just a week before was quickly wasting away.

Two men came to the hospital that morning. They represented the Chinese Saints who had held a special fast and a prayer meeting the day before. Both men had been members of the Church less than a year and neither held the priesthood, but they wanted to help. ... Grant's mom felt the faith of these humble Chinese men as they knelt beside Grant's bed and prayed that this little boy's health might be restored.

As they rose to their feet and left the room, Grant's mother followed them down the hall. She thanked them and then went to the refrigerator where special food for Grant was stored. Just as she opened the door, a familiar voice called from down the hall and she turned around quickly to see Grant coming toward her.

"Look Mommy," he exclaimed with a happy smile, "I can walk!"

The doctors were amazed, but when the polio symptoms did not return, they let Grant go home. ... He doesn't remember his illness in China. His strong legs that helped him make the football team and wrestle for his high school don't remember them either! (*Friend*, Sept 1973)

---

This is the first time I remember participating in a Stake fast. The farmers and ranchers had been severely suffering from a drought. Many throughout the valley pleaded with the Lord through faith, fasting and prayers.

After the fast it started raining almost daily! One day we received over 1" in rain, more than ten times the normal rainfall. Everything started growing up nicely. Many testimonies were strengthened; numerous prayers of deep gratitude were offered. (Journal 5/7/1989)

---

During my mission, my family was trying to sell their home. They were not having much success. Although we weren't required to pay tithing on our mission, we were counseled to pay fast offerings. I hadn't done so and felt a strong prompting to pay fast offerings when I was praying for my family's house to sell.

It was stake conference that weekend and I had my fast offering. The brother I needed to give it to was all the way on the other side of the stake center; I had a feeling to get it to him right away and that I would be blessed. I hurried over and found him and gave him my fast offering.

Sometime later I received a letter from home and found out that our home sold the same weekend I finally paid my fast offering. It was kind of an awesome blessing, because the simple promptings blessed my family. (A relative)

---

I was in the process of going through a divorce and was very sad, worried, discouraged, and didn't know how I was going to make it after the divorce. I needed to find a smaller house to live in, but because I had recently quit my job to start my own business, I could not yet qualify for a home loan. The thought of having to move myself and my teenage kids into a small apartment made me sad. I had no idea what I was going to do.

So, as always, I prayed, fasted, and prayed some more. Not many days had passed when I received a call from my mom.

"This is your fairy godmother."

"Oh, I love fairy godmothers!"

Mom said that she decided to sell her rental property that she had taken off the market because it wouldn't sell. Once that sold, she planned to buy a home in our school district and then rent it out to my family at a "livable rate." Then my children wouldn't have to change schools and I could make ends meet. Once my business was successful, I would have the option to buy the home. I still didn't know what we would do in the meantime.

I continued to pray. My sister and I worked for about a week getting the property ready to sell, and then came the miracle ... they put it on the market Friday afternoon, and by Saturday morning it had sold! We were all shocked and delighted; it was a definite answer to prayers and fasting, and my kids and I now live in that beautiful, little home that is absolutely perfect for us. (A peer)

My first professional job was stressful but rewarding. When I'd been there almost six years, I had the impression to begin putting away large amounts of money into savings. I did not know why, but I did it and found that it was easy since my monthly expenses were low. After I had saved quite a bit of money, my job became more stressful. I felt that my boss had put me in a double bind; he'd shoot me if I did a certain task, but he'd shoot me if I didn't do the task. As I appealed to my boss on multiple occasions, he seemed to ignore my cause, and finally, at my wit's end, I quit and stomped out.

Now I knew why I had saved all that money; I would have to live off my savings until I found another job. I thought it would be a cinch, but it wasn't. I looked every day, but after several months, I still had no job and my money was running low. In desperation, I asked my family to fast for me. We chose a Sunday for a family fast, and that very week I got the interview that landed me a new job at a local college. It was an incredible pay cut, but it was a fun, exciting little oasis for a couple of years. My co-workers all had master's degrees and they inspired me to go back to school. My master's degree then launched the career I've had for the past seventeen years.

Even though I was so blessed, it took me years to forgive my boss until I finally realized that perhaps he had a divine role in spring boarding me into a new and better career. Now when negative feelings crop up about my boss, I remember to bless him instead for the journey he ignited, allowing my family's fast to fan the flame."

It was all in the Lord's hands, every step of the way. He really is in the details of our lives." (A family member)

"The Lord is in the small details of our lives, and those incidents and opportunities are to prepare us to life our families and others and we build the kingdom of God on earth." (Donald A. Rasband, GC, Oct 2017)

————— •◆• —————

And Cornelius said, Four days ago I was fasting until this hour; and at the ninth hour I prayed in my house, and, behold, a man stood before me in bright clothing, And said, Cornelius, thy prayer is heard, and thine alms are had in remembrance in the sight of God. Send therefore to Joppa, and call hither Simon, whose surname is Peter; (Acts 10:30-31)

*When we add sincere prayers to our fastings, the results can be so much more powerful! I recall a teacher telling us that fasting without prayer is like taking a shower with your socks on. You are doing something good yet not gaining the full benefit of your actions.*

————— •◆• —————

One Sunday a friend gathered several of us together after church to suggest a *group fast*. Our ward consisted of a large group of young families who each had two or three beautiful babies and toddlers. There was only one couple our age that did not have any children; the purpose of our group fast would be to pray for the Lord to *open her womb*.

The organizer set a Sunday, other than Fast Sunday, to hold this special family fast for a baby for the barren one. We all desired that the childless couple could experience the blessings and joys we all shared with our respective families. Once all the fruitful couples were contacted, we looked forward to fasting with faith and praying together for a common cause.

A couple days before the group fast, the organizer frantically called everyone she had talked to, exclaiming, "The childless couple found out about our group fast and told me to stop the press and hold our horses!"

This sister also explained to the organizer, "We are intentionally not having children for ten years; that's our family plan. I'm not barren!"

The organizer dialed up everyone and said, "So cancel, cancel, cancel! There will be no special fast; I apologize for the misunderstanding."

Once again, emotions can come into play and be very confusing to us. Sometimes our emotions and spiritual feelings are so similar; we might not know which is which until we know the outcomes. When reasons are not evident, we may never know!

We should never assume things about a couple and/or their children. We should always ask or wait until they tell us something or ask for specific help. Always avoid the "Are you pregnant?" faux pas too.

> "We must ever be on guard against being deceived by our emotions." (Gerald N. Lund, New Era, July 2004)

*I have always been impressed with the people of Nineveh, after Jonah finally carried out his assignment.*

> ... Jonah ... cried ... Yet forty days, and Nineveh shall be overthrown. So the people of Nineveh believed God, and proclaimed a fast ... For word came from the king of Nineveh ... he caused it to be proclaimed and published through Nineveh ... Let neither man nor beast, herd nor flock, taste anything: let them not feed, nor drink water. (Jonah 3:4-7)

*The entire population of Nineveh, including all the animals, fasted. From the least to the greatest, the residents prayed and repented. Because they turned from their sins, their city was preserved and not destroyed.*

There were three different situations in our family that weren't being resolved to anyone's satisfaction: A sister looking for employment for months, a brother-in-law with marriage issues, and an uncle going through some serious surgery.

Our extended family chose to have a large group fast for all three of our loved ones. There were four generations involved in our family fasting and prayers. With the love of an eternal family we all prayed often and then fasted for the blessings of heaven to be showered down upon these three family members.

185

There is a united power that can be felt when holding group fasts. I would describe this as a *synergistic spirit*!

Following the family fast, all three of the family members who had been hampered by different challenges had those problems resolved. Our sister landed a good job, our brother-in-law's marriage healed, and our uncle's surgery's were successful.

These family predicaments were all resolved within the weeks following the fast, seemingly simultaneously! This was a strong testimony of the power of fasting and prayer for our entire family. What a wonderful blessing! (Journal 9/21/1997)

------------◆-------------

*The sons of Mosiah experienced many trials with subsequent success. What did they do to achieve their accomplishments?*

> "...they had given themselves to *much prayer, and fasting*; therefore they had the spirit of prophecy, and the spirit of revelation, and when they taught, they taught with the power of God." (Alma 17:3)

------------◆-------------

A father in our ward was bearing his testimony about their fasting and prayers for a new job. They had been out of work for six months; their money and food storage had run out. Their kitchen cupboards were bare. He was very emotional in describing the large box of food that appeared on their porch one evening. "What was amazing was that everything our children had been asking for was in that box!" he exclaimed. After enjoying some good food once again, a job offer also came. He had been employed for six months and was now reporting their experiences over the past year.

The spirit really ran through my body during his testimony. A year prior to that, my wife suggested we put together a large box of food for this very family who had been unemployed.

She said, "We use to do this more often. And think how thankful we were when the Simpsons brought us a large box of food when you lost your job." At the grocery store as I attempted to put things in the cart, my wife said, "No, not this" and would place the item back on the shelf.

"This is not what we usually buy for people in need."

"Just push the cart dear."

She was an inspired woman on a mission. The Spirit led my good wife to the specific specialty foods and items those children had been longing for—as I pushed the cartful. (Journal 10/12/2008, 10/19/2009)

> "If ye know his things, happy are ye if ye do them." (John 13:17)

# 9. Because of the Prayers of the Faithful

*This is Jesus' promise to all mankind:*

"And I say unto you, Ask, and it shall be given you; seek, and ye shall find, knock and it shall be opened unto you." (Luke 11:9)

"For he that diligently seeketh shall find; and the mysteries of God shall be unfolded unto them, by the power of the Holy Ghost, as well in these times as in times of old as in times to come ..." (1 Ne. 10:19)

*Why should we all be praying?*

"Yea, cry unto him for mercy; for he is mighty to save." (D&C 34:18)

*What should we be praying for?*

"Cry unto him when ye are in your fields ... over all your flocks ... over all your household ... against the power of your enemies ... against the devil ... over the crops ..." (D&C 34:20-24)

*When should we offer prayers?*

" ... when thou liest down at night lie down unto the Lord, that he may watch over you in your sleep; and when thou risest in the morning let they heart be full of thanks to God; ..." (Alma 37:37)

"That your incomings may be in the name of the Lord; that your outgoings may be in the name of the Lord; that all your salutations may be in the name of the Lord, with uplifted hands unto the Most High." (D&C 88:120)

"Pray always, that ye may not faint, until I come." (D&C 88:126)

But behold, I say unto you that ye must pray always, and not faint; that ye must not perform any thing unto the Lord save in the first place ye shall pray unto the Father in the name of Christ, that he will consecrate thy performance unto thee, that thy performance may be for the welfare of thy soul. (2 Ne. 32:9)

*How should we pray?*

And he said unto them, When ye pray, say, Our Father which art in heaven, Hallowed be thy name. Thy kingdom come. Thy will be done, as in heaven, so in earth. Give us day by day our daily bread. And forgive us our sins; for we also forgive every one that is indebted to us. And lead us not into temptation; but deliver us from evil. (Luke 11:2-4)

"But let him ask in faith, nothing wavering. For he that wavereth is like a wave of the sea driven with the wind and tossed." (James 1:6)

"But when ye pray, use not vain repetitions, as the heathen, for they think that they shall be heard for their much speaking." (3 Ne. 13:7)

*After we offer all those prayers, now what?*

"... when you do not cry unto the Lord; let your hearts be full, drawn out in prayer unto him continually ..." (D&C 34:27)

We both felt like my husband needed to go to school. I didn't want to go back to work. I wanted to be a stay-at-home mom and that's what I felt I should be doing. He agreed, but how we're we going to do that. How were we going to make ends meet? Maybe he could work part-time and go to school part-time? We had three small boys and I was pregnant with another boy.
We decided that we were going to have to move in with somebody and that thought is kind of nerve racking in itself. So we decided that we should pray about what we should do. So we prayed together and then we prayed individually. It was really interesting because I got done

praying before he did. I was just sitting there waiting and a voice said, **"You need to go talk to Marilyn Streeter."**

And I said, "No way! I hardly know her. I had only met her maybe 5 times in my life." She was my husband's relative through marriage. I was a little intimidated by her. I thought I'm not going to say anything about this unless my husband says the same thing. I'm not even going to mention it. I wouldn't have thought of her in a million years!

My husband finished his prayer and without saying anything else, he said, *"We need to go see Marilyn Streeter."*

I exclaimed, "Oh! Oh my gosh!" We had the same name come to us from our prayers. So I called her and said, "I don't know if you remember me but I'm married to your husband's niece's brother. We wondered if we could meet with you at Farr's Ice Cream in Ogden."

She said, "Of course I remember you. I came to your wedding." Then she agreed to meet with us at an agreed upon time.

So we met over ice cream and told her about our concerns and our interesting mutual answer to our prayers. We told her we had identical answers to our prayers and that we were suppose to talk specifically with her. And then explained, "We want to know why we're supposed to talk to you."

She told us that she had been praying for someone to come live with her. Her husband was on the road all week driving truck and was only home on the weekends. It was Saturday, so they both were there at the ice cream shop that day.

They didn't hesitant, saying, "Come on over and see the place."

We went to their home and they said, "This is where your boys can sleep and this is where the baby can sleep. You can sleep here. There's the kitchen and your own bathroom and everything you'll need!"

They wanted to help someone out while having company there for the wife. They wouldn't accept any money, so the rent is free.

Sister Streeter said, "You are an answer to my prayers!"

She was definitely an answer to our prayers also!

This woman has taught me a lot about service and charity and there's no limit to what she does. She enjoys buying our children birthday presents and Christmas gifts. This is just what we needed and where we were supposed to be. My husband was supposed to go to school and I was supposed to be home with my babies. (A family friend)

"I knew that it was the Spirit of the Lord and he spake unto me as a man speaketh with another." (1 Ne. 11:11)

———————◆•———————

Following our father's passing our mother decided to sell the family home we had known for forty-five years. Mom was 73 and had recently retired. Mom sent a brief e-mail to her seven children that read, "Everybody pray for a quick sell of the house. Love to all, Mom." She already had a home within another city where she resided. We all prayed for her.

Mother called me, the eldest child, to inform me that the home appraised for $25,000 more than we expected. She was also elated to report that a woman and her two children were praying to find a home in our hometown. They offered above the appraisal and it was only 24 hours since the ad went out! We removed the final things from the basement at 4:30 pm and the future owners were there at 5:30 to inspect it.

This lady said, "I feel like this home is an answer to our prayers!"

We all, likewise, felt like she was an answer to all of our combined prayers. Both sides' prayers were answered. I quickly sent a message to my six siblings and they responded: "Wow! That's amazing!" "Wow! I'm impressed!" "Wow! That was fast!"

My heart was grateful and I thought to myself, "The Lord really WOWED us all!" (Journal 9/22/2007)

"I learned that God worked miracles in the lives of others, and he could work wonders in mine too." (Bonnie D. Parkin, GC, April 1995)

———————◆•———————

A young man came to a turning point in his life. His friends were turning to alcohol and drugs and he wondered just what path he should take.

The Spirit said to him, **"Get away from them."** He agreed to avoid his best friends and their new lifestyle. Then he prayed to the Lord and pleaded that he would place someone in his life that would be a true friend and better him. He wanted someone specific to support and help him. A month later we met when I was 15 and he was 17.

It's amazing that we met because he was in a different school and city. My dad had a friend through his hobby and one time this man's son came with him. That young man said to me, "Hey, you should meet my friend." He literally picked me up and put me in his car and drove over to his friend's house. We became very good friends and married 5 years later, after his mission. (A friend)

*This is another great example of the Light of Christ and the Holy Ghost working together. First ... one's conscious is pricked which causes him to question, wonder, and seek answers. Secondly ... a prayer in one's heart, your mind, or verbally can be answered through personal revelation to the individual/s.*

*When Alma the Younger and the sons of Mosiah were going about destroying the church they were going directly against their king, leaders, and parents. What Alma had built up through blood, sweat, and tears; his son, Alma, was strongly striving to tear asunder, on a daily basis.*

*During these rebellious rants a powerful angel appears to them and explains why he came:*

The angel said: **Behold, the Lord hath heard the prayers of his people, and also the prayers of his servant, Alma, who is thy father; for he hath prayed with much faith concerning thee that thou mightest be brought to the knowledge of the truth; therefore, for this purpose have I come ... that the prayers of his servants might be answered according to their faith**. (Mosiah 27:14)

*May we all continue to pray with similar faith for our loved ones and friends who also need to "be brought to the knowledge of the truth?" We necessarily need to understand that the Lord will answer our prayers on His timeline. Be patient if possible.*

"But we must remember when all is done, it is still up to the Lord to determine when the revelation comes, how it is given, what is revealed, and to whom." (Gerald N. Lund, *New Era*, July 2004)

Following the birth of my fifth child, the doctors were quite concerned. The doctors told me that I should not have any more children. They said my heart couldn't stand it. My heart pounded pretty hard and fast. Sometimes it would race. Often, I had to sit down awhile to quiet my heart or I was afraid I would fall down.

When I got home from the hospital, I closed my bedroom door and knelt down to pray. I said, "God, if I am expected to have more children, take care of my heart. Make my body strong that I may do my duty here on the earth." I had great faith in God and knew He could do all things. (Alta Law Clyde, "Grandma", Life History)

*Our grandmother and her heart were surely blessed by the Lord. She bore nine more children after the doctor's told her she couldn't bear another. Her prayer and faith, along with the subsequent blessing, strengthened her heart and made much more possible. After raising her thirteen living children, she took care of couples in their homes for many years; often her employers were younger then grandma was. She had amazing stamina!*

I was hospitalized for a week and a half while suffering my first major Multiple Sclerosis attack. My wife and I had been married only two years and we were scared! Would I ever be able to return to work? How would we pay for the new home we had recently moved into? Would we ever be able to have children? While in the hospital my eyes weren't tracking so I couldn't read or watch television. I spent a lot of time praying.

I imagine it is human nature, whenever we are struck with an undesirable situation, to pray for it all to go away. I spent hours and days praying. I had complete faith that God would fully heal me. But each time I prayed for this type of healing; it was if the connection with the Holy Spirit was shut off. Every time I intently broached the subject with God, I felt a void. The whisperings of the Spirit were simply absent when I explored that direction.

After several days of this, I came to understand that this was the Lord's way of telling me "No". As I opened myself up to this possibility, I could once again catch the thread of the Spirit's promptings, saying, "**No, you won't be healed.**

**Your MS will not miraculously go away. I have a different plan for you."**

That was one hard pill to swallow. But I knew I had to trust in the Lord. The path forward wasn't clear. My wife and I had to stumble along over the next few years as we worked our way through my health condition. The Lord always offered guidance at critical points. But he allowed us to grow through a lot of trial and error. Sometimes "NO" is the best answer." (A relative)

*This previous story sounds similar to an Apostle's experience, Paul tells us:*

And lest I should be exalted above measure through the abundance of revelations, there was given to me a thorn in the flesh, the messenger of Satan to buffet me, lest I should be exalted above measure. (2 Cor. 12:17) *And the Lord counsels Paul, saying,* **My grace is sufficient for thee: for my strength is made perfect in weaknesses.** (2 Cor. 12:9)

———————

We had a new radiator installed in one of our vehicles that didn't last very long at all. The radiator began irreparably leaking at eleven-and-a-half months on a one-year warranty. We couldn't find the warranty after looking in many places. This was a time-sensitive search.

I recalled that previous searches were much more efficient when not relying on the arm of flesh. Instead of searching our home I began searching heaven for an answer through prayer. Almost immediately a thought came into my mind as to where the misplaced warranty was. I wouldn't have considered that spot.

The sought after paper was easily found once the Spirit showed me where to look. We were able to qualify for a free replacement radiator just in the nick of time; once again, I was very grateful for the power of personal prayers. (Journal 10/16/2006)

"Trust in him at all times; ye people, pour out your heart to him: God is a refuge for us." (Psalms 62:8)

———————

... I began a project to better understand the Bible. I decided to study the teachings of a few religious groups I had heard were not Christian and then compare them with to the teachings of the Bible.

As the next semester began, I started studying the Church of Jesus Christ of Latter-day Saints ... *I prayed for someone with whom I could learn what I needed to learn.*

... Soon a student approached me and asked if I had a partner ... During the next three months I asked questions about the Book of Mormon, temples ... prophets ... I still thought that Mormons weren't Christians.

One weekend our school lost a big game. Some of the teacher's in the lab ... repeatedly used the Lord's name in vain. Lincoln (his lab partner) approached the teachers and asked them if they would please stop speaking about Jesus Christ that way ...

At that moment, my investigation of the Church changed from an intellectual exercise to a question of faith. If this religion produced men like this, it was Christian in every way that mattered ... I investigated the Church for two years. I was baptized and have now enjoyed more than a dozen years of blessings from the restored gospel and its teachings. (Michael Hendricks, Latter-day Saint Voices, *Ensign*, Sep 2015)

---

While working in Hawaii over the summer, following high school graduation, I made some new friends. We would all fly back to Salt Lake City after three months of labor in the pineapple fields. Most of their families lived in northern Utah. My family couldn't pick me up for about a week, so I stayed with an aunt and then with a couple of my new friends.

I was excited to visit one of my new friends, because he had invited me to a young adult activity that involved co-ed volleyball and a BBQ. These were three of my life's loves: Young women, volleyball, and food.

My friend called from downstairs to tell me he was ready to go as I was finishing up in their guest bathroom. All of a sudden my second contact dropped into a tall, thick, multi-green colored shag rug. My contacts were tinted green. I took one look at that green carpet jungle, backed up carefully, thinking: "I don't have time for this!"

So I went down gently on one knee and said a simple prayer, "Dear Heavenly Father, please help me find my contact lens." As I finished my prayer and opened my eyes I saw a little light reflecting within the rug. Light from a small bathroom window made a small contact glisten, which I'm sure, could have only been observed from a kneeling position. I verbally said "Thank You", then carefully cleaned and placed that contact. The youth activity was as entertaining and enjoyable, as anticipated!

Our son was finishing his mission in South Africa and we felt that I should fly over and travel back with him. I went to check my passport, which I mostly ignored. I did make sure that my passport hadn't expired, which it hadn't. My wife dropped me off at the airport and we said our goodbyes.

At the international check-in my passport would not work on any of their machines. We tried different people and different processes and nothing would work. They tried everything time after time and again and again to no avail.

Finally I was distraught, gave up and called my wife to come pick me up. She stopped and said a prayer and I said a prayer wondering why this was happening when I knew I was supposed to go.

Then a supervisor came down from an office and said, "Let me see you problematic passport. I have a son that didn't go on a mission. I am going to find a way to make this work for you." She went back to her office for some time and then came back with the good news that she had found a way to clear my passport through to South Africa (Our peers)

For several months in early 2018 I have added in my prayers: "Please bless the missionaries throughout the world and please bless the missionaries serving within the spirit prison." (For the previous decades I/we always prayed for the missionary elders, sisters, and older missionaries serving throughout the world.)

I have been receiving strange looks and sayings such as: "That was different; I never thought of that; How interesting."

My thoughts were revolving around my patriarchal blessing where it states that I will be serving another mission in spirit prison when I spiritually enter paradise.

I really enjoyed our new prophet's comments in General Conference:

> "Our message to the world is simple and sincere: we invite all of God's children on both sides of the veil to come unto their Savior, receive the blessings of the holy temple, have enduring joy, and qualify for eternal life." (President Russell M. Nelson, GC, April 2018)

Our parents lived in Ashland, Oregon. A sister and I had decided to visit together with our children. While there we decided that we would go up into the mountains to pick elderberries about twenty-five miles from our parent's home. We all piled into the cars and headed for the mountains.

The road we were on had been cut through a series of small hills. Some of the cuts were forty feet or more in height. We picked many buckets of elderberries. To get to them however, you had to climb up steep slopes covered with loose rock. After picking plenty for the day we headed back for the cars.

My brother-in-law was coming down the side of one of these embankments and his wedding ring fell off into the small rockslide we were all creating as we worked our way down. Once at the bottom, we turned around and looked for his ring for thirty minutes. We finally gave up and went home to make jelly.

As we were discussing the events of the day, my brother-in-law said, "I'm going back out to look for my ring!"

I told him I would come and help and my dad said the same. The three of us set off to find the ring. When we arrived back on the mountain we weren't really sure which "cut" we had been climbing last. We picked the most likely one and started there.

I stopped and thought, "I know that Heavenly Father knows where the ring is and I know it is important to Grant." I just asked Him to help us as I prayed. I opened my eyes and flipped over a rock about four inches in diameter and there was his wedding ring! Then I said something to Grant, like, "We sure wasted a lot of time looking around everywhere when we could have just prayed earlier." (A peer)

———◆———

My husband was told he needed to find a new job. We now had six children and just found out *number seven* was on its way. We prayed continually for several weeks and then both felt we needed to go south to Utah and look for work. We left the older five children with my mother in southern Idaho and went on to Salt Lake City, UT.

We thought to check with the Church for a janitorial position which is what my husband had been doing since an industrial accident 13 years prior. The Church told us there were no openings. Then we decided to head down to Saint George, UT, because we also had some family down there.

As we started out of Salt Lake, our car started acting funny. We felt impressed to head back up to Idaho and get the car back in proper working order. As we traveled back north, continuing education came into our minds. We felt my husband should finish school. I had a teaching degree and I could teach while he finished schooling.

We went to the university to see what it would take to finish; we found it would be only two years. We next went to the financial aid office. When everything was said and done, we had enough money for school, rent, and food. We found a home not far from the college and everything fell into place.

We knew this was what we were supposed to do. Then, when our son was born shortly after we moved there, we knew another reason everything worked as it did. He was born with Down syndrome and had an AV canal problem. Where was one of the best hospitals for children with some of the best heart surgeons?—only 80 miles south of our home. Our son received medical help and I received training to help him grow and develop as best he could. We had received answers to prayers in more ways than we ever knew we needed. (Our friends)

In the end you must do in your area what disciples of Christ have done in every dispensation: counsel together, use all resources available, seek the inspiration of the Holy Ghost, ask the Lord for His confirmation, and then roll up your sleeves and go to work. (Dieter F. Uchtdorf, GC, Oct 2011)

We had an elderly friend in Lovina Robson. One Christmas we had a church program with real hay bales, paper animals, and a special light shining on the baby Jesus. Lovina said it was the best Christmas program she had ever seen. She died just three days shy of her 96th birthday.

I was asked to play the organ for the funeral. I only played once-a-month and was still learning, always making mistakes. I prayed to the Lord to help me play well for the funeral. The place was packed!

I sat at the organ praying silently. When I started playing I felt a jolt of power rush through both of my arms. The people sang the first song. Then I was to play a quiet solo, "In the Garden" while everyone contemplated. I didn't make one mistake and I really thanked the Lord for helping me that day. (A relative)

"... he that asketh in Spirit shall receive in Spirit;" (D&C 46:28)

---

The families close by wanted to start a Sunday school and asked us all to meet for the organization. When it came time for the meeting, my husband was very drunk, so I did not want him to attend.

He said, "I want to be there to help organize that Sunday school!"

I tried to get him to stay home, but he wouldn't. I went in the bedroom and knelt down to pray. I asked the Lord to do something to keep him from going to the meeting in that condition. I then said, "Lord, I don't know what? But please do something!"

Just as I came out of the bedroom, our sons came running to the house and said, "We have a flat tire!"

My husband responded, "Oh, we'll fix that in a hurry. You boys take the tire off and get everything ready."

I went back to my bedroom and prayed again, "I know you can keep him home," I prayed humbly and earnestly.

After that prayer, the boys came back into the house, "We cannot pry that tire off the rim!"

My husband went out and pried and cussed and it wouldn't come off. They took turns working on it until they were too tired then they would relieve each other. Nothing worked. The tire would not come loose.

About the time the Sunday school meeting would be over with, the tire came off easily. They were all amazed.

My husband remarked, "Now what do you think was holding it?"

I knew it was the power of the Lord that held it tight. My prayers had been answered. I never did tell him what held that tire; it was secret and sacred to me. (A relative)

"Brothers and sisters, we are at our greatest, not only in the sight of God, but also in our own sight when we are upon our knees." (Matthew Cowley, GC, Oct 1953)

One Sunday after coming home from church I knelt down and prayed sincerely and faithfully for help to quit coffee. We had a lesson on the word of wisdom. I knew the Lord could help me.

The next morning for breakfast, the coffeepot went on the stove along with the hot cereal. After the children were sent off to school I sat down to breakfast and a cup of coffee. When I tasted it there was something wrong. It tasted like musty hay! I tasted the cream and it was okay.

So I dumped the pot, washed and scoured it and made a brand new pot of coffee. It tasted the same; very bad. Then I was reminded of my prayer. I had forgotten, but God hadn't. I quit coffee right then. (A relative)

Prayer in our home was not just words. Daddy talked with the Lord as one speaks to a friend. Both Mom and Dad, separately and together, sought and found direction and guidance and then acted on the answers that came—even when doing so meant making major course corrections in their lives as they endeavored to bring them into closer harmony with their priorities of family and education. (A relative)

"Spirituality comes with prayer. Prayer is the passport to spiritual power." (Spencer W. Kimball, *Ensign*, July 1973, 15)

I was having a hard time and was very down and discouraged. I had been praying just to know that God was aware of my struggles, and I needed some tender mercies.

My brother called later that day and said, "I don't know why, but I feel like I need to tell you that Heavenly Father loves you."

I started crying and told him that the simple sentence he just uttered was an answer to my prayers. Not only was it a testimony builder that Heavenly Father does hear and answer prayers, but that often it is though another person that he answers our prayers.

That is why it is essential that we listen to and follow through with promptings, no matter how simple they may seem, because it may be an answer to someone else's prayers. (A friend)

*I have observed exactly the same thing; prayers are often answered by "earthly angels": our family, peers and even total strangers. Having thought about this much, I believe the Lord often operates this way so that at least two people, or more, are simultaneously enriched through many revelatory experiences.*

———◆———

*I was touched by a young primary girl who said,* "I had this very special small box with some of my things in it and it was lost. I looked all over my bedroom and under my bed and I couldn't find it. I decided to say a prayer for help to find my box. After my prayer, my sister came into my room saying, 'Hey look, I found your box you've been looking for.' I'm glad that Heavenly Father uses people to answer our prayers." (Journal 9/24/2017)

President Monson voiced similar thoughts: "The prayers of people are almost always answered by the actions of others." (Be Thou an Example, *Ensign*, Nov 1996, 45)

———◆———

Several years ago, when my boys were four and eight years old, we went to a reservoir to swim with some cousins. I only wanted to get my feet wet so I went about knee-deep in the water. I wanted to splash water on my shoulders and bent over. This is probably when my prescription glasses fell out of my swimming suit into the water. When I discovered my glasses missing it put me in a panic.

I wouldn't be able to drive the children home without my glasses. We'd have to call someone to come pick us up. They were very expensive glasses and I didn't want to have to buy new ones. I gathered my boys and their cousins around and we decided to begin our search with a prayer. The children all disbursed and began searching in the water, which was difficult because the water was very murky.

After I had basically given up hope, my older son dove into the water and came up with the glasses in his hand. It happened so quick that I accused him of having my glasses the entire time and just teasing me. He reassured me that he found them under the water, even though he couldn't see them.

I immediately said a prayer of thanks to my Heavenly Father. I was humbled. In this experience I lacked faith and doubted. This was an amazing answer to a simple prayer and a very important faith building experience for me and my boys. (A relative)

I was so mad at my husband one day that I packed up some clothes, food, and the baby and drove off after he had gone to work! I said to myself, "I'm through!" When I arrived at the "T" in the road at the highway I pulled over to calm down and decided to say a prayer for direction.

I thought to myself, "If I go left we'll have to find some cheap motel. If I go right I could stay at Dad's, but he'd drive me crazy. Or I could stay at my father-in-laws, but he'd send me right back." (Each of the three choices was at least a two hour drive.)

I was torn between my choices and chose to ask God which direction to go. My prayer was basically, "Lord, which way shall I turn?"

I received an immediate answer, "**Turn around**." I knew the Lord had answered my prayer so I turned around, drove the five miles home, and everything has been peachy for the next thirty-five years! (A relative)

And when Sarai dealt hardly with her (Hagar), she fled from her face. And the angel of the Lord found her by a fountain of water in the wilderness ... and he said ... whither will thou go? And she said, I flee from the face of my mistress Sarai. And the angel of the Lord said unto her, **Return to thy mistress, and submit thyself under her hands. ... I will multiply thy seed exceedingly** ... (Genesis 16:6-10)

Does God have a sense of humor? Many people think so. Our small town had a large, log building that has been used as a roller rink, dance hall, and museum, among other things. During its dancing days, local bands would play for our enjoyment. One weekend, I was leaving the dance hall and wishing I had a steady girlfriend. I wished for someone to hold hands with and talk to. As the dance ended, the crowd funneled through a wide, dark hallway, then out through the large, double doors.

As I was expressing my silent desires in my mind—a warm, soft hand latched onto mine, in the hallway, and gave my hand a friendly squeeze. I squeezed back and she reciprocated. I said in my mind, "That was quick! Thank you!"

As we walked to the front of the building into rather dim light, this girl I was holding hands with exclaimed, "You're not Mark!"

Longingly looking into her eyes I said, "Well?"

She was in no mood to switch boyfriends. So I sauntered home, lonely yet smiling broadly.

------◆------

I had always been taught to pray when I had concerns or needed answers that were beyond my ability to understand. We had three boys at the time and my husband was very happy with "My Three Sons". I had always had a thought and impressions that I would have three boys and a girl.

My husband was teaching at the time and I stayed home with the boys. Money was really tight and things were more expensive and another mouth to feed was not really a good idea at the time. I thought if it was suppose to be it would be. My husband wasn't excited about another child. So for an entire year I would pray daily or weekly that my husband's heart would be softened and he would be okay with another child. So for over a year now I was praying if this was the correct feeling I was having or if I was just hoping I could have a daughter.

My husband got called into the bishopric. I walked into church with our three boys. Before finding a seat and sitting down, a picture appeared in my mind with me holding a baby girl! The only think I could think of was "What is her name?"

A soft spoken answer came, **"Amelia".**

I shared this experience with my husband and he was all for having another child. Within the next year we had our dear daughter, "Amelia." (A relative)

"And the angel of the Lord said unto her, **Behold thou art with child, and shalt bear a son, and shalt call his name**

**Ishmael; because the Lord hath heard thy affliction."** (Genesis 16:11)

---◆---

*A friend of ours shared,*

Oh, I just wanted to share this experience we had skiing with your boy! We got into some deep powder and your son lost one of his skis. The terrain was steep and we figured it had traveled some distance under the powder. We searched all over a large area with no luck. I asked him what he thought we should do and he immediately dropped to his knees and asked the Lord for help.

No sooner had he finished praying than a ski patrol guy stopped by to see why we were all stopped. The ski patrol dude stuck his ski pole into the snow and clunk, it hit something solid. I was so impressed with your boy. He just went down on his knees so quick and we all think that is why we were able to find his lost ski.

*These are the types of stories parents love to hear! Once again, another prayer was answered by an earthly angel.*

---◆---

My wife is an author and has written two books so far. I created a family card game. When our customers, retail or consumers, don't have cash on hand we use a "Square" (small credit card reader) and a smart phone to take payments. I had misplaced the Square and looked all over for the small white thingy.

After useless searching I thought I better pray for additional help. Praying about my simple dilemma created a ready response. The Spirit whispered **"Check your pants pockets."** Thankful the search ended, I started checking my pants I was wearing and then all my pants hanging in the closet, to no avail. Next I checked my suit pants hiding under suit jackets—nothing. I still had not located the Square.

Now I was beginning to doubt the message. We did not find the Square that day. The following afternoon I was mowing the lawn and cleaning up brush in the orchard. Afterwards I brushed off my work jeans and took them directly to the laundry room. Having been taught decades ago to *"check your pockets"*, I did so before dropping the dirty Levis into a laundry basket. To my surprise, there was the Square in the *pants pocket* of my work jeans just like the Spirit said. If I had been obedient and checked ALL my pants pockets, I would have found the Square a day earlier. Once again I had to repent for being of little faith and doubting personal inspiration. (My journal 5/9/2013)

One company I represented held a major contest for all reps nationwide. The prize would be an all-expense paid trip for two to Norway for nine days. The company's goal was to increase sales for all fish oil products that our Norwegian supplier sourced for our company. The sales associate with the highest increase in sales would win; there would be only one prize/winner.

Having served a mission in Scandinavia, I had always desired to return. My plan was to set written goals for each account, on individual sheets in respective files, within my three-state area and then to follow-up with each store regularly. I also planned to physically visit each business, even the ones on the outskirts of the sales territory: Salmon, ID, Mesquite, NV, Moab, UT, Gillette, WY, and Ontario, OR.

Kneeling down in prayer, I laid my plan out before the Lord, along with my hopes and desires. I only asked for strength and support. Then I got up and went to work hard. Halfway through the contest I was informed that I had led all sales people from the start. At that point, I prayed again specifically for this contest, thanking Heavenly Father for his support. I prayed for continued energy and stamina; I got up and went back on the road even more committed.

Near the end of the three-month contest I was physically drained. I had all the accounts statistics on respective papers strewn across a large table. Goals were written on each sheet, along with comments and results. I was searching for other places to possible eke out any possible sales increases, while being too exhausted to go out on the road the final week. I decided to conserve my energy and follow up by phone. Before I finished my thoughts, a call came in to me.

A customer on the phone said, "Hey, I was just thinking, I would like to add all the flavors of your fish products in both the 8 oz and 16 oz sizes, six deep on each. And I'd like to feature them on my radio show!"

I was floored and gratefully replied, "Okay; I'll get that order coming for you. Thank you very, very much!"

While writing up that extremely large order (Accounts normally ordered 3-6 flavors, one or two deep.) my phone rang again. This customer actually scolded me for over ordering eighteen of one flavor of fish oil when they only wanted a dozen of that kind and then revealed, "But that's okay, we sold them all out, send me twenty-four more of that flavor." She reordered very deep on many other flavors of our fish oils too!

I felt like after all I could do, the Lord stepped in and placed little ideas and reminders inside my customer's minds. That last week I was not out selling, yet sent in the largest orders of the quarter! The company said I led the nation wire-to-wire and had won the contest. They gave us $10,000 cash, a $500 Norwegian sweater, and a very nice book!

At that point I prayed again with a heart full of gratitude and thanks. I thanked God for supporting my plan, all the road trips and goals. Sometimes prayers of gratitude are the most important prayers we can offer.

We added an additional week to the trip and were blessed to tour London, Sweden and Norway—a trip of a lifetime! We were also allowed to: Stay where we wanted, eat wherever, buy gifts, take whatever tours we desired and also take our trip anytime we wanted, within a year. Highlights of this, "bucket list"—blessing/trip, were: London temple, Stonehenge, Swedish Temple, and the Norwegian fjords. Norwegian chocolate was to die for too! (Journal 12/15/2013)

> "… Praise the Lord … with a prayer of praise and thanksgiving." (D&C 136:28)

We had been married for many years. We had a temple marriage and because of that I felt like I would never get divorced. My husband had become so verbally and emotionally abusive that I was very unhappy. I understood that this marriage covenant was between three people: myself, my husband, and Lord.

As I was going through my healing process for this and other issues, I took my biggest problem to the Lord. I use to walk on the hillsides and find a quiet place to commune with the Lord. I would pray for one to two hours. Heavenly Father told me to divorce my husband. I began arguing with the God, "Well, what if I try this; what if I do that? I think this marriage can be salvaged."

And the loudest the Spirit ever talked in my mind exclaimed, "**It will not work!**" It was so strong and I had never had the Lord talk to me that way.

I said, "Okay, okay; I get it. I will stop arguing." What was interesting is that I was now filled with joy and that was so amazing because I had been very depressed for so long. It was such a shock to me. I did not think I was supposed to feel happy. I just thought I was a depressed person and my husband added to that daily.

Another interesting thing that happened is that I was told by the Lord to not tell my husband for a month. My husband would do or say things during that month and the Spirit would gently say, "**See ... that is another reason why**." After a month of that I was told to tell him. The divorce process started and was finalized rather quickly.

Now that I was a single mom with five children, I never once looked back and questioned my decision. The Lord was so very, very strong and convincing by telling me "**It will not work!**" (Our friend)

"If they use the same program, but it will not work. The vitality of The Church of Jesus Christ of Latter-day Saints is not in the programs of the Church but in the doctrines of the Church." (Hartman Rector, Jr., GC, April 1975)

———•◆•———

Our washer stopped spinning so I dismantled the beast to find the culprit. The coupler and clutch were fine. With lots of advice from You Tube and a brother-in-law repairman we settled on a bad transmission. I replaced the transmission and was hoping all the pieces were put together right. As I went to reattach the replacement transmission there were no bolts in sight. I looked all over our crowded laundry room and could not find them. I retraced my steps to the bathroom, bedroom, and kitchen with no luck.

I knew I placed them in the room somewhere; I just couldn't remember where. I thought this is ridiculous; I'm going to have to pray for help. I knelt on the cement floor and offered a simple prayer. Still on my knees, I had a thought to move the heavy washing machine motor in front of me. As I tilted it, there were the three bolts I was searching for—obscured the entire time by the motor body.

Oftentimes our thoughts and vision become crystal clear from a kneeling position. (Journal 1/22/2016)

———•◆•———

Our daughter and her two boys were moving from one home to the other. The day she had to move, most of our family was unavailable to help. We had a moving van, trailer, and three vehicles full of belongings. As we helped her, we started tiring out, as grandparents can sometimes. There was no way our daughter, her young boys, or we could carry the heavy things downstairs. My wife and I both prayed for earthly angels.

Not long after that, her ex-husband showed up ready to help.

Then a young, muscle-built man came walking across the lawn demanding, "Where's the heavy stuff?"

That was sweet music to our ears. He could have passed for one of the three Nephites. (Ammon was a neighbor.) These two young men were the relief and help we needed. It was still a very long and exhausting night. We gave earnest prayers of thanksgiving for the heaven-sent help however. (Journal 8/7/2016)

> Nothing would seem more clear than the high premium the Savior put upon selfless service to others as an indispensible element of Christian conduct and of salvation. Helping, giving, sacrificing are, or should be, as natural as growing and breathing. (Marion D. Hanks, GC, April 1992)

---

> Someone close to me committed suicide recently and it has been so hard to understand. I was very upset and frustrated; after four days of turmoil I decided to turn to prayer. As I prayed, I had this wonderful feeling of peace come over me. My answer was calming and reassuring. I still had many questions and did not understand what had happened. Yet, I did have peace given to me over the situation. (Branch member)
>
> Two indicators that a feeling or prompting comes from God are that it produces peace in your heart and a quiet, warm feeling. As you follow the principles … you will be prepared to recognize revelation at critical times in your own life. (Richard G Scott, *GC*, April 2012)

---

Following retirement, I was called and set apart by another stake president to be in a branch presidency at a city care center. This is designated as an out-of-area calling. This necessitated being released from my two stake and two ward callings. Working with those in the sunset of their lives is a rewarding experience. The only drawback for me is that I was having serious withdrawals from holding and cherishing babies every Sunday and/or subbing in nursery.

So I actually earnestly prayed for opportunities, in addition to the hospital I volunteer at, to care for babies. That very evening, a sister in my wife's ward (my former ward) sent a Facebook message asking if I could tend her 5-month-old baby girl on Tuesdays. A little later another sister asked, on Facebook also, if I would watch their young twins and baby so they could attend the temple on Friday night. I felt that the Lord was merciful to my request and very quick to prompt some earthly angels to respond. I quickly affirmed both requests.

We have a different ward from six different stakes support the music, prayers, sacrament, talks, and special musical numbers each Sunday morning at the care center. That Sunday's ward provided a young chorister with a four-month-old baby girl. She sat down next to me in front of the congregation. The baby was smiling gleefully at me.

"What a beautiful, angelic baby girl you have."

"You may have to hold her while I conduct the music."

"I would love to!"

The young mother immediately proceeded to remove her baby girl from her infant car seat and handed her to me. I wasn't conducting, so that worked out superbly. The baby and I bonded quickly and she was so beautiful! I was able to cherish this beautiful angel the entire meeting. The mother thanked me and I likewise thanked her for *making my day.*

Members of her ward that were sitting on the front row came up to me afterwards and remarked:

"How nice for you that your granddaughter could be here with you today; what a coincidence."

"They are total strangers."

"But she was so happy and comfortable with you!"

"I have a sincere love and a gift of love for babies."

"You must!"

I am so grateful that simple prayers are answered. Those tiny things that are important to us become special to our Heavenly Father too. And none of them are coincidences. (Journal 1/25/2017)

> I love the children. They are very much the same the world over. Regardless of the color of their skin and of the circumstances in which they live, they carry with them a beauty that comes of innocence and of the fact that it was not long ago that they lived with their Father in Heaven. How lovely you are, wherever you are, you precious children. (President Gordon B. Hinckley, GC, April 1995)

---

> I was very upset and angered at a family member and thought I would have to end my relationship with them. I found that they had serious sins and kept them a secret and even attended the temple. I went home and knelt by my bed and prayed. I asked for forgiveness for this person and also forgiveness for myself.
>
> I knew my angry thoughts must be banished and that I should love and forgive this person as Christ would. I felt this overpowering love of the Savior, knowing how much he loved the sinner and me. I knew I had to treat others

with love and forgiveness or how could I expect to be treated that way.

The next time the two of us met, this relative didn't expect me to talk to them. They thought I would still be upset and mad at them. I was able to talk with them without any animosity. It was such an answer to prayer. It helped me heal. I am so thankful for the atonement. (A relative)

"I, the Lord, will forgive whom I will forgive, but of you it is required to forgive all men." (D&C 64:10)

————————◆◆————————

My grandmother was 90 years old and had had a stroke a couple of years prior. Since then my mom and her sister have traded days to take care of grandma in her home. Mom was feeling very overwhelmed one week; on her way to take another day serving her mother, she asked the Lord, "This is starting to take a toll on me. How much longer is this going to take?"

The Spirit said just four words: **"Until the lilacs bloom."**

Grandma had a row of lilac bushes in her backyard that she really loved. My mom noticed the lilacs were just starting to bud that day.

When she was caring for her mother, Grandma asked, "When is your dad going to come for me?"

Mom whispered in grandma's ear and softly said, *"When the lilacs bloom."*

The following Saturday, my mother noticed the lilac bushes in full bloom and her mother passed peacefully away the same day. Mom texted me a picture of grandma; a branch full of bloomed lilacs lain across her chest. (Stake member)

"Consider the lilies, how they grow: they toil not, they spin not; and yet I say unto you, that Solomon in all his glory was not arrayed like one of these." (Luke 12:27)

————————◆◆————————

A group of returned missionaries were working together as job foremen on the island of Maui, Hawaii, for the summer. We ran our respective crews during the pineapple field harvest. Four of us were planning to attend BYU that fall. We decided to be roommates and really looked forward to the experience. We had forged great friendships through our mutual toils during our summer labors in paradise.

On the first day of college, for the fall semester at BYU, we had a kneeling prayer together. A good friend of mine was the voice and I only remember one remarkable sentence from that prayer.

Near the end of the prayer he mentioned, "And may we all be blessed to find our eternal companions this semester at school."

After the prayer I quickly queried, "Where did that come from?!"

He replied, "I don't know! I did not intend to say that!"

We all headed off to our first class of the new semester with smiles on our faces. We lived on the corner of 9th North and 9th East in an old home that use to border the BYU campus. (Journal 9/2/1980)

Looking back in hindsight, the four of us all met our wives within the first two weeks of that semester. We were all married in various temples for time and all eternity, within a year's time; with even larger smiles on our faces! Those inspired words were literally fulfilled!

———————◆•————————

After working all summer in Hawaii, I had a few girlfriends to catch up with. We had corresponded through the summer and I had several dates lined up, including a Homecoming date. My favorite extracurricular activities at college were bowling, dancing, and dating. Along with my studies I found time for everything and got back into the swing of things quickly.

One young woman and I had become very good friends over the past several semesters and we dated frequently. She invited me to attend church with her and then over for a nice Sunday dinner at her apartment afterwards. It was a beautiful day. Church was nice, the meal was great; and then we took a stroll to a park with our scriptures. The company was very nice!

We discussed a lot of things and then, as we sat on a picnic bench, she seemed to be interviewing me. She opened her scriptures and was asking me questions about the Gospel and my testimony, etc.

After a couple of hours in the park, she obtained my full attention. "Guy, I think you are a very nice young man and I am attracted to you. You really love children. You have a strong testimony. I think you would make a great husband. I have decided to let you marry me!"

I guess I answered her questions satisfactorily! I said, "I wasn't really expecting that. Why don't we keep dating, go on our Homecoming date, and see how things take shape from there?"

She agreed. We parted with a warm hug and nice kiss. I had a lot on my mind.

That evening a young woman in our ward had invited me over for dinner. We had dated some, off and on. She had her own home, two college degrees, and was teaching school; yet she was only around 25. She was a great cook too. After dinner we sat on the couch and visited.

A little later she shocked me with: "Guy, I'm really attracted to you and you're such a nice guy. You have such a great love for children! I'm glad you finally kissed me. I'm tired of being alone. You'll make a great husband. I would like to marry you."

I was flabbergasted! To say the least! She had no idea what was running through my mind already!! Now my brain was buzzing!

I told her I was rather tired and would have to sleep on this. Now my mind was in a flurry. I rushed home to my roommates exclaiming, "You're never going to believe what happened today!" I explained the two meals with the long discussions afterwards and the two nearly identical proposals.

One roommate shouted, "That's great! You have a choice. Who gets to make a choice like that?"

Another roommate exclaimed, "You got proposed to by two different girls on the same day! That's unheard of! Well, which one is it going to be?" Of the two roommates that were home, one liked the first and the other favored the second young woman.

I told them firmly, "Eternal marriage is a matter of great importance and I have always felt that was more important than any job I will have in the future. I am going to pray about my conundrum and have a solemn talk with God to seek some serious inspiration. As you know the girls are alike in many ways and I need to know which one is best for me. I will let you know my decision in the morning."

> "Remember the counsel of Elder Bruce R. McConkie that 'the most important single thing that any Latter-day Saint ever does in this world is to marry the *right* person in the *right* place by the *right* authority' (*Choose an Eternal Companion,* Brigham Young University Speeches of the Year, Provo, 3 May 1966, p. 2)." (President Ezra Taft Benson, GC, April 1988)

The two similar proposals kept swimming around in my head, doing many laps. It was very uncommon for a girl to propose to a guy in the first place. I tossed around the pros and cons of each young woman. They both: were very nice, attractive, spiritual, and modest. This unprecedented weekend literally changed my whole life. What will the Lord say? He'll probably tell me which is best, but not explain why, was my guess.

Everyone else drifted off to sleep fairly quickly; there were four of us in a long, narrow bedroom. Sleep was hard to come by for me. I knelt in the darkness beside my bed and poured my confused heart out to my Heavenly Father. I explained how nice and similar the two young women were. I had studied them out in my mind and laid out what I felt the pros and cons were. The two young women were quite alike and I desired direction to know which would be the very best choice for me in an eternal companionship. Girl number one or girl number two?

I was summarily surprised and shocked with an immediate response stating, "**Find a third.**" That was totally unexpected!

My first response back was, "You've got to be kidding!" I thought of Joseph Smith's prayer and his unexpected answer.

Paraphrasing in my mind, I pictured Joseph Smith saying:

"Which church should I join myself with?"

"None of them", said God.

... It never had entered my heart that all were wrong ..."
(See *Joseph Smith—History* 1:18)

I was asking which girl to join with and was told neither of them. Then I started thinking about how hard it would be to start from scratch, all over again. I explained to God, "The entire *dating dilemma* is finding a girl that likes you as much as you like her. A girl really likes you and you have no interest. You are enamored with a pretty young thing and she's thinking 'Get lost!' Finding a good match is so difficult!"

Then I thought, "Oh yeah, you know about women, you know about relationships, you know the *dating dilemma*, you know everything." Then I repented for attempting to counsel my Father in Heaven.

"Seek not to counsel your God ..." (D&C 22:4)

Still on my knees I was sensing, as if it were, a gigantic metal door solidly closing shut. The silent impression I received was, *"You asked, you received your answer; deal with it."* I did knock and the door truly was opened, rather quickly at that!

Now another swimmer jumped into the pool. In lane #1 was the first proposal, in lane #2 was the second proposal and in lane #3 was the answer to my prayer. Back and forth they swam; seemingly tireless swimmers they were. "Wow! That's not at all what I expected for an answer! What am I going to do now? What am I going to tell these two girls?" I wondered about all this as I eventually drifted off to sleep late into the night. (Journal, 9/15/1980)

My roommates were anxious for the results the following morning.

"Well, which one is it, its girl number one, isn't it? I think she's the best for you!"

"No, you're wrong, its girl number two. She's the right one!"

I related my prayer to know which girl was the best for me to marry and the quick response to *"**find a third**"* young woman; neither of those two girls was right for me.

"You've got to be kidding!!"

"What are you going to do?"

"What are you going to tell your girlfriends?"

"I can't believe it!"

"I can't believe it either. I guess I'm just going to start all over again, as instructed."

The following day, the swimmers seemed to swim even swifter within my mind's pool. During every class my mind was boggled with those repetitive thoughts, class after class. I could not concentrate on any lecture, reading, or homework. During the last class, I was starting to get a headache due to the constant barrage of competitive thoughts for so many hours. Then a new thought came into my mind. I was subtly reminded of a little piece of paper in my wallet with a girl's name scribbled on it. (Journal 9/16/1980)

Prior to this semester, while working in Hawaii as a job foremen during the summer, the company required us to run crews of young men through pineapple fields at harvest time. Since I had been a successful pineapple planter my senior summer on the island of Lanai, Dole Pineapple gave me a special crew to run in prepared bare fields planting pineapple crowns. There were about 1,000 young men, primarily LDS, flown over from Salt Lake City, UT, to labor in the overly abundant pineapple harvests each summer. There simply was not enough of a local labor pool to handle the demand. They had laborers flown in from the Philippines and other islands too.

We each had a crew that we worked with and slept together in a large bunkhouse, with our respective boys. As foremen, we were additionally the: chauffer, lifeguard, softball coach, teacher, etc. Whatever the exercise, we were responsible to supervise that activity that our young men were involved in 24/7 and to keep them in-line and safe while having fun. On Sundays we would teach the various lessons.

As returned missionaries, three of us were given a special assignment to teach priesthood lessons to the truck drivers, young men that had to be eighteen years of age to qualify as drivers. Our Sunday lessons were to focus on mission preparation. We enjoyed our new assignment: bearing testimonies, sharing positive missionary experiences, and answering their questions.

One Sunday afternoon we were just relaxing after the lesson and shooting the breeze with these older, more mature young men.

One of the young men asked, "Since you guys have already been on missions, what are you looking for in a wife?"

One buddy said he wanted a girl with a wealthy daddy; one that could financially float his business ideas.

My other friend claimed he wanted a young lady with an hour-glass figure.

I said, "I want a: short, slender, green eyed, dark-haired girl with a nice smile, strong testimony, nice personality, and who loves children."

A truck driver from Arizona piped up, "That's a pretty long list; but I know a girl that fits your list perfectly! She's on the seminary council, her dad's the bishop, she's really cute, and she can even touch her nose with her tongue!"

I replied, "She sounds pretty nice."

He responded with, "She's very nice and very cute too. I'll tell her I'm sending a 'Guy' to see her at school." He wrote her name down on a small piece of paper and handed it to me.

I stuck the paper in my wallet and forgot about it ... until weeks later. (Journal 8/9/1980)

Five weeks later, reading this mystery name once again created a new mindset. I was finally able to think about someone else. The small paper had a certain allure to it. Back then, one could look up a peer in college and find their phone, address, home state, and class schedule! This girl's name was a little difficult to find because the first and last name were both misspelled on the paper. I found a similar name, which was from Arizona and seemed to jive with what the young man in Hawaii told me. I jotted down her address and phone number.

I cold called this young woman up early Monday evening and explained that a mutual friend in Arizona suggested we meet. She said that we could come over since her roommate was also home. I asked my roommate if he would mind visiting a new girl's apartment with me. He was game.

It wasn't too far of a drive; we met and hit it off rather well. Luckily, I found out later, her favorite missionary said he would send a guy to check on her and make sure she was still waiting for him. This new girl assumed I/Guy was that guy. The four of us ended up going back to our apartment.

I whipped up an apple-cherry pie and my new friend did the dishes. We all enjoyed a late night fruit pie a la Mode. The new girl and I agreed to go dancing together that Friday. My roommate and her roommate did not hit if off at all. (Journal 9/16/1980)

There was something different about this new girl I had met. I desired to see her every day! In the past, I looked forward to dating girls: once a week or two, every month, or once per quarter. I dated girls and would never see them again on that massive college campus.

Now, I was running into my new friend on a daily basis, unplanned. We would bump into each other in the library, at the campus cafeteria, or on a sidewalk somewhere between classes. It was as if we were being drawn to each other through a heavenly design.

After quite a few dates in a short time I felt like I was falling in love. I had never wanted to be in someone's company all the time before like this. I was praying to know if these feelings were what I thought they were and if she was the right young woman to take to the temple.

We rounded up six couples, 2 gallons of A&W root beer, popcorn, and bags of snacks. The Playhouse Theatre in Springville, UT, would play midnight Hitchcock movies on Saturday nights for $1 and close the snack bar. They allowed their teenage employees to go home so that they wouldn't have to work during the wee hours of the Sabbath.

The show was Hitchcock's *North by Northwest* starring Cary Grant. The twelve of us had a blast being together in the top of the balcony. My new girlfriend and I sat together, holding hands, enjoying the movie.

All of a sudden I felt this energetic wheel spinning in my torso. The wheel's speed would gradually increase. It wasn't painful, yet it was potently powerful. It seemed to be a spinning motion that was also working to draw me closer to my date, like a magnet. Not in any type of physical attraction, yet in a spiritual manner. It was if there was an excitement of our spirits attempting to communicate with each other. I don't know how else to describe it. The revolutions became very strong and felt so good that I leaned over to her and asked, "Do you feel that?!"

She quietly responded, "No."

Then the feeling became extremely stronger. This spiritual wheel spun at an even faster rate and also felt like it increased in volume of spiritual sensation. I have never had such a strong spiritual feeling last for so long, before or since. I sensed she was feeling something and that our inner souls were yearning for each other. I turned to her once again and exclaimed, "DON'T YOU FEEL THAT?!"

As it turns out, she had also been experiencing very similar strong feelings. She leaned out of her chair to give me a huge hug and said unabashedly, "I LOVE YOU!"

We both had such a mutually strong experience that we knew we were getting married, we just weren't engaged yet! We enjoyed many dates during the ensuing weeks and weekends. We would read scriptures together and write in our journals before separating for the evenings. I proposed to Tamara Baughman on September 30<sup>th</sup>, 1980 and she said, "YES!" (I didn't wait for her to propose to me!)

*My wife Tamara's version from her viewpoint:*

I went on several dates with Guy Laing while at BYU in the fall of 1980. He asked me out quite often. So often, in fact, that it was making me a little nervous. It felt like he was getting serious about our relationship rather quickly! I decided to pray about whether I should even keep going out with this returned missionary. I remember having a kneeling prayer about this before he came to my apartment to pick me up one evening. I had accepted to go on a group date with him and several other couples.

About a dozen of us were watching the Alfred Hitchcock movie, "North by Northwest" from the balcony of an older movie theater. We were sharing popcorn and frosted root beer. We were enjoying the movie and good, clean fun! The movie screen had my interest when all of a sudden; my date leaned over with a look of surprise on his face. In the dim light Guy questioned me with a whisper: "Do you feel that? *What is that?!*"

I shook my head and shrugged my shoulders. I had started to feel something, but it was unlike anything I had ever experienced before. I wasn't comfortable talking about whatever was going on that I did not understand *at all*. It was as if unseen swirling sensations—a real, but unseen power—was coursing through and out in front of my torso. Perhaps I wanted to ignore them, but the never-experienced-before feelings didn't go away! Something was going on, unseen. And then, in a flash, glowing bold gold letters were in the air out in front of me. I saw three words in gold, "I LOVE YOU," and instantly I knew they were true.

Guy leaned over again, asking if I was feeling something. Without hesitation, I threw my arms around him and said those words to him. I also confessed that I *had* felt the most unusual sensations. Something invisible was swirling around my torso too. I didn't know what it was, but I did know that I felt it.

Nearly two decades later I would marvel over scriptures verses in Alma chapter 32 speaking about "when you feel these swelling motions" and how they "enlarge [one's] soul" and "enlighten our understanding" *and are discernible.* By studying scriptures and prophet quotes, I began to understand more about the real, yet unseen "light" that was discernible which I experienced strongly that memorable day at the movie theater. I prayed to know whether I should continue to date that young man and I received an answer! We saw each other daily after that date and became engaged that semester.

"And they said one to another, Did not our heart burn within us ...?" (Luke 24:32)

*We have discussed how strongly our hearts burned within us many times since our theatre confirmations to our respective prayers. This was such a long and strong singular experience for both of us that grew into a complimentary dual experience and an eternal companionship.*

We had a houseful of our own children. One of our boys was growing so fast that none of his shoes fit anymore. We had no money, yet had paid our tithing. I went to my knees to pray to my Heavenly Father for inspiration on obtaining a needed new pair of shoes.
Later that morning, there was a knock at the door. A woman I had never seen before, nor since, stood there with a black garbage bag. She said, "I live up on the hill and have noticed you have a lot of children running around. I thought you could use these."
Inside the bag were 10 pairs of nearly new shoes and they were all the same size—the right size! I was only praying for one pair. I felt this was a tithing blessing. (Our friend)

*My all time-favorite story involving faithful prayer comes from a youthful non-member:*

While I was laboring under the extreme difficulties caused by the contests of these parties of religionists, I was one day reading the Epistle of James, first chapter and fifth verse, which reads: *"If any of you lack wisdom, let him ask of God, that giveth to all men liberally, and upbraideth not; and it shall be given him."*
Never did any passage of scripture come with more power to the heart of man than this did at this time to mine. ... I at length came to the

determination to 'ask of God.'.... I retired to the woods to make the attempt. It was on the morning of a beautiful clear day ... It was the first time in my life that I had made such an attempt, for amidst all my anxieties I had never as yet made the attempt to pray vocally.

... I saw a pillar of light exactly over my head, above the brightness of the sun, which descended gradually until it fell upon me.

... When the light rested upon me I saw two Personages, whose brightness and glory defy all description, standing above me in the air. One of them spake unto me, calling me by name and said, pointing to the other—**This is My Beloved Son. Hear Him!** (JSH 1:11-17)

> "But thou, when thou prayest, enter into thy closet, and when thou has shut thy door, pray to thy Father who is in secret; and thy Father, who seeth in secret, shall reward thee openly." (3 Ne. 13:6)

While attending a conference in the East the other day, I listened to the experience of an engineer who joined the Church some months ago. The missionaries had called at his home, and his wife had invited them in. She had eagerly responded to their message, while he felt himself being pulled in against his will. One evening she indicated that she wished to be baptized. He flew into a fit of anger. Didn't she know what this meant? This would mean time. This would mean the payment of tithing. This would mean giving up their friends. This would mean no more smoking. He threw on his coat, walked out into the night, slamming the door behind him. He walked the streets, swearing at his wife, swearing at the missionaries, swearing at himself for ever permitting them to teach them. As he grew tired, his anger cooled, and a spirit of prayer somehow came into his heart. He prayed as he walked. He pleaded with God for an answer to his questions. And then an impression, clear and unequivocal, came almost as if a voice had spoken with words that said, "It's true."

"It's true," he said to himself again and again. "It's true." A peace came into his heart. As he walked toward home, the restrictions, the demands, the requirements over which he had been so incensed began to appear as opportunities. When he opened the door, he found his wife had been on her knees. (Gordon B. Hinckley, GC, April 1948)

# 10. Slow to Hear Their Cry

### Why are my prayers not being answered?

*One might wonder if their prayers are getting through at all. Are my words just bouncing off the ceiling? Another wonders if God has time for her. Am I too sinful to talk to? Additionally he thinks he is unworthy? Why the spiritual silence? Does God really care about me? Why can't I get the answers I want and/or need?*

Have you ever knelt down alone and asked the Lord for something that is really important to you and then gotten up and found that your prayer wasn't answered as you had hoped? I have. Have you ever prayed and prayed for days and days for something special and then found that it didn't work out? I have. In times past, on more than a few occasions, I have gotten up off my knees and wondered in despair, What's the use—He isn't even listening, or Maybe I'm not worthy, or Maybe I just don't understand the signals. (H. Burke Peterson, *Prayer: Try Again*, BYU.SPEECHES.EDU)

*Most all prayers are answered; however, the answers come according to the Lord's timetable and through a variety of delivery systems, some much slower than others. Other prayers are extremely delayed due to God's will, God's plan for us, disobedience, serious sin, and iniquity. Some prayers are actually not answered. Often our own choices and lifestyles determine how our prayers are answered or sometimes not answered at all. Sometimes the best of people do not receive the righteous desires of their hearts; other time the reasons for a "no answer" or "delayed answer/s" are revealed and at other times we/they are left to wonder why.*

*We recently heard a man testify that he received an answer to a prayer he felt was very important. The answer to his prayer came to him 40 years later!*

During his lifetime, President Smith (Joseph F. Smith) lost his father, his mother, one brother, two sisters, two wives, and thirteen children. He was well acquainted with sorrow and losing loved ones.

When his son Albert Jesse died, Joseph F. wrote to his sister Martha Ann that he had pled with the Lord to save him and asked, "Why is it so? O. God why had it to be:"

Despite his prayers at that time, Joseph f. received no answer on this matter. He told Martha Ann that "the heavens [seemed like] brass over our heads" on the subject of death and the spirit world. Nevertheless, his faith in the Lord's eternal purposes were firm and steadfast.

In the Lord's due time, the additional answers, comfort, and understanding about the spirit world came to him through the marvelous vision he received in October 1918. (M. Russell Ballard, GC, Oct 2018) [See D&C 138]

*The prophet Samuel counseled the Israelites not to seek a king to rule over them. The Lord was displeased with the Israelites for **rejecting Him**. After all the miracles shown while saving the Israelites from the Egyptians, the Israelites were **still serving other gods**. The Israelites demanded an earthly king and Samuel prophesied all the hardships that would ensue and lastly, "And ye shall cry out in that day because of your king which ye shall have chosen you; and the LORD will not hear you in that day." (1 Sam. 8:18)*

*Limhi's people were defeated and subjugated by the Lamanites. As prophesied, these Nephites were driven like beasts with burdens lashed to their backs.*

And they did humble themselves even in the depths of humility; and they did cry mightily to God; yea, even all the day long did they cry unto their God that he would deliver them out of their afflictions.

And now **the Lord was slow to hear their cry because of their iniquities**; nevertheless the Lord did hear their cries and began to soften the hearts of the Lamanites that they began to ease their burdens; yet the Lord did not see fit to deliver them out of bondage. (Mosiah 21:14-15)

*Apparently Limhi's people needed more time to be truly humbled and sincerely repent. Their prayers were answered, just not to the degree they were hoping for.*

"But *if it be not right* you shall have no such feelings, but you shall have **a stupor of thought** that shall cause you to forget the thing which is wrong." (D&C 9:9)

*The stupor of thought/forgetfulness is an answer in actuality. Many people have experienced this situation. I have asked for the wrong thing on several occasions.*

---

We had purchased a new home a few years ago; with the addition of several more children, we were growing out of our home. Our contractor would build a new home, 90% by himself on our street. They were beautiful homes with lawns, fences, and garages.

Across the street from ours was the largest house on the street. The owners put up a "For Sale" sign and we quickly made an offer. They said they would have to get back with us.

As time went on, we completely forgot about the offer, and larger home, and that would fit our family and in a neighborhood we loved. We had a spacious new park that bordered our area. About two months later I ran into the seller on the sidewalk and asked, "Weren't you selling your home?"

"Well, we decided not to sell it."

"They're really nice homes aren't they? We sure love ours"

"They sure are; that's why we want to stay."

"Okay, have a nice day."

The thought and desire for purchasing the larger-sized home we needed for our family had turned into a complete stupor of thought.

Not long after that, my boss came into my office for a private conversation. He informed me that the company needed to borrow money after fourteen successful years. "In fact, I'm borrowing money from the bank to pay your salary."

"I had no idea business was that tight? What now?"

"It's fine with me if you search for another job on company time."

"Salary's are being cut 30-50% and I'm taking a very large cut myself.

We began a job search and ended up moving from our 3-bedroom home to a 6-bedroom home in another state that fit our expanding family well. We were so glad the Lord kept us from being saddled with a much larger new mortgage, in the wrong home, city and state, when our benefits and salary were diminished. (Journal, 9/18/1994)

---

"They were **slow to hearken unto the voice of the Lord** their God; therefore, *the Lord their God is slow to hearken unto their prayers*, to answer them in the day of their trouble." (D & C 101:7)

*Again, the answers to our/their prayers are simply slow in coming—on the Lord's timetable.*

"Lord, in trouble they have visited thee, they poured out a prayer when thy chastening was upon them." (Isaiah 26:16)

While finishing up at BYU, Provo, UT, in 1981 I had a pre-graduation job offer. This company desired I begin working for them right away; I had one more semester of school left. Overly tired of doing homework after 19 years of schooling I was looking forward to freedom and paychecks. I was really torn between the two.

As I prayed for a solution I became very frustrated. The only thoughts that would come to me were regarding the ward budget our bishop had requested. It was fifteen dollars for the summer. There was an activity a month planned and we were going to be out of town for two of those. I rationalized, "I'll just pay $5."

My wife encouraged me to pay the full amount.

I had a job offer and I was praying about that; I didn't need to be worrying about the budget right now. Yet again, every time I prayed about finishing up school, that budget issue came into my mind. I decided to humble myself and *follow the bishop's inspiration* and my wife's good advice. I finally paid our full budget assessment.

Once I had humbled myself and followed my local leader, answers to prayers became much clearer. I prayed again about my exciting job offer and the obvious problem of one more semester of college. Now that I had repented, the Spirit revealed my desired answer immediately; the Holy Ghost quickly whispered, "**Home Study**."

I doubted my personal revelation, "But I'm a senior, I cannot do anything with beginning classes and Home Study would not help my cause!"

I checked with my guidance counselor and I soon discovered that the Spirit was very correct and my assumptions fell far short of the truth. I was surely surprised to find that all my upper level classes were completed; all that I needed for graduation was two lower level classes in any subject. There were only six credit hours left to finish up. These classes were available on Home Study. I never dreamed of this sweet solution, nor even pondered this possibility! (Home Study is like old-school online classes.)

I was able to take the job and leave college early, which was quite exhilarating to say the least! BYU would mail me assignments and then mail my tests to the local library. I would study in the evenings after work and then take tests on certain Saturdays at the local library. The librarian would mail my completed tests in a pre-stamped envelope back to BYU. It was the slickest and easiest process—I even finished the semester and all my credits early while I was drawing some nice paychecks! (Journal, Aug 12, 1982)

> "**Believe and repent of your sins** ... and ye shall receive the Holy Ghost, that ye may have all things made manifest ..." (Moses 8:24)

---

> Nevertheless, I did harden my heart, for I was called many times and **I would not hear**; therefore I knew concerning these things, yet **I would not know**; therefore I went on rebelling against God, in the wickedness of my heart ... (Alma 10:6)

> "... Ye have seen an angel, and he spake unto you; yea ye have heard his voice from time to time; and he hath spoken to you in a still small voice, but **ye were past feeling**, that ye **could not feel his words** ..." (1 Ne. 17:45)

*Nephi was explaining the above to his frustrating brothers, Laman and Lemuel. Think the stark contrasts in their future lives; Nephi listening and learning while his older brothers were not feeling or growing spiritually]*

> "Do you suppose that we can enjoy righteousness and peace and joy in the Holy Ghost, if we **fail to keep the Sabbath day holy**?" (Joseph L. Wirthlin, CR, April 1959)

---

*Certain members claim to know answers that are not in the scriptures or even assert they have answers to questions the scriptures indicate are not known by angels or men. A prophet of the Lord comments:*

> Are not the people reaching after that which does not belong to them?...They are looking after something in the future; they are like the fool, whose eyes are wandering to the ends of the earth; like some of the Elders who rise here to preach and want to tell what is going to be in the millennium, and what has been long before the creation of the world, but never think of inquiring as to their duty today. (President Brigham Young, JD 8:188)

"Wisdom if before him that hath understanding; but the eyes of a fool are in the ends of the earth." (Prov. 17:24)

━━━●◆●━━━

*The answer explaining how to "receive any answer to anything through prayer and faith" comes from the teachings of the Savior to the Nephites.*

"And **whatsoever ye shall ask** the Father in my name, **which is right**, believing that ye shall receive, behold it shall be given to you." (3 Ne. 18:20)

*Obviously asking about* the date *of the 2^nd coming fits in the "which is wrong" category.*

*However, looking on the bright side of things,* the signs *of His coming can be revealed to us:*

"And he that believeth shall be blest with signs following, even as it is written. And unto you *it shall be given to know the signs of the coming of the Son of Man.*" (D&C 68:10-11)

*James also teaches us further:* "Ye ask, and receive not, **because ye ask amiss**, that ye may consume it upon your lusts." (James 4:3) *At times our desires through prayer can be self-centered and not in our best interest.*

*Furthermore, Christ teaches us:* "And as surely as Christ liveth he spake these words unto our fathers, saying: Whatsoever thing ye shall ask the Father in my name, **which is good, in faith believing** that ye shall receive, behold, it shall be done unto you." (Moroni 7:26)

━━━●◆●━━━

I had a friend, one time, who went to take a test in school, a test for which he had not studied. Of course he had prayed pretty hard about it. He had asked the Lord to help him remember something he had not bothered to learn. There are some things the Lord cannot do. Other things he can, but he will not. And praying won't work in these cases. I know; I have tried it.

But as this friend went in to take the test, he found he was sitting right next to the smartest girl in the class. He said, "Well, this must be the answer to my prayer. Here she is. The Lord provided her, right here."

But he was a returned missionary. He had been preaching honesty for two years. It is very difficult to go against that which you have been preaching and for which you have had a witness of the Spirit. While he was arguing with himself about what he was going to do, he flunked the test. But as a matter of fact he really passed.

"Remember that without faith you can do nothing; therefore ask in faith. **Trifle not** with these things; **do not ask for that which you ought not.**" (D & C 8:10)

And thus we see that the Nephites did begin to dwindle in **unbelief, and grow in wickedness and abominations**, while the Lamanites began to grow exceedingly in the knowledge of their God; yea, they did begin to keep his commandments, and to walk in truth and uprightness before him. And thus we see that *the Spirit of the Lord began to withdraw* from the Nephites, because of the wickedness and the **hardness of their hearts**. (Helaman 6:34-35)

"And the end thereof, neither the place thereof, nor their torment, no man knows; Neither was it revealed, neither is, neither will be revealed unto man, except to them who are made partakers thereof." (D&C 76:45-46)

"But as it is written, Eye hath not seen, nor ear heard, neither have entered into the heart of man, the things which God hath prepared for them that love him." (1 Cor. 2:9)

*Something's are only revealed to those who actually experience it later.*

*The Prophet Joseph Smith lost answers and spiritual gifts at times, as most everyone does:*

... because you delivered up those writings which you had power given unto you to translate by the means of the Urim and Thummim, into the hands of a wicked man, you have lost them. And *you also lost your gift* at the same time, and your mind became darkened. (D&C 10:1-2)

225

"And likewise also is it counted evil unto a man, if he **shall pray and not with real intent of heart**; yea, and it profiteth him nothing, for God receiveth none such." (Moroni 7:10)

"When you feel blocked or limited, maybe it is stretching. I have shed tears over prayers I did not think were getting very far, but with greater hindsight I could see that was a lesson in maturity and growth." (Elder Jeffrey R. Holland, University of Oxford, Nov 13, 2018)

"Oftentimes He withholds an answer, not for lack of concern, but because He loves us—perfectly. He wants us to apply the truths He has given us. For us to grow, we need to trust our ability to make correct decisions." (Richard G. Scott, GC, Oct 1989)

"… if they speak not according to this word, it is because there is **no light in them**."(Isaiah 8:20)

"Now *Satan had gotten great hold upon the hearts of the people* of the city of Ammonihah; therefore **they would not hearken** unto the words of Alma." (Alma 8:9)

*Amulek's admission to his peers:*

Nevertheless, I did **harden my heart**, for I was called many times and I **would not hear**; therefore I knew concerning these things, yet I would not know; therefore I **went on rebelling against God**, in the wickedness of my heart… (Alma 10:6)

"And GOD saw that the wickedness of man was great in the earth, and that **every imagination of the thoughts of his heart was only evil continually**." (Genesis 6:5)

*Mormon was faced with a similar problem to Noah's time.*
"And there were **no gifts from the Lord**, and **the Holy Ghost did not come upon any**, because of their wickedness and unbelief." (Mormon 1:14)

**A man who continues in his sins**, and who has no living faith in the Son of God, cannot receive the gift of the Holy

Spirit through the ministration of any agent, however holy he may be. The impure spirit of such a one will repulse the pure element, upon the natural laws of sympathetic affinity, or of attraction and repulsion. (Parley P. Pratt, *KST*, 101)

---

As a close relative and I traveled for quite some time by car, we had ample opportunity to reflect and visit. I felt impressed to share a few faith-building experiences. My hope is that he would feel a strong Spirit and increase his desires to seek the same.

"Wow!" He Exclaimed, "I never have experiences like that."

"Do you ever get answers to prayers?"

"Well, I don't really pray much."

"Do you read the scriptures?"

"Not really."

"Have you gone back to the temple?"

"Not since when I first went through."

"Do you think not praying, not reading the scriptures, and not going to the temple could have something to do with your lack of spiritual experiences?"

"Yea, I suppose it might."

"Why don't you give it a try and enjoy those rich blessings that come through obedience? You can get answers to your prayers and your personal quandaries. I know it works!"

He said he would think about it. I prayed that he would follow through.

> ... I spake unto my brethren, desiring to know of them the cause of their disputations. And they said: Behold we cannot understand the words which our father (Lehi) hath spoken ... And I said unto them: Have ye inquired of the Lord? And they said unto me: We have not; for the Lord maketh no such thing known unto us. Behold, I said unto them: How is it that ye do not keep the commandments of the Lord? ... Do ye not remember the things which the Lord hath said?—If ye will not harden your hearts, and ask me in faith, believing that ye shall receive, with diligence in keeping my commandments, surely these things shall be made know unto you. (1 Ne. 15:6-11)

---

At one point in my mission, my assignment and living arrangement was somewhat unusual. I lived in a ranch house, high in the mountains, about 10 miles out of a small town with a senior couple who lived there also. I had become accustomed to receiving the Spirit as I prayed, but one night the door to heaven wouldn't open. I couldn't think of anything I had done to offend the Spirit or anyone else that day. I felt so alone.

After a time of humbling myself and expressing my willingness to do anything the Lord wanted, I received a very clear thought that **I needed to go apologize** to one of the Elders who lived in the town. That confused me, because I hadn't even been around that Elder that day, but I agreed to go right then. It was a dark, windy, and very cold January night. To get to town I had to go through 14 cattle gates.

For those who might not be familiar with this type of gate, this is how they work. The fence is made of 4 or 5 barbed wire strands held up by fence posts. The posts may be made of steel pounded in the ground or often of stout wooden posts. The gate is a section of barbed wire stretched across an opening with a steel or wooden pole attached to the end. This pole is connected to a heavy end post with two loops of wire, one at the top and one at the bottom. It's simple, but effective. To open a gate you get out of your truck, go to the end post where the gate is attached and pull the wire gate tight to release the top loop of wire and then lift the post out of the bottom loop. Then you drag the gate out of the way, across a cattle guard, get back in your truck and drive through the gate. You stop and get out, drag the gate back to the end post, put the post in the bottom wire loop and stretch the gate tight so you can get the pole into the top loop. Then you get back in your truck and drive … to the next gate. That was what I had to do 14 times to get to town.

Once in town, I drove to the Elder's place and knocked on the door. When he answered I said, "Elder, I don't really know why, but I am here to apologize to you."

He invited me in, but seemed troubled. He told me that earlier in the day he had overheard me talking with someone else. Something I said had bothered him.

Had I said something about him? No. Did he feel I was criticizing someone else? No. He wouldn't say what it was, but something I said had struck a tender spot in his heart. I apologized for whatever it was, and though I didn't even remember the moment, I was truly and deeply sorry. It had offended him and that had offended the Spirit, even though it was something I was unaware of.

As we talked, he began to open his heart. He was a young man with a very tender, wounded heart. He was lonely, missed his family, and felt unaccepted by other missionaries. The Spirit whispered, "**He needs a blessing**." I offered to give him a priesthood blessing. Tears began to fall. No one had ever offered to give him a blessing before.

As I laid my hands on his head, God's words flowed freely, bringing His healing power to a lonely son who needed it so desperately.

Two lonely sons were blessed that night. Fourteen cattle gates later I knelt down, and heaven was near again. (Our friend)

———————◆———————

We had served as a bishopric of a brand new ward for several years now. The three of us couldn't have been more different, yet things were finally gelling. We had a wonderful out-of-state two-day temple trip (all of our temple visits were this way) and all positions were filled with great members who were diligent. We had a great bunch of youth and many seasoned members enduring to the end.

On a particular Sunday 7 a.m. meeting, we had an exceptionally good meeting. Afterwards we knelt before the Lord in prayer as a bishopric in the office. This was a prayer of gratitude and the Spirit came into our bodies and seemed to blossom and enlarge to fill the entire room. The experience was phenomenal!

While basking in this wonderful Spirit of love and acceptance; a LOUD BANG on the door resonated in our ears. This knock was so loud and hard that I pictured the door bending in, like one sees in cartoons.

The bishop's face was flush and the veins were popping out on his neck as he madly exclaimed, "Some deacon is going to experience the laying on of hands!"

We cheered, "Go get 'em bishop!", as he dashed for the door.

That wonderful Spirit we were basking in was gone in an instant due to our quick change of hearts!

As the bishop flung open the door our hearts melted as we witnessed Troy, a Down syndrome boy, standing there with the largest smile draped across his face. Troy was sixteen years old with a four-year-old mentality. Troy loved his bishop. We all began the repentance process to attempt to receive the Holy Ghost back into our lives as soon as possible.

Revenge is a surefire method to drive the spirit away in a hurry. When we seek revenge and/or hold grudges it becomes very difficult for one to cultivate a spiritual habitat.

> "If an individual fails to yield to the enlightenment of the Holy Ghost, then the Spirit departs from him, and he is left to his own resources to struggle alone with his problems." (Delbert L. Stapley, GC, Oct, 1965)

*Sometimes we use our prayers to ask for things that shouldn't be prayed for. Some have prayed that certain people would die, for various selfish reasons. Others have prayed for bad things to happen so they themselves could advance in business or relationships. Still others have prayed for special blessings and endowments ahead of their time.*

*The second prophet Nephi had found Christ by giving his own life through steadfast service:*

> Blessed art thou, Nephi, for those things which thou hast done; for I have beheld how thou hast with unwearyingness declared the word, which I have given unto thee, unto this people. And thou hast not feared them, and hast not sought thine own life, but hast sought my will, and to keep my commandments.
>
> And now, because thou has done this with such unwearyingness, behold, I will bless thee forever; and I will make thee mighty in word and in deed, in faith and in mighty works; yea, even that all things shall be done unto thee according to thy word, for **thou shalt not ask that which is contrary to my will**. (Helaman 10:4-5)

> I have had prayers answered. Those answers were most clear when what I wanted was silenced by an overpowering need to know what God wanted. It is then that the answer from a loving Heavenly Father can be spoken to the mind by the still, small voice and can be written on the heart. (Henry B. Eyring, GC, Oct 2000)

> Behold, I, the Lord, was angry with him who was my servant Ezra Booth, and also my servant Isaac Morley, for **they *kept not the law, neither the commandment*; They *sought evil in their hearts***, and I, the Lord, *withheld my Spirit*. (D&C 64:15-16)

*We are all familiar with the ball of curious workmanship, the Liahona. When Lehi's family **wasn't living right** they were unable to receive direction or revelation from the Liahona; similar to our not being able to get answers for heaven sent questions when we are disobedient.*

"… I, Nephi, beheld the pointers which were in the ball, that they did work according to the faith and diligence and heed which we did give unto them." (1 Ne. 16:28)

*When we give faith, diligence, and heed to the scriptures and our leaders we are much more likely to receive personal revelation and answers to even the simplest prayers in faster fashion.*

Laman and Lemuel did take me and bind me with cords, and **they did treat me with much harshness**...after they had bound me insomuch that I could not move, the compass, which had been prepared of the lord, did cease to work. (1 Ne. 18:11-12)

*Anger is another sure fire way to quickly drive the Spirit away from ourselves. When one is vengeful or vindictive, his thoughts and/or actions become a venomous poison. The Spirit flees from an angry soul and evil spirits are quick to take up any available space. Repentance and righteousness reject that evil one while welcoming the return of the Holy Ghost.*

———— •◆• ————

… we wait for light, but behold obscurity; for brightness, but **we walk in darkness**. We grope for the wall like the blind, and we grope as if we had no eyes: we stumble at noonday as in the night; we are in desolate places as dead men. (Isaiah 59:9-10)

*The people of Israel had separated themselves from light and truth due to their iniquitous lives of sin and idol worship.*

———— •◆• ————

A son of Bishop Wells [Presiding Bishopric member] was killed in Emigration Canyon on a railroad track … Sister Wells was inconsolable. She mourned during the three days prior to the funeral, received no comfort at the funeral, and was in a rather serious state of mind. One day soon after the funeral services while she was lying on her bed relaxed, still mourning, she says that her son appeared to her and said, Mother, do not mourn; do not cry. I am all right. He told her that she did not understand how the accident happened and explained that he had given the signal to the engineer to move on, and then made the usual effort to catch the railing on the freight train; but as he attempted to do so his foot caught on a root and he failed to catch the hand rail and his body fell under the train. It was clearly an accident. Now listen! He said that as soon as he realized that he was in another environment, he tried to see his father but **he couldn't reach him. His father was so busy** with the duties of his office he could not respond to his call. Therefore, he had to come to his mother. He said to her, "You tell father that all is well with me and I want you not to mourn anymore." President McKay made the statement that the point he had in mind was that when we are relaxed—in a private room we are more susceptible to whisperings of the Spirit. (Harold B. Lee, *TPC*, 19)

I fear this supernal gift is being obscured by programs and activities and schedules and so many meetings. There are so many places to go, so many things to do in this noisy world. We can be too busy to pay attention to the promptings of the Spirit. (Body K. Packer, GC, April 2000)

"Be thou humble; and the Lord thy God shall lead thee by the hand, and give thee answer to thy prayers." (D&C 112:10)

We learn of the dedication which was given to the seminary program in its very beginning by reading from a diary of John M. Whitaker, one of the early instructors of the seminary program. In April of 1915 ... So I did as I have always done when presented with a task, went in humility and prayer to my Father in Heaven and in my simplicity told him my problem and asked for inspiration, guidance, wisdom and courage for the task before me. (L. Tom Perry, GC, Oct 1960)

*Learning humility will push away pride; our prayers will be answered much quicker.*

"God had often sealed up the heavens because of the covetousness in the Church." (*TPJS*, 9)

...when we undertake to **cover our sins**, or to **gratify our pride**, our **vain ambition**, or to **exercise control or dominion or compulsion** upon the souls of the children of men, in any degree of **unrighteousness**, behold, the heavens withdraw themselves; *the Spirit of the Lord is grieved; and when it is withdrawn, Amen to the priesthood or authority of that man.* (D&C 121:37) (Underline added)

For behold, if you have **procrastinated the day of your repentance** even until death, behold, ye have become subjected to the spirit of the devil, and he doth seal you his; therefore *the Spirit of the Lord hath withdrawn from you, and hath no place in you,* and the devil hath all power over you; and this is the final state of the wicked. (Alma 34:35) (Underline added)

*The lack of the spirit was a great part of the destruction of the Nephites and the "great slaughter".*

"Making a mock of that which is sacred, denying and disbelieving the spirit of prophecy and of revelation." (See Helaman 4:11-13, 23)

*There are even times when all revelation to a person and/or people is stopped. King Saul was relying more on the arm and mind of flesh and disregarding the prophet Samuel, in turn placing less importance on the Lord. We read:*

"And when Saul inquired of the LORD, **the LORD answered him not, neither by dreams, nor by Urim, nor by prophets**." (1 Sam. 28:6)

To be sure, there may be times when you feel as though the heavens are closed. But I promise that as you continue to be obedient, expressing gratitude for every blessing the Lord gives you, and as you patiently honor the Lord's timetable, you will be given the knowledge and understanding you seek. Every blessing the Lord has for you—even miracles—will follow. That is what personal revelation will do for you. (President Russell M. Nelson, GC, April 2018)

———————◆———————

Draw near unto me and I will draw near unto you; seek me diligently and ye shall find me; ask, and ye shall receive; knock, and it shall be opened unto you. **Whatsoever ye ask the Father in my name it shall be given you, <u>that is expedient for you</u>;** and if ye ask anything that is not expedient for you, it shall turn unto your condemnation. (D&C 88:63-65)

"There is a difference between aspiration and the inspiration that comes from prayer. Both relate to desire; but aspiration is merely subjective, while inspiration includes divine help." (David O. McKay, Gospel Ideals, 24)

*Therefore, we can pray and have "anything" revealed that: Isn't contrary to God's will, is not asked awry, isn't bad, is expedient for us, is not trifling, is not asked amiss, is not wrong, or that which we ought not ask— and then it will be revealed to us on the Lord's timetable.*

# 11: Called of God by Prophecy

Imagine the miracle of it! *Whatever our Church calling*, we can pray to our Heavenly Father, and receive guidance and direction, be warned about dangers and distractions, and be enabled to accomplish things we simply could not do on our own. If we will truly receive the Holy Ghost and learn to discern and understand His promptings, we will be guided in matters large and small. (President Russell M. Nelson, GC, April 2018)

I remember Elder Bednar talking to our stake in the adult meeting on a Saturday evening. I will paraphrase what he said. This Apostle of the Lord taught us: "The General Authorities do not come to pick a new stake president; the General Authorities come to find the stake president whom the Lord has chosen." End paraphrase.

This is the procedure that should and most often does take place in every presidency within the church; there are an extremely large number of presidencies when you think about it. I did wonder one time when a new adult presidency in a ward was staffed by a man and his two very best friends. Then I had the thought that the Lord knew this brother would choose his best friends without even praying about it; those three brethren were supposed to serve together at that time and they did a most wonderful job.

"Surely the Lord God will do nothing, but he revealeth his secret unto his servants the prophets." (Amos 3:7)

The bishop wanted to talk to me. I was thinking, "Anything but the music director." He called me to be the Primary chorister. I dreaded it. However, I learned the meaning of those songs as we would sing them. Once I understood the songs I would bear testimony to the children about the message within them. It was the most spiritually rewarding calling I've ever had. And it was in the Primary, being the chorister! (A friend)

"… Attend to thy calling and thou shalt have wherewith to magnify thine office …" (D&C 24:9)

In our bishop's meeting, the bishop said, "I believe we need to find a new Relief Society president." The bishop asked us, his counselors, to pray during the week for inspiration as to who our next Relief Society president should be. The bishop would be praying for direction likewise. During the week I prayed nightly and in part sought inspiration regarding the bishop's request. During the middle of the week, one sister's name came clearly to my mind.

We met up as a bishopric the following Sunday at our weekly 7 a.m. meeting.

"So did you pray about a new Relief Society president?"

"Yes, the name '**Millie Kelley**' came clearly to my mind."

"That's the same name that came to me, '**Sister Kelley**'s,'"

"Well, there's no argument here; that is also the same name I came up with too. There's no doubt who the Lord wants to serve as our new Relief Society president! I will extend the call and ask her to pray and submit names for her counselors."

Sister Kelley did a wonderful job as she related really well with the needs of the sisters within our ward!

"And we know that all things work together for good to them that love God, to them who are called according to his purpose." (Romans 8:28)

When I was in high school there was one teacher that I just did not like at all. It may be partly because she was the teacher and I was the student. She was my least favorite teacher and I avoided her whenever possible.

After marriage we bought our first home and moved into a new neighborhood and ward. To my surprise there was the teacher I despised, sitting in our new ward! Again I tried to avoid her.

A couple of years later this former teacher of mine was put in as the Relief Society president. Just after that I had a hysterectomy and I did not want anybody to know of my personal grief. Of course my immediate family knew about this; they also knew they were sworn to secrecy regarding the matter.

My mother was watching our children while we were at the doctors making an appointment and discussing my procedure. When we arrived back home my mother reported that the Relief Society president had called to see when she could drop off a dinner for our family.

I asked my mother why she had shared the secret she was told not to. My mother hadn't said anything. Then I was mad at my children who were supposed to be sworn to secrecy. None of the children had told anyone!

This inspired woman had sensed that I needed special care at the time, with no idea what my issues or problems were. I was impressed with her being in tune to understand the known and unknown needs of the sisters in our ward. I realized that I had judged this woman without ever really knowing her. I now know her and cherish and love my former teacher and sister in the gospel. (Missionary peer)

"As surely as you can tune in on the radio and hear voices from afar, so sure am I that God our Father lives, and the soul of man can commune with him through the Holy Spirit." (David O. McKay, CR, Oct 1950)

--------◆•-------

When I was serving in the Stake Young Women's presidency I needed a new counselor and I was praying for inspiration as to who that might be. I was sitting in the temple one day and I just saw the back of one woman's head and the Spirit said, **"That is who you should call."** But I had no idea who she was and no idea where she was from. She was several rows ahead of me and I did not see her later.

Our stake consisted of several towns. I started describing her to different people over two weeks trying to discover who she was. Somebody thought they knew her by my description. I attended a stake meeting and this person pointed her out and I said, "Yes, that's her!"

She was from a town thirty miles away, but she was the one. She had the perfect talents and gifts that we needed at that time in our presidency. She was perfect for the job! (A friend)

"... we shall finally all have to come to the same conclusion that Paul did—'No man knows the things of God but by the Spirit of God;'" (*TPJS*, 247)

--------◆•-------

*There's a wonderful woman that we home teach, who teaches us more than we will ever teach her. She shared this story:*

We were being stationed in Germany with a young family. We lived at a United States military base. We belonged to an LDS Branch there and were attending for only the 2nd time since we'd moved overseas.

I was sitting in the Sunday school class when the Branch President appeared in the doorway and motioned for me to come see him. I got up and as we walked down the hall he said, "Sister, the Lord would like you to be our new Primary president."

"Okay."

"Thank you; you can go back to your class now."

As I sat down, two names came to my head and I wrote them on a little piece of paper. I had no idea who they were. After class the Branch President approached me again and informed me that I needed two counselors for the Primary Presidency.

I replied, "I know. Here are the names;" as I handed him my little piece of paper.

The names I submitted were contacted and accepted. The next week a new family moved into our branch. All three members of our new Primary Presidency had simultaneous impressions that this was our new Primary pianist. I told the Branch President we knew who our pianist was supposed to be, as I pointed her out.

"Does she play the piano?"

"We have no idea; we just know she is the right one!"
(Ward member)

"When Elder David E. Sorensen extended to me the call to serve as stake president, he gave me an hour to select counselors. Through tears, I indicated that the Lord had already provided that revelation." (M. Joseph Brough, GC, Oct 2018)

---

I faced a great fear of mine today—teaching the Gospel Doctrine class. But the lesson material was fantastic, Ezekiel 34, 36 & 37: the valley of dry bones, two tribes coming together, and shepherding.

Heavenly Father truly answered my prayers; I hardly coughed at all. Yesterday I had cough attacks all day long. My stomach muscles hurt from coughing so much. I couldn't have done it without His help. I learned a lot." (A relative)

————————◆•———————

Right out of college we moved to a new job and into a great Ward. I was called to be the Young Men's President. I really enjoyed that calling, except there were too many meetings at times. We had wonderful young men and young women. We had held many joint activities, including: Youth Conference, Out-of-state temple trip, Road show, etc.

After around one year of full activities the bishop called me into his office. He proposed, "I feel it is time to make a change with the first assistant in the priest's quorum."

I was verbally hesitant saying, "Oh bishop, our current leader is the best young man I have worked with. He's service oriented, sings, dances, plays sports, and is the best example for the other young men. He's positive and encourages the others. I would just hate to make a change now."

The bishop replied, "Yes, I know what you mean. What I want you to do is to go home and seriously pray about it and then you can come back and visit with me."

I agreed. I prayed seriously for a couple of weeks, more or less pleading with the Lord that He not make a change. I even went as far to suggest that God change the bishop's mind.

One night I had a clear dream. I was out with the older Scouts working on Eagle projects with them. (We were doing an Eagle project about every two to three weeks during the summer, in reality.) All of the Priests were gathered where we had built a fence for a school and also laid a cement sidewalk. (These were two recent Eagle projects we had actually finished.) We were all inspecting the work and everything looked very well done. I complimented the young men on their fine Eagle projects and also for supporting their peers on their respective Eagle projects. The boys informed me that they had come across one tough issue they were unable to resolve. Near the end of the new sidewalk was a large healthy weed that they had not been able to remove.

The Scouts would try one-at-a-time, and encourage each other, as they pulled their hardest to no avail. I asked them to watch me tackle the beast. I couldn't budge it! We would cut it, chop it and the dream ended without success.

A few days later I had a follow-up dream; a continuation of the same dream. We were at the same spot on the sidewalk facing the goliath weed. Only two of the older young men were there this time. My wonderful 1st assistant came up to give it a tug. He was a very large and strong young man, much bigger than all the boys, including myself.

As he began to grip the base, grunt, and groan the large weed started slowly coming up. He kept pulling and working at it. It looked like a long hose being pulled up from a hole in the ground. The root was extremely long and his effort took quite some time, but he remained determinedly steady and strong. Finally the entire monstrous weed was laid out on the side walk with a thick root at least twenty to twenty-five feet long! We congratulated him for a job well done! And the dream ended there.

I visited the bishop after church the following Sabbath and shared the dream with him.

"So, what do you think?" the bishop asked.

"You are right; it is time to make a change. He's done a fine job, but he has finished up."

I shared my interesting answer through dreams with my bishop.

With a wry smile the bishop said, "Oh, I knew it was right to make a change right away; I just wanted to see how long it took you to catch up with the Sprit of Truth!"

I love this bishop! (Journal, 6/10/1984)

I have a dear friend who was the Scoutmaster for these same young men four-five years ago. We had a lot of fun sharing stories with each other about *our* fine Scouts, at different ages. My friend, also one of our home teachers, came over for a visit and we were talking about inspiration in callings. I shared the above story with him and his eyes lit up and I could tell he was entertaining a thought. I expected him to complement me on my prayerful faithfulness in seeking inspiration in my calling and the ensuing answer coming through dreams.

I was truly blown away when he exclaimed, "Why that was an alfalfa plant. Their roots can go on forever: 20 … 25 … even 30 feet!"

I love my good friend the farmer too!

Encyclopedia Britannica confirms that, "In porous sub soils, alfalfa taproots as long as 50 feet have been recorded in plants over 20 years old! (https://www.*britannica*.com plant/alfalfa/)

Reflecting on his experience with the young men in his ward, President Benson said: One of the joys of working with boys is the fact that you do get your pay as you go along. You have an opportunity to observe the results of your leadership daily as you work with them through the years and watch them grow into stalwart manhood, accepting eagerly its challenges and responsibilities. Such satisfaction cannot be purchased at any price; it must be earned through service and devotion. What a glorious thing it is to have even a small part in helping to build boys into men, real men. (Ezra Taft Benson, *TPC*, 7)

When I was a young father with five children I was serving on the High Council. Our Stake was divided and they called me to the High Council of the new Stake. I did not know the people of my own Ward very well at all.

One Wednesday evening the stake president asked me to visit with him. He told me I was to be the new bishop and that I would be sustained that Sunday along with two counselors. I explained to the stake president that I didn't really know the people in my home ward because I had served in the Stake so long.

He confided in me and said, "Oh, you will know who your counselors are. Now, you need to let me know right away, because I need to approve them, extend their calls and have them accepted before Sunday too!"

I don't think I have ever prayed harder in my life. Following intense prayer I had two names come to me, but I had no idea who they even were! I gave the names to our stake president and we were all sustained that Sunday. They turned out to be the best men I could have worked with; they were perfect! The Lord really knew who needed to serve at that time." (Our 90-yr. old friend)

And it came to pass in those days, that he went out into a mountain to pray, and continued all night in prayer to God. And when it was day, he called unto him his disciples: and of them he chose twelve, whom also he named apostles. (Luke 6:12-13)

As a Relief Society president, my counselors and I would pray together and often receive the same answer. One time I needed a new 2nd counselor, and we were going through the list of sisters and none of them seemed right. We went through the list three times, and we still felt that none were right. We could not get an answer this time.

Finally it dawned on me that my Relief Society secretary was to be the new 2<sup>nd</sup> counselor. It was then fairly easy to know who was to be the new secretary. (A family member)

"You hearken to the still small voice that whispers eternal truth." (President Brigham Young, *JD* 15:7)

━━━━━━◆━━━━━━

I had some wonderful experiences when I had to choose new counselors at the branch. I had been inspired to keep the original counselors when I was sustained as the new Branch President. After a few months I felt impressed to seek a new first counselor. I prayed about this impression and it was confirmed.

It was quite an overwhelming task because I had seven stakes to choose from. I prayed about it for two weeks and did not receive any guidance. I decided to change my prayers and asked instead, "Is it someone I have seen today?" Immediately, Gary's face came into my mind, and I felt that unmistakable burning feeling.

I called the stake president to tell him the first counselor needed to be released and that I had a name for his replacement.

He told me he would review this with his counselors and get back with me. He called back a few days later and asked me to keep the current counselor.

I was very disappointed, but I learned a lesson about supporting our leaders. We need to support them even when their decisions don't go our way.

Several months later my first counselor told me he needed to be released. Once again, I prayed about Gary's name and it was confirmed to me again. This time Gary was approved.

Several months after that, the stake president contacted me at 10 pm, informing me that my 2<sup>nd</sup> counselor needed to be released.

As I lay in bed, I was going over men in the seven stakes who were retired. This was important because we made regular visits during the week to the care center. I thought of several people and then Don's faced came to my mind. I didn't know him very well at all, I just knew of him. As soon as Don's face came to my mind I was filled with a warm, burning feeling, and I knew he was the one. I called the stake president in the morning and he was thrilled with my choice. Gary, Don, and I made a really good team while we were serving together. (A family friend)

But I know what that voice is like, because I have had it come into my mind and give me names when I have had to select stake presidents. There is nothing mysterious about it to people who learn to be guided by the spirit. The voice of the Lord has come into my mind, in sentences, in answer to prayer. (Marion G. Romney, GC, Oct 1961)

*As a new prophet Heber J. Grant experienced the following in choosing a new apostle:* As he pondered this responsibility, his thoughts turned repeatedly to his lifelong friend Richard W. Young, a faithful Latter-day Saint and a proven leader. ... When he finally felt confident with this course of action, he wrote his friend's name on a piece of paper and took the paper with him to the weekly temple meeting with the First Presidency and the Quorum of the Twelve. However, when he was about to present the name for the approval of his Brethren, he was unable to do so. Instead of presenting the name of Richard W. Young, he presented the name of Melvin J. Ballard, a man whom he hardly knew. President Grant later told of the impact this experience had on him: "I have felt the inspiration of the living God directing me in my labors..." (*TPC*, 20:181-182)

While serving as the ward YM President as a newlywed I found the calling to be very rewarding. It was winter time and we were having a joint activity with the young women in the gym. I had a distinct impression to leave the activity and go to the parking lot. On each end of the hallway, were matching parking lots behind the church.

As I went to the middle of the west parking lot I starting looking around for any lights, exhaust from cars, while listening for any sounds. There was no sound anywhere. There were no cars running. No brake, parking, or car lights were on. I started wondering why I was prompted so strongly to stand in a parking lot where nothing was happening. Then I thought to myself, maybe I went to the wrong parking lot.

I looked at nearly a foot of snow around the building and I was not going to trample around to the other side. I could just walk back into the building, down through the hall, and out into the other parking lot. As I looked to do that, I noticed one of the young men looking for something in his coat. As I secretly spied from the darkness outside, I realized he was looking for something in everybody's coats. It was a cold Wyoming winter and every youth and adult had left their coats hanging up in the hall coat racks.

Now I knew why I was prompted to go outside during our activity; so that I could see inside and witness an activity that shouldn't be going on, from the outside. I rushed in and said, "Hey, how's it going? You'd better get back to the activity."

He was surprised, kinda mumbled, and said, "Sure." I passed my discovery on to the bishop for further handling.

During the summer, while still serving as YM President, we held another combined activity in the cultural hall. Once again, I received a strong prompting to leave the activity. This time I was prompted to remain in the building and to take the perpendicular hall that led pass the kitchen to the chapel.

Once again, I was on the Lord's assignment, yet clueless as to what or why. I came to a stairwell and a small closet door under the stairwell stood out to me. I had never really noticed it before. I assumed it was locked.

Being drawn to this small closet, I unlocked the door to peek inside and was sorely surprised. Yet nowhere near the surprised look of the cramped occupants! I discovered a young man and young women tucked in the small space with shirts unbuttoned and pants undone. I put an end to that right away. I believe I was sent to stop an event that nearly had serious consequences for both of the participants. "Get dressed and get back to the activity!" I commanded. Once again, I turned over my spirit-led find to the bishop for further action.

During this YM's calling I was prompted a third time to leave a combined activity in the gym and go to the parking lot. I went to the same west lot as before, since that worked out last time. No vehicles were running and no lights were on. I looked back into the hallway between the parking lots and saw no activity inside the church hallway this time.

Then I heard a whimpering sound. I found a young woman, from our ward, between two cars and she was acting very strange. I thought she might be on drugs. Then I discerned she was having a mental breakdown. My first impression was to take her into my arms and console/comfort her. The Spirit said, "**Unh Uh**!" as I started to step towards her.

Then I looked at her more closely and saw a fifteen-year old who looked twenty, with an extra blouse button undone, and wearing a very short red skirt. I understood why I should not be giving her a hug. "Avoid the very appearance"; I ran to the bishopric to inform them of this serious situation. I was elated to be relieved of that responsibility.

When we receive an impression in our *heart,* we can use our *mind* either to rationalize it away or to accomplish it. Be careful what you do with an impression from the Lord. (Richard G. Scott, GC, Oct 1989)

———————•◆•———————

I was up in our pear tree admiring all the beautiful fruit before picking them. Then I noticed a straight branch lying horizontally across the other branches. It was about three feet long and had dried up black leaves with little black pears on it.

I just stared at the dried up branch and kind of felt sorry for those little pears. The Spirit said to me, "**Take this to Primary and teach the children**."

During my next Primary class, I had a nice bowl of fresh pears alongside this dried up branch. I explained to the children what could happen if we break away from our family and/or leave Jesus Christ's church. It was the best object lesson I believe we ever had in our class. (A friend)

———————•◆•———————

*The saints from South Africa share the following story:*

The sunny skies of Cape Town were dark with rain clouds ... the boys and girls bake sale would be ruined by the storm ... But they knew grandmother Fourie would expect them regardless ... Sister Ouma greeted them ... and then explained that the sale must be held that day ... also she said the sale must be held outside so people would stop to buy.

"We'll pray for the rain to stop," she directed, "and we know it will, for we need the money to continue holding our Primary. This is what our Father in Heaven wants, so of course he will help us."

... as each child bowed his head and she prayed for the rain to stop, everyone just knew it would. And it did!

The rain that had pelted unceasingly for several days stopped ... The sun smiled on the children ... After a most successful sale, the empty tables were carried back into the chapel, and the rain began again and continued steadily during the next three days.

"But what would you have done, Sister Fourie," asked a Primary worker later, "if it hadn't stopped raining?"

This woman, who for thirty-four continuous years loved and taught the boys and girls of South Africa, answered very softly, "But we all knew that it would." (*Friend*, Apr 1972)

---

I still remember the mutual lesson on Wednesday evening, over forty-five years ago. Brother Rex Reasch was bearing a strong testimony of the Sabbath Day. He was a retail clothier whom we visited for our prom and homecoming attire. That night he fervently testified of the blessings his family had enjoyed because they always kept closed on Sundays. From the lesson he brought to our young minds, things we could be doing and other activities we should be avoiding. During his lesson the Spirit burned within in me and I knew in my heart his witness of Sabbath worship and its inherent blessings were true.

Afterwards I told my LDS friends that I would no longer be playing basketball with them on Sundays. I followed with, "I'll be glad to play pickup-ball after school or on Saturdays with you guys."

This lesson had not touched my buddies in the same way. We all gain our own testimonies of gospel principles and truths on various time schedules, "line upon line and precept upon precept; here a little and there a little." (2 Ne. 38:30)

Because of my conversion to the Sabbath observance, at a young age, we can also now testify of the blessings we have enjoyed. I have noticed from my journal that many of the promptings and whisperings that have come to me have been on quiet Sunday afternoons.

When we were engaged, one of our mutual goals for the Sabbath was the avoidance of the media on Sunday. Even though I have competed heavily in sports and won various awards, I have never watched a Super Bowl. We have enjoyed quiet family games together on some Sundays.

We also had a goal to not shop or work on the Sabbath Day. Over the years we have had to work during special occasions and shop about once every five years on Sunday, usually for a prescription emergency. We have done our best to make Sunday a day of devotion, peace, rest, and service and this decision has blessed our family, marriage, and our lives.

When we moved to a new state we were looking for some family friends late one January, 1996. I was reminded of "spiritual tracting" in the mission field. I looked through our new ward's phone directory until I found a family that *felt right*. I cold called them and introduced myself and our family. Our children were similar ages. When I explained that we liked to worship and visit on Sunday and do not watch sports or the Super Bowl, our newfound friend explained, "Come on over! We don't either!" (Journal 2/11/1996)

For well over twenty years now our two families have enjoyed a Soup n' Sundaes get together on Super Bowl Sunday and have developed an eternal relationship. We thought some of each other's children might marry one another, but that's not usually how it works out—nor did it.

––––––––•◆•––––––––

A brother at church was sharing an experience when he was the Ward Mission Leader in a Hawaiian Ward. He was helping the sister missionaries with a part-member family. Only the husband was not a member. He had done everything he needed to do to get baptized, yet he still had some questions that he felt hadn't been answered.

This young leader prayed for a solution to the father's questions. As the sisters taught, a thought came to the mission leader to open the scriptures. The scriptures fell to a perfect selection of verses which answered the questions the father had. The investigator received exactly what he needed. Following that he was baptized. (Ward member)

"That ye may be prepared in all things when I shall send you again to magnify the calling whereunto I have called you, and the mission with which I have commissioned you." (D&C 88:80)

––––––––•◆•––––––––

I was called to be the ward Relief Society president and needed to choose my counselors. I prayed about this and a few people came to mind. I went to the temple with a couple of names I was thinking of. When I got out of the temple, I went to pray for these two sisters and I couldn't even remember their names!

I prayed again to ask Heavenly Father what happened with those sisters I was thinking of and the Spirit responded, **"Think younger."** When I changed my thinking to consider the younger women in our group, two sisters came clearly to my mind. It was confirmed to me that they were the ones who should be my counselors at this time. (A family friend)

*I remember, when that Relief Society presidency was sustained, turning to my wife and commenting, "Boy those are young counselors, aren't they?" She replied, "Yes, that's the same thought I had." (And just what God had in mind.)*

––––––––•◆•––––––––

247

*We had a Stake Conference in Cody, WY, in 1981. Elder Loren C Dunn of the First Quorum of the Seventy presided. It was always thrilling to have visiting general authorities, because they seemed to be a rarity outside of Idaho and Utah decades ago.*

*Elder Dunn was closing the conference after speaking for one hour. He had shared many stories and interesting experiences that we all loved. Then he paused … and said:*

> You know those spiritual messages or when people say the Spirit has influenced them to say something? Well, this is one of those times. I wasn't planning on ending this way, but there's a man in the audience with a member wife and the children are members. Haven't you waited long enough? Isn't it time to pull your family together? Surely you know it's true; you've lived in that house for so many years with them. Isn't it time father?

*We were very impressed and wondered who he was inspired to touch personally.* (Journal 2/8/1981)

———◆———

The bishop asked me if I would extend a call to a ward member. I gladly agreed and set up an appointment in the home. As I visited with this member I got an earful of difficulties, confusion, and some despair regarding the past, present, and future. After lending a listening ear I reminded them that I was on the bishop's errand and needed to talk to them about something important.

"What is that?" they questioned.

"The bishop would like you to be our new '_____'."

"Oh, Brother Laing, that's not the Lord, that's just the bishop wanting me to do this."

"All the callings the bishopric makes in our ward are done through prayer and inspiration, every single one and this call is no different."

"No, no … it's just the bishop. And I have all these issues to deal with. I have been praying so hard to get an answer to my problems."

"This calling is the answer you are seeking. This calling is the answer to your prayers! Magnifying this calling will greatly ease your issues and concerns."

I strongly testified to her since I knew it was true. I surely did not plan to say that! This was a very surprising discernment. Her prayer was not revealed to me, only the answer she was seeking from God.

This member chose to not accept the new calling, feeling it wasn't from the Lord and those personal issues and problems festered and literally tore her family apart. Obviously I cannot say all the challenges hinged on accepting or rejecting a church calling; the Lord did confirm however that the calling was the answer she was seeking. Oftentimes we don't like or agree with the answers that come from our pleadings and prayers.

> "Be thou humble; and the Lord thy God shall lead thee by the hand, and give thee answer to thy prayers. I know thy heart, and have heard thy prayers …" (D&C 112:10-12)

*It is very uncommon to know someone's prayers or the answer to someone's prayers. I believe the Lord reveals this in rare instances, only as needed. There are a few examples in the scriptures of similar revelations:*

> Then came the word of the Lord to Isaiah, saying, Go, and say to Hezekiah, Thus saith the Lord, the God of David thy father, I have heard thy prayer, I have seen thy tears: behold, I will add unto thy days fifteen years. And I will deliver thee and this city out of the hand of the king of Assyria: and I will defend this city. (Isaiah 38:4-6)

*Hence, the Holy Ghost did not answer Hezekiah's prayer directly. The Lord's servant/messenger, Isaiah, went to Hezekiah knowing both Hezekiah's prayer and the answer to Hezekiah's prayer.*

*Alma and Amulek, a recent convert, were granted a powerful spiritual gift also:*

> … for power was given unto them that they knew the thoughts and intents of his heart; for power was given unto them that they might know of these things according to the spirit of prophecy. (Alma 12:7)

*An angel of the Lord explained to Alma the younger that his visit was the answer to the prayers of the saints and his father Alma:* "Behold, the Lord hath heard the prayers of his people, and also the prayers of his servant, Alma, who is thy father; for he has prayed with much faith concerning thee that thou mightest be brought to the knowledge of the truth; therefore, for this purpose have I come to convince thee of the power and authority of God, that the prayers of his servants might be answered according to their faith." (Mosiah 27:14)

The new Primary president knew of my love for little children; I had gently cared for her babies, along with most of the other young mother's babies in our wards, through the years. (Through my gift of love for babies and toddlers I have been bountifully blessed to care for, hold, and cherish over 2,000 babies and toddlers.) The Primary president requested that I be her nursery leader. I was thrilled with the calling and never have I looked more forward to fulfilling my calling than this one.

We started with twenty-four two year olds; an additional dozen were in junior nursery. I had seven people under me, with two rotating off each week. I never wanted to take a single week off and I didn't. I loved the children and they loved me. This was the perfect calling for me because it was the hardest time in my life involving my immediate family. I really relied on the unconditional love of those precious angels!

They would run up and hug me in the hall and at ward activities. Many of them would crawl around, over, and under the benches to come sit in my lap during sacrament meeting. At our Ward Christmas party, there were more two-year olds lined up to see me than Santa! I had two in my lap and one at each knee. I had grown to love them all so much!

I went through three Primary Presidents and they all asked me if I needed to be released and I emphatically told them to please not release me from a calling I loved so much. They didn't release me.

While dressing for the late block meetings in December I noticed a wrapped hotel mint that had been sitting on my dresser for many months. I had a petite prompting to place the mint in my pocket. I remember thinking, "Oh, maybe I'll have bad breath later at church and need a breath freshener."

After five years of pure joy, I was once again sitting in front of these Celestial little boys and girls and saddened because they had turned three and would soon be moving on to Sunbeams. Yet, my disappointment was replaced with excitement to be receiving a new class of younger children in a few weeks. I looked at each of their faces, one by one, and saw brightness, hope, and love. After we sang some fun songs, we moved into the playroom. The nursery had a lesson room, playroom, and dining room, next to a kitchen. We would rotate the two large classes, junior and senior nursery, on a timed schedule, in and out of the three rooms. The playroom and the lesson/singing room had a folding curtain between them which allowed us to move a group without having to go into the hall and deal with noisy toddlers and runaways.

We had been enjoying the tots in their playtime; it was soon my turn to give the lesson. I informed the adults that I was going to set up the lesson a little early. As I left the playroom to go a short distance in the hallway to the lesson room, I was unable to turn left and do so. An unseen, physical force was preventing me from going to the room on the left. This gentle, yet strong, force kept me close to the wall moving to the right and forward to the dining room and kitchen and away from the lesson room.

I was fretting, "I really should be getting my lesson ready." There was nothing bad or evil about the force, so I wasn't worried that way. "Why can't I get to where I'm supposed to be?' This force was determined and as I attempted to turn back to the left several times, I simply physically could not do it. "But I need to do the lesson." I was firmly directed past the *dining room*.

This unseen angel directed me right to the door to the kitchen, which we only used to fill a pitcher for little water cups. I entered the kitchen which had a walkway to the left, in front of a straight parallel counter. The main counter and sinks were to the right. It was mid December and we had the late church, so it was rather dark outside. I noticed the token single fork or glass cup one often finds weren't even on the counter. The kitchen was spotless.

I then thought there might be a small scared child hiding around the corner or by the cove where the two large "garbage cans on wheels" fit under the counter. I slowly inched forward, watching and listening for a sign of anything. "Why was I in the kitchen and not doing my lesson like I promised my peers I would be preparing?" I didn't find any little child, leak, or problem of any sort. Then I heard a whimper coming from behind me near the door I had just entered.

Behind me there was one of the junior nursery sisters with her nose in the corner. She was between the doors to the hallway from the kitchen and another from the kitchen to the dining room. I never did turn on the kitchen lights. I thought, "I must have walked right past her, or maybe she followed me into the kitchen as I entered?"

I asked her if she was okay and if she needed any help. She was unresponsive. She was leaning into me, her back to my chest, and mumbling. The situation was rather peculiar; I now knew why I was firmly led to the kitchen. She would make little sounds now and then and slight movements. I had an impression to support her, so I pressed my torso against her back and placed my hands on her shoulders. I never could get a response from her and had no idea what was wrong with her.

I then thought, "This could look bad if someone came into the kitchen." "Oh bishop, you wouldn't believe Brother Laing pressing himself against this young sister in the dark kitchen corner!" I do not know if that thought came from the Spirit or me; either way it got me moving to a new location.

I decided to slowly move her into the dining area and hoped to get some help from the other workers. I had to practically carry her forward,

251

since she couldn't walk. As we entered the room, the junior primary was sitting down enjoying treats. A very young married couple was helping them. The couple and the kids just looked bug-eyed at our situation.

One adult asked, "What's wrong with her?"

I responded, "I don't know." This sister I was supporting then took her left foot out of her shoe and put her foot back into the shoe three times. "Hmm" I thought? Then this young mother I was supporting started to move more. She tried to throw her head hard into the concrete wall. That would have been a losing battle. I had enough of a grip on her that I prevented her from injuring herself against a very sturdy wall.

I hurriedly looked around the two of us and noticed the very sharp metal corner of the eraser holder ledge, the corner of the table, the doorknob, and whatever else she could unwittingly injure herself on. I then made an executive decision to take her down to the floor for protection. I gripped her shoulders tighter and forced her down. She sat on her folded legs. I was impressed when she pulled her very modest ¾ length skirt down over her calves. She was not in control of her own faculties, yet exhibited enough inner will to remain modest.

When she made noises and sharp movements it scared the little ones. The other workers decided to skip the lesson and place both groups of children in the nursery playroom, leaving me again, alone with this poor young mother. Now I was kneeling behind her with my torso tightly against hers; still gripping her shoulders for her protection.

Then she cried out the only audible words of the incident, "My BOYS!" Now, as if that angel was still there directing, each of her two boys came slowly and separately to the open door and made eye contact, respectively smiled, and waved at her. Then the nursery workers closed that door. Now we were totally alone again and I obviously hoped she would come around or snap out of it.

One leader popped her head in and said, "Do you need anything?"

I requested, "Go to the Relief Society and see if there's a nurse in the group."

Pretty soon, a nurse who is a friend of ours came in. She asked, "What's wrong with her? What has she been doing?"

I explained our experience up to that point in time and she said, "I don't know what's wrong with her! Where's her purse?"

I suggested she ask one of the female nursery workers.

A primary worker came in stating, "A young mother's purse is her diaper bag!"

The nurse rifled through the diaper bag and found something. She exclaimed, "She's diabetic! She's in diabetic shock! Who lives close to the church? We need a spoonful of honey or something really sweet, right away!"

Then the spirit reminded me of a hotel mint in my pocket. I gripped the young mother's right shoulder strongly and used my left hand to find, unwrap, and present a candy mint whose first three ingredients are: Sugar, sugar, and sugar of one sort or another.

"That's perfect, just place it in her mouth!"

"But won't she choke on it?"

"It will be fine—just put it in her mouth."

I placed the *inspired candy mint* in her mouth and she began to calm down. During that calming she went into convulsions for awhile. I could not control or hold her then and just let it play out on the floor while protecting her from coming in contact with anything dangerous or sharp. After the convulsions stopped I got her back up and started supporting her again.

One of the Relief Society sisters peeked in on us and really freaked out and got the EMTs there pronto. By the time the professionals arrived, this young mother revived and was able to tell them her name, address, and other vitals. The EMTs said she was fine now and just needed to be monitored. They asked if someone could stay with her. A friend of hers informed us that her husband was out-of-state on business and her mother was also out of town.

One of the Relief Society sisters said she would be able to take this recovering young mother and her two young boys home and then stay with them. I was very grateful that I listened to an unusually quiet prompting to place a candy mint in my pocket; a sweet hotel wrapped pillow mint that had been lying atop my dresser for five-six months simply collecting dust. (Journal 10/22/2006)

Bonding with a beautiful angel girl

*I love how President Monson puts it:*

"The sweetest spirit and feeling in all of mortality is when we have an opportunity to be on the Lord's errand and to know that He has guided our footsteps." (Thomas S Monson, *To the Rescue*, 482)

During the Saturday session of the conference, as President Monson stood to speak, the Spirit whispered "Suffer the little children to come unto me, and forbid them not: for of such is the kingdom of God." (Mark 10:14) His notes became a blur. He attempted to pursue the theme of the meeting as outlined, but the name and image of [the little girl] would not leave his mind. He listened to the Spirit and rearranged his schedule. Early the next morning, President Monson left the ninety and nine and traveled many miles to be at the bedside of the one. (Dieter F. Uchtdorf, GC, April 1970)

True, every man, every officer in the Church has the right to inspiration and revelation as to how he should conduct himself and how he should carry on his office and his duties. But when that inspiration and revelation come, they will never be out of harmony with Church discipline, nor with the revelations of the mind and will of God made known to His prophet on earth. The president of the Church, not a bishop of a ward, nor the president of a stake, lays down the rule for the Church. Whenever any Church officer gets any other impression than to follow the president of the Church, that impression is not coming from the right source. (J. Rueben Clark, CR, April 1944)

To all who hold positions of leadership, to the vast corps of teachers and missionaries, to heads of families, I should like to make a plea: In all you do, feed the spirit—nourish the soul. ". . . the letter killeth, but the Spirit giveth life" (Gordon B. Hinckley, GC, Oct 1967)

# 12. Blessed with a Multiplicity of Blessings

> "Blessed be the God and Father of our Lord Jesus Christ,
> who hath blessed us with all spiritual blessings in heavenly
> places in Christ:" (Ephesians 1:3)

One winter afternoon as we were visiting with friends their parents called to see if they could come over for priesthood blessings since there were two Melchizedek Priesthood holders present. After the grandparent's arrival to their children's home we shuffled eleven children into a sunroom, along with two chairs in the middle of the room for their parents. There was a long wooden bench running under the windows for everyone else to sit upon.

We proceeded with the simultaneous blessings for these choice grandparents. Golden rays of sun were streaming through the window panes and the Spirit of God absolutely filled that room to capacity! The experience was a real testimony building experience regarding faith and the power of the priesthood.

I had discerned that everyone in that room had felt some portion of that most abundant and wonderful spiritual outburst. I just knew they all had felt the Spirit in strength too. Sensing this was a great teaching moment; I asked all the children if they had felt that very special feeling. As I glanced individually to each of the children, parents, and grandparents there were many tear-filled eyes.

Then I testified: "That special feeling that we all felt and are feeling so strongly is the power of the Holy Ghost bearing testimony to each one of us that: this was a true priesthood ordinance, God approved those beautiful blessings, and those blessings were sealed in the name of Jesus Christ. This special feeling testifies to each of us that God lives, that this is a truth and that it is right." This experience turned a good day into a wonderful day. Having your entire family share bountifully in the Spirit of Truth is a very rewarding blessing.

> "... When a man speaketh by the power of the Holy Ghost
> the power of the Holy Ghost carrieth it unto the hearts of
> the children of men." (2 Ne. 33:1)

> "If ever there was a time when the Spirit of the Lord was
> indubitably manifest, it was on that occasion. Everyone
> present thrilled to it. Everyone present was aware, beyond

doubt, of the absolute rightness of it." (Patriarch to the Church Joseph F. Smith, CR, Oct 1945)

*During his first mission, Mathew Cowley had been ill for several months; he gave this report:*

There were sixty-five of us there then. We were in a big native hall and as soon as the opening exercises were over the grand old mission president put his chair down in the center of the hall and he motioned for me to come and sit in it. ... I could hardly make it I was so weak. I sat down there and sixty five of my brethren put their hands on me. If they couldn't get them on me they put them on the shoulders of each other, and the mission president blessed me.

His name was William Gardner, a man seventy-three years of age ... He hadn't been to school, but he was full of common sense and the Spirit of God. He got up every morning at four o'clock and went out to a secluded spot and prayed to the Lord. He lived right with him all the time. He put his hands on my head. It is the shortest blessing I believe I ever received. He said, 'In the name of Jesus Christ and by virtue and authority of the Holy Melchizedek Priesthood we command you to be made well immediately.' That was all. I stood up out of that chair perfectly well. The old strength came right back through me from head to foot just as if it were being poured into me, and it was, by the gift and power of God. (Mathew Cowley, *Man of Faith*, 142-144)

On my mission, one evening I suddenly got really sick and my companion had to take me home. I think it was the flu. I could barely get out of the car and into bed. I asked my companion to call the elders and they came over and gave me a blessing. As soon as their hands touched my head, before any words were said, I could feel the sickness leave me, and I was totally well. (Sister missionary)

"Now faith is the substance of things hoped for, the evidence of things not seen. For by it the elders obtained a good report." (Hebrews 11:1-2)

I was humbled to be asked to administer to our stake patriarch prior to his prostate surgery out-of-state. Patriarch Mark Robertson was the saint whom I visited as a young man for my patriarchal blessing. I had always looked up to him. Now he made me nervous with his request, yet I was honored. I was a young father serving in our bishopric. Our high priest group age averaged around 65 years old (They were referred to as the *Prostate Group*). The stake patriarch was one of our many older members. The Spirit attended that blessing in abundance, likely due to the great faith of this servant of God, our patriarch. The surgery was successful; all went well. Our patriarch was sitting in church the following Sunday with a generous smile. (Journal 9/26/1993)

> Patriarchal blessings contemplate an inspired declaration of the lineage of the recipient. A patriarchal blessing also includes an inspired and prophetic statement of the life possibilities and mission of the recipient. It may include such blessings, promises, advice, admonitions, and warnings as the patriarch may be prompted to give. It should always remain clear that the realization of all promised blessings is conditioned upon faithfulness and the Lord's will. (*Information and Suggestions for Patriarchs* [1970], 3-4). (Richard D. Allred, GC, Oct 1997)

> Many decades ago I went to receive my Patriarchal Blessing when I was a young married man. I had another obligation one hour later, yet I knew that visits with the Patriarch were long sometimes. I calmed myself down and decided I would be available for however long this would take.
> As I entered his home, he started visiting with me and asked me a few questions. I wasn't nervous at all, but he surprised me when he commented, "You have to be somewhere, so we better get started." I received a wonderful blessing and through his inspiration was able to make my other appointment on time. (Ward member)

> While serving as a Stake Mission President in Oregon I had an unusual experience. My counselors were great men, both with strong spirits and good counseling abilities. We met at the stake center once per week to correlate our activities for the coming period and discuss any new programs, problems, or changes needed in our missionary activities.

257

This particular evening one counselor reported that one of our member missionaries was having some personal problems and on a leave of absence. We were impressed to go visit with her that night in her home. We loaded up our material and continued our planning as we drove to her home. We arrived unexpectedly without having called her in advance.

As we entered her home we noticed her coat lying across the end of the couch as if she had just arrived home or was planning to go somewhere. After several minutes of visiting we realized she was very unhappy in her marriage. Her husband was not LDS and he resented her being a missionary. It was the second marriage for both of them. It was difficult for us to counsel her with these problems. We asked her if she would like a blessing.

One counselor anointed her and I pronounced the priesthood blessing upon her. Within the framework of the blessing I was prompted to say to her, **"Sister _____, do not do what you had planned to do this night. The Lord will not be pleased if you carry out your plan."** This was so pronounced that the words came fast and with elevated voice, as a voice of warning. More of the blessing was pronounced including a blessing for her to gain strength and to continue to do the Lord's work.

As we concluded the blessing she was in tears and as she stood up, she put her arms around my neck and sobbed for some time. We concluded our visit and headed back to the stake center to return to our respective homes. On the way back, my counselors questioned the blessing part about canceling her plans that evening. I told him that I was at a loss, just as he was. I had no idea why I was prompted to do so.

I arrived home about 11:00 pm. When I walked in the door, my wife informed me that this sister we had blessed had called me and was in tears and wanted to talk to me the minute I arrived home. I called her and through a sobbing voice she requested that I return to her home, she needed to talk further. I felt uncomfortable going alone, so my wife agreed to come along with me.

When we arrived, this sister was waiting at the door for us. She opened the door before we could knock. She then unfolded to us an incredible story, which answered the questions my counselors and I had.

That evening she had a heated argument with her husband. He had stormed off in a fit of anger. She felt so despondent that she made plans to end her life. She had already written a note to her children. She was just getting ready to pick up her coat from the couch and walk to a tall bridge over the Willamette River and there end her life by jumping off. This bridge is a very high suspension bridge similar to the Golden Gate Bridge near San Francisco.

She read the suicide note to us. She thanked me for interceding in this plan. She wanted to know how I knew what she was going to do. Why did our presidency come to her home and warn her about this ill conceived idea? I explained that no one had warned me. My counselor was inspired to say you needed visited right away, not another time. The Holy Spirit directed the three of us to come and to offer a blessing. It was the Spirit putting words in my mouth as we pronounced that very special and tender blessing upon her head.

Years later my family moved to the Salt Lake City area.

In a discussion about places in Oregon we had been, one of our neighbors said, "My mother lived in that very area." He wondered if we had ever met her.

This dear sister missionary was his mother we discovered back in the days! I thank the Lord for the Spirit that moved us that night to do the Lord's work. (A peer)


I know that the sweetest experience in all this life is to feel His promptings as He directs us in the furtherance of His work. I felt those promptings as a young bishop, guided to the homes where there was spiritual—or perhaps temporal—want..." (President Thomas S. Monson, GC, April 2008)

———— •◆• ————

When I was a senior in high school my dad had a sudden heart attack. He almost died and was very sick after that. No one in the family had health problems until then.

I am the second oldest of seven children. I was very scared of my dad dying and was upset for a long time. I went to the temple all of the time, prayed, and read my scriptures; I was still afraid of my dad leaving. I had a difficult time finding comfort. Suddenly school and extra activities didn't matter much. I only wanted dad to stay here and help raise all of us.

Awhile after his heart attack his doctors felt a pacemaker would be best for him. Prior to the pacemaker's installation we went on a family trip with my cousins. During this vacation my uncle gave my dad a blessing. I don't remember much of what was said, except for, "You will be here on earth until your work is finished." I knew right away that my dad was going to be okay. I knew he would still be here to take care of all of us.

That was a huge tender mercy for me. It still wasn't easy but, I knew the Lord had a plan for my dad on the earth still. I am very grateful for priesthood blessings. They always comfort me with what I need at the time. My dad is still with us, many years later and I am so grateful to have him with us." (A young friend)

During my mission to Sweden, the Church decided to divide the country into two missions. Our mission president's younger brother was called to serve. Our new mission president, Paul Oscarson, was only 30 years old! His wife was only 25! We had four elders that were actually older than our mission president. Many Elders were older than the mission president's wife. (Our original mission president was Richard Oscarson who was around 40 years old at the time of his call to serve in Sweden.)

One of these older elders, all were converts, was already a practicing doctor. Many of us younger elders had not even started college. This doctor elder became quite ill and he was experiencing consistent nosebleeds. Nothing the "doctor" tried, or that his Swedish doctors recommended, worked. He had received a priesthood blessing from the Assistants to the President and from our Mission President also. This bloody nose nuisance had been going on for about one month and the elder was unable to do any missionary work. This situation was difficult for his companion, obviously, who had to stay indoors with his constantly sick missionary companion.

President Paul Oscarson gave him an ultimatum, informing the sick elder that he would be sent home to America to heal, if his problem persisted pass thirty days. This elder's final request is that I give him a blessing. I was surprised at the request. We had never been companions nor really worked together. I only knew this elder from Zone Conferences and Mission meetings. He was already a doctor and I felt like "a nobody"... coming from a poor family in a small town in Wyoming.

The sick Elder and I did not even work in the same area of the country. The Assistants to the President informed my companion and me of this situational problem and this elder's special request. We scheduled time for a special visit. They brought the sick elder to us in the only car in the mission. (We were all on bikes and an infrequent bus.)

But why did he want me to administer to him? When they arrived we set about to honor his request.

The main thing I remember about the blessing from his Heavenly Father was "I bless you to be healed so that you can fulfill your mission and the righteous desires of your heart."

Well, I couldn't believe it and I'm not sure my leaders could either, but this sick missionary, that had been sick for 4 weeks, was healed on the spot! The bleeding totally stopped. He had no further issues as he completed his full mission assignment with gusto. I knew the righteous desire of his heart was to finish his mission with honor and I desired that for him also. This was a real testimony to me of the power of simple faith and the priesthood. (Missionary journal)

> And a woman having an issue of blood twelve years, which had spent all her living upon physicians, neither could be healed of any. Came behind him, and touched the border of his garment: and immediately her issue of blood stanched.
>
> And Jesus said, Somebody hath touched me: for I perceive that virtue is gone out of me. And when the woman saw that she was not hid, she came trembling, and falling down before him, she declared unto him before all the people for what cause she had touched him, and how she was healed immediately. And he said unto her, Daughter, be of good comfort: thy faith hath made thee whole; go in peace. (Luke 8:43-44, 46-48)

> During the fall of 1941 we and our small baby moved from Durango, Colorado to Salt Lake City, Utah. We moved to an apartment across the road from the city cemetery. We became active members of a ward in the Emigration Stake. Our elder's quorum was responsible for going to the hospital to bless the sick. I was a very *green elder*, having not been active for too long. I shall never forget my first visit to the hospital.

My companion, a member of the elder's quorum presidency, and I had administered to several sick persons. As we were walking down the hospital hall a nurse came rushing out of one of the rooms. She passed us, then wheeled around, and asked us if we were Mormon elders. She then asked if we could administer to a young mother who had lost her baby and was very distraught.

The nurse was concerned about the mother's well being. Because of her tragedy she was rolling and tossing and causing hemorrhaging. As we entered the room there was definitely a young woman pulling at her hair, rolling back and forth and sobbing. As we walked to her bed, the counselor grasped her hand and patted it gently. He assured her that the Lord loved her and that we were servants of the Lord sent there to attend to her needs.

He handed me the oil. With great anxiety I performed the anointing on her head and promised she would be made whole.

We both laid our hands on her head. As soon as my companion addressed the Lord, a peace descended upon the room. The mother relaxed completely. You could feel the tenseness subside in her body. What a beautiful blessing she received.

The counselor traced the purpose of life and reassured her that the blessings of motherhood extended beyond this mortal life. He promised her that one day, in the Lord's due time, she would see this lovely baby who was perfect and only needed to obtain a body to go to the Celestial Kingdom. He promised her that she would rear her child. Then with great feeling he promised her that she would yet have other healthy sons and daughters that would bless her life.

Tears were pouring down my cheek bones as I felt the hand of the Lord. She felt the hand of the Lord and thanked us. The nurse was still dabbing at her eyes when we left. The mother was now at peace. She knew that the Lord loved her because she felt His presence.

I have always been grateful to this elder for showing me the true power of the priesthood. (Fellow missionary)

---

While serving in a branch on my mission, we rented the Catholic Church for our services. In the branch there was a man with two daughters; the mother had left the family. We got to know them pretty well. Anyway, he was sick and in the hospital and asked for us Elders to come and give him a blessing.

I was voice for the blessing and it was the oddest blessing I had ever given. What was odd about it is that it really wasn't a blessing but a rebuke. I rebuked this man pretty straightforward. I just knew he was involved in illegal drugs. I told him to cease and desist! I warned him that if he did not quit that he would lose his family and his salvation; that it would all be taken away from him.

Then I blessed him with a promise, "If you will turn your life around, you will be blessed with the blessings of eternity." When I got done with that blessing I was shocked! What did I just say? Soon after that I was transferred out of the area. A little over one year later I ended up serving in the same stake as this branch was in. We were attending stake conference and when they read the names of new elders in the stake, they asked this man I had rebuked to stand up.

I went over to talk to him and as it turned out, I was able to ordain him an elder. It was a sweet full-circle experience. It was so cool; he had turned to the Lord. (A relative)

---

A great friend invited me to go and help administer to his brother's newborn baby at the hospital. Glad to oblige, we met up in a hospital room. The little baby boy wasn't breathing on his own, yet his color looked good.

As we laid fingers on the tiny infant's head (hands wouldn't fit) my friend tried to offer a blessing. There was a cold, dark, humid feeling—very unusual and almost hard to describe as far as blessings for children go.

There was a long pause in the blessing and then my good friend blurted out, "Lord, if it be thy will, send a spirit to this child!" And that was it, no more, no less.

His brother and sister-in-law looked at him with hopeful eyes. With a grim look strewn across his face, he shook his head "no." Next, they looked at me and I gave a little shake of my head as well as we all began to shed tears together.

Afterwards, my friend explained, "Words just wouldn't come!"

Later my buddy questioned, "Did you feel that?"

"Yes!" I replied, "I have never felt so much coldness, hopelessness, and darkness during a blessing."

The feelings are completely opposite of the usual blessings for babies and those accompanying little children. We had experienced and felt the same; having a mutual witness that the baby would not be healed nor survive.

Three days later, the professionals unhooked the machines due to no sign of life. I hoped to never have this experience again.

The Lord teaches us: "… he that hath faith in me shall be healed, and is not *appointed to death*, shall be healed." (D&C 42:48)

This situation, "appointed to death" is difficult to describe, yet the feeling is so tangible—one could cut it with a knife. (Journal, 7/22/1990)

————— •◆• —————

A young couple in our ward had a small one-year old baby girl. She was a beautiful thing. One day she developed a small water blister on her face. At first her parents thought she had somehow been burned. But the next morning it had spread over most of her face. They took her to the family doctor. Upon examination he had her immediately committed to the UCLA Medical Hospital. The little girl had contracted a rare disease which was nearly always fatal. The water blisters, similar to a 2nd degree burn, would spread over her entire body. The heart would not be able to handle the load. The water would not allow the skin to function properly as a cooling mechanism.

I was asked to go to the hospital and give her a priesthood blessing. Her uncle, a ward member, was there to assist me. We scrubbed down as though we were to help in a delicate operation. We then removed our clothing and put on surgical trousers, tied at the ankle along with a green surgical gown. We slipped on some sterile slippers. We scrubbed down again. With hair covered and masks over our faces we went into the room. I sealed the anointing and gave her a blessing.

I shall never forget what happened. I confirmed the anointing and began to give her a blessing that she would get well. I felt that I had the right and obligation as a priesthood holder to make such a promise. I had faith she would get well.

During my blessing I heard a voice as clearly as could be saying firmly, '**NO!**'

Then I began to plea with the Lord. I prayed that professional staff would be inspired to find a cure for this child.

Again, as clearly and distinctly as before I got the same message, '**NO!**'

I was devastated for I knew she would not live; that beautiful child just beginning the sojourn of her life. She was going back to God's presence as an innocent sweet spirit.

After leaving the room we placed all our surgical clothes in a cleaning hopper, scrubbed down again to avoid passing the "bug" on to some other child. I tried to console the parents and drove home. As I walked up to my front door I could hear our phone ringing inside the house. I sensed who it was and knew the message would be that this special little girl had peacefully passed to paradise. I was informed that she died peacefully within minutes of our leaving the hospital.

The Lord does not always say, "YES" He can say "NO." (A peer)

As I experienced the death of loved ones, including my father, my mother, and my wife, the comforting revelations of the Holy Ghost gave me the strength to carry on. The Spirit affirms that there is purpose in mortal adversities and gives assurance of the resurrection and the reality of family relationships sealed for eternity. (Dallin H. Oaks, GC, April 2002)

On a beautiful Saturday morning, a family in the ward asked me to come and administer to their father who was not doing very well. The home was all abuzz with activity because a daughter in the home's upcoming wedding and reception were that very day. One of my daughters was asked to come over earlier to fix up the triplet-girl's hair. We had cherished the triplets since newborns.

This family lived down the street so I walked on over to their home. As I arrived there were paramedics driving up in an ambulance. Working in tandem with the EMTs, I administered to this grandpa. The interesting thing about this blessing is that all the words spoken were meant for grandpa's children and grandchildren only. Nothing at all was said about grandpa in his own blessing.

Once again, a very cold and empty feeling came over me as I ended the blessing. And again, there were hopeful eyes gazing at me for a positive report, from his daughter and son-in-law.

I pursed my lips, showed sorrow in my eyes, and shook my head "No." At which time the EMTs pronounced him dead as they recorded that exact minute as their father's "time of death" for the record.

The family and I had a good long cry and hug. (Journal, 2/03/2002)

---

I have not only used my priesthood to bless others but have been the recipient of multiple priesthood miracles. In 1984, I became seriously ill while we were on a family vacation in the Tetons. We aborted the trip, returned home immediately, and I was taken to LDS hospital, where I was diagnosed with *coccidio mycosis meningitis*, a fungal form of that illness that is not only rare but nearly always fatal!

The only antidote that could help was a drug called Amphotericin-B (dubbed "Ampho-terrible"), necessitating that a shunt be implanted into the ventricle of my brain to deliver the drug, since at that time there was none capable of crossing the blood-brain barrier. It is a risky procedure that often results in severe brain damage. The surgeon was Dr. LaVerne S Erickson—who would, a couple of weeks later, also be part of a team that would successfully separate a set of Siamese twins at the University of Utah.

Knowing what we were facing, my wife's mother asked Elder Boyd K. Packer, whom she knew well, if he would be willing to give me a priesthood blessing prior to the surgery. He came in the early morning hours the day of my surgery and in the blessing petitioned the Lord that the surgeon's hands be guided. Dr. Erickson later told me that instead of the multiple probes often required to locate the passage way to the ventricles, he had placed the shunt perfectly on the "very first pass", something that never happens. This was the first of many miracles that have occurred for the more than 30 years since contracting the illness.

For more than 20 of those years I've been on a protocol at the National Institutes of Health with the nation's leading fungal authority, Dr. John E Bennett, who says he's never seen anyone but me survive this illness with a functioning brain. He so frequently expressed his amazement that I survived with no brain impairment that I finally told him about the blessing I'd received from an Apostle of God.

Dr. Bennett immediately threw his hands in the air and said, "Well! That explains it!" Then he added, "It's certainly not anything we've been doing." (A relative)

"... The Spirit of the Lord ... to guide you in wisdom's paths that ye may be blessed, prospered, and preserved—" (Mosiah 2:36)

---

Today we were asked to give a special blessing to a brother in our Care Center Branch. Although healthy and active less than two years ago, his family had made the difficult decision to turn off the machines that were now keeping him alive.

A dear friend, who would often wheel the brother suffering from Lou Gehrig's disease, had requested that we give this dear brother a blessing of "release from this life and mortal body." The family had preapproved the same.

The family reported to us that he had lost all motion and could not even open his eyes anymore. As we approached him in his room and lovingly touched his hands and shoulders to comfort him, prior to the blessing, he opened his eyes and actually tracked and looked at each one of us (three).

The Spirit that attended this blessing was very somber and serine. When we had finished this singular blessing, the good brother's eyes were firmly closed, as before, and he appeared very peaceful. (Journal 9/30/18)

> President George Albert Smith suffered a light stroke that paralyzed his right arm and slightly impaired his speech. ... He continued to slip downhill, losing more functions and contracting new fevers. On April 1, he calmly told his family that he felt the end was approaching and repeated his gratitude for his blessings. On April 4, 1951, he wrote his last journal entry: "Today is my 81st birthday. The day dawned clear and beautiful." David O. McKay, his first counselor, administered a *blessing of release*. Surrounded by his children and grandchildren ... he died peacefully and without pain in the early evening. (*Journal of Mormon History*, Vol. 34, No 4)

*In my estimation, blessings of release are proper when guided by the Holy Spirit. Blessings of release are not listed nor mentioned in the Church's official Ordinances and Priesthood Blessings.*

---

> This is the miracle story in my family: I was a young baby and very sick in the hospital. The doctor sent word to have all of my family come and say goodbye to me. The doctor

told my parents and grandparents there was nothing more they could do to help me.

My grandfather gave me a priesthood blessing and then held my hand and wouldn't let go. He said, 'If they come to take her to the other side, I'm not letting her go!" Everyone else eventually went home, except my wonderful grandpa. He held my hand all night long.

In the morning, the doctor came in my hospital room, expecting to find a dead baby. He got out a shiny pocket watch on a chain and made it swing above me. I reached up and grabbed the pocket watch. The astonished doctor exclaimed, "Something much better than medicine has healed this baby!"

That was really a miracle and my grandfather was such a great man. (Our friend)

My grandparents had a baby that was not doing well and became very sickly. One afternoon the baby stopped breathing and started to turn blue. They called the elders to come and administer to their child. The baby's fingertips were turning purple.

The elders arrived and exclaimed, "This baby is dead!"

My grandmother was totally deaf, yet very inspired. Though unable to hear her husband's and the elder's conversation, she spoke out, "I called you over to give our baby a blessing."

At this point the elders complied and blessed the baby, yet only gave a blessing of comfort to the parents.

Somewhat frustrated, the pleading deaf mother said, "I asked you to bless the baby, I don't need the blessing!"

Surprised that she knew what was happening even though she couldn't hear them, the elders complied again and administered to the baby once more. The second blessing promised a recovery and full, long life to the lifeless baby's body. Soon the color came back into the child and he returned to normal health and grew up strong.

That baby was my father. (A family friend)

As I was servicing a smaller account in Bountiful, Utah, I had the distinct impression to share a recent General Conference talk with the buyer. We had become friends through bi-monthly visits over the years. I knew she was a faithful woman. I asked for her permission to go off topic and she agreed to the same.

I explained to her how impressed I was with Elder Dallin H Oaks priesthood talk on blessings. I paraphrased; "There are five main parts to a blessing and the words of the blessing were the least important part and often it doesn't matter what the blessing says."

She excitedly responded, "That is the very topic my inactive son is hung up on! That's perfect! I can't wait to read it. When he blessed his father and then lost his father to an early death; he felt that the blessing was useless and took it very hard!"

She thanked me immensely; I now knew why that talk came to my mind just at the right moment. (Journal 4/17/2010)

———————◆———————

Patriarch Eldred G. Smith frequently shared a story about an independent young woman with little opportunity that was promised a good education in her patriarchal blessing:
She was elated, and she went out of the office feeling very happy. Before she had gone half a block ... she fell to earth out of her cloud with a realization that going to college cost money, and she did not have any, nor the means to get it.
The thought came to her to **go visit her aunt**. Without stopping to analyze that impression ... she went to visit her aunt and told her aunt of her experience—and cried on her shoulder.
Her aunt said, "I know an elderly woman who lives down the street a few blocks. She has at various times helped young girls get through college in return for the help the girls can give to her." The young woman went on the run to this elderly woman's home, and within two weeks from the time she received her patriarchal blessing, she registered at the University of Utah.
But she did not stop to analyze that impression; she acted upon it. As a result she met the woman who gave her the opportunity of receiving her education. (CR, April 1952)

*It is intriguing to note that the impression was to visit her aunt, who was not the actual answer—yet her aunt was the conduit to the earthly angel who fulfilled the young woman's blessing's promise.*

———————◆———————

When I was the bishop of a small town in Wyoming, we were many miles from any temple. The Idaho Falls Temple had recently been built (1945) and was designated as our temple. It was still over seven hours away. There were many people in our ward who hadn't attended the temple for many years or not at all. We decided to organize a "temple excursion" and travel as a group.

One young couple with two children was among those desirous to attend since they hadn't been since they were married several years before. We all stayed at the same hotel and planned to attend an early evening session.

That evening the young husband came to my hotel room to tell me that their baby was very ill. He had been throwing up all day and not able to eat anything. He was afraid they wouldn't be able to leave the sick baby with a sitter as they had planned. He also suggested that I assist him in giving the baby a blessing. After the blessing, the father hadn't made any further plans to attend the session.

I returned to my hotel room and offered a prayer that the young father would be able to have the faith that his child would be healed so that he and his wife could attend the temple. I asked the Lord to cause a smile to come on the baby's face so we would know he was healed.

My wife and I then returned to our friend's room. He met us at the door with the baby in his arms. When the baby saw my wife he reached out to her with a big smile on his face! The father was overwhelmed at the baby's reaction and said that this was the first time the baby had smiled in over two days. I explained to him about the prayer I had offered and how the Lord had answered my prayer. His response was, "Bishop, I have just seen the priesthood in action." (Ivin Lynn)

*Ivin and Julia Lynn were the first living examples for me of a couple "enduring to the end." They were snowbirds in Phoenix when we were sealed in the Mesa, AZ, Temple. These angelic, white-haired sweethearts blessed us with their surprise presence at our temple wedding. (1980)*

We had the unique opportunity to pray and seek inspiration weekly to fully staff a brand new ward. First we needed to visit all the people the Lord had inspired us to choose for leadership callings. It seemed like we set people apart for and hour or two every Sunday for several months.

The bishop would bless the Relief Society president, then I would bless the first counselor, after which my peer blessed the 2nd counselor; and likewise throughout all the other presidencies. As I was thinking about blessings being rather rote or similar, the Lord proved me wrong again, once more. The individuality and uniqueness that was apparent throughout each respective blessing was a great testimony to me of the Lord's inspiration and the faithfulness of His members. What a wonderful witness of Heavenly Father blessing his children through the Holy Ghost's inspiration to the bishopric. (Journal, 4/12/1992)

We were out with extended family on a Friday night enjoying laser tag and a nice dinner in Salt Lake City. After an hour drive home, arriving at 11:30, we finally got to bed by midnight, which is very late for us. Early in the morning our youngest son, in the next room, started violently throwing up. He hit everything! We rushed out of bed: one taking the boy, PJ's, and pillowcase; the other taking the blanket, sheets, and treating the carpet. It was a massive mess.

Our little one felt better after losing everything. We finally all got back to bed and back to sleep comfortably once again. At 3:45 am Saturday morning our phone rang. A friend in the ward asked me to come over and assist in blessing his wife.

After I arrived, she was obviously in great pain, exclaiming, "My back hurts! It's worse than childbirth!"

We administered to her atop the large bed. She calmed down, but felt prompted to go to the emergency room. I could sense that she was very tired and scared. I suggested that her husband go with her and promised that I would take care of their six small children. I knew all their little ones and their names.

When their family first moved into the ward, we invited them over to get to know them. The young mother questioned:

"Brother Laing, we have six children, six and under, and NOBODY ever invites us over. Why did you?"

"Because—I absolutely adore little children!"

"Oh."

We became friends from that day forward.

Back to the middle-of-the "short night" bedroom blessing: they agreed to let me tend their flock, thanked me, and left for the hospital. I attempted to get back to sleep and wondered what the morning would bring.

A few hours later the morning brought a bunch of surprised children (six), three or four of them in soiled diapers and one was a "blowout!" I didn't know where anything was. Luckily the six-year old was able to show me where the diapers and wipes were. Then it was cold cereal. I was rifling through all the cupboards to find where they stored cereal boxes.

My inspired wife knew of my very short night and sent our two girls, eleven and thirteen, to rescue me at 8:30 am. I was a zombie and my daughters helped get the children cleaned and dressed, which I was very grateful for. Our friends came back that morning and the husband had to leave to work in SLC, while the wife needed bed rest. Our daughters volunteered to stay all day. A neighbor brought in dinner and my wonderful wife went over also. We then helped bring some of the little ones to church on Sunday. I took a Saturday and Sunday nap that weekend! (Journal 2/23/1997)

Nearly two years later we were going to serve in the Ogden, UT, Temple with this fine young couple. We had to wait in the car awhile for them because the real estate agent in our ward was visiting with them. When they came to our car I commented, "I hope that was your home teacher."

They quietly told us they were selling their home and moving to another city in two weeks! We were sad to be losing such a wonderful couple and family from our ward and friendship circle.

There are five or six arteries to get to Ogden from Roy, UT. We chose to take the least traveled which turns through an industrial section. As we rounded the bend things just didn't look right. It was dusk and harder to see. We realized that there was a train stalled on the tracks blocking the entire road. Then we noticed a "pancaked" car. We could determine that she had run under the train and hit the wheels on the other side and then bounced back. The train tracks cross the road at an angle, not perpendicular at this location. There were no lights or bells or anything.

We got out and found a young girl, amazingly still alive, pinned tightly inside. She must've ducked down or was pushed down by an angel to save her from the crushing roof. We called 911. She was lucid and we discovered she was LDS.

We asked her if she would like a blessing and she agreed. I had some consecrated oil in my suit. We had to finagle our arms through the wreckage, both of us only able to get one arm inside. We knew that would suffice under the circumstances. Our friend wrote down the girl's mother's phone number and called her. Her mom screamed. We gave her mom the address of the accident as the emergency vehicles arrived, indirectly due to the blocked road. We hurried to backtrack and connect to one of the other arteries into downtown Ogden.

We had missed our planned dinner (no one was hungry now) and made our temple session. After the temple, we decided to go to the hospital and check on the young girl. Her family was at her bedside and she was already on the mend. They thanked us.

I had the thought, "Boy, I'm really glad the realtor was there and slowed us down five minutes. We could have been the ones to wreck into the stalled train with no lights or warnings!" (Journal 12/12/1999)

---

We were living in Texas on a military base. I had been raised Presbyterian and always attended church as a girl and read the bible often. As a teenager I even had a desire to become a youth minister. But I felt that my prayers were too rote; just say it and you're done. It did not feel like I was talking to anyone. I often felt that there was something more and I desired to find it.

One evening we were visiting with some new friends we had made. We discussed faith and religion a little bit. This man got up saying, "There's something I need to read to you. It's very personal and sacred." He came back later with a long paper and said, "This is my Patriarchal blessing and I feel that I must share my blessing with you."

That blessing touched my heart so strongly and my emotions showed the same. I exclaimed, "I want to get baptized now!" I had felt that feeling I had been searching for over the years.

Our friend informed me, "You cannot just be baptized right away; you need to take the missionary lessons and learn about the church." So I did meet with the missionaries and was baptized not long after that.

I do not remember a thing that was in his patriarchal blessing, yet I will never forget how I felt. This was a major turning point in my life and in the proper direction. I am grateful our new friend followed this inspiration that came to him. (Ward member)

---

We were at a large family reunion in the wilds of southern Utah. There were around eight four-wheelers that kept the children and adults quite entertained.

One of our daughters and her husband were out for a long ride on individual machines when she had a strong impression to slow down. She obeyed the prompting as a large deer crossed in front of them. After that they both had an impression to turn around and head back. Not sure why, they followed the direction.

After I felt the children all had enough time on the toys, I decided to take a ride, since there was one idle machine.

No matter what I tried the four-wheeler would not start. I checked everything and found: gas in the tank, the power on, and the fuel line was "on." I wore myself out trying to start it and was getting a bit frustrated. Just about then my daughter came running down from the cabin and gasped, "Can you come and give a blessing to Tommie? He drove his four-wheeler off the road into a 30' ravine and it snapped the axel and he's really hurting!"

I told her I would be glad to administer to him and that I would be right up. As I walked up the hill I said a prayer and sought heaven's inspiration. I was thinking the young man must have internal injuries from such a serious wreck.

He was moaning and in pain and felt like he'd broken ribs. After the blessing he obviously felt better and later there were no injuries or broken bones, yet a bunch of various body pains and scrapes. What was most amazing to me was that I walked back down to the four-wheeler that just wouldn't start, still sitting there—now the engine started up easily on the first try! (Journal 7/21/2008)

---

Our youngest son had made an appointment to receive his Patriarchal Blessing. We were pleased that he invited us to join him for his special blessing. He informed us that the Patriarch and he were fasting. We chose to fast along with them. On the appointed day we met in the Patriarch's home, where he taught us. This humble brother was very spiritual and a servant of the Lord. He had served as a bishop three times prior to becoming a permanent patriarch.

I had forgotten how powerful fasting and praying with a purpose could be. We felt an outpouring of the Spirit before, during, and after the blessing. His home was rife with the Holy Spirit. It is absolutely fascinating in how many different positive forms the Holy Ghost can touch us. During the blessing it was as if slender sheets of the Spirit were raining down upon us and passing through our bodies from top to bottom. It was akin to a spiritual shower; an overall cleansing! The experience was one of those that physically tires you out, yet you wish it would never stop. This was one of the more unique feelings of the Spirit in my life.

Our son's blessing was amazing and we thanked him again for the invitation to attend. We had a great discussion about the Holy Ghost obviously ratifying the patriarch, the priesthood, and the blessing, among other things. (My journal 6/2/2012)

It was a great day for Nate. He received his patriarchal blessing. He was promised awesome blessings, such as: witnessing the second coming, being a judge in Israel, a wife and children, gifts, and talents. It was such a spiritual occasion. (My wife's journal 6/13/2012)

*Sharing this special experience with our friends in the ward, they added the following:*

We took our son to the same Patriarch and I have never been in a more spiritual home. When our son was receiving his blessing it was as if the room was totally filled with the Holy Spirit, while we were wrapped in an extremely soft, thick blanket of the Spirit. The feelings were so amazingly wonderful. (Their journal 12/23/2017)

"... were wrought upon and cleansed by the power of the Holy Ghost ..." (Moroni 6:4)

My uncle was dying from advanced cancer and I felt impressed that he should receive a priesthood blessing. He was not a member, yet he believed in Christ and he also believed in healing by the laying on of hands. I had recently moved to Pennsylvania.

I tried to contact the Branch President, but could not find him. I finally looked up the mission home, twenty-five miles away and called them. I explained my situation and asked for help finding the local leader.

The mission president said, "Oh, I'm so sorry sister, but this man is no longer a member of our church." (The local leader had recently been excommunicated.)

So the mission president contacted some of his missionaries in my area and they got in touch with me. I gave them the contact information and they were able to give my uncle a blessing. Afterwards I spoke with the missionaries and the one that gave the blessing was just beside himself.

"Oh sister, what have I done?"

"I don't know; what have you done?"

"I promised that there would be no pain, in the blessing. How could I have said that to a man in the advance stages of cancer?"

"Did you intend to say that?"

"No."

"Don't you worry; it's from the Lord."

The next weekend my aunt told me that my uncle was pain-free for this last week and it was such a wonderful blessing. He passed away the next day. (A friend)

---

We were attending the baptism and confirmation of the triplets, on our street, which we had known and cherished since their births. What I felt when participating in the confirmations describes similar feelings to temple prayers and administrative blessings, all involving the Holy Priesthood, after the Order of the Son of God.

From my journal we read:

The Spirit was so strong at the beginning of the confirmations. It feels as though my spirit stands to attention and, along with the Holy Ghost, wraps my body with an encircling energy that enthralls my entire bosom. Then this tangible tingling holy power runs through my arms to my hands and to/through the person being confirmed, set apart, blessed, ordained, etc. (Journal 5/28/2006)

"This burning in the bosom is not purely a physical sensation. It is more like a warm light shining within your being." (Body K. Packer, *Ensign*, Nov 1994)

---

*Harold B. Lee shares his experience with a remarkable blessing:*

I was suffering from an ulcer condition that was becoming worse and worse. We had been touring a mission; my wife, Joan, and I were impressed the next morning that we should get home as quickly as possible, although we had planned to stay for some other meetings.

On the way across the country, we were sitting in the forward section of the airplane. Some of our Church members were in the next section. As we approached a certain point en route, someone laid his hand upon my head. I looked up, I could see no one. That happened again before we arrived home, again with the same experience. Who it was, by what means or what medium, I may never know, except I knew that I was receiving a blessing that I came a few hours later to know I needed most desperately.

As soon as we arrived home, my wife very anxiously called the doctor. It was now about 11 o'clock at night. He called me to come to the telephone, and he asked me how I was; and I said, 'Well, I am very tired. I think I will be all right.' But shortly thereafter, there came massive hemorrhages which, had they occurred while we were in flight, I would not be here today talking about it.

I know that there are powers divine that reach out when all other help in not available. (GC, April 1973)

*My wife and I have also had the privilege of being blessed through the veil, for lack of a better term. If our spiritual eyes were opened, we would be able to see who was graciously blessing us. Mine felt like a good-sized man's hands being gently laid on my head, pressing down upon my hair. This happened a few times. I looked up expecting to see someone and no one was there.*

*Mark E. Peterson shares the following:*

One of the bishop's brought his mother to the stand, as she wished to shake hands and send a message back home.

"Will you give a message from me to Brother Thomas E. McKay?"

"I shall be very glad to."

"Two years ago Elder Thomas E. McKay was down here to our stake conference. I was blind. I knew that if he would lay his hands upon my head I would receive my sight again. I sent over to the conference and had him come. He and the other brethren laid their hands upon my head and blessed me. Now you see that without even the use of glasses I have been able to read ... will you tell him what I have done here today and express to him the gratitude I feel? ... Whereas I was blind two years ago, now I can see and I can read without glasses." (CR, Oct 1951)

A young father and neighbor in our ward called me over to help administer to their sick baby. I anointed the baby and the father sealed the anointing and administered the blessing. I had held their baby several times and had a great love for him and his family. As the father began speaking I could feel mild electrical charges waving down through my arms and into the baby. I have often felt this when giving the blessing, but only occasionally when assisting in the blessing. The baby calmed down and according to his dad was healed from the point of the blessing. I literally felt the power of the priesthood during that administration.

The law of spiritual fluid, its communicative properties, and the channel by which it is imparted from one person to another, bear some resemblance or analogy to the laws and operations of electricity. Like electricity, it is imparted by the contact of two bodies, through the channel of the nerves. (Parley P. Pratt, *KST*, 100)

*The following story, (fall of 1833) of my fourth-great-grandfather has been printed several times in the Church News and church manuals:*

When the mob first began to gather and threaten us, I was selected to go to another county and buy powder and lead. Soon after I returned, a mob of about 150 men came upon us in the dead hour of night. I was aroused from my sleep by the noise caused by the falling houses and had barely time to escape to the woods with my wife and two children when they reached my house and proceeded to break in the door and tear the roof off ... The next day we heard firing down in the Whitmer settlement. Seventeen of our brethren volunteered to go down and see what it meant. When these 17 men arrived at the Whitmer settlement, the mob came against them and took some prisoners. Brother David Whitmer brought us the news of them and said, "Every man go, and every man take a man."

We all responded and met the mob in battle in which I was wounded with an ounce ball and two buckshot, all entering my body just at the right side of my navel into my stomach. Several others were also shot. After the battle I took my gun and powder horn and headed for home. When I got about halfway I became faint and thirsty. I wanted to stop at Brother Whitmers house to lay down. The house, however, was full of women and children, they were so frightened. The mob threatened that wherever the found a wounded man, they would kill men, women and children.

I continued on and arrived home, or rather at a house in the field that the mob had not torn down. There I found my wife and children and a number of other women who had assembled. They assisted me upstairs ...

The next morning I was taken further off from the road, that I might be concealed from the mob. I bled inwardly until my body was filled with blood. I remained in this condition until the next day at five p.m. I was then examined by a doctor who said I could not possibly live and was pronounced dead. David Whitmer, however, sent me word that I should live and not die...

After the doctor had left me, brother Newell Knight came to see me and sat down on the side of my bed. He laid his right hand on my head, but never spoke. I felt the Sprit resting upon me at the crown of my head before his hand touched me. I knew immediately that I was going to be healed. It seemed to form like a ring under the skin and followed down my body. When the ring came to the wound, another ring formed around the first bullet hole, also the second and third. Then a ring formed on each shoulder and on each hip and followed down to the ends of my fingers and toes and left me. I immediately arose and discharged three quarts of blood or more, with some pieces of my clothes that had been driven into my body by the bullets.

I then dressed myself and went outdoors and saw the falling of the stars ... It was one of the grandest sights I ever beheld. From that time on not a drop of blood came from me and I never afterwards felt the slightest pain from my wounds, except that I was weak from the loss of blood." (Philo Dibbles diary and life history, 1806-1895)

(See *Church News*, Oct 1978 *Ensign* - The Joseph Knight Family, *Aaronic Priesthood Manual* 3 – Lesson 37 – 1995; Primary 5 – Lesson 27 – 1997, *Church History* - Lesson 7 – 2003, D&C Lesson 15 – 1999; and *Our Heritage* - Lesson 4, 1996)

*This great "great grandpa" of ours lived a full and rich life in the Gospel and he also lived 63 more years following the mob shooting!*

# 13. He Will Guide You into All Truth

The Holy Ghost speaks with a voice that you *feel* more than you *hear*. It is described as a "still small voice." And while we speak of "listening" to the whisperings of the Spirit, most often one describes a spiritual prompting by saying, "I had a *feeling* ..." (Boyd K. Packer, *Ensign*, Nov 1994)

When I was living in Phoenix, AZ, the summers had 110-117 degree weather which required short routes for errands; otherwise the heat would overtake me. For efficient trips to the city, I had to plan each stop, including where to park and how to get in and out of the car quickly. After such planning one morning, the thought occurred to call a lady in my ward. This lady was one of the most talented women in the ward. She knew how to do everything and was usually the one who helped others. I felt so small next to her and thought, "What could she possible need from me?" Besides, I had planned my day out so perfectly; I decided that I would call her after my errands. After all, I wouldn't be gone that long.

Unfortunately, I miscalculated the time it would take to do a few simple things, and I wasn't finished until 4 p.m. I went straight to the lady's house on my way home. She opened the door looking ragged and said, "My father-in-law passed away. We've been working in the house all day and we will fly out tomorrow for the funeral."

I asked if I could help, but she said they were done with all the cleaning. All I could do was give her a hug. I drove home feeling ashamed. As competent as this lady was, she could have used a cheerful helper that day, and it could have been me. It was supposed to be me.

I resolved not to delay a prompting again. After I moved back to Utah, I had another strange prompting to call a lady in the ward—someone I didn't know at all. I felt uncomfortable calling her, but I dared not disregard the prompting. I explained to her that I felt that I should call and had no idea why.

"Can you sing?"

"Yes, I sing alto."

"Well I'm in charge of the stake production of *The Ten Virgins*. It's a musical and I'm having the hardest time finding singers."

"I'd love to do it! I also know some other people in the ward who sing." I couldn't believe how good this was turning out.

"Actually, I just need one more person. I'm waiting on another lady, and I think she'll say yes, so if you do it, I think we'll be OK. Oh, I'm so relieved!'

Once again, I was the right person to help someone in need; she didn't want anybody else but me. Responding to this prompting helped me as well, because I loved being in the inspired program where I gained new insights into the parable of the ten virgins. In fact, I felt as if the lady in charge helped me much more than I helped her. That's usually how it goes when we serve, but we miss opportunities when we delay. (A relative)

"We watch. We wait. We listen for that still, small voice. When it speaks, wise men and women obey. We do not postpone following promptings of the Spirit." (Thomas S. Monson, GC, April 1985)

---

One evening I was coming home from a sales trip on the road and had a strong impression to stop by our retail health food store, which was my moonlight business. I was responsible for handling all financial matters and maintaining our major product line. The orders were up to date, I wasn't scheduled to fill in for anyone, and all the bills were current. I had no reason to stop that evening, other than the impression to do so. As I pulled into a parking spot, my focus was directed to a lady moving confusedly on the broad sidewalk in front of our store.

She looked very concerned as she paced back and forth rather aimlessly. Thinking she might have locked her keys in her car or something; I approached her and asked her if she needed any help.

She said, "I don't know! I'm just so confused. I have a teenage son who is cutting himself and suicidal and just not the boy we knew. It's so difficult!"

Having gone through a strikingly similar challenge already I now knew why the impression to stop at our store came.

I was able to share with her the pros and cons of medications, natural remedies, psychologists, psychiatrists, and alternative medical facilitators. I was able to give her names, references, and hope. I explained to her what worked so-so and what worked best for our child that suffered very similar trials. We visited for about an hour and a half. She thanked me, we parted, and I drove home without ever even entering our store.

Often we can support and strengthen others through our own challenging experiences. This is one of the silver linings amongst the murky clouds of anguish, darkness, and grief we had waded through. (Journal 10/15/2005)

"God will use you to make the lives of others better." (Dieter F. Uchtdorf, GC, Sep 2017)

---

We were unable to have any children after years of trying so we began the adoption process. The hardest part of adoption for me is that the agency of the baby is totally out of your hands. And that's a hard place to be because you feel like you have no control of any situation. When we first started adopting, we had been on the waiting list for two years and it was really getting old.

We had a Relief Society activity that was planned for an evening but we were in the middle of pouring concrete for a patio, so it was a really bad time for me to go anywhere. But I had this feeling that I just had to be there. So I told my husband I felt very strongly I needed to go to my activity and left him to finish up the concrete.

So I went to Relief Society and as part of the activity we had to talk about things that were very important to us. So I talked about our inability to have children and difficult in adopting a child. A woman came up to me and said that she was a nurse at the Davis Hospital. Sometimes we have women in there that have babies and they have no plan of what to do.

The nurse said, "Just give me your card and if anything comes up I'll give you a call."

Another six months went by and nothing had happened. There was this one day when I was going to go down to the U of U and meet my younger sister and her new boyfriend. I got in the van and started the car and I got this terrible feeling that I definitely shouldn't go to the U. So I immediately turned the car off, returned to the house, and sat down. I wanted to sit down and pray to try and figure out what was going on.

As I sat there the phone rang right away. It was my neighbor and he said, "Stay home, don't go anywhere. This sister, the nurse from the hospital, is trying to get hold of you." So I just sat there and waited for half-an-hour.

Then this nurse contacted me and said they had a baby from a mother needing a good home for him. This young mother had come from the southeastern United States and had not been in Utah long. The mother had no plan; in fact, she had hidden the pregnancy from her entire family. So no one knew or prepared for the baby, including the new mother.

This young woman came to the closest hospital and up to the desk, prior to delivery, and asked for a newspaper. She said, "I need to place an ad for someone to adopt my baby."

The nurse told the expectant mother that she did not need to place an ad. The nurse at the desk was the same nurse at the Relief Society activity. So she called us and we met with the mother and agreed to adopt the baby.

When you find a baby to adopt on your own you call Family Services. They came and kicked the process into gear. Family Services takes care of all the paper work for you. And we had the baby the next day! (The nurse at the desk got sick the next day and wasn't back to work for a week. This all had to happen on that day!)

The great thing that I learned from this is that even though it seemed so out-of-our-control, Heavenly Father was really in control the entire time. So it was just those two simple promptings: first to go to that Relief Society meeting and second to not leave my house the day the phone rang. That whole adoption process was just from two tiny promptings. Of course, God did a lot of work behind the scenes getting that little one from the southeast to our family in Utah. (A family friend)

"And whoso is enlightened by the Spirit shall obtain benefit therefrom." (D&C 91:5)

As I packed for a day at the beach with our family, I had a prompting to *"throw in a hammer."* We did not need one for our wave runners or trailers; so I tossed one in the vehicle—just in case. Later in the day a sizable group of young men and women showed up. They looked like young adults. The group was trying to set up volleyball standards in the sand with little luck. I recalled the *hammer prompting* and went up to retrieve it from our vehicle.

As I walked over to the group with my hammer in hand they excitedly said, "We were just praying for a hammer! Thank you for bringing us one. Would you like to play with us?"

I informed them that I loved volleyball and would really enjoy playing with them. It was a win/win situation derived from a combination of simple faith through a small prompting in my mind and a quick prayer from the young adults. (Journal 8/25/1996)

> "Other times, without beckoning, counsel and instruction and assurance have come through the power of the Holy Ghost …" (Richard G. Scott, GC, April 1970)

> I had a day off from my more than fulltime job at the hospital. I decided to drive to a nearby town where both my mother and mother-in-law lived. They were within thirty minutes of my home, yet I hadn't visited them lately. My mother was exhibiting signs of early dementia.
>
> As I pulled into town I was prompted to visit my mother-in-law first. I shrugged it off and drove to my mothers and had a nice visit. Afterwards I went to my mother-in-law's home, where she lived alone, and it was dark. Her TV was not on so that meant she had gone somewhere. Maybe someone took her out for dinner.
>
> I checked around the house, peeking in the windows and tugging on the doors. After awhile a neighbor came over and asked if I was looking for his neighbor. I confirmed the same. He informed me that she had become very ill, was suffering from pneumonia, and was taken to the hospital. I rushed to the hospital and found out that she had unfortunately passed away suddenly.
>
> If I had listened to the Spirit I would have been able to help her in her final hours on earth and to say goodbye. (A peer)

> "I have learned in my life to never postpone a prompting."
> (Thomas S. Monson, GC, Oct 1996)

Promptings come to us as such soft tones: finite feelings in our hearts, quite ideas in our minds, simple thoughts to call, visit, or write someone, etc.

I stopped for lunch while working on the road. As I was exiting the vehicle I had a petite prompting to grab a couple of order forms and a pen. Normally I would try to enjoy my meal and avoid working for a spell. As I sat down in a restaurant booth my cell phone began to go off. I received one large order after another before I could even place my order for food. The nice thing about this was that I was prepared and ready to take those customers orders because I had heeded a small thought. I did not mind waiting a little later to eat one bit.

On a different morning I noticed my "New Accounts" folder sitting atop my desk, as it had for several weeks. There was a post-it note reminding me to *Update this Folder*. It really stood out and even though I had not set up any new stores for several months, the task seemed important.

With the folder now rife with all my lines' brochures, credit forms, and new account applications, I headed north for a day of sales. I was very surprised when I arrived in Logan, UT, and discovered a new health food store had quietly opened up without putting out any notices. I was sure pleased to look professional and prepared with every document and paper needed to help them fill their store with the quality products I represented. I thanked the Lord for His simple reminders. (Journal 5/7/2006)

> "Thus, the Spirit of the Lord usually communicates with us in ways that are quiet, delicate, and subtle." (David A. Bednar, GC, April 2008)

---

> My mother, grandmother, son, and brother's dog were traveling from Salt Lake City, UT, to Minot, South Dakota to visit my brother and bring him some of his belongings. We decided to make the fifteen-hour one-way trip in one day/night. The roads were long; it was hot and there really wasn't much to look at.
>
> We passed the time with simple conversations and music. My mother and I traded off driving every few hours so the other could rest or nap, if needed. The day became night and we were traveling through the middle of "Nowhere", Montana. We were tiring and debating about pulling over to take a quick nap before continuing.
>
> I was driving at the time and both my mother and I were too tired to keep driving. I kept weaving in my lane and knew it was time to pull over. The very next exit was literally an exit to nothing. There was a big open, flat, empty dirt parking lot just off the exit. There wasn't any

lighting and it seemed like the perfect place to pull over and nap. Out-of-sight of the road, we shouldn't be bothered or be bothering anyone else.

As soon as I brought the truck to a stop I was wide awake. I had a very uneasy feeling, but I thought my mind was playing tricks on me. If there were any real danger the dog was in the back and he would bark and warn us. So I tried to get comfortable and close my eyes. Still, the feeling would not go away and I was feeling an urgency to leave. The feeling was so heavy I decided to ask my mom how she was feeling. She, too, did not feel right.

My son and grandmother were fast asleep so I wasn't going to bother waking them. We said a prayer, knowing I was too tired to keep driving. I was in need of a nap for the safety of my family. Again, the feeling persisted and became urgent, **"Start the car and do it NOW!"**

I looked at my mom and said, "I can't sleep; I can't shake this feeling." My comment was immediately following by a deep long drawn out howl from the dog. He had never in his life made that kind of noise.

It was the final warning to get moving. I immediately started the engine and began to drive. We left in a huge hurry! I felt like we barely made it in the nick of time, not knowing what was out there, but having the feeling that there were no more warnings left. We needed to act fast and I'm grateful we did.

To this day, we have no idea what or who was there. The promptings to leave were stronger than any I had ever felt before. It was clear we were to keep moving; even the dog gave us a clear warning. Heavenly Father helped me stay awake long enough to get my family to a safe place where we could pull over. To this day I will never forget those feelings and how blessed we are to have felt and listened when we were being prompted. (A peer)

"The promptings that come to us to flee evil reflect our Heavenly Father's understanding of our particular strengths and weaknesses and His awareness of the unforeseen circumstances of our lives." (Robert D. Hales, GC, April 2006)

Subtle promptings solve the simplest situations in our lives if we will but listen. We were preparing to travel to southern Arizona for our Thanksgiving vacation with my wife's family. As I packed I had the littlest of promptings to toss in a second bathing suit, so I did.

It was unseasonably warm, even for the dessert, and the temperature hit 88 degrees in late November. We all decided to go swimming in the family pool. One brother-in-law asked me if I had a bathing suit and I told him I did but was just getting ready to put it on and jump in the pool. Then I remembered the earlier thought to toss a second suit in. I dug out the extra bathing suit and chased him down and said, "Here, I happen to have an extra bathing suit." The suit fit and everyone that wanted to swim was able to enjoy that family activity at the same time.

That experience reminds me of a similar occasion back in college. Three of us newly married college couples were staying in a cabin above Salt Lake City and would later be going down to the Capitol Building for a semi-formal dance Saturday night. As we all took turns changing in the bathroom. I soon discovered that my suit pants were not on the hanger with my suit. I couldn't wear blue jeans to that dressy dance. My wife and I were disappointed.

I shared the dilemma with our small group and one friend piped up saying, "Oh, I don't know why but I had a thought to bring two pairs of dress pants. Well, I know why now! I think we're about the same size. Here try these on."

I was amazed and pleased; the pants actual fit quite well. Following a simple thought from above allowed us all to enjoy the dance together that evening. All in all it turned out to be an awesome weekend! (Journals 10/9/1981, 11/26/2017)

> "Whether they are direct promptings or just impulses to help, a good deed is never wasted, for "charity never faileth"—and is never the wrong response" (Michelle D. Craig, GC, Oct 2018)

> We lived out in the country with homes, sheds and a shop. Two of our adult children lived on the property with us and the grandchildren loved running around and playing their simple games. We would watch through the window and check outside for them also.
> One day my daughter blurted, "We need to find the children!" We ran outside and saw the little ones, except, *where was Emmy*?

We asked the children where she was and they said, "She's in the chocolate shop" (One son was developing a special candy bar line.) We rushed over to the chocolate shop and could not find her. So we left and looked around.

My daughter blurted again, "No he said she's in the chocolate shop! We need to go back and look." We could not find her and were starting to leave the shop.

My daughter heard the Spirit say, "**No she's in here, you find her.**"

As we looked around, my daughter thought she heard a noise. We found Emmy had climbed up somehow and locked herself in the refrigerator! She had screamed and screamed but no one could hear her. That was a lifesaving prompting my daughter had and we are all eternally grateful she listened and followed it. It was a time-sensitive event. When the Spirit prompts or speaks that is when we should start in motion. (Our friend)

"Brothers and sisters, it is of utmost importance that we exercise our agency and act, without delay, in accordance with the spiritual promptings we receive." (David M. McConkie, GC, Oct 2010)

*It has been proven time and again that when Angels, the Godhead, the Holy Spirit, or Translated Beings, etc. prompts or speaks, that is the optimal time, in our current environment, to act and get going immediately, if not sooner!*

———— •◆• ————

I had a tedious twelve hour day of work and wanted to just come home and crash. Only our youngest was still at home but out with friends. My wife was in a planning meeting with her presidency. Now I could really relax in total quietness.

For some reason I was not able to relax and found myself pacing the floors, which is not normal for me. Thoughts came to me about Uncle John being in one of the local hospitals. I couldn't get him or his wife out of my mind. I felt an urgency to visit them in the hospital.

I tried getting a hold of my wife and wasn't sure where she was because it was later in the evening. I discovered afterwards that they had conveniently planned their meeting at an ice cream shop and were necessarily taking more time than usual. She arrived home about fifteen minutes later and I told her I had a long and strong impression to visit Uncle John in the hospital.

We left around 9:30 p.m. and it took us about thirty minutes to get there and into his room. It was apparent that he was in the final moments of his life. I asked myself, "Why are we here? What is so important?" Then my attention was turned to my sweet aunt instead and I realized that she was the one that needed comfort and love. We took her into our arms and she really appreciated that through her sobbing. Some of her sons, my cousins, were on their way and just hadn't arrived yet.

I am thankful for the strong prompting that moved me from relaxation to service. My dear aunt needed some sustaining support at this difficult time in her life, prior to her own family's arrival. Uncle John passed away peacefully a few hours later.

My cousin's wife commented, "That must have been your Dad (my aunt's brother) that came to you in spirit. I remember he was always antsy waiting at the crossroads for us to stop and pick him up for our weekly out-of-state temple trip." (Journal 6/8/2008)

Recently I had an impression to visit my wife's aunt in Saint George, UT. We were planning on attending a "cousin's reunion" in Cedar City, UT. (Our cousin's reunion is unique and very enjoyable with the simple rule of *no children or grandchildren allowed*.)

I suggested to my wife that we leave a day earlier and go on down to Saint George and take her Aunt, a recent widow, to the temple and out to dinner. My wife agreed then made the call to her aunt.

Her aunt agreed to the visit and dinner and offered us a bed to sleep in the night we would visit.

We had a great visit with this aunt, her son-in-law, her granddaughter, and great grandsons. We all talked about the other fun family reunion we had planned in Kanab, UT, scheduled in just a few weeks.

We immensely enjoyed the new Cedar City, UT, temple and the cousin's reunion and June 7th-9th, 2018.

My wife's family reunion was three weeks later on June 30th. My wife's aunt was not feeling well and couldn't attend. She went into the hospital with pneumonia then suddenly died unexpectedly. Most of the family was staying in the Kanab/St. George area for a week and we were all able to attend the funeral that no one had planned for.

We were very grateful for the prompting to spend a last good evening and morning with this wonderful woman before she peacefully passed into paradise. (Journal 7/15/18)

I had an unusual prompting to put a cough drop in my toiletries in preparation for a flight. I had a lot of things in this bag because it was before the airlines limited what one could carry and the sizes didn't matter.

As we were flying I noticed this man across the aisle from me. He was blind and had a travel companion that assisted him. He started coughing and his companion did nothing to help him. I looked in my travel bag and that cough drop was sitting right on top of everything!

I took the cough drop out and handed it to the blind man. Then his cough subsided. (A friend)

Prior to attending the conference, before leaving the United States, I felt the prompting to buy three cartons of chewing gum. I purchased three flavors: Doublemint, Spearmint, and Juicy Fruit. Now, as the gathering of the youth was concluded, I distributed carefully to each youth two sticks of gum—something they had never before tasted. They received the gift with joy. (Thomas S. Monson, GC, April 2002)

———— •◆• ————

I had a miniscule prompting to *tie a double knot* in my shoestrings as we were preparing to rake up thousands of nefarious bean pods that had fallen from our diabolical trees. These bean pods are 10-14 inches long. I shrugged it off and forgot about the simple suggestion until I found myself face down on the grass. I had tripped; and what did I trip upon? — My untied shoelace. (Journal 3/28/2018)

———— •◆• ————

In late 1941 we had our first child; a baby girl. The ongoing preparation for war now required a priority certificate to get such things as copper wire and electrical components. Material and jobs were getting very difficult to find.

We lived in Durango, Colorado. My brother and father had driven to Denver and then on to Salt Lake City to look for work. A large ammunition factory was under construction in SLC.

We decided to follow suit and move to SLC for work. I loaded all of our earthly possessions in the trunk of our 1936 Chevrolet Coupe and onto an old homemade 2-wheeled trailer. The trailer was made from the front end of a 1925 Dodge automobile.

With our newborn baby, my wife and I started out for Salt Lake City in hopes of finding work. We had less than $100. As we began driving, the trailer wasn't tracking straight and started whipping behind the car. About 10 miles out of Durango, I stopped to check the load, tires, and trailer. The tires were wearing out at an alarming rate.

I knew there was a service station on down the road in a small community in Colorado called Hesperus. We drove slowly so that the trailer wouldn't whip around and then a trailer tire blew out with a large bang! I stopped, unloaded the trailer, lifted up the trailer and rested the axle on a large rock. I removed the wheel and rim assembly. The wheels were wooden spokes (like a wagon wheel) including a thin metal tread on the outside of the spokes just like a wagon metal surface. The tire was small and measured 2.75 X 21.

I placed the tire with its own rim on my shoulder and walked about one and a half miles to the service station.

The attendant was sympathetic to my problem but said, "Son, that tire is totally gone. I could patch the tube but look there's nothing left of the tire." With that he pushed the tire in one spot and his finger punched right through it like thin paper!

I asked him if he had a replacement or knew where I could get one.

He again said, "Son, I haven't seen that tire for years now. They just don't make them anymore!" He then suggested I might find one at a junk dealer back in Durango.

With a feeling of bitter defeat I started back to the car with the tire on my shoulder. On the way I was praying mentally to the Lord for help. Just off the road in the field I caught the glimpse of a tire. I thought to myself, "No, that can't possibly be the right size!" I continued up the road, but something kept drawing my eyes back to that tire. I stopped and stared; it did look smaller than a regular tire. Again, I said to myself "No—there is no way that can possibly be a 2.75 by 21 tire!"

Again, I continued up the road. I had only taken a few steps and was almost compelled by the Spirit to walk down to the edge of the road bed. I laid the damaged tire down, climbed through the barbed wire fence, and wended my way through the sagebrush. As I approached the tire I could see that it was an old one and might fit. I picked it up and had to pour water from inside the tire. I then had to scrape all the mud off from the side lying on the ground.

My heart leaped with joy as I saw the magic number "2.75 X 21!" I couldn't believe it! I just had to stare at it. Then I noticed the tire was weather checked and had a hole through the side of the carcass. I put my arm through the newfound tire and nearly ran back to the service station.

As I returned to the station, the attendant exclaimed, "Son, where in the world did you find that tire!"

I explained to him how I'd found it and he proceeded to put patch over patch on the "inner tube" until it held air. Now I was headed up the road a second time to my car, wife, and new baby.

The tires, both old and weak, carried our few possessions all the way to Salt Lake City, where I sold the used trailer to a neighbor for $25.

It wasn't until several years later that I realized what a great faith-promoting experience this was. The Lord, through the Holy Ghost, had to almost shout in my ears and turn me to the field where the answer to my prayers lay. As we go through life we each have our "2.75 X 21" experiences, where the Lord is prompting and leading us in order to obtain the answers we seek through prayer. (A friend's father)

———— • ◆ • ————

Harvey Cluff was a member of the First Rescue party. When they reached Willow Creek, the storm that caught the Willie and Martin Companies was upon them, and it was so intense that they left the road and moved down stream about three miles to be in the protection of some willows.... Brother Cluff was impressed to go back to the road and leave a sign telling of their where abouts. He made his journey into the face of the storm and placed the sign and returned to camp.... Captain Willie and John Elder, who had gone ahead of the Willie Company came into camp frozen, hungry, and tired. They would have never found the camp had Brother Bluff not followed the promptings of the Spirit and placed his sign at the road. (*Remember*, Riverton Wyoming Stake Members, 147-148)

———— • ◆ • ————

I leaned close to her and asked, "Grandma, tell me how the gospel has blessed your life." She whispered softly and shared her gratitude for the promptings and guidance she had received from the Holy Ghost.

When her second child, James, was 18 months old, he and his older brother were playing outside and she was watching them from the window. Suddenly, she couldn't see him and ran from the house calling and searching frantically. There was water in the irrigation ditch that shouldn't have been there, and she searched along the edge of the ditch and could see nothing. She ran for the hired hands to come and help and ran back to where the ditch went through a long culvert. Running to the other end of the culvert, she saw two little shoes, and pulled on them. When she had her son in her arms, she was prompted to clasp her hands together and place them under his stomach and carry him in front of her in this way, using her knee to hold some of his weight. She ran toward the road crying for help. The promptings she received to carry him in such an unnatural manner saved his life. (Patricia P. Pinegar, GC, Oct 1999)

I was asked to repair the washing machine of a single mother with small children. We found the error code on the washer and ordered the part to replace the defunct part. We googled the diagram and repair instructions.

When the part came, I felt ready to tear into it and fix the problem. As I prepared to go, there came a tiny thought to **"take screwdrivers."** The home I was going to was very disorderly and there may have been screwdrivers there, yet who knew where they were. I decided a pipe wrench would be very helpful to unscrew the water hoses and grabbed my entire toolbox.

I left early to run a couple of errands first. On the way to my first errand I received a text that read, "Please bring your screwdrivers." (Journal 8/19/18)

Now, brethren, I want to make it very clear that I am not prophesying, that I am not predicting years of famine in the future. But I am suggesting that the time has come to get our houses in order. So many of our people are living on the very edge of their incomes. In fact, some are living on borrowings. We have witnessed in recent weeks wide and fearsome swings in the markets of the world. The economy is a fragile thing. A stumble in the economy in Jakarta or Moscow can immediately affect the entire world. It can eventually reach down to each of us as individuals. *There is a portent of stormy weather ahead to which we had better give heed.* (President Gordon B. Hinckley, Ensign, Jan 1999)

*Our prophet wasn't prophesying seven years of famine, yet he was definitely counseling us to get our houses in order ahead of stormy weather. The reader may likely remember the "dot.com crash" in 2000-2002 and might also recall the "Housing Market Crash" in 2008-2012. Those who heeded a prophet's voice, for the most part, weathered those financial storms well. There are many who did not follow the prophet's advice that should be retired now; they find it unfortunately necessary to continue working during their sunset years.*

———◆——

We flew to New York to help our husbands at a trade show. What a busy place!

While our husbands attended a business meeting, my friend, Sylvia, and I were to iron the clothes after a long flight. Our husbands had *both* taken off with their respective luggage keys.

Then I remembered that earlier that morning I was prompted to **put a bobby pin in my purse**. I NEVER use them and thought that was quite silly, but obeyed. Well, that bobby pin unlocked our huge suitcase and one of Sylvia's too!

In addition, the bellman had hung our clothing bag upside down and the weight of everything made the zipper pop off! We each tried, but could only get half of the zipper reattached. Then something told me to **put some soap on it.** I was stubborn at first and didn't admit that I could get a prompting about such a thing. But when I did apply some soap to the zipper, it went right back on.

It pays to listen. We got the ironing done after all. (My wife Tamara's journal)

"Don't postpone a prompting rather, act on it, and the Lord will open the way." (Thomas S. Monson, GC, April 2003)

———◆——

Oftentimes the promptings are very quiet and simple. I did not hear a voice in my head; only a small impression came to my mind to **bring a flower home** for lunchtime. I followed the idea, picked up a rose, and presented it to my wife.

She commented, "That was good timing; I really appreciate it." She explained that she had been real busy and especially frustrated at the children.

I was thankful that I listened. Oftentimes we get so rushed that we don't take time to listen or our lives are so noisy that we cannot hear quiet promptings. I know I have been guilty of that myself many times over. (Journal 10/16/1988)

> Each of us should be careful that the current flood of information does not occupy our time so completely that we cannot focus on and hear and heed the still, small voice that is available to guide each of us with our own challenges today. (Dallin H. Oaks, GC, April 1982)

I called my sister in a distant state for no reason, just to talk. She said I must have been inspired because she had a week from Hades. She needed to visit with someone she could trust and be understood by. She finally came out and said she had not been getting along with her husband for three years and they were at a low point. They had actually considered divorce for the first time in their marriage of many years.

After lending a long listening ear I suggested that they both read their patriarchal blessings and that admitting the problem was a big first step to doing something about it. I am grateful that things improved within their relationship. (A relative's journal)

It was just after 9 a.m. when I felt these strong hunger pains. Turning away from my home PC, where I was editing a book, I sauntered downstairs. I determinedly told myself, "I'm not going to eat breakfast; I just ate a big breakfast! Why am I so hungry?" My wife was out-of-state visiting a relative.

I decided to just fill up with water. It did not make sense to eat again so early. As I filled up my water cup I sensed something strange. Turning to look at the stove I noticed a stove light still on. Then I was shocked to see a forgotten frying pan that was very hot and sported blackened hash browns.

The bacon and eggs were done first and I started with those for breakfast, totally forgetting the hash browns on the stove, which were now inedible. I did not need to eat again; I needed to be in the kitchen to prevent a fire. That "hunger prompting" placed me where I needed to be at the right time. (Journal 11/11/2018)

> He who fashioned this world can calm the seas with His word and can steer both Alma and Amulek and Nephi and

Laban to be at the right place at precisely the right time. (Ronald A. Rasband, GC, Oct 2017)

———————◆◆◆———————

One summer I was invited to go to Laramie, WY, with my neighbor to pick her daughter up from summer music camp. We were invited to the group's ending concert before returning. While watching the concert, I noticed a girl who looked like she was hiding something. Her brunette hair was hanging over one eye. She had on a calf length skirt with a long top over it.

I heard the Lord tell me to say three words to her: **'Jesus loves you.'**

I argued with the Lord in my mind saying I would never be able to get close enough to talk to her. After the concert we went to the dormitories to collect their things. We used the elevator to help carry things. On the way up the elevator, we stopped on a lower floor. Unbeknownst to me, my young son stepped off the crowded elevator on the wrong floor.

When we arrived at her daughter's floor, I discovered my little boy was missing. I panicked and went back down to that floor we stopped at. When the door opened, there was that girl standing right in front of the elevator. I finally located my son and we headed back up. During the moving I saw that same girl in the dormitories again.

We headed to the car and once again, the girl was right there on the grass in front of where we were parked. I had already made up my mind that I wasn't going to talk to her. God showed me he could get me close enough to talk to her three times! I learned to act more quickly the next time He told me to do something. (A relative)

"In our day ... we too must be careful not to hinder, disregard, or quench the Spirit in our lives." (Keith K. Hilbig, GC, Oct 2007)

———————◆◆◆———————

Our youngest son inherited a car from his grandfather's estate. Over a year's time we fixed the car up and drove it from out-of-state. I would be working near the motor vehicle department soon and planned to apply for a new title. I figured they would be suspicious of a "free car" from another state.

Following that thought of suspicion I had an impression to ***"bring a death certificate."*** I would have never thought of this, with Dad having passed away over a year ago. I fumbled through an old briefcase of Dad's and found a few death certificate copies. I placed one copy with the emissions and inspections records.

Upon arriving to apply for a new title, the clerk's first question surprised me when she questioned, "Do you have a death certificate?" Thankfully I listened, which saved me from making an additional trip and taking extra time again in those very long lines at the DMV.

The impressions that trickle down to us are often so simple in nature. (Journal 9/22/2007)

We are very apt through our traditions, former associations, and notions of things and ideas, to attribute every act of man and every manifestation of mankind to an invisible source—the good or the evil. God is the author of all Good; and yet, if you rightly understood yourselves, you would not directly attribute every good act you perform to our Father in Heaven, nor to his Son Jesus Christ, nor to the Holy Ghost; neither would you attribute every evil act of a man or woman to the Devil or his spirits or influences; for man is organized by his Creator to act perfectly independently of all influences there are about or beneath. Those influences are always him, and are ready to dictate and direct—to lead him into truth or to lead him to destruction. But is he always guided by those influences in every act? He is not. It is ordained of God that we should act independently in and of ourselves, and the good is present when we need it. (President Brigham Young, JD 9:122)

"Verily I say, men should be anxiously engaged in a good cause, and do many things of their own free will, and bring to pass much righteousness;" (D&C 58:27)

While working on the road, specifically Hwy 89 in Utah, I stopped to see an associate in the small, quaint town of Fairview. Realizing I had overstayed my visit, I excused myself and headed south to service more of my accounts. It was several hours past lunch and I was starving.

"I've got to find someplace to eat soon!" I said out loud. As I began to turn back onto Main Street, I said a prayer in my heart, "Where am I going to eat?" I rounded the corner, looked up, and there was a 4' X 8' piece of plywood attached to the side of a two-story brick building. On the plywood in very large, bright red, block letters it read: EAT HERE. I exclaimed, "Thanks!" out loud and pulled up to the small restaurant.

This really seemed like a definite coincidence, however I no longer believe in coincidences. I know President Thomas S. Monson has said that he doesn't believe in coincidences either. Our Heavenly Father directs our paths more than we know or realize.

As I entered the business it became readily apparent that the bulk of the retail space was used for a second-hand store. It was several hours past noon and also evident that no one else was seated at the few booths they offered. A young couple with a fussy baby greeted me. I asked them if they could whip me up something quick. Then I started grilling them about their child, "Is this your first child? How old is he? What's his name?"

They answered my questions and appeared very tired and drawn out. They explained that their baby was very fussy, not eating or sleeping. I could see they needed a break.

I promised, "I'm very good with children. I would like to hold and comfort your baby while you make my lunch." I figured the two of them would get my food faster and I always enjoy holding babies: fussy, crying, or sleeping ... it doesn't matter to me.

Bonding with a beautiful baby boy

298

So they agreed and I cuddled the baby, held him close, and simply sent him love. He went to sleep quickly in my arms and I thoroughly enjoyed his sweet little spirit. When they brought my food, I told them that we were both so comfortable that I would like to still hold him; I ended with "You two can go get some needed rest." I ate slowly and enjoyed the moment. Although I was two hours behind on my work schedule, nothing bothered me because our meeting each other was heavenly orchestrated. This was definitely not a coincidence, no way!

———•◆•———

Many promptings are very simple thoughts and/or reminders. Recently we replaced a tire pump for our bikes. I went to throw the receipt away and a thought entered my mind to "**Keep the receipt**." We normally do not keep receipts for anything under $50 cost.

Not long after that, my son went to use the tire pump for the very first time and it broke in two on the first pump. He came in and exclaimed, "Dad I used new tire pump on my bike and it just fell apart!" I assured him that was not a problem because I had the receipt handy. (Journal 8/7/2016)

———•◆•———

We lived about twenty miles out of town and would come in for supplies and food about once a week. I made my usual stop at the hardware store for a few things. A firm prompting came to me in my mind "**Buy a box of nails**". My first thought was how unusual of a prompting that was. I had purchased a new box of nails for my nail gun previously. I already had more than enough nails waiting at home to complete the project we were starting that afternoon. I thought, 'I've already got a full supply of new nails'; yet the prompting was so clear. Not understanding why, I purchased an additional supply of nails.

When I arrived home I now had two large supplies of nails. I thought, "Well I can have some for my storage." I placed the original nails into my nail gun and they wouldn't work, no matter what I tried! So I opened the new box of nails and they worked fine and we were able to finish the job up without any problem.

The next time I was in town I returned the first box of nails. The hardware store owner told me, "We've had a lot of those nails come back. They were made wrong and won't work in any nail gun." (Our friend)

"But there is a spirit in man: and the inspiration of the Almighty giveth them understanding." (Job 32:8)

---

I had borrowed the store truck to take a couple of loads of branches and garden waste to the recyclers. I received a distinct premonition to "**Gas up.**" My two round trips would be twenty miles total, at the most. The gas gauge red ¾ full. I really had no reason to refuel at the time, other than a strong feeling to do so. I would only use/need 1-2 gallons of gasoline, at the most, for my brief runs.

I decided to follow the feeling however, against my better judgment. After pulling into a gas station and fueling up, I was surprised how much gas the truck took. Maybe my partner had installed a larger or second gas tank on the store vehicle?

After dumping the two loads, I received a text from my business partner: "By the way, the gas gauge in the truck broke and it's really empty! Make sure you get gas right away."

Had I not listened to the prompting, the truck and I would likely have been stranded along the road somewhere awaiting assistance.

---

Our washing machine was having some issues. My wife started the first load of the week and then I asked her if she had stayed around to listen to how it was running. She had not.

I started the second load in the washer. Later, my wife asked me if I had stayed downstairs to listen to it. I had already forgotten. On the third load, I felt I should just stand in front of the washer and listen to the cycles.

As I listened there was a loud metal clicking sound. It reminded me of the noise on kid's bicycles when we would clothespin a playing card to the frame; the spokes would flip it and make it sound like a motor. My son rushed in from his room and said, "What's the matter with it?"

I replied, "I don't know." Then there was a loud pop, like a gunshot! Then lots of white smoke began pouring up from the bottom of the washer and we could smell melting wires.

I immediately unplugged the washer and we were able to prevent any further damage. I kind of shudder to think what would have happened if I had not been right in front of the washing machine when it was overheating. The laundry room is down in the basement behind a closed door. I was thankful for a very simple prompting to watch over the washer. (Journal 3/9/2017)

---

Often women will let me hold their babies after I compliment their little angels. I always take the opportunity quickly, before mamma has a chance to change her mind. When the little ones hug me tightly, smile brightly, or comfortably fall asleep in my arms, this quickly puts their parents at ease. I was out of town on business and had finished the day. In the hotel hallway I met up with a young woman cradling a newborn. Their room was right across the hall from mine.

I complimented her baby and she quickly replied, "Would you like to come in the room and hold her?" I liked the idea and was looking forward to holding her baby. I was actually turning to go towards her open door when the Spirit gave me a strong "**UN-HUH**!"

Then I explained to her, "I'm sorry but I have a dinner appointment I need to get to." I didn't tell her my dinner meeting was just between me and a juicy steak at the local hotel steakhouse.

> "... the Spirit *constraineth* me that I must not ..." (Alma 14:11)

We enjoyed tubing the South Fork River in Weber County, UT, with some family friends. We would all ride over mild rapids, in individual tubes, while attempting to protect our tubes from the bushy banks on both sides. It was often hard to stay in the middle when the current had a strong mindset and pull of its own!

Our friend had an impression to "**put your diamond ring in your mouth**."

She thought to herself, "Well I don't want to swallow it. It's an expensive wedding ring." Soon after that, the strong current was drifting her toward some bushes along the riverside. She reached up to grab some limbs and pushed herself away to avoid a tube puncture. She was successful in protecting the tube, but she noticed her ring was gone from her finger.

She exclaimed, "I think the cold water shrunk my finger and the ring slipped off. Because I was so stubborn with the Spirit, I lost my nice wedding ring forever!" (Journal 7/28/2013)

> "The reason some people don't accept revealed truth from heaven is because they are afraid or too stubborn to give it an honest trial and thus find its worth." (Paul H. Dunn, GC, Oct 1966)

The Primary has me down as a *permanent nursery sub* which I am delighted to do quite often. Occasionally they need me in the older classes. Many of the various class members are children I have worked with in nursery. The Primary president called Saturday evening to see if I would sub in an older class the following morning. I agreed to help out.

As I went to print the assigned lesson, nothing would print out. The unit just stopped working. The printer and computer were not communicating with each other very well at all. I rebooted the computer. Then I checked the HP website for advice; which said to reboot the printer; still nothing. I used the *HP Doctor* for diagnostics and the next step was to reboot the router, which I did, to no avail.

Then one of our children called up at the last minute to see if we could watch two grandsons for four hours that evening. These are very active boys, so the computer issue had to wait. I was a little miffed about the late notice interrupting our printer fix. However, I felt I needed to be forgiving and work on my patience. The boys were not picked up until about an hour past our usual bedtime and we were beat.

In the morning the idea came into my mind "**work from the printer to the computer**." Everything we had done the night before was working from the computer to the printer with no results. Within a few minutes my Primary lesson was printing out, along with other delayed print jobs from the queue.

After all we can do, the Lord will step in and help even with simple matters that are important to each of us, at the time; especially following our service to Him through others. (Journal 11/16/2014)

I was just finishing the day at my last account in downtown Ogden. I got a phone call from one of my daughter's and she quickly said, "Dad, where are you?"

I told her I was in Ogden and she replied, "Oh, good. There's been an accident and I'm on a stretcher. A big truck rear-ended me at a stop sign."

I let her know I would be right over. We were only about three blocks apart at that time. I am confident I was prompted to plan my schedule exactly how I did that day. I could have been in Ontario, OR, Sheridan, WY, Mesquite, NV, or Moab, UT. I could not have been closer during my work day than when her phone call came.

As I approached, I witnessed our precious daughter lying on a stretcher sporting a neck/head brace. I don't know why we always imagine the worst, but I did. "Oh, no, she's paralyzed! She won't be able to have children. She's brain damaged!" I frantically flew through negativity land.

I held her hand and prayed for her until the ambulance took her away. Thankfully, she only had some discomfort and light pain. There was no major damage. Her little truck was totaled however. I again thanked God who prompted me to be finishing my work at the right time and place to give comfort to a frightened young lady. (Journal 12/16/2001)

"For I the LORD thy God will hold thy right hand, saying unto thee, Fear not, I will help thee." (Isaiah 41:13)

After returning home from my mission, a high councilor asked me to travel to Meeteetse, Wyoming, to speak with him in their sacrament meeting. I agreed and told him I would meet him there. I decided to fast that day. It was around 55 miles away. We had a large Stake geographically.

When a friend noticed my name on their program, she called ahead and invited me over for dinner after the meeting. Her father was the bishop in Meteetsee. I knew her brother from track meets, yet did not know her parents, other than by sight.

Church went fine and got better from there. The bishop's wife is an amazing cook and I still had the appetite of a missionary. Everything was so delicious and then this fantastic dessert surfaced. After the large dinner this young woman and I took a leisurely stroll afterwards. Then I started not feeling very well. Her brother was still on his mission, so she allowed me to relax in his room. My friend had choir practice and surprised me with a gentle goodbye kiss. That didn't help much though; I was still feeling terrible.

Her mother got me some Pepto-Bismol and I laid down in grief. Once I finally started feeling a little better I told the family I should be off for home, over an hour drive. I was ten miles from home when my stomach would not allow me to go on. It felt as painful as food poisoning. It wasn't food poisoning, but a near cousin I'm sure! I pulled over to the side of the road.

As I got out I had to lean against the car for support and then worked slowly over to the roadside and knelt down on one knee, in a three-piece suit, with severe gastrointestinal pain. A station wagon with a large family pulled off the highway and asked if I needed some help. I tried to respond and all I could do was to throw up all over the side of the road. This happened three times! I was hoping they would stop asking me questions! Every question was responded to with nasty upheavals. Their children's faces were pasted against the car windows with their eyes and mouths agape.

After losing everything in my stomach in three large vomits, they offered to drive me home. The father helped me up and got me into the passenger seat of the station wagon. He then drove my car. While chauffeuring me, his wife shared something very interesting.

"We are visiting from out-of-state and were headed to grandmas for Sunday dinner. **The Spirit prompted *both of us* to drive in the opposite direction**. We had no idea why, yet knew we should follow the Spirit since we were both prompted to do the same thing. We turned around, driving in the wrong direction until we found you!"

They ended up going more than many miles out of their way with all those hungry children and a dinner waiting upon their Christian acts. I am thankful that these earthly angels were both in tune. (Journal, Aug 1978)

———————◆———————

I had made a gallant effort but had been unsuccessful in finding the address. Instead, I offered a silent prayer for help. The inspiration came that **I should approach the area from the opposite direction**. I drove a distance and turned the car around so that I was now on the other side of the road. Going in this direction, the traffic was much lighter. As I neared the location once again, I could see, through the faint light, a street sign that had been knocked down—it was lying on its side at the edge of the road—and a nearly invisible, weed-covered track leading to a small apartment building and a single, tiny residence some distance from the main road. As I drove toward the buildings, a small girl in a white dress waved to me, and I knew that I had found the family. (Thomas S. Monson, GC, April 2007)

———————◆———————

Not too long ago I was beginning to plan my day to visit several accounts. One of the companies I was representing at the time was Burt's Bees, which is a very popular line. I was my own boss and could set my route and schedule as I saw fit. I would try to contemplate and plan, in a quiet place—often within my car in the garage, prior to heading out for the day. I had decided to work in Bountiful and SLC, Utah, on this day. The thought came to service the Smith's Foods in Bountiful first, prior to the other three accounts there and then proceed to downtown Salt Lake City.

As I approached the buyer at Smith's Grocery she was abnormally excited to see me. This is not usually the typical reception a salesman receives.

She exclaimed, "Your timing is impeccable! I'm just getting ready to leave for a two-week vacation and I wouldn't have stocked up on Burt's Bees had you not showed up right now."

I thought to myself, "The Lord's timing is truly impeccable" and silently thanked my Father in Heaven for the simple direction of where to begin business that day.

The buyer continued, "If you hadn't shown up I would have lost out on thousands of dollars in sales. Let's place an extra large order, just in case."

Well that was *music to my ears* and I likewise thought, "I would have lost out on hundreds of dollars in commissions too." Was this ever a nice start to my sales day!

———◆———

During the weekend I was determining where I would go and just how far the travels would be the following week. My sales trips ranged from fifty to 1,050 miles and included parts of five states. Being my own boss offered ample latitude. I have always loved sales/marketing and have never had a problem getting up and hitting the road with gusto on Monday mornings.

The start of this week was very different. I could not come up with a business plan and actually felt like going nowhere. Was I getting lazy or coming down with something? I did not know what was going on; it was as if I was overwhelmed by a stupor of thought.

On Sunday night my wife started to experience some severe pain. She received a priesthood blessing and was comforted, but not healed. She ended up needing to be hospitalized after surgery that week. I was thankful for my promptings to not go out on the road. This way, I was "there for her" in her time of need. This was an outpatient surgery and we had anticipated she would be recovering at home the same evening.

That afternoon I attempted once more to plan the four days ahead; which accounts should be serviced along with their respective priorities? Now there was this continual emptiness of thought; nothing seemed right. I was unable to plan anything in the near future again. I thought, "Man, I really am getting lazy!"

During her surgery for gall bladder removal the surgeon irritated her pancreas and this became a much more serious problem. Now she had a four-five day hospital stay for pancreatitis!

There were neither hotel reservations nor any appointments with any accounts made. My schedule was clear; I was able to take the week off to help comfort my eternal companion. I wasn't lazy after all; I was simply spiritually detained for a higher purpose. She couldn't eat or drink anything at first. After two days the doctor moved her to an ice-chip only diet!

I was available to run home and get her clean clothes, reading material, and whatever errands she needed me to run for her. All in all, it was a slow process, but she healed up nicely. (Journal 4/29/2008)

———◆———

I had the wonderful blessing of serving as a branch president at a care center. During our weekly visits, the high point of my weeks, my counselor and I made our rounds to visit with all our friends. One day as we finished our visits and headed for the doorway to leave, I felt a prompting that told me, "**You are not finished yet.**"

I told my companion to go and ahead and leave because I was going to stay for awhile. I didn't know what I was going to do or who I was going to see, I just knew I wasn't finished yet. I paced in the lobby for a bit and decided to walk through the halls again.

I started up the first hall and as I got to the second room on the left I looked in and saw our dear friend Sheila. She had not been in her room when we came through visiting previously. I stepped in the door and asked her how she was doing. She replied, "Oh, I don't feel very good. Can you give me a blessing?" Then I knew why I wasn't finished.

I found a male orderly, who was a member, and we administered to Sheila. After which, I felt I could go home.

A few years later Sheila shared this story, "I had been praying that day and asked the Lord to send someone to give me a blessing. As soon as I finished my prayer I opened my eyes and saw you standing in the doorway." Her prayer was answered immediately! (A friend)

On my way home from the office, I had an impression to stop at the house of a widow whom I home taught. When I knocked on the sister's door, she said, "I have been praying for you to come." Where did that impression come from? The Holy Ghost. (Robert D. Hales, GC, April 2016)

---

Later, while still working for the novelty candy company, I was sitting at my desk pondering what task to tackle next. Then I had a distinct prompting to "**Check the mail bin.**" As the small company grew from 100 to over 15,000 accounts we sent tons of bulk mail, invoices, and promotions, etc., through U.S. Mail. This was the only time in fourteen years I was spiritually directed to the mail bin. Because of the uniqueness of the message/feeling, I immediately grabbed all the stacks of outgoing mail to take a look.

Unbundling all of the letters, I noticed two fat envelopes I had prepared. These letters were addressed to our two major accounts who could account for up to 15 -25% of our total business, at times, due to their hundreds of respective retail stores. Each major account had specific terms and each was different. The terms were tailored to what was important to each company. One liked extended dating and free displays. The other's hot buttons were discounts and free products.

Opening these two special letters up I discovered that I had inadvertently put the wrong letters in the wrong envelopes! You never want competitor's to know what each other's terms are, unless legally required. If those letters had gone out, each of the two major companies would have asked for MORE deals from us and our profit margin would have been cut very slim. This was a big enough mistake to possibly cost me my job!

I was so very grateful for the heavenly curtailing of catastrophe! The Lord can protect us in so many different aspects of our lives if we but prepare ourselves to hearken. (Journal 4/15/1984)

> "It can come as personal inspiration and guidance to assist us in our daily life—in our homes, in our work." (Rex D. Pinegar, GC, April 1993)

I had finished up the day servicing accounts in the Sun Valley, ID, area. Now I had a quiet two-and-a-half hour drive across ranchlands to Boise, ID; I would start my morning servicing that city's accounts. On this drive, I was really looking forward to a comfortable bed and relaxation after a long day. I would probably arrive after dark, between seven and eight pm.

About halfway through the drive, I had a distinct prompting to call the hotel. I have stayed in hotels thousands of nights, yet never had this prompting before. I had time on my hands and a hands-free phone, so I called. I was really surprised to hear the desk agent inform me:

"I'm sorry Mr. Laing, but we do not have a room reserved for you tonight or tomorrow."

"But I reserved the rooms on the hotel's website. I specifically remember doing it and I have the confirmation here in my car."

"Please hold on while I double check. Here's what happened, you booked the room for next month, not this month."

"Oh my ... I'm a little more than an hour away and I need a room tonight and for the next two days!"

"We do have a room with a king bed available for the next three nights. Will that work for you?"

"Thank you so much. That is a great relief!"

They even upgraded me to a suite when I eventually arrived.

I was very grateful for that impression. If I had not called, the hotel could have easily been sold out by the time I arrived that evening. It is fascinating how our Father in Heaven and our Savior watch over us through many miniscule details throughout our respective lives; when we are not too busy or noisy to listen.

I was preparing to speak at a business conference. I was up first at nine a.m. and I got this distinct impression to go right away at 8:15. I had planned to go set up my laptop for my PowerPoint at 8:45. I left our booth; telling my daughter I felt I needed to go early.

When I arrived in the large presentation room, the building's tech guy was there. He was so glad to see me. He said, "I have all the wires and connections, I just needed a computer to make sure the audio and video are working for the day." He hooked the cables to my laptop and was now confident that everything was working properly. I came at just the right time because I followed a little prompting. I believe we are becoming a people who will eventually be guided all the time; when we need to be instructed or led. (Our friend)

"If we were more alert to the promptings of the Holy Ghost, we would see them before we reach them and thereby be guided more effectively. This process requires self-mastery, self-control, and a heart willing to accept change." (Richard G. Scott, GC, Oct 1979)

As a teacher, I take every summer off. Since I had a family reunion *and* surgery one year, I was looking forward to a long, eventless summer the following year; I didn't want to worry about a thing. During spring break, however, I contemplated feeling a bit lonely since I am single and most of my friends are at work all year round. That same day, I was also wondering about the **new ministering program**. How could I minister to a new sister I was assigned to? She was the type that didn't accept help well because she felt she could do things herself and also felt that others deserved help more. However, she had five children and I wondered if she might like some of them out of the house for a while.

Then a thought popped into my head: "**Have a drama day camp.**" I know this thought was a spiritual prompting because it was way beyond my desires for that summer. Next, I remembered my childhood of attending a fun parks and recreation program in the summer. The more I thought about it, the more excited I became, and I called my

**ministering companion** to tell her about it; it would prevent me from backing out. Sure enough, the next time we visited the sister with five kids, my companion told her of my plans. Now I was committed.

Although I knew it was God's will to have the camp, I still had many doubts about how to pull it off. It took me weeks to type up a flyer and registration form for children from four families, all who seemed right for the camp.

One thing that stuck with me was to make it fun, not at all like work, so I didn't do a play; we did short skits and had a blast; all of the children benefited from the camp. For example, some of them made new friends. One boy's confidence grew considerably in just two weeks. Two of the children were experiencing their parents' divorce, and my home was a good getaway. All of the kids wanted the camp to last longer, and they all wanted to return the following summer.

As for me, for someone with no kids, it was sheer joy to hear my house filled with happy, noisy youngsters rehearsing their lines, and some of their own, original skits were laugh-out-loud funny. Plus, getting to know three of the kids from **the ministering family** made it so much more comfortable when I visited their home.

Now the background story: Several months before my inspiration came, I had been missing my theater experiences of high school and decided to get my feet wet again. I tried out for a play and totally bombed. I was devastated, because I was trying so hard to find a new outlet. You know the old saying, "Those who can't, teach." That's not always such a bad thing, because the drama camp healed me from the disappointing audition and was the most enjoyable teaching I'd ever done. The Lord, in his tender mercy, gave all the children and me so many blessings. (A relative)

"And it came to pass that he did teach them and minister unto the children ..." (3 Ne. 26:14)

The city had received a foot of fluffy white snow overnight. We woke up Saturday morning to a marshmallow world. Everywhere one looked was a beautiful, pure, winter wonderland. Having been raised in

Wyoming, I enjoyed breaking drifts with my body, bike, sled, motorcycle, car, jeep, truck, snowmobile, etc.

That morning, following the storm, we had something that needed to get up to the post office. I quickly volunteered and was eager for some fun in the deep snow. I enjoyed "fishtailing" and doing "doughnuts/cookies" in safe areas. This was a simple drive on major roads, once I got out of our neighborhood. As I slowly plowed through the deep snow and looked at all the snow covering everything in sight, a road I had never before been on looked appealing to me.

No one had driven into this neighborhood that was nestled up against a steep hill, at all. There was not a single track in the snow. I had to zigzag through, continually making left and right turns towards the main road. There was virgin snow everywhere; when there were no vehicles parked on the streets, or fire hydrants, I started playing around. (This was much easier accomplished in the older model rear-wheel drive vehicles).

I turned a full 360 (doughnut or cookie) in an intersection and headed to a new street when the shocks bottomed out hard. There was a deep gutter for water runoff hidden by the heavy snow coating. All the intersections had pretty deep gutters and even with all that snow my backbone still rattled hard. Stopping in the middle of the road to regain my composure, I thought "I'm never taking this route again!" As I shook my head from side to side I sited something out of character to the left.

There was a home with no snow around its chimney. The sight looked strange and it took a minute to register because everything else was covered in deep whiteness. A large oval space showed snowless shingles. Then I noticed flames licking the bricks of the chimney and the roof. That took an enormous amount of heat to melt that much snow off the roof area. I jumped from the car and ran through the deep snow to the house. Luckily in small towns people don't lock their doors. I knocked hard and then rushed inside, yelling, "YOUR HOUSE IS ON FIRE!! YOU NEED TO GET OUT NOW!!"

Their home was full of white smoke. The tallest old couple I have ever met were holding onto each other for stability and slowly shuffle-stepping towards me. They looked in their eighties. He looked at least 6'7" and she was around 6'4", if not taller. They were in their bathrobes and slippers. I yelled, adrenaline rushing and thinking they might be hard of hearing also, "Grab your coats and go to your neighbors! I'll call the fire department!"

They seemed oblivious to the white smoke swirling around them and throughout their rooms. If God hadn't led me there I am confident they would have surely succumbed to the smoke and died. Their old style phone was right there on the wall. I quickly found some mail with the couple's home address on it and dialed 911. The volunteer fire department was there in less than 5 minutes! I moved my car, parked in the middle of the street with the door wide open, out of the way of the fire department vehicles.

I waited and watched until the elderly couple made it slowly and safely to the porch of their neighbors' home and saw the door open. They were safe and away from the smoke and fire and out of the deep snow. I find it very interesting that Heavenly Father will use our idiosyncrasies for His special errands in assisting His embodied spirit children here on earth. He used my habits to stop me precisely in front of that home, knowing I would turn my head and notice the fire! (Journal 11/3/1991)

> "The sweetest spirit and feeling in all of mortality is when we have an opportunity to be on the Lord's errand and to know that He has guided our footsteps." (President Thomas S. Monson, *BYU Magazine*, Spring 2008)
>
> ————————◆•◆————————
>
> Shortly after our marriage in the Salt Lake Temple, Jim and I found ourselves living in a rented cottage on the Oregon coast. Jim was a topographical engineer … His work was difficult because the coast was heavily forested … One evening I was about to start dinner, a strong impression came into my mind that my dinner preparations were not important … Jim was in trouble and needed my help!
> I did not hear a voice, but the message came as clearly to my mind as if it had been spoken … I felt impelled to get on the main highway … I felt that I should turn south … I passed many side roads, any one of which could have been Jim's area of work.
> I was impressed to leave the highway and follow one of the single-lane roads. It was raining, and after a mile or two the road became a muddy trail. I decided to turn around and head back … I thought, "It was silly of me to have come."
> But no sooner had I turned onto the highway than I came upon two tired, despondent engineers, so covered in mud that no one else would have wanted to pick them up.
> "How did you know where we were?" they wondered … I explained how I had been guided by the Spirit.
> As Jim and I knelt in prayer that evening, we gave thanks for the influence of the Holy Ghost, which had come to me in answer to my husband's prayers for help. (Latter-day Saint Voices, *Ensign*, Sep 2010)

Our oldest son did very well in school. I had a late season Elk permit and asked the school if I could take him and a friend, on an activity with me after lunch. Tyler and Jame were both ten years old. It was a snowy wintery Wednesday. I felt like there would be very few hunters during the middle of the week and we might have more of our pick of places and wild game.

My father, in a nearby town, had a 1961 Willy's box-style Jeep. He would remove the back bench seat during hunting season. This allowed room to lay our wild game: antelope, deer, or elk on the cold floorboards. Dad was done with his season, so he loaned his Jeep to us. It was a rattletrap and if you went over 45 mph one would think that the rivets were going to pop right off!

On the other hand, the Jeep was low geared and great for traversing steep mountainsides and snow. Our hunting area for deer and elk was west of Cody, WY, and butted up against Yellowstone National Park. My friends and I had multiple successes finding large buck deer and our choice of elk in these expansive, mountainous terrains. I picked my son and his friend up from their elementary school. There was a light snow falling, which seemed to increase in density as we continued deeper into our area. The main road was plowed, but all the side roads had about six inches of snow on them that had fallen during the day.

We kept watching for game and looking for the "right road" that would bring us success. Nothing seemed right until we arrived nearly at the East entrance to Yellowstone. There was a last road that went off to the left for miles. That one felt right. We went through all the snow effortlessly in the Jeep. We were looking for a place to park, get out and walk or watch for elk. There was already around 1 ½—2' of snow on the mountainside.

We came to a clearing on the right side where it was very steep. I thought, "I'll show my son how great this old Jeep is at driving straight up through snow." My father had shown me something similar when I was a boy and it was impressive. The jeep was slow, but very steady in those low gears. We drove above the tree line and parked in the deep snow. There was a large bald mountain in front of us. This would be a great place to watch for elk to come across. The snow was really too deep for hiking through though, especially for young boys.

Then I had the thought to turn off the engine. I told my son it would be best if the jeep and we would be very quiet. I then thought about my hunting partner (Jame's dad) who would actually *smell elk* and told the boys. I said, "Let's get out and look around and sniff around. Maybe something will show up. The snowflakes continued to increase in size.

As we looked around we notice something dark coming across the ridge towards us. I was putting my rifle scope up to get a better look when my son yelled, "Dad, I think that's a man!" (I think my scariest hunting experience was watching a trail on an opposing ridge and finding, in my scope, a gun with a scope looking at me! He was watching his opposing ridge trail also. Our big game rifles were pointed directly at each other. That made my heart jump!)

I put my rifle down after spotting the man atop the mountain frantically waving his arms. He was too far away to be able to hear his muffled sounds. We were so surprised to see someone on this snowy mountaintop during a major snowstorm in the middle of the week. Soon, two other men came over the ridge. It took them quite a long time to make their way down to our jeep through the heavy snow, which was now between two or three foot deep. They had spent most of their energy huffing it up the opposite side of the mountain through heavy snow.

They told us they had a brand new, four-wheel drive truck, with all the bells and whistles, buried up to the axles in the valley on the other side of the mountain. They had a large wench but there were no trees anywhere near to secure to. They told us they hurried up the mountain when they heard our Jeep climbing up the other side.

They were physically exhausted when they got to us and the snowstorm was very severe now. They were so excited to see us and gladly sat on the cold metal floor of the jeep. They exclaimed, "You saved our lives!!"

We were about three miles down this last road in our area. By now it was dark and it was snowing several inches per hour. The snowflakes were so thick and large that we could barely see the road. And there was a steep drop off on the right side. What really startled me was that there was a foot of snow on the road now and you couldn't even see any evidence of our driving on it. Our previous incoming tracks were all completely covered. If someone had been looking for us or our vehicle; they would have no idea where we were in this snow-blanketed massive hunting area!

We carefully and slowly made our way back to the main road through well over a foot of snow over three miles. These men were staying in a cabin that was another seven miles further down the main road. When we finally got to their cabin, they hugged us and thanked us for saving their lives. They were so pleased they were safe in their cabin that they offered us cash, gifts, and rewards.

"All I'd like is a cold drink."

"We have ice tea, coffee, Mountain Dew, Coke, beer, wine, and whiskey!"

I had to laugh inside my head and then replied, "How about just a cold glass of water?"

After downing our waters, they said, "Isn't there anything we can do for you?"

"Yes, just help someone else out in the future that needs saved."

As we drove back with our eyes very wide open, I began to think back about how Heavenly Father directed my thoughts every step of the way. We were directed to the last road on the left; then drove three miles through snow precisely to a small clearing in the trees on the right. The thought came to climb that steep snowy mountain above the timberline. Another thought came to turn off the engine, which stopped the heater. Then an additional idea trickled in to go outside the Jeep so we could view the entire mountainside to listen and watch. We never would have even spotted those stranded hunters had we not exited the vehicle at that precise spot.

I explained to the young boys that Heavenly Father puts good thoughts in our heads so we can help and serve other people. God showed us which road to take, the last road. He told us exactly where to stop on that long road. God put the thought in my head about grandpa showing off the Jeeps climbing skills. That idea made me want to show you how well the Jeep climbed in steep snow. Then He made me think about being quiet and turning off the Jeep, even though it would be cold. Then God placed the thought of your dad's (Jame's father) ability of smelling elk, so we got outside the car. Because we could see the whole mountain we were then able to see the stranded people.

If you knew how large these mountains and this area is, it was literally like being directed from heaven to directly find a small needle in a humongous haystack! I explained this to my son and his friend and exclaimed to them, "We didn't save those men's lives—God saved their lives! He led our every move and guided each thought; taking us to the only place amongst all those big mountains and all that snow where we could have possibly even seen one another. That is really amazing, isn't it?!" I hoped they would remember this experience; I sure haven't forgotten it! (Journal 11/29/1992)

> "Go your way whithersoever I will, and it shall be given you
> by the Comforter what you shall do and where you shall
> go." (D&C 31:11)

# 14. A Still Small Voice

It was not a harsh voice, neither was it a loud voice; nevertheless, and notwithstanding it being a small voice it did pierce them that did hear to the center, insomuch that there was no part of their frame that it did not cause to quake; yea, it did pierce them to the very soul, and did cause their heart to burn. (3 Ne. 11:3)

"No man can receive the Holy Ghost without receiving revelations. The Holy Ghost is a revelator." (*TPJS*, 328)

---◆---

"I felt this soft electrical charge run down my body like sparkling rain." (Our friend)

In our meetings, the majority never rules! We listen prayerfully to one another and talk with each other until we are united. Then when we have reached complete accord, the unifying influence of the Holy Ghost is spine-tingling! (President Russell M. Nelson, GC, April 2018)

And their meetings were conducted by the church after the manner of the workings of the Spirit, and by the power of the Holy Ghost; for as the power of the Holy Ghost led them whether to preach, or to exhort, or to pray, or to supplicate, or to sing, even so it was done. (Moroni 6:9)

*This pure revelation while conducting meetings that Moroni talks about is exactly what the Church, led by President Russell M. Nelson and Jesus Christ, are leading us back to—understanding and utilizing the workings of the Light of Christ and the Holy Ghost's powers in order to best minister to His children and to bless our families.*

And the light which shineth, which giveth you light, is through him who enlighteneth your eyes, which is the same light that quickeneth your understandings. Which light proceedeth forth from the presence of God to fill the immensity of space. (D&C 88:12-13)

For the word of the Lord is truth, and whatsoever is truth is light, and whatsoever is light is Spirit, even the Spirit of

Jesus Christ. And the Spirit giveth light to every man that cometh into the world; and the Spirit enlighteneth every man through the world, that hearkeneth to the voice of the Spirit. (D&C 84:45-46)

---

*Jehovah instructed the prophet Elijah to go and stand on the mountain in front of him.*

... And the Lord passed by, and a great and strong wind rent the mountains, and brake in pieces the rocks before the Lord; but the Lord was not in the wind: and after the wind an earthquake, but the Lord was not in the earthquake: And after the earthquake a fire; but the Lord was not in the fire: and after the fire *a still small voice.* (1 Kings 19:11-12)

The Holy Ghost is a member of the Godhead, yet He has no physical body ... but is a personage of Spirit. Were it not so, the Holy Ghost could not dwell in us." (D&C 130:22)

*The Holy Ghost is a testator of all truths. The main mission of the Holy Ghost is to witness to all of God's children that Jesus is the Christ and that Heavenly Father is our God.*

"... By the Holy Ghost, which beareth record of the Father and of the Son." (D&C 20:27)

"... Moses lifted up his eyes unto heaven, being filled with the Holy Ghost, which beareth record of the Father and the Son." (Moses 1:24)

You may believe that Jesus is the Christ, you may have been trained up in that belief; but you cannot know it unless God shall reveal it to you. It is only by the power of the Holy Ghost, that this knowledge can come to the children of men, neither can knowledge come to anyone concerning the things of God, except by the same spirit. (Charles Penrose, JD 22:82)

*The Holy Ghost is not the Light of Christ; these are two separate beautiful bounteous blessings to mankind. We have heard members testify over the pulpit that the two are the same; one personage that can touch all mankind. That is simply a falsehood.*

*President Joseph F Smith said,* "The Holy Ghost should not be confused with the Spirit [Light of Christ]" (*DS*, 1:49–50)

*Everyone on earth is blessed by both; however the Holy Ghost can be given as a companion gift through those with proper priesthood authority. Those that have not received the gift of the Holy Ghost can receive the influence of the Holy Ghost. There are some notable "non-members" who received the Holy Ghost's influence, including: Alma, Columbus, Cornelius, Joseph Smith, King Lamoni & the Queen, Saul/Paul, our nation's founders, millions of missionaries' investigators, etc.*

"... that I may pour my Spirit upon all flesh." (D&C 95:4)

There is a difference between the Holy Ghost and the gift of the Holy Ghost. Cornelius received the Holy Ghost before he was baptized, which was the convincing truth of the Gospel, but he could not receive the gift of the Holy Ghost until after he was baptized. (*TPJS*, 199)

*Ironically, there are many non-members who actually have more experience with the influence of the Holy Ghost than many members who have received the Gift of the Holy Ghost. It is simply a matter of life's choices. We have all probably had learning experiences with darkness when the Holy Ghost leaves and the resultant joy when He returns, in our own lives and/or in the lives of our loved ones. There are so many wonderful people throughout the world that receive answers to their prayers, promptings for their respective problems, and many personal revelations. A number of stories in this book are from faithful inspired non-members.*

"A man may receive the Holy Ghost, and it may descend upon him and not tarry with him." (D&C 130:23)

*The Light of Christ is given to every person born as a gift from God.* "And that *I am the true light that lighteth every man that cometh into the world.*" (D&C 93:2) "That was the true Light, which lighteth every man (woman) that cometh into the world." (John 1:9) *Many believe the Holy Ghost works in tandem with or even through the Light of Christ. I tend to agree with that school of thought. Even though everyone has the wonderful gift of the Light of Christ, that light can vary from "no light in the ... only*

*darkness" to "that light groweth brighter and brighter until the perfect day"*
*We all lay somewhere in between those two extremes.*

"But if a man walk in the night, he stumbleth, because there is no light in him." (John 11:10)

"… And because of meekness and lowliness of heart cometh the visitation of the Holy Ghost, which Comforter filleth with hope and perfect love …" (Moroni 8:26)

"How many of you have had the Spirit of God whisper unto you—the still small voice. I would have been in the spirit world a great many years ago, if I had not followed the promptings of the still small voice." (Wilford Woodruff, *JD* 21:189)

"As we faithfully live the gospel, we will have power to be virtuous in every thought, feeling, and action. Our minds become more receptive to the promptings of the Holy Ghost and the Light of Christ." (Robert D. Hales, GC, April 2017)

---

Our children all loved learning how to swim, except for our youngest. He loved to splash around in the beginner's swim class, but his progress was so slow that he remained in the beginner's class.  He was tall for his age and looked funny at 5, playing with the 3-year-olds.
Every year, when it was time to sign up for summer swim lessons; he would whine and try to talk me out of it. But I was determined that all of my kids would learn how to swim. His swim teachers would try to pass him off to another teacher because he was so difficult and this was discouraging to all of us. One time it took 3 teachers, one in the water and two by his side, to get him to do a squat dive. He cried and cried and hated it!
When he was in 4th grade, he started clear back in December to try to convince me not to make him take swimming lessons in the coming summer.  I never heard the end of it! I signed him up anyway and the night before his lessons started he was so upset.  He cried and begged me not to take him to swimming lessons.

I was so distraught and had all kinds of thoughts going through my mind: "Maybe I was wrong in forcing him to go? Maybe he has an unconscious thought about drowning in the future? Maybe I should give in to him?" In desperation I walked into my room and stood with my arms folded and said a prayer. "Heavenly Father, Devin doesn't want to take swimming lessons. Am I wrong to make him do it? I need an answer—right now, because he starts in the morning." As I had my eyes closed, I heard a voice as distinctly as if He was standing next to me say, "**A weakness can become a strength**." I was so surprised that I was immediately given such a clear and unquestionable answer to my prayer, that I said out loud, 'Thank you!'

Then the Lord put in my mind some names of people that I had learned about over the years, who have overcome weaknesses by turning them into strengths. I went immediately back into my son's room and sat on the edge of his bed. I told him that I had prayed and shared what Heavenly Father had told me. I told him about other people who were able to turn their weaknesses into strengths.

One of these was James Earl Jones who did the voice of Darth Vader in Star Wars. I shared with Devin, "When James was a boy he stuttered and was so ashamed of it that he would never raise his hand in class, even when he knew the answers. Now he is one of the most famous voices in the world!" I shared other stories and this comforted him. I told him I knew he could learn to be a strong swimmer.

I explained to the new teacher about his weakness and how I believed we could turn it into a strength. That was the year Devin finally learned to swim. A gentleman who had been watching his grandchildren over the years during their swim lessons commented to me, regarding Devin, 'You'd never know that was the same kid!'

Because of this experience, I have a very strong testimony of prayer. I know that if it is that important that you receive an answer, you can receive it right now. (A family friend)

And if men come unto me I will show unto them their weakness. I give unto men weakness that they may be humble; and my grace is sufficient for all men that humble themselves before me; for if they humble themselves before me, and have faith in me, then will I make weak things become strong unto them. (Ether 12:27)

In the twenty years I have kept the books for a retail store, the Spirit came to me only once throughout two decades of bookkeeping. In February of 2010 I was entering large credit card expenses, from January of the same year, into QuickBooks. This computer program takes all your data and puts batches of information entered and places everything into the *"right places"* for business and tax purposes.

As I was entering these credit card charges for large inventory purchases, the still small voice quietly said, **"Wrong year."** With that in mind, I reviewed the year slots and realized I had put in the wrong date of 2009, instead of 2010, on those major expenses. These large charges would have gone back into the previous year's records and been lost and unaccounted for; the 2009 records were already finished and sent off to the feds. (Journal 2/4/2010)

Our young family was visiting the grandparents one Sunday afternoon. A voice said clearly to me, **"Gather your family and go home"**. The voice was just like someone was standing by my side and visiting. I asked me wife to gather the children up because we needed to leave earlier than usual.

She sensed the importance in my voice, yet neither of us knew what exactly was important at the time. As soon as we walked in the door of our home the phone rang. The executive secretary of our ward was on the line and wanted us to come down immediately to visit with the stake president. We changed and went to see what was needed. I was called to serve in a bishopric and to be ordained a high priest. (A missionary peer)

... the angel of the Lord appeareth to Joseph in a dream, saying, Arise, and take the young child and his mother to Egypt, and be thou there until I bring thee word ... When he arose, he took the young child and his mother by night, and departed into Egypt. (Matthew 2:13-14)

One quiet Sunday afternoon the Spirit surprised me succinctly stating, **"Talk to Sam and Lisa about the temple."** The command was so specific and direct, that I called them right up. I asked them if I could come and visit them in about three weeks on my next business trip to their area. I explained that I wanted to talk to them about the temple. They agreed.

They are relatives that have always been members and were less active. They had been married for 23 years up to this time. They were inactive in the church as teenagers when they met and semi-active after marriage.

In a few weeks I set the appointment. When I visited, they provided a nice dinner and opened the rest of the evening for my counsel. The conversation was basically a 'temple preparation class.' I went over the details without being too specific. We discussed the sacred nature of the temple, ordinances and clothing. I bore testimony of the Lord's House. We talked about the eternal nature of temple covenants and its inherent blessings for families.

We discussed eternal families and the sealing power that binds us all together. I informed them of the necessary requirements for obtaining temple recommends and what they might need to change or do differently. The Spirit was definitely in their home that night and I felt confident the Holy Ghost touched all our hearts. We talked about the Holy Temple for three hours. Near the end of our discussion I committed them to talking with their bishop and setting an actual goal to be temple ready that summer. It was an awesome evening! (Journal 2/5/2006)

I followed up with this couple over the coming months to make sure they were staying on task. That summer our family gathered together in the Saint George Temple and this couple was sealed for time and all eternity. Some of their children were also sealed to them forever. Times like these are what we like to refer to as gospel *"paydays."*

When I shared my story of the specific prompting to talk to this couple I was pleasantly surprised to discover that several other people also received the same prompting: four or five members if I remember correctly. So after twenty-three years of marriage this couple was ready to make a spiritual commitment. No one really knew this, except the Godhead. They weren't ready at 20 years and probably wouldn't be at 25 years. When the time was optimal, Heavenly Father assigned the Holy Ghost to reach out and touch those people who were closest to this couple. Hence, the Spirit of God was moving across the land and creating a synergistic response to affect the couple from all angles at the appropriate and perfect time in their lives. (Journal 5/7/2006)

Curious about this event, I asked the couple at a later date, "Who all talked to you about the temple earlier in the year?" They informed me that people just started talking to them and they all wanted to talk about the same thing—the temple: Myself, her father, his weight-lifting partner, a former stake presidency member, etc.

"Indeed, we cannot have true faith in the Lord without also having complete trust in the Lord's will and in the Lord's timing." (Dallin H. Oaks, The Right Thing at the Right Time, *New Era*, JUL 2005)

---

*Amanda Smith shares her heart-wrenching experience at Haun's Mill:*

We sold our beautiful home in Kirtland for a song, and traveled all summer to Missouri—our teams poor, and with hardly enough to keep body and soul together. We arrived in Caldwell County, near Haun's Mill, nine wagons of us in company. Two days before we arrived we were taken prisoners by an armed mob that had demanded every bit of ammunition and every weapon we had. We surrendered all. They knew it, for they searched our wagons. A few miles more brought us to Haun's Mill, where that awful scene of murder was enacted. My husband pitched his tent by a blacksmith's shop. Bro. David Evans made a treaty with the mob that they would not molest us. He came just before the massacre and called the company together and they knelt in prayer.

I sat in my tent. Looking up I suddenly saw the mob coming—the same that took away our weapons. They came like so many demons or wild Indians. Before I could get to the blacksmith's shop door to alarm the brethren, who were at prayers, the bullets were whistling amongst them. I seized my two little girls and escaped across the mill-pond on a slab-walk. Another sister fled with me. Yet though we were women, with tender children, in flight for our lives, the demons poured volley after volley to kill us. A number of bullets entered my clothes, but I was not wounded. The sister, however, who was with me, cried out that she was hit. We had just reached the trunk of a fallen tree, over which I urged her, bidding her to shelter there where the bullets could not reach her, while I continued my flight to some bottom land. When the firing had ceased I went back to the scene of the massacre, for there were my husband and three sons, of whose fate I as yet knew nothing.

As I returned I found the sister in a pool of blood where she had fainted, but she was only shot through the hand.

Emerging from the blacksmith shop was my eldest son, bearing on his shoulders his little brother Alma. "Oh! my Alma is dead!" I cried, in anguish. "No, mother; I think Alma is not dead. But father and brother Sardius are killed!" What an answer was this to appall me! My husband and son murdered; another little son seemingly mortally wounded; and perhaps before the dreadful night should pass the murderers would return and complete their work! But I could not weep then. The fountain of tears was dry; the heart overburdened with its calamity, and all the mother's sense absorbed in its anxiety for the precious boy which God alone could save by his miraculous aid.

The entire hip joint of my wounded boy had been shot away. Flesh, hip bone, joint and all had been ploughed out from the muzzle of the gun, which the ruffian placed to the child's hip through the logs of the shop and deliberately fired. We laid little Alma on a bed in our tent and I examined the wound. It was a ghastly sight. I knew not what to do. It was night now. There were none left from that terrible scene, throughout that long, dark night, but about half a dozen bereaved and lamenting women, and the children. Eighteen or nineteen, all grown men excepting my murdered boy and another about the same age, were dead or dying; several more of the men were wounded, hiding away, whose groans through the night too well disclosed their hiding places, while the rest of the men had fled, at the moment of the massacre, to save their lives. ... Yet was I there, all that long, dreadful night, with my dead and my wounded, and none but God as our physician and help. "Oh my Heavenly Father," I cried, "what shall I do? Thou seest my poor wounded boy and knowest my inexperience. Oh, Heavenly Father, direct me what to do!"

And then *I was directed as by a voice speaking* to me. The ashes of our fire was still smouldering. We had been burning the bark of the shag-bark hickory. **I was directed to**

323

**take those ashes and make a lye and put a cloth saturated with it right into the wound.** It hurt, but little Alma was too near dead to heed it much. Again and again I saturated the cloth and put it into the hole from which the hip joint had been ploughed, and each time mashed flesh and splinters of bone came away with the cloth; and the wound became as white as chicken's flesh.

Having done as directed I again prayed to the Lord and *was again instructed as distinctly as though a physician had been standing by speaking to me.* Nearby was a slippery-elm tree. From this **I *was told* to make a slippery-elm poultice and fill the wound with it.** My eldest boy was sent to get the slippery-elm from the roots, the poultice was made, and the wound, which took fully a quarter of a yard of linen to cover, so large was it, was properly dressed. It was then I found vent to my feelings in tears, and resigned myself to the anguish of the hour. And all that night we, a few poor, stricken women, were thus left there with our dead and wounded. ...

... I removed the wounded boy to a house, some distance off, the next day, and dressed his hip; *the Lord directing me as before.* I was reminded that in my husband's trunk there was a bottle of balsam. This I poured into the wound, greatly soothing Alma's pain. "Alma, my child," I said, "you believe that the Lord made your hip?"

"Yes, mother." "Well, the Lord can make something there in the place of your hip, don't you believe he can, Alma?" "Do you think that the Lord can, mother?" inquired the child, in his simplicity.

"Yes, my son," I replied, "*he has showed it all to me in a vision.*"

Then I laid him comfortably on his face and said: "Now you lay like that, and don't move, and the Lord will make you another hip." So Alma laid on his face for five weeks, until he was entirely recovered—a flexible gristle having grown in place of the missing joint and socket, which remains to this day a marvel to physicians. On the day that he walked again I was out of the house fetching a bucket of water, when I heard screams from the children. Running back, in affright, I entered, and there was Alma on the floor, dancing around, and the children screaming in astonishment and joy. It is now nearly forty years ago, but Alma has never been the least crippled during his life, and he has traveled quite a long period of the time as a missionary of the gospel and a living miracle of the power of God. (*LDS Biographical Encyclopedia*, Andrew Jenson, Vol. 2, p.792-796)

---

*A most important conversation between two pregnant women:*

And it came to pass, that, when Elisabeth heard the salutation of Mary, **the babe leaped in her womb**; and **Elisabeth was filled with the Holy Ghost:** And she spake out a loud voice, and said, Blessed art thou among women, and blessed is the fruit of thy womb. And whence is this to me, that the mother of my Lord should come to me? For, lo, as soon as the voice of thy salutation sounded in mine ears, the babe leaped in my womb for joy.
And Mary said, My soul doth magnify the Lord. And my spirit hath rejoiced in God my Saviour. For he hath regarded the low estate of his handmaiden: for, behold, from henceforth all generations shall call me blessed. (Luke 1:38-44, 46-48)

---

When I was dating I decided to just date and have fun because I had run into so many dead ends in the past. So as soon as I stopped looking for someone to marry, I met a girl and we became friends through a lot of fun experiences. I really started liking her and prayed to Heavenly Father about her. This was probably one of the more clear thoughts I've had from Heavenly Father in my life. The voice that came into my mind was, **"Well, what are you waiting for then?"** That gave me the courage to go forward and propose to her. We've had a great marriage ever since. (A young friend)

---

I was once concluding a talk I had given at the funeral of a fine Latter-day Saint mother and was almost ready to say amen and sit down. There came into my mind the words, **"Turn around and bear your testimony."** And this I did. I thought no more about the event for several months until my sister, then living in a neighboring stake, paid us a visit and told us this incident:

She said: "There lives in our ward a woman who for many years has taken no interest in the Church. Our efforts to activate her have been fruitless. Recently she has completely changed. She pays her tithing, attends sacrament meetings regularly, and participates in all Church activities. When asked what caused the reformation, she said: 'I went to Salt Lake City to the funeral of my mother. During the services a man by the name of Romney spoke. After he had given an ordinary talk, I thought he was going to sit down; but instead he turned around to the pulpit and bore a testimony which greatly impressed me. It awakened in me a desire to live as my mother had always taught me.'" (Marion G. Romney, GC, April 1978)

---

One late Sunday afternoon, our family was relaxing and the Spirit simply said, **"Check on the store."** I got up and grabbed my keys and told my wife I was told by the Spirit to *check on the store*. She asked if I needed anyone to tag along and I thought that wouldn't be necessary. We co-owned this business and it was a large, stand-alone building. One of my pre-opening stipulations was that we never open or work on Sundays, which I am grateful my partner agreed to.

Arriving at the front of our retail health food store, I noticed nothing was amiss. There were no broken windows and nothing out of the ordinary. I got out and checked the front door to find it locked solid. Then I looked through the large plate glass windows to find the cash registers, computer, safe, shelves and product all sitting in their respective spots. At least what I could see looked in order.

Finding nothing out of the ordinary I was beginning to wonder why I was clearly prompted to come check things out. Then I moved to the back of the store and could immediately see that the large metal rear door was ajar; it was not secured! Now I had a bit of fright run through me, thinking: "Somebody could be inside, vandals could have damaged things, and people might have stolen things from the back room: computer, scales, equipment, etc.

Opening the back door slowly and quietly, I listened for any sound or activity. Not hearing anything, I entered the back of the business and grabbed a steel rod. Proceeding towards our deli, I carefully rounded the corner and saw nothing out of the ordinary. Then I slowly went by the end of each long aisle with my crude weapon. There was no product lying on the floor, not a thing was out-of-order, and everything checked out fine.

Finding nothing wrong whatsoever, I braced the metal doors in the back with the long metal bar that should have been set on Saturday night while closing. Then I went back to the front of the store and unlocked, then relocked the front doors and went home. I am confident that something seriously wrong would have happened to our business and/or business property that evening; because some *hoodlums* would have noticed the door to the store ajar, as I had. This was the only time over fourteen years that I felt a need to *check on the store*."

---

*Our fourth great grandfather bears his testimony of the Holy Ghost:*

> When I came out of the water, I knew that I had been born of water and of the spirit, for **my mind was illuminated with the Holy Ghost.**
> I spent the evening at Dr. F. G. Williams. While in bed that night I felt what appeared to be a hand upon my left shoulder and a sensation like fibers of fire immediately enveloped my body. It passed from my right shoulder across my breast to my left shoulder; it then struck me on my collar bone and went to the pit of my stomach, after which it left me. I was enveloped in a heavenly influence, and could not sleep for joy.
> The next day I started home a happy man. (Philo Dibble, *Early Scenes in Church History*, p. 76)

> "Words cannot describe the happiness that comes into our lives when the Spirit of God is with us. This happiness includes a peace that passeth understanding except to the person that receives it." (Franklin D. Richards, CR, Oct 1965)

---

> Therefore it is given to abide in you; the record of heaven; **the Comforter**; the peaceable things of immortal glory; the truth of all things; that which quickeneth all things, which maketh alive all things; that which knoweth all things, and hath all power according to wisdom, mercy, truth, justice, and judgment. (Moses 6:61)

*The Holy Ghost is most comforting and purely powerful.*

---

While living in California we moved to a new home and ward within our stake. After being there only two weeks, the Spirit brought my attention to a woman and said to me, **"Take dinner to her on Tuesday."**

I could see that she had several young children, just like we did. I did not know her name or anything else about her. I asked someone where the stranger lived.

I was so busy going to school, fulfilling my callings, and being a wife and mother. However, because of the unique prompting, I committed to bring her dinner. That Tuesday I had not even had time to go to the store. I had some canned beans, which I never used to make dinner for anyone else before.

I put something together with the canned beans and took a meal to this sister. At the door, I explained, "I felt impressed to bring you dinner today."

She was very grateful and explained that someone had asked her to take care of their children for the day and it was all she could do to take care of all the small children in her home. She had not even had time to think about dinner.

A couple of weeks later was our "temple anniversary" and that was such a special date that we could return to the temple to remind us of our eternal family bond. Unfortunately, my husband was not able to attend the temple at this time and I was very sad and heartbroken. It was as if my dreams were being shattered.

During my discouragement, a knock on the door brought me to discover the sister I had made dinner for standing on my porch. She had a little pot of flowers and said, "I was impressed to bring these to you today."

No one except the Lord knew what I was going through. Then the Lord sweetly said unto me, **"I brought you flowers."** (A relative)

---

I felt the unmistakable prompting to park my car and visit Ben and Emily, even though I was on the way to a meeting. It was a sunny weekday afternoon. I approached the door to their home and knocked. Emily answered.

When she recognized me, her bishop, she exclaimed, "All day long I have waited for my phone to ring. It has been silent. I hoped that the postman would deliver a letter. He brought only bills. Bishop, how did you know today was my birthday?"

I answered, "God knows, Emily, for He loves you." (Thomas S. Monson, GC, April 1985)

———————◆———————

Working as a national marketing manager required many flights across the country, to trade shows in most every major metropolitan area. I quickly discovered the benefits available to frequent flyers. I was blessed to make most of my own reservations in advance. After learning the ropes, I started throwing all of our company's travel business to Continental and Delta. I soon found myself at the premium levels of both airlines' frequent flyer programs, landing at the top 1% of their frequent flyer's category/level respectively.

The choicest benefit was the First Class bump; if there was an open First Class seat available it became mine, with no extra fees. Should my wife be traveling with me and there were 2 seats open in First Class, we both enjoyed the benefits. From perusing my journal I noted I was bumped to First Class seating on every single flight to and from all major cities back in 1988 and 1993 and most flights the other years; those were numerous trips. (We were able to fly First Class to Hawaii for free as a benefit.)

The airlines literally spoiled me; treating me/us like royalty. We could board first, middle, or last; it was our option. There were many other amenities also. The airlines soon began bumping me up to First Class in advance. I didn't even have to request it.

I was traveling east from Los Angeles on business and seated in 1D. I was surprised to see a young Hispanic girl, with a baby, sit down next to me in 1C. I thought, "I wonder how she can afford First Class? Maybe she has a rich grandma? Maybe her dad's a sports star?" Then I thought to myself, "Well that's very judgmental of me. I'm from a poor family and am flying First Class." Still, one does not often see young people riding in the front of an airliner, and very rarely does one discover a baby in First Class seating.

Her baby boy was so cute, with curly black hair, glistening dark eyes, dimples, etc. I was flirting with the baby and he was smiling back at me. Normally First Class is more reserved and quiet. There's not a lot of visiting between passengers. With a yearning desire to hold her baby, I simply said a silent prayer in my heart and mind, "I'd really love to hold that baby."

Immediately, in response to my heartfelt prayer, the Spirit simply suggested, **"Ask her."**

So I turned to the young mother with renewed confidence and asked, "May I hold your baby?"

She quickly responded in a soft voice, "Oh would you please, I don't feel well at all! Here's his food and his diapers and wipes … here are some toys." She promptly handed him over to me along with all his things.

I explained to her that I was really good with babies and that I would be glad to take care of him for her while she rested. He came gleefully into my arms. He was eight-months old. (I love all babies and toddlers; 8-10 months being my most favorite age). His mother immediately drifted off into a long sound sleep. I informed the First Class stewardess of the situation and requested she not interrupt the ill mother's rest for anything. We all allowed the young mamma to sleep.

This was the most enjoyable flight I have ever been on! The bouncing bundle of boy cooed, smiled, and we elated each other. As we soared across America, I fed him, changed him, and entertained him. He mostly wanted to bounce up and down in my lap. He would smile and his entire face would glowingly light up, which pleased me to no end. I'm sure my face was lighting up in reciprocating response. I was actually glad he didn't take a nap because this baby boy was so invigorating! He was also entertaining me.

Eating the meal was tricky because he was so active. I was just glad I wasn't cramped in coach with an active baby and food. I cared for her baby boy the entire flight. His mother sorely needed deep sleep. In fact, she did not wake up when we landed, taxied, and arrived at the gate. Not until we all heard the loud clank of the exit door opening did she stir.

She could not stop thanking me and exclaimed, "You must really love children!"

I confirmed her comment and then suggested I continue to hold her precious package until she had everything together and we deplaned. Then a thought came, "Nobody on that plane had any inkling that the young mother was under the weather, not the baby, stewardesses, me, or any other passengers."

Only Heavenly Father knew his daughter's dilemma. There is no doubt in my mind as to why we were seated together on that jet. She needed an earthly angel that day. I actually pray to be seated near or next to cranky babies on airplanes. I doubt if many men or women in the world even desire or hope for what I pray for! On this flight, the baby was anything but cranky!

"Yea, and when you do not cry unto the Lord, let your hearts by full, drawn out in prayer unto him continually for your welfare, and also for the welfare of those who are around you." (Alma 37:27)

My parents had five children and then they had a late surprise, which was me. During Mom's last pregnancy, and only this one, *both of my parents heard the Spirit whisper,* **"You will have a girl, her name will be Maria."**

When they went to the hospital for the delivery, the nurse asked them to write down a boy's name and a girl's name, which was common then. They explained to her that they were having a girl named Maria.

The nurse was persistent and suggested they have a boy's name also.

My Mom said, "Ok, um … Joe, I guess." (Our friend Maria)

*In the scriptures we find similarly striking stories:*

**"Fear not Zacharias: for thy prayer is heard; and thy wife Elisabeth shall bear thee a son, and thou shalt call his name John"** (Angel Gabriel, Luke 1:13)

**"And she shall bring forth a son, and thou shalt call his name JESUS …"** (Angel in a dream to Joseph, Matt 1:21)

I was headed out to work on the road one day and stopped first at our credit union. After dealing with the teller, I turned around and was surprised to see our oldest son standing there, right in front of me. He had some paperwork in his hand and sounded rather anxious.

"Dad, I want to buy this car and all I need is for you to cosign for me and I can get it!"

I had the impression **"Do not cosign"**

I told him I was sorry but I was not supposed to do that for him.

He couldn't understand why not. He persisted and pestered me.

I told him it was a firm feeling I had inside, along with a gut feeling, and I was going to stick to my impressions.

He walked off in a disappointed huff.

As I traveled from account to account I had forgotten about our discussion at the credit union.

When I arrived home and visited with my wife about our day's doings, she shared, "I had the most interesting experience on the porch deck today while I was eating my lunch.

"A voice said, **'Do not cosign.'**

"I thought that was the most unusual message I'd ever received! Then 'he' came home right after that and came out on the deck and he asked me to cosign on a car for him. I explained to him that I was told not to, by God. He wasn't very happy at all."

I then shared my previous experience at the credit union with her, that very morning, where I received an identical message from the Holy Ghost. We do not have any idea why we weren't suppose to cosign, we just both absolutely knew we were not supposed to for some unknown reason.

It is an awesome blessing when couples receive similar or identical personal revelations. The quiet whisperings become a couple's revelation. It's so wonderful when we are on the same page! (Journal 5/13/2001)

We had several projects to print out personally and for church assignments to no avail. We had carpeted and painted our office; after putting everything back together and hooking up all the cords, the printer was not functioning.

Accessing the "Print and Scan Doctor" app did not work. The "Doctor" found the printer and claimed it was connected and working. We couldn't obtain a "second opinion." I tried working from the PC to the printer and vice versa, with no luck.

We decided to go to the temple to serve and forget our worries. As we drove towards our temple, we both had identical promptings. My wife said, "I think we need to restart the printer."

"That was the same idea I just had!"

"Well, let's try that when we get home."

"Okay."

We had unplugged the printer recently when we modernized the room and it would have restarted then—so I wondered. After our temple time, I simply unplugged the printer and then plugged it back in 30 seconds later—and things started printing again! (Journal 2/24/19)

Because Adam and Eve were obedient, the Holy Ghost led them. As husband and wife, you can receive direction in your lives by qualifying for the gift of the Holy Ghost through obedience to the teachings of the Savior. (Richard G. Scott, GC, 1996)

*On other occasions we can receive the same revelation/words for two separate, yet similar, situations:*

When I was helping take care of our dying father I found myself consumed by his needs. This strong man had to have everything done for him. Dad had such a big heart and had helped and served so many people in different ways that he made numerous friends over many decades. He was a Seventy in the Stake for a long time and his sincere love for people made him very successful in his missionary labors. He helped support children, nephews, and others on missions. He gave big discounts when doing extended family's graduation, wedding, and other pictures in his photography business. He befriended people with physical and mental disabilities that most other folks commonly avoided and shunned.

When he fell ill there were so many of his family and friends that would call or come over. The phone seemed to ring constantly along with Dad's call outs for this or that. Many people would come to the door. If the phone wasn't ringing, the doorbell was. I was run ragged. After awhile I realized that I had forgotten to use the bathroom, eat, shower, comb my hair, and brush my teeth. I prayed for extra strength to serve our father and the Holy Spirit clearly instructed **Take care of yourself first."**

After taking the heavenly counsel, I found that I felt better and had more energy to serve our dying father when I took care of my needs first. It was so simple, but I was not even taking time to think of any of my own needs. (Journal 5/8/2007)

My wife was spending an inordinate amount of time nurturing a child with a chronic illness. This nearly constant service was consuming her. She pleaded and prayed for God's help on how to best assist our child. The Holy Ghost responded to her question for help likewise with this sage advice, **"Take care of yourself first."**

*When we are strengthened we can strengthen others.*

"But I have prayed for thee, that thy faith fail not: and when thou art converted, strengthen thy brethren." (Luke 22:32)

---

I have used a "verbal battering hammer" on myself in silent despair, as I've compared us and ours to: all good people doing their best, though far from perfect against other's faultless selfies posted on Facebook or whose accomplishments are described in detail in the Christmas letters we receive from friends and family, justifiably touting the accomplishment of their grandchildren—*all* serving missions, *all* marrying in the temple, *all* staying active in the Church, and *all* gathering together *every* Sunday evening for dinner.

With our mixed bundle of children and grandchildren (who are every color of the rainbow, none of whom we would give away), we have watched them suffer through multiple divorces, cope with confused gender identity, and grapple with doctrinal doubts while also seeing them all do their best to deal with a tangle of hectic work schedules and other demands. We rarely get to be together. We wish it were different. But, when we do see them, we always have a great time!

For years, as our kids were growing up, we sought diligently to ensure obedience and tried consistently to hold Family Home Evening, say family prayers, and read the scriptures. We often failed in our efforts. But when our kids' choices bordered on rebellion, we all too often exercised authority in a manner that surely didn't echo God's commitment to agency, as expressed in the hymn 240, *"Know This, That Every Soul is Free"*—wherein one verse proclaims that "God would force no man to heav'n." Well, that wasn't always our approach, but, with children now grown we are learning that our job instead is to pray for them, listen to them (when they do call), encourage them, and, mostly, just love and accept them.

My hope is strengthened as I serve each Friday morning in the Salt Lake Temple. Not all who so serve are perfect or have perfect families, but we are trying. A widowed friend, perhaps sensing my family failures and recognizing them in her own, shared with me a recent experience. She had just attended a missionary homecoming for a nephew (the *fifth* and last in her brother's family to "return home with honor") followed by a joyous family gathering.

Truly happy for her brother and his family, still upon going home to her empty apartment, she felt "lesser than," hurting with thoughts of her own inactive, wayward, and sometimes distant children. Getting ready to crawl into bed and just pull the covers over her face, the Spirit whispered to her, **"Your children aren't finished yet**." No verbal battering hammer here!

The comforting message that had blanketed her in God's love for less-than-perfect progeny, offered me, second-hand, that same balm to my own soul. I felt a great comfort knowing that my own children and grandchildren *"aren't finished yet"* and neither am I."

We *can* all be perfect "eventually." We just need to keep going, keep trying, keep trusting, and keep loving until we are all "finished." After all, Jesus is our "author and *finisher"* (see Hebrews 12:2) (A relative)

*This story was shared with my wife and me at a most needy time when we also struggled with striving to do all that the Lord has commanded and then having none of our sons serve missions and a daughter and son not marrying in the temple. This was followed by multiple divorces, financial disasters, doctrinal disagreements, and four-generations of mental illnesses. We and our children are also "not finished yet" and are eternally grateful for Heavenly Father and the Savior reaching out now and in the future, as a hen gathereth her chickens under her wings. (See 3 Ne. Chapter 10)*

"These things I have spoken unto you, that in me ye might have peace. In the world ye shall have tribulation: but be of good cheer, I have overcome the world." (John 16:33)

Since one of our daughter's divorce I have struggled with it and wondered how in the world God can fix that we make down here. I love my former son-in-law to death and wish it could be fixed and mended. Then our daughter married another guy. It was such an emotional rollercoaster in our family for some time.

There are so many situations like this and how are they all going to be fixed? All these messes are all over the place! So I went to cross the yard one day and it was like being in a stuffy room when you open a window and a fresh breeze comes in and you smell everything; an entirely different environment comes upon you.

It was like what Joseph Smith described as pure intelligence pouring into my mind. It is too hard to describe, but the knowledge was amazing. **"I can fix it. Relax,"** I heard in my mind. I'm fine now. God settled my mind, He can fix those things. I don't know how He's going to fix them but I did know that He would do it somehow with proxies.

I got the impression that some people would raise other people's children; different people would do things for other people. We also are adopted into so many things within the Gospel: the family of Christ when we get baptized, the sons of Moses and Aaron when we receive the priesthood, the House of Israel, if we are not a literal descendant, etc. He is going to arrange families as to how they are suppose to be and we will be okay with it.

I was on the way to the my shop and not even thinking about this when my eyes filled with tears and I understood that God could and would fix all these messes through adoptions and proxies, which He uses a lot. I had to compose myself so the five welders there wouldn't see me crying; so I ducked into the office. My wife was there and I was able to share my personal revelation with her. (Our friends)

"In the Millennium, a duration of one thousand years, we shall be actively engaged **administering for the dead**, and *assisting God to fix up accounts* with the inhabitants of the earth." (John Taylor, *JD* 19:150)

I speak to those who are facing personal trials and family struggles, those who endure conflicts fought in the lonely foxholes of the heart, those trying to hold back floodwaters of despair that sometimes wash over us like a tsunami of the soul. I wish to speak particularly to you who feel your lives are broken, seemingly beyond repair.

To all such I offer the surest and sweetest remedy that I know. It is found in the clarion call the Savior of the world Himself gave. He said it in the beginning of His ministry, and He said it in the end. He said it to believers, and He said it to those who were not so sure. He said to everyone, whatever their personal problems might be: "Come unto me, all ye that labour and are heavy laden, and I will give you rest. Take my yoke upon you, and learn of me; for I am meek and lowly in heart: and ye shall find rest unto your souls." (Matt 11:28-29) (Jeffrey R. Holland, GC, April 2006)

In 1990 my husband was having a difficult time. He was overwhelmed with life: school, coaching, husband, father, and trying to do a church job! He received a new calling to work in a Ricks College Ward. The circumstances were that he actually was called to the wrong calling at first. Later the correct calling was issued. He was having feelings that the leaders were in desperation verses inspiration.

As he vented to me, I worried about his attitude. The "mother in me" felt the need to correct him. This only fueled the fire, so to speak. I tried to tell him how he should think and feel. My actions were understandably met with resistance. We struggled in our relationship. There was much contention.

I went to the canal in Sugar City, Idaho, to be alone. It was here that I had a personal revelation.

Clearly, in my mind, I heard the words: "**It is not your job to make him be good!**"

It amazes me how the Holy Ghost can help us understand like no one else can. I knew this is what I had been doing. If anyone else had said this to me, it wouldn't have struck me in the same way.

This helped me to back off. I was more able to just listen and give support. I realized that each of us has to seek our own salvation. I can lead by example, encourage, and listen, but it isn't my job to force anyone to act or think in a particular way." (A friend)

"Behold, this is not my doctrine, to stir up the hearts of men with anger, one against another; but this is my doctrine, that such things should be done away" (3 Ne. 11:30) 'Let us think seriously about that scripture: the spirit of contention is the spirit of the devil, who is the father of contention! Can we suppose that any of us can do the work of Christ if we have the spirit of contention in our hearts or in our homes? ... We are engaged in the Lord's work. Then we should be guided by the spirit of the Lord and not by some contrary spirit. We should not invite into our homes the spirit of Satan himself by engaging in family quarrels, contention, and arguments.'" (Mark E. Petersen, CR, Oct 1961)

One of the members of our ward had a mental breakdown. He would always come to church and be found pacing around behind the overflow chairs during sacrament. He would quietly mumble. He was asked to give the opening prayer for sacrament meeting one Sunday. As this brother made the long walk from the very back of our long narrow chapel, he was softly mumbling.

I simply asked a quiet question internally, "What is it with Charles, Lord?"

I was quite surprised to receive a firm and quick verbal response, **"He is a man of God."**

Charles Hawkins and his wife Olive had both served missions, as did all of their children, five boys and two girls. They are a wonderful family. I was humbled and looked at Brother Hawkins under an entirely new light. This experience taught me to look at others in a new light also. It has been a lifelong process for me to attempt to see people as their Heavenly Father and Christ sees them. The following scripture came to mind: "... for the Lord seeth not as man seeth; for man looketh on the outward appearance, but the LORD looketh on the heart." (1 Samuel 16:7)

> "And the angel said unto me **he is a holy man**; wherefore I know he is a holy man because it was said by an angel of God." (Alma 10:9)

———— •◆• ————

Many times we have seen the Lord's hand active in our lives through the inspiration that has come when answers were needed and unavailable in any other way. In 1996, I spent a summer in Yorkshire, England, doing family history research and e-mail was a still new technology.
Being able to regularly be in touch with my husband at home in Maryland was vital to my homesick heart. During my first week in England, I spent hours on the phone with a CompuServe tech in Ireland, who tried repeatedly to figure out why my laptop was unable to connect. Nothing worked!
Then came the quiet whisper of the spirit, that I should "**replace the capital 'Os' in the string of logon numbers with zeros.**" I did so and the connection was instantly successful. Tears of gratitude spilled over as I thanked God for heaven's help. (A relative)

> "Rejoice in the Lord always, and again I say, Rejoice." (Philip. 4:4)

———— •◆• ————

And, behold, there was a man in Jerusalem, whose name was Simeon; and the same man was just and devout, waiting for the consolation of Israel: and the Holy Ghost was upon him.

And it was revealed unto him by the Holy Ghost, that **he should not see death, before he had seen the Lord's Christ.**

And he came by the Spirit into the temple: and when the parents brought in the child Jesus, to do for him after the custom of the law,

Then took he him up in his arms, and blessed God, and said, Lord, now lettest thou thy servant depart in peace, according to thy word: For mine eyes have seen thy salvation ... (Luke 2:25-30)

We rented four-wheelers, snowmobiles, and wave runners as a family over the years. We chose to buy wave runners and that was a great decision. These big water toys brought all the children and grandchildren together to the beach as we created enjoyable memories. We feel like the water toys have been a very worthwhile investment for our entire family.

One Saturday morning, my youngest son and I were preparing to tow the wave runners to the reservoir and then meet his married siblings and nephews at the beach. He mentioned that he had watched me hook up the trailer and lights and thought it was about his turn to do it. I said, "Sure", as I loaded other things into our vehicle. We got away and stopped to gas up several blocks from home.

As we pulled out from the gas station, I had one of my more unique spiritual whisperings, simple saying "**Hitch Pin.**" I immediately pulled over to the side of the rode to inspect the hitch.

"Why are we stopping dad?"

"The Spirit suggested I check the hitch pin."

The hitch pin is what keeps the hitch locked onto the ball so that the hitch and trailer don't pop off and cause damage to your own vehicles and others. Rounding the back of the SUV, I spotted the hitch pin lying atop the back bumper, obviously unattached. I secured the hitch pin properly and now had a choice to make.

Though it has taken me decades, I am finally starting to make much better choices when responding to these types of situations. I could have blown my top or lost my cool with my son. I could have berated him for not locking the hitch. Then I could have explained how it would be entirely his fault that the trailer and machines were damaged and worse, how he could have caused a serious accident on the freeway or even killed someone!

Instead, choosing the higher road, I said, as we drove off, "Isn't it neat how the Holy Ghost can tell us simple things that can protect others, ourselves, and our belongings?" We had a nice discussion about inspiration and how to be worthy to hear the same. It was a very nice drive to the reservoir and a great day. Had I come down on him hard, it would have been a most different mood and ride to the mountains and nothing positive would have been gained therefrom. (Journal 6/24/2012)

> Rather than being judgmental and critical of each other, may we have the pure love of Christ for our fellow travelers in this journey through life. May we recognize that each one is doing her best to deal with the challenges which come her way, and may we strive to do *our* best to help out. (President Thomas S. Monson, GC, Oct 2010)

God speaks to us in our language. He also doesn't always say "YES" or "NO" even when it's really important. I was asking Heavenly Father whether or not I should serve a mission as a sister missionary. I had thought of the pros and cons and always planned on going.

These words entered into my head, **"is this what you want?"**

"Yes this is what I've always wanted and looked forward to it."

Then more words came into my head, **"If this is what you want, then I would love if you served."** Funny though, He left the choice to my desires, totally up to me.

Imagine my surprise when the same council came when I was praying about a young man I was dating. Once again Heavenly Father asked, **"Is this what you want? Then I'm behind you."** Sometimes, rather than telling me the answer he trusts me to make my own decisions. (A relative)

Not too long ago my wife, Tamara, came into the room and excitedly exclaimed, "I'm going to write a talk!" She seemed so happy about this. Such excitement about a talk has never occurred during our decades of marriage.

"Really— Why?"

"The Holy Ghost told me to!"

"So, did He give you a topic too?"

To my surprise she confirmed the same stating, "Yes, He did, I'm suppose to **prepare a talk on the Savior.**"

Little did she know that our bishop had asked me that very morning if we would speak as a couple in sacrament. I wasn't going to share this with her until after dinner. Usually when she has a speaking assignment it causes some anxiety and trepidation. When I called the bishop later that evening to let him know we accepted the speaking assignment, I asked him if there was a topic he would like us to touch on.

The bishop replied, "I'd like you both to speak on 'Keeping Christ as the focus of my life.'"

She is so in tune that she already knew she would be speaking and what the topic would be!

I am eternally grateful for an inspired companion! (Journal 3/3/2013)

> "I am grateful for my companion and for her inspiration, strength, and help. I know that I could not have accomplished the little that I have achieved, without her great faith, devotion, and support." (Ezra Taft Benson, GC, April 1947)

---

*A great story from Wilford Woodruff:*
While on the road there, I drove my carriage one evening into the yard of Brother Williams. Brother Orson Hyde drove a wagon by the side of mine. I had my wife and children in the carriage. I had not been there a few minutes when the Spirit said to me, **"Get up and move that carriage."** I told my wife I had to get up and move the carriage. She said, "What for?" and I said, "I don't know." That's all she asked me on such occasions. When I told her I did not know, that was enough. I got up and moved my carriage four or five rods and put the off fore *[sic]* wheel against the corner of the house. I then looked around me and went to bed. The same Spirit said, **"Go and move your animals from that oak tree."** They were two hundred yards from where my carriage was. I went and moved my horses and put them in a little hickory grove. I again went to bed.

In thirty minutes a whirlwind came up and broke that oak tree off within two feet from the ground. It swept over three or four fences and fell square in that dooryard near Brother Orson Hyde's wagon and right where mine had stood. What would have been the consequences if I had not listened to that spirit? Why, myself, wife, and children would have been killed. That was the still small voice to me. No earthquake, no thunder, no lightning but the still small voice of the Spirit of God. It saved my life. It was a spirit of revelation. (*Discourses of Wilford Woodruff,* 295-96)

---

While flying from Salt Lake City airport on Southwest Airlines, a quiet thought suddenly popped into my head as I boarded the plane, **"first open window seat."** So I found just that, and sat down—although I wouldn't normally have chosen a row with a man already seated there.

All I wanted to do was sleep with my head against the window. With five children to care for, I was exhausted from all the preparations I had made ahead of time to make my absence easier on my husband. I leaned against the window and hoped for a lengthy rest.

A few minutes later the man laid a book down on the seat in-between us. I became abruptly alert by the surprise that he was reading a book relating to subtle energy. I pulled my copy of a similarly-related book and he got a big grin on his face. As it turned out, that prompting had led me to a seat by a Materials Scientist who was on the board chairing the forthcoming Whole Person Health Summit in Baltimore, Maryland.

When he found out I intended to write a book about the incredible help I had found for my daughter using alternative health modalities, he started suggesting websites and recommending authors and scientific research that could help me.

We talked all the way across the country to Baltimore, which was entirely out of the ordinary for my quiet nature. I got off the plane with fourteen pages of notes from a complete stranger who had become an esteemed acquaintance. A few weeks later my new friend offered me a complimentary entrance ticket to the Whole Person Health Summit worth several hundred dollars. My husband and I prayed about it and I KNEW I was supposed to attend the event." (My wife Tamara)

*Preparing meals ahead of her absence is simply the type of Christ-like person Tamara is. She takes care of us, even when she's not here! In no way do I demand or request this; although I have come to graciously and thankfully expect prepared meals, she continually ministers to me and our family whether she's home or abroad.*

---

I was at a meeting in Chicago for three days. We ended up finishing early and I wondered if I could get home to my husband and children quicker. I called the airlines and they did have an earlier flight with plenty of room, so I changed my plans.

I was excited to get home earlier and looked forward to relaxing on the plane. When I boarded it was "open seating." The Spirit suggested, **"Sit by him,"** as I glanced at a young man with many open seats around him. I would never sit by a single male unless directed to do so.

He seemed frustrated and sad, so I thought I would try to cheer him up. We were flying to Salt Lake City and I thought he might be a member of the Church.

I asked him if he was and he said, "Yes."

"Have you thought about serving a mission?"

"I don't know. I've been so frustrated and confused!"

"What is causing all this?"

"I received my patriarchal blessing and I did not like what it said at all! The blessing made me feel mad, not glad."

I immediately knew why I was supposed to sit with him on the flight. I had had the very same experience when I was a teenager, with my seemingly frustrating patriarchal blessing.

I was able to share with him the very same frustrations and problems I experienced. Then I explained how I had gotten over them and was able to understand my blessing better through prayer. I also told him that our lives are normally long and the blessings can be meant for the near future and also far into the future, maybe even into the next life. When we parted, his entire countenance had changed. He was happy and light on his feet. He thanked me for sharing my story. I am so grateful that I followed the Spirit to sit by a boy and to buoy him up instead of just taking a nap on the plane. (Stake member)

We had always done our best to catch every session of General Conference and made extra efforts and planning to do such, every year. Conference had become a priority in our lives and we so enjoyed being richly taught be the Lord's servants, especially the Lord's prophet. I was decidedly displeased when our elder's quorum president organized a service project on conference weekend.

Knowing how important service was, I agreed to help on that Saturday morning. There were half-a-dozen of us that showed up at this country cabin. Some older members needed help getting their home and property ready for a Wyoming winter.

"Why would our leader think to take us away from the Prophet and Apostles?" I thought. "He probably doesn't even watch Saturday conference!" I continued murmuring.

Our leader said, "Hey, Brother Laing, you can crawl through this hole and brush off all the bad spots. You're best for the job since you have experience taking the Scouts inside all those caves."    I was assigned to go through a small opening and clean the inside of a 30,000 gallon gas storage tank; which was being converted into a water storage tank. I was totally isolated and went to work scrubbing.

I was still ruffling my own feathers though and thinking, "I should be listening to a Prophet's voice instead of being stuck in here. What if some joker closes the lid?! What's wrong with this elder's quorum president? I wouldn't make that call if I was in charge!"

Alone in the giant metal drum, I was lucky to even hear the Spirit amidst my grumblings; the Holy Ghost said very calmly and clearly, "**This is what it's all about**." That awesome advice kept resonating in my head. I exclaimed to myself, "Oh, so the elder's quorum president is actually inspired and I'm the one suffering spiritual shortsightedness!" I began the repentance process, once again, and asked God for forgiveness.

Feeling much better about the overall situation, I started scrubbing the inside of the large drum with gusto and vigor. Our small group accomplished a lot that morning for the needy family. I had also learned a valuable lesson! Whenever tackling a tiring service project or other church assignments, I can always go back to **"This is what it's all about."** This is so true, because we serve God by serving our fellowman. (Journal 10/4/1987)

"When ye are in the service of your fellow beings, ye are only in the service of your God." (Mosiah 2:17)

Someone very close to me passed away and that really affected me. To clear my mind I like to take long drives in my car. I was having a hard day with my loss and decided to go off by myself. I just kept driving around and finally in frustration I said out loud, "Does it really have to be this hard?!"

The still small voice responded, "**I know**."

With those simple, quick words I knew that my Heavenly Father was aware of me and my situation. I knew that

Christ had atoned for our sins and that They already know all we go through. This was more calming to me than the drive. (Stake member)

---

During the week, all the children were in school and my wife decided to go shopping after she made sure I had everything I needed. My temperature had been peaking at 104 and I was absolutely miserable. My eyes hurt, so the computer, television and reading were out. My torso was terribly tender so that I couldn't sit back against any chair nor lie down. I had been on sick leave a couple of days suffering in total misery. The only "rest" I could find was to sit on the front edge of a chair with my eyes closed and my hands folded in my lap. It was helpful to have no one home making any noises.

I hadn't showered for a couple of days and my beard was rough but I could have cared less. I felt a bit like Moses: "Now, for this cause I know that man is nothing, which thing I never had supposed." (Moses 1:10) I realized that if my temperature went up just two more degrees I could easily expire. I felt so weak and helpless.

After sitting silently for a couple of hours I felt a tad better and needed to visit the bathroom. I slowly walked by a stack of videos on the table. Through painful eyes I noticed the deadline to avoid a fee was noon of that day. I made it back slowly from the bathroom and thought, I could maybe drive these four blocks and not have to talk to or see anybody. The video store wouldn't be open yet and I could just drop the videos in the return slot and get back home to rest in my only "comfortable" position. I lifted the steering wheel up as far as it would go and pushed the seat back as far as it would go so that I wouldn't have my sore body against the seatback or steering wheel. I sat on the edge of the car seat and drove slowly.

Two blocks from home I rounded the corner and there was a nice, new vehicle stopped in the middle of the road. The Spirit whispered, "**Help her.**"

"Really" I thought? "But my plan was to avoid any human contact."

So I stopped, slowly rolled down the passenger window, leaned over very slowly, and looked up at the "lifted" SUV, through my open passenger window. "What's wrong?"

In a high-pitched, squeaky voice she exclaimed, "I can't make it go!"

I hadn't noticed any leaked fluids and the beautiful vehicle was too new to lose a water pump or timing chain. "How's your gas?"

"My tank is full."

"Where did you come from?"

"I just backed out of that driveway right there and then I couldn't go any more!"

It was too new of a car for any transmission trouble. Then the thought came to me, "**Parking brake**."

I asked her to check her parking brake; the brake was on and once disengaged she squealed, "Thanks!" and was on her merry way. The videos were returned on time.

Even though I was very ill, the Lord used my thrifty nature to put me in the right place at the right time. Being under the weather also humbles us, making us more alert and susceptible to hear and receive that still small voice. (Journal 3/30/1997)

> "The voice will be as soft as a whisper, coming as a thought to our minds or a feeling in our hearts." (Robert D. Hales, GC, April 2006)

---

> We had built our dream home, with all the bells and whistles, and lived in it for approximately eight years. Back in 2008 the Spirit whispered to me **"Sell your house."** It was so clear that I thought we should and my wife agreed. But I dallied and thought I'll fix this and work on that. Then the housing market crashed and our home lost $60,000 in value almost overnight! I so wished I had been responsive to the Holy Ghost when I was prompted.
>
> We ended up moving to another state for a job and did sell our home for a greatly reduced price. This was a very expensive lesson for me. I determined to follow promptings much quicker from then on and have had bounteous blessings from doing so." (A peer)

---

My brother was at the top of the hill outside town and headed back to the farm one day.

The Spirit said **"Go to the church."**

He had not been to the church, nor was there anything going on at the church that day. But because the prompting was so strong he turned the pickup around and drove back to the church in town. It didn't look like anyone was there. Then he came upon our former stake president and his wife. They were quite elderly now. This sister had fallen hard and was unable to get up. Her husband was elderly and unable to help her up either.

My brother was able to take care of both of them because he turned back when the Spirit asked him to. (A friend)

---

I was going to the hills almost every day for one to two hours. I was healing from terrible abuse as a girl and a married woman. I would write in my journal, read the scriptures, and pray in an attempt to get closer to God. I had felt worthless. Now I was a single mom and talking to God every day. This was a time before there were any cell phones.

On this day I had dropped my daughter off at some stables where she volunteered to work, and then I went to the hills. I was there about one half hour and the Spirit said very clearly, "**Go home now!**" So I immediately headed back home, which was about fifteen minutes.

As soon as I walked in the door, the phone rang.

My daughter said, "Mom, please come pick me up. Everyone else left on a long ride and there's just me and an older man. I got a very uncomfortable feeling."

My daughter said a prayer when she starting feeling uncomfortable. While brushing a horse, she said, "Dear Heavenly Father, I know my mom is out in the hills talking to you. Can you please get a message to her that I need her to come get me? I know she will hear you." My daughter exclaimed to me, "Mom, thanks for having your *beeper* on!"

She was thirteen and said, "I knew it was a sure thing." What a cool experience to know that my daughter knew I was communicating with the Lord and that she could get Him to talk to me for her needs! (Our friend)

*What a special tender mercy for a distraught daughter and her inspired and tuned in mother!*

How did the missionaries know to knock on the door of someone who had been praying for them? or the home teacher to call a family that was in desperate need? or the young woman to stay away from a situation where her values could be compromised? In each of these situations they were guided by the influence of the Holy Ghost. Similar experiences happen repeatedly to members throughout the world on a regular basis, and there are those who desire to feel the Spirit guiding them daily in their lives. While each person can learn to recognize the whisperings of the Spirit, that learning process can be facilitated as others help us understand about the Holy Ghost, share their personal testimonies, and provide an environment where the Spirit can be felt. (Vicki F. Matsumori, GC, Oct 2009)

---

We had six children and my wife convinced me to go in and get fixed. I had the operation scheduled for Monday.

The Sunday before, we were sitting in church and my wife turned to me and said, "You can't get that operation. There's another child waiting to come down to us."

His wife replied, "I was just sitting on the bench in church and the Spirit said, '**You cannot let your husband have that operation.**'" So I turned to him and told him he couldn't go through with the surgery. We need to have another baby.

After church he said, "You're a crazy woman! You just imagined the whole thing."

He went to work the next day and I didn't know if he was going to go through with the surgery or not. He decided not to and then we had another daughter and two more children after that! (Family friends)

---

On a Sunday afternoon our family was all relaxing after a nice dinner and cleaning up. Our small children were napping or playing quietly in their rooms. My wife and I were reading the scriptures and catching up on our journals. As I sat back in the recliner to think what to write next in my journal, the still small voice came through very clearly and succinctly stating, "**Go to the Emergency Room.**"

I immediately got up out of the chair and grabbed the car keys. Upon hearing the jingling of the keys, my wife questioned,

"Where are you going?"

"I'm going to the Emergency Room."

With some anxiousness in her voice she asked, "Why?"

"The Spirit told me to go but didn't say why. My guess is that there is some small child or baby that needs a blessing."

Because of my great love for children I am often asked to bless or participate in the blessing of babies and toddlers.

Going out the door, I left with, "I'll let you know *why* when I get back home." I hurried to the only hospital on the other end of town and found a nearly empty parking lot. As I entered the emergency waiting area I discovered lots of empty chairs and a receptionist doing paperwork in a nook off to the left, around a corner. Then I spotted the only other person in the entire room; sitting in a fetal position in a chair against the wall; underneath a courtesy phone.

I recognized her as one of the great-grandmothers from our ward; Stella Dunn. I was surprised to see her like this because she was so energetic, strong, and very independent. We would see Stella high up in one of her trees sawing off dead branches. Another day we would find her atop her roof replacing shingles. She did not want or need any assistance. We wished to have her energy and vigor when we became that old.

I asked her if she needed any help.

She was sobbing and simply beside herself. She was having an anxiety attack. After regaining her composure, she replied through tears, "My third husband is dying and I've already buried two husbands. I don't know if I can go through this again! *I was praying to Heavenly Father for someone to come and take me home.*"

Putting my arm around her for comfort, I assured her, "I will be glad to take you home and then my wife and I can come back and pick up your car and park it in your driveway for you."

She said, "That would be nice."

I helped her to my car and chauffeured her home. I got her a drink of water and she lay on top of her bed; I covered her with a blanket. I asked her to please let us know if she needed anything else and she never asked; she truly was independent. My wife and I drove to the hospital and brought her big, bright red Cadillac home for her.

I was honored to be an earthly angel delivering that tender mercy to a heartbroken daughter of God that Sabbath. (Journal 6/16/1991)

> "... I began to pray unto the Lord that he would have mercy
> on me, according to the multitude of his tender mercies."
> (1 Ne. 1:8)

*This is how a church leader describes a tender mercy:*

> Of all the blessings Elder Monson treasures in his life, he
> has said that one of the greatest is 'that feeling which the
> Lord provides when you know that He, the Lord has
> answered the prayer of another person through you.'
> (Thomas Monson, *To the Rescue*, 385)

*My fondest quote in my missionary journal comes from Parley P. Pratt:*

> The gift of the Holy Spirit adapts itself to all these organs or
> attributes. It inspires, develops, cultivates and matures all
> the fine toned sympathies, joys, tastes, kindred feelings
> and affections of our nature. It inspires virtue, kindness,

goodness, tenderness, gentleness and charity. It develops beauty of person, form and feature. It tends to health, vigor, animation and social feeling. It develops and invigorates all the faculties of the physical and intellectual man. It strengthens, invigorates and gives tone to the nerves. In short, it is, as it were, marrow to the bone, joy to the heart, light to the eyes, music to the ears, and life to the whole being. (Parley P. Pratt, *KSY*, 101-2)

———•◆•———

Through the holy scriptures we are taught that the Holy Ghost/Holy Spirit: Anoints, appoints, authorizes, awakens, bears record, befriends, bestows spiritual gifts, blesses, buoys up, calls, calms, carries truths, casts out devils, cautions, ceases striving, clarifies, cleanses, comforts, commands, communes, confirms, constrains, convinces, delivers, departs, descends, directs, discerns, edifies, educates, elevates, empowers, encourages, enlarges, enlightens understanding, entices, exhilarates, explains, falls upon, fills, forbids, frees, gives utterance, guards, guides, heals, helps, influences, informs, inspires, instructs, justifies, leads, liberates, lifts, makes known, manifests, moves, opens eyes, pierces, pours, prepares, prevents, profits, promises, prompts, prophecies, protects, proves, purifies, reminds, reveals, sanctifies, seals, shows, smoothes, softens, solves, speaks, stills, stops, strengthens, substantiates, teaches, testifies, translates, unfolds mysteries, verifies, visits, warms, warns, whispers, withholds, and witnesses; just to name a few!

Each of these blessings has come as a result of seeking and heeding the promptings of the Holy Ghost. Said President Lorenzo Snow, "This is the grand privilege of every Latter-day Saint ... that it is our right to have the manifestations of the Spirit every day of our lives." [Lorenzo Snow, TPC, 76] (President Russell M. Nelson, GC, April 2018)

———•◆•———

*The Godhead's plan:*
"... the Lord God prepareth the way that the residue of men may have faith in Christ, that the Holy Ghost may have place in their hearts." (Moroni 7:32)

"I declare unto you ... that there is nothing which can bring more joy into our lives or more peace unto our souls than the Spirit which can come to us as we follow the Savior and keep the commandments." (President Thomas S Monson, *Ensign*, Nov 2018)

# 15. The Lord is in His Holy Temple

I was sitting in the corner of the celestial room by the organ during the dedication of the Memphis Tennessee Temple. President James E. Faust (1920-2007), a member of the First Presidency from 1995-2007, had come to dedicate the temple … A young woman I visit was a member of the choir.

Throughout the meeting, I prayed that she would receive what she had come for. She had confided in me that she came to the temple dedication that day to find out her standing with the Lord. She had committed serious sins … though she had repented; she still struggled to feel good about herself ….

I stared at President Faust, feeling that he, as a representative of the Lord … ought to be able to do something. But how could I tell him … I understood that he was busy … but still I prayed.

President Faust, deep in thought, looked at me for a while … When the meeting ended, a happy expression flooded his countenance with light. He looked at me again and then suddenly stood up, turned around, and stretched his arm forward as far as it would go. He pointed directly at my friend. Then he said firmly and loudly, 'The Lord loves you!'

President Faust's gesture was small and simple yet so powerful that it could have come only from the Holy Ghost communicating to him what I could not. Those few words blessed my friend and continue to sustain my faith that the Lord is mindful of the details of our lives and "that by small and simple things are great things brought to pass" (Alma 37:6). (Latter-day Saint Voices, *Ensign*, Oct 2014)

"It has been said, that words fitly spoken are like apples of gold in pictures of silver. This is especially true when they are accompanied by the Spirit of the Lord, carrying with them life and salvation to the people." (President Brigham Young, JD 25:117)

Often we attend the temples with someone else in mind. We go there to pray for our loved ones. We place people's names on the prayer rolls and seek blessings for them. Many times we can feel a kinship with the people we do proxy for. Occasionally we attend the temple seeking the Lord's blessing in our own lives.

This was the case when I was a young adult. As I focused on my need to heal and prayed for that blessing, I could actually feel the sickness leave my body and the swelling in my glands go down. My throat wasn't sore and my glands were no longer swollen. I could hardly believe it! I know the Lord can do all things; my own weak faith had surprised me though. I am thankful my parents and teachers taught me to pray as a child. (Journal 12/10/1980)

---

> We have heard tributes paid here to the leaders of this Church, these great men who stand before you every six months and manifest to you their great leadership, but never have they been raised to greater heights of leadership than when I have knelt with them in the temple of God and listened to each one open up his heart and appeal to God for his sustaining influence and power to enable him to carry on as your servant in his divine ministry. How high, brothers and sisters, these men are raised when they are on their knees in a circle, claiming sanctuary from the outside world in God's holy temple. (Matthew Cowley, CR, April 1952)

---

One evening, while serving as the baptistry coordinator in the Jordan River, Utah, temple, one of the temple presidency brought a lady to me. He told me she was visiting from China with some of her friends. She had a limited-use recommend and could do baptisms. He said that she didn't speak any English and asked if we would assist her. I said we would be happy to help her.

It was a busy evening and we already had a number of ward youth groups waiting. Using hand signs to communicate, I began to try to help her with limited success. At that moment a large youth group came down the steps and filtered into the clothing area, where we were, because the waiting area was full. This group was not on the schedule.

Two of the young women approached me, saying, "We speak Chinese, can we help?"

"Really, you speak Chinese?"

I asked the young women to accept an assignment to take the Chinese sister through the baptistry and confirmation. They agreed and kindly assisted this sister in an unfamiliar and foreign land. Afterwards I asked the young women if they had noticed any miracles during their visit. They said they hadn't. I asked them what were the chances that a person from China, who spoke no English, was here at the very moment you two girls, who could speak Chinese and were willing to serve, showed up in the room?

The Spirit testified to them that they were part of a divinely orchestrated miracle in the temple that evening. I asked them to testify of their miracle when prompted to do so. (A peer)

---

One summer day I had the opportunity to go on a long drive with a relative. As we made our way back, over several hours, she surprised me with a story about her marriage.

She stunned me by saying, "The first three weeks of my marriage were just great; the last thirty years have been miserable!" She then went into stories of abuse: mental, emotional, physical, and sexual.

I was dumbfounded. I knew her husband was very selfish, but I was clueless and floored, to say the least.

She told me how she wished so hard she had married one of her other boyfriends back in the day.

I tried to express how sorry I was for her.

She asked me for advice.

I suggested she pray sincerely, read the scriptures, and attend the temple. She always went by herself to the temple, unless it was a family wedding.

I told her to talk with her bishop and stake president. I forewarned her that they would give advice very similar; the leaders are strongly counseled to not tell anyone to get divorced. Instead, they will tell you to try and work things out, but more importantly to get your answers for yourself through personal inspiration. Under the circumstances, no one in her immediate family and circle of friends believed she had any other choice than divorce. I felt it was inevitable, yet knew that it was her own decision—just between her and the Lord.

*After attending the temple many times,* she confided in me that she could not get an answer to split up.

I thought about it and prayed that I could help her, following decades of her wallowing in sorrow and sadness. I told her, "You have had a stupor of thought and *not getting divorced* seems to be your answer, as hard as that is to believe."

She agreed with me and said that's what she thought too. "I guess I got my answer, but it seems like the wrong answer. I don't understand it!" she passionately exclaimed.

I suggested she run with it and see what the Lord has in store. (I couldn't believe it either, but I wanted to keep positive during this very confusing and critical period.)

Within a year, her husband recognized the errors of his ways and made a complete turnaround! He talked with church authorities, set out on a long road of repentance, and became a gentleman. He's courteous to her and like a totally different person. By thinking of her and responding to her needs, she loves him more.

No one could see this or believe this awesome outcome; however, the Lord knows his children and their hearts and minds. (Journal 5/7/2006)

> "Behold, happy is the man whom God correcteth ..." (Job 5:17)

A few years ago my wife, Dorothea, and I were walking across the grounds of a temple in a foreign land when we met a very radiant, cheerful, silver-haired sister. Her cheerful, Christlike countenance seemed to set her apart from those around her, and I felt inclined to ask her to explain why she looked so happy and content with life.

"Well," she said with a smile, "several years ago I was in a hurry to get married, and quite frankly, after a few months I realized I had married the wrong man." She continued, "He had no interest in the Church as he had initially led me to believe, and he began to treat me very unkindly for several years. One day I reached the point where I felt I could go on no longer in this situation, and so in desperation I knelt down to pray, to ask Heavenly Father if He would approve of my divorcing my husband.

"I had a very remarkable experience," she said. "After I prayed fervently, the Spirit revealed a number of insights to me of which I had been previously unaware. For the first time in my life, I realized that, just like my husband, I am not perfect either. I began to work on my intolerance and my impatience with his lack of spirituality.

"I began to strive to become more compassionate and loving and understanding. And do you know what happened? As *I* started to change, my *husband* started to change. Instead of my nagging him about going to church, he gradually decided to come with me on his own initiative. "Recently we were sealed in the temple, and now we spend one day each week in the temple together. Oh, he's still not perfect, but I am so happy that the Lord loves us enough to help us resolve our problems." (Spencer J. Condie, GC, Oct 1993)

———◆———

We were all very excited for the new temple opening up in our area. We looked forward to taking our family and non-member friends through the open house. On this particular evening, my husband brought two business associates along to share our beliefs with them.

We got our little "white booties" on and proceeded into a large seating/waiting area. Only the last two rows were available. I was lagging behind while my husband visited with his friends.

I noticed a man in the back corner of the last row. He was the most frightening and scariest man I had ever seen. He wore this odd looking wig, had a black trench coat, his face was painted white, and he had red blood-like drips coming out from his eyes.

The Spirit whispered to me "**talk to him**." I slowly walked over, behind the last row and kind of peeked into the backpack beside him, afraid I might spot a knife or gun. Once again, the Spirit gently said, "**talk to him**." As I leaned over I introduced myself and asked him where he was from.

He explained that his family was active members, but he had left home and was accosted. He took off his big wig and showed me the scar on his skull. He said that when he dressed up like he did, no one dare bother him. He was very grateful that I took time to visit with him. (A kindred spirit)

———◆———

My wife and I attended a temple session. As I pondered the temple I felt as if I was encircled by the Spirit. As I further considered our eternal friends and the many temple trips we enjoyed together, the encompassing Spirit became even stronger. I love the Lord's House! (Journal 3/7/1997)

———◆———

In late 2002 the LDS church changed the questions for the temple-recommend interviews. Along with this change the recommends were extended to every two years instead of annual renewals. When we went in for our interview I noticed that we received the first two recommends from the brand new book our bishop had. At many of our gatherings with friends and church groups the topic of change with temple recommends often came up.

I would take the opportunity to inform everyone that we knew all about this because we were the first in our ward and stake to hear the interview changes and receive the extended recommends.

Friends would always ask us, "So what were the new questions like?"

Every time, my answer was the same, "You are not going to believe it! The three new questions that really grabbed our attention were: Do you shop on Sunday? Do you watch R-rated movies? Do you drink caffeinated sodas?"

Eyes would pop out and chins would drop. One could just see the wheels churning within many members minds!

After the heart palpitations settled down and they stopped profusely sweating, I would admit, with a wry smile, "No, you don't really have anything to worry about; the questions are quite similar but a little different than they were before." Boy-oh-boy, were they ever relieved! (Journal 12/1/2002)

When I left for my American Sign Language mission, the movie, *Children of a Lesser God*, came out. It starred Marlee Matlin, an actress who was deaf, and it was a big deal among the deaf community, as the movie was one of the first of its kind. Everybody in the deaf community was talking about it and I debated whether I should see it or not because it was R-rated.

When I arrived home from my mission, *Children of a Lesser God* was on TV, and I thought some of the bad parts would be cut out, so I watched it. The movie wasn't very good— not much of a plot, and I felt it misrepresented most people who are deaf. Worst of all, the bad parts did not seem edited; I felt guilty for watching the movie because I was going to the temple the next day.

After that temple session, I was putting away my things and a tiny, wrinkled, white haired temple worker started talking to me. She went on and on, yapping about this and that, and I wondered how I was going to get rid of her. Then suddenly she locked eyes with me, shook her finger, and said, "And don't you watch those R-rated movies!"

This experience helped me in the following years with many situations with friends who wanted to see R-rated movies. I was able to stick to my guns and say no. (A relative)

━━━━◆━━━━

We had finished a session and were basking in the beauty of the Celestial Room. As we contemplated eternal things we saw a light and heard a voice! Unfortunately it wasn't the "Rapture." The revolving blue flashing light was a warning; the voice over the intercom was a soft female voice asking everyone to evacuate reverently.

We noticed some fire trucks driving up. After a few minutes there were around 200 matrons, patrons, and workers all dressed in white, standing in the Tabernacle parking lot in Ogden, Utah. The group looked similar to paintings of large groups of saints clothed in white in the Spirit World.

It was rather cold and we obviously had no coats or jackets. We were told later that there was some overheating and excessive smoke discovered in the laundry area. (Journal 4/24/2015)

━━━━◆━━━━

We were enjoying a ward temple night in the Ogden, Utah, temple one evening. It was a full house and very busy. I think nearly half of the group was our own ward, which was rather nice. As we were sitting there being taught, I received a strong impression that a sister in our ward wanted to participate in the prayer. She was wheelchair bound since a car wreck years ago and was serving as our Relief Society president.

I scanned the males, looking for her husband and discovered he wasn't in attendance. I wondered why not, but knew he had a good excuse. They were an honorable couple enduring to the end. I was able to get my wife's attention and ask for her permission to take another woman up for the prayer through my weak attempt at sign language, which actually worked.

She approved.

When it was time I walked over to this sister and stated, "You would like to go up front and participate in the prayer, wouldn't you?"

"I sure would, thank you."

"May I wheel you up?

"Yes, I would appreciate that."

All in all, it was a very nice session. After that night, this good sister called me over a few times to offer blessings for her family.

━━━━◆━━━━

After being married for several years, my wife and I were frustrated about our apparent inability to produce children.

We had sought competent medical help and had followed the best qualified counsel we could find. But month after month my wife did not get pregnant. We prayed about this constantly and fasted frequently, but still no pregnancy. I was confused. The words of our patriarchal blessings made it sound as if we would have children born to us, but no child was forthcoming. We married later in life than many of our contemporaries and several years had gone by. Our body clocks were ticking away.

One day I went to the temple in a spirit of fasting and prayer. I pondered deeply our situation and our desires.

As I did so I felt the Sprit whisper to me, "**you will have children**." As I followed the Spirits' promptings I gradually received increasingly greater understanding, **"you will have five children: four boys and a girl."** This was not a cymbal crashing; it was a calm, quiet assurance. I did not tell my wife about it at first, but I did go home and write down my experience. Although I did tell my wife that I felt she would get pregnant, I wasn't sure it was my place to tell her that she had to endure five pregnancies.

The following months and years tested my faith. The first pregnancy came only after a variety of failed infertility treatments and a surgical procedure. The second pregnancy occurred naturally just about as planned. Then it took four years of various treatments before our third child was born. Then another three years of various approaches for our fourth son to arrive. Her OBGYN was retiring soon. During labor my wife expressed concern because she felt certain there was a fifth soul that was supposed to come to our family. The nurses were surprised, saying they never heard a woman in labor expressing a desire for an additional child!

Two-and-a-half years later we welcomed our daughter to our family and my wife felt that our brood was complete. What the Spirit had told me in the temple that day had come to pass. God told me he was going to do miracles and He did, over and over again! (A friend)

---

We had a wonderful reunion at the new Vernal, Utah, temple. My first group of Eagle Scouts was all off their missions; the first one to be married was the reason for our reunion. All of those Eagle Scouts were in attendance to everyone's delight. The bride was one of my wives' former YW girls.

"The bride and groom have asked you two to come sit up front;" a temple worker said and inquired, "what is your relationship with this fine young couple."

"Let us count the wonderful ways!" I joyfully replied.

A lot of our friends from the old ward were there too. This is what I refer to as a church service *pay day*. The day was full of high emotions and spiritual outpourings. Events lasted the entire day; the reunion and new temple were so fulfilling and rewarding. I wouldn't have missed that experience for anything! (Journal 2/15/1998)

In my mind's eye I could see these two young men three or four years after completing their missions. I visualized them as having found their eternal companions and serving in an elders quorum or teaching a group of young men. (Paul E. Koelliker, GC, April 2012)

Who doesn't remember the excitement and spirit of the great temple revelation/expansion President Hinckley announced in General Conference? Think of all the saints who have not traveled out of their own country and now have a temple close enough for them to serve and worship in. What an immense blessing to the worldwide membership of the LDS church.

But there are many areas of the Church that are remote, where the membership is small and not likely to grow very much in the near future. Are those who live in these places to be denied forever the blessings of the temple ordinances? While visiting such an area a few months ago, we prayerfully pondered this question. *The answer, we believe, came bright and clear.* We will construct small temples in some of these areas, buildings with all of the facilities to administer all of the ordinances. (President Gordon B. Hinckley, *Ensign*, Nov 1997)

Within the Kirtland, Ohio, temple a major portion of the restoration of the Church of Jesus Christ was revealed by celestial angels to the Prophet Joseph Smith and Oliver Cowdery:

**... Moses appeared before us, and committed unto us the keys of the gathering of** Israel from the four parts of the earth, and the leading of the ten tribes from the land of the north.

After this, **Elias appeared, and committed the dispensation of the gospel of Abraham,** saying that in us and our seed all generations after us should be blessed.

After this vision had closed, another great and glorious vision burst upon us; for **Elijah the prophet, who was taken to heaven without tasting death, stood before us** and said: Behold, the time has fully come, which was spoken of by the mouth of Malachi—testifying that he [Elijah] should be sent, before the great and dreadful day of the Lord come—To turn the hearts of the fathers to the children, and the children to the fathers, lest the whole earth be smitten with a curse—Therefore, **the keys of this dispensation are committed into your hands** ... (D&C 110:11-15)

**We saw the Lord** standing upon the breastwork of the pulpit, before us; and under his feet was a paved work of pure gold, in color like amber. His eyes were as a flame of fire; the hair of his head was white like the pure snow; his countenance shone above the brightness of the sun; and his voice was as the sound of the rushing of great waters, even **the voice of Jehovah, saying: I am the first and the last; I am he who liveth, I am he who was slain; I am your advocate with the Father.** (D&C 110:2-4)

———————•◆•———————

*We found time on vacation to attend the fairly new Gilbert, Arizona temple with one of my sisters. The Gilbert temple has a unique "agave" theme throughout.*

*We choose to do proxy sealings. After a very spiritual session the sealer opted to visit longer with us.*

*He was a seasoned Samoan sealer. This fine brother shared the following experience:*

When we were newlyweds back in Samoa, we were delighted to be visited by President Spencer W. Kimball. After one meeting he placed his hand on my shoulder and shared something special with our small group.

The prophet said, "You are Nephites!"

We all felt a strong spirit from his statement.

I wondered, how can this be possible? Weren't all the Nephites finally destroyed by the Lamanites? I searched the Book of Mormon thoroughly and found my answer.

… Hagoth, he being an exceedingly curious man, therefore he went forth and built him an exceedingly large ship … and launched it into the west sea … there were many of the Nephites who did enter therein and did sail forth with much provisions, and also many women and children. … this man built other ships. And the first ship did also return, and many more people did enter into it; and they also took many provisions, and set out again … they were never heard of more. … one other ship did also sail forth … (Alma 63:5-8)

"So you see … we are descendants of the Nephites on those ships, just like our prophet revealed to us!" (Journal 11/27/17)

———◆——

I was in the temple because we worked there. As I sat pondering I was able to see many hundreds of people outside of the temple. They were waiting to have their work done. They were dressed in everyday clothing. They appeared very orderly and very patient and were waiting for the completion of their names.
I'll have to admit I got discouraged … because how could we get all that work done? Yet, it motivates me. So I keep working. I believe these people's names are already in our temple, on either temple files, or in the stake files. They were just all out there waiting. (A friend)

"But the primary goal of ponderizing is to provide an uplifting place for your thoughts to go—a place that keeps you close to the Spirit of the Lord." (Devin G. Durrant, GC, Oct 2015)

———◆——

While doing proxy sealings for a great American Indian friend of ours, the sealer stopped to discuss the names on the card: Jim Bridger and Miss Flathead.
The sealer commented, "You know … this could be the real Jim Bridger that discovered the Great Salt Lake? He did marry an Indian wife."
The other sealer said, "I feel like it is the real Jim Bridger."

I spoke up and promised, "I'll Google it and get back with you on my findings."

Another patron perked up with a wry smile and suggested, "Just ask Siri!"

I was rather pleased, after Googling later, and surprised to discover that Jim Bridger married three Indian women; the first being an Indian woman from the Flathead tribe. His last two wives were chief's daughters in the Shoshone tribe. (The first two wives both died: one several years after their marriage and the other during childbirth.)

The sealers' discernment was correct; it was truly the famous Jim Bridger and his first wife, Miss Flathead sealed. (Journal 3/27/2018)

When I was a young girl, my parents weren't supportive about the church or religion in any form. I had a good neighbor next door that would help me get to church and back. Later in my teenage years I had the right kind of similar support from my grandparents. When I first went to do baptisms for the dead in the Ogden, Utah Temple, I wasn't quite sure what to expect.

When we were dressed in white and waiting around the baptismal font I had an amazing experience. I saw a group of people: men, women and children standing across from us. What surprised me is that they were in their street clothes. I felt like they were the people we were doing the names for in the baptistery. (Our friend)

"And he shall turn the heart of the fathers to the children, and the heart of the children to their fathers ..." (Malachi 4:6)

One of the great highlights of our temple marriage in Mesa, AZ, was the throng of family and friends in the Celestial room afterwards. There seemed to be a combination of the Spirit in full strength along with high emotions. I felt so loved by all: my new wife, her family, my family, our friends, the temple workers, and Heavenly Father, Jesus, and the Holy Ghost. This was surely a snapshot of *heaven on earth*—a true glimpse of heaven. (Journal 12/20/1980)

How President Benson and his beloved wife, Flora, enjoy attending the temple each week! His feeling for the temple is found in his statement: "I love the temples of God. This is the closest place to heaven on earth—the house of the Lord." (Thomas S. Monson, GC, April 1990)

---◆---

There was a brother that served in a former bishopric with us that I really liked. He was about twenty years older, but that didn't matter. Some of his daughters were our babysitters and his son was a great assistant Scoutmaster who served with me. We had a lot of connections. He had moved to Meridian, Idaho and then his dear wife, of many years, had recently passed away. When I was working in the Boise area every two to three months we would get together on one of the evenings.

We met up at the Boise Idaho Temple and enjoyed serving together again. We would go to a steakhouse afterwards and have long visits while sharing family photos and experiences. We also enjoyed talking about our missions to Europe and our old ward.

As we were sitting in the Boise temple together, I felt such an overwhelming peace. During that temple sessions I heard angelic music that sounded like a small beautiful choir. My first thought was a radio or IPod. Then I remembered where I was and decided it was definitely beautiful enough music to have come through the veil that normally keeps us from hearing and seeing the *other side*. (Journal, 11/9/2014)

---◆---

Heber C. Kimball, a member of the Quorum of the Twelve, recalled: "About the first day of June 1837, the Prophet Joseph came to me, while I was seated in … the Temple, in Kirtland, and whispering to me, said, 'Brother Heber, the Spirit of the Lord has whispered to me, "Let my servant Heber go to England and proclaim my gospel and open the door of salvation to that nation."'" Elder Kimball was overwhelmed by the thought of such an undertaking: "I felt myself one of the very weakest of God's servants. I asked Joseph what I should say when I got there; he told me to go to the Lord and He would guide me, and speak through me by the same spirit that [directed] him. (Joseph Smith, TPC, 28:327)

---◆---

One of the best activities one can do with one's family and friends is to tour new Temples, prior to their respective dedications. We were able to travel with our children to the new Mount Timpanogas Temple in American Fork, UT.

Anytime one can collectively feel the Holy Spirit is a very welcome event. We felt a "serene spirit" during the open house and also thoroughly enjoyed the intrinsic beauty. Don't pass up such an opportunity.

We acquired about twenty five names to take to the temple. We started with our two oldest in the baptistery. I was able to baptize my wife and son for these family names. Afterwards, I confirmed those names using my son and daughter as proxies. Then the worker asked if someone could pronounce Spanish names. I told him that I could and they had my son and I do fifty Spanish names. What an awesome spirit there is when a family works together on their own ancestors. There was a calming, peaceful, and satisfying feeling throughout my soul. (Journal 8/25/1996, 11/30/1997)

My wife and I were doing proxy sealings in the beautiful Bountiful, UT, Temple. The family names we were working on were from my wife's line and over 400 years old! When I was kneeling at the altar, being a proxy son sealed to his proxy parents, I had an amazing experience.

I could feel that son kneeling at the exact some spot at the altar where I was kneeling. His spirit resonated within my entire body. It felt like his arms, torso and legs were inside my arms, torso and legs. His vibration was at such a high frequency that I became very emotional. I looked up at the proxy mother through tear-filled eyes and she commented, "It's wonderful, isn't it?" Overcome and speechless, with trembling lips I could only nod in agreement.

This all encompassing feeling continued through the entire sealing and then this spirit left as quickly as he'd come. I felt a great loss and so desired to feel that good again. All of a sudden one of the witnesses mumbled as if he'd been sleeping and rudely awakened. He blurted out, "That name was wrong!"

The sealer looked at the name card and agreed that the witness was correct, so the sealer started the sealing over again. That awesome spirit came back! He was kneeling right there within me again and the amazing light of a very righteous person emanated through every cell in my body!

I believe the spirit of this son/man left me in order to whisper to the witness so that the ordinance would be correct, since the spirit of the son made the effort to attend his own proxy sealing. Once he delivered the message, the spirit returned to the altar. This is one of those experiences that feels like it could have been just yesterday. I like to think he was a just man made perfect. He was definitely a very righteous individual; because of the different spirits I have sensed/felt, this spirit personage vibrated at such a higher level and frequency than any other. This valiant spirit/man purely radiated righteousness. (My journal 1/15/2012)

When I was kneeling as a proxy son, as soon as my hand was laid on the proxy parents hands I felt the spirit of that boy/man kneeling with me. I was taken aback. I was not sure if someone else's spirit could be inside my body. As soon as I laid my hand down, he was right there! My eyes were so full of tears that I could not see. It was a most wonderful experience. (A peer, 6/29/2018)

*The feelings of the Holy Spirit in the temples of our God are often very strong and witness truths to us in various manners that we will individually understand. The Spirit usually increases in intensity when you are working with family names. I testify of this. I have heard many saints testify of the same, when taking family names through the temples.*

> "... I can testify that heaven was very close, that there were others with us that day who had previously passed through the veil of mortality." (Elder Dale G Renlund, GC, April 2018)

My wife and I were doing baptisms and confirmations in the Bountiful, Utah temple. We were working on family names and had over twenty names to be baptized. After completing all the baptisms we moved to confirmations in order to finish our family names for that portion of their proxy temple work.

In the middle of confirming those names, on the tenth or eleventh name, we both stopped on one name and nearly simultaneously stated to the officiator, "We didn't do that name!"

He acted surprised and after rechecking the card he discovered that this name was not baptized, therefore that person could not be confirmed yet.

We honestly felt like this sister relative was there in the spirit prodding both of us to handle her ordinances correctly. It is very comforting when a couple is on the same page spiritually. (Journal 12/20/2009)

> "You have felt it in the temple when the name on a card seemed like more than a name, and you couldn't help but sense that this person was aware of you and felt your love." (President Henry B. Eyring, GC, April 2017)

We can be inspired all day long about temple and family history experiences others have had. But we must do something to actually experience the joy ourselves. I would like to extend a challenge to each one of us so that the wonderful felling of this work can continue and even increase. I invite you to prayerfully consider what kind of sacrifice—preferably a sacrifice of time—you can make in order to do more temple and family history work this year. (Russell M. Nelson, *Ensign*, Oct 2017)

---

When President Brigham Young first arrived in Salt Lake City and decided that there should be a temple, he marked the spot where the temple would be, and then proceeded to erect a building that was entirely beyond their means, but within the power of God. That building was built on the faith of a people who were poverty-stricken. They didn't have money, but they did have the spirit of cooperation and welfare, and so they built the building, and it took many years (*Forty years*).

It wasn't for immediate use; and somebody said to Brigham Young, "Where's the provision for heating this immense stone building? Stone is always cold. How are we going to keep warm, with no fireplace, with nothing provided for heating the building?"

He said, "Before this building is completed, there will be some heating system invented that will take care of the heating of this great building," and before it was finished, furnaces had been developed and steam heating, and all that had to be done was to build a little building outside the temple and install a large furnace, and run the pipes in, and heat the building that way. What he couldn't see with his own eye, he had faith that God would see with his eyes the ways and means for looking after the construction of that great temple." (Mathew Cowley, *Man of Faith*, 253-254)

---

When I stayed to help my father in the last weeks of his mortal life he allowed me to have power of attorney to handle all his business and other affairs. He had many collections with the most valuable being his large gun and pistol collection and tons of silver dollars. In his wisdom, two years prior to his demise, he passed out identical lists to Mom and their seven children.

The lists were of all his different collections followed by empty lines for those who were interested to place their names on. As the oldest child and executor it was so simple to easily divide everything per the predetermined list requests. This eased a lot of the anger, tension, and issues that arise in many estate settlements.

As for stocks, bonds, and other accounts, they were to be divided up equally ... which I later did. Interestingly enough, his largest mutual fund account was with a company in New York City and no beneficiary was listed on that account. Even though I had power of attorney, the company would not let me touch or handle that account. My goal was to have every financial investment cashed into his hometown bank account; then I could easily divide all the assets after death because the power of attorney would also be expired. (The home and life insurance went to our mother and the collections and cash/investments were designated for the seven children per our father's will.)

While serving our father I was on the phone every day with this investment company. Each of those days they required me to jump through another hoop. I would get the documentation they needed from different banks and a notary and go to the town library to fax the information to New York from the small Wyoming town or send it overnight by UPS.

The first day was simple: a "Notary" verifying my signature. The next day was a copy of the "power of attorney." Then that was not enough and they wanted a "Signature Card" from our local bank. Another day was a "Green Medallion Signature" which I had never heard of. They informed me that only one bank per county has the approval to do this. So, I found which bank had that and hopped through yet another hoop. Doing all this along with everything else, I was frazzled on Friday after five days of legwork and housework.

Then the New York investment company called me and said, "It's not enough."

I replied, "You have got to be kidding. I've done everything you've asked me to do!"

"Sorry" they replied.

I was exasperated and exhausted and thought to myself, "I just can't do this anymore along with shopping, paying bills, caring for dad, handling his finances, cleaning the home, etc."

I dropped down on a bed and hoped for a solid nap.

Then mom called out, "I can't lift dad up, come and help me!"

So I got up like a zombie and helped out. I told my mother I had to have a little rest or I might pass out. I lay back comfortably on the bed and just started to doze off when the phone in the bedroom rang. I thought, "No way! This can't be happening!"

I did not answer it, yet felt I should. I picked up the phone and was most pleasantly surprised:

"Hi, this is so-and-so representing the New York financial company. We have an office in Billings, Montana, and have noticed that you have been going through a lot of hoops on your father's behalf. My boss worked with your father in the Billings Temple. He knows him well. He has signed off on this account as a personal reference and your funds will be transferred within twenty-four hours."

Wow! I never expected this type of a blessing from temple service. Now we could keep the largest funds out of probate. The most interesting fact is that the money from this "no-beneficiary account" arrived before any of the other accounts with beneficiaries! I dropped off into a sorely needed deep sleep with sweet satisfaction strewn across my face. (Journal 5/25/2007)

———◆———

During one temple visit, we enjoyed a soul-enriching prayer. This humble brother gave a rather long prayer replete with gratitude. He was so sincere and this brought an immense, rich outpouring of the Spirit into that room of the temple. He was a great example and reminder for us to exhibit greater gratitude in our personal prayers. This was one of our more spiritual temple experiences.

———◆———

When I went to do baptisms for the dead as a Beehive I had a most interesting experience. As I was being baptized for a list of girls names, I noticed a girl in a white dress that was crying a lot. I wondered why someone wasn't helping her. When I was baptized for the fifth name, I came up out of the water and this girl disappeared in front of my face. The name I was just baptized for was Martha Hale. That is my family name.

Later when I was older and in institute, my teacher helped me with my genealogy and we came across one of my relatives: Martha Hale. (Our friend)

———◆———

One of the richest outpourings of the holy temples is actually found outside the temples for many of us. During temple dedications and rededications many members across the world have enjoyed strong testimonies of The Lord's House and the importance of all work done there within.

Each temple dedication ceremony can be a spiritual feast for each respective event and prayer that fill one's soul to over flowing. One that was very special to our family was the dedication of the Oquirrh Mountain Temple in the Salt Lake valley on August 21st, 2009. All Utah stakes replaced their block meetings with the temple dedication that Sunday. The event was dotted with light humor and filled with the spirit through word and song. (Journal 8/23/2009)

———◆———

*One of my all-time favorite General Conference talks was given in 1877 by President Wilford Woodruff:*

> I will here say, before closing, that two weeks before I left St. George, the spirits of the dead gathered around me, wanting to know why we did not redeem them.
> Said they, "You have had the use of the Endowment House for a number of years and yet nothing has ever been done for us. We laid the foundation of the government you now enjoy, and we never apostatized from it, but we remained true to it and were faithful to God."
> These were the signers of the Declaration of Independence, and they waited on me for two days and two nights, I thought it very singular that notwithstanding so much work had been done, and yet nothing had been done for them. The thought never entered my heart, from the fact, I suppose, that heretofore our minds were reaching after our more immediate friends and relatives. I straightway went into the baptismal font and called upon Brother McAllister to baptize me for the signers of the Declaration of Independence, and fifty other eminent men, making one hundred in all, including John Wesley, Columbus, and others. I then baptized him for every President of the United States except for three; and when their cause is just, somebody will do the work for them. (*JD* 19:229)

*Since this exceptional event, I'm not sure why but every time I read or hear this miraculous experience, that occurred in the St George temple, the speakers and writers always seem to leave off the important women who were also there in spirit and had their temple work done. We cannot make it without the sisters, brethren! (And neither can they make it without us.) Think deeply about the new and everlasting covenant.*

*There were seventy eminent women also baptized. Brother McCallister also baptized Lucy Bigelow Young as proxy for those righteous female spirits awaiting their important work. That is the rest of the story.*

*If you should get a chance to do sealings in the Saint George, Utah, temple you will find paintings of J.T.D McAllister and Wilford Woodruff on opposing walls, just outside the sealing office. I thought it looked like they were "looking across the room at each other in approval". Elder Wilford Woodruff was the first temple president from 1877-84; Elder McAllister was the second temple president from 1984-93, in St. George, Utah.*

For some time President Woodruff's health had been failing. Nearly every evening President Lorenzo Snow visited him at his home. This particular evening the doctors said that President Woodruff could not live much longer, that he was becoming weaker every day. President Snow was greatly worried. We cannot realize today what a terrible financial condition the Church was in at that time—owing millions of dollars and not being able to pay even the interest on its indebtedness.

My father went to his room in the Salt Lake Temple, dressed in his robes of the priesthood, knelt at the sacred altar in the Holy of Holies in the House of the Lord and there plead to the Lord to spare President Woodruff's life, that President Woodruff might outlive him and that the great responsibility of Church leadership would not fall upon his shoulders. Yet he promised the Lord that he would devotedly perform any duty required at his hands. ...

... [On September 2, 1898, after receiving word of the death of Wilford Woodruff, President Snow] went to his private room in the Salt Lake Temple.

President Snow put on his holy temple robes, repaired again to the same sacred altar, offered up the signs of the priesthood and poured out his heart to the Lord. He reminded the Lord how he plead for President Woodruff's life to be spared, that President Woodruff's days would be lengthened beyond his own; that he might never be called upon to bear the heavy burdens and responsibilities of the Church. "Nevertheless," he said, "Thy will be done. I have not sought this responsibility but if it be Thy will, I now present myself before Thee for Thy guidance and instruction. I ask that Thou show me what Thou wouldst have me do."

After finishing his prayer he expected a reply, some special manifestation from the Lord. So he waited,—and waited—and waited. There was no reply, no voice, no visitation, no manifestation. He left the altar and the room in great disappointment. Passing through the Celestial room and out into the large corridor a glorious manifestation was given President Snow which I relate in the words of his grand-daughter, Allie Young Pond. ...

*Alice Armeda Snow Young Pond (1876–43), heard her grandfather, President Lorenzo Snow, share his experience of the Lord's visit in the Salt Lake Temple.* NOTE: Alice Armeda Snow Young was also a granddaughter of Brigham Young.

One evening while I was visiting grandpa Snow in his room in the Salt Lake Temple, I remained until the door keepers had gone and the night-watchmen had not yet come in, so grandpa said he would take me to the main front entrance and let me out that way. He got his bunch of keys from his dresser. After we left his room and while we were still in the large corridor leading into the celestial room, I was walking several steps ahead of grandpa when he stopped me and said: "Wait a moment, Allie, I want to tell you something. It was right here that the Lord Jesus Christ appeared to me at the time of the death of President Woodruff. He instructed me to go right ahead and reorganize the First Presidency of the Church at once and not wait as had been done after the death of the previous presidents, and that I was to succeed President Woodruff."

Then grandpa came a step nearer and held out his left hand and said: "He stood right here, about three feet above the floor. It looked as though He stood on a plate of solid gold."

Grandpa told me what a glorious personage the Savior is and described His hands, feet, countenance and beautiful white robes, all of which were of such a glory of whiteness and brightness that he could hardly gaze upon Him.

Then [President Snow] came another step nearer and put his right hand on my head and said: "Now, grand-daughter, I want you to remember that this is the testimony of your grandfather, that he told you with his own lips that he actually saw the Savior, here in the Temple, and talked with Him face to face" (LeRoi C. Snow, "An Experience of My Father's," *Improvement Era,* Sept. 1933, 677)

*The holy temples are "Houses of the Lord." The temples are peaceful places for pondering and prayer. Within the holy temples we can feel the Spirit of the Lord and often sense the spirits of our kindred dead. The Holy Ghost can be experienced in abundance, as He testifies of eternal truths.*

# 16. Behold this Dreamer Cometh

Just after my grandpa and grandma Laing passed away; only one month apart from each other, I had a dream full of realness and clarity. (Grandpa had passed away first.) I was standing among a large group of people. It felt like a party or celebration. Families were standing around and visiting in a most beautiful room.

Suddenly I looked up and saw my grandpa Laing standing next to me. I thought, "Wait, how can that be?" Then in the corner of the room a beautiful casket was rolled in. I began to wonder at everyone's excitement. But my grandpa Laing hurried right over there. He reached his hand into the casket and lifted my grandma Laing up from lying there, and they embraced.

Taking her hand again he said, "Come on, we have work to do." And off they hurried, running with excitement as they exited the room. It was so appropriate. They were together. They were happy doing the Lord's work, just as they'd done so well for so many decades. (A relative)

---

I had always been bothered by scriptures that said man was nothing and that we couldn't do anything without God or Jesus. I came back with: we should do many things of our own choosing and free will, running that we may obtain the prize; being a literal son of God, belonging to a royal priesthood, and working with faith. (All previous phrases paraphrased from the scriptures.)

Then I received my personal solid answer through a unique dream:

In a crystal clear dream I found myself on a groomed football field. I was standing in the center of the field on the 50-yard line inside a huge stadium. It looked like a professional football field. So clear was the answer to my thoughts that I remember this dream vividly to this day.

There was an angel host, in white—yet not bright, directing me. He had me turn to one side and I was asked to observe.

As my eyes adjusted I could see thousands of families, friends, and loved ones filling the stadium seats from one end zone to the other! They were all smiling and happy as they waved to me, blew me kisses, and sent me well wishes. They were a joyous crowd to witness. I felt like this was surely my fifteen minutes of fame.

I came to understand that this large crowd consisted of all the people I had buoyed up, helped, served, prayed over, cheered up, loved, and simply smiled at. There was a large group of thousands I had done proxy work for in the Holy Temples. There were thousands more that I had cherished and tended their babies and/or toddlers. I recognized many of the faces in the front seats; the majority of the people I did not recognize nor see clearly. All in all, I was basking in the bright accolades and filling with pride. I was thinking to myself, "Yes, this is what it should be like … being recognized for all those quiet simple acts, multiple service projects, and all those fulfilled callings."

As I was basking in my newfound glory, my host directed me to turn around to the opposite side of the stadium.

I thought to myself, "Oh boy! There will be thousands more of my fans!" My mind was contemplating multitudes of people I had been an example to and had unknowingly helped and served. My ego began growing even larger in anticipation. My guess was correct; the stadium, on that side, was completely full off folks filling up every single seat similarly in the large arena on the opposite side—stretching to both end zones once again!

However, my swelling pride quickly turned to humility and sorrow as my joy melted into sadness when I was shown all the people I had not helped that I could have. Many persons were not served because I opted out of the activity. People I had: frowned at, criticized, ridiculed, and been angry with. Those I had sinned against through sins of commission and omission. The most hurtful and revealing observation was that many of my family and friends were represented on both sides of the large stadium. I had chosen to hurt and not serve those I loved the most, from time to time.

How could I have ignored and shamed so many? The joyous group and disappointed group in the stadium were roughly equal in number and therein laid my answer: I was about as good as I was bad. Without God and the Savior I literally am nothing. I now understood the scriptures' meanings much better. I titled this dream the *Stadium of Pride*.

> But even though man is nothing, it fills me with wonder and awe to think that "the worth of souls is great in the sight of God." (D&C 18:10) … This is the paradox: compared to God, man is nothing; yet we are everything to God. (Dieter F. Uchtdorf, GC, Oct 2011)

> "For we labor diligently to write, to persuade our children, and also our brethren, to believe in Christ, and to be reconciled to God; for we know that it is by grace that we are saved, after all we can do." (2 Ne. 25:23)

"For if a man think himself to be something, when he is nothing, he decieveth himself." (Galatians 6:3)

———◦◆◦———

Not long ago a friend recounted to me an experience he had while serving as a mission president. He had undergone surgery that required several weeks of recuperation. During his recovery, he devoted time to searching the scriptures. One afternoon as he pondered the Savior's words in the 27th chapter of 3 Nephi, he drifted off to sleep.

He subsequently related: I fell into a dream in which I was given a vivid, panoramic view of my life. I was shown my sins, poor choices, the times ... I had treated people with impatience, plus the omissions of good things I should have said or done. ... A comprehensive ... review of my life was shown to me in just a few minutes ... I awoke startled and instantly dropped to my knees.

Prior to the dream, I didn't know that I had such great need to repent. My faults and weaknesses suddenly became so clear to me that the gap between the person I was and the holiness of God seemed like millions of miles. (D. Todd Christofferson, GC, Sep 2017)

And now I ask, can ye say aught of yourselves? I answer you, Nay. Ye cannot say that ye are even as much as the dust of the earth; yet ye were created of the dust of the earth; but behold, it belongeth to him who created you.

And I, even I, whom ye call your king, am no better than ye yourselves are; for I am also of the dust ... (Mosiah 2:25-26)

———◦◆◦———

We are a family of eight that has grown quite large with many grandchildren that are scattered in a few states. I sent some family name cards to my daughter-in-law, when our oldest grandson turned twelve, so that he could help with the proxy baptisms. My daughter started perusing the name cards and noticed this family of Samuel and Sallies had 12 children, the oldest born in 1876.

She called me with this crazy idea about having the whole family meet together at one temple and doing the proxy work for this entire family. Within six weeks we managed to have our 6 children and all of our grandchildren meet in

Utah to help with our family temple goals, with many small miracles along the way.

Our plan was to do most of the work in the new Provo City Center Temple and then to finish the sealings in the Bountiful Temple the next day. I had the privilege of doing the endowment work for Sallie, the mother.

Two of our daughters wouldn't be going to the temple: Our youngest wasn't endowed yet and our other daughter had distanced herself from the church. These two watched all the grandchildren for us.

Our less active daughter was pregnant, going through a divorce, and often had severe depression. She had a major meltdown between our Friday and Saturday temple visits. In her distressed state, she spewed out hatred against me, our family, and the Church.

I knew she didn't really mean those hurtful things, yet my heart was really hurting for her. So it was bittersweet to be in the temple to seal a family together, but aching also for our family that seemed to be ripping apart! That night I cried myself to sleep. Then, about four in the morning, I awoke because Sallie, the mother of those twelve children, had come in my dream to tell me something.

Her message was, "I know how you feel. Not all of my family accepted the Gospel either."

I pray consistently and steadily for my children and I am sure Sallie does too. Perhaps there is still time for Sallie's wayward children to accept the truth on the other side. I pray for them too.

We are connected when we do work for our kindred dead, sometimes more closely than we can imagine. (A friend)
*Amen to that!*

"And he shall turn the heart of the fathers to the children, and the heart of the children to their fathers ..." (Malachi 4:6)

———————◆•———————

I had been serving in the Swedish mission for about 6 months. Our mail was slow coming back in the 70's. Sometimes we'd receive nothing for days, while at other times a bundle of letters would arrive. On one of these bulk deliveries I received eleven letters, 8 of which were from different young women. That started a reputation in the mission about my many "friends" and the talk did go to my head.

That week I had a strong, shocking warning come to me in a clear dream.

**"My Savior was the world"** was the main message. The dream was about all those enjoyments of life I cherished back home: Motorcycles, best buddies, girl friends, dancing, hunting, fishing, pizza and root beer, etc. I received a stark reminder as to where my loyalties and thoughts were residing.

This is preciously what Satan seeks to evoke upon us: a love of worldly things, doubting deity, a reliance on the arm of flesh, and inflated egos. We are eating right out of Satan's dirty hands when we worship worldly idols.

I woke up with a fresh resolve to refocus my entire missionary activities in order to place the true Savior of the world in my life, thoughts and, words. I decided to answer letters to young women much slower, while bearing testimony of Joseph Smith and Jesus Christ through short, succinct replies.

I found that the days became brighter and our success surged. I was very grateful for the warning to me in a clear dream, not realizing how much I was dragging the work and our companionship down. (Missionary journal)

> "Set your affection on things above, not on things on the earth." (Col. 3:2)

> Speaking about worldly Idols:... but every man walketh in his own way, and after the image of his own god, whose image is in the likeness of the world, and whose substance is that of an idol, which waxeth old and shall perish in Babylon ... (D&C 1:16)

> ... Not only images in the form of God or man, but the likeness of anything which is earthly in any form. It would include both tangible and intangible things, and everything which entices a person away from duty, loyalty, and love for and service to God. (Spencer W. Kimball, *The Miracle of Forgiveness*, 40)

---

> I was really upset and very mad that I got pregnant prior to my senior year of college basketball. Through my frustrations I had a most interesting dream one night. A small girl walked up to me and smiled.
> She said her name was ***"Jasmine."***

This made me feel better and I shared the dream with my husband.

He said, "We are going to have a boy so it doesn't matter and there's no way we're going to name a child Jasmine!"

I admired her beautiful young daughter as we sat together around a table discussing her mother's dream.

Then she shared the following:

"This young lady you're eating breakfast with is our beautiful daughter Jasmine." (Journal 10/15/2017)

———————◆———————

*A new friend of ours told me,* "We had five children and were done.

"Five years later I had a very clear dream and an angel appeared and succinctly stated, **'You will have a son and his name will be David.'**

"My husband didn't have a direct confirmation, but felt my dream was validating and he was supportive. What was surprising to us is that after we took this personal direction with gratitude it took fifteen months to conceive!"

*Then she said to me,* "That beautiful baby you're holding is *David*, our sixth child." (Journal 9/17/2017)

"And God said, **Sarah *thy wife shall bear thee a son indeed; and thou shalt call his name Isaac*:** and I will establish my covenant with him for an everlasting covenant, and with his seed after him." (Genesis 17:19)

———————◆———————

I had a dream in the fall of 1928 that always impressed me. I dreamed the children and I were walking in the Blackfoot River bed. It was mostly dry and we were collecting pretty rocks and picking flowers along the banks. I looked up and saw a large stream of muddy water coming up the river. (I say coming up the river because this stream was coming in the opposite direction than the river usually ran.)

I hurried and helped all of the children up over the bank to safety; then I looked again and there was a little baby in front of that stream and it was taken under. This dream made me feel like someone in the family was going to die. I didn't see how it could be the baby I was expecting. I felt really well and the baby seemed so strong.

My eighth child was born March 1st, 1929, and this was my easiest pregnancy. He lived one day. (Grandma Alta Law Clyde, Family History)

———————◆◆———————

I was awoken in the night by a young girl's voice and heard, "Daaaaaaaadddd....Daaaaaaaddddyyyy.....Daaaaaaaaaddddd....Daaaaaaaddddyyyy"

This repeated several times and I shrugged it off. Our two youngest boys were 5 and 9 at the time and this was a younger female voice.

Then I heard the same "Daaaaaaddd...Daaaaadddddyyy" again two more times.

So I got up in the middle of the night and searched the house. My wife and our five children were all sound asleep. The TV was not on and the windows were all closed tightly. I deliberated because I had heard the call in my sleep and also while awake.

After thinking about the repetitive voice for a day I felt like it was a voice from behind the veil. Someone was trying to make contact. I suggested to my wife, "Maybe we're not done with our family?"

That next night I prayed for an answer and had an interesting response in a dream. This little, dark-haired, girl appeared clearly in my dream in our bedroom and then she climbed atop our tall dresser. She was so cute that I couldn't get mad at her for standing where she shouldn't be. She smiled and said, "*My name is Mary*." She looked around 3 or 4 years old. That's all I found out.

So my prayer about a dream was partially answered in another dream. We actually tried for some time to have another baby, thinking that might be the message, yet it wasn't. We both felt like our family was complete. We are still unsure where sweet little Mary fits in the eternal scheme of things. I did want eight children—my wife gave birth to five beautiful babies and had three miscarriages. Time will tell. (Journal 4/27/2003)

———————◆◆———————

I remember on a certain occasion in Liverpool we were told not to say anything about the gathering. A lady came to me and said she had had a singular dream. "I dreamed," she said, "that the whole Church was going off to America, and that you were there; we were going on board of a ship and leaving for America." What was the reason of this singular dreaming? She had embraced the Gospel, and it revealed certain things to her that she could not know in any other way.

———————◆◆———————

Early on the morning of April 11, 2011, I was awakened by a vivid dream. In my dream, I was hiking with several friends and a group of young men who were ahead of us on the trail, and with two friends from our ward that I admire and look up to. We were on a mountain trail that ascended upward. We were headed towards a mountain lake. It was late and it was getting dark.

Twice I asked my friends, "Where are we going?" I had never hiked this mountain or been to the lake before.

Both times they patiently explained where we were headed and what the lake was like.

After he explained this for the second time, I turned to my left, and there, walking beside me was the Savior. His feet did not touch the ground. He had on a dark red tunic and wore a prayer shawl over his shoulders. His hair was dark, a sort of brown auburn color. He was looking at the ground in front of Him.

When I realized that it was the Savior, I fell on the trail on my hands and knees and began to weep. My friends could not understand what had overcome me, and I could not explain it.

In the midst of my tears, I woke up and wrote my experience in my journal. That evening after work, I shared my dream with my wife and daughter during family night. I was filled with incredible warmth and peace and a sense of safety, protection, and assurance as I shared it.

I had been sick for several weeks and was barely holding my life together. The dream could not have come at a more perfect time. Two days later, I came home from work and collapsed on the living room couch. I was not able to walk after that for nearly a week. I had never been sicker, and I despaired of my life. Could it be that the Lord had prepared me for what I was about to experience and that the Savior was right there beside me, though I could not always see Him? (A peer)

"Because when the Spirit testifies to each of us that God is our Father and Jesus Christ is our Savior, it is *that* revelation that will invite true reverence born of love and profound respect." (Margaret S. Lifferth, GC, April 2009)

When three different women contacted me during my early marriage, over a couple of years, my mind became sidetracked as my ego was bursting. Two were former girlfriends and one was a complete stranger. Thoughts came to me such as: "You're still in demand. Women love you. Think how much fun so-and-so would be."

I must admit that I entertained these thoughts and pondered *what ifs*: "What if I'd married her? What kind of wife would she be? What kind of mother would she be? What kind of a companion would this one be?

As I went to into a deep sleep one night thinking those thoughts, I had a crystal clear dream.

We were in SLC, Utah, at the top level of some skyscraper downtown. There was a very nice restaurant with large glass windows overlooking the Salt Lake valley. A row of long tables were set with fine white tablecloths and adorned with sparkling china. The silverware was glistening. The guests at the multi-course meal were our family members. My wife was to my right; we were seated at the far left of the extended table. The chairs directly across from us were empty; all the family, from both sides of our families, was seated. We anxiously awaited a tasty five-course feast.

Just before the servers started bringing in the first course, a stunningly elegant woman pleasingly walked the length of this very long table, finally gracefully sitting down directly across from me. Everyone in the room couldn't help but stare at her.

She was perfect in every way. Her dark hair was full and long with attractive large waves and a slight bounce. Her cheekbones and nose were captivating. One could easily become lost in her emerald green eyes. Her clothing was modest, yet very tasteful. Her shoes were just right. Her lips were luscious and when she spoke it was most genuine and loving, with perfect words emanating between those snow white teeth of perfection.

I, along with everyone else, just thought, "WOW!" I was nervously fidgeting with my fork as she gracefully walked the length of the room to the seat in front of me. Of all the beautiful women of the earth, she seemed to have each of their best attributes and qualities. She was like a combination of Ava Gardner, Bo Derek, Farah Fawcett, Kate Moss, Beyonce, Reese Witherspoon, and more!

No one could take their eyes off of her. I paraphrase one of the earlier leaders, who said something to the effect of, "You're not a man if you don't look once at a beautiful woman. You're not a saint if you look more than once!" Well, I only looked once—it was just one extremely long stare!

After the beautiful woman was seated, she leaned over the table towards me and in the softest, prettiest voice clearly stated, "I love you."

She was sincere and her words sunk deep within my core. I had found a *pearl of great price* and was ready to give up everything I owned to obtain her.

Her comment shocked me and I dropped my fidgety fork onto the empty chinaware, causing quite a racket. Then I said, "Well if YOU love me, then I love you!" That was all she wrote.

That was that and we headed to the SLC Temple to be sealed. As we rode the short distance in a car, we were circling Temple Square for a parking spot; I looked at her and my wife as I sat in between them in the back seat. I was thinking to myself, "How can this be? I cannot be sealed to two women who are both alive! Am I going to be the poster child for the reintroduction of approved polygamy? Or, are we going to get in a car wreck; will my wife be killed?"

Sure enough, someone T-boned our vehicle at high speed—causing horrendous noises as metal scraped and screeched on metal. There was a fatality. The crash left the most beautiful woman in the world dead in the back seat. The rest of us finally made it to the temple, after everything settled down.

As we sat in the temple, God taught me loud and clear through the Spirit, "**You have the perfect woman already**."

That was the definitive message of the dream, which taught me that I needed to refocus clearly on my marriage and to rededicate my life so as not to entertain adulterous thoughts. The evil thoughts will still appear on the stage of my mind, I just need to replace them much quicker; immediately, if not sooner! (Journal 9/23/1984)

"Revelation can also be given in a dream when there is an almost imperceptible transition from sleep to wakefulness. If you strive to capture the content immediately, you can record great detail, but otherwise it fades rapidly." (Richard G Scott, GC, April 2012)

*A little humor from Gordon B. Hinckley:*

Which brings to mind the story of the boy who came down to breakfast one morning and said, "Dad, I dreamed about you last night."

"About me? What did you dream?"

"I dreamed I was climbing a ladder to heaven and on the way up I had to write one of my sins on each step of the ladder."

"And where did I come into your dream?" the father asked.

Said the boy, "When I was going up, I met you coming down for more chalk." (GC, Oct 1972)

———————— •◆• ————————

One Sunday I shared an interesting dream from the night before with my wife:

I was at the care center serving in the branch presidency, which I actually do. We begin by moving everything from the recreation room aside and then setting up the chairs, placing a hymnal for everyone, setting up the sacrament table, a podium, microphones, a piano, etc. [Which we actually do in reality too.] None of the other three members of the branch presidency were there, however a couple of ward members showed up.

The few of us there were scurrying to move everything out before setting everything else up. These members hadn't been there before, because we are blessed with a variety of different people from many wards from six different stakes to help out each Sunday. Finally the other counselor showed up and we had everything set up except for ourselves. We had messy clothes and hair and were sweating. Then we went to the four different halls to hurriedly help push those in wheelchairs that desired to attend sacrament meeting. [End of my dream]

That very afternoon the branch president called saying, "By the way the secretary and I are going to be gone for two weeks and we'll be missing the next two Sundays. Can you please conduct in my absence?"

Dreams can prepare us for future needs, warn us of possible dangers to body and/or spirit, answer our prayers, bless and calm our souls, etc. I believe the message from that dream was simply to remind me to show up much earlier the next two Sabbaths. (Journal 3/18/2018)

———————— •◆• ————————

A sister in the ward had a warning come to her in a dream. She was warned to avoid the "spiritualist sisters." The very next morning these rebellious sisters came to her home and asked her to join them.

They challenged her, "You need to choose a side!"
She explained to them, "I am on the Lord's side!"

*A perfect answer!*

And if it seem evil unto you to serve the LORD, choose you this day whom ye will serve; whether the gods which your fathers served that were on the other side of the flood, or the gods of the Amorites, in whose land ye dwell: *but as for me and my house, we will serve the LORD.* (Joshua 24:15)

---

Now the birth of Jesus Christ was on this wise: When as his mother Mary was espoused to Joseph, before they came together, she was found with child of the Holy Ghost. Then Joseph her husband, being a just man, and not willing to make her a publick example, was minded to put her away privily. But while he thought on these things, behold, <u>the angel of the Lord appeared unto him in a dream</u>, saying, Joseph, thou son of David, fear not to take unto thee Mary thy wife: for that which is conceived in her is of the Holy Ghost.

<u>The angel of the Lord appeareth to Joseph in a dream</u>, saying, Arise, and take the young child and his mother, and fell into Egypt, and be thou there until I bring thee word.

But when Herod was dead, behold, <u>an angel of the Lord appeareth in a dream to Joseph</u> in Egypt, Saying, Arise, and take the young child and his mother and go into the land of Israel: (Matthew 1:18-20; 2:13, 19-20)

---

I was having very rough weeks at work. While working in my office I would have these thoughts about being unworthy and unacceptable to God for the sins I had committed during my life. I was too bad and sinful for repentance. They were all very discouraging and perpetual thoughts. These negative thoughts played out in my mind, now and then, day after day.

To top that off, every night I would have a reoccurring dream where I was the hero fighting the bad guys. I was able to overcome my enemies due to my ability to fly and due to super strength. However, the leader of my foes seemed undefeatable. I would slice, dice, burn, crush, and discombobulate him, to no avail.

After a couple of weeks of discouraging thoughts at work and continuous struggling dreams, I was finally able to unveil my main foe's face. Why it was Satan! No wonder I couldn't kill him. He didn't have a body to kill. The Devil cannot be destroyed physically. (He took care of that on his own.) Then I realized that it was Satan buffeting me every day and night for two to three weeks at work and at home.

*Elder Heber J. Grant explained:*
There are two spirits striving within us always, one telling us to continue our labor for good, and one telling us that with the faults and failings of our nature we are unworthy. … That spirit followed me day and night telling me that I

was unworthy to be an Apostle of the Church, and that I ought to resign. (CR, April 1941)

Now that I had finally figured out who my fiendish foe was, I was ready to fight him along with the Captain of God's army. I uttered an urgent prayer pleading for deliverance from this strong evil power that was encompassing me day and night. I asked for a witness that my sins had truly been forgiven—that I was truly cleansed through the repentance process and the atonement.

That night I had a most interesting dream that clearly answered my cries to Heavenly Father. This dream was another one that seems so crystal clear and fresh in my memory; it could have happened last night!

I found myself walking with an attractive escort. I thought I might know her from somewhere, but wasn't sure. She shook my hand and I felt a slight twinge of pain in my palm. Her congeniality and warmness got me over that quickly. She wrapped her arm gently in mine as we strolled down a very long street with no cars. It was like a promenade, somewhat similar to walking into Disneyland, yet much longer. The buildings, here though, were all multi-storied apartments on both sides of the promenade. There were no alleys, as the buildings each shared a common wall and there was no space between any of them. These buildings seemed similar to some Boston, Massachusetts, areas, yet even more tightly spaced. The structures were all different light, pretty, pastel colors—their abodes were so pristine and clean. All the buildings boasted balconies on the upper levels.

There was no pollution or garbage anywhere in sight. There were also no animals, birds, fountains, trees, etc. The sky was a beautiful blue with white puffy clouds. I kept gawking at the promenade's peculiarities as my guide was attempting to hurry me along. The entire scene and neighborhood was really quite sterile. The temperature was perfect.

There were people upon all the balconies and in front of the bottom level apartments. All of them wore solid, clean, attractive clothing and they looked so happy and welcoming. They were waving and smiling at us. I would stop and wave back and shoot them a smile.

Once again, my escort pulled me gently along. "Come on, I want you to meet someone really important."

As I analyzed the residents more, I noticed there were no babies, children, pets, or teenagers. They were all adults, and somewhat similar in height, weight, and size. The further we walked, the friendlier the community's greeters became and the quantity of people seemed to increase from a couple per balcony to four or five per balcony. I continued to slow down and respond to them while my escort persisted in prodding me gently onward.

Once again, my less-patient escort, said, "Come on now. You have just got to meet him!" as her eyes lit up with excitement.

I was curious as to how this would all end up. Finally, up ahead, I could see an end to this extensive promenade. The pristine pastel apartments came to a stop and there was actually some foliage: flowers, bushes, and trees. There was a town square with graduating wide cement steps eventually leading to a pinnacle platform. After arriving at the base, we gradually climbed many levels to reach the apex. (This area reminded me of the Whoville town square in *The Grinch* movie.)

An amazing man stood on the top level; he was overlooking everything. He was sharply dressed, very attractive, and appealing. He had blond wavy hair and looked like an all star. People were drawn to him and seemed to be worshiping him. He offered a very welcoming smile. He warmly offered me a hand up as my pretty little escort disappeared. I was interested to see what all the ado and excitement was. My curiosity was short lived.

As soon as we clasped hands I sensed that I shouldn't be there. A large sharp barb, like an oversized fishhook, pierced my right palm and I could not pull away from his solid grasp. I was snagged by something sinister. I soon figured this fiendish foe was Satan himself and that I was ensnared. The barb in my palm was very painful and even worse than the pain was the spiritual entrapment. He was very powerful and convincing— all the beauty and light quickly melted away though.

As I looked up at him, all the light was replaced with darkness. All the pretty pastel colors and foliage disappeared. The earth opened up into a deep chasm where I heard awful noises coming from dark depths very far below. There was very minimal light, if any. Everything appeared dismal dark gray to black. It seemed as if I was perched atop the precipice of hell which was waiting to swallow me up. I felt I had been given a view through the window to hell itself! It was ghastly frightening!

> "... and above all if the very jaws of hell shall gape open the mouth wide after thee ..." (D&C 122:7)

*The Lord explains about the sons of perdition as follows:*

> ... they shall go away into everlasting, punishment ... to reign with the devil and his angels ... And the end thereof, neither the place thereof, nor their torment, no man knows ... neither will be revealed unto man, except to them who are made partakers ... Nevertheless, <u>I the Lord, show it by vision unto many, but straightway shut it up again.</u>

385

> Wherefore, the end, the width, the height, the depth, and the misery thereof, they understand not, neither any man except those who are ordained unto this condemnation. (D&C 76:44-48)

The despair and darkness I felt was incomprehensible. My helplessness and fright levels were *"maxed out."* The feeling of darkness was worse than viewing the darkness. My pierced hand was throbbing—my mind was darkened and I felt as if my body's total destruction was imminent!

I attempted to raise my arm to the square, yet I was too weak and overcome to do so. I closed my eyes and in a desperate and frantic cry for help I pleaded, "God, please save me from the Devil and his darkness! I am trapped! Please set me free! Bring me back to the light! Save me!!" I also called out to Jesus and the Holy Priesthood, after the Order of the Son of God. At that point I gained strength to raise my arm to the square and rebuke the devourer. I still had great doubt of my ever being released from Satan's power due to his amazing strength; yet he did disappear. What a tremendous relief!

> And it came to pass that Moses began to fear exceedingly; and as he began to fear, he saw the bitterness of hell. Nevertheless, calling upon God, he received strength, and he commanded saying: Depart from me Satan, for this one God only will I worship, which is the God of glory. (Moses 1:20)

After the prayer and casting out darkness, in the name of Christ, I found myself released from Satan's tight grasp. Even though I felt like I blacked out in preparation to be consumed by Hell, I came to ... finding myself abandoned all alone in an uninhabited wasteland. I was in the bottom level of a humongous building that resembled a gigantic parking garage. It was a half basement of sorts, with slotted openings in the cement wall that allowed one to see outside, at ground level. I looked around, inside and out, and saw no vehicles or life whatsoever. It was a massive empty shell of a building. There was a little water dripping here and there with a few shallow water puddles in spots. A few weeds were growing in the cracks of concrete. I did not find, nor hear, any birds or bugs.

Once I checked out my inner surroundings my eyes began adjusting to the brighter landscape outside. As I looked out across the surface of a flat land, I began noticing small mounded hills all over the place. They seemed to be shorter than a termite hill yet taller than an anthill; the mounds/hills were somewhere in between those types of hills in height. They looked somewhat similar to the shape of those rounded salt shakers with the silver-domed lids. The hills were all light tan in color, as was the ground, wider at the base and mounded on the top. As my eyes adjusted even better, I could see these mounds were kind of close together and went on forever in every direction as far as one could see. I estimated there were millions of mounds.

Then some movement above the mounds surprised me. I started witnessing these dark wispy spirits floating horizontally in the air and occasionally diving into various domed hills. I noticed that some of the domes boasted broad holes while others had tiny openings. Still there were many other domes that were sealed, some with light repair while others had heavy patchwork. The dark spirits could only descend into the hills with openings in their domes. However, they would hover around sealed domes in a type of frustration. As I continued to view this curiosity, the dark spirits increased in number and they became very active. Some would perform a flyby past the opening I was looking through and that was very unnerving.

> "Behold, we are surrounded by demons, yea, we are encircled about by the angels of him who hath sought to destroy our souls. ... Oh Lord, canst thou turn away thine anger from us?" (Helaman 13:37)

I began feeling that powerful, frightening dark spirit again in my isolated and lonely world. I continued to feel trapped in an undesirable environment, but at least now I was free from pain. Once again I called in mighty prayer for the salvation of my body and soul. "God please save me again!" I cried out.

Immediately I found myself in the arms of our Savoir. I was in a frightened fetal position as he held my whole weight effortlessly. We continued to stay in the bottom of the large building and to watch all the activity amongst the mounds. I felt safe and protected. I basked in the warmth and love of our Lord.

Then a very dark and evil spirit did a flyby and stopped right in front of the window and shot evil from dark, yellowish eyes. I shook and shivered and felt terrible. I despaired, "Oh, me of little faith! I'm in the arms of the Savior and I still get frightened." I felt like that darkest evil spirit was going to consume me! The Lord knew my unspoken thoughts and He comforted me with love and the evil one departed out of sight.

I asked Him the meaning of the millions of mounds.

He said that each one represented a person on earth. Those that are unrepentant leave themselves open to receive multiple evil spirits.

Those that repent have their mounds covered and protected through obedience and repentance.

"This is your mound. You have relied on my Atonement and your sins are forgiven you."

The Spirit ran through my body and there was light and relief once again in my mind, heart, and soul. There was hope!

I was quite humbled and so eternally grateful for the atonement because "my mound" had many patches on it, yet it was securely protected. This was quite an extensive dream to receive the answer I was seeking, to know that I was truly forgiven. The daily torments and repetitive nightmares also ended immediately.

An interesting observation I made from this dream was how Satan pierced my palm so that I experienced pain, darkness, and entrapment. That was the adversary's way.

While the Savior had his palms pierced in pain and agonized for us so that we could be free from pain, darkness, and snares. What extreme polar opposites these spirit brothers are. Jesus' way is God's way! (Journal, 5/6/1984)

> And now, for three days and for three nights was I racked, even with the pains of a damned soul. ... I cried within my heart: O Jesus, thou Son of God, have mercy on me, who am in the gall of bitterness, and am encircled about by the everlasting chains of death. And now behold, when I thought this, I could remember my pains no more; yea, I was harrowed up by the memory of my sins no more. And oh, what joy, and what marvelous light I did behold; yea, my soul was filled with joy as exceeding as was my pain! (Alma 36:16, 18-20)

> "...mine Only Begotten Son, who is full of grace and truth, which is Jesus Christ, the only name which shall be given under heaven, whereby salvation shall come unto the children of men..." (Moses 6:52)

> My English grandfather was a man of great faith. As a young man he had the feeling in his heart that the gospel of the Lord Jesus Christ must be upon the earth somewhere, and that the Church of Jesus Christ could be found.

So he prayed to the Lord earnestly that he might find the Church and the gospel. Finally one Saturday night before retiring, he knelt down and asked the Lord in faith whether or not the Church was upon the earth, and if it was, could he find it.

During that night he had a dream, and in the dream he saw a street in the city where he lived, and in that street there was a hall, and in that hall two men were preaching the gospel of the Lord Jesus Christ.

When he awoke the next morning he was so impressed by the dream that he got up, dressed, and went to the street, found the hall, and there found two servants of God preaching the gospel of the Lord Jesus Christ. He came to this country amidst hardships. Because of the faith of these forefathers of mine, I am here, living in peaceful valleys, in the shadows of great mountains, and, above all, within hearing of the voice of the latter-day prophets. (Joseph L. Wirthlin, CR, April 1952)

———————◆◆◆———————

I listened to President George F. Richards [of the Council of the Twelve] one time as he told of a dream. In the dream he saw the Savior. There came to him at the moment of that seeing such a feeling of love, he could not describe it. It overpowered him, and he said that he made up his mind that if that was the love of Christ, he was going to do all he could to keep it all his life and through all eternity. We need to love the Lord too. (S. Dilworth Young, GC, April 1969)

———————◆◆◆———————

"And he said, Hear now my words: If there be a prophet among you, I the LORD will make myself known unto him in a vision, and will speak unto him in a dream." (Thorp B. Isaacson, CR, April 1960)

389

# 17. Where There is No Vision, the People Perish

*In my mind, a vision is a revelatory view of God's messages to mankind while one is awake. A prophet's vision would be for everyone, in most cases. A vision given to a person would be only for him/her and their respective responsibilities at the time. Whereas, dreams are revelations revealed while one is sleeping. (Dreams and visions are very likely interchangeable terms found throughout the scriptures and in journals however.)*

*A Lamanite servant named Abish was present and alert when all the other servants, Ammon, King Lamoni, and his Queen, fell to the ground as if they were lifeless.*

> "… they had all fallen to the earth, save it were one of the Lamanitish women, whose name was Abish, she having been converted unto the Lord for many years, on account of **a remarkable vision** of her father …"(Alma 19:16)

*Abish was instrumental in preserving Ammon's life, while stabilizing the dangerous mob that had gathered. They were rightfully concerned upon finding their King, his Queen, and most all of the royal household seemingly lying dead upon the ground, along with this one Nephite man, the shepherd servant, who was also motionless.*

*Abish was obviously prepared for this vital experience in her life. Her Lamanite father must have been prepared for a special mission too, which we know not of. Hearing her father's report of his remarkable vision and the Spirit of God solidly converted Abish.*

When I was in high school we had early morning Seminary before school. We had to "plug in" our cars and throw canvas sheets over the front and rear windshields during Wyoming winters. A head bolt/block heater is used to keep an engine's coolant warm for easier car starting on freezing mornings. A head bolt heater was critical when it was five, ten, or twenty below zero, unless you had a heated garage; we didn't even have an unheated garage or a carport. I was a 16-year-old sophomore.

We were studying the Doctrine & Covenants in Seminary that year. Early in the year I began reading these scriptures on a Friday after school. I could not put the book down. The revelations and information on the pages came alive. Over the weekend I immersed myself in the Doctrine & Covenants and nothing else.

My mother would periodically call downstairs,

"Guy, are you hungry?"

"No thank you."

"Guy, are you sick?"

"No, I'm okay."

"Don't you want to go hang out with your friends?"

"No. I'm fine. I'm studying."

I did not eat, yet I was full; I did not drink, and I was not thirsty. I hung out in my corner basement bedroom and ate and drank scriptural doctrine.

"And Jesus said unto them, I am the bread of life: he that
cometh to me shall never hunger; and he that believeth in
me shall never thirst." (John 6:35)

I was a little embarrassed and didn't want my family or friends to know I was being a *scripture nerd* for three days. Hence, until now, no one knew except the Godhead and I.

I absolutely loved what I was reading! I was gaining a testimony of Joseph Smith, God's prophets, revelation, and the scriptures. I even developed a testimony of the truthfulness of the Book of Mormon from reading the Doctrine & Covenants. I knew within my heart that the Gospel of Jesus Christ was true. I knew that Joseph Smith was a prophet of God. This wonderful feeling was burning within my bosom. It was most pleasing and joyful.

Then **a vision open up to me** on Sunday evening after church as I was reading the last sections. I witnessed what appeared to be a large conduit extending from heaven down to earth. Within this conduit flowed a plethora of symbols representing the prayers of people and prophets, ascending to heaven. Within the same giant conduit were answers to these prayers descending in the shape of even different symbols. The symbols going up and coming down were in many different colors and shapes. The symbols seemed to represent innumerable little packages of prayers and answers to those and other prayers/revelations being transported between the two realms.

Within the busy, controlled conduit was a constant stream of scattered symbols that ascended up while other symbols came down simultaneously. There was a lot of action. It was bright and busy, but not noisy at all. The mass of messages were not in a specific order, yet they were orderly. Pure revelation was being poured down upon earth's faithful masses. It was a smooth operation full of light and positive energy.

To my young mind this vision represented, for me, the "Conduit of Revelation." I was witnessing pure revelation and my whole body felt an intense spirit of the truthfulness of Heavenly Father hearing and answering everyone's prayers, including mine. This was an intense and emotional experience. I committed myself to being active in the Gospel of Jesus Christ, serving a mission, and marrying in the temple.

*Following Moroni's first visitation to Joseph Smith, the future prophet explains:*

> After this communication, I saw the light in the room begin to gather immediately around the person of him who had been speaking to me, and it continued to do so until the room was again left dark, except just around him; when, instantly I saw, as it were, *a conduit open right up into heaven*, and he ascended till he entirely disappeared ... (JSH, 43)

*Additionally, the twelve apostles gave their testimony to The Book of Doctrine and Covenants:*

> We ... bear testimony to all the world of mankind ... that the Lord has borne record to our souls, through the Holy Ghost shed forth upon us, that these commandments were given by inspiration of God, and are profitable for all men and women and are verily true. (Introduction: Doctrine and Covenants)

———◆◆◆———

*Alexander Neibaur was introduced to the Gospel of Jesus Christ and taught by a "dream team": Elders Heber C. Kimball, Willard Richards, Orson Hyde, and Joseph Fielding:*

> One of the first questions he asked, was, "You have a book?" And nothing could satisfy that eager, inspired question till he had a copy of the Book of Mormon in his own hands, for **he had seen it, so he declared in his night visions** and recognized the Book on sight. He was waiting for this great message.
>
> His was the swift conversion of the spirit that demanded baptism on the spot. He was advised by the elders to wait and investigate further. He said later that he could not eat nor sleep till he had mastered all the contents of that wondrous volume. When he returned the book he offered himself up for baptism. He answered, "Gentlemen, I am prepared." And his subsequent life found him always

prepared. (*Genealogical and Historical Magazine*, April 1914, 53-63)

———◆———

*Prior to Peter's vision to take the Gospel to the Gentiles, a devout Gentile, Cornelius had his own vision following fasting and prayer:*

> **He saw in a vision** evidently about the ninth hour of the day an angel of God coming in to him, and saying unto him, Cornelius, And when he looked on him, he was afraid, and said, What is it Lord? And he said unto him, Thy prayers and thine alms are come up for a memorial before God. And now send men to Joppa, and call for one Simon, whose surname is Peter (Acts 10:3-5)

*Peter was praying on a housetop and became very hungry. He had a vision, obviously very important, repeated three times in a row.*

> ... heaven opened, and a certain vessel descending unto him, as it had been a great sheet knit at the four corners, and let down to the earth. Wherein were all manner of fourfooted beasts of the earth, and wild beasts, and creeping things, and fowls of the air. And there came a voice to him, **Rise, Peter; kill, and eat.** But Peter said, Not so Lord; for I have never eaten any thing that is uncommon or unclean. And the voice spake unto him again the second time, **What God hath cleansed, that call not thou uncommon.** Then Peter ... said, Of a truth I perceive that God is no respecter of person. (Acts 10:11-15, 34)

*As Peter pondered what this vision meant, Cornelius' men showed up at Peter's gate.*

> "... The Spirit said unto him, **Behold, three men seek thee. Arise therefore, and get thee down, and go with them, doubting nothing: for I have sent them.**" (Acts 10:19-20)

*Thus began the many missionary journeys to the Gentiles as Peter, doubting nothing, was commanded to in his triple vision.*

———◆———

I was serving as the Branch President at the Heritage Park Care Center. I was driving the local missionaries around for their preparation day activities in February of 2004. After dropping them off I was on my way home and had a really strong prompting to stop by Heritage Park. I felt like I needed to go in there NOW.

I entered the facility and started down one of the halls where I met Sterling, one of the residents, coming toward me in his wheelchair. Sterling and his wife had both been living there about three months.

"Hi Sterling, how are you doing today?"

"President Taylor, I have some great news for you. My wife died at about noon today."

"Oh Sterling, I'm so sorry."

"Don't be sorry, she doesn't have to hurt anymore. I didn't lose anything!"

A week later, at his wife's funeral, I visited with their daughter. She informed me that Sterling had been mugged and severely beaten many years earlier, and he had been pronounced dead in the hospital. **While his mortal body was dead his spirit went to the spirit world.** He knew what was going on there and exactly what his wife would be experiencing. He was so excited that day he could hardly stand it. In fact, we met in the hall because he was on his way to get some popcorn to celebrate. They had been married for 63 years!

I have always had a knowledge and testimony of our Father's plan, but not the firsthand knowledge like Sterling's. Sterling's testimony was much deeper; he had been there—he KNEW! (A family friend)

---

A lot is said about the fairest Virgin Mary, and rightly so. Her husband Joseph was definitely foreordained for his special calling in life. Joseph received revelations through dreams and visions that protected Mary and baby Jesus: "... **An angel of the Lord appeared to him in a vision** ...."—"And being warned of God in a dream,"—"... **The angel of the Lord appeared in a vision** to Joseph ...," and—"... **being warned of God in a vision**...." (See: Matthew 2:3; 3:13; 3:19, 3:22) I believe Joseph is a very obedient and righteous soul from before the foundation of this world and beyond.

---

Through the years as we raised our large family, we planted a garden with lots of vegetables and other produce. Every summer we'd work together to harvest and can many of the vegetables, especially the green beans.

One summer we had a bumper crop of beans and I borrowed my mother's pressure cooker so I could get them canned as the other family members snapped the beans.

The two pressure cookers each held twenty pints and had to cook for twenty minutes at twelve pounds pressure, just a little above the ten pound mark on the gauge. After cooking, the pressure had to return to zero before you could take off the lid to do another batch. Since I was simultaneously using two cookers, I had to be watchful so that I did everything right.

As I turned off the heat on one pressure cooker full of beans, I observed that it didn't take very long for the pressure gauge to return to zero. **Suddenly "in my mind's eye" I could see** the pressure gauge as it really was and it was only at seven not twelve. I had cooked the twenty pint batch at the wrong temperature and they would have spoiled because of the error.

At first I doubted that I would make that mistake, but then I realized that the Holy Ghost had given me that visual prompting so I could remedy the situation and avoid losing the beans we spent so much time preparing.

I am thankful for the help we receive from the Holy Ghost even though it may seem trivial at the time. The Lord knows our needs and is willing to help us if we are in tune." (A friend)

"... **the vision was opened to my mind** that I could see the place where the plates were deposited, and that so clearly and distinctly that I knew the place again when I visited it." (Testimony of the Prophet Joseph Smith/Book of Mormon)

---

Through the manifestations of the Holy Ghost, the Lord will assist us in all our righteous pursuits. I remember in an operating room, I have stood over a patient—unsure how to perform an unprecedented procedure—and **experienced the Holy Ghost diagramming the technique in my mind.** (President Russell M. Nelson, GC, April 2018)

---

Now, I will refer to a thing that took place with me in Tennessee. I was in Tennessee in the year 1835, and while at the house of Abraham O. Smoot, I received a letter from Brothers Joseph Smith and Oliver Cowdery, requesting me to stay there, and stating that I would lose no blessing by doing so. Of course, I was satisfied. I went into a little room and sat down upon a small sofa. I was all by myself and the room was dark; and while I rejoiced in this letter and the promise made to me, **I became wrapped in vision**. I was like Paul; I did not know whether I was in the body or out of the body. A personage appeared to me and showed me the great scenes that should take place in the last days. One scene after another passed before me. I saw the sun darkened; I saw the moon become as blood; I saw the stars fall from heaven; I saw seven golden lamps set in the heavens, representing the various dispensations of God to man—a sign that would appear before the coming of Christ. I saw the resurrection of the dead. What does this mean? It was a testimony of the resurrection of the dead. I had a testimony. I believe in the resurrection of the dead, and I know it is a true principle. (Wilford Woodruff, *JD* 22:330)

———————•◆•———————

I owned a full-size Bronco which had a rear tailgate window that quit working. I had looked into it several times, including testing the motor and simply could not find the problem. On my day off I decided to find and fix the problem even if it took all day to do it. Early in the morning I laid out my tools and removed the cover from the tailgate. I was only in the carport a few minutes when my wife informed me that my sister-in-law had a blown water heater and needed a replacement right away. Her husband was at work. I finally agreed and got my tools then picked up a new water heater at a plumbing store. I figured I could finish this job in two to three hours tops.

When I previewed the job, there was a new wall built around the furnace and water heater. They had also cemented the legs of the water heater to the floor! I had to tear down the wall and break the cement up to remove it. I then dragged the water heater up the stairs and wrenched my back doing so. I gently let the new water heater slide down the stairs. Because of the uneven concrete, I had to solder new pipes due to the uneven heights.

As I was leaving that night it was nearly ten! I had spent the entire day and evening. I was feeling a bit sorry for myself with a sore back and my wiring problem still looming. As I traveled back home, **a vision of the problem with the wiring opened in my mind** and I knew exactly where the problem was and how to fix it! It was a ground wire screwed into the wheel well of the truck. I would have never looked there. I had not prayed about my problem, yet Heavenly Father taught me a great lesson about service. Even with my grumbling heart, He came to my aid. The scriptures are right; there is not a sparrow that can fall from the sky that He does not know about. (Our friend)

———◆———

While awake and in deep prayer **I had an interesting vision**. I became aware of my wife's grandpa nearby, dressed like a temple worker and involved in some calling. He seemed quite happy. I also noticed grandma in another area of the structure. She was also dressed like a temple worker. She was smiling that same smile that used to come frequently to her in earth life, talking and quietly laughing as she interacted with other workers while fulfilling some calling. Grandma was clearly the happiest I had ever seen her.

My focus then went to their son who was never gung ho about the church and the gospel, but had also passed on. I marveled about him being there.

Then I heard a voice that resounded in my soul with authority and love say, **"Do not judge my servant for I have forgiven him. I know him."**

"I have laid before every woman this principle and let her have her choice. Why deprive a woman of being sealed to her husband because he never heard the Gospel? What do any of us know with regard to him? Will he not hear the Gospel and embrace it in the spirit world?" (Wilford Woodruff, *Messages of the First Presidency*, 3:257)

At this point, my mind turned to some of my own sins that I struggle with. The Spirit said, **"Forgive yourself and move ahead."** I wondered about that, because it sounded like an easy way to excuse continuing with the same sin. I guess I had also always somehow figured that forgiveness of self was the final step of the repentance process, after recognition, remorse, restoration, etc. The Spirit then gave me to understand that forgiveness of self is really the beginning of the repentance process. You're not excusing your disobedience; your recognizing that Christ has willingly accepted and taken upon himself the eternal consequences of your misbehavior.

The Spirit communicated that the *steps* aren't really steps; per se. rather, they occur in an intertwining and upward spiraling manner. So forgiveness of self is a process. (A relative)

When the Lord requires that we forgive all men, that includes forgiving ourselves. Sometimes, of all the people in the world, the one who is the hardest to forgive—as well as perhaps the one who is most in need of our forgiveness—is the person looking back at us in the mirror. (Dieter F. Uchtdorf, *Ensign*, July 2013)

A couple of my friends wanted to leave our ward dinner being held in our chapel's cultural hall and go outside with a few boys our age, when I was around thirteen years old. It was late evening and dark outside. My friends wanted to meet in the parking lot in the back of the church.

We were heading to the outside door when my father saw me and suggested that we come back and join the ward activity. Competing thoughts inside my head were having a war of words. "He *is* my father and I should respect him. But didn't he want me to have a good time?"

"Why should I listen to my father?" I asked myself. After all, he was "only" the scoutmaster at the time, my mind reasoned. I justified this line of thinking by judging my father for having become an active member of the church only years previous.

As I debated whether to follow my peers, **it was as if a vision came to view** and I saw in *gold words* **"MAN OF GOD"** in block letters in the air above my head. The all capital golden letters declared to me the real nature of my father and his standing in the Lord's eyes. I immediately turned around and followed my dad back to our ward family.

The closest thing these letters resembled, I discovered years later, were large gold letters found inside the Arizona temple. They were a beautiful sight! I am grateful that bold words in gold helped me make a wise choice about following my father's counsel that evening and on into the years that followed as he served as bishop of our ward. (My wife, Tamara)

*On one other occasion, my wife had a similar experience where she saw gold words in the air as an answer to another prayer. This is somewhat similar to Elder David O. McKay who shares this remarkable vision while sailing to Samoa:*

Toward evening, the reflection of the afterglow of a beautiful sunset was most splendid! ... Pondering still upon this beautiful scene, I lay in my [bed] at ten o'clock that night. ... I then fell asleep, and **beheld in vision something infinitely sublime**. In the distance I beheld a beautiful white city. Though it was far away, yet I seemed to realize that trees with luscious fruit, shrubbery with gorgeously tinted leaves, and flowers in perfect bloom abounded everywhere. The clear sky above seemed to reflect these beautiful shades of color. I then saw a great concourse of people approaching the city. Each one wore a white flowing robe and a white headdress. Instantly my attention seemed centered upon their leader, and though I could see only the profile of his features and his body, I recognized him at once as my Savior! The tint and radiance of his countenance were glorious to behold. There was a peace about him which seemed sublime—it was divine!

"The city, I understood, was his. It was the City Eternal; and the people following him were to abide there in peace and eternal happiness.

"But who were they?

"As if the Savior read my thoughts, he answered by pointing to a semicircle that then appeared above them, and on which were written in gold the words:

**"These Are They Who Have Overcome the World—Who Have Truly Been Born Again!"** (*TPC*, 1-2)

━━━━◆•◆•◆━━━━

*Elder Melvin J Ballard, an Apostle, shared his cherished experience:*

I lost a son six years of age **and I saw him a man in the spirit world after his death**, and I saw how he had exercised his own freedom of choice and would obtain of his own will and volition a companionship, and in due time to him and all those who are worthy of it, shall come all of the blessings and sealing privileges of the House of the Lord. (*Three Degrees of Glory*, 31)

———◆———

Our family had just experienced a devastating house fire … our family faced challenges and discord.

My husband was not active in the church … our two teenage sons were making choices that would lead only to sorrow … I was serving as YW President in our ward … several of the young women were struggling, some of the parents faced struggles.

I knew the young women needed me … my six sons needed me … my good husband depended on my strength … Yet there seemed to be nothing but darkness around me, and I felt empty, weak, and incapable…

Late one night as I rocked our infant son in the stillness of our temporary home … I prayed with all my heart that Heavenly Father would show me the way to help them despite my inadequacies. He answered immediately and showed me the way. **I seemed to see myself** in our ward's large cultural hall, which had no windows. It was late at night, and there was not even a glimmer of light. Then I lit a tiny birthday candle. It seemed so insignificant, yet the power of that miniscule light was enough to displace the darkness.

That was my answer! The quantity of darkness surrounding us in the world simply does not matter … This simple insight has carried me through the past 25 years with the knowledge that with the Lord's help and guidance, we can do—and be—all that He needs us to be in this world of darkness. (Susan Wyman, Latter-day Saint Voices, *Ensign*, Feb 2014)

"Now we have received, not the spirit of the world, but the spirit which is of God; that we might know the things that are freely given to us of God." (1 Cor. 2:12)

———◆———

A few months ago, I was kneeling in prayer with a young family in Albuquerque. I had a wonderful warm feeling as I opened my eyes and looked around that circle. **It was as if I**

**imagined families in homes throughout the world** having that same experience. Hopefully, if the pattern of prayer is established in our homes, individual family members will help reproduce that pattern for others as my roommates did for me. (Janette C. Hales, GC, April 1991)

•◆•

Our dryer was making funny noises and then the cycle would stop. It would start again and then suddenly stop again. After checking Google, which listed four possible culprits, I called my brother-in-law, who repairs appliances in a distant state. He was 99% sure it was the drive motor. I ordered a drive motor on line; the dryer was totally disassembled awaiting the motor's arrival. I worked a day putting it all back together with help from an online video and texts to our relative. Finally, feeling exhausted, I decided the dryer was ready to start again. There was unusual noise and a smell of something burning. I shut it off, unplugged the dryer, and threw my hands in the air, exclaiming, "Lord I need some help here!"

Going upstairs I chose not to share the bad news. We then had our nightly ritual of *Come Follow Me*, family prayer, and a family hug. The *Come Follow Me* program has blessed our lives. That evening we had a great discussion on the interesting lesson that involved transfiguration and translated beings. As we ended our family hug, a short vision opened in my mind—my spiritual eyes saw the solution. I saw the pulley between the dryer drum and its motor and discerned that I needed to move the pulley frame over to another slot. I fixed our dryer within minutes the next morning! (Journal 3/2019)

•◆•

*Brother Benjamin F. Johnson wrote of his experience:*

President Rigdon was called upon to put forth his claim before the people, which he did, and after his closing remarks, which were void of all power or influence, **President Brigham Young arose and spoke. I saw him arise, but as soon as he spoke I jumped upon my feet, for in every possible degree it was Joseph's voice, and his person, in look, attitude, dress and appearance was Joseph himself, personified; and I knew in a moment the *spirit and mantle of Joseph was upon him.***

President Wilford Woodruff, who was also a witness to the event, said: **If I had not seen him with my own eyes,** there is no one that could have convinced me that it was not Joseph Smith speaking. It was as the voice and face of

Joseph Smith; and anyone can testify to this who was acquainted with these two men (President Brigham Young, *TPC*, 2.18)

———————————•◆•———————————

After our beloved prophet President Gordon B. Hinckley passed away, our new prophet—Thomas S. Monson was speaking at his first General Conference. Even though Elder Monson had been at the general conference pulpits for 45 years, this was his first talk as our newly sustained Prophet of the Lord. As my wife and I watched him, **we had a simultaneous vision of the** *mantle of a prophet* *slowly and solidly descending upon him*. The Holy Spirit ran tingling through our bodies and we had our amazing individual witnesses that Elder Thomas S Monson was truly called of God as our new prophet, seer, and revelator. (Journal 4/9/2008)

*Another Apostle testifies with a strikingly similar witness:*

Of the many privileges we have had in this historic conference, including participation in a solemn assembly in which we were able to stand and sustain you as prophet, seer, and revelator, I cannot help but feel that the most important privilege we have all had has been **to witness personally the settling of the sacred, prophetic mantle upon your shoulders, almost as it were by the very hands of angels themselves.** Those in attendance at last night's general priesthood meeting and all who were present in the worldwide broadcast of this morning's session have been eyewitness to this event. (Jeffrey R Holland, GC, April 2008)

———————————•◆•———————————

One day ... **I lost consciousness of my surroundings and thought I had passed to the Other Side**. I found myself standing with my back to a large and beautiful lake, facing a great forest of trees. There was no one in sight, and there was no boat upon the lake or any other visible means to indicate how I might have arrived there. I realized, or seemed to realize, that I had finished my work in mortality and had gone home.

I began to explore, and soon I found a trail through the woods which seemed to have been used very little, and which was almost obscured by grass. I followed this trail, and after I had walked for some time and had traveled a considerable distance through the forest. I saw a man coming towards me. I became aware that he was a very large man, and I hurried my steps to reach him, because I recognized him as my grandfather [George A. Smith]. In mortality he weighed over 300 pounds, so you may know he was a large man. I remember how happy I was to see him coming. I had been given his name and had always been proud of it.

When grandfather came within a few feet of me, he stopped. His stopping was an invitation for me to stop. Then—and this I would like the boys and girls to never forget—he looked at me earnestly and said, **"I would like to know what you have done with my name."**

Everything I had ever done passed before me as though it were a flying picture on a screen—everything I had done. Quickly this vivid retrospect came down to the very time I was standing there. My whole life had passed before me. I smiled and looked at my grandfather and said: "I have never done anything with your name of which you need to be ashamed.

He stepped forward and took me in his arms, and as he did so, I became conscious again of my earthly surroundings. My pillow was as wet as though water had been poured on it—wet with tears of gratitude that I could answer unashamed. (George Albert Smith, TPC, xxv-xxvi)

*The disciple Ananias was taken far away from his comfort zone due to a vision. During that vision, the Lord revealed to Ananias that Saul had also seen a vision and that Ananias was in Saul's vision!*

And there was a certain disciple at Damascus, named Ananias; and to him **said the Lord in a vision**, *Ananias*. And he said, Behold, I am here, Lord. And the Lord said unto him, *Arise, and go into the street which is called Straight, and inquire in the house of Judas for one called Saul, of Tarsus: for, behold, he prayeth, And hath seen in a vision a man named Ananias coming in, and putting his hand on him, that he might receive his sight.* Then Ananias answered, Lord, I have heard by many of this man, how much evil he hath done to thy saints at Jerusalem. And there he hath authority from the chief priests to bind all that call on thy name. But the Lord said unto him, Go thy way: for he is a chosen vessel unto me, to bear my name before the Gentiles, and kings, and the children of Israel: For I will shew him how great things he must suffer for my name's sake. And Ananias went his way, and entered into the house; and putting his hands on him said, Brother Saul, the Lord, even Jesus, that appeared unto thee in the way as thou camest, hath sent me, that thou mightest receive thy sight, and be filled with the Holy Ghost. And immediately there fell from his eyes as it had been scales: and he received sight forthwith, and arose, and was baptized. (Acts 9:10-18)

Now, it is very important, my brethren, that we each live so that we can have this spirit of the Lord. Its importance did not cease with the death of the Prophet Joseph Smith. In 1879, two years after the Prophet Brigham Young had died, President Wilford Woodruff was down in the mountains of Arizona traveling with Lot Smith. On one occasion, **he had a vision or a dream** in which he saw Brigham Young and Orson Hyde, and he asked Brigham Young if he would not come with him to Arizona and speak to the people. Brigham Young answered that he had done his talking in the flesh and that work was now left for Elder Woodruff and others to do. In his diary, President Woodruff quotes President Young as saying: "Tell the people to get the spirit of the Lord and keep it with them." (Marion G. Romney, CR, April 1944)

"That we through our faith may begin to **inherit the visions** and blessings and glories of God." (The Spirit of God, Hymns, no. 2)

... I, Nephi, having heard all the words of my father, concerning the things which he **saw in a vision**, and also the things which he spake by the power of the Holy Ghost, which power he received by faith on the Son of God—and the Son of God was the Messiah who should come—I, Nephi, was desirous also that I might see, and hear, and know of these things, by the power of the Holy Ghost, which is the gift of God unto all those who diligently seek him, as well in times of old as in the time that he should manifest himself unto the children of men. (1 Ne. 10:17)

# 18. Of Necessity They Feel After Me

"In the day of their peace they esteemed lightly my counsel; but, in the day of their trouble, of necessity they feel after me." (D&C 101:8)

*This scripture was referring to persecutions of the Saints from the mob and the Saints questioning of why they had to persevere such torment. Praying in dire circumstances is much more pleasing to the Lord when we are also praying when everything is going well. Death-bed repentance would be an example of feeling after Him out of necessity.*

*The following experiences are from Christians who do have prayerful hearts of gratitude and pleading during the challenging as well as the peaceful times.*

"Yea, and when you do not cry unto the Lord, let your hearts be full, drawn out in prayer unto him continually for your welfare, and also for the welfare of those who are around you." (Alma 34:27)

My friends and I were breaking snowdrifts just outside of town through the rolling hills of northern Wyoming for fun. It was the winter of 1974 and we had a big-bodied Oldsmobile, one Saturday, to plow through big natural drifts. Due to Wyoming's windy nature, large drifts were common and would sometimes close down schools. In the valleys of these hills, the drifts were huge and snow would fly everywhere as we careened through them at fairly high speed. We really enjoyed it.

We saw our next big drift and barreled down the hillside. There was more snow than usual flying around us and then suddenly the car came to a complete stop. The engine was still running, but the car was wedged tightly inside an enormous snow drift. We were packed inside the large drift and encased! Once we realized what had happened, a panic came upon the three of us sixteen-year-olds. We thought all the exhaust might come back into the car and kill us since we were in an enclosed pocket, so we shut it off. "Now the car won't kill us!"

"We're going to run out of air anyway!"

"We'll just die slowly and no one will even know where we are!"

"What are we going to do?"

We were tucked inside a giant snowdrift that was taller than our car. There was solid snow around all our windows and the car, including the roof. We were buried! We were all members of our ward's priest quorum. We had a panicked prayer: "God save us!"

Then we went to work. I rolled down my window and started frantically punching the snow really hard. The snow would only give a few inches at a time so I punched it like a punching bag. I was able to finally make a narrow path between the car door and the massive snowdrift. I worked my way up, punching away and finally—standing on the door's window frame; I could see sunlight and the top of the snowdrift. I also witnessed a whole lot of snow in every direction. This was a very large drift; a gigantic one. So maybe there was hope?

I was able to wiggle myself on top of our car and then atop the drift, lay out spread eagle, and then move in a military crawl across the snow surface for quite some distance. I yelled—instructing my nervous travel companions on how to keep from sinking into the snowdrift. We had to walk quite a distance down a country road. Tuckered out, we finally reached a main road and we were able to hitchhike back to town. Later it took two four-wheel drives and some long chains to dislodge the Olds' from its snowy impound!

> The great plan of happiness includes a proverbial roller coaster of challenging times along with the most joyful times. Yes, we all have our moments of difficulty and heartbreak. Occasionally, they are so difficult for us that we just want to give up. There are times when our steps are unsteady, when we feel discouraged and even reach out in desperation. (W. Craig Zwick, GC, Oct 2003)

> A friend and I took a couple of young men snowmobiling in Cooke City, Montana, about a three-hour drive from Billings, Montana. The boys were just learning to ride and had a lot of fun. It was dark by the time we headed over the Chief Joseph Highway.
> The road had been clear when we went over it that morning. Now the road consisted of hard packed snow. After the sun settled, ice formed on the highway. We had to go over Dead Indian Pass and were heading down it when trouble began. I was driving our 1967 two-wheel drive Chevy. We had one sled in the back and two on the trailer I was pulling behind us.
> As we started down the hill, I geared the truck down to hold it back. This portion of the grade had a dirt surface and would have been fine had it not snowed. It was a long

hill with a curve at the far end. About halfway down the hill I could feel the truck starting to lose traction and beginning to slide. Braking would have only made it worse; at this point I had no control over the truck and told the boys to tighten their seatbelts. They were getting quite concerned and I rushed off a prayer under my breath.

Now the trailer started to come around on the driver's side and "jackknifed!" If we kept sliding as we approached the curve, we would go off the road and down several hundred feet of mountainside and most likely find death.

Just before we reached the curve, I felt the wheels on the driver's side catch traction and slow us down. I was then able to give the truck enough throttle to pull in front of the trailer and straighten it out.

From there we all made it home safely. I breathed a sigh of relief and knew that an unseen power was watching over and protecting us. (A peer)

———◆———

Our priest group took some snowmobiles atop the Bighorn Mountains in northwest Wyoming. We were above timberline and there were miles of virgin snow surrounding us. It was a winter playground with few obstacles if any. We all had a blast driving every which way and all over the place.

I became separated from the group and was having fun in some deep snow. Unfortunately the snow became even deeper and I was heading downhill and was unable to turn around. I was stuck.

I jumped off the machine to physically turn it around and immediately sunk in the deep snow up to my armpits! Needless to say I was quite alarmed and frightened. Now the snowmobile and I were both stuck. This was a time for emergency prayer. I prayed quickly and anxiously waited for some time.

After a while one of my more experienced peers discovered my plight. He had me grab onto the back of the machine while he only had his left foot on my snowmobile as he leaned far to the right. His momentum and skill slowly pulled the machine and a rescued rider out of a snowy grave. I am so grateful that Heavenly Father answered my panicked prayer.

———◆———

Maybe sixty-five is too old for this kind of thing. At the time I didn't think so. We were on a Book of Mormon tour visiting ruins in Mexico and Guatemala. When our tour guide gave us the option of a massive zip line I jumped at the chance. This was definitely on my bucket list.

The zip line had nine stations and covered a few miles. It went under, through, and over the jungle canopy. We could see howler monkeys, exotic birds, and other wildlife not seen in the U.S. I felt confident, especially after seeing ninety-year-old Joe in line ahead of me. Granted, he went tandem with a worker.

Being in a third world country, OSHA regulations were definitely not met at this thrill ride. The third link required carefully negotiating one's way between two trees just a few feet apart. On a zip line it is easy to get turned sideways or even backwards; I managed to do both! The guides had given us instructions on what to do if that happened but we did not have an opportunity to practice before they turned us loose.

I left the platform and immediately picked up way more speed than what I was comfortable with. I turned sideways, backwards and sideways again. I looked ahead and saw the two trees that we were warned about and I panicked big time. This was not looking good. If I couldn't straighten out I would lose both legs and that was not a good option.

I said a quick prayer as I kept attempting to turn myself. To me it was a miracle; I managed to get turned around about two seconds before I went screaming between the two trees. (A peer)

---

We were traveling north from a family reunion along I-15 in Utah. Our son-in-law worked at an RV dealership and one of the perks was a free rental for vacations. There was plenty of room for us and their young family in the large motor home. As we traveled along, everybody else on the freeway passed us by easily.

Then we all had an eerie feeling and noticed something strange: There were no more cars passing us and there were no cars or trucks going south on the interstate. There was absolutely no traffic in either direction on the interstate. It was a surreal feeling—similar to what one would experience in a "twilight zone."

As we came around a turn we noticed a very tall and wide fire on the left. This immense and intense wall of high hot flames was heading down the hillside for the freeway and was obviously large enough to jump all lanes and start burning the other side—or anything else in its way. We had never seen anything like this and were all in fear.

We all prayed in desperation and floored the big unit as the fire wall and motor home raced simultaneously. As the fire reached the edge of the southbound lanes we were just slowly sailing by in the northbound lanes, FAR right, before disaster. No one was comfortable cutting it that close. Safely passing, we felt that our prayers of desperation had surely been answered. All the traffic behind and ahead of us was completed stopped in both directions. Our oversized vehicle had been just slow enough to be left lingering in between both roadblocks. The fire did cross the road behind us and burned brightly on both sides of the freeway!

———◆———

When my kids have a swim meet, I put my bike on the back of my van and away we go. I ride my bike during the hour-long warm-ups they have. I have been blessed to ride my bike all over Utah and enjoy many beautiful vistas. The pool we meet at the most often is in Bountiful, UT. I love riding my bike there because I grew up in Bountiful and know the area. Call me crazy, but I do enjoy a good uphill bike ride that really gets my heart pumping. I like to ride above the Bountiful Temple high upon the mountainside.

I was coming down this steep hill in Bountiful during March of 2016. I had really enjoyed my ride that day and as I picked up speed I discovered that my brakes were not working. I started to panic and thought of my options. There was a stoplight at the bottom of the hill and I could hit or be hit by a car. I was going too fast to make any turns off the road. I really didn't know how I was going to stop. In my panicked state, I started praying really hard. I said a loud prayer, at the top of my lungs, "Dear Heavenly Father, please help me be able to stop my bike so I can get back to my husband and my kids safely!!"

The very instant I uttered the screamed prayer, I heard a loud pop and realized that my bike had a flat tire. Wow, just like that, my prayer was answered; an instant answer to a prayer! I knew Heavenly Father answered my prayer. I never dreamed in my years of biking that a flat tire would ever be an answer to prayer. The flat slowed my bike down and I was able to prevent an accident. I was immensely glad to walk the remainder of the way down the hill.

I arrived back at the swim meet in time to see all my children's races without a scratch. I know that God knows my name, knows my challenges, and what I am going through at any given moment of my life. All I need to do is ask, and He will be there for me—not always in the way that I want, but in the way that is best for me. (A friend)

"In times of urgent need, after meditation and prayer to receive confirmation of a selected course of action, those promptings have given the comforted feeling that it was right." (Robert D. Hales, GC, April 1977)

My knees starting wearing out following twenty years of competitive volleyball in church and city leagues and competitive tournaments. We were competing in the co-ed tournament's championship games and I went up to spike a perfect set. As I slammed the ball around the blocker, his knee came in contact with my right knee, through the net. I wore thick knee pads for protection, so I thought, (I was 37 at the time.)

As I fell to the floor, I did not feel so well. My knee was funky. I placed my finger where my kneecap should be and it was all squishy, like Jell-O! In terror I thought, "My kneecap has either split in two, shattered to pieces, or moved somewhere else!" There was no bone or hardness whatsoever in my right knee.

We went to the hospital and they confirmed that I had torn my anterior cruciate ligament (ACL). The surgeon informed me that everything on the bottom and sides of the patella (knee cap) were sheared. My kneecap was intact; it was just pulled up my leg by the quadriceps tendon. Next, I was placed on this very cold metal table for preoperational x-rays. This was positively painful as the nurse twisted my leg into various positions to obtain the desired angles for x-ray photos, causing my knee horrendous hurt.

I went home and slept in a recliner since surgery was scheduled for the next morning. My leg stayed propped up in one place all night. The knee and my ankle were both extremely swollen. Many of you know how painful a sprained ankle can be. My knee hurt so much worse that I could not even feel the sprained ankle at all. When I got up to use the bathroom, I hobbled on my crutches and intense pain began radiating from that damaged leg as blood rushed to the damaged areas. I got to the toilet and plopped down and the pain had increased to such an unbearable level; so excruciating—that I passed out.

I woke up to my wife slapping me across the cheeks, one side and the other, back and forth. She was exclaiming, "Oh Heavenly Father, please don't let him die! Please don't let him die!"

That's a prayer of desperation along with faith in action! (Journal 4/28/1993)

... I was a new Aaronic Priesthood holder with an assignment to pass the sacrament. Terrified that I would make a mistake, I went outside the chapel before the meeting started and prayed in desperation that God would help me. An answer came. I felt that the Lord was with me. I felt His confidence in me, and so I felt confidence in my part in His work. (Henry B. Eyring, GC, April 2017)

One Saturday morning, in late spring, there was a stack of rental videos on the edge of the kitchen table staring back at me; a sign that the videos needed to be returned soon. Looking at the receipt, we had about an hour to get them back to avoid late fees. We had rented two movies and earned one free. However we didn't have time to watch them all. There was no way I was going to pay a penalty for a free movie I hadn't even viewed.

I was always looking for a reason to take the motorcycle for a spin, so I zipped over to the video store with time to spare. I had a habit of putting down the kickstand and throwing my helmet onto the mirror simultaneously as I dismounted. As I went through this familiar routine, a voice quickly said "LOOK!" and my head seemed to be turned along with the command—to look back behind my motorcycle. I was strongly impressed to turn and go the opposite direction I was initially heading. Everything happened in mere seconds.

Here was the scene: There was a large, 4-door Oldsmobile slowly backing out of the sloping parking lot. Not too exciting actually. However, the startling situation was that there were only two small toddlers at the wheel. They were rolling towards a perpendicular road at the bottom of a steep hill where cars generally came careening at higher speeds than normal. On the opposite side of that road lay a full, uncovered irrigation canal teaming with rushing water ... there were no fences. This is the danger the two tiny tots were unknowingly headed for. Their worst case scenario would be getting T-boned by a fast car and then being pushed sideways or upside down into that rushing canal water and having the water begin filling the car through its shattered windows.

As I dashed to the runaway vehicle, I rushed a prayer or plea off to God for HELP! I seemed to be able to reach the car quite quickly and grabbed for the door handles and then braced my feet. It helped that these older cars had large metal handles. I was expecting the momentum of the car to just slide my shoes, and me, over the gravel atop the sloped cement parking lot. To my amazement, I was able to quickly stop the large car! It was as if my feet were cemented to the ground and my arms were made of steel. I exclaimed, "Thank you God!"

Then I had to just laugh out loud because the two young drivers, around 2 and 3 years old, were jumping up and down on the front seat with extreme excitement! They were bouncing and playing with the shifter and steering wheel. They would hang onto the steering wheel with one hand and then touch every button, knob, and lever within their grasps! Each boy would quickly go from the stereo knobs to the heat controls and anything else that protruded or looked shiny. They were elated and overjoyed!

I imagined them saying, or at least thinking, "We made it go! We made it go!"

It all happened so fast. I firmly believe it was a case of the Lord placing me at the right place and at the right time in order to be allowed to save the little toddlers from unnecessary danger and harm. I find it most interesting that our Father in Heaven uses our habits, one of mine being thriftiness, to accomplish His desires.

Now that the large vehicle was at rest I noticed that all the doors were locked. I decided to grip tighter with one hand and use my other hand to play games through the window to get the toddler's attention. I used simple sign language to encourage the young giggling boys to unlock the door. They were touching everything else, why not the door locks too? When they finally unlocked it, I threw open the door, slammed the shifter into Park and jerked the emergency brake on as hard as it would go. I shook my finger while sharply saying to the little drivers, "Now don't you touch anything! Just sit down on the seat!"

I then rushed into the video store and loudly announced to the customers and employees, "Who has a large tan car with two little boys in it?"

A woman came towards me screaming and questioning, "Are they all right!"

I explained to her that they had shifted her car into neutral and were headed for the road and canal; but I was able to stop her car and that the toddlers were just fine.

She exclaimed, "Oh those two!! They are going to be the death of me!"

By this time I had only minutes to spare as I pulled the rental videos from my backpack and returned them to the video counter, with no extra charges. (Journal 5/6/1990)

"And I was led by the Spirit, not knowing beforehand the things which I should do." (1 Ne. 4:6)

# 19. We Wrestle Against the Rulers of Darkness

*One can search the scriptures to discover some of Satan's many tools he uses to sadden, stress, and seduce us with, such as: Arrows, strong bands, awful chains, flaxen cords, darkness, devices, fetters of hell, fiery darts, handcuffs, strong holds, mists of darkness, possessions, scales of darkness, secret combinations, shackles, shafts in the whirlwind, dark veils of unbelief, iron yokes and all manners of secret works of darkness.*

*Lucifer is the enemy of all righteousness and would that we would be miserable like he is. He is the father of all lies. The Devil makes war against the saints of God. Lucifer has one third of the hosts of heaven as his army of evil angels; unembodied dark spirits that tempt and try mankind through diverse measures.*

> "... also a third part of the hosts of heaven turned away from me because of their agency; and they were thrust down, and thus came the devil and his angels." (D&C 29:36-37)

> Who has not heard and felt the enticing of the devil? His voice often sounds so reasonable and his message so easy to justify. It is an appealing, intriguing voice with dulcet sounds. It is neither hard nor discordant. No one would listen to Satan's voice if it sounded harsh or mean. If the devil's voice were unpleasant, it would not persuade people to listen to it. (James E Faust, *Ensign*, Jan 2007)

**Satan's Great Lies:**

*Satan commanded Moses,* "... saying: I am the Only Begotten, worship me." (Moses 1:19)

*The devil deceived Korihor, saying,* "... There is no god ..." (Alma 30:53)

*Nephi warns us:* "... for the evil spirit teacheth not a man to pray, but teacheth him that he must not pray." (I Ne. 32:8)

> "If the Devil says you cannot pray when you are angry, tell him it is none of his business, and pray until that species of insanity is dispelled and serenity is restored to the mind." (Brigham Young, *JD* 10:170)

President Kimball taught me an unforgettable lesson. He pulled my coattail and said, "It has always troubled me what the adversary does using the name of our Savior." (Robert D. Hales, *GC*, April 2006)

*Korihor the anti-Christ claimed:*

... there shall be no Christ ... for no man can know of anything which is to come ... ye look forward and say that ye see a remission of your sins ... it is the effect of a frenzied mind; and this derangement of your minds ... there could be no atonement made for the sins of men ... whatsoever a man did was no crime. (Alma 30:12-13, 16-17)

"Korihor the anti-Christ, ridicules Christ, the Atonement, and the spirit of prophecy—He teaches there is no God, no fall of man, no penalty for sin, and no Christ—" (Alma Chapter 30 Heading)

*From the combatant Nehor:*

And he also testified unto the people that all mankind should be saved at the last day, and they need not fear nor tremble, but that they might lift up their heads and rejoice; for the Lord had created all men, and had also redeemed all men; and, in the end, all men should have eternal life. ... Now because Gideon withstood him with the words of God he was wroth with Gideon, and drew his sword and began to smite him ... therefore he was slain by the sword. (Alma 1:4, 9)

*Christ reveals what Satan says:*

"Deceive and lie in wait to catch, that ye may destroy; behold, this is no harm ... it is no sin to lie that they may catch a man in a lie, that they may destroy him." (D&C 10:25)
"And behold, others he flattereth away, and telleth them there is no hell; and he saith unto them: I am no devil, for there is none—" (2 Ne. 28:22)

When I was on my mission in the mid 70's, I worked to be dutiful and obedient. After I had been out 6-7 months, I was thinking, "You know, I don't really feel like I've been inspired. It's me that makes the decisions and choices for what I dictate." So I decided I would fast and pray for inspiration, so I did.

We were going to a movie, *The World's Greatest Athlete*, because it was P-day. I was still fasting. After the movie it was raining and there were six of us Elders crammed in an American Motors Hornet. That's what we had to drive. And, what happened is that the Spirit completely left me. I don't think many people experience this. I know President Eyring mentioned a similar experience and I think the Savior had this experience in the Garden and on the cross.

When the spirit was fully departed, I felt like a ruthless person. I could do anything, even murder and not feel any consequences whatsoever. It was a most scary experience. I felt like I could do whatever I pleased, as long as it benefited me. Then I was looking for a way to get out of the car.

I was looking out the window and it was as if the Lord had taken the top of my head off and was filling me up with the Spirit, pouring down like water. The Spirit just filled me up from my toes back up to my head. Then I was back to normal. What I realized was that I had always had the Spirit; I just wasn't recognizing the Spirit. I had been blessed with a conscious of what's right and wrong. I had just been taking it all for granted. (Our friend)

"But behold, the Lord God poured his Spirit into my soul ..." (Jacob 7:8)

While serving my mission on some islands, we came across a landlord that frightened us. We felt that he was evil. We used our large housing to live in and also to host church meetings. My companion and I felt that we should move to another location. Our mission president said he would like to meet our landlord. He felt that things could be worked out.

One day our mission president visited from another island. He met with our landlord. Afterwards he told us that we needed to immediately find another place to live and hold our meetings. He said, "I have never felt such evil as I did when shaking that man's hand!" (A friend)

"... That ye may not be seduced by evil spirits, or doctrines of devils, or the commandments of men; for some are of men, and others of devils." (D&C 46:7)

———————◆———————

With my frequent flyer upgrade status I was allowed to board my flights first, in the middle, or last. I would frequently board last, shortening my duration sitting on a waiting plane. At the final call I would slip into First Class seating.

On this morning I was flying from Los Angeles, CA, to Columbus, OH. The only downside to boarding last is that there were no good magazines left to peruse, if any. I wanted to read that day, so I boarded first and hurried down the long aisle, surrounded by hundreds of empty seats, to the very back of the large airplane where the magazines rested in the last overhead bins on the right.

As I approached the back of the jet, an armed air marshal barked, "What are you doing?"

I meekly replied, "I just want to grab a few magazines in the overhead."

He roughly replied, "Okay, well hurry up ... then go to your seat!"

As I leaned forward to reach for the magazines I was able to see the last row of seats on the right. There were two more, armed-to-hilt, federal air marshals sitting down. In between them was a skinny, young, blonde boy. He was wearing handcuffs and leg shackles and those shackles and cuffs were chained together. I thought, "Oh my!" as I hurried the full length of the large plane back again. I needed to get to the front of the jet before people with early boarding needs began blocking both aisles for my return. I made it back to the front and the flight was very pleasant.

Upon arrival, as was my option with no overhead luggage, I jumped out of my seat and was lined up to be the first passenger to disembark. First Class passengers are allowed to deplane before the remaining travelers. As I worked my way up the jet way I heard some unusual noises and commotion. I walked out to TV cameras, reporters, and lots of lights. I knew they weren't interested in me. There was this *dressed to kill* female TV reporter with her cameraman alongside, just like in the movies, front and center. So I simply stood directly in front of her and her cameraman out of curiosity.

She exclaimed, "Sir, you are going to have to move!"

I shot back with, "Well I'm not budging until you tell me why you're here!"

She obliged my curiosity and explained that two radical religious groups in Ohio were infighting; one family was expelled because they were too radical for the radicals! So much animosity brewed between these two families that one family killed the other family and buried their bodies underneath a barn floor. The radical couple, their son, and conspirators split to: Seattle, Los Angeles, and Miami in order to hide out separately and hopefully avoid detection. The parents and son had been captured, in different cities, and were being brought back separately to Ohio for their respective murder trials.

Well, I wasn't expecting that on a magazine run! I thanked her and quickly moved out of her way. (Journal 4/8/1990)

This story surfaced once again at the execution of Jeffrey Lundgren in October of 2006. His wife and son (the boy in chains on the airplane) were serving life sentences.

Mr. Lundgren claimed to the jurors at his trial for five heinous murders, "I am a prophet of God. I am even more than a prophet." (Foxnews.com/2006/10/24cult-leader)

*Fanaticism never works well within the true Gospel of Jesus Christ. Most all of the fanatical members I have come in contact with over the decades have been excommunicated as they summarily begin breaking both the laws of the land and the laws of God.*

A man must have the discerning of spirits before he can drag into daylight this hellish influence and unfold it unto the world in all its soul-destroying, diabolical, and horrid colors; for nothing is a greater injury to the children of men that to be under the influence of a false spirit when they think they have the Spirit of God. (*TPJS*, 205)

---

Elder Boyd K. Packer of the Quorum of the Twelve has likened the fulness of the gospel to a piano keyboard. He has told us that a person could be "attracted by a single key," such as a doctrine he or she wants to hear "played over and over again." ... Some members of the Church who should know better pick out a hobby key or two and tap them incessantly, to the irritation of those around them. They can dull their own spiritual sensitivities. They lose track that there is a fulness of the gospel ... [which they reject] in preference to a favorite note. This becomes

417

exaggerated and distorted, leading them away into apostasy. (Dallin H. Oaks, *Ensign*, Oct 1994)

---

*An older reader might remember the man who claimed he was the Holy Ghost and successfully convinced his family to follow him in death. He committed suicide and two days later his family followed him in death. They were fully committed to their husband/father and followed him blindly. On August 3, 1978, Rachel David persuaded or threw her seven children off of an 11th-floor balcony of a hotel in Salt Lake City, UT. One daughter amazingly survived the fall.*

*Immanuel David was a self-proclaimed prophet who at times claimed to be any member of the Godhead.*

> "And thus we see the end of him who perveteth the ways
> of the Lord; and thus we see that the devil will not support
> his children at the last day, but doth speedily drag them
> down to hell." (Alma 30:60)

*Others have counseled the brethren regarding "what they really should be focusing on" and have been excommunicated for public dissent.*

*Now it is okay and fine for anyone to have any opinion about whatever one wishes; it is the public display of anti-doctrine/anti-leadership that brings church courts right to that member's doorstep.*

*Some people get so full of themselves while pounding on one piano key that it consumes their lives. Their own doctrine becomes so important to them that they believe that it is the most important subject for everyone and for the leading brethren and sisters at the time. They believe the brethren—church leadership, are not focusing on the true priorities. This is a tool the great tempter knows how to use very well.*

*Once again, "seek not to counsel God, but take counsel from his hand." (Jacob 4:10)*

*Come on now, it really isn't a group of elderly men making the decisions and calling the shots; in reality it is the Lord Jesus Christ at the helm, the very oldest of men and the only perfect man. Our Savior operates under the direction of Heavenly Father, an even older perfect God.*

> "... My word shall not pass away, but shall all be fulfilled,
> whether by mine own voice or by the voice of my servants,
> it is the same." (D&C 1:38)

*If someone claims the brethren aren't focusing on the right doctrines or subjects, they are, in reality, claiming that the Godhead isn't realizing what's really important and necessary for our salvation. I testify that Heavenly Father, Jesus Christ, and the Holy Ghost are in full control with our best interests in mind—our best earthly and eternal interests. The Godhead is at the holy helm—steering us towards eternal felicity, while hoping and praying we don't abandon ship!*

---

*Korihor admitted,* "But behold, the devil hath deceived me; for he appeared unto me in the form of an angel ..." (Alma 30:53)

"And this Zeezrom was a man who was expert in the devices of the devil, that he might destroy that which was good." (Alma 11:21)

And thus we can plainly discern, that after a people have been once enlightened by the Spirit of God, and have had great knowledge of things pertaining to righteousness, and then have fallen away into sin and transgression, they become more hardened, and thus their state becomes worse than though they had never know these things. (Alma 24:30)

---

One summer day, while visiting my mom and sister in Wyoming, we took our small children to the rest stop on the outskirts of town to play. They ran around enjoying the sun and playground equipment while my sister and I visited. It wasn't too long when I became nervous about a man that was walking towards us. I had a distinct impression to **"Leave NOW!"**

I commented to my sister that we should leave and she felt the same way. Hurriedly we gathered up our children, got in the car and left. Of course, we'll never know what would have happened. But I will always remember the distinct impression to "**Leave NOW!**" (A friend)

---

During my mission to Sweden we would sometimes hand out literature at town squares, visit with locals, and attempt to set up appointments. In one city there were a couple of teenage girls that expressed some interest. We explained that we teach families. They gave us a phone number along with their parent's names. They suggested we call their home and ask their momma and papa's permission. In the meantime the girls said they would talk to their parents also about a possible visit from us.

Within a few days, we did make contact with the parents and set up an appointment to teach this family of four. We were elated because it was quite rare to teach a family. We primarily taught college age or elderly people. So we hopped on our bikes and rode about five miles to this new contact's home. They were expecting us and even had a few gospel-related questions, which was also rather uncommon. We gave the family the first discussion. They seemed a little odd and were quite humorous. The first discussion went okay.

When we asked for an appointment to come back to teach more and to answer more of their questions, they agreed. This appointment was about two weeks later. We allowed time to bike the five miles again. Many Swedes ride bicycles and there are bike racks everywhere. We parked in a bike rack across the street from the family's home on a corner lot.

As we approached the front of their yard there was a massive field of darkness emitting from and surrounding their home and property. I had never felt anything so powerful. The hairs on our bodies stood on end, and a shrill scare ran up our spines as we sprinted back to our bikes! We jerked the bikes quickly out of the bike rack, mounted and raced away! We were so surprised and frightened that we never spoke a word to each other. I have never peddled so hard for so long in my life. All we wanted to do is escape the powerful plume of evil; to get far away as fast as possible in order to avoid our destruction.

After we arrived home huffing and puffing, we shared with each other the same feelings and frights. Then we went to our knees and prayed long and hard for protection and freedom from all evil. We both prayed one after the other and drove any hint of any evil spirit(s) away from us and our apartment.

> I have always been specially [sic] impressed with the doctrine relating to the power of Satan, as well as with the doctrines relating to the power of God. I have always felt that no Saint fully comprehends the power of Satan as well as God's Prophet; and again I have thought that no Saint could fully understand the power of God unless he learn [sic] the opposite. (Jedediah M. Grant, JD 2:10)

Sharing this harrowing experience with another elder on a split was most enlightening.

He was familiar with this family and exclaimed, "I see they're up to their old tricks! These girls will approach every new set of elders that comes to town and express interest. Their family will have the elders over and get to know them. The girls have permission from their parents to do *whatever it takes* to get an American husband!"

I'm so grateful my companion and I were sensitive to the spirits and acted accordingly. If our egos had convinced us to try and tackle that evil and powerful adversary, the results could have been devastatingly disastrous and even ended our missions. (Missionary journal)

> "What I say unto one I say unto all; pray always lest that wicked one have power over you, and remove you out of your place." (D&C 93:49)

Mom became physically and spiritually depleted and disheartened ... she wrote, "I am struggling against blackness." She did not gain ground when Daddy left to take her mother from Ohio back to Utah. With the priesthood gone, she felt an evil presence enter our home and it struck her with terror!

Our branch president took her to the hospital and called Daddy ... without resting, he headed back to Dayton, OH. He brought mom home and she was emotionally and spiritually lost.

She wrote: "Somewhere in my soul was born a conviction of the Savior's tender mercy in sparing us from the horrible power of the evil one." She knew that He was aware of her and that He cared about her and stood ready to help.

With effort, she knelt and covenanted that if He would forgive her and strengthen her she would willingly serve Him all the days of her life. Almost immediately she felt His forgiving power within her. Her full recovery was gradual, but she was now building on bedrock. Through her suffering she had come to know that the Savior is there and He cares; that Joseph Smith spoke truth—embodied evil is a reality; that there is a means by which souls can be strengthened and helped. (A relative)

And why should I yield to sin, because of my flesh? ... That the evil one have place in my heart to destroy my peace and afflict my soul?... Rejoice, O my heart, and give place no more for the enemy of my soul. ... Rejoice, O my heart and cry unto the Lord, and say: O Lord, I will praise thee forever; yea, my soul will rejoice in thee, my God, and the rock of my salvation. (1 Ne. 4:27-28, 30)

━━━━•◆•━━━━

We received a frantic call at three in the morning exclaiming, "I feel like I'm being choked to death by evil spirits! Can you please rush over right away?"
We hurried into some clothes, rubbed our eyes, and drove as fast as we thought safe to her home. My wife used prayer to cast out the evil in Christ's name and I used the priesthood, commanding the evil spirits to depart in the name of Jesus Christ. The person who called had a mental illness and could not seem to handle many challenges independently. (A relative)

It is a great matter to act firm, for one of the main objects that the Saints should accomplish is to be perfectly calm and serene, no matter how sudden accidents may occur. If you find that you are surrounded by a host of evil spirits that are choking you to death, have presence of mind enough to call upon the Lord; but some have not had presence of mind enough for that. (Lorenzo Snow, *JD* 4:181)

━━━━•◆•━━━━

With no temples in Wyoming or Montana, back in the day, it was necessary to carpool to Idaho Falls and stay in motels due to long distances; including traveling through Yellowstone Park, which has a 45 mph speed limit. (It's much slower when bears, buffalo, elk, and/or moose are spotted along the roadways.) For the youth it was exciting to be on a trip, stay in a motel, and eat in restaurants—not something most of our families did much at all. (Our family usually stayed with relatives on trips.)

My group of friends was around sixteen and seventeen. When we finally arrived at the temple in the late afternoon, we prepared for proxy baptisms. This is the only time I have felt a dark spirit or maybe it was a lack of the Spirit of Light. It was not a good experience. We felt more depressed than enlightened. Why did I/we feel so terrible?

Thinking back about the day and our long travel I realized the source of the darkness in our minds. The three of us older young men, in the back seat of a passenger van, were talking inappropriately about young women. These whisperings, seemingly exciting at the time, ruined the temple trip for my friends and me.

Everyone else appeared much happier than we were and they also enjoyed the experience more. We vowed to clean up our conversations,

422

especially whenever going to the temple. The Light of Christ and the Holy Ghost have presented themselves throughout the temples ever since.

Many have adopted President Boyd K Packer's advice, as I have, on replacing bad thoughts with a hymn. I had often heard about our minds being a stage and that we can only entertain one thought at a time. Let's keep those thoughts positive and replace the bad thoughts with favorite scriptures or hymns. I personally use, "**I am a Child of God**" (*Hymns,* no. 301)

> This is what I would teach you. Choose from among the sacred music of the Church a favorite hymn, one with words that are uplifting and music that is reverent, one that makes you feel something akin to inspiration. Remember President Lee's counsel; perhaps 'I Am a Child of God' would do. Go over it in your mind carefully. Memorize it. Even though you have had no musical training, you can think through a hymn.
>
> Now, use this hymn as the place for your thoughts to go. Make it your emergency channel. Whenever you find these shady actors have slipped from the sidelines of your thinking onto the stage of your mind, put on this record, as it were. (Boyd K Packer, GC, 1973)

This has worked thousands of times throughout my life. I like to alternate singing "I Am a Child of God" between English and Swedish. If it is a pervasive evil thought I will sing the song twice, once in each language. Most often I sing the song quietly in my mind. Elder Packer's advice works wonders!

We should do whatever it takes: Three X's, the hook, open the trap door, bang the gong. Whatever works best for you to remove the evil actor/s from the stage of your mind and your mind's eye.

———————◆————————

> "These signs shall follow they who believe. In my name," says Jesus, "they shall *cast out devils*."... Devils and unclean spirits frequently took possession of the human tabernacle, tormenting individuals in various ways. Jesus promised believers that they, in his name, should cast them out. Now one object which Jesus had in view in granting this power was to benefit the one possessed. Another object was to confirm the believer, that they, by having power over the devil in this life, might be more fully assured that they should obtain a complete victory and final triumph over

him in the world to come. <u>That person who cannot obtain power in the name of Jesus to cast out devils in this life has great reason to fear least the devil have power over him in the next.</u> (*Masterful Discourses and Writings of Orson Pratt*, 604)

———————•◆•———————

After work, while my wife was making dinner, I read "The Atonement" section from *Mormon Doctrine* aloud. We marveled at the description of an infinite atonement. We understood that the Lord Jesus Christ atoned for all living things and even an infinite number of earths under the direction of our Heavenly Father. We then prayed about the atonement with gratitude and thanked God for all our other blessings too.

Later that night an unexpected visitor was knocking on our door. An old friend from high school was standing in the cold and he looked terrible. It was cold, yet he did not want to come inside, so I grabbed a warm coat and stood on the wooden porch and visited with him.

He explained how he had totally messed up his life and broken about every law of the land and every law of God there was. And he was not exaggerating! I had never seen a person so low and hopeless. He felt like he had gone too far and could never, ever, be forgiven. Though not a very huggable person, he needed and accepted a warm hug that evening.

I testified to him that the atonement of Jesus Christ was more powerful than all sins and crimes. I assured him there was light at the end of what seemed to be very long and exceptionally dark tunnel. I explained that it would not be easy, yet forgiveness was definitely possible when traveling on the rugged road of repentance.

I gave him some comfort and hope and we parted with another handshake and warm hug. (Journal 2/13/1981)

> ... however late you think you are, however many chances you think you have missed, however many mistakes you feel you have made or talents you think you don't have, or however far from home and family and God you feel you have traveled, I testify that you have *not* traveled beyond the reach of divine love. It is not possible for you to sink lower than the infinite light of Christ's Atonement shines. (Jeffrey R. Holland, GC, April 2012)

Later in life I visited and stayed at this good friend's home in a far away small town. He was happily married, living in a nice house, and we had an awesome visit. They were active in the church, he had a leadership position, and they took members on distant temple trips in their large vehicle.

This friendship reminded me of the sinful Saul converting to the great missionary Paul. Similarly, Alma repented, because of Abinidi's teachings, and became a prophet and leader after living amongst the vilest of sinners, which he once was. There is hope for all; never succumb to doubting the Atonement's eternal ramifications.

"... I promise you that whether it's in the boardroom or the bakery, at some point, as a disciple of Christ, you will be called upon to articulate what you know and believe." (General Primary President Joy D Jones, BYU Women's Conference, May 2018)

---

We were married in the temple and looking forward to the arrival of our first baby. When I was home so much with our newborn I came across some pornography in my husband's things. When I asked him about it he apologized and said it was a fluke and that he would never do that again. I told him that I was there for him and that we could make this work.

When I was eight months pregnant with our fourth child I got a phone call from a telemarketer asking if my husband, mentioning him by name, wanted to renew his pornography subscription.

I told her, "Oh, my husband would never do anything like that; it must be a mistake" and hung up on her. She called right back and said, "I'm sorry honey but he has been ordering these magazines" and she hung up on me! That night he didn't come home until two a.m. and he found me awake on the bed, reading.

I told my husband, "Beware, I will leave you if I ever find pornography again!" I was distraught and felt that our family was unstable and didn't know what I was going to do. I came to realize that he had been lying and was exposed to this filth our entire marriage. I told him as a team we could overcome this. I also told him we would have no more children if I felt like we were bringing them into an unstable environment.

I knew we were supposed to do our best to sustain temple marriages, but I was really struggling with what to do. I suggested we needed to go to counseling and he refused. I knelt down to God in prayer and asked Him, 'What would you have me do in this difficult situation?'

I got a real clear answer, **"Throw your energy and your life into the lives of your children."**

Then I asked God, "But what happens when this child turns eighteen and graduates from high school and I'm forty-eight? What do I do then?"

Again I got a really clear answer, **"Let forty-eight take care of itself."**

I thought, "really, that's a peculiar answer; alright then."

I followed the advice and thoroughly enjoyed my children. They were age newborn to seven and I threw myself into them and their lives. My husband came in after midnight ("had to work late") and started going on vacations without me. We grew further apart. I still hoped to work things out. My children do not even remember him being around. He had a habit of being home the three hours that we were in church. He was mentally and physically absent most all other times.

One day I came home and had the strongest craving for chocolate. I'm a nutritionist and avoid most sweets. This craving was so strong yet I could find nothing in the cabinets. I finally went to my husband's closet where he hid chocolates all for himself. I did not find any chocolate there. The only thing I found was an old briefcase that looked out of place. I thought, "That's strange, nobody uses this old style anymore." The briefcase had a combination lock so that I couldn't open it.

I heard a voice tell me, **"The combination is his birthday."**

His briefcase was packed full with porn in French and English! I took pictures with my phone for proof because I knew he would totally deny it all. I felt like he had become a pathological liar and he was serving on the High Council! And then I realized that my children were grown and I was forty-eight years old. I discovered porn on his phone and laptop. Our storage shed was full of it. He was very, very addicted!

I prayed everyday for what to do for this marriage. Every answer I got was a way to prepare for a separation and divorce. I was hoping to still talk with my husband and work it out. The Lord kept saying, **"NO!"** I finally received a vision that showed me what my life would be like if I stayed in the marriage. If I stayed I would have a nice: home, car, clothes, and travel ... yet I would be miserable. If I left I would not have all the material I things in life, but I would find joy!

Then God said to me, "**Which do you prefer? I love you either way.**"

I chose *joy* and am so happy with my choice, even though I don't have those worldly things. (Our friend)

"Wherefore take unto you the whole armour of God, that ye may be able to withstand in the evil day, and having done all, to stand." (Ephesians 6:13)

*The First Presidency described Satan:*

He is working under such perfect disguise that many do not recognize either him or his methods. There is no crime he would not commit, no debauchery he would not set up, no plague he would not send, no heart he would not break, no life he would not take, no soul he would not destroy. He comes as a thief in the night; he is a wolf in sheep's clothing (*Messages of the First Presidency,* comp. James R. Clark, 6 vols., Salt Lake City: Bookcraft, 1965–75, 6:179).

Our daughter met a nice young man at work and they began dating. After awhile he expressed some interest in the Church and would occasionally attend church with us and stay for Sunday dinner. In a couple of months he was over often and was attending church nearly every Sunday with our family. Our daughter indicated she was really starting to like him. Her siblings were also becoming enamored with this new young man in our family's life. He had some interesting experiences that we all found quite fascinating.

Our family was wrapped around his finger as we made plans to make trips and do things together with James. He had many connections and some well-to-do friends. We were planning a trip to San Diego, CA, and then to Yuma, AZ, to see the grandparents; James was part of our travel plans now.

On one of these Sunday afternoons, I was alone in an upstairs bedroom and the Spirit clearly said, "**Ask James to get baptized.**" I immediately went down into the living room and found James standing there all by himself, which was unusual. I guess all the rest of the family had gone down to the basement for something. Anyway, the two of us were alone.

"How would you like to take the missionary discussions?"

"I think I would like that."

"That's great! If you would like to, we would gladly open up our home to you, 'our daughter', and the missionaries. I believe this would provide a nice environment for studying the Church and its doctrine."

"That would be nice. I think I'd like that. Thank you."

Our daughter was very excited now, along with the rest of the family. The local missionaries set up a weekly meeting in our home. The discussions were going well. I was pleased that one of the Elders suggested we have a group prayer about Joseph Smith; this was something we did on my mission decades ago. All six of us would say a prayer, one after the other, asking for a witness that Joseph Smith was a prophet of God. Once again I had this feeling of a large spirit encompassing the entire group. Additionally, I had a very strong confirmation of the importance and mission of the Prophet Joseph Smith. The group prayer was an emotional experience for everyone.

One of the Elder's blurted out, "James, I feel like you are WHY I came on my mission! I wasn't going to go and didn't really want to go. Now I know why I'm out here!" James and this Elder embraced each other. After some discussion a baptismal date was set. Our daughter drew about 50 circles around that day, which you could see from across two rooms; one thick dark circle carved on the calendar. Everyone was elated!

The following week, my daughter was talking to me in my office as I set at my home computer after a successful day on the road. She was concerned about me, explaining, "Dad, everyone in the family has told James that they love him, except you? James is kind of sad because of that. Mom told him that she loved him last night. What's the problem? Don't you love him too?"

I responded, "I don't know why, but something is definitely not right with this situation. I'm discerning a serious issue but don't know exactly what it is yet. We simply need to get the facts first. Something doesn't feel right."

In the middle of my declaration to my daughter, the phone rang. It was our bishop on the line and he said, "Brother Laing, we need to talk. Are you alone?"

I replied, "Not really."

"Well, I'll give you a short message and then you and your wife need to call me later … I received a call from another bishop, in a different stake and city, and we agree that the young man dating your daughter is not who he says he is. She may be in danger!" he exclaimed.

428

I simply said, "Okay" attempting to show as little emotion as possible, even though the gears were churning hard in my head.

Following that call my mind was spinning as my daughter immediately questioned:

"Was that the bishop on the phone?"

(How could she know that?)

"James said people were spreading lies about him and those lies would eventually get to our bishop! This is exactly what he told me would happen."

"I need to discuss something with your mom first and get back with you."

Thereafter our other daughter and my wife returned. They soon had me cornered in the kitchen and all three girls were hammering me with "You need to let James know that you love him too! What's wrong with you, dad? Not loving James is like not loving your own daughter!"

I was harboring this terrible secret while being trounced upon by hormones from Hades! I stated to my girls, "I need to talk privately with your mother about something!" I finally pulled my wife, who was confused and resisting, away for a private conversation. I told her there was somewhere very important we needed to drive to. I finally got her in the car and we drove to a large park and settled under a shade tree. Then I dropped the BOMBSHELL on her. She was confused, shocked, and wondered what the truth really was. I told her we were alone here to call the bishop in private and that he would explain things to both of us.

"Really?!" she questioned.

We called the bishop and held my phone up to both of our ears. I either didn't have a speaker phone or didn't know how to turn it on.

The bishop shared the following: "A bishop from another city has sent me an envelope with pictures of a young man from his ward and they look like the young man that has been sitting with your daughter in church. I have been communicating with this bishop and have given him a description of James. We are now in agreement that James is actually a returned missionary and member of this bishop's ward. He's obviously been through the temple. His bishop said that James had been caught following and stalking girls. We both feel like your daughter may be in danger; although he hasn't hurt anyone yet, that we know of. He's a returned missionary posing as a non-member and he has a lot of issues. We would strongly advise that your daughter cut off all ties with James immediately and to never talk to or see him again!"

We thanked the bishop as we sat in bewilderment, shock, and fear! It was quite a while before we could regain our composure and return home with heavy hearts.

Afterwards, we had a private conversation with our daughter; she was very upset and would not accept any of it at all, not a word!

She informed us that, "James told me this would happen! He told me that lies were out there to destroy him and he predicted this very thing. Some of his friend's dad was a bishop and that leader had a serious vendetta against him for years!" She was in disbelief. She was confident that this was all a lie to defame James.

She confronted James with the information and she soon discovered, to her horror, that all his tales, stories, and life were truly BIG FAT lies. In fact, he was a pathological liar. He had convinced almost everyone, including himself!

Our daughter's resulting comment was, "This is a freakin' nightmare!!!"

Once James confessed, our daughter was able to bring everyone in the family around to the truth of the situation. That was the end of it, except for a few things James would mail to her and then that thankfully stopped.

I felt awful though, because I was sure my corrupt thinking of counseling the Lord had drawn this suffering out for our precious girl. The Holy Ghost clearly told me to "**Ask James to get baptized.**" With my carnal thinking I surmised that the means justify the ends and he obviously needed to take the missionary discussions first. I honestly believe if I had been obedient to the instruction from God and actually asked James straight out to be baptized, like I was commanded; the situation would have erupted and ended much sooner than it did. (Journal 2/24/2004)

> ... For the Spirit speaketh the truth and lieth not. Wherefore, it speaketh of things as they really are, and of things as they really will be; wherefore, these things are manifested unto us plainly, for the salvation of our souls. (Jacob 4:13)
>
> ———————————◆———————————
>
> After I had retired to the place where I had previously designed to go, having looked around me, and finding myself alone, I kneeled down and began to offer up the desires of my heart to God. I had scarcely done so, when immediately I was seized upon by some power which entirely overcame me, and had such an astonishing influence over me as to bind my tongue so that I could not speak. Thick darkness gathered around me, and it seemed to me for a time as if I were doomed to sudden destruction.

But exerting all my powers to call upon God to deliver me out of the power of this enemy which had seized upon me, and at the very moment when I was ready to sink into despair and abandon myself to destruction—not to an imaginary ruin, but to the power of some actual being form the unseen world, who had such marvelous power as I had never before felt in any being—just at this moment of great alarm, I saw a pillar of light exactly over my head, above the brightness of the sun, which descended gradually until it fell upon me.

It no sooner appeared than I found myself delivered from the enemy which held me bound ... (JSH 15-17)

If you're praying for something that really matters, you can count on the fact that the devil will get involved ... He will do his best to thwart you from going forward. He'll give you such thoughts as "You can't do it. You're not worthy enough. Your family has too many problems. You can't do what the Lord requires." He'll engineer whatever he can to try to make you doubt ... When you attract the devil's attention and he starts to give you more opposition than you normally have, that's a great sign that you're on a course that pleases God and displeases Satan. (Gene R. Cook, *Receiving Answers to our Prayers*, p 136, 1996, © Deseret Book Company, Used by permission.)

... Satan came tempting him, saying: Moses, son of man, worship me ... But I can look upon thee in the natural man. Is it not so? ... where is thy glory, for it is darkness unto me? ... Get thee hence Satan ... Depart hence Satan ... Moses began to fear, he saw the darkness of hell. Nevertheless, calling upon God, he received strength, and he commanded, saying; Depart from me Satan, for this one God only will I worship, which is the God of glory. And now Satan began to tremble, and the earth shook; and Moses received strength, and called upon God, saying: In the name of the Only Begotten, depart hence, Satan ... Satan cried with a loud voice, with weeping, and wailing, and gnashing of teeth, and he departed hence. (Moses 1:12-22)

*This is a great example for us should we ever need to cast out evil/evil spirits. Remember, not until the fourth time did Satan depart. The final time Moses called upon the power of Jesus Christ, which Satan responded to.*

---

I had been on my longest sales trip I had ever planned. I started in Denver, then on to Los Angeles, Dallas, Atlanta, Miami, New York, Pittsburgh and Detroit, before returning home to the Rocky Mountains. I would spend roughly three days, at each town, visiting various sales groups' trade shows and their permanent showrooms. My job was mainly to train the sales teams on our product lines while answering any questions they might have regarding our company's products and policies. I would also meet with major accounts within their respective areas to answer their questions and concerns while also introducing our new products and line extensions to their buying teams.

The last business leg of my sales journey was flying from Pennsylvania to Michigan in the evening. I had called home to check in with the family from the Pittsburgh airport. I looked forward to getting back to my wife and children after three weeks. I was very lonely and tired of eating alone all the time. I had never been gone for so long.

Enjoying my frequent flyer status, I was bumped to the front of the plane, as usual. The airline placed me in 1-B on this flight. Next to me, in 1-A, was a college-age blond girl. We visited only briefly. Then she asked me if I was visiting Detroit to return home or just on business. I told her just for business.

She gently grabbed my arm, leaned into me and softly started whispered in my ear. She shocked me with the following, "I've got my own place and if you'd like to come home with me I will show you the time of your life!" Let's just say she he had my full attention.

As I mulled her salacious proposition over the "spirits" started working on me immediately. Just like one sees in many movies and cartoons, I had the Holy Spirit whispering in my right ear and the evil spirit whispering in my left ear; a little white angel resting on one shoulder and a little red devil dancing upon the other. The young woman was also whispering in my left ear.

I thought about her and she was cute and had very little makeup, if any, and no jewelry—just what I like, and I was really lonely. She was very soft, gentle, and smelled pleasant. I discerned some would say, "Oh men! Why can't they use their brains to think with?"

My reply is, "Satan will tempt one with their strongest weaknesses during their most vulnerable moments and he knows what and when those are too; your temptations are not my temptations."

What was most interesting is how similar the two opposing voices are/were. Both were soft, smooth, and suggestive.

Then the young woman leaned into me and softly said, "I can take you wherever you need to go in the morning."

The Spirit was basically giving me suggestions of what I would be giving up if I chose to visit the girl's home. The Holy Ghost would say, "You'll lose your temple recommend." "You're abandoning the priesthood." "Your membership would be in jeopardy." "You could lose your family."

The voices from opposite sides were literally alternating short sentence salvos one after the other and so forth.

The evil spirit would gently whisper: She's beautiful without makeup." "She would be a lot of fun!" "You would really enjoy this; you already called home and checked in, you don't have to be to work until ten or eleven in the morning, etc." Please note that everything the girl, the Holy Ghost and Satan were whispering was all true. One would say a truth, then the other, followed by another truth. The main difference was that the Holy Ghost was talking about eternal things; whereas, the girl and the evil spirit were talking about very temporary, yet tantalizing truths.

Then to make sure I did not misunderstand her intentions—she leaned gently and softly into me once again and whispered quietly, yet assertively, "You can have anything you want!"

At that point the evil spirit softly said, "And you can have everything you want again in the morning." And then, after all the truths, Satan's only lie slipped out—"No one will know."

I had an interesting discernment at that point; I was made aware that if I chose to go through with this temptation, in actuality, my wife, my mother, and our bishop would know that I had fallen hard.

At that juncture the Holy Spirit gave me a choice and privileged vision of my beautiful family kneeling in prayer and praying for my safe return! That brought tears to my eyes and I was so sorry that I was even considering the younger woman's inappropriate offer.

The two soft-speaking spirits and the girl had finished launching their alternating artillery; I turned to the pretty young thing and said, "Thanks, but no thanks; I have a beautiful wife and four beautiful little children, and I'm already having the time of my life!"

While teaching the high priests, years later, on how to prepare in advance to avoid the fiery darts of the adversary, I shared a synopsis of the previous story. One wide-eyed brother exclaimed, "That wasn't a fiery dart—that was a javelin!!"

> And now my sons, remember, remember that it is upon the rock of Christ, the Son of God, that ye must build your foundation; that when the devil shall send forth his mighty

winds, yea, his shafts in the whirlwind, yea, when all his hail and his mighty storm shall beat upon you, it shall have no power over you to drag you down to the gulf of misery, and endless wo, because of the rock upon which ye are built, which is a sure foundation, a foundation whereon if men build they cannot fall. (Helaman 5:12)

*Satan tempts us when we are at our most vulnerable and weakest points in our lives. That is why it is so important to be safely shod with the armor of God; to be able to withstand temptations and trials when we are downtrodden, hungry, and tired.*

But ye are commanded in all things to ask of God, who giveth liberally; and that which the Spirit testifies unto you even so I would that ye should do in all holiness of heart, walking uprightly before me, considering the end of your salvation, doing all things with prayer and thanksgiving, that ye may not be seduced by evil spirits, or doctrines of devils, or the commandments of men; for some are of men, and other of devils. (D&C 46:7)

Our daughter was having all kinds of serious issues. I knelt down for strength. I must have asked for courage and added faith because I walked to my teenage daughter's bedroom, commanded devils and evil and unclean spirits to leave in the name of Jesus Christ, and ran upstairs.
I hadn't been upstairs but a few minutes when my husband came rushing over exclaiming, "She is suddenly up and getting ready for school! What happened? Did you do something?"
I told him all that I had done. My husband was in awe at the difference it made. Our daughter got out of bed, dressed, ate breakfast, and left for school without any of the coaxing that was usually required of us." (A relative)

*Evil and unclean spirits know Jesus Christ; they understand His power and His place in the Godhead.*

... there met him two possessed with devils, coming out of the tombs, exceeding fierce, so that no man might pass by the way. And, behold, they cried out saying, What have we to do with thee, Jesus, though Son of God? art thou come hither to torment us before the time? (Matthew 8:28-29)

*We must, even as Moses needed to, cast out all and any evil in the name of Jesus Christ. One cannot rely on the arm of flesh when dealing with evil personages; one must call upon Christ to cast out evil spirits*

"And whoso shall *ask in my name in faith*, they shall cast out devils..." (D&C 35:9)

As a girl, my room was always across from mom and dad's room until I was married. One night I felt this strong evil presence all over my room and it was very frightening. I don't know what it was but I felt paralyzed and could not move or talk. With all the strength I could muster, I called out, "Daddy!"
I could hear dad shuffling towards my room. As soon as my father crossed the threshold, that evil presence left me and my room. I was so grateful for my father and the priesthood.
This scripture made me think of my dad and driving away evil. (A relative)

Yea, verily, verily I say unto you, if all men had been, and were, and ever would be, like unto Moroni, behold, the very powers of hell would have been shaken forever; yea, the devil would never have power over the hearts of the children of men. (Alma 48:17)

*The Tree of Life is such an awesome vision that we often forget or pass up the beginning of Lehi's vision:*

I saw a man and he was dressed in a white robe ... he bade me follow him ... as I followed him *I beheld myself that I was in a dark and dreary waste. After I had traveled for the space of many hours in darkness*, I began to pray unto the Lord that he would have mercy on me, according to the multitude of his tender mercies ... after I had prayed unto the Lord I beheld a large and spacious field ... I beheld a tree, whose fruit was desirable to make one happy. (1 Ne. 8:5-12)

Serving in a bishopric was challenging at times because there were many things we did not see eye to eye on. I came home from church so frustrated from our pre-church meetings that I made a derogatory comment about our bishop in front of my wife and five children. As soon as I allowed those awful words to fly from my lips, the Spirit swiftly departed and I felt a dark, powerful presence replace the empty space. It was a strong and impressive presence that I found somewhat attractive. The power of evil was surprising and did seem to offer appealing strengths.

I additionally felt terrible as soon as I said those improper things in front of my family. I was the bishop's first counselor; I was to suppose to be supportive, not demeaning! Then I gathered myself and began repenting, because light is much more pleasing and powerful; even though darkness can seem more powerful in the moment. I apologized and asked my wife and children for their forgiveness. I explained to them what I had done wrong. Then I proceeded to apologize to my Heavenly Father. I prayed earnestly to get the Spirit back so that this evil presence would depart and I was blessed with a return of the Holy Ghost, who at times does not always tarry with us. (Journal 3/18/1995)

> For the natural man is an enemy to God, and has been from the fall of Adam, and will be, forever and ever, unless he yields to the enticings of the Holy Spirit, and putteth off the natural man and becometh a saint through the atonement of Christ the Lord, and becometh as a child ... (Mosiah 3:19)

A single sister in the ward called me to get a priesthood blessing because she felt evil in the new home she had recently moved into. As a Seminary teacher, we are instructed to not be the first line of help in this regard. I suggested she call her home teachers, which would be following protocol.
She explained that her home teachers wouldn't come over because it wasn't a blessing for an illness.
Next, I suggested she call the elder's quorum president; he told her that "such a thing isn't a real problem."
Finally, I asked her to talk with her bishop. Sadly, her bishop did not believe in offering such assistance either.
I told her that I would locate a "believer" and come assist her in this matter. We were able to give her a blessing and also cast out the evil in the name of Jesus Christ; cleansing her home, possessions, and property." (A peer)

Thirty-six natives came to the mission home one time. They were all relatives and said they all wanted a blessing. I said, "That is quite a job—the hardest thing I do in this Church." They answered, "We don't want you to put your hands on us—just stand up in front of us," the spokesman said. "Many years and generations ago one of the chiefs put a curse on our family, and every generation since someone would produce a leper, and the last one in the last few days has been taken off to the leper colony. We want you to stand up and rebuke that curse and take away the leprosy." There was no doubt in my mind when those people spoke. (Maoris')

I blessed them and commanded the power of God to cleanse that family of the curse; and I know as well as I am standing here there will never be another leper in that family. (Matthew Cowley, *Man of Faith*, 140)

The stake president asked the high council what important items we had omitted on a list to teach the priesthood brethren. One council member asked, "What about casting out evil spirits?" The room became deathly quiet. The stake president didn't know what to say. The suggestion was not added to the list.

I am not sure why so many members, including leaders, are so doubtful and unsure about evil spirits. Was this not the most common miracle Jesus performed—casting out evil spirits? Have the billions of Satan's angels been sent anywhere else besides on this earth to constantly try and tempt us? The only real change that has occurred over time seems to be member's/leader's opinions regarding evil and casting out the same. There is a large war waging all around us! (A relative)

*I have had the very same thoughts, questions, and concerns regarding casting out evil from among us. Why is it so common in the scriptures and church history yet almost taboo to discuss in wards and stakes in our day? Even within the awesome new book, "The Saints", casting out an evil entity is the first miracle recorded by the Prophet Joseph Smith.*

Amongst those who attended our meetings regularly, was Newel Knight son to Joseph Knight. He and I had many and serious conversations on the important subject of man's eternal salvation: we had got into the habit of praying much at our meetings and Newel had said that he would try and take up his cross, and pray vocally during meeting; but when we again met together he rather excused himself;... he replied that provided he had got into a mudhole (sic) through carelessness, he would rather wait and get out himself, than have others to help him, and so he would wait until he should get into the woods by himself, and there he would pray.

Accordingly he deferred praying until next morning, when he retired into the woods; where (according to his own account afterwards) he made several attempts to pray but could scarcely do so, feeling that he had not done his duty, but that he should have prayed in the presence of others. He began to feel uneasy, and continued to feel worse both in mind and body, until upon reaching his own house, his appearance was such as to alarm his wife very much. He requested her to go and bring me to him. I went and found him suffering very much in his mind, and his body acted upon in a very strange manner. His visage and limbs distorted and twisted in every shape and appearance possible to imagine; and finally he was caught up off the floor of the apartment and tossed about most fearfully. His situation was soon made known to his neighbors and relatives, and in a short time as many as eight or nine grown persons had got together to witness the scene.

After he had thus suffered for a time, I succeeded in getting hold of him by the hand, when almost immediately he spoke to me, and with great earnestness requested of me, that I should cast the devil out of him, saying that he knew he was in him, and that he also knew that I could cast him out. I replied "if you know that I can it shall be done," and then almost unconsciously I rebuked the devil; and commanded him in the name of Jesus Christ to depart from him; when immediately Newel spoke out and said that he saw the devil leave him and vanish from his sight.

This was the first miracle which was done in this church or by any member of it, and it was done not by man nor by the power of man, but it was done by God, and by the power of godliness: therefore let the honor and the praise, the dominion and the glory be ascribed to the Father, Son, and Holy Spirit for ever and ever Amen. ("History of Joseph Smith," *Times and Seasons*, vol. 4 (November 1842- November 1843), Vol. 4 No. 1 November 15, 1842, p.13)

Whatever causes our spiritual ailments, they all have one thing in common: the absence of divine light.
Darkness reduces our ability to see clearly. It dims our vision of that which was at one time plain and clear. When we are in darkness, we are more likely to make poor choices because we cannot see dangers in our path. When we are in darkness, we are more likely to lose hope because we cannot see the peace and joy that await us if we just keep pressing forward.
Light, on the other hand, allows us to see things as they really are. It allows us to discern between truth and error, between the vital and the trivial. When we are in the light, we can make righteous choices based on true principles. When we are in the light, we have "a perfect brightness of hope" because we can see our mortal trials from an eternal perspective.
We will find spiritual healing as we step away from the shadows of the world and into the everlasting Light of Christ. (Dieter F Uchtdorf, *GC*, Oct 2017)

*Elder F. Enzio Busche was a member of the First Quorum of the Seventy and served from 1977-2000, teaching in 41 different countries:*

The following experience was probably one of the most sacred in my life … I began a tour of a neighboring mission and stayed in the basement of the mission home that night. I was very tired when I went to bed around 11:00 … I woke up with a start when, at about 1:00 A.M., the mission president came into my room.
He said that in the evening, a missionary had been possessed by an evil spirit. His companion had called the assistants to help cast it out. The assistants had done that, but as they got back to their own apartment, the evil spirit

had entered one of the assistants. The other was so shocked that he did not know what to do, so he went straight to the mission home.

The mission president was appalled ... this was one of the stalwart, experienced missionaries who was speaking gibberish and not in control of his physical movements. The mission president had tried to cast out the evil spirit but had failed. He began to panic, but then he realized that he had a General Authority in the basement.

... I was very uncomfortable and asked the mission president to give me a little time ... I immediately began to pray with a deep, fervent plea for help. I felt so helpless because I had never been in a situation like that ... As I went upstairs I heard noises and unintelligible sounds, and fear began to creep into my heart. I felt that fear come from the ground, from below, trying to sneak into my system.

As I entered the room, it was like a voice said to me, **'Brother Busche, you must make a decision now.'** I knew immediately what decision it was, I had to decide whether to join the fear and amazement and helplessness or to let faith act and let courage come in ... I wanted to have the power, the priesthood power, and I wanted to know what to do to save the situation.

In that moment, *two scriptures came into my mind*. One scripture was very simple: Moroni 8:16, 'Perfect love casteth out all fear.' And the other was the same: 1 John 4:18, 'Perfect love casteth out fear.' But I did not have love, I had fear. What do we do when we have fear but not love? My mind was drawn to Moroni 7:48, where the Lord points out how we gain love: 'Wherefore ... pray unto the Father will all the energy of heart, that ye may be filled with this love.'

I prayed with all the energy of my heart, 'Father, fill my soul with love.'... it was if my skull was opened and a warm feeling poured down into my soul—down my head, neck, my chest ... It drove out all of the fear. I still did not know what to do. As I stood there, it was as though someone came and put his arm around me and said, **'Let me do this for you. I can take it from here.'** I was very happy with that idea. Then I watched myself do something very strange and surprising because I did not know what I was doing. I went to the young man who was sitting on a chair shaking uncontrollably. I knelt in front of him and put my arms around him, pulling him gently to my chest. I told him, with all the strength of my soul, 'I love you, my brother.'

In the very moment I did that, the evil spirit left. The missionary came to his senses, looked at me and said, 'I love you too.' He snapped right out of it and asked what had happened. For about an hour after that, we had a spontaneous sharing of testimonies, jubilantly praising God and singing and praying. It was an exuberant experience of the workings of the spirit of love, which is the Spirit of Christ and by it overcoming all evil. (F. Enzio Busche, *Yearning for the Living God,* 268-271)

"There is no fear in love; but perfect love casteth out all fear." (1 John 4:18)

When I was sixteen, I really enjoyed the motorcycle I had worked two summers to purchase. I was on a long ride in the summertime between Shoshone and Casper, Wyoming. (It is over 100 miles between these cities) I was about halfway between a spot in the road and one of Wyoming's "largest cities." There is not much on that long stretch there now, and back in the early seventies there was even less. One might find antelope, jackrabbits, rattlesnakes, and scorpions amongst millions of sagebrush covering rough hills. It is a dry, barren, and merciless land.

About in the middle of nowhere and nothing I noticed something out-of-place out in the sagebrush-infested badlands. This person was walking northward as I headed south on the highway. He was a giant of a man walking in a straight path where no human can walk straight. He did not seem to go up or down, nor around. This did not make sense at all. Sagebrush is unforgiving; they are one bush you simple cannot walk through. Sagebrush is nearly as tough as thick rubber rods! Yet this large, hairy person was walking as if he were on a bike path.

[On a side note, one Eagle project our Scout troop completed outside of Cody, WY, was to clear sagebrush at a women's archery range. The female archers were sometimes surprised by rattlesnakes when retrieving their arrows. They desired a clear path between themselves and the targets in order to easily detect anything possibly harmful. The Scouts brought shovels, weed whackers, an axe, and a chain saw. The axe would just bounce off of the rubbery trunks and the small chain saw just wouldn't cut it. None of these tools would work on the tough sagebrush.

We had to reschedule the Eagle project until we could borrow industrial-sized chain saws from the U.S. Forest Service. Only then could we begin to dismantle the stubborn plants and afterwards begin to dig out the newly uncovered roots. (Journal 8/19/1990)]

I couldn't tell where this creature's long black hair and beard started or stopped. The hairy mess was kind of matted together and sort of intertwined. He had thick, old, crude leather clothing hanging from his mammoth torso. He was taller than normal and wider than usual. I have met a couple of "giants" (people who suffer from gigantism) and they are clumsy and cannot move around easily. This monster of a man moved as if he was a teenager out on a leisurely stroll. This situation did not make any sense at all!

This personage was out there some distance from the highway, walking freely in the opposite direction. It was as if he had control over the elements or something. He was human and not an animal. He was white yet looked dark and dirty—severely weatherworn.

As I arrived about even with him, he turned his large hairy head and stared at me. It seemed as if his eyes were bright yellow and shot evil rays out into my eyes and soul. All of the hair on my body stood straight up and a shrill shriek ran up and down my spine. I gulped, my heart probably skipped a few beats, and I was very frightened, to say the least! Of any *evil eye* someone has thrown at you, it would not compare to the depth and height that this dark personage's evil stare consisted of!

I gunned the bike up to 100 mph—feeling like I had to get away as fast as possible. My body was still tingling with fright and my hair continued standing on end. This personage simply did not compute in my mind. How could someone that large walk so easily and do so where there are no paths or roads? How old were those thick, leather sheets of crude leather hanging from his hairy body? Who was that? Why did he frighten me so? All kind of questions swirled in my mind, with no clear solution or answer surrounding the sum total of the oddities I witnessed.

I did not drink, smoke, or take any drugs and I was not sick. I was an honor roll student and active in many organizations and sports. I was healthy and alert, yet clearly confused. I kept this to myself until a certain time during my foreign mission in Sweden.

During our mission we had a very strict reading list in addition to the Holy Scriptures. There were only four other books we were allowed to read. Those limited, approved books were: *Jesus the Christ* and *The Articles of Faith* by James E. Talmage; *The Miracle of Forgiveness* by Spencer W Kimball; and *A Marvelous Work and a Wonder* by LeGrand Richards. I enjoyed reading all four books on my mission, having to look up in the dictionary the meaning of many of Brother Talmage' words!

442

My experience with the frightening personage in the Wyoming badlands all came clearly back to me through Elder Kimball's book; I was wide-eyed and surprised while reading and rereading the following on my mission:

> As a punishment the Lord consigned the wicked Cain to be a fugitive and a vagabond and placed a mark upon him which would reveal his identity.
>
> On the sad character Cain, an interesting story comes to us from Lycurgus A. Whitman's book on the life of David W. Patten. From the book I quote an extract from a letter by Abraham O. Smoot giving his recollection of David Patten's account of meeting "a very remarkable person who had represented himself to be Cain."
>
> As I was riding along the road on my mule I suddenly noticed a very strange personage walking beside me ... His head was about even with my shoulders and I sat in my saddle. He wore no clothing, but was covered with hair. His skin was very dark. I asked him where he dwelt and he replied that he had no home, that he was a wanderer in the earth and traveled to and fro. He said he was a very miserable creature, that he had earnestly sought death during his sojourn upon the earth, but that he could not die, and his mission was to destroy the souls of men. About the time he expressed himself thus, I rebuked him in the name of the Lord Jesus Christ and by virtue of the Holy Priesthood, and commanded him to go hence, and he immediately departed out of my sight ... (Spencer W. Kimball, *Miracle of Forgiveness*, 127-128)

My thoughts were, "Wow, could this be possible? Could Cain still be alive? Was the peculiar creature I saw five years ago really Cain wandering the earth? How could this be? Why would that humble servant Spencer W. Kimball put such an outlandish story in his wonderful book? I determined that President Kimball must have had a witness that the experience of Apostle Patten was true? I could think of no other rhyme or reason for an Apostle of the Lord to include a false story in his own book. (I and others felt Elder Kimball knew the experience was factual. Why would the missionary committee, governed by apostles approve this book for missionaries?" I continued to keep the experience to myself for the most part. [Other missionaries, in different missions, felt the same way I did about Elder Patten's experience: Church approved reading for missionaries, Apostle's story in an Apostle's book, obvious belief.]

I wondered what kind of a man David W. Patten was?

On February 14, 1835, Brother Patten was called to the Twelve Apostles. In the Introduction to the Doctrine & Covenants, after the Title Page, David W. Patten is listed second on the list of the Twelve Apostles. His name follows that of Thomas B. Marsh and precedes Brigham Young's name.

"On May 2, 1835, the Prophet Joseph Smith directed the seniority of the Twelve be determined according to the member's ages ... in early February 1838, Thomas B Marsh and Patten were appointed as Presidents pro tem of the Church in Missouri. On April 6, 1838, Patten and Brigham Young were sustained as assistant presidents of the Church in Missouri, with Thomas B. Marsh as President pro tem. (*Encyclopedia of Mormonism*, Patten, David W.) A President *pro tempore* would act as President in that area during the absence of the currently sustained President.

"... Patten served almost continuously as a missionary for the Church. He established numerous branches of the Church on each of his proselytizing journeys and was renowned for his spiritual gift of healing." (*Encyclopedia of Mormonism*; Patten, David W.)

*From Elder Wilford Woodruff's journal:*

"Brother [David] Patten was a man of great faith, and performed many miracles in the name of Jesus Christ; he had many visions and dreams, and was very valiant in the testimony of Jesus and the word of God." (*Millenial Star*, 1864)

On April 11, 1838 Elder Patten was called on a mission.
Verily thus saith the Lord: It is wisdom in my servant David W. Patten, that he settle up all his business as soon as he can, and make a disposition of his merchandise, that he may perform a mission unto me next spring ... (D&C 114:1)

David W. Patten was the first martyr of the Restoration. He was killed from a wound in the battle at Crooked River on October 25, 1838. Even though Apostle Patten's earthly work was finished and he could not serve his mission call, he did have all his things in order. He no doubt was assigned new missions on the other side of the veil.

If Elder Patten had not been martyred he would have been in line to replace Joseph Smith as President and Prophet due to his seniority in the Quorum of the Twelve Apostles and Thomas B. Marsh' apostasy. Obviously Brigham Young was foreordained to be the prophet that would lead the Saint's westward migration.

> David Patten is mentioned in a future revelation also:
> "That when he shall finish his work I may receive him unto myself, even as I did my servant David Patten, who is with me at this time ..." (D&C 124:19)
> *David Patten could very well be a Just man made perfect.*

*Later in life, I perused Elder Pratt's educational book and read with interest the following:*

> A person on looking another in the eye, who is possessed of an evil spirit, will feel a shock, a nervous feeling, which will, as it were, make his hair stand on end, in short, a shock resembling that produced in a nervous system by the sight of a serpent. (Parley P. Pratt, *KST*, 121)

*This described my experience exactly!*

I shared my experience with an Area Authority; I wanted to "bounce it off of him."

He was aware of David Patten's experience and commented, "I don't know what you saw; it was definitely an evil personage!"

I agreed; I didn't know for sure what I saw either. I also knew that the person was purely evil. I also felt even more convinced later in life that the evil personage actually was Cain.

*What do the scriptures say about Cain?*

> "And the Lord said unto Cain ... For from this time forth thou shalt be the father of his lies; thou shalt be called Perdition ... and this is a cursing which I will put upon thee ..." (Moses 5:22, 24-25)

"And now thou art cursed from the earth ... a *fugitive* and a *vagabond* shalt thou be in the earth." (Genesis 4:11-12)

*A fugitive is described as being a roaming, fleeting, elusive thing. A vagabond is a person who moves from place to place, with no fixed abode; an: idle, disreputable, or shiftless person.*

*Cain's response to his punishment was*, "My punishment is greater than I can bear." (Genesis 4:13)

The Orthodox Jewish Bible refers to Cain as "a *restless fugitive* and *wandering nomad.*" (Genesis 4:12)

The New International Version of the Bible says Cain will be

"a *restless wanderer* on the earth." (Genesis 4:12)

I started thinking that these scriptures could actually be literal in this case. This would explain all the sightings of a large, elusive, hairy man/beast wandering all over the world as Big Foot, Sasquatch, Yeti, etc. Those looking for these elusive creatures say that they have never found any bones. The "Beast" seems to be able to elusively appear and disappear, similar to translated beings abilities. A translated being has no offspring, has power over the earth and death. Translated beings will not be buried nor have any funerals, "never tastes death", yet be changed in the twinkling of an eye in the future. We know there are great blessing in the resurrection and that God's children will be assigned to several different kingdoms. There could similarly be different levels of translation; for example, a higher and lower degree of the same.

In my mind I thought, "Well, if there is truly opposition in all things, maybe Cain has been translated to a damned state. A translated person does not die, cannot kill himself, and is able to survive any disaster, even a large flood!" I bounced this idea off of a regional Seminary and Institute Coordinator and he disagreed. Saying, "In the flood all flesh was destroyed."

His statement is scripturally correct, yet not all encompassing. I responded with, "So how did Enoch survive the flood?"

"Well he was translated of course."

"Exactly!"

"The bible is also clear that only 8 people survived the flood."

"The bible and modern scriptures are very clear that an entire city survived the flood. I also believe Cain was translated. Maybe when Enoch was taken up—Cain was taken down; both being translated and both surviving? Many men, women, and children were translated within the City of Enoch."

"Translation is a blessing of righteousness."

"If there's truly opposition in all things, Cain could have been translated as a punishment for unrighteousness."

"I don't think anyone could live that long."

"Well, the Three Nephites and John have lived for 2,000+ years, why not 6,000 years? Translated people do not age or die, per se. If God decides a very long life for any of his children, it happens."

"Possible, but not probable," were his parting words.

I had to agree. We parted as friends. (Journal 7/15/2016)

Eliza R. Snow wrote an interesting poem in 1884:

As seen by David Patten, he was dark
When pointing at his face of glossy jet
Cain said, "You see the curse is on me yet."
The first of murderers, now he fills his post
And reigns as king o'er all the murd'rous host.

Recently I read from the diaries and journals of LDS leaders in the late 1800's, after becoming available. A member of the First Presidency wrote that Apostle Patten's experience with Cain totally changed his way of thinking.

Bro. J. F. Smith told about David Patten having seen and walked with Cain. Cain is described as being a very large man, his head being even with that of David Patten when the latter was seated on his animal. I always entertained the idea that Cain was dead, but my attention was called to the passage of scripture concerning the curse of God which should fall upon whoever should slay Cain. I supposed this meant whoever should kill his seed. (Abraham H. Cannon, Journal Excerpts, Nov 9, 1893)

According to Matthew Bowman's article published in the Journal of Mormon History, "A Mormon Bigfoot: David Patten's Cain and the Concept of Evil in LDS Folklore," the night before the Laie Hawaii Temple was dedicated in 1921; E. Wesley experienced the following events:

A man came through the door. He was tall enough to have to stoop to enter. His eyes were very protruding and rather wild looking, his fingernails were thick and long. He presented a rather unkempt appearance and wore no

447

clothing at all. . . . There suddenly appeared in [Smith's] right hand a light which had the size and appearance of a dagger. . . . A voice said, "This is your priesthood." He commanded the person in the name of the Lord Jesus Christ to depart. . . . Immediately when the light appeared the person stopped and on being commanded to leave, he backed out the door" ("Experiences with Cain," n.d., MSS 5273, Archives, Family and Church History Department, Church of Jesus Christ of Latter-day Saints, Salt Lake City (hereafter LDS Church Archives).

Thoroughly disturbed by the encounter, E. Wesley wrote to his brother, the then-Apostle Joseph Fielding Smith, about his experience.

*According to Matthew Bowman's article, Joseph Fielding Smith wrote to his brother that the strange visitor was "Cain . . . whose curse is to roam the earth seeking whom he may destroy."*

*Joseph Fielding Smith went on to say that there was "always unusual evidence . . . for a period just prior to the dedication of every temple and Cain was representative of the spirit of the adversary."*

*In Apostle Spencer W. Kimball's own words:* "On the sad character of Cain, an interesting story comes to us..."

"Possible—but not probable."

————————◆•◆————————

*We must all double down with determined diligence in order to defeat and defy the Destroyer!*

# 20. A Lamb without Blemish

… For I, the Lord God, created all things spiritually, before
they were naturally upon the face of the earth. (Moses 3:5)
… God said: Let the waters bring forth abundantly the
moving creature … and fowl which may fly above the earth
… great whales, and every living creature that moveth …
Let the earth bring forth the living creatures after his kind,
cattle, and all creeping things, and beasts of the earth after
their kind, and it was so … and I, God, saw all these things
were good. (Moses 2:20-25)

"… I, God breathed into them the breath of life, and
commanded whatever Adam called every living creature,
that should be the name thereof." (Moses 3:19)

*Did a 500-year-old man building an ark really have time to collect
all those animals, after determining their gender, to fill that behemoth
boat? Many believe the creatures, male and female, were inspired by God
and led to Noah and the Ark.*

*One scripture hints at this school of thought because of what the
Lord promised Noah:*

"Of fowls, after their kind, and of cattle after their kind, of
every creeping thing of the earth after his kind … **shall
come unto thee**, to keep them alive." (Genesis 6:20)

*Obedient animals had already set a precedent:*

And out of the ground I, the Lord God, formed every beast
of the field, and every fowl of the air; and commanded that
they should come unto Adam, to see what he would call
them; and they were also living souls, for I, God, breathed
into them the breath of life, and commanded that
whatsoever Adam called every living creature, that should
be the name thereof. And Adam gave names to all cattle,
and to the fowl of the air, and to every beast of the field …
(Moses 3:19-20)

*When the great flood subsided, Noah used a raven and a dove to
determine the earth's status. Three times, once per week, he sent this dove
out; and the dove did not return the last time it was sent. So they prepared*

449

*to exit the ark, along with its many passengers. Being the obedient servant he was Noah waited to disembark until the Lord spoke.*

"... God spake unto Noah, saying, **Go forth of the ark...**" (Genesis 8:15-16)

———————— ◆ ————————

*King Darius inquired if Daniel's God had delivered Daniel in the den of lions. A surviving Daniel replied:*

"My God hath sent his angel, and hath **shut the lions' mouths,** that they have not hurt me ..." (Daniel 6:22)

*Two of the Nephite disciples, Nephi & Lehi, had a similar experience:*
"And twice were they cast into a den of wild beasts; and behold **they did play with the beasts as a child with a suckling lamb,** and received no harm." (3 Ne. 28:22)

*During the millennium the wild animals will all become peaceful and vegetarian.*

**The wolf shall also dwell with the lamb,** and **the leopard shall lie down with the kid;** and **the calf and the young lion and the fatling together;** and a little child shall lead them. **And the cow and the bear shall feed; their young ones shall lie down together; and the lion shall eat straw like the ox.** They shall not hurt nor destroy in all my holy mountain ... (Isaiah 11:6-7, 9)
"And in that day the enmity of man, and the enmity of beasts, yea, **the enmity of all flesh, shall cease before my face.**" (D&C 101:26)

*A similar terrestrial lifestyle must have existed in the Garden of Eden and after the great flood. Herd and flock strengths would have had to build up for a long period of time to provide for our current circle of life in the animal kingdom.*
*Disembarking from the ark, if the fox ate the hen, the wolf devoured the ewe, the bear killed the cow, and the eagle feasted on the buck rabbit, we would have many more extinct species. All the animals must have been blessed to be herbivores for an extended period of time while their strength in numbers increased. Now days we have carnivorous birds, fish, insects, mammals, and reptiles, etc.*

*Jonah ran away from his assignment and nearly drowned avoiding the Lord's bidding. Through a terrible tempest Jonah asked his shipmates to cast him into the sea. He promised them that the storm would be calm after they threw him into the tempestuous waters. They complied and cast Jonah overboard into a watery grave.*

"Now the Lord had prepared a **great fish** to swallow up Jonah. And Jonah was in the belly of the fish three days and three nights." (Jonah 1:17)

*Being stuck in a large fish's tummy must have been very dark, slimy, and frightening! Jonah prayed hard and long with promises of repentance, gratitude, faith, and sacrifice.*

"And the Lord spake unto the fish, and it vomited out Jonah upon the dry land." (Jonah 2:10)

*I cannot think of a more harrowing experience than that to grab one's attention!*

Balaam was in close communication with Jehovah and Balaam also rode an inspired ass. On one journey the Lord attempted to persuade Balaam from taking we read, "the ass saw the Angel of the Lord ... **the Lord opened the mouth of the ass**, and she said unto Balaam, What have I done to thee, that thou has smitten me these three times? (Numbers 22:27-28) Later in the story, the Lord open's Balaam's eyes so that he can also see the angel his ass saw standing in the trail—with a drawn sword in the angel's hand! Balaam became sorrowful for beating his beast and for being disobedient.

*The Lord used asses to bring Saul and the prophet Samuel together. Saul was sent to find their wandering asses.*

Kish ... had a son, whose name was Saul, a choice young man, and a goodly: and there was not among the children of Israel a goodlier person than he: from his shoulders and upward he was higher than any of the people. (1 Samuel 9:1-2)

*Kish sent Saul and his servant to search for the wandering asses. They went to several locations and could not find any. Saul desired to*

451

*return, however his servant counseled him to stay and suggested they meet a man of God in the next city.*

*Samuel was close to the Lord from a young aged-boy living with the priest Eli.*

> "And all Israel from Dan even to Beer-sheba knew that Samuel was established to be a prophet of the Lord." (1 Samuel 3:20)

The Holy Ghost told Samuel a day in advance:

> "To morrow about this time I will send a man out of the land of Benjamin, and thou shalt anoint him to be captain over my people of Israel, that he may save my people out of the hand of the Philistines ..." (1 Samuel 9:16)

*Without Saul even telling the prophet why he came, Samuel calmed his concerns by prophesying:*

> **"And as for thine asses that were lost for three days ago, set not thy mind on them; for they are found** ..." (1 Samuel 9:20)

———•◆•———

*Prior to Jesus' triumphant ride into Jerusalem he said to two of his disciples:*

> Go ye into the village...in the which at your entering **ye shall find a colt tied, whereon yet never man sat**: loose him, and bring him thither ... And they brought him to Jesus: and they cast their garments upon the colt, and they set Jesus thereon. (Luke 19:30,35)

———•◆•———

*One of the purest animals in the world would have to be a white dove. When John the Baptist had the unique privilege of baptizing Jesus Christ, Heavenly Father said from heaven:*

> "... **Thou art my beloved Son; in thee I am well pleased** ...
> And the Holy Ghost descended in a bodily shape like a dove upon him ..." (Luke 3:22)

The Prophet Joseph Smith gives us great clarity on this pure dove symbolism, "The sign of the dove was instituted before the creation of the world, a witness for the Holy Ghost, and the Devil cannot come in **the sign of the dove** ... The Holy Ghost cannot be transformed into a dove; but the sign of a dove." (*TPJS,* 276)

———•◆•———

*Prior to the Savior's great sacrifice, many animals without blemish were sacrificed in similitude of the same.* **"Your lamb shall be without blemish"** (Exodus 12:5) "... he shall bring his offering, a kid of the **goats, a male without blemish."** (Leviticus 4:23) "... **A ram without blemish from the flocks."** (Leviticus 5:15) **"Thou shalt not sacrifice unto the Lord any bullock, or sheep, wherein is blemish,** or any *evilfavouredness* ..." (Deuteronomy 17:1)

───────◆·•───────

*When Jesus came to be baptized by John the Baptist, John exclaimed,* **"Behold the Lamb of God,** which taketh away the sin of the world." (John 1:29)

*An angel shall sound his trump saying* **"The Lamb of God"** hath overcome and trodden the wine-press alone ..." (D&C 88:106)

*In revelations John sees "...* **a white horse** ... another **horse that was red** ... lo **a black horse** ... **a pale horse** ...."* (Revelation 6)

*The riders of these horses had great powers from God to assist with prophecies of the end of times.*

───────◆·•───────

Most everyone, especially boys and young men, remembers the exciting story of Ammon saving the King Lamoni's flocks of sheep by slicing off the avenger's arms in order to save the sheep from scattering. His courageous actions eventually led to the conversion of that entire Lamanite kingdom! (See Alma 17)

───────◆·•───────

The reader has likely heard stories from time-to-time when animals, often dogs, have saved people from serious harm or house fires:

*USA Today* reported in May of 2017 that a Pinscher-Chihuahua saved a family of ten. The dog would not stop barking, nor would he go to anyone. He made them come to him and the mother discovered the fire and woke up her nine children. Her husband was away driving truck. The home was a total loss. No animals or people were lost.

In September of 2017 the *Tallahassee Democrat* reported a Chihuahua-Dachshund woke up their family and saved their lives. Most everything was lost in that fire. All the animals and people were safe however.

In Clermont-Ferrand, France a fox terrier dog dragged a brown paper parcel along the streets, laid it at the feet of a policeman and gazed up as much to say, "Have a look at this." The policeman opened the package and found a newly born baby! The dog had apparently heard the baby crying and started pulling it along the sidewalk.

There are numerous stories of dolphins coming to the aid of humans in distress, but none quite as harrowing as surfer Todd Endris's. While out trying to catch some waves, Endris instead got caught in the jaws of a Great White shark. Describing it like "trying to fight a car," the already badly wounded surfer was saved from the shark coming back for seconds when a group of dolphins created a wall between him and the beast, allowing him and his friends to swim back to shore. (*Viralnova*, April 19, 2015)

A parrot has been honoured (sic) by the Red Cross for saving the life of a toddler. It was Willie's cries of alarm which alerted his owner that the toddler she was baby-sitting was choking on her breakfast. Megan Howard had left the room last November when the Quaker parrot noticed something was amiss with Hannah and began to raise the alarm by yelling **'Mama, baby'** and flapping his wings. (*Mail Foreign Service*, March 24, 2009)

In 2007, this smart tabby cat saved her human family—Kathy Keesling, her husband, and their teenage son—from carbon monoxide poisoning when a water pump malfunction in their basement created a leak in the middle of the night. Winnie sensed the change in air and rushed to Keesling's bed to wake her up. Her husband and son were completely unconscious by the time she found the strength to keep herself upright long enough to dial 911. Without Winnie, there's little chance the family would have survived. (*Viralnova*, April 19, 2015)

*I can guarantee you that many dogs and other animals have been/will be considered "earthly angels/animal angels!"*

———◆◆———

Doth not your master pay tribute? ...Notwithstanding, lest we should offend them, go thou to the sea, and cast an hook, and take up the fish that first cometh up; and when thou hast opened his mouth, thou shalt find a piece of money: that take, and give unto them for me and thee. (Matt. 17:24, 27)

———◆◆———

We were on vacation and visited a local Ward for their services. In Gospel Doctrine, the lesson was on the Willie and Martin Handcart companies. The Gospel Doctrine teacher, through inspiration, had recently discovered two missionary couples who had served four to five missions each at Martin's Cove and/or Sixth Crossing. The teacher invited them to share special experiences along with a history of the two companies that lost so many lives.

While we were serving at Martin's Cove during one of our missions, we learned to love a special dog. His name was Roscoe and he was from the Sun Ranch. Roscoe would come for a visit every time the busses pulled up. He would look at the children unloading. Roscoe would then find a special child, usually a handicapped child and remain with that child for the entire trek.

At the end of one of these treks, Roscoe laid right in front of the front tire of the bus. The bus couldn't back up, so the bus driver waited with all their precious cargo aboard. Attempts were made to move Roscoe, but he would not budge. After awhile a smaller girl emerged from the bathrooms and got on the bus. They had miscounted, thinking everyone was already boarded. As soon as the young lady was on, Roscoe got up and went back to the Sun Ranch—until the next group of busses rolled up. (Journal 9/17/2017)

---

My friend and others have told me when looking for a dog, "don't pick the dog—let the dog pick you." Perhaps God helped Winkie walk toward me and melt into my lap. I had been interested in his darker brother, but Winkie has been the perfect dog for me! (A relative)

---

Years ago when our children lived at home, I was upset and disappointed with the kids for spreading tree bark pieces from around our trees out onto the grass. Prior to mowing the lawn, we needed to pick, throw, or kick the tree bark pieces back into the 4'-square wood around each tree.

One early morning I was glancing outside and noticed some movement from the corner of my eye. I turned and saw a lovely red-breasted robin flipping tree bark pieces like crazy onto the grass. This was a beautiful creature of God fulfilling the measure of her creation. She was gathering worms from the moist dirt—both were hidden by the tree bark.

I was misjudging my children. Hence, I found myself again upon my knees repenting for falsely accusing my children for something they obviously did not do. A Robin was doing what they do to simply feed her young chicks.

This is why we must not judge others. We often misjudge because we have not heard both sides of the stories. Sometimes both sides of the stories are not all true too. We must not judge unless we are set apart as a judge in Israel by the proper authority. Remember that when we point a finger at someone there are three fingers pointing back at us!

There is an important reason for this wise counsel from Jesus on the Sermon on the Mount: "Judge not, that ye be not judged. For with what judgment ye judge, ye shall be judged …" (Matthew 7:1-2)

———•◆•———

Recently at the Care Center a couple brought in a miniature horse. This was a big hit amongst all the residents and the workers. The tiny horse ("Not a Shetland pony!" they exclaimed,) was an awesome service animal. (Journal 1/12/2019)

In 2002, 78-year-old Australian farmer Noel Osborne slipped on manure while outside attending to his animals. Though that may sound like the beginning of a hilarious slapstick sketch, it was anything but for the man who <u>suffered a broken hip and became unable to move</u> from his stinky situation for the next five days while waiting for someone to find him. He survived those days thanks to his goat, Mandy, who curled up with him during the cold nights and allowed him to drink her milk. (*Viralnova*, April 10, 2015)

———•◆•———

The terrific storm which caused the immigrants so much suffering and loss overtook me near the South Pass, where I stopped about three days with Reddick N. Allred, who had come out with provisions for the immigrants. The storm during these three days was simply awful. In all my travels in the Rocky Mountains both before and afterwards, I have seen no worse. When at length the snow ceased falling, it lay on the ground so deep that for many days it was impossible to move wagons through it.

Being deeply concerned about the possible fate of the immigrants, and feeling anxious to learn of their condition, I determined to start out on horseback to meet them; for this purpose I secured a pack-saddle and two animals (one to ride and one to pack), from Brother Allred, and began to make my way slowly through the snow alone.

After traveling for some time I met Joseph A. Young and one of the Garr boys, two of the relief company which had been sent from Salt Lake City to help the companies. They had met the immigrants and were now returning with important dispatches from the camps to the headquarters of the Church, reporting the awful condition of the companies.

In the meantime I continued my lonely journey, and the night after meeting Elders Young and Garr, I camped in the snow in the mountains. As I was preparing to make a bed in the snow with the few articles that my pack animal carried for me, I thought how comfortable a buffalo robe would be on such an occasion, and also how I could relish a little buffalo meat for supper, and before lying down for the night I was instinctively led to ask the Lord to send me a buffalo.

Now, I am a firm believer in the efficacy of prayer, for I have on many different occasions asked the Lord for blessings, which He in His mercy has bestowed upon me. But after praying as I did on that lonely night in the South Pass, I looked around me and spied a buffalo bull within fifty yards of my camp—my surprise was complete; I had certainly not expected so immediate an answer to my prayer. However, I soon collected myself and was not at a loss to know what to do. Taking deliberate aim at the animal, my first shot brought him down; he made a few jumps only, and then rolled down into the very hollow where I was encamped.

I was soon busily engaged skinning my game, finishing which, I spread the hide on the snow and placed my bed upon it. I next prepared supper, eating tongue and other choice parts of the animal I had killed, to my heart's content.  After this I enjoyed a refreshing night's sleep while my horses were browsing on the sage brush.

Early the next morning I was on my way again, and soon reached what is known as the Ice Springs Bench. There I happened upon a herd of buffalo, and killed a nice cow. I was impressed to do this, although I did not know why until a few hours later, but the thought occurred to my mind that the hand of the Lord was in it, as it was a rare thing to find buffalo herds around that place at this late part of the season. I skinned and dressed the cow; then cut up part of its meat in long strips and loaded my horses with it.

Thereupon I resumed my journey and traveled on till towards evening. I think the sun was about an hour high in the west when I spied something in the distance that looked like a black streak in the snow. As I got near to it, I perceived it moved; then I was satisfied that this was the long looked for hand-cart company, led by Captain Edward Martin.

I reached the ill-fated train just as the immigrants were camping for the night. The sight that met my gaze as I entered their camp can never be erased from my memory. The starved forms and haggard countenances of the poor sufferers, as they moved about slowly, shivering with cold, to prepare their scanty evening meal was enough to touch the stoutest heart. When they saw me coming, they hailed me with joy inexpressible, and when they further beheld the supply of fresh meat I brought into camp, their gratitude knew no bounds.

Flocking around me, one would say, "Oh, please, give me a small piece of meat"; another would exclaim, "My poor children are starving, do give me a little"; and children with tears in their eyes would call out, "Give me some, give me some."

At first I tried to wait on them and handed out the meat as they called for it; but finally I told them to help themselves. Five minutes later both my horses had been released of their extra burden—the meat was all gone, and the next few hours found the people in camp busily engaged in cooking and eating it, with thankful hearts.

A prophecy had been made by one of the brethren that the company should feast on buffalo meat when their provisions might run short; my arrival in their camp, loaded with meat, was the beginning of the fulfillment of that prediction, but only the beginning for them, as we journeyed along. (Ephraim Hank's journal: Martin's Cove) "Grammar and punctuation modernized."

# 21. The Ministering of Angels

Angels speak by the power of the Holy Ghost; wherefore, they speak the words of Christ. (2 Ne. 32:3)

*Angels have great power that they are assigned to use at times:*

*As Alma and the sons of Mosiah went about actively destroying the Church,*

> "… the angel of the Lord appeared unto them; and he descended as it were in a cloud; and he spake as it were with a **voice of thunder**, which caused the earth to shake …" (Mosiah 27:11)

*Peter's escape from prison was so magical that he believed it was a vision:*

> "… the angel of the Lord came … a light shined in the prison … his **chains fell off** from his hands … past the first and second ward … **the iron gate … opened** to them of his own accord …" (Acts 12:7-9)

*Prior to this miracle prison escape, the church members were praying to God without ceasing for their brother Peter.*

*Abraham was strapped to an altar in preparation to be sacrificed to the Egyptian idols of the day, by the wicked priest of Elkenah and Pharaoh.*

> "… the Lord filled me with a vision of the Almighty, and the angel of his presence stood by me, and immediately **loosed my bands**;" (Abraham 1:15) "… and **smote the priest** that he died …" (Abraham 1:20)

*The reason Balaam's beast was beaten:*

"And the ass saw the angel of the Lord standing in the way, and his **sword drawn** in his hand." (Numbers 22:23)

"So the Lord sent a pestilence upon Israel … and there died … seventy thousand men. And David spake to the Lord when he saw the angel that **smote the people** …" (2 Samuel 24:15&17)

My father was a very independent farmer. As he aged in his older years he found it necessary, following a hospital procedure, to recuperate in a care center. The first thing my dad said to me upon visiting him was, "Get me out of here!"

I could see he was very frustrated and unhappy. As soon as he healed up, we brought him back home for about one year. After that it was necessary to place him in a care center permanently. His doctor's gave him 6-12 months; he lived about nine more years!

I would go over and visit him every night and help feed him his dinner. After visiting regularly I realized that several of my friend's parents were also residents at this care center. We all had lived in the same town all our lives. Now that I knew more people, I would also visit these other residents when I finished visiting my father.

After doing this regularly for about eight months; I came into the care center and was working my way to the dining hall. Something or somebody had my attention as I approached the door. Then **I felt a firm, yet gentle hand on my shoulder and the pressure was turning me around** to the residents in the dining area. First I looked to see who was trying to get my attention. There was no one there that I could see.

**While that hand remained firmly on my shoulder, my spiritual eyes were opened.** I could not see any apparatus or wheelchairs or anything except for the Lord's children as they really are/were!

This experience gave me a whole new perspective about people, especially those with extreme challenges. This was probably the greatest spiritual experience of my life and it literally changed my life! (A peer)

"By the power of the Spirit our eyes were opened and our understandings were enlightened, so as to see and understand the things of God—" (D&C 76:12)

On another occasion a phone call came when I was a bishop—this time from the police. I was told that a drunk driver had crashed his car through the glass into the lobby of a bank. When the bewildered driver saw the security guard with his weapon brandished, he cried, "Don't shoot! I'm a Mormon!"

The inebriated driver was discovered to be a member of my ward, baptized only recently. As I waited to speak to him in the bishop's office, I planned what I would say to make him feel remorseful for the way he had broken his covenants and embarrassed the Church. But as I sat looking at him, I heard a voice in my mind say, just as clearly as if someone were speaking to me, **"I'm going to let you see him as I see him."** And then, for a brief moment, his whole appearance changed to me. I saw not a dazed young man but a bright, noble son of God. I suddenly felt the Lord's love for him. That vision changed our conversation. It also changed me. (Henry B. Eyring, GC, April 2017)

———————— •◆• ————————

My father was living alone in his family home in Powell, Wyoming, at the age of 85. He had started getting really weak so we took him to a heart specialist in Billings, Montana. The heart surgeon called me and my sister in for a private visit after dad's checkup.

The doctor said, "Your father's heart has massive damage and he's too old for the type of surgery we would need to perform. He's only going to get increasingly weaker and may even die on the drive home (two hours). I know this is hard to hear, but you need to know how serious his situation is."

That was one of the most difficult things my sister Ginger and I ever had to do: Tell our strong father that he was dying and wouldn't be able to do many of the things he had planned for the coming year. He had hoped to go pheasant and elk hunting one last time; not at the same time. He had gone elk hunting on a horse the previous year and was successful!

We went back to Wyoming in a fairly quiet car, as dad slept and we contemplated life and the words from the heart surgeon. Dad made it home okay. My father taught me to shoot straight on the range, in the field, and through life; and I'm eternally grateful for his patience with me.

Ginger, her son Zac, and I spent a few months caring for Dad, spelling each other, as his health gradually declined. During that time he was placed on hospice. A hospice bed was set up in his living room for him, while I slept in his bed; which felt odd at first. He got to the point where he stopped eating and was so weak that we couldn't tell if he was nodding or shaking his head to answer our questions. "Was that a yes, or a no?" we would ask each other. He was so weak that he could neither talk to nor respond to us.

Near the end of his life, I was alone with him in his makeshift room. I felt the strong presence of a radiant being in the room, yet saw nothing. I sensed that it was my fraternal grandmother and asked, "Dad is your mother here in the room?"

He nodded his head strongly three times!

The Spirit surged through my body as **I felt Grandma getting closer to us** in the room. Dad's energy level was only around 1-2%. I thought, "Maybe grandma, as an angel from paradise, loaned him the strength to react so vividly?" Nevertheless, Dad witnessed what I felt and that was a choice and memorable experience for both of us. Our dear father passed not long after that under his grandson Zac's loving and watchful care.

---

*President Heber J. Grant testifies of comfort from the spirit world:*

I have been blessed with only two sons. One of them died at five years of age and the other at seven. My last son died of a hip disease. I had built great hopes that he would live to spread the Gospel at home and abroad and be an honor to me. About an hour before he died I had a dream that his mother, who was dead, came for him, and that she brought with her a messenger, and she told this messenger to take the boy while I was asleep; and in the dream I thought I awoke and I seized my son and fought for him and finally succeeded in getting him away from the messenger who had come to take him, and in so doing I dreamed that I stumbled and fell upon him.

I dreamed that I fell upon his sore hip, and the terrible cries and anguish of the child drove me nearly wild. I could not stand it and I jumped up and ran out of the house so as not to hear his distress. I dreamed that after running out of the house I met Brother Joseph E. Taylor and told him of these things.

He said: "Well, Heber, do you know what I would do if my wife came for one of her children—I would not struggle for that child; I would not oppose her taking that child away. If a mother who had been faithful had passed beyond the veil, she would know of the suffering and the anguish her child may have to suffer; she would know whether that child might go through life as a cripple and whether it would be better or wiser for that child to be relieved from the torture of life; and when you stop to think, Brother Grant, that the mother of that boy went down into the shadow of death to give him life, she is the one who ought to have the right to take him or keep him."

I said, "I believe you are right, Brother Taylor, and if she comes again, she shall have the boy without any protest on my part."

After coming to that conclusion, I was waked by my brother, B. F. Grant, who was staying that night with us, helping to watch over the sick boy. He called me into the room and told me that my child was dying. I went in the front room and sat down. There was a vacant chair between me and my wife who is now living, and **I felt the presence of that boy's deceased mother, sitting in that chair.** I did not tell anybody what I felt, but I turned to my living wife and said: "Do you feel anything strange?" She said: **"Yes, I feel assured that Heber's mother is sitting between us, waiting to take him away."**

Now, I am naturally, I believe, a sympathetic man. I was raised as an only child, with all the affection that a mother could lavish upon a boy. I believe that I am naturally affectionate and sympathetic and that I shed tears for my friends—tears of joy for their success and tears of sorrow for their misfortunes. But I sat by the deathbed of my little boy and saw him die, without shedding a tear. My living wife, my brother, and I, upon that occasion experienced a sweet, peaceful, and heavenly influence in my home, as great as I have ever experienced in my life. (*Improvement Era,* June 1940, pp. 330, 383.)

On the morning of the Book of Mormon conference for Saturday my plan was to get there early so that I could have a better parking place. I was able to get there early because **I had someone gently shake my shoulder and wake me up**. I looked at the time and realized that I had slept in and I needed to hurry. I thought it was my husband at first thought, but he was still in bed. Then I called him later that day and asked him if he had touched my shoulder and moved it back and forth to wake me up for the conference and he said he had not. (A family friend)

"And, behold, **the angel of the Lord came upon him**, and a light shined in the prison: and he smote Peter on the side, and raised him up, saying, Arise up quickly." (Acts 12:7)

463

O what an unspeakable blessing is **the ministry of angels** to mortal man! What a pleasing thought, that many who minster to us, and watch over us, are our near kindred, our fathers who have died and risen again in former ages, and who watch over their descendants with all the paternal care and solicitude which characterize affectionate fathers and mothers on the earth." (Parley P. Pratt, *KST*, 119)

"And as he lay and slept under a juniper tree, behold, then **an angel touched him**, and said unto him, Arise and eat." (1 Kings 19:5)

We were headed south from Ogden, UT, to see family for the Christmas holidays in Saint George, UT, and eventually Yuma, AZ. A snowstorm started and it grew heavier as we drove. By the time we passed Salt Lake City snowfall was heavy on the roads. The snowplows could not keep up. It was a major storm.

When we slowly arrived at Provo, UT, there was half a foot of snow on the freeway. The traffic was getting lighter and everyone still on the freeway had slowed down to a crawl for safety. We had prayed as a family for safety for our trip that morning.

I was going about 10 mph and came upon a van going only 5, so I decided to use my momentum to plow through the heavy snow in the "fast lane." So we got up to a healthy 15 mph and passed them okay. Before we could get back into the slow lane an impatient driver, coming up behind us, was in a white minivan like ours and weaving between cars.

This van passed the vehicle we had just passed and then went back into the slow lane to go around us. He might have been going 25 or 30, really speeding for the conditions. The next thing we witnessed was the faster van right in front of us, perpendicular to our car, as we prepared to T-bone their vehicle. White knuckles and wide eyes around, we braced for the impact.

"Hold on everybody!" What a terrible start to our long drive and we were still in Utah County! The impact would surely take out our lights and the radiator, at the very least.

**If angels can push handcarts, they can surely push minivans.** That van seemed to be quickly shoved out of our way and into the deep snow, to our left, into an extra wide median. We didn't hit it! Why didn't we wreck? We couldn't believe it! The movement of that van was with such force that it moved perpendicular to our vehicle and slid through the deep snow clear over near the edge of the oncoming lanes and lodged in deep snow. They were securely stuck and safe from any oncoming traffic.

We said a pray of gratitude and also prayed for the "speeders" who were really stuck now in deep drifts. After that, it was white knuckles all the way down I-15 through Utah as the storm raged. The snow finally quit just outside of Saint George, UT. That storm ended up dumping over two-and-a-half feet of snow in northern Utah on the valley floors and much more in the mountains! (Journal 1/4/2004)

I had been driving on winter roads for many years, so I felt very capable driving around town. I was not too concerned one chilly day heading down 800 North in Orem, Utah, a road that slopes considerably from the upper elevation of Provo Canyon westward to the freeway on lower ground. Unfortunately, I was in a new car and was not used to the rule to *not* pump the brakes.

I was planning to turn right at a light at the bottom of the hill just before the freeway. As I neared the turn, I realized that although I wasn't breaking the speed limit, I was going way to fast for the slippery road. I habitually began to pump the brake pedal. It did nothing, but I dared not apply full pressure on the brake for fear of losing control of the car.

The light was red so going straight would bring me head on with cars coming off the freeway. However, there was no way to stop then turn right. The best plan was to make the turn without stopping. As I tried to turn, to my alarm, the car remained straight, so I turned the steering wheel hard all the way to the right. A van was stopped at the intersection and I was headed straight for it at a T. I was already praying intently, mostly begging that I would not kill the people in the van; it didn't matter what happened to me. There was no way I could not hit them; my car was not turning but only sliding to the right, not enough to make a clean turn. I found myself wondering why my life wasn't flashing before my eyes, as happens when people are about to die. Instead, I imagined broken glass and my bloody, lifeless body.

In the last seconds, I relinquished my control; I could do nothing to stop myself from plowing into the van. I would have to accept my fate. Upon these thoughts, I soon found myself sailing north along the road. It was surreal; to this day, I have no memory of turning or passing the van. I had to blink and look over my shoulder to make sure it wasn't a dream! I don't know how I got onto the road safely; I must have come within inches of that van. I know that in my own wisdom and strength, I could not have made the turn. **Heavenly Father orchestrated a miracle** for me and the people in that van. (A relative)

---

We lived in Eagle, ID when I was nine. We lived in the country outside of Boise, ID. I would help my friend during the hay harvest. He had a small tractor that he used to pull a slip. It was simply a wooden platform that lay on the ground. As the tractor slowly pulled it along you could walk alongside and drag or carry hay bales on to it. I wasn't big enough to lift the bales, but I could drag them onto the slip.

I had wandered into the hay field and was dragging bales and lining them up so the slip could follow along when it came. Suddenly I heard a snorting noise and turned around to see a large bull pawing at the ground and looking at me. It had long horns and looked meaner than anything I had ever seen. Although I was a considerable distance away from the tractor, all I could think to do was run. When I took off on a dead run the bull decided to come after me and chase me down.

Looking behind me as I ran I could see the bull getting closer and closer and just knew he was going to catch me before I could reach safety. Out of nowhere I heard a man yelling at the bull. I turned to see a man dressed in farm clothes with a pitchfork in his hands. He was running at the bull and jabbing the fork at him while yelling at him to get away.

I kept running and made it to the tractor and my friends. When I looked back behind me the bull was running off in the opposite direction; **the man with the pitchfork had disappeared and was not to be seen again**. He had vanished and nobody knew who he was or where he came from. (A peer)

*Often unseen powers help fellow sojourners on earth. They are most likely angels or translated beings.*

"Be not forgetful to entertain strangers: for thereby **some have entertained angels unawares**." (Hebrews 13:2)

*The reference to the topical guide for "angels" refers to two categories: Angels and Translated Beings. We understand there is great help from across the veil and from heaven; we are not sure which group of **angels is ministering** to us unless they introduce themselves and/or we utilize those three grand keys of handshaking. (See D&C 129)*

---

I noticed the neighbor kids playing out in the country where we lived. They were members of our ward. I decided to go back in the house and it was as if I was frozen and couldn't move!

Then I saw one of the neighbor boys fall backwards into a swift running part of the canal. At that point I could do nothing but move and dashed to the canal to search for the little boy. I frantically searched all around with no success. My heart sank. Then I noticed the little boy standing up on top of the bank, dripping wet.

**A protective power removed him** from that fast running water and sustained his life! (A friend, Journal 6/22/1986)

---

My sister was dying of cancer at the age of 21. This was really hard on the family. Our family surrounded her during her final hours in her bedroom. The family was wondering who would come to take her through the veil. Our parents and grandparents were all living. My sister wasn't married yet.

A lady, whom we did not know, knocked on our door and she explained, "I don't know why but I felt impressed to come to your door and tell you that **your home is glowing**!"

My sister passed away a couple hours after that knock on our door.

My father said, "It makes sense that our house was blessed and sanctified. For our Savior can visit Holy places. I believe our home was prepared for His visit to take our daughter through the veil." (A peer)

---

I was on a motorcycle with a guy and we hit a vehicle at high speed. I was launched off the back of the motorcycle and thrown into oncoming traffic. Neither one of us had helmets on. We were probably going 75 miles per hour. But **I literally felt there were angels carrying me and laying me down on the pavement and then protecting me**. I didn't roll or flop around. I just ended up lying on the ground or being laid down. No cars were in the lane at that time.

I had minor injuries to my leg and wrist, but just a few scrapes. The road rash I got was about like when I fell off my tricycle as a child. I felt like this was a real miracle and started examining my life to see where I could improve.

The motorcycle driver/young man was killed in the accident. I could have easily been killed too. I was protected and saved for some reason. (A friend)

————————————◆•————————————

Back in 1994, we had a close call. We had just dropped our son off at the MTC in Provo, UT, and were driving in rush hour traffic. We were in bumper-to-bumper traffic near Layton, UT, as we headed on our way home to Montana.

I was driving a 1988 Subaru XT6, a small sports car. We got up to around seventy miles per hour, in heavy traffic, when both of us noticed a truck tire rolling along the freeway … headed in our direction. It started bouncing in the median and then back into our lane of traffic. We were in that lane, next to the median and totally freaked out and knew we were dead!

We could not slow down or move over due to the traffic around us. Then the Holy Ghost let me know for sure that the tire would hit us! If the tire hit the windshield we would have both been killed. As the tire approached I yelled at my wife and we both ducked down in the small car. The sound of the tire hitting the car sounded like a cannon had just been fired! I looked in my rearview mirror and saw the tire ricochet back into the median. I envisioned the entire left side of our car being caved in.

Within a few miles were able to work our way over and then get off on an exit to survey the damage. The only damage was a rubber smudge mark on the center of the rear wheel. The runaway truck tire could not have hit our vehicle in a better place. **We knew there had been divine intervention.** (A peer)

————————————◆•————————————

Early in 1884 the beautiful Mormon temple in Logan, Utah, was almost ready to be dedicated. ... While the temple was being built, Bishop Henry Ballard, who had worked on the temple from the beginning, prayed earnestly that in some way he would receive names of ancestors who had lived in far-off England. On the day before the dedication of the temple and while several of Bishop Ballard's daughters were playing ... two strange men suddenly approached!!!

One of the men gave the oldest girl a folded newspaper saying ... "Give this to your father and no one else, go quickly and don't lose it."

The girl hurried to take the paper ... so her father. It was the *Newberry Weekly News*, printed in his hometown in England just three days before. One full page was filled with birth and death dates of people buried in the Newberry Cemetery.

The temple president said, "Bishop Ballard you are authorized to do work for these people, **you received the record through messengers of the Lord**." (*Friend*, Oct 1977)

These young girl's brother comments:

We looked in vain for these travelers. They were not to be seen. No one else saw them. The newspaper ... was printed in my father's old English home, May 15th, 1884, and reached our hands May 18th, 1884, three days after publication. We were astonished, for by no earthly means could it have reached us ... (Melvin J. Ballard, *Three Degrees of Glory, 24*)

*The newspaper the young girl brought to her father contained over 60 names with complete birth and death dates! My money is on translated beings for delivering a recent newspaper printed in England all the way to Utah in the 1800's.*

---

I was a crossing guard for the local district for two years. I would sit in my car on Center Street and wait for students. When students approached the crosswalk, I stopped the traffic and the children would cross safely.

One afternoon I stood in the road with my stop sign raised. It soon became apparent that the high school boy in the gray pickup was not paying attention. Surely he can see me here! But, he didn't see me. I needed to get out of the way fast, but everything seemed frozen. Finally, I jumped backwards to avoid being hit!

It was only later that I realized what had actually taken place and what could have happened. As I reflected on the events, I realized that it wasn't me that had jumped backwards. There was no way I could have jumped that high and that far back. I realized that I had been **protected by some other *force*.** My 6th grade son came to the crosswalk just a few minutes later. I cringed to think what he would have had to deal with for the rest of his life had I been hit that afternoon. I was so grateful that no children were in the crosswalk at the time the pickup barreled through.

It was an amazing feeling to actually understand that Heavenly Father truly knows me personally; to know that he protected me and my son from a possibly terrible day. My patriarchal blessing told me that my life would be prolonged so that I could fill the measure of my creation in righteousness before our Father in Heaven. (A friend)

————— •◆• —————

When I was a young teenage mother, I was driving to my mom's place to pick up our baby. I was driving over the viaduct and stopped at a light to turn left. Across the intersection I noticed a single man parked by the side of the road and then our eyes met. I got this real yucky feeling.

This was the time when Ted Bundy was killing all those young girls. After I turned left, the man in the car pulled up right after me and was following quite closely. Then I noticed another car pull up close behind him. I thought, "Great! Now there are two cars after me!"

There were not a lot of other homes on this desolate road my mother lived on. Frightened, I pulled into the driveway and the car behind me slowly rolled by. Then the second car pulled into the driveway. I didn't know what to think at first because I was so scared!

Then I recognized it was my Uncle Pete. He exclaimed, "Girl, that man was after you! I was across the road at the light and I saw him pull after you, so I turned to follow you and protect you."

He happened to be right there at that intersection at the same time. **Uncle Pete was my guardian angel that day!**

*There's no doubt that the Lord influenced her earthly angel, Uncle Pete, to be at the intersection at the very critical time.*

———•◆•———

I have spoken here of heavenly help, of angles dispatched to bless us in time of need. But when we speak of those who are instruments in the hand of God, we are reminded that **not all angels are from the other side of the veil.** Some of them we walk with and talk with—here, now, every day. Some of them reside in our own neighborhoods. Some of them gave birth to us, and in my case, one of them consented to marry me. Indeed heaven never seems closer than when we see the love of God manifested in the kindness and devotion of **people so good and so pure that *angelic* is the only word that comes to mind.** (Jeffrey R. Holland, GC, Oct 2008)

———•◆•———

As we sat in sacrament meeting on the third row, our toddler began begging us to let her sit on the front row. We succumbed to her pleadings and I said, "As long as you can sit still and be quiet up there, it's okay." The row was empty.

She crawled under the benches, climbed on the bench, and sat there through the meeting very quietly, staying in her seat. The only movement she made was to keep looking up to the right.

She came back to sit with us before the closing song. Our little one said to her mother, "Grandpa had to leave." (Grandpa's funeral was just three weeks ago.)

"Yes dear, it was Grandpa's time to go and he's gone to heaven."

"No mom, Grandpa and Johnny had to leave."

"What do you mean, dear?"

**"Johnny and Grandpa were sitting with me and they had to go."**

My parents had a stillborn son many decades ago. The next time we were on Family Search, we changed my brother's name from "STILLBORN" to Johnny! (Our friend)

"And now, he imparteth his word by angels unto men, yea, not only men but women also. Now this is not all; little children do have words given unto them many times, which confound the wise and the learned." (Alma 32:23)

As I was journeying to see a very near kindred, behold **an angel of the Lord appeared unto me and said: Amulek, return to thine own house,** for thou shalt feed a prophet of the Lord; yea, a holy man, who is a chosen man of God; for he has fasted many days because of the sins of the people, and he is an hungered, and thou shalt receive him into thy house and feed him, and he shall bless thee and thy house; and the blessing of the Lord shall rest upon thee and thy house. (Alma 10:7)

And it came to pass that while he was journeying, thither, being weighed down with sorrow, wading through much tribulation and anguish of soul, because of the wickedness of the people who were in the city of Ammonihah, it came to pass while Alma was thus weighed down with sorrow, behold **an angel of the Lord appeared unto him, saying, Blessed art thou Alma;** therefore, life up they head and rejoice, for thou has great cause to rejoice; for thou hast been faithful in keeping the commandments of God from the first time which thou receivedst thy first message from him. Behold, I am he that delivered it unto you." (Alma 8:14-15)

*This angel identified himself as being the same angel Alma first saw when he was in his rebellious stage. He is likely the same angel that talked to Amulek. Maybe these angels glow with such intense light that it is hard to distinguish between them? On another note, it is interesting that Amulek was traveling to see relatives while Alma was leaving Ammonihah after being rejected. The angel commanded both of them to return to Ammonihah where they met each other before ending up at Amulek's home where they ministered to Alma. Once Alma regained his strength he, in turn, ministered to Amulek's entire household, which greatly blessed them.*

And as he entered the city he was an hungered, and he said to a man: Will ye give to an humble servant of God something to eat? And the man said unto him: I am a Nephite, and I know that thou art a holy prophet of God, for **thou are the man whom an angel said in a vision: Thou shalt receive.** Therefore, go with me into my house and I will impart unto thee of my food; and I know that thou wilt be a blessing unto me and my house. (Alma 10:19-20)

For behold, he hath blessed mine house, he hath blessed me, and my women, and my children, and my father and my kinsfolk; yea, even all my kindred hath he blessed, and the blessing of the Lord hath rested upon us according to the words which he spake. (Alma 10:11)

*When the angel told Amulek that Alma would "bless thee and thy house," that was an understatement!*

———————◆———————

When our son was four years old, his two-year-old brother got really sick with croup. We were going to take him in to get breathing treatments because we were afraid his little lungs were going to collapse. My sick boy was crying and screaming and we were all being kind of loud. We worried that we might wake up our older son.

The next morning I said, "Buddy, you slept really well even though it was real crazy last night. Good job!"

He said, "I did wake up; but **a man came to my bed and he told me that 'everything was going to be okay.'** Then he stayed with me and I was able to go back to sleep."

I asked him what the man looked like and he couldn't really describe him. (A family friend)

———————◆———————

A nephew flew up to SLC and stayed with us for a few days prior to entering the MTC in Provo, UT. We were so impressed with this young man. His maturity in the Gospel was evident. He was actually better read and prepared than some missionaries I have seen at the end of their missions! He carried a spirit of goodness about him. He was a blessing to us and our home for those few short days. (Several years later he was called to be the *new elder's quorum* president in his ward, after general conference April, 2018.)

I drove him down to the MTC on the designated day. As we arrived at that large sweeping drive we observed a lot of activity. There were a lot of excited elders and sisters acting as escorts to the new missionaries. The *system* would allow four cars at a time to pull in where the greeters were waiting. The entire operation was very impressive and orderly.

The message from my nephew to me was that we were supposed to have a quick goodbye in order to allow the next four cars to enter. We enjoyed a quick hug and pat on the back and then his two escorts whisked him away. The other elders had their mothers with them and they were taking much longer to say goodbye.

This allowed me to ponder, while peacefully waiting in my car, and I thought about what a fine young man this was. He was so prepared and faithful; he would have a successful mission. Then I thought back to the sweetness during my mission to Sweden. As I meditated on missionary labors a SWOOSH of strong wind came through the car from back to front. The presences elated my torso with a super strong spirit. To my mind and body **it felt like angels came down and flew** horizontally through the four parked vehicles and through my body and spirit. I quickly looked at all the windows to see where this strong wind came from. All the windows were rolled up! I have no idea what passengers in the vehicles behind me felt; I hoped that they also basked in the Spirit and experienced the same phenomenal feelings.

I thought, "If this is what it feels like in the driveway, the Spirit must be absolutely amazing inside!" My hypothesis is that these were missionary-minded angels protecting the precious participants at the MTC. This was a super special singular experience. (Journal 4/21/2011)

> Joseph recalled that during the dedication of the Kirtland Temple, George A. Smith arose and began to prophesy, when **a noise was heard like the sound of a rushing mighty wind**, which filled the Temple, and all the congregation simultaneously arose, being moved upon by an invisible power; many began to speak in tongues and prophesy; others saw glorious visions; and I beheld **the Temple was filled with angels**, which fact I declared to the congregation. The people of the neighborhood came running together (hearing an unusual sound within, and seeing a bright light like a pillar of fire resting upon the Temple), and were astonished at what was taking place. (*HC*, 2:428)

> On the day of Pentecost everyone in the room experienced the following: "And **suddenly there came a sound from heaven as of a rushing mighty wind**, and it filled all the house where they were sitting." (Acts 2:2)

> "Sometimes when I feel the Spirit it comes as a *swoosh of peace*." (A peer)

*After King Belshazzar, his princes, and concubines drank wine from temple vessels and worshiped idols, an angel visited them and left a message on a palace wall.*

In the same **hour came forth fingers of a man's hand, and wrote** over against the candlestick **upon the plaster of the wall of the king's palace**: and the king saw the part of the hand that wrote. Then the king's countenance was changed, and his thoughts troubled him, so that the joints of his loins were loosed, and his knees smote one against another. (Daniel 5:3-6)

*Daniel was brought in to interpret the writing on the wall, which no other expert in the kingdom could read.*

This is the interpretation of the thing: MENE; God hath numbered thy kingdom, and finished it. TEKEL; Thou art weighed in the balances, and art found wanting. PERES; Thy kingdom is divided, and given to the Medes and Persians." (Daniel 5:26-28)

*This reminds us of another scripture story:* "...it was Aminadi who interpreted the writing which was upon the wall of the temple, which was **written by the finger of God**." (Alma 10:2)

———————◆———————

Mother tripped and went down hard on her knees. She thought that fall brought the baby early. The baby had difficulty breathing. Mother said, "In the night **I saw my Grandma Wing, who passed away years before, carry a little bundle and pass through the wall**." Mother then knew that the baby had died.

Ralph Lewis Clyde was born on March 1st and died the next day in 1929. Grandma Sophia Anena Bohne Wing passed away in 1895. (Our mother)

———————◆———————

Grandpa Joseph Smith Wing was a doctor and converted in the East. He rode a one-horse buggy to Utah where he acquired four wives. When polygamy was stopped my Grandpa Wing said, "If I cannot have all of my wives, I won't have any of them!" He did not want to show favoritism to any of them. Three of his wives remarried other men and the fourth remained single.

I always loved Grandma Wing. She acquired pneumonia. Grandma got the chills and they kept piling quilts upon her. Dr Wing (Grandpa) told them they needed to start a fire because the quilts were too heavy for her frail body and she wouldn't be strong enough to support the weight. Doctor Wing, now the ex-husband, was kicked out of the house by the new husband.

Grandma Wing kept looking up at the corner of the room and then said, **"Jehovah's come for me,"** and was gone. She was only forty-four." (Alta Law Clyde, Life History)

*Alta is my grandmother and Grandma Wing my 3ggm.*

... A short time before the end, **his face suddenly lit up and his countenance brightened**. He cast his eyes upward as if he could see far into upper distant spaces. "What do you see, father?" they asked. (Alexander Neibaur) murmured clearly, "Joseph—Hyrum—" (Genealogical and Historical Magazine, April 1914, 63)

———— •◆• ————

We were coming back to Utah from seeing the kids and grandkids in Phoenix. It was late and dark. We were on a long straight stretch of road heading north. I was driving and I guess I fell asleep.

**I felt a strong hand on top of mine that was helping me** to move the steering wheel to the left. As I woke up I was being directed back onto the freeway. I had fallen asleep and we had driven off the road!

After I caught my breath, I turned to Uke (her husband) to thank him for keeping us on the road. He was sound asleep, leaning away from me against the passenger door! (Great Grandma)

A strong crosswind was blowing, creating a ground blizzard of snow that made the road difficult to see and to navigate. We were without a heater in the car and were wrapped deep in quilts. We must have been going about fifty miles an hour.

Suddenly out of the darkness and the storm there loomed two horses, crossing the highway from right to left. They were just starting to cross into the left lane when I saw them. Without my thinking—there was not time for that—my hands turned the steering wheel left. In a second we were on the far left, the left wheels on the shoulder of the road. As we whizzed by, the lead horse jerked his head high and back, and we brushed by his nose. Another split second and we were back into our proper lane. I remember no thought that caused me to turn the wheel just enough to clear the horses yet not enough to roll us over into the borrow pit. **I know that it wasn't I who did the driving**. (S. Dilworth Young, *New Era*, Oct 1971)

————————◆•◆•◆————————

*Parley P. Pratt described his wife, Thankful, as tall and slender, having large dark eyes and black glossy hair:*

> ... Thankful had very poor health and was unable to conceive ... Heber C. Kimball gave her a priesthood blessing, she regained her health and became pregnant ... Thankful died a few hours after giving birth. ...
> Parley was imprisoned on bogus charges in Richmond, Missouri, along with several other brethren ... the jailers seemed content to keep them indefinitely ... Parley began to wonder if that was to be his fate as weeks of imprisonment turned into months.
> Kneeling in the dark, cold and filthy dungeon, Parley began praying daily to know if he would ever be released to preach the gospel ... Finally, during one of those prayers; **a sweet angel brought him a comforting answer** ... I seemed carried away in the spirit and no longer sensitive to outward objects ... a heaven of peace and calmness pervaded my bosom; a personage from the world of spirits stood before me with a smile of compassion ... with the tenderest love and sympathy.
> A soft hand seemed placed within my own, and a glowing cheek was laid in tenderness and warmth upon mine. A well-known voice saluted me, which I readily recognized as that of the wife of my youth, who had then for nearly two years been sweetly sleeping where the wicked cease from troubling and the weary are at rest ... Shall I ever be at liberty again in this life, and enjoy the society of my family and the saints, and preach the gospel? ... She answered definitely and unhesitatingly: Yes! (*Autobiography of Parley Parker Pratt*, p 166.)

————————◆•◆•◆————————

I was covering five states as a salesman for mechanical supplies. After spending two days in Las Vegas, NV, I was headed north to Salt Lake City, UT. About five miles outside of Vegas, I noticed a car off to the side of the road with its hood up. I have seen hundreds of cars like this over the many hundred thousand miles I've logged.

As I passed this car, **a loud audible voice said, *"STOP!"*** I looked over into the empty passenger seat expecting to see someone. It was that loud. So what did I do; I pulled over. I had lots of tools in my car. This family's car would start, but when they turned the lights on the engine would die. I knew they needed a new alternator and removed it for them.

Then I drove back to Vegas to my nearest client. They did not have the right alternator but their warehouse on the other side of Vegas did. Weaving through the heavy traffic I arrived just as they were locking up the shop. I was able to obtain the correct alternator and reinstalled it and gave their battery a jump.

They had been to the Los Angeles, CA, area for a meeting and some family vacation time. They were headed back to Rexburg, ID when their car died. They sat there for about fifteen minutes trying to figure out what to do. Then they decided to pray. When they said, "Amen", I drove by and was told to stop. This was decades before we had cell phones. They arrived home safe and sent me a nice thank you note. (A peer)

We lived in a double-wide trailer home in northwestern Wyoming. Everyone living in trailers would use "heat tape" to wrap around the water pipes running between the ground and trailer frame. This prevented one's pipes from freezing up when the temperatures dipped below zero, which was not uncommon.

We had been vacationing in southern Utah and Arizona. Upon returning from these warm climes we were disappointed to find our pipes froze up, meaning our heat tape had broken. We no longer had water to our: Sinks, shower, bath tub, toilets, dishwasher, and washing machine. It was Saturday afternoon before the big-box store-era and I went out on a snowy evening to search for an open hardware store. Back then many of these small stores would close up at noon on Saturday. I drove through heavy snow around the large parking lot of an industrial area. Nothing was open at all. No indoor lights were noticeable and hardly any outdoor lights were even on.

I was quite concerned for my wife, toddler, and baby. The neighbors were nice enough to let us use their bathroom periodically. I sat there and pondered for a solution. Nothing would be open at all on Sunday. We would just have to wait until Monday morning.

As I inched the car forward to return home unsuccessful, a loud voice called out, "**WHOA!**" I immediately stopped the car and looked behind me to see if someone else was in the parking lot. I saw no one. Next I checked to see if the radio was on. It was not. Then I looked around for any other cars or lights on. There were none. In the severe cold my windows were obviously rolled up. I got out of the car and looked back around the entire parking lot to see if there was a lone person in the snow somewhere. There was just a lot of snow everywhere and no sign of any life or activity. "Hmm," I said out loud as I wondered?

As my eyes adjusted to the dimly lit snowpack, I noticed a shift in the pattern in front of the car. As I moved forward I was surprised to now notice a deep drop off into a concrete loading dock. I believe that an angel was sent to keep me from totaling our car, which probably would have been more than we could have handled at the time. I was so grateful for the warning. (Journal 6/6/1985)

*My hypothesis and personal belief is that when there is a loud audible noise, shout, and/or warning that an angel, of some magnitude, is the source.*

> I was chiefly tagged as a recruiting officer ... I visited branches of the Church in Ohio, Indiana, Illinois and Missouri ... On one occasion, I traveled all night to overtake the camp with some men and means ... At noon I had turned my horse loose from the carriage to feed on the plain.... I sank down overpowered with a deep sleep, and might have lain in a state of oblivion till the shades of night had gathered about me, so completely was I exhausted for want of sleep and rest; but I had only slept a few moments ...when **a voice, more loud and shrill than I had ever heard before, fell on my ear, and thrilled through every part of my system**; it said: **"Parley, it is time to be up and on your journey."** In the twinkling of an eye I was perfectly aroused; I sprang to my feet so suddenly that I couldn't quite tell where I was ... I related the circumstance afterwards to brother Joseph Smith, and he bore testimony that it was the angel of the Lord who went before the camp, who found me overpowered by sleep, and thus awoke me. (Autobiography of Parley P. Pratt, 122-123)

"Ye are swift to do iniquity but slow to remember the Lord your God. **Ye have seen an angel ... he has spoken unto you like unto the voice of thunder**, which did cause the earth to shake as if it were to divide asunder." (1 Ne. 17:45

*I, along with President Harold B. Lee, believe that the Holy Ghost may never raise His voice. The Holy Ghost, at times, can be very loud and moving within our body, heart, mind, and/or soul. The majority of the time feelings and messages come as quiet directions and promptings. Angels can be loud and strong.*

"All too often when God speaks in this still, small voice, as he did to Elijah in the cave, it may not be audible to our physical hearing ..." (Harold B. Lee, *TPC*, 6)

"I know for example, what Enos was talking about when he said, '... the voice of the Lord came into my mind again' (Enos 1:10). He did not say it came into his ear, but that it 'came into my mind again, saying ...'" (Marion G. Romney, GC, Oct 1961)

Yesterday Elder Marion G. Romney mentioned the matter of the Holy Spirit and said that one does not hear it with our ears. May I read to you a verse of scripture which verifies that.... "Ye have seen an angel, and he spoke unto you; yea, ye have heard his voice from time to time; and he hath spoken to you in a still small voice,"—and this is the part I would like to have you hear—"but ye were past feeling, that ye could not feel his words." (I Ne. 17:45)
I used to wonder why Nephi didn't say "hear his words." Now I know that one doesn't hear them with his ears, as brother Romney said. But into a person's mind there come words. (S. Dilworth Young, GC, Oct 1961)

If you will heed the voice of warning of the Holy Ghost and will follow His direction, you will be blessed with **the ministering of angels**. This blessing will add wisdom, knowledge, power, and glory to your life. This is a sure blessing promised to you by the Lord. (L. Tom Perry, GC, Oct 2010)

# 22. All These Gifts Come From God

Now there are diversity of gifts, but the same Spirit. But the manifestation of the Spirit is given to every man to profit withal. For to one is given by the Spirit the word of wisdom; to another the word of knowledge by the same Spirit. To another faith by the same Spirit; to another the gifts of healing by the same Spirit; To another the working of miracles; to another prophecy, to another discerning of spirits ... But all these worketh that one and selfsame Spirit ... (1 Cor. 12:4, 7-11)

*This ability to discern what is in the mind or heart of another is a remarkable manifestation of the Holy Spirit. Stephen L. Richards, a member of the First Presidency, explained what this gift is:*

This gift ... when highly developed arises largely out of an acute sensitivity to impressions—spiritual impressions, if you will—to read under the surface as it were, to detect hidden evil, and more importantly to find the good that may be concealed. *The highest type of discernment is that which perceives in others and uncovers for them their better natures, the good inherent within them.* (CR, April 1950)

Over the years I have discovered that one of my spiritual gifts is the gift of discernment. This gift has taught me so much about unconditional love and Christ-like charity. When one discerns a truth it is simply that, pure truth. Caustic criticism, judgmental jargon, and all of the natural man's traits are missing. God-like love is present due to the source. This is very similar to feelings of those who have had near-death experiences. While experiencing a glimpse through the veil, these people frequently feel an abundant, all-encompassing, and pure Christ-like love that is judgment-free. To me, discernment also is rife with heavenly traits.

During the middle of a week I was leaving the Boy Scout office in South Ogden, UT. As I came down the long hill I noticed my car was starting to overheat and then white smoke began billowing from under the hood. Turning off the air conditioner and radio, and putting the vehicle in neutral I coasted as far as possible down the long hill. The car dealership was only about a mile away. Hopefully I could roll into the shop prior to doing any serious damage to my car's radiator and/or engine.

The dealership's mechanics were able to inspect my car right away. Afterwards, the service manager informed me that my radiator was leaking from the seam.  Such a problem was not reparable; however, they could hook me up with fresh anti-freeze and a new radiator in two hours time, for just $650. The time frame sounded great, but the price didn't.

Then I immediately *discerned that I did not need a new radiator.* However, this idea was going directly against the experts.  I really had a struggle within myself and felt like I was disregarding authority when I suggested, "Just fill the radiator up with water and I'll limp home and work on it myself."

They hesitantly agreed and warned me that I was making a possibly big mistake that could lead to serious damage and even more costly issues.

"You might need a new engine instead of just a radiator if you don't fix it right away," was the head mechanic's parting words.

As mentioned, they were the experts and I was going against professional judgment. However, on any given day, conventional wisdom never stacks up to Heavenly Father's perfect knowledge.

I still wondered what the eventual outcome would be, though.  I drove slowly home, needing to climb one long hill up out of Riverdale, UT. The car made it home okay.  I decided to take half a day off from work to tackle this problem.  After removing the radiator from the car, I called the radiator shop in Ogden, UT.  The company's voicemail informed me that they had closed their Ogden location and moved everything to their main facility in Salt Lake City.  So I loaded the radiator in my wife's car and headed to their new location in SLC.

The radiator shop ran a high-pressure test on my radiator and came back with the damage report.

This professional commented, with a chuckle, "You don't need a new radiator.  There were no leaks anywhere at high pressure.  Your only problem is that you need a stronger radiator cap.  Here's a better cap, (as he tossed it over the counter to me) you can just have it!"

Well if that wasn't the sweetest music to my ears!

I now knew for sure that my discernment was true and factual, even though I spurned the experts and had seriously doubted my own feelings. What I found extremely educational, from this event, was that the spiritual discernment was simply "You don't need a new radiator." There were no feelings or ideas whatsoever regarding the truthfulness and intentional or unintentional responses at the dealership. They could have made an honest mistake. The service manager might have been trying to increase sales dishonestly? Maybe it was just a stupid error? Regardless of the real reason, the spirit of truth doesn't judge people in a natural manner, as we are prone to do. There was no condemnation—only truth.

True discernment is simply pure love and charity without judgment and that is a goal of mine that I am far from achieving.

> "There are a great variety of spiritual gifts given; but none of these gifts are given for the exclusive benefit of the individual possessing them …. They are commanded to give, not part, but the whole, to the pure in heart, that all may be equal in the enjoyment of these precious gifts." (*Masterful Discourses of Orson Pratt*, 644)

During the reception line we were standing in, at a large wedding in Salt Lake City, Utah, Elder Boyd K. Packer came through shaking hands. As he firmly grabbed my hand, the Apostle stopped and stared into my eyes for some time; I felt as though *he could see directly into my soul*. Elder Packer then questioned me, "Elder, what have you done with your life?"

"Well—I served a two-year mission in Sweden, married this beautiful young girl (pointing to my wife in the reception line) in the temple, and we are attending BYU."

"Well, elder, that's a good start." (Journal, Aug 28, 1981)

> Jesse N. Smith, the Prophet's cousin, said: "[Joseph Smith was] incomparably the most God-like man I ever saw. … I know that by nature he was incapable of lying and deceitfulness, possessing the greatest kindness and nobility of character. I felt when in his presence that *he could read me through and through*. I know he was all that he claimed to be." (Joseph Smith, *TPC*, 499)

I was waiting patiently as a salesman, at a store for the owner/buyer to be free. There was a great-grandpa type and a young couple with a baby also waiting for the owner to finish talking to a customer. A salesman is generally last on the totem pole, hence patience.

As we stood there in a small group, the baby lunged out of her mother's arms and reached for me. Afraid she might fall, I grabbed her, lifter her up, and she snuggled tightly to my neck. The older gentleman remarked, "What a beautiful granddaughter you have."

"Oh, these are total strangers." (The young couple nodded).

"What an amazing gift you have; what do you do with your gift?"

"Well, I babysit a lot for young couples, for free, so that they can attend the temple or go out for dinner."

"But what do you really do with your gift?"

"Well, I tried to volunteer at the major hospitals in Ogden, Utah, and Layton, Utah, but they do not allow you to touch the babies unless you are a doctor or registered nurse. I told them, 'I cannot volunteer here if I cannot snuggle the babies!'"

"I have a hospital where you can snuggle the babies."

"Really!"

"Here's my card; stop by and set up an interview."

"I definitely will. Thanks!"

Following an hour-and-a-half oral interview, a six-page written interview, and an intense FBI background check—I have been allowed to hold brain-damaged babies, alone in their rooms, and snuggle them at the South Davis Community Hospital (Specialty Hospital of Utah) in Bountiful, Utah. I'll cuddle one precious package for about half-an-hour and then get a fresh gown and lift another beautiful baby from their crib or highchair.

The older gentleman was a hospital administrator. I know that Heavenly Father directed all of us to that little gathering to bless my deep desire to help babies. This has been a most enjoyable service as I have held, cherished, and nurtured these celestial babies and toddlers ever since. (Journal 1/18/2015)

"The innocence with which children come into the world is one of the awesome responsibilities of all who, in any way, influence their lives." (Richard L. Evans, GC, April 1969)

———————◆———————

Unlike others who have—only after great effort—come to know that The Church of Jesus Christ is true, I did not have to fight for my conviction concerning the truths of the restored gospel. Why I never had to struggle I do not know, but I am *grateful for that gift*. Though at times, I have wondered if, had I not been born into the Church, I would have recognized and accepted its doctrines, as familiar and sweet as they are to me now. I have to believe that I would have, since life would be empty for me without them. (A relative)

———————◆———————

We had purchased a large solar generator and the two 12-volt batteries were not recharging well. We thought they had seen their lifespan and were near expiration. I took the batteries to an auto parts store and had them tested. The employee did the usual free test and explained that the batteries were no longer any good and would need to be replaced. Once again, I felt like this was not the truth. I thanked him and told him I would have to think about it.

I had discerned that the batteries weren't expired. As before, there was no feeling of impropriety, stupidity, system error, or flat out cheating. It did not matter why and I did not care. What I care about is being in tune with the Holy Spirit to allow truths and facts to be revealed as they really are.

The next stop for the batteries was a battery store in the industrial part of town. Following their tests they informed me that one battery was at 95% and the other at 105%!

"Well that's a solid 100% average", I commented. I was very pleased, especially since this style of battery goes for $315 each. We could have experienced a very expensive, yet unnecessary expense. (Journal 8/27/2017)

———————————•◆•———————————

*Elder Bednar also brought up another spiritual gift, "to be quick to observe."*

> Another seemingly simple and perhaps underappreciated spiritual gift—the capacity of being 'quick to observe' (Mormon 1:2) is vitally important for you and for me in the world in which we do now and will yet live.
> The gift of discernment opens to us vistas that stretch far beyond what can be seen with natural eyes or heard with natural ears. Discerning is seeing with spiritual eyes and feeling with the heart—seeing and feeling the falsehood of an idea or the goodness of another person. Discerning is hearing with spiritual eyes and feeling with the heart— hearing and feeling the unspoken concern in a statement or the truthfulness of a testimony or doctrine. (David A. Bednar, BYU Devotional, May 10, 2005)

*Additionally Elder Bednar complimented his wife's charitable habit of quickly following promptings with her gift of being able to quickly observe. Elder Bednar also shared the following story with our Stake in Roy, UT, when he spoke 12-13 years ago.*

> Before attending her sacrament meetings, Sister Bednar frequently prays for the spiritual eyes to see those who have a need. Often as she observes the brothers and sisters and children in the congregation, she will feel a spiritual nudge to visit with or make a phone call to a particular person. And when Sister Bednar receives such an impression, she promptly responds and obeys. It is often the case that as soon as the "amen" is spoken in the

benediction, she will talk with a teenager or hug a sister or, upon returning home, immediately pick up the phone and make a call. As long as I've known Sister Bednar, people have marveled at her capacity to discern and respond to their needs. Often they will ask her, "How did you know?" The spiritual gift of being quick to observe has enable her to see and act promptly and has been a great blessing in the lives of many people. (Elder David R Bednar, *BYU/Magazine*, Fall 2005)

---

The bishop called my wife and asked us both to meet with him on a Thursday evening. After twenty to thirty minutes of waiting for the bishop I convinced my wife to bag it and go home. Upon arriving home I called the bishop's wife to see if he was okay.

She replied, "I'm sorry, this is only the third time in five years that he has forgotten an appointment."

Although anxious to find what her new calling was, our next meeting with the bishop wasn't until Sunday. My wife was currently serving in the Primary. The next morning while showering I discerned her new call would be serving as a secretary to the Relief Society. That was I calling I never even considered or thought of before. After my shower I mentioned my feelings to her.

My wife told me that she already knew what her new calling was too and that it was revealed to her while I was showering—so basically we simultaneously discerned identical answers through the Holy Spirit. (Journal 11/17/1984)

"And all these gifts come from God, for the benefit of the children of God." (D&C 46:26)

---

*Patriarch of the Church, Eldred G. Smith shared one of his spiritual gifts:*

In the middle of our discussion of reminiscing, I turned to the lady of this couple and said, "Would you be surprised if you had Jewish blood in your line? You have, don't you?"
"How did you know?"
"Well, if you had asked me out in the street I couldn't have told you. There's not any Jewish mixture in your husband's line, is there—just yours?"
"Yes, that is correct."

I could tell you three or four very similar experiences, definite experiences I have had where it has just come to me that there was a mixture of certain lineage in an individual and I stated it to them before they told me. (University of Utah Forum Address, Jan 17, 1964)

After sacrament meeting, as I entered the foyer, I noticed a sister standing all alone in the center of the foyer. She appeared to be very deep in thought. I had privately nicknamed her "the model" because she was tall, slender, and beautiful. We had never spoken before, except for a "thank you" at the nursery door when she picked up her boys.

I was drawn to her for some reason other than her beauty; she seemed to need help. I simply asked, "How are you doing?"

"I'm doing fine."

"How is your husband doing? Didn't he have a brain tumor?"

"He had a procedure done and we have been blessed. He has no residual effects."

"That's awesome!"

I sauntered off to Sunday school class. After that class I was drawn back to the same foyer. To my surprise, there was this same sister standing all alone again! I was drawn to speak with her once more. Having had her always very busy boys in nursery, I asked: "How are those rambunctious boys doing?"

"Oh—they're full of maximum energy as ever!"

"Yes, that's what I remember—like little Energizer bunnies!"

"Yes!"(Laughing)

"My wife and I like to give busy parents a break and take their children for 3-4 hours. Maybe we should do that for you and your husband? I just sense that you two need a break."

"That might work some time."

"I hope it does."

Off to priesthood meeting I went. And afterwards, a third time, I was prompted to return to that same foyer and there stood "the model" a third time, all alone again! I discerned I was not done communicating with her and as I approached her I boldly blurted: "Here's what we're going to do, tomorrow at 4 pm have your vehicle ready with the children's car seats. We'll leave you our car and keys. Then we'll take your children out for dinner and entertain them until 7 or 8. When is their bedtime?"

"Eight o'clock."

"Okay, we'll have them back by 7:30."

"Okay."

That afternoon I notified my wife what our next home evening involved. We did this for other stressed families once or twice a year and always enjoyed doing it. My wife was on board.

The next day at 3:30, the father of the busy boys called me to make sure we were going to be there at 4. I confirmed the same and reminded him to have all the necessary car seats for each young one buckled in their car. He gladly agreed.

When we arrived at the home, the father rushed the children out and strapped them in their seats. When he was out of earshot I commented to my honey, "Boy—he's really looking forward to some alone time with his good wife!" We were surprised to have one extra passenger, whereas we did not know that this sister babysit a girl for another sister in the ward. This little girl was one of my favorite nursery students and I was her favorite too; no one sat in my lap, during sacrament meetings, as much as she did for a five-six year period. So she was not a problem at all.

At four o'clock we handed over our keys and the couple explained their urgency. That afternoon they got an urgent call from a relative that had a sudden heart attack and was in a local hospital. These ward members were the only relatives in the area and their uncle was asking for them whereas they were the only family that could possible visit him right away. They needed to leave for the hospital ASAP!

Once again, my trying to outguess people and the Lord is fruitless! The Lord's timing is immaculate. This surprise call, that did not exist the day before, came at a time when they needed to farm out their three boys, plus a girl they tended. Heavenly Father saw to it that the babysitters were already lined up in their time of urgent need.

I think this couple left before we did. We would always take a group of small children to a fast food joint with the largest play area. That was our *modus operandi*. We would then turn the children loose and after about 45 minutes they would gather back at the table, where we were visiting, and questioned, "Aren't we going to eat?"

"Sure, we're going to eat. What would you like to eat?"

"Kids meal— hotdog— hamburger—soda."

"Okay, go back and play and we will call you when your food is here."

"Okay"

We would order our meals and then they would eat about 1/3 of their food and be off to the play area again. A little later they would come back and nibble and then play again. Once they were finally bored we would take them to a nice park with lots of swings and contraptions for younger kids.

The only hiccup in the event was that the sister in our ward came to pick up her little girl and no one was home. The parents were at the hospital and we had their boys and her girl. When the girl's mother finally found out who her baby girl was with, she was greatly relieved!

Once again our Heavenly Father utilized our habits to fulfil His righteous ways. We were very grateful to be earthly angels to this young family's urgent needs through the Lord's spiritual promptings.

> Jesus gave us a clear pattern to follow in fulfilling our responsibility to nurture and teach children ... We can know their needs and minister to them *when we spend time with them* ... **We are their ministering angels on earth** if we follow the Lord's example. (Michaelene P. Grassli, GC, Oct 1992)

---

> Gray shadows of disappointment nagged at Karl as he walked home in the dark between the two elders who had just baptized and then confirmed him ... He had prayed that he might know whether the church had been dreamed up my a man or whether it had truly been established by the Lord ... he had fully expected the horizon to lighten ... No sign had been given.
>
> As the three returned home through the dark together ... One of the elders spoke German and interpreted for Karl, who only spoke German, and then interpreted for the other elder, who spoke only English. Suddenly there was no need for an interpreter! For a short time both elders understood Karl's questions and comments, and Karl understood their answers whether spoken in German or English.
>
> Karl now felt that his prayer at the time of his baptism had been answered ...
>
> ... Twenty-one years later ... Dr. Maeser was teaching in Salt Lake City when a blast destroyed the building. (Dr. Karl Maeser informed President Brigham Young that the school would have to be closed.)
>
> "That is exactly right, Brother Maeser," President Young replied, "For I have another mission for you." And that is how Karl G. Maeser was told of his call to establish the Brigham Young University in Provo, Utah ..." (From Dark to Light, *Friend*, Dec 1971)

*An event during the Pentecost reads as follows:*

And they were all filled with the Holy Ghost, and began to speak with other tongues, as the Spirit gave them utterance ... Now when this was noised abroad, the multitude came together, and were confounded, because that every man heard them speak in his own language. (Acts 2:4 & 6)

———◆———

With my gift of love for children I find myself in somewhat uncomfortable situations at times. I was at a splash pad with my two daughters and grandsons. I was away from the water, standing in the grass, watching them. I heard some laughter from the picnics tables on the far side of the large grassy park. I turned around and noticed a small toddler who hadn't been walking long. The little one was working his way across the expansive grass. I assumed a mother would come and get him before he finally reached the splash pad unattended. He came all the way over directly to me and wanted me to pick him up. I had no impression not to so I did take him into my arms; he was too cute to resist! He hugged on me, I laughed with joy, and once again, another baby really brightened my day.

I decided to carry him back across the grass towards the picnic tables. I prayed that no one would think I was running off with him. His mother finally noticed him in my arms and thanked me for watching after her baby boy. I was relieved.

On a different day, I popped into a mall to shop for new tennis shoes. I stopped and looked down the two hallways for the right type of store. As I stood there wondering which way to go, I felt a small child tightly hugging my left leg. He had wandered out from the play area, some distance, and wanted me to pick him up. I thought to myself that some big farm boy is going to come out of one of those shops and yell, "Hey, what are you doing with my kid!" and then thump me. So, I didn't pick him up.

The little boy continued holding on very tightly and he would not let go. Instead of holding him, I got him to stand on my shoes and then I used my legs to *walk him* back over to the play area. He liked that "game." I sat down as he continued to cling tightly to my leg. This is one of the very few children I have not picked up, as much as he and I both wanted to. He finally became distracted by some other little ones and I quickly ran away from him and the play area and then found some new tennis shoes.

Part of my service area included Colorado City, Arizona/Hildale, Utah, which is a large polygamous community. I was in the back of one store inventorying my product in their cooler. I heard some noise down the long aisle and then noticed a small girl running hurriedly towards me. The polygamist toddler finally reached me and jumped into my arms and clung tightly to my neck.

Eventually her mother reached us in her full-length dress and very long hair, saying only, "Sorry."

I explained that children loved me and I loved them and that this happens to me all the time. She took her toddler and walked away, saying no more than that one word. The polygamist people don't usually talk to outsiders at all, except for the store manager whose business purposes necessitated discussions with me.

"We believe in the gift of the Holy Ghost, the power of faith, the enjoyment of the spiritual gifts according to the will of God ..." *TPJS*, 121)

Recently I attended a trade show with my wife at the Salt Palace in Salt Lake City, UT, where she had a display booth for her books she authored. A young mother, visiting the next booth, had a fussy baby girl in a backpack that caught my attention. I had an impression that I could calm her down. Stepping out from my wife's table, I approached the little one and she grabbed my finger tightly. I complimented the cuteness of the little one and her mother challenged, "See if you can get her to sleep."

I caressed the baby's forehead and nose gently and whispered softly into her ear as she gripped my finger firmly. She stopped crying almost immediately and started dozing off. Finally her head dropped back, she was totally out—leaning back so far that I was concerned and let her mother know.

Mommy took the baby out of the backpack and handed her into my awaiting arms with a "Thank you." Then this young mother proceeded to stare into my eyes for a very long time. I hadn't had a stare like that since meeting Boyd K. Packer nearly forty years ago.

Then she stated, "I can see that you are an honest, good man. If you'd like to keep her for awhile, we are in a booth in the far corner." I nodded in gleeful agreement. The mother, a total stranger, contentedly walked away.

I was more content and felt the baby's spirit emanating and held her until I needed to grab some lunch quite a while later. It took some time to find her mother. When I finally found her she tried to get me to keep her baby. When I explained about a lunch break, she said, "Well come back and get her after you eat your lunch!"

That was a shocking statement of surprise. I enjoyed caring for her beautiful baby a couple more times during that day. (Journal 4/29/18)

Little ones will come up to me and climb in my lap or want a hug at funerals, on airplanes, during church, around campgrounds, throughout outdoor events, at retail stores, and in restaurants, etc. I feel it is a most wonderful gift!

"I bear testimony that God has given us the gifts of the Spirit do allow us to be drawn more closely into His circle of love." (Robert D Hales, *Gifts of the Spirit*, BYU Speeches, Aug 1, 1993)

———— •◆• ————

As members of the church and kingdom of God on earth, we enjoy the gifts of the Spirit—those wonders and glories and miracles that a gracious and benevolent God always has bestowed upon his faithful saints. The first of these gifts listed in our modern revelation on spiritual gifts is the gift of testimony, the gift of revelation, the gift of knowing of the truth and divinity of the work. This gift is elsewhere described as *the testimony of Jesus, which is the spirit of prophecy. This is my gift.* I know this work is true (Bruce R. McConkie, GC, Oct 1972)

———— •◆• ————

One Sunday during sacrament meeting a brother made a moan, stood up stiff, and his eyes rolled back into his head. He was a good size man, so two even larger brethren rushed to his aid and helped escort him out from the chapel pew and into the foyer.

I said a prayer in my mind, asking if I should help with this brother who was also our neighbor and friend. I received nothing in response.

After the next talk, the bishop stood up and asked everyone to use the two doors on the west side of the chapel only, when exiting for their callings and classes following the closing prayer.

Then during the opening of the closing song, I discerned an immediate need to leave the meeting and help. It was as if there was a gentle jolt internally. I stood right up and excused myself, leaving through the proper door to the west. I did a walking run through the hallways around to the opposite foyer.

Our friend lay on a stretcher as paramedics were working on him. Two of the larger men from the stake and bishopric had their heels dug against the bottom of the two doors on the east side. You would hear occasionally loud clanks of the door handle as people/children attempted to come through those doors, in spite of the Bishop's council.

I saw our bishop standing there and thought maybe we needed to administer to the brother. The bishop confirmed that a blessing had already been given. Then I heard these deep guttural noises from the brother in pain and thought to myself, "Oh my! Is that what they call the *death rattle*? Is he dying in the foyer!?"

Now I wondered just why it was so urgent to leave the sacrament meeting. I then noticed his wife standing alone in the middle of the foyer. There were no other sisters in the area, just priesthood leaders. I had another thought, "These brethren are admonished to keep an arm's length. I am the nursery leader and give hugs all the time! This worried wife needs a good hug."

I discerned that our friend was in dire need of comfort. As I approached her, she enveloped me and I comforted her in an extremely long embrace for 8-10 minutes; she was convulsing and sobbing a lot until she finally gained control.

Once she had some composure, she said, "He is having esophageal spasms and they are extremely painful. He's had this before and needs a certain drug for relief. Here are my car keys and his suit coat. Give these to my daughter and instruct her to take the triplets home for us. When we are finished at the hospital can you come and get us and bring us home?"

I assuredly replied, "Sure! Don't worry." Around four hours later we received a call to pick them up from the hospital and they both were much better and relieved.

> Try to live, brethren, so that you can have the Spirit with you in all your activities. Pray for the spirit of discernment that you may hear the promptings of the Spirit and understand them and then pray for courage to do them, to follow the guidance of the Spirit. (Marion G. Romney, GC, April 1980)

> Behold, I, the Lord, will give unto my servant Joseph Smith, Jun., power that he shall be enabled to discern by the Spirit those who shall go up unto the land Zion, and those of my disciples who shall tarry. (D&C 63:41)

On the way to my 41st mission reunion, traveling between Ogden & Salt Lake City, Utah, I commented to my wife, "I feel like there's going to be a new temple between Layton and Farmington, UT." Two days later President Nelson announced seven new temples, one in Layton, Utah! I love this new prophet, as well as the last ones. (Journal 4/1/2018)

> "And it came to pass, as the voice was still speaking, Moses cast his eyes and beheld the earth, yea, even all of it; and

there was not a particle of it which he did not behold, *discerning it by the Spirit of God."* (Moses 1:27)

———————•◆•———————

When I had an awesome experience of feeling another spirit within me in the holy temple I shared my experience. When my wife had a similar sacred experience she drew no attention to herself.

As we knelt across the altar from each other while doing proxy sealings, for American Indian names, my wife became extremely emotional. I knew she was feeling something special which I did not sense or see. The sealer was also very visibly touched and he had to stop several times on this specific female name. For all I know they may have actually witnessed the deceased sister's spirit.

All my wife would say about the experience was, "Did you see how touched the sealer was? He could hardly finish the ordinance!"

My sweet wife has the gift of humility, I don't! (Journal 4/22/2018)

"You have the spiritual DNA of God. You have unique gifts that originated in your spiritual creation and that were developed during the vast span of your premortal life." (Dieter F. Uchtdorf, GC, Oct 2017)

———————•◆•———————

*Elder David W. Patten had the gift of healing:*

When we found any sick I preached to them faith in the ordinances of the Gospel, and where the truth found place in their hearts, I commanded them in the name of the Lord Jesus Christ to arise from their beds of sickness and be made whole; in many instances the people came after me to lay hands on their sick, because of this gift which the Lord had bestowed upon me, and *almost daily, the sick were healed under my hands*: a woman who had an infirmity for nearly twenty years was instantly healed. (David Wyman Patten's journal, Millenial Star, 1864)

———————•◆•———————

*Martin Harris was given one specific spiritual gift in order to help translate from the gold plates—with no other spiritual gifts given until later:*

And you have the gift to translate the plates, and this is the first gift that I bestowed upon you; and I have commanded that you should pretend to no other gift until my purpose is fulfilled in this; for I will grant unto you no other gift until it is finished. (D&C 5:4)

I have recently had the experience, under the direction of the First Presidency, of going through the missions of the Orient. I cannot deny the miracles of God, and I think many of the things I have seen are truly miracles.

Not long ago, I sat in an old high school gymnasium in the city of Seoul, Korea. Just a short time earlier the blood of the young people of Korea had been running in the streets of that strife-ridden city. In our meeting that evening there were over 500 young Koreans. I was told that we have only two married couples who are members of the Church in all of the Seoul District. Our members there are young, forward-looking people. Conducting that gathering was a sandy-haired, Utah farm boy. He conducted with dignity and spoke with ease the language of those people, and after the meeting, as they came up and put their arms around him, and he put his arms around them, I marveled at the power of the gospel of Jesus Christ to change men's hearts.

We then went down to the sad city of Pusan on the southern tip of Korea. We held a street meeting in the park overlooking the harbor. Within a few feet of a great anti-aircraft gun emplacement we opened our meeting, and about 150 curious, intelligent-looking people gathered. A boy from Florida, a missionary of this Church, began to speak. I then wandered down into the crowd with an army sergeant—one of our boys who was taking us around.

A Korean who spoke some English said in substance to the sergeant,

"How long that young man been here?"

"Two years."

"No—he here longer. Americans here fifteen years and not speak our language. Americans not speak Korean like that."

I thought of the words of the Savior as recorded by Mark: "... they shall speak with new tongues" (Mark 16:17) (Gordon B. Hinckley, GC, Oct 1960)

*We have heard many stories over the years of the blessings to brothers and sisters in the mission field and their testimonies which they have given regarding the gift of tongues. When one experiences this wonderful gift, the knowledge of that language is greatly enhanced and flows beautifully. All around are edified.*

495

The Prophet Joseph Smith warns us: "You may speak in tongues for your own comfort, but I lay this down for a rule, that if anything is taught be the gift of tongues, it is not to be received for doctrine." (*TPJS,* 229)

"Speak not in the gift of tongues without understanding it. The devil can speak in tongues." (*TPJS,* 162) *Great advice!*

———————◆———————

My wife, some extended family members and I were attending some meetings for a new multi-level product. The presenter was very convincing as she was sharing some amazing, tear-jerking stories. My extended family and spouse asked what I thought about this impressive woman. I replied, "She has lying eyes. There is something wrong here."

The responses from my family back to me were, "You are so judgmental!—Why do you always have to be so critical?" among other things.

As we proceeded to work with the company a little further, many problems emerged. Too many promises were unfulfilled. People were losing money instead of making money. Those folks with larger investments at risk began to investigate this woman and opened *Pandora's Box.* The impressive presenter was actually a convicted felon. We discovered that all her special stories were tall tales—flat out lies! Her great promises were meant to impress, yet never intended to fulfill. It was all a well-disguised devious ruse to enrich her at the expense of others. She was simply up to her old tricks. (Journal)

We knocked on the door of the drug dealer. The suspect opened the door, and upon seeing us, tried to block our view. But it was too late; we could see the cocaine on his table....His eyes and disarming smile gave me the impression that he was harmless, so I quickly left him and started to move toward the table. The suspect was now behind me. At that instant, I had the distinct, powerful impression come into my mind: **"Beware of the evil behind the smiling eyes."** I immediately turned back toward the suspect. His hand was in his large front pocket. Instinctively I grabbed his hand and pulled it from his pocket. Only then did I see, clutched in his hand, the semiautomatic pistol ready to fire. A flurry of activity followed, and I disarmed the man. (Neil L. Andersen, GC, April 2005) *Elder Anderson shared a friend's story.*

"That I may proceed to bring to pass ... and perform my work ... that men may discern between righteous and the wicked, saith your God." (D&C 101:95)

In 1967 I was asked to translate the pamphlet *The Testimony of Joseph Smith* into Vietnamese ... I was not very good at reading English. I took the pamphlet home and stayed up all night reading it. As I read, something strange happened to me. It was as if someone unseen was helping me understand. The first translator translated word for word; but as I finally understood part of the testimony, I put it aside and wrote my translation in my own words. I translated according to the thoughts and feelings impressed upon me. I did not know it at the time, but I was translating by the spirit.

... the members read it and said they understood what it meant. They said, "It communicates feelings—it affects us." ... So then I translated four or five pamphlets. They were all accepted.

As I worked on those pamphlets, I began to love the Church and the doctrines and teachings of the Gospel. I asked Brother Lewis to send me some missionaries. They taught me for three months and I was baptized.

... I was extended a calling to translate the Book of Mormon ... That night I prayed, "How can I translate this book and still earn a living?" I had ten secretaries, drivers and helpers ... I had a five-story building, but my six children and their families lived there.

Soon after, my son ... came to me early one morning. To my great surprise he gave me a large cash gift he had won in a government contest ... I quit my job to work in some remote area ... After the Book of Mormon, I translated the Doctrine and Covenants and the Pearl of Great Price. Then I started on some more books but was not able to finish because South Viet Nam fell to North Viet Nam ... in 1975 ... when all the missionaries left Viet Nam, they took my translations ... to Salt Lake City. I was not able to see the printed books until 1985. (Cong Ton Nu Tuong-Vy, Out of the Tiger's Den, *Ensign*, June 1989)

Article of Faith #7 "We believe in the *gift of tongues*, prophecy, revelation, visions, healing, interpretation of tongues, and so forth."

We had an interesting experience at the orthodontist. We took our four school-aged children for a checkup due to their crooked teeth. The orthodontist looked over all their choppers and then met with us for a consultation. He explained that all four of our children would need to continue and/or receive full braces immediately.

I stated, "That's quite a financial burden to place on a family all at once. How could all of our children possibly need braces at the very same time? What'd you do, buy a new boat?! Here's what we're going to do; we'll bring one of our children in every 18 months for their full braces."

As we were leaving the facility, the receptionist stood up and grabbed my shoulder, stopped me, and whispered in my ear, "You were right; he did just buy a new boat!"

Once we started *our braces plan* I received a positively pleasing notice from the company I worked for. The company's new benefit plan would provide an extra $2,000 cash/year for any family member's dental/orthodontic needs. What was interesting is that this plan was in place for all the years our children had those high expenses. Once the expenses were gone, the great dental policy also vanished.

I believe this was a blessing of paying tithes and offerings. The windows of heaven often pour out a variety of blessings, such as: A better job, good health, wealth, debt reduction, reduced expenses, nothing breaking down, increased love, peacefulness, a variety of blessings, etc.

"The Spirit of the Lord spake by me, and his was in my tongue." (2 Samuel 23:2)

Sometimes your spiritual gifts can work synergistically to bless your fellow sojourners upon the earth. With my spiritual gifts of discernment and the love for babies/small children, I find these gifts work in tandem at times. Not by choice however, yet only when heaven chooses to combine them and presents the options to the spiritual end user are many spiritual gifts available. During those special times I am able to discern a mother's future needs for her baby/babies.

We were in a booth at a conference my wife attended. A young mother stopped by with twin 5-month-old baby girls. I just had to ask her their age and their names and compliment their angelic beauty. Then I felt impressed to share with the mother, "If you find you have a need for either one of your babies or both, don't hesitate to ask me. I'm very good with infants and have a lot of free-time here." She thanked us and was off to other booths.

During the lunch hour we took turns to eat. Crowds really aren't my thing, so I bought some food and headed up to the stage. (The booths were all set up in a college gymnasium floor.) I was on stage left at a cafeteria table, enjoying being all by myself. I could watch the crowds at a distance. I was able to view my wife's booth to see if she needed my assistance.

As I was eating, I heard a cry and looked over to stage right and saw the young mother with the twins sitting against the wall by the curtains. The first thing I recognized was actually the colorful double stroller.

I observed that she was scanning the gym floor and looking for someone. When her eyes finally reached me, she called and waved me over. I went immediately to see what she wanted. Both of her baby beauties were fussing.

She explained, "My babies are hungry and I can only nurse one at a time. Would you mind taking her while I feed her sister? When she's through; we can switch babies and I'll feed the other one."

I told her that sounded awesome and that I was more than glad to help. The second baby was much easier to care for whereas she had just eaten and was content.

"And all these gifts come by the Spirit of Christ; and they come unto every man severally, according as he will." (Moroni 10:17)

On a beautiful spring afternoon we were in the Ogden, UT, airport terminal waiting with a bunch of other passengers to fly to Phoenix, AZ, on Allegiant Air. I noticed in the waiting area there was a young woman with a toddler and a baby. Of course she had all the paraphernalia that goes with little ones: stroller, baby seat, diaper bag, and toys.

I stopped to visit with her and said, "Boy, you have your hands full! I'm traveling with my wife and two sons and we would be glad to offer you assistance, should you need any. I love children and would love to help."

She replied, "Thank you but I am used to handling them. We probably won't see you again because our seats are clear up on row 2."

I came back with, "Well that's perfect actually because we will be sitting in row 1!" I complimented her little ones and walked back to my family.

As we walked outside to go up the stairs to the plane, a young father with a baby was having a heck of a time folding up a stroller. I offered to take the little one or the stroller and he handed me the latter. I folded the stroller up for him and we all boarded. We sat comfortably in the front of the plane and were looking forward to seeing lots of family on my wife's side. Her father was celebrating his 75th birthday at a resort.

As we visited, someone tapped me on the shoulder. It was the young mother from the waiting area. She said, "Could I impose upon you to hold my baby? My little boy has to go to the bathroom really bad."

I replied, "I would love to!" She handed me her little bundle of joy. The two of us bonded quickly and I enjoyed the baby for quite a while. This all happened before we taxied to the runway. I find it interesting in that the Lord, only, knew this young woman would need some help in the near future. I was able to discern a future need through the Lord's grace when He activated my gifts.

"... We believe in the gift of the Holy Ghost, the power of faith, the enjoyment of the spiritual gifts according to the will of God ..." (*TPJS,* 121)

We had six wonderful years serving in our Stake Young Men's presidency. Our presidency met at least once a month in order to keep on top of a multitude of various youth activities. One evening the other counselor and I were assigned to inventory our stake closet prior to an upcoming event. As we walked down the long hallway, to the other end of the church, I clearly discerned that my peer would become our new stake president.

Seemingly out of the blue I blurted, "We're sure going to miss you in Young Men's."

"Why's that?"

"Well you're going to be our new stake president!"

He looked very serious as consternation ran across his face. I could imagine him thinking, "I haven't told anyone. I don't think my wife even knows him! I'm sure she hasn't told anybody. He wasn't around any of our meetings. How could he know this?" He kind of mumbled and then quickly changed the subject.

One-and-a-half weeks later, he was sustained as our new stake president. He served valiantly during his calling. (Journal 2/12/2006)

At times we receive interesting revelations that should only be shared with those involved, if anybody. I did receive the same discernment on his replacement. I mentioned this to my wife only, telling her that our bishop was going to make a great stake president right away. Within a week, our bishop was called to be our stake president and he's served superbly in both leadership callings. I am not sure why these truths come and definitely cannot predict when, nor where, discernment will exhibit its truthful light.

These discernments were not prophecies in any way; they were simply truths being revealed. Those two great brethren had already been "called of God by prophecy." For some reason their new callings were revealed to me between the times they were respectively called by God and being sustained by their leaders and peers.

> "... for all the gifts of the Spirit are not visible to the natural vision, or understanding of man; indeed very few of them are." (*TPJS*, 244)

We received an abnormally high water bill one month. I had a strong discernment that the bill was not correct at all. I called the city water department to question our bill.

She replied, "Have you checked your toilets? One or more must be draining or leaking."

"No, but I'll check and call your back." Upon several flushes and quietly listening there were no drains or leaks in any of the toilets.

"I checked our toilets and they are solid and there are no leaks. Do you think the problem could possibly be on your end?"

"Nope; everything's in order here. Check under your sinks, the dishwasher, the water heater and anything else in your home that water pipes are linked to. There must be a serious leak."

"I checked everything in the house and there are no leaks. Are you sure the issue isn't on your end?"

"You need to go under your home and check all the other water pipes. That must be where the leak is."

Under our home everything was bone dry. There was not a leak or drip anywhere.

"Why don't you just humor me and have the water meter guy come back and recheck? I am confident the problem is on your end, not ours."

"Um, sir, I'm sorry to report that the meter reader transposed the numbers on your meter. It was 317 and he wrote the number down as 731! When he arrived at your home and saw the meter actually at only 450, he realized his error. I am issuing you a $200 credit."

"Thank you!"

The gift of discernment has saved us thousands of dollars from many companies' errors and mistakes. This special gift has protected us from the evil designs of people also. It is a great spiritual gift I hope to never loose. We can never be too careful, however, regarding our spiritual gift/s.

Remember that the wisest person on earth was blessed with a double-dose of wisdom and squandered his wonderful spiritual gift by worshiping other God's through his marriages to non-Israelite women.

*Note: Jesus is actually the wisest being next to Heavenly Father, however they are both Gods.*

> And God gave Solomon wisdom and understand exceeding much, and largeness of heart, even as the sand that is on the sea shore. ... For he was wiser than all men ... And there came of all people to hear the wisdom of Solomon, from all kings of the earth, which had heard of his wisdom." (1 Kings 4:29, 31, 34)

> And the LORD was angry with Solomon, because his heart was turned from the LORD God of Israel, which had appeared unto him twice. And had commanded him concerning this thing, that he should not go after other gods: but he kept not that which the LORD commanded." (1 Kings 11:9-10)

———— •◆• ————

When I was on my mission, the branch president had served for many years and the word got out somehow that he would be released. Excitement rippled through the branch as members speculated who would be the next branch president.

Most people thought it would be the first counselor, who had served a long time and knew the ropes. He himself felt confident that he would be called; he argued that it was the logical choice. He seemed to have a following since many people agreed with him.

However, out of the blue, a name came to my mind and I knew it was not my own thought. I was sure the first counselor would not be the new branch president. Instead, a humble man, a convert of just two years, was called.

It was no surprise to me since I had already been told. Some people were shocked and some were very disappointed, saying, "How can he know what to do? He's a new convert!" I testified that this man was called of God. I never doubted that he was the right person for the calling. (A relative)

*I remember being in various church meetings over the years where similar feelings were voiced. Members would often believe the choice of leadership was wrong or not the best. Those that have doubts in this area should go to their knees and ask for the understanding of callings and how they work. I know from many experiences that Heavenly Father and Jesus Christ lead this Restored Gospel and direct their work in righteousness. Callings come through inspiration from heaven the high majority of the time.*

President Kimball provided this quote, from his predecessor (President Harold B. Lee), to a national newspaper: "The Lord directs the affairs of his church through continuing revelation. To those who do not believe in revelation, there is no satisfactory answer, to those who believe in revelation, there should be no question." (*New York Times*, Sept 10, 1974)

*Think of the struggle the prophet Samuel had when he was asked to select a new king to replace King Saul from Jesse's family—Samuel:*

"... looked on Elias and said, Surely the Lord's anointed is before him. But the Lord said unto Samuel, Look not on his countenance, or on the height of his stature ... the Lord looketh upon the heart." (1 Sam 16:6-7)

*As David was out tending sheep, Elias was admiring David's seven brother's countenances and statures. It's simply human nature!*

———————◆———————

We were newlyweds living in a, new to us, married student ward at BYU in 1981. On the second Sunday, the bishop invited me to come to his office and visit. I wondered what calling he had for me already. To my surprise, that was not the case at all.

The bishop started with questions like: "So how is school? Are you getting good grades? How is your marriage? Are you happy?"

"Everything's great! School is going very well and I am really enjoying married life."

"Is your wife in school? How is she doing? Is she happy? Does she feel like you have a good marriage?"

"Yes, she is enjoying school, life, and marriage. She seems very happy."

Then he dropped the bombshell, saying, "We have a matter of great concern and I need to discuss it with you privately. Are you aware that your wife was married before and has had a child? And another problem is that she is still married to her original husband!"

I discerned that the information the bishop shared was an untruth. Yet, how was I supposed to deny what the bishop was telling me. How could I tell my bishop he was wrong?

I replied with a small chuckle, "No, I don't believe that's right."

The bishop retorted, "This is not a laughing matter! You must look at this situation seriously!" The bishop then explained, "We may be looking at some serious consequences here. Not only are we looking at church action, but legal action too! Bigamy is against the law in the state of Utah! I'm sorry to have to tell you all this."

My confidence swelled with those remarks and I surprised myself. I did not want to tell the bishop he was wrong but I could tell him his information/source was wrong. "bishop, I'm sorry but you must have incorrect information. This is an untruth! I am very confident that I married a virgin! Please go back and check your records and sources then get back with me when you find the true answers!"

The Bishop was only trying to save an innocent young elder from starting life with a humongous skeleton hidden in the closet.

A couple of weeks later, the bishop invited me to visit with him in his office once again.

Following a few pleasantries, he said, "We investigated deeper into your wife's situation and we found a problem with the Church membership records. Somehow, the Church had given the same ID number to two different members, one being a single mother with a child and a separated husband. The other, is obviously your wife. So, you don't have anything to worry about now."

I thanked our bishop and asked if his membership clerk couldn't please take care of this serious record issue and put this problem to bed. He affirmed that that would be the case.

About 6 months later we found a better apartment to live in while we finished out our schooling. We found ourselves in another married student ward. After a few weeks attending, the bishop of our new ward called me into his office for a visit. Again, I wondered what my new calling was going to be—until I saw his face.

He had a look of consternation strewn across his face. He thanked me for coming in and told me he had a serious matter to discuss with me.

I replied, "Let me guess; my wife was married to someone else, is not divorced, and has already given birth to a baby!"

This bishop shot back with, "Oh good, you're already aware of the situation!"

He was really shocked that I was laughing so I quickly related the experience with our previous bishop and then asked, "Do you have a really, really good membership clerk?"

He confirmed the same and this time the membership clerk actually did get the incorrect records issue taken care of. Once again, emotions can easily be mistaken for spiritual feelings.

———————————————

I remember one young man who asked for counsel about his educational choices. He was a freshman at a very good university. A week after I had given the advice, he scheduled an appointment with me.

When he came into the office, he surprised me by asking, "Bishop, could we pray before we talk? And could we kneel? And may I pray?"

His requests surprised me. But his prayer surprised me even more. It went something like this: "Heavenly Father, You know that Bishop Eyring gave me advice last week, and it didn't work. Please inspire him to know what I am to do now.

Now you might smile at that, but I didn't. He already knew what the Lord wanted him to do. But he honored the office of a bishop in the Lord's Church and perhaps wanted me to have the chance to gain greater confidence to receive revelation in that calling.

It worked. As soon as we stood up and then sat down, the revelation came to me. I told him what I felt the Lord would have him to do. He was only 18 years old then, but he was mature in spiritual years. (Henry B Eyring, GC, Oct 2017)

"... being filled with the Spirit of God, therefore he perceived the thoughts ..." (Alma 18:16)

———————————————

After finishing up a semester at BYU, our final grades came in. I received a B in one class and discerned that it was wrong; my grade should have been an A. I contacted the professor and voiced my concern. He told me everything was in order and no grades were missing. Professors are not big fans of anyone telling them they made a mistake. He suggested that my B was a decent passing grade.

After I arrived back at my apartment I had another distinct discernment that the grade definitely was incorrect. I didn't have any idea why, I just knew it was wrong. I connected with my professor again and explained my strong impressions. After basically bearing my testimony to him, he agreed to take a closer look.

As it turned out, he called me to apologize. My final test had 48 of 50 questions right and I was credited one point per correct answer. I was supposed to be credited 2 points for each correct answer on that major test for a 96%. The erroneous 48% grade on my final took my A average for the semester down to a B. It is not easy to get a final grade changed in college. Because it was fully his department's fault, they did do what it took to change my grade and GPA records even though the semester was over.

The following year in college, a nearly identical event occurred when my final grades arrived. Once again I received a B grade in a class and discerned that this was not the actual grade earned. I immediately contacted this professor and met up with him to review my concerns.

I shared with him my gift of discernment. He wasn't buying it! He claimed I hadn't turned in my final test and that brought my A average down to a B. (I humorously thought, "I've got to stop getting F's on my final tests at BYU!")

I explained to him that I was present during the final exam and that I did turn my final in to him. I distinctly remembered it.

He wouldn't budge, explaining, "It is almost impossible to change a final grade after the semester is over."

The previous professor had set precedence with the first final grade error; I knew that it was possible to change a grade after the fact. I asked the professor, "When can I meet with you again? I will prove to you that I took my final exam!"

He set up a time; acting like it was only to humor me and would likely be a waste of his time.

This was a religion class, so I grabbed my personal journal and brought that to our next meeting. I kept a daily journal and had recorded each exam and how I felt my performance was respectively. To the doubting religion professor I said, "These are my personal scriptures and here is the verse proving I took your final. Following is the verse regarding my guesstimate of performance and outcome on your final exam to us."

He actually read my journal entries.

Once again, I was bearing testimony of the truthfulness of my actions. I finalized my comments with, "Why on earth would I attend class all year, maintaining an A average and then skip the final test? That does not make sense … because it is not the truth of what really happened."

The Spirit of Truth must have touched this professor of religion.

He turned 180 degrees and came around to my side. He promised, "Well, I cannot deny that. I will see if I can get your grade changed to an A. Great job on keeping a journal; you have already been blessed by doing so!

Your final was either stuck to the back of someone else's paper or mislaid somewhere." That felt like the real truth.

I believe we separated both feeling a lot better. I felt best when he later confirmed he was able to change my grade to an A. I thanked him for believing in me and my journal.

I thought, "It's kind of weird to have to use a journal, testimony, and spiritual promptings to keep your GPA up at *the Lord's University!*" I have been grateful for my journals on multiple occasions and have witnessed bounteous blessings, not to mention both B's rightfully becoming A's. (Journal 7/8/1981)

> "There is no perfect operation of the power of discernment without revelation from God. That is why the righteous are given the power of the Holy Ghost." (Joseph Smith, Gospel Doctrine, 61)

Being in sales all my life necessitated extensive travel throughout the U.S. and Canada. Not only did I enjoy the perks of being a frequent flyer; I soon relished the benefits of also being a frequent hotel guest. I gave all the business I could to Marriott and Holiday Inn, receiving free nights or suite upgrades, respectively.

Most of the towns I visited had a Holiday Inn Express and they would upgrade me to very nice suites three out of four stays. My stays were usually two-four days. I had pulled in for a three-day stay in southern Utah. I showed the desk manager my platinum card.

He explained, "I'm sorry sir, we don't have any suites available; thank you for staying with us again."

I immediately discerned his statement was not reality or truth.

Pulling out my Ipad, I quickly logged onto the hotel's reservation site and pretended to rent a suite for the next three days at that hotel. Not one, but two suites were actually available to choose from. I showed my findings to the manager and asked if he would please explain this.

Glancing at his computer screen he came back with, "Oh, I guess a suite just became available." He extended a free upgrade.

Not pushing the issue, nor being critical, I simply replied, "Thank you very much!" The suite was very nice. (Journal, 11/16/2014)

*We are all blessed with varying gifts; otherwise the Church would be rather boring. We are meant to bless and serve one another, in and out of the Gospel, with our multiple spiritual gifts from God.*

*I have heard a loud audible voice, had prayers answered through clear dreams/visions, have sensed and felt righteous and evils presences nearby (at different times), and been blessed to hear the still, small voice on multiple occasions. Yet, I have never seen an angel, spirit, nor had a visible visitation from any beings. I do know of people who are visually gifted and see spiritual things.*

> *Elder Lund confided:* I am not hesitant to say that I have never seen an angel, heard an audible voice speak to me, seen any kind of vision, or had any kind of remarkable dream. Nor have most people I know. *The Lord has chosen to speak to me through quieter, more subtle, forms of revelation,* and my life has been continually blessed by that. (Gerald N Lund, *Hearing the Voice of the Lord*, 41)

> "During my life I have heard and read of people's hearing a voice and obeying it. I believe these experiences, even though I have never heard the voice speak out loud to me. ... when you are inspired, a certain confirming feeling accompanies the thoughts in your mind. You learn to recognize and understand that the Holy Ghost does bear witness. He does speak in a still small voice—which is not always words. (S. Dilworth Young, *New Era*, Oct 1971)

> I did not live in the days of our Savior; he has not come to me in person. *I have not beheld him.* His Father and he have not felt it necessary to grant me such a great blessing as this. But it is not necessary. I have felt his presence. I know that *the Holy Spirit has enlightened my mind and revealed him unto me,* so that I do love my Redeemer. (Joseph Fielding Smith, *TPC*, 49-50)

*Elder Joseph Fielding Smith had been an Apostle over 38 years when he wrote the above statement found in our church manuals.*

> "I have had the administration of angels in my day and time, though I never prayed for an angel. *I have had*, in several instances, *the administration of holy messengers.*" (*Discourses of Wilford Woodruff*, 289)

> President Heber J. Grant testified, "Four times in my life *I have been permitted to read the thoughts of people.*" (*Gospel Standards*, Improvement Era, 1969, 193)

When Alma and Amulek were testifying to the unrighteous lawyer Zeezrom; Alma revealed the following:

"... thou has not lied unto men only but thou hast lied unto God; for behold, he knows all thy thoughts, and thou seest that *thy thoughts are made known unto us by his Spirit;*" (Alma 12:3)

————◆◆◆————

Coming home from work late one evening I was approaching our Stake Center and had a strong prompting to pull into the parking lot and go into the church. I was surprised because it was after 7pm on a Wednesday, Mutual night, and there was no noise coming from the halls, nor the gym. I walked down a long quiet hall and then opened the door to the gymnasium.

As I opened that door another door, kitty corner from me, started to open. The gym was completely empty. I was pleased to see one of my daughters appear in the doorway. We walked towards each other and met at mid court and embraced. She appeared very concerned.

We then began conversing and I explained to her what her predicament was, what the ramifications of her choices would be, and the best road she should choose to travel.

She exclaimed, "Dad! How could you possibly know all that? I haven't told anyone!"

I replied that I had the gift of discernment that comes from God and that the Godhead knows all things. Sometimes they choose to reveal actual truths, even though no one else knows about them, for the benefit and betterment of mankind and sometimes for reasons unknown to us.

"For it shall be given you in the very hour, yea, in the very moment, what ye shall say." (D&C 100:6)

————◆◆◆————

During our mission in Sweden we had only five dinner appointments over eighteen months. Two of these were on Christmas and one was a lunch meeting, when as a greenie I got in trouble for *putting the lid on the sandwich!* The Swedes enjoy their sandwiches open faced.

We came across two inactive sisters and they greeted us at the door with, "Oh, Elders, you look famished! You must be hungry. Come in and let us feed you."

That offer was sweet music to our ears and stomachs after the "meal drought." Their names were Thea and Helga. One had worked as a cook and the other as a baker for their entire careers. (They both had been brokenhearted as young women and never married—now in their late sixties. One was shafted by her best boyfriend and the other's beau had died during a war.)

I had never known anyone to whip up a five-course meal so quickly. The Swedish meatballs and new potatoes were absolutely divine. Their desserts were heavenly. We set up a weekly discussion/feast and became good friends through feasts following famine.

We were attempting to discern why these two giggly sisters stopped going to church about twelve years prior. As we would show them a film and/or give them a lesson after dinner, they would come up with an excuse as to why they stopped attending any church meetings or services. I had a firm discernment that their excuse was not the real reason.

I would tell them, "No, that is not why you stopped going to church." We would still part with hugs and smiles while setting our next week's appointment. Every week, for six weeks, they would give us a new excuse. Each week I would discern this was not the true reasoning and I would firmly tell them, "That is not why, that is not it!" They would smile and send us off. They were so cute because they could finish each other's sentences, having lived together for so long. We nicknamed them "Chip and Dale."

After running out of excuses, they finally confessed to the real reason. They had a third sister. The three of them had a big argument and to spite the one, these two stopped going to church.

I asked them if their sister still attended.

They affirmed that she did.

I asked them if they thought she was happy.

They said she probably was.

I asked them if they might be happier attending church again.

They thought it was possible.

We testified of the same.

After two months of enjoyable visits and fantastic feasts we were able to get them back to church and make amends with their sister. This was in Malmö, Sweden where there was an actual real chapel. As we sat in the middle of the congregation, the sun was streaming in large rays through the tall slender windows.

The branch president asked us to stand and sing, "*Jag är Guds Lilla Barn/I am a Child of God.*" There was not a dry eye in the audience. The branch president, the three sisters, and two elders began crying heavily. The tears freely falling from the branch president's cheeks caused us to be even more tearful.

It was a warm spiritual welcoming for these two sisters and they felt the love of the members, their sister, the Elders, the branch presidency and the Godhead! This had to be the most glorious day on my mission. I can still feel the Spirit of this occasion in strength to this day! (Missionary journal, 1978)

> "There Is Sunshine In My Soul Today … More glorious and bright." (*Hymns*, no.227)

———— •◆• ————

*Elder Marvin J. Asthon shares some ideas on spiritual gifts:*

One of the great tragedies of life, it seems to me, is when a person classifies himself as someone who has no talents or gifts. … Let me mention a few gifts that are not always evident or noteworthy but are very important. Among these may be your gifts—gifts not so evident but nevertheless real and valuable. Let us review some of these non-conspicuous gifts: the gift of asking; the gift of listening; the gift of hearing and using the still, small voice; the gift of being able to weep; the gift of avoiding contention; the gift of being agreeable; the gift of avoiding vain repetition; the gift of seeking that which is righteousness; the gift of not passing judgment; the gift of looking to God for guidance; the gift of being a disciple; the gift of caring for others; the gift of being able to ponder; the gift of offering prayer; the gift of bearing a mighty testimony; and the gift of receiving the Holy Ghost. (GC, Oct 1987)

"The gifts of teaching wisdom, teaching knowledge, exceedingly great faith, healing with exceedingly great faith, working mighty miracles, prophesying all things, beholding **angels and ministering spirits**, etc." (See Moroni 10)

———— •◆• ————

We co-owned a retail health food store for thirteen years. About the middle of our tenure, we had two business men present a management program to improve our business. Both were likeable and I felt they were honest and sincere. Their business model looked fine. There were no red flags whatsoever.

Then I received a definite discernment—that this business model would not be right for our store. Following the presentation my partner and I discussed the offering. I told him of my strong feeling. Even though I was the minority shareholder he respected my position; we told them "Thanks, but no thanks."

They were surprised and asked, "Well why not?"

I told them I was not sure why, but there was a strong *gut feeling* not to run with it. I had the impression that something beyond their control would have affected our business relationship in a harmful and negative way.

> "Thus we see that the Holy Ghost is a witness of the Father and the Son, a comforter, a teacher, and the bearer of valuable gifts of the spirit, such as wisdom, knowledge, faith, discernment, and direction." (Franklin D. Richards, GC, 1973)

———◆——

*Because of his great faith, Brigham Young enjoyed many of the gifts of the Spirit, such as revelation, prophecy, and speaking in tongues. He wrote:*

> A few weeks after my baptism I was at Brother Kimball's house one morning, and while family prayer was being offered up, brother Alpheus Gifford commenced speaking in tongues. Soon the Spirit came on me, and I spoke in tongues, and we thought only of the day of Pentecost, when the Apostles were clothed upon with cloven tongues of fire (Brigham Young, *TPC*, 2.8).

———◆——

My morning started in Dillon, Montana. I was on a longer than usual sales trip and working my way through eastern Idaho to get to two accounts each in Jackson and Pinedale, Wyoming. That afternoon, after finishing up in Pinedale, my wife called and said she was at a retreat in Lava Hot Springs, Idaho. She wondered if I would like to come stay with her in Lava. I explained that I was really tired and that it was a long drive. (There was no quick way to travel between where we both were. The route is decent for an eagle flying, but I would have to take 5 or 6 different highways to make the connection.)

She had a carrot on a stick and explained, "There are three or four babies here that you will really like! And the conference people are providing a nice warm dinner for all of us. You should come."

I must admit that, unlike most men, babies wake me up and are exciting vs. being tiring and needy.

I arrived just in time to enjoy a great dinner before they cleaned it all up. While my wife was off visiting with peers, I went to a large empty room that had a wall length padded bench along it. I sat on the left side just to relax and rest from a long tiring day on the road. A woman with an eighteen-month old girl in a harness, with a leash, sat a ways down from me. I heard the little girl making noises and noticed that she had the rope stretched to the max as she was leaning towards me and reaching out for me. The toddler's smiled glowed.

I smiled and waved at her and then went back to my rest. She made some more noises and this time the mother released her. The toddler came running over to me and jumped into my arms and gave me the longest loving hug. I must absorb little ones energy because I wasn't tired anymore.

I turned to her mother and asked, "So, why did you finally decide to let her go?"

She surprised me with, "I said a little prayer and asked God if you were a weirdo or a creep. I got the answer that you were safe."

"Oh."

"She sure likes you!"

"I really love all babies and children—and most of them really love me."

Now the mother was resting and I enjoyed her little girl for about one hour. After this mom and toddler left, I found the other babies and toddlers and held all but one of them, a newborn girl. I got to know their names and found out a little about each one of them from their mothers.

Later my wife and I went off to a very old hotel room. The original cupboards were metal and in colors our grandparents would like. At least the bathroom and bed were updated. We were quite tired that night and hoped to sleep in because there was no reason to get up early. Don't you absolutely hate it when you need and want a good night's sleep and then you cannot sleep in? We were wide awake at 5:30 am. There was no noise, we just woke up two hours before we needed to and I mean wide awake and alert. So we decided to take a shower and wait for the town to open.

I always like to read a newspaper in the morning; this was one of President Gordon B. Hinckley's habits also, so it seemed like a good thing to do. We were ready for the day real early and just read scriptures and visited while we spent our sleep time as alert as chipmunks. I got this strong urge-like impression to immediately go and get my newspaper. The little café across the side street didn't have any newspapers, but they directed me to a place down the road and across the main street.

Cars were parked bumper to bumper and you had to carefully peek around a truck or vehicle with tubes tied to the top and sides to watch for oncoming traffic. Every intersection was a blind spot. This reminded me of Park City, UT, during major events; Cody, WY, during the July 4th celebrations; or Jackson Hole, WY, in the summer. Small towns with limited parking and excess tourist vehicles also describe Lava Hot Springs' summers. I carefully found a clearing and quickly crossed the street.

As I was crossing the dirt road, about two blocks long, which intersected with the main drag and led to the event my wife was and would be attending, I noticed one of the toddlers I had befriended the night before. She was headed directly for one of the dangerous busy road's blind spots and that put me into action. I ran over and stopped her before she could walk onto the main street.

She was sobbing, trembling, and muttering: "M...m...mommy? M...m...mommy?" She was in stocking feet and a little nightgown. Her white socks were now black on the sides and bottoms from the dew drenched dirt road.

She recognized me, so that was obviously comforting to her—no *stranger danger* here. She was happy with me versus being more freaked out and frightened. She still did not stop quivering or asking for her mommy though. I asked her where her mommy was. She shook her head no. I was glad I could call her by name after learning it the night before.

I got her back to her nervous mother who was nursing a newborn. The mother had gone in the bathroom to feed the baby and her little daughter did not see mommy go in there. She assumed her mommy had gone to the car and that's why she was walking to the road to look for mommy's car and mommy. Now the mother needed to comfort her little angel which gave me an opportunity to finally hold the content newborn angel.

Once again, Heavenly Father used my habits (daily newspaper), an early wake-up call, along with a *do it now* prompting to prevent a serious accident from happening to this sweet little girl. It could have been a deadly mishap from a blindsided accident. I feel confident that our Heavenly Father, through the Holy Ghost, and using me as an instrument saved her life that early morning. (Journal 8/31/2008)

> "And this is the blessing which hath been bestowed upon
> us, that we have been made instruments in the hands of
> God to bring about this great work." (Alma 26:3)

We had a conversion van with four "captain's chairs" and it was packed to the gills with suitcases, sleeping bags, quilts, blankets, books, toys, food, and cleaning supplies (some child/children would lose their lunch on each road trip). My wife said she had a prompting to **"leave it in"** when she tried to replace our large first aid kit with a much smaller version. Our son's Scout leader worked at the local hospital and he was able to outfit each of the Scout's with these oversized "has everything-you-might-need kits."

My wife obeyed the prompting and packed around the large first aid kit. We loaded our five children up, after running them through the bathroom, and headed south on Highway 89. All three of my wife's living grandparents lived in Kanab, UT, which is just above the Arizona line. We were all looking forward to seeing their great grandparents, enjoying a delicious meal, and then sleeping soundly in their dark, comfortable basement.

After we gassed up in Panguitch, UT, we soon started toward the canyon where the road followed the path of the winding Sevier River. (The road is much wider and somewhat straighter now days.) It was a dark, cold winter night and hardly anyone was on the road. There was just an hour-and-a-half left to travel. We had the cruise control set at 60 mph as we inched ever closer to grandmas. We had no issues on our trip so far.

Finally a group of cars approached from the opposite direction. As they passed, by a few small rocks flipped up and hit our car. I thought, "Great, another chip in the windshield." As I now watched the cars in my rearview mirror I discerned that something was severely wrong. I had no idea what, yet it was an extremely strong feeling. We kept on down the highway at a steady speed nevertheless.

First I checked all the gauges on the instrument panel. We had plenty of gas, the car wasn't overheating, and the oil pressure looked good. There were no warning lights on whatsoever. Then I asked my wife, "Is everything okay?"

She replied, "Yes, why!"

Without replying to her, I loudly asked the children, "Is everyone okay back there? Is something wrong with any of you?"

One of the teenagers shot back with, "What's wrong with you dad?"

Tamara confirmed that all the children were fine. "What's wrong?" she questioned me.

"I don't know, but somebody needs help somewhere."

The best way I can describe this feeling is in the Star Wars jargon "I felt a disturbance in the Force." I knew for a surety that someone needed help. I looked back at the cars disappearing into the darkness. Through periodic mirror checks I never saw any brake lights or flashers. I was clueless as to where the problem lay. There were no warning signs inside or outside the vehicle, only internal feelings.

I looked up towards heaven and pleaded, "What is it?"

A clear and calm voice quickly responded, stating, "**Someone has gone off the road**."

I immediately hit the brakes and finally came to a stop in the canyon. I did a slow seven-point turn while being yelled at by my family.

"You're going to kill us all!"

"You can see lights bouncing off of canyon walls at night, nobody's coming right now."

"Why are we going the wrong way?"

"Someone has gone off the road."

"How do you know? Did you see something?"

"No. I felt something was wrong, prayed about it, and the Holy Ghost told me '**Someone has gone off the road.**' That's how I know."

I then pleaded inside, "Please don't let them be in that icy river. I'll go in if I have to, but, please not the icy water!" There was a thick blanket of frozen snow on the ground and it was very cold.

We drove back slower and looked off to the right side, where the road drops off. After about five miles we all saw a car some distance from the road and saw "stuff" strewn all over the crusted snow. I was sorry for them, yet very grateful the car was in a spot where the river bowed away from the highway. It was a very cold night with some moonlight.

We found two young oriental couples and only the driver was moving. He got out of the car with a small flash light and was in shock.

He was walking slowly in a big circle, crying, "Mena … oh, Mena."

We didn't know if that was his girlfriend's/wife's name or a foreign phrase. Our main concern regarding him was to periodically check on him to make sure he didn't climb up to the road or go towards the icy river. Their air bags had deployed and as far as we could tell they were all wearing seatbelts. From what we could gather later, they were four Japanese students or young adults from Los Angeles in a rental car.

As we approached the crash, we could see that all of the windows were broken out. The passenger door was ripped completely off. The hood and trunk were both wide open. The car roof was caved in on the right side. There were open suitcases and personal belongings strewn everywhere across the snow. One young woman was hanging out the front right door-less side, retained only by the seatbelt strap.

We had our oldest daughter keep the smaller children in the van and off the highway. A single man in a pickup came upon us and he came down to help too. Our oldest son helped us carry our quilts, blankets, and sleeping bags down to the injured four. The couple in the back made painful moaning sounds. We put things around them to help them keep warm. We got a blanket and wrapped it around the driver who was still mumbling while plodding in circles in shock.

We were not sure if the young woman hanging from the passenger seat was even alive. She made no sound or movement. I was shocked to see her face so full of large glass shards that it was difficult to distinguish her features. Thinking she may be dead or possibly alive, we made a decision to lay her out on a sleeping bag and quilt and cover her with a couple of blankets. My wife knelt beside her, held her hand, and prayed for her. I looked down at the girl's legs because something looked out of kilter. One foot was pointing skyward while the other pointed to the ground, 180 degrees in the opposite direction. I thought, "Oh my goodness, her leg is totally twisted the wrong way!"

As we did our best to keep them stable and warm I learned two great lessons:

First, blood makes me pass out. I missed all five of our children's births intentionally. In this instance, the Lord turned my weakness into strength and the blood didn't affect me. I always thought the scripture meant a weakness could become a permanent strength. Now I know one could be strengthened temporarily, as needed, "in the moment." My wife gets antsy at times and she carried herself cool, calm, and collective as a summer morning; she was likewise strengthened for the specific occasion.

Secondly, we were very prepared for ourselves by packing all the sleeping bags, quilts, blankets, large first aid kit, and food. I did not realize that we would be using our preparations for total strangers. I had the impression/thought, "Having good food and preparation storage may be used by someone else, but we'll be blessed for being obedient; even if we don't use the other supplies and eat the stored food ourselves."

All of the crash victims were very bloody. That large first aid kit came in very handy. There was an ample supply of gauze and tape. We patched the four up on all their bloody spots that were visible. The cold weather also helped the blood to coagulate quickly. At this time, the blankets, quilts, and sleeping bags were priceless to them; we didn't really need them. The inspired first aid kit with everything came in very handy.

This was prior to the cell phone craze so we had no way to contact anyone. All we could do was comfort them as we attempted to keep them from freezing and as we continued praying for the crash victims.

After about twenty five minutes my wife exclaimed, "She squeezed my hand; she's alive!"

At thirty minutes later, a highway patrol man came upon the scene and asked us for an update on this accident. He radioed the volunteer ambulance in Panguitch, Utah. It was another twenty minutes before the ambulance arrived.

Upon arriving the EMT's enlisted us as volunteers as we all helped place and hold on oxygen masks, checked blood pressure, strapped them to gurneys, and whatever else they directed us to do. It took four of us (teenage son, myself, highway patrolman, and the man helping) with some effort to slowly take each gurney up the steep hillside, one after another.

They were able to place one gurney on each side, another on the floor, and the last hanging from the ceiling of the ambulance.

After the ambulance was gone, the highway patrolman asked me to fill out an accident report. I did not realize how cold it was. I could not physically grip the pen to write anything.

The patrolman turned up his heater and said, "Sit in my car for awhile and warm up until you can write."

I marveled at all the bells, whistles, and big shotgun surrounding me in the car. I understood it was around 20 degrees Fahrenheit that evening.

I finally warmed up and was ready to fill in the questions on the patrolman's report:

"Did you witness the accident?"

"NO."

"If you didn't witness the accident, how did you find out about it?"

"God told me, '**Someone has gone off the road.**' I felt someone needed help and turned our car around to find them and the spot I was led to."

"Did someone tell you about the accident?"

"The Holy Ghost."

I thought, "This is going to be an interesting police report to read. I hope someone feels the spirit of it."

After checking out the area, the patrolman said, "Their car flipped once and then rolled several times."

We all thanked each other and parted ways. We had a family prayer before taking off. We called our grandparents to explain the accident and our hour-and-a-half delay. We shouldn't have called; they assumed we'd been in an accident! We were cold and tired, but wide eyed as our minds went over the incident. I was glad to have an experience with discernment and personal revelation on my wife's and my part that the entire family could share.

Another interesting observation was that our children did not say: "How much longer? I need to go potty! Are we there yet? I'm hungry!" When others needs are greater, your needs shrink in size. I am most extremely grateful that my wife and I both followed the Holy Spirit on this family vacation. (Journal 1/5/1997)

About six weeks later I was working in Southern, UT, and was curious as to how the young adults from the crash ended up, especially the young lady that was severely injured. I stopped by the hospital in Panguitch and ran into a nurse in the back hallway. I asked her if she was aware of the serious accident six weeks ago and wondered if any of our quilts or sleeping bags were retrievable. She explained that all of our things were covered in blood and had to be cut off; everything was trashed.

Sensing my real purpose, gently grabbing my arm, she shared,

"Because of HIPAA laws I'm not supposed to share information with you, but they all survived. You saved their lives!"

"Actually God saved their lives. Do you want to hear the story?"

"Yes, I'd like that."

I shared with her my wife's experience of being prompted to leave an extremely large first aid kit in our packed car. Then I explained a discernment of an unknown problem, silent prayer, and quick answer: **"Someone has gone off the road**." The Spirit richly ran through my body from top to bottom. I could tell that she felt it too. This nurse and I had a choice spiritual experience in the back hall of the Panguitch, Utah, hospital that day.

We thanked and hugged each other as we parted and she further added, "The one that was injured the most had a broken pelvis and other broken bones, but survived. They all survived!"

We were all truly grateful. (Journal 3/16/1997)

"For by my Spirit will I enlighten them, and by my power will I make known unto them the secrets of my will ..." (D&C 76:10)

———————◆———————

For all have not every gift given unto them; for there are many gifts, and **to every man is given a gift by the Spirit of God**. To some is given one, and to some is given another, that all may be profited thereby. (D&C 46:11-12)

Wherefore, beware lest ye are deceived; and that ye may not be deceived **seek ye earnestly the best gifts**, always remembering for what they are given. (D&C 46:8)

If thou wilt do good, yea, and hold out faithful to the end, thou shalt be saved in the kingdom of God, which is the greatest of all the gifts of God; **for there is no greater gift than the gift of salvation**. (D & C 6:13)

# 23. The Spirit Said Unto Me Again

*At times we are commanded or prompted to carryout assignments that are uncomfortable, seemingly impossible, and some even going against our moral compasses.   This fact was evident with Nephi's experiences in finally obtaining the brass plates from Laban.*

And I was led by the Spirit … **I was constrained by the Spirit that I should kill Laban** … And the Spirit said unto me *again*, **Behold the Lord hath delivered him into thy hands** … the Spirit said unto me *again*: **Slay him, for the Lord hath delivered him into thy hands … Behold the Lord slayeth the wicked** to bring forth his righteous purposes. **It is better that one man should perish than a nation should dwindle in unbelief.** (1 Ne. 4:6, 10-13)

*Following serious, deep thought, soul searching, and relying on previous teachings from the Lord, Nephi finally obeyed and slew Laban with Laban's own sword.*

*Due to the difficulty in our minds, of some promptings and whisperings, we need to be reminded time and again to carry out what the Lord asked us to do the first time.   We are a lot like our children.   Often children need to be told two or three times, or more, before they actually carry out their responsibilities. Are we any different when responding to our Heavenly Father's requests to His children? Often we are not.  I'm as guilty as anyone in this regard. This is a common thread I have found woven throughout many of the experiences our family, friends, and I have had.*

One Sunday after church and dinner, we were all relaxing.  My wife and I were reading our scriptures and writing in our journals. Our four small children were napping or playing quietly in their rooms. As I sat in the recliner, the Spirit whispered to me, "**Check on Tyler**" (Tyler being our oldest son).

I listened for anything out of the ordinary and heard no: coughing, choking, crying, or whining, etc. Everything seemed and sounded as calm as it had for the last thirty minutes. I went on with studying the Gospel.

Then the Spirit said to me again, "**Check on Tyler**." Once again I heard nothing that would make me think anything was wrong, ignored the prompting, and went about my business.

Now, for a third time, the Spirit said once again, **"Check on Tyler"** and I guess He finally got the message through to my carnal skull after knocking on it three time.

I got up out of the recliner and went to Tyler's room to *check on Tyler*. I was surprised to find the screen removed from the window and the window cranked wide open. A very cold breeze was coming into his room whereas it was winter. Tyler was nowhere to be found! I called for him and there was no answer whatsoever.

We had a good amount of fresh snow; looking down from the window I could see his little footprints in the snow. I anxiously announced the news to my sweetheart and we quickly attired with boots and coats. We ran outside and still couldn't find our little boy. So we tracked him, which wasn't too hard. He had gone to the end of the block and was hiding behind some apartment buildings. He wasn't dressed for the cold and was shivering. He was very stubborn and would never tell us what drove him to run away from home in the bitter cold of a snowy Wyoming winter. We were grateful for the snow.

I am very confident that if had I listened to the first prompting and been more obedient to the Spirit I would have discovered Tyler taking the screen off and he never would have gone out in the cold. When the Lord says we are slow to hearken, he isn't kidding! (Journal 3/3/1991)

"Yea, thus saith the still small voice, which whispereth through and pierceth all things ..." (D&C 85:6)

One day the spirit said to me, **"Write Uncle Rufus."** I brushed it off and one week later the Spirit whispered again to me, **"Write Uncle Rufus."** I said to myself, "Okay, I'll go ahead and do that." Each time the Spirit would say the exact thing, **"Write Uncle Rufus"** except the frequency of the reminders increased from one week ... to few days ... then one day ... to just hours apart. I finally said out loud, "Okay, I'll write to him so you stop pestering me!"
We didn't live close enough to visit him at that time, so I sat down and wrote that letter. Uncle Rufus was really sad and distraught because his son and son-in-law had both drowned in an accident. The letter really helped him because he was at a very low point in his life. The letter meant a lot to him." (A family friend)

*The Lord said to Jonah:*

> **"Arise, go to Nineveh, that great city, and cry against it;
> for their wickedness is come up before me. "** (Jonah 1:2)

After Jonah's experience of near shipwreck and drowning, not to mention being stuck in the smelly belly of large fish, likely a whale, for three days—the Lord spoke to him once again:

> **"Arise, go unto Nineveh, that great city, and preach unto
> it the preaching that I bid thee."** (Jonah 3:2)

The city of Nineveh with over 60,000 inhabitants fasted, repented, and turned from evil back towards God; they saved themselves with faith.

───────◆◆◆───────

I had grown up in the church in California. After high school I landed a good job. I found myself enjoying life several years later. As I was driving cars for a company that I really enjoyed working for, the Spirit said clearly to me, **"Go on a mission."**
I replied, "But I don't want to go on a mission!"
Later in the afternoon the same voice said, **"Go on a mission"** and I couldn't get this thought out of my mind. After work I called our bishop and we met that night to start my mission plans. I did not serve until I was twenty four. It was the best decision God helped me make in my life." (Ward member)

───────◆◆◆───────

Friday evening, after a busy day, I noticed there were no leftovers in the fridge. My wife was finally relaxing after bottling pear jam most of the day. I sauntered over to her and said, "Let's go to our favorite soup and sandwich shop for dinner." There was no arm twisting involved.

We enjoyed relaxing to a freshly prepared meal. As we were finishing up, my mind was drawn to a young mother standing in a long line. **Three times the Spirit prompted me to help this young woman.** She also had a diaper bag, baby, and toddler. It became apparent that daddy wasn't there. I had the impression that she desired help, yet would not ask anyone for help.

It seemed rather brazen to approach a stranger in a busy restaurant. I asked my wife what she thought. She gave me an impression and permission: "It's your idea, deal with it."

I suggested to my honey that we could just leave, yet felt inclined to help again. Overcoming my trepidation and fear, I got up an approached the young mother.

"Could you use some help? I could carry your food tray."

"Oh that is so kind. Aren't you still eating though?"

"No, my wife and I just finished up."

"Would you mind taking the baby?"

"I would love to hold your baby!"

As I now waited in line along with them, the baby started getting fussy. I suggested to her mother that the baby was hungry. She set her toddler on the counter and took the baby. Fearing the toddler might lean forward and fall off; I gently grabbed her to set her down on the floor.

She immediately grabbed onto me like her best friend in the world and did not want to be let down for anything. Now I was carrying the sweet toddler, to my delight. The young mother paid for her tab and then turned with the baby and diaper bag. I now had the toddler and the heavy tray of food. Luckily, the little girl was clinging on so snuggly that I could use both hands to carry the tray.

My wife came over and grabbed the heavy tray to set it down on their table. This little angel I was holding was so sweet, I didn't want to let her go and she didn't seem interested in the table or her food either.

The mother thanked me sincerely and began to tear up. I told her that her little angels made my day! Gently setting the toddler down in a chair, we said our goodbyes.

We often need to leave our comfort zones when following the Spirit *when ministering* to our fellow brothers and sisters on this earth. Listening to and obeying, the still, small, voice will lead us to multiple ministering experiences that are outside our typical assignments or callings. (Journal 9/7/18)

> What will matter is that we came with a desire to serve ... reaching out with friendship even though we *aren't* assigned to minister to them. And it will certainly matter that we do all that we do with the special ingredient of service coupled with love and sacrifice. (Cristina B. Franco, GC, Oct 2018)

————— •◆• —————

This was when I was in college before my mission. I had just bought this brand new bicycle for $500 and it had dual-suspension and everything I wanted in a mountain bike. I would take the bus to school because it was free for students. I would bring my bike along because the bus stop was some distance from my classes.

There was this one day I was sitting in my computer class and I got the prompting, "**Just go home and finish your**

**work there**." Everything we were doing in class I could have been doing at home that day; we were just working on some packets. The prompting was like, "**Go home right now**." So I packed everything up and was walking out; the teacher says, "Hey, where do you think you're going?"

So I sat back down, laid out my material and opened the books up. This was my last class. After class, I gathered my things up and went to get my bike and it was stolen. The lock was there, but not the bike; they had just snipped it. I had just placed my bike there before my last class at that building.

I had the thought, "Well if I had just followed that prompting when I heard it, I would still have my bike." I had let the fear of man overtake me and I didn't follow the voice of God. That was a $500 mistake and lesson for me. I was glad I could learn this at that level and follow the Spirit more closely in the future to avoid costlier mistakes. I chose not to repeat this misstep and decided to follow promptings quickly no matter what, eliminating the fear of men.

That became my goal for my mission and life. If I didn't learn anything else, I wanted to be really good at following the promptings of the Spirit. (A peer)

"For, behold, you should not have feared man more than God." (D&C 3:7)

---

Our bishop's wife was working as a shipping manager. I was the sales manager and we worked together on fulfilling large and/or special orders. One day we both needed the copy machine at the same time. The copy machine didn't work for either of us because the last paper available had jammed. I worked to get the jammed paper dislodged and upon success refilled the paper tray.

At this point I said something offensive to this sister that I wish I had never uttered. I was embarrassed and felt terrible. She felt awful too, but for different reasons.

"For thy mouth uttereth thine iniquity, and thou choosest the tongue of the crafty." (Job 15:5)

After several days of frustration with myself and **persistent reminders to repent**, I finally mustered the courage to apologize to her for my misstep.

She replied, "Oh, I forgave you right away. I must admit I did sorta' enjoy seeing you suffer for a couple of days."

Following that apology we have been great friends for decades.

Years later in a different Stake and State I offended a brother from another ward by losing my cool. He sadly withdrew from my presence and I could tell that my brash mannerisms really affected him harshly.

Once again, I felt awful and wished I'd never said anything to this good brother. Following **repetitive urges from the Spirit over many days**, I called him up and sincerely apologized in person for my misbehavior.

He thanked me, forgave me, and invited me to go on a cruise with him and his wife. We were now BFF's!

> "Go thy way unto thy brother (sister), and first be reconciled to thy brother, and then come unto me with full purpose of heart, and I will receive you." (2 Ne. 12:24)

This simple scripture works so well in accessing the power of the atonement when repenting for offenses rendered. The offender, offended, and the Lord are all happier and pleased. The charity and love that spring forth from the atonement are eternal and real!

Like millions of others, I am eternally grateful God granted us the gift of repentance.

———•◆•———

> I was a soccer player all through high school. During my senior year I kept getting the idea **to NOT try out** for soccer that year. I shrugged it off; thinking how funny that was and not seeing a reason for it. The idea **"not to try out"** came softly and quietly a few more times.
>
> Finally, on the way out the door to the first soccer practice, even though I had an open door, car keys in hand, soccer ball and cleats in my bag, it was if there was a brick wall before me. I felt like I couldn't move. I was unable to go forward.
>
> It so happens that I had underestimated the work load and stress that my school year and family held for me that coming year. I almost drowned in the strain of everything! Had I placed soccer on top of everything else, who knows what would have happened? Well obviously Heavenly

Father knew. I grew a great trust in that God would not lead me astray. (A relative)

My four-year old was really clinging to me all day, so I figured he wasn't feeling well. He wasn't eating or drinking much. He seemed kind of warm, yet nothing was alarming enough to take him to the doctor. His symptoms seemed like he had a cold. Besides, the co-pay is $45 a visit; and those add up fast! I can't just take my kids to the doctor every time there's a sniffle or a fever.

I was still debating whether to take him in or not. I prayed that he would get better and decided to sleep with him so I could easily give him breathing treatments every four hours with the nebulizer. I remember waking up because his fever had spiked and he was burning hot. I gave him some children's Tylenol.

That night, I don't know if it was a dream or while I was awake, but a voice said "**Take him in**" During the night the same message repeated itself, "**Take him in**" three times as clear as day. By morning his fever had broken and he felt much cooler; he hadn't needed any more breathing treatments. As soon as I was awake though, I remembered the words I heard in the night: **"Take him in."**

I immediately called and made an appointment for our son. When my son woke up he seemed so happy and I thought about cancelling the appointment due to his improvement. Once again, I quickly remembered the words: **"Take him in."**

So I took him to the Instacare and it turned out that he had strep throat and a temperature of 104 degrees! They gave him three different prescriptions. He was much sicker than I had thought. I hadn't specifically prayed to know if I should take him to see the doctor; I prayed that he would get better. In this instance in order to get better he needed to be seen and get those prescriptions. I thought it was interesting that my answer was in my own language. I had asked myself and my husband if I should *take him* so when those exact words came to me I knew what I was to do. (A family member)

I was a single and self-employed when I was new in the Church, so I had days when I had extra time. ... I called the

Relief Society president and asked if anyone needed help that afternoon. She mentioned an elderly sister ... I had met Anita before and was happy to visit her.

I called and then went to her apartment. She asked me to make lunch for her; afterward we had a great visit. ... After lunch she said she was tired and asked me to help her from her wheelchair to her bed. Soon I had her tucked in. Suddenly, the still, small voice I had heard so much about spoke to me: **"Get her to the hospital now!"**

I moved away from her bedside and knelt. As soon as I started to pray, the voice repeated, **"Get her to the hospital, and get her there now!"**

Anita was angry that I would even mention taking her to the hospital, but I called an ambulance anyway. ... I followed in my van. ... Soon the doctor came out.

"She didn't tell you that she had fallen before you came to her apartment, did she?"

"No"

He told me that Anita had injured her spleen and was bleeding internally. Without immediate medical attention, he said, she might have died. (Gayle Y. Branvoid, *Ensign*, Aug 2015)

———◆———

The missionary was indeed very ill. Fervent prayer was followed by administration, during which the impression came very strongly to **get him back to the hospital on the main island, and to do it now!**

The weather had deteriorated to the point of a small gale. The seas were heavy, the clouds were thick, the wind was fierce, the hour was late, and the sun was sinking rapidly, betokening a long black night ahead. But the impression was strong—**"Get back now"**—and one learns to obey the all-important promptings of the Spirit. (John H. Groberg, GC, Oct 1976)

———◆———

Our family was in the midst of crisis. My youngest daughter suffered from depression, mood swings, and excessive anxiety. She was diagnosed with a bipolar type of illness. She was cutting, repeatedly suicidal, and had to be hospitalized three times.

527

We endured years of living nightmares—in daylight as well as darkness. The illness was affecting my entire family. We lived on a roller coaster of her emotions from day to day as we dealt with explosive mood swings while trying to shelter our young children from the worst emergencies. Our oldest daughter didn't live in the same house with her sister for several months due to a terrorizing encounter.

Adding to the stress was a set of parents who didn't always agree on how to discipline a chronically ill child experiencing such upsets. Simply put, there was more trauma than one could understand—unless you've lived this close to this kind of illness yourself. It didn't seem like the chaos would ever end.

The answers the medical field had to offer were drugs and counseling. I took my daughter to conventional methods for four years, trying one prescription drug "cocktail" of medications at a time, one after another. There was no lasting improvement; the medications still left her ill and even suicidal. Additionally, the side-effects of the drugs were horrendous. Suddenly gaining forty pounds in a couple of months is *never* a good thing for an already depressed teenage girl. We erroneously thought that the traditional medicine route was our only option.

We took opportunities to have priesthood blessings given. I asked our new, young bishop for advice. He gave my daughter a blessing of comfort, telling her to pray and read her scriptures, because "answers were to be found there." To be honest, I was disappointed with such advice; she had enormous trials, and I felt this was a very generic blessing. However, I repented of that thought and took the Lord's counsel to heart.

Our bishop was right, answers were found in the scriptures. In time, I came across *many* educational and helpful answers to health problems in the scriptures. Scripture stories even revealed that certain emotions were contributors to health issues. I often put my daughter's name on the prayer roll at the temple and fasted every Sunday during the most difficult months. I prayed frequently for the Lord's help.

A quiet voice in my mind **prompted me repeatedly to call the wife of a past bishop of ours**. I didn't understand how a stay-at-home mother with seven perfect children could possibly be of much help for trials as major as a daughter with suicidal tendencies. It was the **insistence of the Holy Ghost** that convinced me to call her. I didn't understand why I was supposed to call her, so I felt a little silly. I finally dialed her long-distance phone number.

She listened as I tearfully recounted some of the trials we'd been through. Then she said something that still stands out as being profoundly important.

She asked, "So, you've only looked for help in the medical field?"

"Startled, I answered, "Yes, of course. What else is there?"

"Oh," she said, "there is a whole other field of medicine."

"Really?" I asked incredulously.

"Yes, it is called Energy Medicine," she replied in a matter-of-fact-way.

She said it was an alternative but complementary treatment. In today's language, it is considered integrative medicine. We could continue to follow the doctor's orders while investigating its effectiveness. I believed her because she was a woman of complete trustworthiness. "Energy Medicine" is a field of medicine that takes into account that our bodies are complex systems of energies.

What a huge blessing finding this kind of help was for our daughter! And the Rapid Eye Technology sessions the bishop's wife did for our daughter didn't come with side effects. (My wife Tamara)

I find it interesting to compare stories in our journals to see how we view and handle similar situations. I wrote about our thirteen-year-old daughter being in Cedar City, UT, attending EFY (Especially for Youth). Our family traveled on further south for a family reunion involving some camping. It was very enjoyable to be with our eternal families in the outdoors.

Then we picked up our daughter and her friend from EFY. Our daughter wasn't acting normal. She was very "huggy" and apologetic. She was confessing things. "What happened?" we asked her friend that attended EFY with her. Her friend wasn't sure if our daughter had been acting strangely for attention— or what was going on.

Our daughter seemed to get worse as time went on that day. She became weak. The next day when we drove home, her greatest desire was to talk to our bishop. She talked less and less to us. It was becoming difficult for her to even speak, yet she could sing songs at length. She sang "I am a Child of God" several times along with other church songs. My wife and my daughter's friend sang songs along with her as we drove along and sometimes her siblings joined in. Singing church music seemed to help her somehow and her face brightened.

Our daughter felt overwhelmed and experienced a physical reaction not unlike Alma's. "...for the space of three days and three nights ... I could not open my mouth, neither had I the use of my limbs." (Alma 36:10) Our daughter got to the point that she could hardly answer a yes or no question. She sobbed instead and lay in bed. By the time we could get her to the bishop's office we had to physically help her to walk. As she met with the bishop she was sobbing, weak, lethargic, and wouldn't respond to questions. She said Satan was bothering her. Our bishop gave her a really nice blessing. Tamara and I both called on the power of God to get Satan away from her. We began to wonder if she was having a nervous breakdown, but didn't have any idea of what that meant or might look like. We wondered if she was hallucinating.

> A recent General Conference talk explains the 'norm': "Thousands and thousands of young men and women spent a week strengthening their love of the Savior and then returned home to their families and friends, radiating the light and love of Christ." (GC, Mark A. Bragg, May 2017, 37)

Our family's post EFY experience over the next couple of years was: many of our daughter's friends dropped her and some adult members dropped us. Our home teachers never came the entire year—during the greatest time of emotional and financial need in our lives! The usual meals never came. There were a few members with mental illness in their families that also experienced this unique ostracizing who became friendly peers, however. Some inspired members of the ward offered various types of support.

This started many prayers, much fasting, and frequent temple visits seeking understanding. We made an appointment with the bishop, hoping for inspired advice and healing. This was the first time our bishop had seen a person in this condition, also. As he got up from behind his desk and made his way around to our seated daughter, I could see him sweating and sense him desperately seeking for inspiration as he prepared to give her a blessing. He had an obvious concern and love for her. She was not healed. The bishop said if it was his daughter he would take her to the ER right away.

Later the bishop did inform us about LDS Family Services and we began visiting them. After this she spiraled down and became lethargic in speech and movement.

About half a year later, we had gone to bed one evening and just drifted off to a sound sleep when our lights (five of them under our ceiling fan) came on and we heard a noise. As we groggily looked up, there was our daughter with bloody cuts all over her arms and legs, a piece of flab hanging from her bicep, and a BBQ fork starting to stick into her stomach. She said, "I want to shove this all the way through me! Get me a knife, I want to kill myself!"

Talk about a living nightmare!!

We were paying $1,000 per month for health insurance premiums and the insurer wouldn't pay a dime for her ambulance, emergency visits, doctors, hospital stays, psychologists, psychiatrists, behavior health unit of the hospital, etc. (All of which were very expensive!) There was no parity, equality coverage for all medical expenses that aren't optional, in Utah at that time. One slight glimmer of help came when the insurer's paid 50% on her expensive psychotic meds. The financial strain was a real concern for me.

Our children would complain at dinner, because they had to use butter knives to cut their meat. We had all the sharp knives and razors hidden away and locked up tight. One day after we took our daughter's car away, our daughter locked herself in our bathroom and broke the window. I was working out-of-state and my wife frantically called the neighbor who came over and broke the door down before she cut herself.

After such major incidents with suicidal tendencies she would be taken to the hospital and sometimes end up in the hospital's behavioral health unit. We had every vehicle with flashing red lights in front of our home on multiple occasions: Police, Sheriff, Highway Patrol, Ambulance, and Fire Truck—everything except Search and Rescue! We stopped caring what the neighbors thought.

Then our oldest son moved out, wanting to live closer to his college, because he did not want to deal with the drama. Our oldest daughter was threatened with a knife by our ill daughter, and this older sister moved into her boyfriend's home. Her boyfriend was serving his mission at the time. We were concerned about our two young boys; would she threaten or hurt them? Would she harm or stab anyone during our sleep. Would we find her dead? So many worrisome thoughts crossed my mind day and night. My wife didn't worry about this like I did.

I thought to myself, "If she threatens or harms anybody else in the family, I am shipping her off to the state mental hospital." I then experienced the coldest, strongest feeling in the very center of my soul that resonated strongly, "No!" It actually felt like it was deeper inside my actual body, maybe at a spiritual level.

> "I Daniel was grieved in my spirit in the midst of my body ..." (Dan 7:15)

I then discerned that she would be drugged and taken advantage of in that type of facility, because she is a very pretty girl. She would actually lose her agency. So I dropped that thought of sending her away immediately and never entertained the idea again.

I am so grateful for **my wife listening to her repetitive promptings** and finding the additional help that is out there. On a sales trip to southern Utah I took this challenged daughter along with me to counsel with a "Stress Management Counselor"; we were very pleased with the results.

After a couple of hours of his integrative help, which involved teaching her to forgive out loud very specifically using present tense the doctor said, "I think you have your daughter back." She looked radiant with light in her face, something I hadn't seen since before her unique EFY experience. She said every physical pain in her body was gone along with all of the mental anguish! Jan Graf also taught her how to cast out evil spirits which was incredibly helpful. I was astounded at the changes forgiving out loud and casting out evil had brought about in two hours time.

What was equally amazing were her pricey prescription medications falling under the seat of the car. They were lost for over a week and she didn't seem to need them anymore! She did not ask for her medicine and we got permission from her doctor to experiment with no RXs for awhile.

This one appointment was able to bring her to a place of belief and self worth that enabled her to greatly improve her life.

———◆———

While I was thus in the act of calling upon God, I discovered a light appearing in my room ... when immediately a personage appeared by my bedside, standing in the air ... he was a messenger ... his name was Moroni ... after this communication ... I lay musing on the singularity of the scene ... the same heavenly messenger was again by my bedside. He commenced and **again related the very same things** ... I lay overwhelmed in astonishment at what I had both seen and heard. But what was my surprise when again I beheld the same messenger at my bedside, and heard him **rehearse or repeat over again to me the same things as**

**before** ... in attempting to cross the fence ... my strength entirely failed me, and I fell helpless on the ground ... I looked up and beheld the same messenger ... he **then again related unto me all that he had related** to me the previous night. (JSH, 30, 43-46, 49)

*Four times the angel Moroni related God's world-changing restoration message to emphasize its eternal importance to the future prophet Joseph Smith, Jr.*

————————◆————————

As part of his work duties, Dad would go out at 2 a.m. and check various pieces of electrical equipment. His usual route included walking down a set of railroad tracks that went through a tunnel. This tunnel went under a building where coke was loaded onto railroad cars.

One night, Dad walked about 30 feet into the tunnel when he heard a voice say, **"Don't go through there."**

He stopped for a second, thinking he was just being spooked. After all, it was an eerie place to walk around alone in the middle of the night. He laughed at himself, but only walked a few feet farther when a louder voice repeated, **"Don't go through there."**

He stopped again, but told himself to not be so nervous. Then the loud voice said, **"Jack, don't go through there!"**

This third warning scared him enough that he retraced his steps out of the tunnel entrance and instead used the asphalt road that paralleled the tunnel.

He reached the other end of the tunnel and walked back over onto the railroad rails. Just then there was a tremendous crash right behind him. A thick cloud of coke dust hit him and he couldn't see anything.

... then he saw a 40-foot-long conveyor belt system—with all of the structural steel supporting it—had fallen from 20 feet above the ground. It landed on the tracks where he would have been walking if he hadn't following the promptings. (Chad Daybell, *Living on the Edge of Heaven*, Pgs. 25-26, used with permission.)

————————◆————————

Four times I have had **multiple promptings to call or write someone** and I put them off. Most recently I felt I should contact an old friend from school. She had moved to another state. I found her cousin working in a box store I shopped at.

Every time I was prompted to contact her, I would ask her cousin for her address. Finally, after about three months, he got me her address.

Then I procrastinated and thought, 'I'll contact her at Christmas and send a card and nice letter." She was killed in October. I sure wish I had sent that letter. (A family friend)

———— • ◆ • ————

My son and I were pulling a trailer with all our camping supplies for a stay in the mountains with three generations of our family. As we started up Ogden Canyon in Utah, we came to a line of stopped cars going around a large curve. We had no idea what the delay was. Only a few cars were sporadically coming down the canyon in the opposite direction. We surmised there was construction or an accident.

Two other cars with family members would meet us up there, and the first vehicle would actually be arriving early to select a large campsite for a 3-day stay; we had all the equipment and the food. We were stuck and I began receiving *multiple gentle promptings* to **"turn around."**

My son and I began a conversation regarding our "parked situation" on the canyon road.

"I feel like we should turn around."

"Maybe the cars will be moving pretty soon."

"I believe those few cars we see coming down the road are actually people who've already turned around."

"Just give it some time. It would really slow us down to go back around."

"I think we need to turn around."

"It would be dangerous to make a U-turn with a trailer on this canyon curve.

Due to the few cars that were turning around, the vehicles ahead of us would slowly inch forward. I barely inched forward until there was a wider than normal spot and stopped, leaving ample space between the car ahead of us. When that car inched forward, I remained still.

Then with the *fourth prompting to turn around*, I put on my left blinker and moved to the right before turned back left and stopping to check for oncoming traffic. Not seeing any activity on the road ahead, I pulled the trailer around and headed the other way.

"Dad, what are you doing?"

"We're going the other way."

"We should have waited, the line will probably move while we're taking the long way around."

"So what if we're an hour later, we'll still get there."

"Oh, Dad, I just got a news update on my phone. There is a downed power line across both lanes of traffic and Ogden Canyon is closed until at least 10pm tonight!"

"Good thing we turned around, huh?"

"Yes, it was."

If we had driven ahead into the tight curves of that canyon there is no way we could have turned around for many miles and we would have been stuck for untold hours. We were able to drive south through town and drive up the next canyon over.

As we drove over Trappers Loop, which is a steep climb, the lanes were limited to one lane in each direction due to construction. Orange cones lined most of the entire long pass.

A vehicle behind us seemed impatient and he passed us going over the double yellow lines and through the orange cones. Then he would drive to the right and the tires on the right would be off the road kicking up dirt and gravel. Then he would veer to the left.

"What's wrong with that dude?"

"I don't know; he's either on drugs, alcohol, or medication."

"Should we call him in?"

"Probably."

"Drive up closer so I can take a picture of his license plate"

"Okay."

Then this crazy driver went totally into the left lane again and came very close to causing a head-on collision. The oncoming car had to swerve hard left and into an orange cone to prevent an accident! The erratic driver was on the far left of the opposite lane!

"Call 911!"

"OK!"

Since there are no coincidences, I believe we were prompted to turn around, take the long route, and then follow behind an impaired driver so that he could be legally removed from the road before people were killed.

When we arrived at the large campsite, my wife and grandsons were waiting at a perfect site for the group. We were setting up a day early to secure a better site prior to a busy holiday weekend. We got all set up when a forest fire broke out. We rushed to the camp host and he said that the fire was burning from the canyon, from which we witnessed large plumes of thick smoke emitting high into the sky, burning east towards Powder Mountain Ski Resort. So we were okay for now.

We had a good afternoon and evening with one of our sons and two of our grandsons. The next day we were playing in the creek with the boys and there were lots of sirens and then dual-propeller helicopters with large water buckets flying constantly back and forth just north of us. Then a county sheriff drove up and said that we needed to evacuate because a second forest fire had lit up and it was even closer than the first.

We are not sure why we had to cut 2 days off our family campout; the balance of the family was called and never came up at all! I'm confident there's a reason we weren't suppose to be there. The ban was lifted later and the campgrounds (187 spots) were fine. (Journal 9/2/18)

––––––◆––––––

There is another story I would like to tell you that President Grant often told…. And the President of the Church called on Brother Grant to go out and collect funds that they might put into the bank to save it (the bank) from disaster.
…
He asked Reed Smoot for $2,000 and he asked Jesse Knight for $5,000. They were both men of means …

"I'll give you $1,000, but I won't give you $2,000."

"I'll not take it, but you go home tonight and get down on your knees and pray to the Lord and ask him to give you an enlargement of heart and give me $2,000."

"Brother Grant, why didn't you ask me to pray?"

"Oh why should I ask you to pray? You didn't offer me anything. No use of asking the Lord to give you enlargement of heart."

"I'll tell you what I'll do. I will go home tonight, and I will pray to the Lord about that."

And so, two or three days later there came through the mail two checks—on from Jesse M. Knight for $10,000 and on from Brother Smoot for $2,000.

"What happened? I didn't ask you for $10,000. I only asked for $5,000.

"I'll tell you this Brother Grant. When you come to me again with a mission from the President of the Church to raise funds, I'm going to pay without any question…. I got down on my knees, and it just kept going through my mind like a tune: 'Give Heber $10,000.' And I got into bed and that tune kept going through me mind: 'Give Heber $10,000. Give Heber $10,000'

"I got down on my knees again and said, 'Lord, Heber didn't ask me for $10,000. He only asked me for $5,000. The tune kept going through my mind. 'Give Heber $10,000. Give Heber $10,000. And so, in order to satisfy the situation and have peace of mind, I told the Lord,

'Alright, I'll give him $10,000.'" (Joseph Anderson, BYU, Speeches of the Year, "Prophets of the Living God," June 29, 1969)

———•◆•———

There were a couple of different trails behind our home that lead to the countryside. I planned to go for a long walk and head north. As I approached the "Y" in the trail, **I was prompted to go east.** But I did not want to go east—my plan was to go north. I started on the north trail and **was again prompted to go east** instead. So I changed my plans and headed eastward.

As I made my way down the trail, I was wondering why I was prompted to take it. **Then I was prompted to stop and turn myself around.** As I looked back, I saw a single horse just standing off in the grass. There shouldn't have been any loose horses or cows in this area. I slowly approached the horse and then heard a moan.

As I got closer, I found a woman with blood all over her. She had apparently fallen off the horse and injured her head. I went over to her and held her in my arms and prayed for her. I remembered there were some stables in the area and assumed that's where she came from.

I was able to assist her in slowly walking until we finally found a couple on the trail. I asked one of them to go for help and asked the other to take the horse back to the stables. Soon an ambulance came and the paramedics took care of her and rushed her to the hospital. I don't know, but she might have died had I not been told to take the east trail. (Our friend)

But the Comforter, which is the Holy Ghost, whom the Father will send in my name, he shall teach you all things, and bring all things to your remembrance, whatsoever I have said unto you. (John 14:26)

———•◆•———

I was called to serve as the elder's quorum president of a student ward while in college. As such I was focusing on the young men in our ward that were prospective elders. There was one man that fit the mold but he wasn't sure he even wanted to be an elder. I was reading to him the *Oath and the Covenant of the Priesthood* as I was trying to encourage him to become an elder. Doctrine and

Covenants 84 ends with some damning references for those who do not accept this priesthood.

The Spirit told me, **"don't read that scripture—the damning part"** I ignored the prompting and read it anyway; which just brought up more concerns and issues. I was upset with myself that I wasn't helping his testimony grow.

I was very pleased however to see this young man get up on Fast Sunday and stand in the long line to bear testimonies. As you might remember, in college wards, it's like everybody wants to bear their testimony. Anyway, I'm sitting in the congregation and hear the Spirit say, **"go tell the bishop not to close the meeting until that young man bears his testimony."** I was like, "What?" Then **the same prompting came again**. And then **a third time the exact same prompting came** as this young man was next in line. The bishop got up and closed the meeting.

The young man was not able to bear his testimony and he needed to. I was the one with the keys to help that young man and I didn't follow those promptings. So while he was under my stewardship, he did not become an elder. I was reminded of an excellent talk by Elder Bednar when he stressed that we need to heed promptings quickly. (A relative)

"In our individual study and classroom instruction, we repeatedly emphasize the importance of recognizing the inspiration and promptings we receive from the Spirit of the Lord. We should seek diligently to recognize and *respond to promptings as they come to us*." (David A. Bednar, GC, April 2006)

As the session dragged on, he kept watching the clock, trying to balance a growing sense of urgency with the uneasiness of leaving in the middle of the meeting. During the closing song, he bolted. Arriving at the hospital, he hurriedly checked at the desk … then raced up the stairs … he could see a cluster of people …

The nurse looked at him and said, 'Are you bishop Monson?

"Yes," he replied heavily.

"The patient was asking for you just before he died," she said.

Remorse consumed him. He had not responded immediately to the promptings of the Spirit ... From this experience Thomas Monson learned a lesson and a truth that has defined his life: *"**Never postpone a prompting**."* (Thomas S. Monson, *Errand*, 133, emphasis added)

*The great lesson here for all of us to seek is to emulate President Monson's example in responding to the Spirit immediately. I know of no other person who has responded so quickly and so often for the rest of their life, no matter how uneasy the task made them feel. He is truly inspiring! If you desire to truly enjoy a spiritual feast, while being educated on obedience to the Spirit and promptings, please peruse: Thomas S. Monson's Biography, TO THE RESCUE.*

After my mission I had a desire to marry a returned sister missionary when the time came. At college I dated returned missionaries and there were just a few because this was a two-year college and most young women had gone to college and then on a mission. When these sister missionaries returned, they were off to full universities.

The returned missionary I was dating seemed like she would make a wonderful wife and mother. When I prayed about marrying her I got this uneasy feeling. I brushed it off as Satan trying to discourage me from dating, so I proposed and she accepted. I attended the temple a lot and every time I prayed about my fiancée that **same uneasy feeling returned**. I finally realized it was the Spirit communicating with me and that this relationship was not the right one for me.

This was not the returned sister missionary that I should marry. **I could no longer discount the repetitive feelings** and I broke off the engagement. It was a hard thing to do. I finished college and returned home to look for a job.

At this time, a local sister had just come home from her mission. Ironically, I had talked to her before her mission outside the SLC temple as her mother and she came out. The young woman, from my home town in another state, told me she was starting her mission soon. So I saw her just before and after her mission.

I was driving home from work and stopped at a stoplight. This young woman came to mind and the Spirit simply said,

**"This is a good decision."** I gave her two weeks home and then I asked her out. I truly felt that she was *the one* and we started dating and the rest is history. I couldn't ask for a better mom for my kids. She's perfect!

I feel like you marry another family and I couldn't ask for better grandparents for our children. They are such great examples, as are my parents. (A relative)

We must be confident in our first promptings. Sometimes we rationalize; we wonder if we are feeling a spiritual impression or if it is just our own thoughts. When we begin to second-guess, even third-guess, our feelings—and we all have—we are dismissing the Spirit; we are questioning divine counsel. The Prophet Joseph Smith taught that if you will listen to the first promptings, you will get it right nine times out of ten. (Ronald A. Rasband, GC, April 2017)

"Your name kept popping into my mind and that's why I called you."
"I'm so glad you did!" (Missionary peers)

*This is one of the best ways to properly minister to God's children. Utilize those inspired thoughts that pop into our heads and/or touch our hearts—then act upon them accordingly. Our Heavenly Father knows who needs cherished, loved, and served; the Godhead will direct daily those willing to listen and follow Them.*

I was set apart by Elder Orson Pratt to go on a mission to New England and the Eastern states to preach the gospel to the living, but more especially to procuse (sic) the records of the dead kindred of Latter-day Saints. I was profoundly impressed by the blessing Elder Pratt gave me.

...

One of the first genealogies I undertook to trace on this mission was that of a Williams family. ... The clerk gave me directions for finding Judge Williams residence, and I started to go to it. I soon came to a marble yard which had a sign extending over the sidewalk. The sign gave the name of the proprietor. It was Williams. [Not Judge Williams] Something seemed to say to me, **"This man belongs to the family you are tracing, and you had better speak with him."**

A lady customer was selecting a gravestone, and the proprietor of the marble yard was walking about with her, directing her attention first to one monument and then to another ... As it would have been impolite to interrupt them, I waited. The lady could not decide. It was getting late in the afternoon and I was uneasy at losing time. Mr. Williams had not noticed me, and I decided to go on to Judge Williams' residence. But something seemed to say to me: **"This is the man you want to see."**

"But," I argued with myself, "the clerk of the surrogate's office advised me to see Judge Williams, and the clerk is likely to know whom I had better see." For about an hour this debate continued in my mind. The lady was about that long in choosing a stone and I chafed at losing time. Again and again I started to leave the marble yard, but each time came the same prompting: **"This is the man for you to see; do not leave until you have talked to him."**

Yielding to my unseen adviser, I waited. When the lady had selected a stone, Mr. Williams approached me and asked what he could do for me. I told him I desired to trace genealogy of the Williams family for that vicinity ...

"I am the man for you to see," he said promptly. I was struck with his words. ... As he spoke he turned on his heel and without another word walked to a desk some distance away, opened it at took two sheets of foolscap paper. ... he had traced his father's line back to the first settler of the name in New Jersey ... he had made two copies ... which he held in his hands as he spoke, and said that I was welcome to one of them. So saying he handed me one of the sheets, to my great surprise and delight. (Benjamin F. Cummings, early missionary)

---

Back in 1983, I became frustrated trying to find information on my Edward and Ann (Wood) Wheeler family in the Willie Handcart Company of 1856. A family history library missionary in Salt Lake City suggested I go into the Special Collections. In that card file I was excited to find a card for the Willie Co. Journal! Handing the librarian the card, I waited for her to get the journal. She didn't return and didn't return. I needed to get home to our six small children and relieve the baby sitter. But something kept me there for an agonizing 45 minutes until she finally came, apologizing for making me wait so long. She said she didn't understand why it was so hard to find.

I realized I didn't have time to read it. The words came to my mind, **"Copy it!"**

"I don't even have time to copy it."

**"Copy it!"**

"I think I used all my money for lunch."

**"Copy it!"**

"I'll just copy it when I come back next week."

**"What if it's not here?"**

The Spirit spoke strongly so I stayed and copied the journal pages. I was so certain that my Wheeler family <u>must</u> be there!

After relieving the sitter and making sure all the children were in bed, I began pouring over the copied journal pages. No Wheeler family was even mentioned. I must have missed it, so I carefully reread the copied pages. Nothing! What a waste of time and money, not to mention the devastating feeling that I must not know what the Spirit feels and sounds like!

That very next Sunday, I saw Allen Willie in church; he was a member of our ward for the past 15 years, whom I have never said more than "Hi" to. The Spirit said, **"Tell Allen."**

"I don't know what to say."

**"Tell Allen."**

When he came by me, I stopped him and asked, "Allen, are you related to Captain Willie?"

He told me he was a direct descendent of Captain James G. Willie and also a member of the Willie Family Association. He got excited when I told him about my search for the Wheeler records and asked if he could come over to our home and visit after church.

At our home, he told me that in 1981, he and Paul Willie met at Rock Creek Hollow and were surprised to discover the entire Riverton, WY, Stake there celebrating the July 24th pioneer day.

He said, "When members of the wards discovered we were 'Willies', they invited us to speak to their large group."

On their way home from Wyoming, Allen told Paul that Captain Willie's descendents should donate a granite marker at Rock Creek Hollow to honor the 13 handcart pioneers who were buried there in a common grave. At the

Willie family reunion, on May 31, 1982, Paul told the family of their experience and Allen's idea. The Willie Family Association voted to make that dream a reality.

Allen then asked me if we would like to join with the Willie family by donating to buy the granite marker.

"What will be engraved on the marker?"

*"In Honor of the 13 Handcart Pioneers Who Perished Here"*

"Why don't you put their names on the marker?"

"Nobody knows their names. We've searched everywhere. Nobody knows them."

"I do!! I just read them in the Willie journal!"

As I handed the journal pages to Allen he was extremely excited! He begged me to let him copy the journal pages and I complied.

When Allen gave the journal copies to Paul Willie, he exclaimed, "How did she GET THIS!"

The granite marker was then engraved with the names of the 13 who were buried in a common grave along with the two men who died after they had dug the grave for the others.

In 1985, Allen asked me to go with them to present the stone to the Riverton, WY, Stake, telling me I was an important part of it. I longed to go, but couldn't. It seemed like a wild dream of fantasy, yet my heart longed to be there with them.

On July 20, 1985, Paul and Allen Willie met at Rock Creek Hollow where the Riverton, WY, Stake was having another July 24th pioneer celebration. Paul Willie, representing the Willie family as their elected president, presented the marker to Stake President DeMar Kay Taylor. President Taylor was also presented a copy of the Willie 4th Handcart company's records of births, marriages, and deaths from the 1856 document I created from the copied pages that I gave to Allen Willie in 1983.

Paul asked that the granite marker be mounted on the ground in some way. At that time, Rock Creek Hollow was privately owned by Yellowstone Ranch and no one had permission to place the marker anywhere. President Taylor didn't know what to do with it, so he placed the marker in his garage, where it sat for over a year, waiting to be rescued.

One day President Taylor's counselor, Robert Scott Lorimer, suggested they give the job of mounting the marker to a young man in the stake who was looking for an Eagle project. The Stake leaders did receive permission for the Boy Scouts to place the marker next to the Rock Creek monument. The marker remained in the young man's car trunk until he was too old to complete his Eagle project.

One day, the young man found the marker while cleaning out his trunk and gave it back to President Taylor who then passed it on to President Lorimer.

Another Scout was headed to West Point and was determined to finish his Eagle project. The marker remained as a winter weight in his trunk for six months. In the spring of 1988, he got on the ball and started writing letters and getting everything lined up. The first week of September, they laid the wooden concrete frame for the marker, dug a 30" plug beneath it, poured cement into it, tied rebar through the rebar on the underside of the marker, and inserted river rock on the back side to give it an angle. The Boy Scout remarked, "I knew this was more than the typical Eagle project, more than doing service. This is part of our history. We boys grew up in this country at the old River Rock monument on the 24th of July celebrating the sacrifices of the pioneers. Doing it just seemed right." In later years he commented, "I had no idea it would affect so many people."

When President Taylor was released and President Lorimer was called as the new stake resident on Sep 20, 1987, he heard himself close the stake conference by asking the saints to "Pray for the Willie Project." When he sat down, his councilor, John L. Kitchen, asked him, "What's the Willie Project?"

President Lorimer replied, "I don't know … but I guess we are suppose to pray for it.

Before that stake presidency found out what the "Willie Project" was, the other councilor, Kim W. McKinnon, had unlikely encounters at key moments with individuals who ignited within him a burning drive for the Riverton, WY, Stake to obtain from Church headquarters two of the first computers equipped with the first Temple Ready Program. They tell of miracles that actually did bring those first two computers to Wyoming.

President McKinnon said, "After we received the computers and set them up in the Family History Center, President Lorimer and I took a drive to Lander, WY, to meet with the Wind River Branch. On the way, we discussed my strong drive to obtain the computers and their miraculous delivery to us."

Suddenly, President Lorimer stated, *"It's the Willie people! Their temple work hasn't been done!"*

*"His revelation was a surprise to both of us!* We felt the Spirit confirming the prompting and looked forward to verifying the names with the resources on the computer. After finishing our business at the Wind River Branch, we headed straight for the Stake Center."

President Lorimer testified, "All at once, in a way I'd never received revelation before, I KNEW what the 'Willie Project' was, and when I knew what the 'Willie Project' was, I remembered the picture of the granite marker I had. Back at the stake center, I found that picture in my desk and read the name on the marker of Bodil Mortenson. We shouted for joy when her name appeared having no temple work done for her. Then I gave him the name of James Kirkwood and he hadn't had his work done either! From these two names on that granite marker began the "Second Rescue.""

I remember being sad as a child when my Primary teacher told me that nobody knows the names of the people buried at Rock Creek Hollow. There was no marker at the time. Allen Willie had told me they had tried and tried to find out the names to no avail.

I was intrigued to hear President Lorimer explain that once they began their "Second Rescue," the Family History Department tried to prove the names on the granite marker were not real people. When they found out the names were real, they tried to prove those 13 were not members of the church. When that proved false, the history department attempted to prove these people were not members of the Willie Company #4. After discovering they were in the Willie Handcart Company, they tried to prove they hadn't been buried at Rock Creek. Still determined, they suggested their temple work was already done. The Family History Department found only a few whose temple work was completed. Most of these valiant pioneers were still waiting for temple blessings.

The Lord put all the pieces in place to inspire the Willie family, the missionary at the Family History Library, the Special Collections Library, myself, Presidents Lorimer and McKinnon, along with many others—so began the "Second Rescue" from this granite marker donated by the Jame G Willie family. From the special copied journal pages came the names found on the three monuments dedicated by President Hinckley on Aug 15, 1992.

Allen Willie called me again and begged me to come for President Hinckley's dedication of Rock Creek Hollow and the granite marker on Jul 24, 1994. "You have to come. You are the one that got the ball rolling on all of this!"

My heart ached to go, but I knew I couldn't. A quiet assurance came to my heart and mind: **"One day you will see it."** So I believed and was comforted.

What a delight it was to later be called by the Lord as a Missionary at Sixth Crossing (The Willie Company rescue site). That promise was fulfilled. My husband and I looked down through the rain at the 15 names on this granite marker. I wept in gratitude for the fulfillment of God's promise; another confirmation that He lives and keeps His promises!

"And ye must give thanks unto God in the Spirit for whatsoever ye are blessed with." D&C 46:32

Overwhelmed with emotion, I wondered "What if I hadn't listened to the Spirit?" Suddenly in my mind's eye, the names faded away and I saw instead: *"In Honor of the 13 Handcart Pioneers Who Perished Here"* How many things could have changed if I had left the Family History Library early, or did not **"Copy It"**, or had been too shy to stop brother Willey and **"Tell Allen."** "By small and simple things are great things brought to pass." (Alma 37:6)

How thankful I am to know for certain that the Spirit of God truly was guiding me and how grateful I am to have listened! It was a small thing for Allen Willie to think of putting a marker at Rock Creek Hollow. Yet he spoke that thought. Paul Willie could have ignored the suggestion, yet he acted. Such a small thought, "Copy the journal." How I argued with that one. It was a small thought to ask Allen Willie if he was related to Captain Willey. What if I had let him pass by without speaking up? A small thought promised one day I'd be here looking down at this monument made by the Willie Family with the names the Lord led me to that were provided in that journal—names in granite that have burned into the hearts and lives of countless multitudes. Promises were fulfilled.

How grateful I am for the marker being brought to Wyoming during the Riverton Stake Pioneer Day Celebration. How eternally grateful I am for Presidents: Lorimer, Kitchen, and McKinnon; for their many sacrifices. These wonderful leaders acted on the thoughts and feelings of their hearts. They were guided like pawns by the mighty hand of God.

Many small impressions have been heeded and have helped build the kingdom of God, bringing about great and marvelous blessings. Each year, over 23,000 people, mostly youth, trek here (Sixth Crossing and Martin's Cove, both in Wyoming.)

Truly the Lord is planting "in the hearts of the children the promises made to the fathers" and the hearts of the children are turning to their fathers. How important is this? "... if it were not so, the whole earth would be utterly wasted at His coming." (JSH 1:39)

We all have had a thought come into our mind of something we should do. If there's nothing wrong with it, just do it. Over time, you will come to know which thoughts are from the Lord. I promise you that as you act on these good thoughts, one day either in this life or in the next, you will rejoice as you are shown the great and marvelous things resulting from your small acts. You will feel such joy knowing that you played a part in establishing the kingdom of God upon the earth.

This experience has truly taught me that "by very small means the Lord doth confound the wise and bringeth about the salvation of many souls." (Alma 37:7) (Our eternal friend)

**"For behold, again I say unto you that if ye will enter in by the way, and receive the Holy Ghost, it will show you all things what ye should do." (2 Ne. 32:5)**

IN MEMORY OF THOSE MEMBERS OF THE WILLIE
HANDCART CO. WHOSE JOURNEY STARTED TOO LATE
AND ENDED TOO EARLY AND WERE BURIED HERE IN
A CIRCULAR GRAVE OCTOBER 24 & 25, 1856.
WILLIAM JAMES, 46          BODIL MORTINSEN, 9
ELIZABETH BAILEY, 52       NILS ANDERSON, 41
JAMES KIRKWOOD, 11         OLE MADSEN, 41
SAMUEL GADD, 10            JAMES GIBB, 67
LARS WENDIN, 60            CHESTERTON GILMAN, 66
ANNE OLSEN, 46             THOMAS GURLDSTONE, 62
ELLA NILSON, 22 JENS NILSON, 6  WILLIAM GROVES, 22

### Rock Creek Hollow Plaque

*President Gordon B. Hinckley dedicated the granite marker of Rock Creek Hollow on Jul 23, 1994:* "Brethren and sisters you have a great inheritance. We have a tremendous responsibility to live up to it. God bless us to be faithful, to be true to that which meant so much to those who died here and their associates who died along this long and wearisome trail."

Rock Creek Hollow was acquired over a long period of time through the leadership and inspiration of Robert Scott Lorimer, former president of the Riverton, Wyoming Stake. President Lorimer did much to initiate what has come to be known as the "second rescue," or researching the names of the handcart saints and seeing to it that their temple work was completed. Because of his years of service in this connection, President Larimer was awarded the Junius F. Wells Award by the Mormon Historic Sites Foundation. His efforts were continually approved and encouraged by President Gordon B. Hinckley of the First Presidency. President Hinckley considered the site of Rock Creek to be holy ground and was known to become emotional at this and other sites in the area. (Mormonhistoricsites.com)

*For the complete and awesome story of the "second rescue" see the book: **Remember** The Willie and Martin Handcart Companies and their rescuers—past and present, 1997.)*

Made in the
USA
Lexington, KY